ALL·IN·ONE

AWS

Certified Developer Associate

EXAM GUIDE

(Exam DVA-C01)

ABOUT THE AUTHOR

Kamesh Ganesan is a cloud evangelist, seasoned technology professional, cloud security subject matter expert (SME), author, speaker, and coach with over 23 years of IT experience in all major cloud technologies, including AWS, Azure, GCP, Oracle, and Alibaba Cloud. He has over 50 IT certifications, including 5 AWS, 4 Azure, 3 GCP, 6 OCI, and an Alibaba cloud certification. He has played many roles, including certified multicloud architect, cloud-native application architect, lead database administrator, programmer analyst, and developer. He architected, built, automated, and delivered high-quality, mission-critical, and innovative technology solutions that helped his enterprise, commercial, and government clients be very successful and significantly improve their business value using a multicloud strategy.

About the Technical Editor

Rajat Ravinder Varuni provides consultations to customers in the public sector that include architectural design and deployment of solutions that reduce the likelihood of data leakage, web application, and denial-of-service attacks. He is a subject matter expert who provides ongoing support for achieving regulatory needs such as the Health Insurance Portability and Accountability Act (HIPAA), Federal Information Security Management Act (FISMA), and Federal Risk and Authorization Management Program (FedRAMP) attestation and authorization. Currently, he holds the GIAC Penetration Tester certificate, as well as a host of AWS certifications. He also participates in the development of AWS certification exams, including the Security specialty. Additionally, he has contributed to the AWS Security Blog found at https://aws.amazon.com/blogs/security/author/varunirv/.

Rajat serves as an academic advisor for the Global Information Assurance Certification (GIAC), a graduate-level cybersecurity program. He is also on the editorial board for the *Journal of Information Systems Education* (JISE) and serves as a journal reviewer at Information Systems Audit and Control Association (ISACA) and the Association for Computing Machinery (ACM).

Rajat holds a master's and a bachelor's degree in computer science from The George Washington University and Michigan Technological University, respectively.

In his free time, Rajat enjoys having a single-threaded conversation and exploring nature.

ALL·IN·ONE

AWS
Certified Developer Associate
EXAM GUIDE
(Exam DVA-C01)

Kamesh Ganesan

New York   Chicago   San Francisco
Athens   London   Madrid   Mexico City
Milan   New Delhi   Singapore   Sydney   Toronto

AWS Certified Developer Associate All-in-One Exam Guide (Exam DVA-C01)

1 2 3 4 5 6 7 8 9   LCR   24 23 22 21 20

Library of Congress Control Number: 2020946006

ISBN   978-1-260-46017-9
MHID   1-260-46017-7

Sponsoring Editor
Lisa McClain

Editorial Supervisor
Patty Mon

Project Manager
Parag Mittal,
    KnowledgeWorks Global Ltd.

Acquisitions Coordinator
Emily Walters

Technical Editor
Rajat Ravinder Varuni

Copy Editor
Lisa McCoy

Proofreader
Tricia Lawrence

Indexer
Ted Laux

Production Supervisor
Thomas Somers

Composition
KnowledgeWorks Global Ltd.

Illustration
KnowledgeWorks Global Ltd.

Art Director, Cover
Jeff Weeks

I would like to dedicate this book to my mother, father, all my teachers, and God Almighty.

CONTENTS AT A GLANCE

Part I   Getting Started on the AWS Journey

Chapter 1   Overview of Cloud Computing and AWS..................................... 3

Chapter 2   Interacting with AWS Using API, SDK, and CLI......................... 37

Chapter 3   Networking Using Amazon Virtual Private Cloud 79

Chapter 4   Creating a Virtual Machine Using Amazon EC2...................... 107

Part II   AWS High Availability and Fault Tolerance

Chapter 5   Elastic Load Balancing and Auto Scaling 137

Chapter 6   Distributing the Contents via AWS CloudFront...................... 161

Chapter 7   Domain Name System and Amazon Route 53 185

Part III   Working with Cloud Storage

Chapter 8   Working with Simple Storage Service 221

Chapter 9   Amazon EBS, Amazon EFS, and Amazon S3 Glacier 249

Part IV   Authentication and Authorization

Chapter 10   Securing AWS Resources with Identity
and Access Management 285

Chapter 11   Web Identity Federation and Amazon Cognito
for User Authentication 309

Chapter 12   Protecting Your Data Using Server-Side
and Client-Side Encryption 327

Part V   Creating SQL and NoSQL Database in AWS Cloud

Chapter 13   AWS Relational Database Services...................................... 349

Chapter 14   AWS NoSQL Database Service: Amazon DynamoDB................. 371

Part VI   AWS Application Integration and Management

Chapter 15   Amazon Simple Queue Service and Simple Notification Service 395

Chapter 16   Amazon Simple Workflow Service, Amazon API Gateway,
and AWS Step Functions 415

Chapter 17   Monitoring Using Amazon CloudWatch, AWS CloudTrail,
and AWS Config.. 437

Chapter 18   Infrastructure as Code Using AWS CloudFormation................. 457

Part VII   Developing Cloud Native Applications in AWS

Chapter 19   Developing Serverless Applications with Lambda 481

Chapter 20   Deploying a Static Website on Amazon S3 Bucket 499

Chapter 21   Deploying a Web Application Using AWS Elastic Beanstalk 529

Chapter 22   Migrating Your Application and Database to AWS 545

Part VIII   Building, Deploying, and Debugging Cloud Applications

Chapter 23   Hosting Secure Repositories Using AWS CodeCommit 571

Chapter 24   Building an Application Using CodeBuild........................... 595

Chapter 25   Deploying Applications Using CodeDeploy and CodePipeline 615

Chapter 26   Building a Scalable and Fault-Tolerant CI/CD Pipeline 641

Part IX   Appendixes and Acronyms and Glossary

Appendix A   AWS Certified Developer - Associate Exam Objective Map
(DVA-C01) 673

Appendix B   About the Online Content.. 675

Acronyms and Glossary... 679

Index.. 691

CONTENTS

Acknowledgments xxv

Introduction xxvii

Part I Getting Started on the AWS Journey

Chapter 1 Overview of Cloud Computing and AWS 3

Cloud Computing Overview 3

Cloud Computing Benefits 4

Cloud Deployment Models: IaaS, STaaS, PaaS,
DaaS, FaaS, SaaS 5

Cloud Services Types: Public, Private,
Hybrid, and Community 7

AWS History 9

AWS Regions and Availability Zones 9

AWS Services 11

AWS in Action 25

Chapter Review 28

Questions 28

Answers 33

Additional Resources 35

Chapter 2 Interacting with AWS Using API, SDK, and CLI 37

Create a New AWS Account 37

Explore AWS Free Tiers 42

AWS Management Console 44

AWS Command Line Interface 49

Installing and Setting Up a Profile in the AWS CLI 50

Getting Help with CLI Commands 53

Working with EC2 Key Pairs Using the AWS CLI 53

Creating Security Groups Using the AWS CLI 54

Launching an Instance Using the AWS CLI 56

Creating an S3 Bucket Using the AWS CLI 57

AWS Software Development Kit 57

AWS SDK for Java 2.0 58

AWS SDK for .NET 59

AWS Tools for PowerShell 60

In Windows 60

On Linux and macOSX 61

AWS Serverless Application Model 62
 Using the AWS SAM CLI 62
 Installing Docker on Linux 63
AWS IDE Toolkits 63
 The AWS Toolkit for Eclipse 63
 The Toolkit for Visual Studio 65
 AWS Tools for Visual Studio Team Services 66
Chapter Review 67
 Exercises 68
 Questions 71
 Answers 75
Additional Resources 76

Chapter 3 Networking Using Amazon Virtual Private Cloud 79
Amazon Virtual Private Cloud 80
 Subnets 81
 Route Tables 81
 Network Access Control Lists 82
 Security Groups 82
 Internet Gateways 83
 Dynamic Host Configuration Protocol Option Sets 84
 Elastic Internet Protocols 85
 Endpoints 85
 Network Address Translation Devices 87
 Egress-Only Internet Gateways 88
 Peering Connections 88
 Virtual Private Gateways 89
 Customer Gateways 89
 Site-to-Site Virtual Private Network 90
 Point-to-Site Virtual Private Network 90
 Direct Connect 90
 Transit Gateways 91
Chapter Review 91
 Exercises 92
 Questions 103
 Answers 105
Additional Resources 106

Chapter 4 Creating a Virtual Machine Using Amazon EC2 107
Elastic Compute Cloud 107
Amazon Machine Image 108
 Bundle Tasks 108
 Root Device Types 109
 The AWS Marketplace 109
 AMIs Generated from Existing Instances 109

Tenancy Options 109
    Shared Tenancy 110
    Dedicated Tenancy 110
Instance Types 110
    General Purpose 111
    Compute Optimized 111
    Memory Optimized 112
    Storage Optimized 112
    Accelerated Computing 113
Pricing Model for EC2 113
    On-Demand 114
    Spot Instances 114
    Reserved Instances 114
    Dedicated Hosts 115
EC2 Instance Virtualization Types 115
    HVM AMIs 115
    PV AMIs 115
Storage Options for Amazon EC2 116
    Instance Store–Backed Instances 116
    Amazon EBS–Backed Instances 116
The EC2 Instance Lifecycle 117
    Launching 118
    Bootstrapping 118
    VM Import/Export 118
    Instance Recovery 119
    Instance Metadata 120
    Instance Stop and Restart 121
    Instance Hibernate 121
    Instance Reboot 122
    Instance Retirement 122
    Instance Termination 122
Generating Security Keys 122
Launching an Amazon EC2 123
    Creating an Amazon EC2 Instance 123
    Connecting to the Amazon EC2 Instance Using SSH 125
    Connecting to an Amazon EC2 Instance
        Using a PuTTY Session 125
Security Groups that Protect the Instances 126
Best Practices for Amazon EC2 127
Chapter Review 128
    Exercises 129
    Questions 131
    Answers 133
Additional Resources 134

Part II	**AWS High Availability and Fault Tolerance**	
Chapter 5	Elastic Load Balancing and Auto Scaling	137
	Elastic Load Balancing	137
	Types of Elastic Load Balancers	138
	Application Load Balancer	138
	Network Load Balancer	138
	Classic Load Balancer	139
	Elastic Load Balancing Concepts	140
	Load Balancer Subnets	140
	Load Balancer Security Groups	140
	Load Balancer States	140
	Deletion Protection	141
	Connection Idle Timeout	141
	Load Balancer Listeners	141
	Listener Configuration	141
	Listener Rules	142
	Rule Condition Types	142
	Load Balancer Target Groups	143
	Routing Configuration	143
	Target Type	143
	Registered Targets	144
	Deregistration Delay	144
	Slow Start Mode	144
	Sticky Sessions	144
	Load Balancer Monitoring	145
	Elastic Load Balancer Best Practices	145
	Amazon EC2 Auto Scaling	146
	Advantages of Auto Scaling	146
	The EC2 Auto Scaling Lifecycle	147
	Scale Out and In	148
	Attach and Detach	148
	Lifecycle Hooks	148
	Enter and Exit Standby	148
	Launch Templates	149
	Launch Configurations	149
	Auto Scaling Groups	149
	Scaling the Size	150
	Maintaining the Number of Instances	150
	Manual Scaling	150
	Scheduled Scaling	150
	Dynamic Scaling	151
	Cooldown Period	152
	Monitoring Auto Scaling Groups	152

Chapter Review 153
   Exercises 154
   Questions 156
   Answers 159
Additional Resources 160

Chapter 6   **Distributing the Contents via AWS CloudFront** 161
Amazon CloudFront 161
CloudFront Origin Servers 162
CloudFront Pricing 163
Regional Edge Caches 164
   Adding Content 164
   Removing Content 164
Securing Content 164
   HTTPS with CloudFront 165
   Restrict Access in the Origin 165
   Restrict Access in Edge Caches 165
   Signed URLs and Signed Cookies 165
   Origin Access Identity 167
   AWS WAF to Control Access 167
   Restricting Geographic Distribution 167
   Field-Level Encryption 168
CloudFront Distributions 168
   Distribution Contents 168
   Origins for Web Distributions 169
Alternate Domain Names 170
WebSocket Protocol 171
Optimizing Content Caching 171
   Cache Hit Ratio 171
   Cache Lifetime 171
   Query String Parameters 172
   Caching Based on Cookie Values 172
   Caching Based on Request Headers 172
Content Expiration at the Edge Cache 172
CloudFront Origin Groups 173
Domain Fronting 173
Custom Error Pages 173
   Request and Response Behavior 173
Lambda@Edge 174
Chapter Review 174
   Exercises 175
   Questions 178
   Answers 182
Additional Resources 183

Chapter 7 Domain Name System and Amazon Route 53 185

    Domain Name System 186
        How DNS Works 186
        Domain Names 186
        Name Servers 187
        DNS Resolution 187
        DNS Records and Zone Files 189
        Types of DNS Records 189
    Amazon Route 53 194
    Route 53 Concepts 194
    Domain Registration 197
    Routing Traffic 198
    Hosted Zones 199
        Public Hosted Zone 200
        Private Hosted Zone 200
        Split-View DNS 200
        Routing Traffic for Subdomains 200
    Choosing a Routing Policy 201
        Simple Routing 201
        Failover Routing 201
        Geolocation Routing 201
        Geoproximity Routing 201
        Latency-Based Routing 201
        Multivalue Answer Routing 202
        Weighted Routing 202
    Amazon Route 53 Health Checks 202
    Chapter Review 204
        Exercises 205
        Questions 215
        Answers 217
    Additional Resources 217

Part III Working with Cloud Storage

Chapter 8 Working with Simple Storage Service 221

    Amazon Simple Storage Service 222
    Buckets 222
    Creating a Bucket 223
        Accessing Your Bucket 223
    Bucket Configuration Options 223
        Cross-Origin Resource Sharing 223
        Cross-Region Replication 224
        Amazon S3 Event Notifications 224

Amazon S3 Transfer Acceleration 224
Billing and Usage Reporting for S3 Buckets 225
Requester Pays Buckets 225
Static Website on Amazon S3 225
Amazon S3 Server Access Logging 226
Folders 226
Objects 226
Object Key and Metadata 227
Storage Classes 227
General-Purpose Amazon S3 Standard 227
Unknown or Changing Access: Amazon S3
Intelligent-Tiering 228
Infrequent Access: Amazon S3 Standard-Infrequent Access ... 228
Amazon S3 One Zone-Infrequent Access 228
Archive: Amazon S3 Glacier 228
Amazon S3 Glacier Deep Archive 229
Object Lifecycle Management 229
Lifecycle Transitions 229
Configuring Object Expiration 229
Object Versioning 230
Identity and Access Management in Amazon S3 234
Operations on Objects 234
Getting Objects 234
Uploading Objects 234
Copying Objects 234
Listing Object Keys 235
Deleting Objects 235
Selecting Content from Objects 235
Restoring Archived Objects 236
Data Protection in Amazon S3 236
Access Control Lists 236
Amazon S3 Object Lock 237
Retention Periods 237
Legal Holds 237
Best Practices for Amazon S3 238
Chapter Review 240
Exercises 241
Questions 244
Answers 246
Additional Resources 247

Chapter 9   Amazon EBS, Amazon EFS, and Amazon S3 Glacier 249

Amazon Elastic Block Store 249
Create an Amazon EBS Volume 251

Working with Amazon EBS Volume 252
    Detach an Amazon EBS Volume 252
    Delete an Amazon EBS Volume 252
Monitor Amazon EBS Volumes 252
Amazon EBS Snapshots 253
    Multivolume Snapshots 254
    Delete an Amazon EBS Snapshot 254
    Copy an Amazon EBS Snapshot 255
    Amazon EBS Snapshot Lifecycle 255
Amazon EBS Elastic Volumes 256
Amazon EBS Encryption 256
    Key Management 256
    Restoring and Copying Snapshots 257
RAID Configuration on Linux 260
Amazon EBS Metrics 261
Amazon EBS Best Practices 261
Amazon Elastic File System 262
Amazon EFS with Amazon EC2 263
Amazon EFS with AWS Direct Connect and VPN 264
Data Consistency 265
Storage Classes 266
Amazon EFS Backup 266
Amazon EFS Encryption 266
Lifecycle Policy 267
Monitoring Amazon EFS 267
Amazon EFS Performance 267
Amazon EFS Best Practices 268
Amazon S3 Glacier 268
    Vault 269
    Archives 269
    Jobs 270
    Notification Configuration 270
Glacier Operations 271
    Creating and Deleting Vaults 271
    Archive Operations 272
    Data Retrieval Policy 273
Vault Lock 273
Data Protection 273
Logging and Monitoring 274
Chapter Review 274
    Exercises 275
    Questions 278
    Answers 281
Additional Resources 282

Part IV   Authentication and Authorization

Chapter 10   Securing AWS Resources with Identity
and Access Management 285
Identity and Access Management 285
Users 288
Users and Credentials 288
Password: Configure a Strong Password Policy 289
Multifactor Authentication 289
Groups 290
IAM Roles 291
AWS Service Role 292
AWS Service-Linked Role 292
Role Chaining 292
Delegation 292
Federation 292
Role for Cross-Account Access 292
Policies and Permissions 293
IAM Policy Types 293
Permissions Boundaries 294
IAM Policy 294
IAM Policy Structure 295
IAM Policy Versioning 296
IAM Best Practices 297
Chapter Review 298
Exercises 299
Questions 303
Answers 305
Additional Resources 306

Chapter 11   Web Identity Federation and Amazon Cognito
for User Authentication 309
Identity Federation and Providers 309
Web Identity Federation 310
Amazon Cognito 311
Cognito User Pools 312
Identity Pools 312
Amazon Cognito Sync 313
Amazon Cognito for Mobile Apps 313
Federating Users with SAML 2.0 318
Session Policies 319
Chapter Review 321
Exercises 321
Questions 323
Answers 325
Additional Resources 326

Chapter 12 Protecting Your Data Using Server-Side
and Client-Side Encryption 327
Data Protection 327
Server-Side Encryption 331
Server-Side Encryption with Customer-Managed
Keys in KMS 332
Server-Side Encryption with Amazon S3–Managed
Encryption Keys 333
Server-Side Encryption with Customer-Provided
Encryption Keys 334
Client-Side Encryption 335
CMK Stored in AWS KMS 335
Master Key Stored in the Application 336
Command-Line Encryption and Decryption 336
Encrypt a File 336
Decrypt a File 338
Data Protection Best Practices 339
Chapter Review 340
Exercises 340
Questions 342
Answers 344
Additional Resources 345

Part V Creating SQL and NoSQL Database in AWS Cloud

Chapter 13 AWS Relational Database Services 349
Amazon Relational Database Service 349
High Availability (Multi-AZ) 351
Multi-AZ Failover Process 352
The Amazon RDS Lifecycle 353
Modify 353
Maintain 353
Upgrade 353
Rename 354
Reboot 354
Stop 354
Start 355
Delete 355
Read Replicas 355
Create a Read Replica 356
Promote a Read Replica 356
Monitor Read Replication 356
Option Groups 356
DB Parameter Groups 357
Storage 357

Billing 358

Backups 358

Snapshots 359

Security 359

Encryption 360

Monitoring 360

Amazon Resource Names 361

Tagging 361

Best Practices 361

Chapter Review 363

Exercise 363

Questions 366

Answers 368

Additional Resources 369

Chapter 14 **AWS NoSQL Database Service: Amazon DynamoDB** 371

Amazon DynamoDB 371

Data Types 373

Control Plane Operations 373

Data Plane Operations 373

SQL vs. NoSQL 374

DynamoDB Transactions 375

Read Consistency 376

Read/Write Capacity Mode 376

Isolation Levels 376

DynamoDB Accelerator 376

DAX Components 377

DAX Read 377

DAX LRU 377

DAX Cluster and Nodes 377

DAX Control 378

DAX Write 378

DAX Encryption 379

Auto-Scaling 379

Data Distribution 379

DynamoDB Local 379

DynamoDB Web 380

Secondary Indexes 380

DynamoDB Stream 380

Backup and Recovery 381

DynamoDB Global Tables 381

NoSQL Workbench 381

Data Protection 382

Maintenance Window 383

Logging and Monitoring 383

Infrastructure Security 384
Security Best Practices 384
Chapter Review 385
    Exercises 386
    Questions 389
    Answers 391
Additional Resources 392

Part VI AWS Application Integration and Management

Chapter 15 Amazon Simple Queue Service
               and Simple Notification Service 395
Amazon Simple Queue Service 395
Amazon SQS Architecture 396
    Queue Lifecycle 396
    Standard Queues 396
    First In/First Out Queues 397
    Short Polling 399
    Long Polling 399
    Dead-Letter Queues 399
    Visibility Timeout 399
    Inflight Messages 399
    Delay Queues 400
    Temporary Queues 400
    Virtual Queues 400
    Message Timers 400
    Large Messages 400
Data Encryption 401
    Virtual Private Cloud Endpoints 401
    Logging 401
    Monitoring 401
Amazon Simple Notification Service 401
Amazon SNS Architecture 402
    Fanout 402
    Alerts 402
    Push Message 402
    Push Notifications 403
    Message Durability 403
    Message Delivery Status 403
    Message Delivery Retries 403
    Delivery Policies 403
    Creating a Delivery Policy 404
    Dead-Letter Queues 404
    Message Attributes 405

Message Filtering 405
Tags 405
Data Encryption 405
Logging 406
Monitoring 406
Infrastructure Security 406
Chapter Review 407
Exercises 408
Questions 411
Answers 413
Additional Resources 413

Chapter 16   Amazon Simple Workflow Service, Amazon API Gateway,
                 and AWS Step Functions 415

Amazon Simple Workflow Service 415
Development Environment 416
Tags 419
Monitoring 419
Logging 420
Amazon API Gateway 420
REST API 423
API with Lambda Integration 423
Create a REST API 424
AWS Step Functions 425
Standard Workflows 425
Express Workflows 425
Standard vs. Express Workflows 425
Step Functions Local 426
Tagging 428
Monitoring 428
Logging 428
Security 428
Chapter Review 429
Exercises 430
Questions 432
Answers 434
Additional Resources 435

Chapter 17   Monitoring Using Amazon CloudWatch,
                 AWS CloudTrail, and AWS Config 437

Amazon CloudWatch 437
Metrics 438
CloudWatch Agent 442
Data Protection 442
Logging 442

AWS CloudTrail 442
   The CloudTrail Lifecycle 443
   Control Access 444
   AWS CloudTrail Security 445
AWS Config 445
   Security Analysis 446
   Resource Configuration 446
   Managing AWS Config 447
   AWS Config Managed and Custom Rules 448
   Monitoring AWS Config 448
Chapter Review 448
   Exercises 449
   Questions 451
   Answers 455
Additional Resources 456

Chapter 18   Infrastructure as Code Using AWS CloudFormation 457

AWS CloudFormation 457
   Templates 459
   Stacks 465
   Change Sets 466
   Export 466
   AWS CloudFormation Registry 467
Chapter Review 467
   Exercise 468
   Questions 475
   Answers 477
Additional Resources 478

Part VII   Developing Cloud Native Applications in AWS

Chapter 19   Developing Serverless Applications with Lambda 481

AWS Lambda 481
   AWS Lambda Functions 481
   AWS Lambda Applications 487
   AWS Lambda Layers 487
   AWS Lambda Security 487
Chapter Review 488
   Exercise 488
   Questions 495
   Answers 497
Additional Resources 498

Chapter 20 Deploying a Static Website on Amazon S3 Bucket 499

Amazon S3 499
Deploy a Static Website Using Amazon S3 500
Deploy a Static Website Using Amazon S3 and Amazon Route 53 . . . 510
Deploy a Static Website Using Amazon S3, Amazon Route 53,
    and Amazon CloudFront 515
Chapter Review 523
    Exercise 523
    Questions 524
    Answers 526
Additional Resources 527

Chapter 21 Deploying a Web Application Using AWS Elastic Beanstalk 529

AWS Elastic Beanstalk 529
Deploy an Application in AWS Elastic Beanstalk 530
Migrate and Deploy an Application to AWS Elastic Beanstalk 534
Chapter Review 540
    Exercise 540
    Questions 541
    Answers 543
Additional Resources 543

Chapter 22 Migrating Your Application and Database to AWS 545

AWS Migration 545
Application Migration 546
    AWS Server Migration Service 556
Database Migration 557
Chapter Review 564
    Exercises 565
    Questions 566
    Answers 568
Additional Resources 568

Part VIII Building, Deploying, and Debugging Cloud Applications

Chapter 23 Hosting Secure Repositories Using AWS CodeCommit 571

AWS CodeCommit 571
Chapter Review 589
    Exercises 589
    Questions 590
    Answers 592
Additional Resources 593

Chapter 24	**Building an Application Using AWS CodeBuild**	595
	AWS CodeBuild	595
	Build Projects	595
	Build Environment	595
	Working with AWS CodeBuild	596
	Test Reporting	610
	Chapter Review	610
	Exercises	611
	Questions	612
	Answers	614
	Additional Resources	614
Chapter 25	**Deploying Applications Using CodeDeploy and CodePipeline**	615
	AWS CodeDeploy	615
	AWS CodePipeline	625
	Chapter Review	635
	Exercises	635
	Questions	637
	Answers	639
	Additional Resources	639
Chapter 26	**Building a Scalable and Fault-Tolerant CI/CD Pipeline**	641
	CI/CD Pipeline	641
	Chapter Review	665
	Exercises	665
	Questions	667
	Answers	669
	Additional Resources	669
Part IX	**Appendixes and Acronyms and Glossary**	
Appendix A	**AWS Certified Developer - Associate Exam Objective Map (DVA-C01)**	673
Appendix B	**About the Online Content**	675
	System Requirements	675
	Your Total Seminars Training Hub Account	675
	Privacy Notice	675
	Single User License Terms and Conditions	675
	TotalTester Online	677
	Technical Support	677
	Acronyms and Glossary	679
	Index	691

ACKNOWLEDGMENTS

A special thanks to my wife, Hemalatha, and my kids, Sachin and Arjun, for their continuous support in all my pursuits. I would like to express my gratitude to my father, Ganesan, my mother, Kasthuri, and my brother, Gandhi, for their motivation. I want to thank my friend, Prithviraj Padmanabhan, who always supported me unconditionally. I would like to thank Jennifer Scott for her encouragement and Yujun Liang for his inspiration. Also, I would like to thank everyone at McGraw-Hill, especially Senior Editor, Lisa McClain, Editorial Coordinator, Emily Walters, Copy Editor, Lisa McCoy, Project Manager, Parag Mittal, Editorial Supervisor, Patty Mon, and Technical Reviewer, Rajat Ravinder Varuni.

INTRODUCTION

Many small, medium, and large enterprises and government agencies around the world are adopting a public cloud and hybrid strategy for enhanced scalability, availability, security, and cost savings. There is a great need for certified AWS developers who can create secure applications in AWS Cloud using the most popular programming languages and build serverless applications, protecting the data in AWS using encryption, help migrating enterprise applications to AWS, and build scalable CI/CD pipelines in AWS. This hands-on, all-in-one guide helps anyone who wants to achieve AWS Certified Developer – Associate certification and to develop cloud-native applications in AWS.

This book is for anyone who wants to change their career path to AWS Cloud or begin their career in AWS Cloud as a developer, whether you have basic or even no prior knowledge of AWS Cloud technology. If you want to pass the AWS Developer Associate Exam with flying colors and have a passion for developing cloud-native applications, this book is ideal for you. If you already have some experience with cloud-native development in AWS, this book can help you speed up your cloud development in a fast-paced way in addition to passing your AWS Certified Developer - Associate (DVA-C01) Exam.

About the Exam

The AWS Certified Developer - Associate exam is intended for professionals who perform a development role and have one or more years of hands-on experience developing and maintaining an AWS-based application. By achieving this certification, you demonstrate an understanding of core AWS services, uses, and basic AWS architecture best practices and demonstrate proficiency in developing, deploying, and debugging cloud-based applications using AWS. Although this exam does not have specific prerequisites, AWS recommends one or more years of hands-on experience developing and maintaining an AWS-based application.

The exam has 65 multiple-choice questions and a duration of 130 minutes. Multiple-choice questions will have one correct response and three incorrect responses or two or more correct responses out of five or more options. You may take the exam at a testing center or through online proctoring. Candidates should visit the AWS Certified Developer Associate page (https://aws.amazon.com/certification/certified-developer-associate/) for the most current details and to download the exam guide.

As outlined in the AWS exam guidelines, AWS developers focus on a wide range of responsibilities. The AWS Certified Developer - Associate certification is built to test your knowledge of the five developer domains:

Domain	Exam (percentage)
Domain 1: Deployment	22%
Domain 2: Security	26%
Domain 3: Development with AWS Services	30%
Domain 4: Refactoring	10%
Domain 5: Monitoring and Troubleshooting	12%
Total	**100%**

In addition to explaining all the domains of the exam, this book will help you learn the different building blocks of AWS with which you can create a secure, scalable, cloud-native application in order to be successful as an AWS developer in the real world.

About the Book

The AWS Certified Developer Associate All-in-One Exam Guide is your one-stop preparation guide for the latest exam with a focus on hands-on development. This book is intended for cloud developers, architects, consultants, DevOps engineers, managers, and leaders who are using AWS Cloud to provide services to their end clients. This guide covers all exam objectives and provides the detailed steps to code, build, deploy, migrate, monitor, and debug cloud-native applications using AWS. It helps you gain the technical knowledge and skills necessary with best practices for building secure, reliable, cloud-native applications using AWS services. This book is your all-in-one exam preparation guide, providing all the knowledge you need to pass the exam, with many questions and answers to practice with.

This book starts with an introduction to cloud computing and AWS. To quickly immerse you in your hands-on journey, it shows the steps to create an AWS free account, setting up developer tools such as AWS Command Line Interface (CLI). You will then create your first Amazon Virtual Private Cloud (VPC) and Amazon Elastic Compute Cloud (EC2). This book will take you on a journey of using some of the important services such as Elastic Load Balancing, Amazon EC2 Auto Scaling, AWS CloudFront, Amazon Route 53, Amazon EBS, Amazon EFS, Amazon S3 Glacier, Amazon RDS, and Amazon DynamoDB from the exam point of view, as well as building your experience for working in real-world scenarios.

This book will prepare you much more than just passing the AWS Developer exam—you will be able to perform the expected tasks of an AWS-certified developer in the real world.

- Part I starts with taking the first step of your exciting AWS Cloud journey by providing an overview of cloud computing and AWS Cloud. You will then create an AWS free account and install the necessary developer tools, such as AWS CLI, to interact with AWS programmatically, in addition to teaching you tasks such as creating Amazon VPC and Amazon EC2 using the AWS Management Console.

- Part II introduces you to the core cloud concepts such as Elastic Load Balancing and Auto Scaling, which help you build highly scalable applications. Then you will learn about AWS CloudFront, which is a fast content delivery network (CDN) that securely delivers your application data to your worldwide customers, and Amazon Route 53, which is a managed, highly available cloud domain name system.

- Part III describes various cloud storage services such as Amazon S3, which offers high availability, scalability, and security with 99.999999999 percent durability for the data stored in Amazon S3 buckets, and Amazon S3 Glacier, which is used to easily archive your data using simple life cycle policies. Then you will learn about Amazon EFS, which is a managed elastic network file system, and you will also learn about EBS volumes and how to use them for your mission-critical applications and the most demanding workloads that require block storage.

- Part IV discusses authentication and authorization, where you will learn to secure your AWS resources using Identity and Access Management (IAM) and configure users, groups, and policies to allow or deny access. You will learn to use Amazon Cognito, which lets you use third-party identity providers, such as Amazon, Facebook, and Google using SAML 2.0. Then you will learn to protect your data at rest and while in transit using server-side encryption and client-side encryption.

- Part V teaches you the steps to create a SQL database using AWS Cloud and AWS Relational Database Services, which automates many administration tasks such as backup, patching, and replication, and then you learn to create Amazon DynamoDB, which is a managed key/value pair and document NoSQL database with built-in security and in-memory caching for your applications.

- Part VI discusses the application integration and management services such as Amazon Simple Queue Service, which is used to decouple your distributed systems and serverless applications, and Simple Notification Service, which is a managed publication/subscription messaging service. You will learn about continuous monitoring for your applications and databases using Amazon CloudWatch to monitor operational health and optimize resource utilization using AWS CloudTrail to track user activities and AWS Config to assess and audit your AWS resources. Then you will learn to automate and build your AWS infrastructure using AWS CloudFormation, which uses a JSON and YAML format infrastructure as code.

- Part VII moves into an in-depth, practical approach of developing cloud-native applications in AWS. You will build a few serverless applications using AWS Lambda, and you will learn the step-by-step instructions to deploy and migrate a web application using Amazon Elastic Beanstalk. You will learn detailed instructions to deploy a highly available and secure static custom website using Amazon S3, Amazon Route 53, and Amazon CloudFront with Secure Sockets Layer (SSL) certificate enabled, which can be utilized in the real world. You will gain important experience by performing an actual migration of a web application and database to AWS.

- Part VIII gives you step-by-step instructions to manage your application source code repositories using AWS CodeCommit, automatically build a web application using AWS CodeBuild, and automatically deploy a web application using AWS CodeDeploy. At the end of this part, you will gain the actual experience of creating a fully managed continuous integration and continuous delivery pipeline using AWS CodePipeline that you can use to automate your releases for faster application and infrastructure delivery in the real world.

This book will guide you to fully prepare for this new AWS Developer exam using real-world knowledge and the latest content, chapter review questions, and additional resources. The comprehensive content and robust step-by-step exercises and examples in this book will assist you to distinguish yourself as an AWS expert by obtaining the necessary practical experience and the highly recognized AWS certification. The skills that you will learn in this book are in great demand by many companies who are migrating their resources to AWS Cloud and building cloud-native applications. As many experts say, there is no better preparation than hands-on experience—which you will gain in this book and will be helpful both on the exam day and throughout your career as a valuable on-the-job reference guide. Your decision to purchase this book is your first step on your exciting journey in AWS Cloud and achieving the AWS Developer certification, which boosts your chances of landing a cloud job.

Using the Objective Map

The objective map included in Appendix A has been constructed to help you cross-reference the official exam objectives from AWS with the relevant coverage in the book. References have been provided for the exam objectives exactly as AWS has presented them, including the chapter and section that covers that objective.

Online Content

This book includes online content, featuring the TotalTester exam software that allows you to generate a complete practice exam or to generate quizzes by chapter or exam domain. See Appendix B for more information.

PART I

Getting Started on the AWS Journey

■ **Chapter 1**   Overview of Cloud Computing and AWS
■ **Chapter 2**   Interacting with AWS Using API, SDK, and CLI
■ **Chapter 3**   Networking Using Amazon Virtual Private Cloud
■ **Chapter 4**   Creating a Virtual Machine Using Amazon EC2

Overview of Cloud Computing and AWS

In this chapter, you will learn

- Cloud computing overview
- Benefits of cloud computing
- Cloud deployment models: IaaS, STaaS, PaaS, DaaS, FaaS, and SaaS
- Cloud services types: public, private, hybrid, and community
- AWS history
- AWS regions and availability zones (AZs)
- AWS services
- AWS in action

Congratulations on purchasing this *All-in-One Exam Guide*! You are one step closer to learning how to build applications for the cloud. I am excited to join you on this journey toward developing cloud native applications for Amazon Web Services (AWS) and of course becoming an AWS-certified developer associate. You will learn everything you need to create, automate, migrate, and monitor applications in the AWS cloud.

Cloud Computing Overview

Cloud computing is the on-demand delivery of computing resources, such as servers, storage, networking, databases, and other services, over the Internet. Its pay-as-you-go pricing means that you pay only for the services you use, which reduces or eliminates your organization's total cost of ownership and lowers operating costs. Cloud computing enables you to run your infrastructure more efficiently: it enables faster business innovation, offers flexibility to scale as your business needs change, and helps create economies of scale.

Cloud Computing Benefits

Cloud computing creates a major shift from the traditional methods used to access IT resources in organizations. Here are few basic benefits of migrating to cloud computing services:

- **Global scale** Cloud computing enables you to deploy your IT infrastructure in other parts of the world quickly and easily. Suppose, for example, you operate a chain of successful stores in the United States and want to expand your business to other countries across the globe. Using traditional IT methods, this could take a few months to a year, based on the size and complexity required to build datacenters in those countries for operation. In contrast, if you use a public cloud provider such as AWS, you can deploy similar infrastructures in different countries or continents within a few hours. You can even set up a global disaster recovery system with only few mouse clicks.

- **Cost** Cloud computing reduces or eliminates the costs of purchasing server hardware and software; setting up datacenters; providing power supplies, cooling, and security; and hiring IT experts to manage your infrastructure. Suppose your startup company creates and markets a big data analytical solution that handles petabytes of data. With a traditional IT infrastructure and on-premises datacenter, this could require upfront costs of $200,000 to $300,000. Using cloud computing, however, you simply create an account with AWS and start building your infrastructure; then you can scale up or down as needed and pay for only the services you actually use.

- **Speed** In a traditional onsite infrastructure, capacity planning for each IT resource takes much time and effort. In AWS cloud computing, you can provision IT services on demand and within few minutes using the AWS self-service portal. You can also use automated scripts to provision a complex infrastructure quickly in different regions and scale it up or down to accommodate demand.

- **Security** You are responsible for the end-to-end security in a traditional on-premises datacenter, where the disconnected security and monitoring tools used by the many teams that manage different infrastructures can make security management difficult. In cloud computing, security tools are interconnected and mostly driven by the developer. The cloud's shared security model can help relieve some of the organization's security responsibilities.

- **Performance** The top cloud computing providers use high-speed networks to provide secure datacenters around the world in different regions and continents. These providers regularly upgrade their infrastructures with the latest generation of fast and efficient hardware and software. This offers great advantages over running your workload on a single corporate datacenter, including reduced latency for applications and global content delivery systems.

Cloud Deployment Models: IaaS, STaaS, PaaS, DaaS, FaaS, SaaS

Cloud deployment models represent a specific, prepackaged stack of various types of services. Figure 1-1 shows the IT resources that are managed by cloud vendors based on their cloud deployment model offerings. The following sections are descriptions of each of the deployment models.

Infrastructure as a Service (IaaS)

IaaS provides virtualized computing resources over the Internet, such as virtual servers with scalable CPU, memory, storage, network, security, and more. With IaaS, customers don't need to manage or control the physical cloud framework; however, customers have full control over the operating systems, storage, and applications they deploy.

On-premise	IaaS	PaaS	STaaS	FaaS	SaaS
Functions	Functions	Functions	Functions	Functions	Functions
Data	Data	Data	Data	Data	Data
Application	Application	Application	Application	Application	Application
Runtime	Runtime	Runtime	Runtime	Runtime	Runtime
Middleware	Middleware	Middleware	Middleware	Middleware	Middleware
Security	Security	Security	Security	Security	Security
Database	Database	Database	Database	Database	Database
Operating System	Operating System	Operating System	Operating System	Operating System	Operating System
Virtualization	Virtualization	Virtualization	Virtualization	Virtualization	Virtualization
Servers	Servers	Servers	Servers	Servers	Servers
Storage	Storage	Storage	Storage	Storage	Storage
Networking	Networking	Networking	Networking	Networking	Networking
Datacenters	Datacenters	Datacenters	Datacenters	Datacenters	Datacenters

Figure 1-1   Cloud deployment models and the IT resources provided

Because the IaaS customer doesn't need its own physical datacenters, it can use IaaS as a fast, disposable, cheap infrastructure that can be expanded or terminated according to business requirements. If you are traditional organization on a tight budget, IaaS is a good choice, because you pay only for the services you use. The most popular cloud platforms that offer IaaS are Amazon Elastic Compute Cloud (Amazon EC2), Azure Virtual Machines, and Google Compute Engine, along with open source alternatives Open-Stack and Apache CloudStack. (For more information, see `https://www.g2.com/categories/infrastructure-as-a-service-iaas`.)

Storage as a Service (STaaS)

With STaaS, a platform such as AWS offers its storage infrastructure (in AWS, it's Amazon Simple Storage Service, or S3) to another organization or individual to store files, objects, and backup data. Organizations and individuals find this very convenient, because they don't need to manage the underlying storage infrastructure, which is highly available. STaaS works through a web-based application programming interface (API) that is remotely implemented through its interaction with the customer's on-premises applications and the provider's cloud storage infrastructure. If the organization ever loses its local data, it can be retrieved from the cloud storage. STaaS could be used as disaster recovery storage for an on-premises application infrastructure. The most popular enterprise-level cloud storage platforms are Amazon S3, Google Cloud Storage, and Microsoft Azure Storage, along with popular open source alternatives ownCloud and Cozy Cloud.

Platform as a Service (PaaS)

PaaS offers tools and services to help customers develop and deploy applications rapidly and efficiently. A PaaS cloud provider hosts and maintains the hardware and software for you. This helps your developers spend more time doing what they do best, developing solutions, rather than spending time installing and managing the hardware and software required to develop or run new applications. PaaS providers manage and control the underlying cloud infrastructure, including network, servers, operating systems, and storage, while cloud consumers control the deployed applications as well as configuration settings for the application-hosting environment. The most popular examples of PaaS platforms are AWS Lambda, AWS Elastic Beanstalk, Google App Engine, and Microsoft Azure App Service, along with open source alternatives such as Red Hat OpenShift, OpenPaaS, and Cloud Foundry.

Data as a Service (DaaS)

DaaS is a more advanced, fine-grained form of SaaS, in which data (as opposed to files) is readily accessible through a cloud-based system. Data in the form of databases or object containers is supplied on demand via cloud platforms. The DaaS cloud vendor provides tools that make it easier to access and explore the data, regardless of the user's geographical location or organizational separation. This offers a number of significant opportunities. DaaS eliminates the single point of failure by providing redundancy and makes the data available for multiple users using different database tools. Popular enterprise-level DaaS database platforms are Amazon DynamoDB, Microsoft Azure Cosmos DB, and

Google Cloud Datastore, along with open source alternatives such as Apache Cassandra, CockroachDB, and Apache CouchDB.

Function as a Service (FaaS)

The idea of running serverless computing is behind FaaS, which means customers don't have to provision or scale their servers. As a developer, you run a piece of business logic or deploy an individual function without worrying about the underlying infrastructure. The function will start executing your business logic within a few milliseconds, and after successful completion, it terminates the infrastructure in the background. The functions are event driven and scalable instantaneously in the background. FaaS completely abstracts the servers away from developers, and customers are billed based on their consumption and number of executions. FaaS is extremely popular among developers and was introduced by hook.io in 2014, followed by AWS Lambda, Google Cloud Functions, and Microsoft Azure Functions, with open source alternatives OpenWhisk and Fn project Functions.

Software as a Service (SaaS)

If you use e-mail, you are using SaaS. The vendor manages everything from the infrastructure side, and access to the applications is provided on a subscription basis, via a web browser, programming interface, or mobile platform. You don't have to install any software with SaaS, and SaaS lets you access software from any device via the Internet, from any place, at any time. Installation, maintenance, security, and compliance are managed by the SaaS provider. The cloud giants AWS, Azure, Google Cloud, and many others offer SaaS services. Popular SaaS products include Google G Suite, Microsoft Office 365, and Slack.

Cloud Services Types: Public, Private, Hybrid, and Community

The cloud has increasingly become a default platform for developers. Cloud computing resources are built to provide abstraction from the management, architecting, and scaling requirements of a core infrastructure. Cloud-native applications are fully deployed on the cloud, and all related application services are running in the cloud.

Four popular cloud service types vary significantly based on how the services are offered and by whom: the public cloud, private cloud, hybrid cloud, and community cloud.

Public Cloud

In the public cloud, resources such as servers, databases, storage, and networking are owned and operated by third-party cloud service vendors and delivered through the Internet. All the hardware, software, and other supporting infrastructure is owned and managed by the cloud vendor. Each customer organization shares the same hardware, storage, and network devices with other customer organizations, or cloud tenants. As a customer, you can access the cloud services and manage your account using a web browser. You don't need to purchase hardware or software, and you pay only for the services you use. Your cloud vendor provides the maintenance and enables you to scale on-demand to meet your business needs. The public clouds are usually built on massive hardware installations distributed in different locations throughout the country or across the globe. Their size enables economies of scale, which allows for maximum scalability to meet company requirements to expand or contract and to meet surges in demand in real time, and provides maximum reliability in case of hardware failures.

Private Cloud

In a private cloud, computing resources are used exclusively by one business or organization. The entire infrastructure is physically located at your organization's on-premises datacenter, or it's hosted by a third-party service provider. In a private cloud, the entire IT infrastructure is maintained within a private network and not shared with anyone. All the hardware and software are dedicated exclusively to your organization. A private cloud makes it easier for an organization to customize its infrastructure resources to meet specific IT and business requirements. Financial institutions, government agencies, and other midsize to large enterprises with business-critical operations use private clouds, which offer full control and security over their infrastructure environment. In a private cloud, the infrastructure sits behind your company firewall, which is accessed only through an intranet via encrypted connections. Private clouds provide enhanced levels of security and privacy since the entire IT infrastructure is dedicated to a single client. Private clouds are more expensive to install, maintain, and operate than public clouds, and organizations are limited to using only the current infrastructure unless they procure, install, and configure a new infrastructure to meet demands.

Community Cloud

A community cloud is similar to a private cloud, but it provides a cloud solution for particular business communities, such as banks or trading companies. The members of the community cloud share similar security, compliance, privacy, and performance requirements. Community cloud members normally own private cloud space that is built to meet the security, privacy, and compliance needs that are common in the community. Organizations involved in financial, health, and legal activities require community clouds that adhere to strict regulatory requirements. The community cloud service provider often combines different types of clouds with different service models to provide businesses with attractive cloud solutions to meet organization requirements.

Hybrid Cloud

The hybrid cloud offers the best of both worlds; it combines on-premises infrastructure with public and community clouds so organizations can reap the advantages of all three. It provides a way to secure sensitive data that remains within the private cloud, where high security standards can be maintained. Applications that do not contain sensitive data or that are not bound by compliance requirements use the public cloud, where infrastructure can be scaled to meet demands at a reduced cost. Hybrid clouds are most suited for running big data operations on nonsensitive data in the public cloud, while keeping sensitive data secured in the private cloud. In a hybrid cloud, it is easy to migrate the data and applications between private and public clouds for greater flexibility and more deployment options.

AWS History

Amazon Web Services (AWS), one of the world's most popular cloud computing platforms, emerged as a side business of Amazon.com in the early 2000s to help developers deal with the burgeoning growth of the company's online presence and to improve the efficiency of Amazon's own infrastructure. The beginnings of AWS as a development tool can be traced back to 2002, when an underlying beta was released that offered SOAP and XML interfaces for the Amazon product inventory database. It provided an amazing platform for developers and was the first step by Amazon in grasping the capability of developer-friendly tools, especially in an infrastructure area, as an actual cloud product.

 NOTE For more on AWS history, see https://www6.software.ibm.com/developerworks/education/ws-aws1/ws-aws1-ltr.pdf.

In 2003, Amazon leadership brainstormed to identify the company's top qualities to differentiate the company from the other similar organizations. One thing was abundantly clear: its infrastructure service—now known as AWS—gave the company an enormous advantage over its competition.

From that point, a more remarkable idea arose to blend an infrastructure framework and development tools to create a pseudo-operating system framework that could be used over the Internet. The infrastructure framework was separated into different components, such as compute, storage, and database, and could be managed using a variety of developer tools. Amazon's first acknowledgment of AWS was in a blog entry of AWS Chief Evangelist Jeff Barr in 2004, alluding to the development of AWS cloud computing.

AWS launched Amazon Simple Storage Service (S3) and Amazon Elastic Compute Cloud (EC2) along with Amazon Simple Queue Service (SQS) on March 19, 2006. Amazon launched S3 and EC2 services in Europe in 2009. Along with the Amazon Elastic Block Store (EBS), the Amazon CloudFront content delivery network (CDN) became part of its formal AWS offerings. These developer-friendly services attracted enterprises such as Dropbox, Netflix, and Reddit along with all the cloud-ready customers in 2010 as early adopters. AWS continued innovating and spreading its footprint, attracting organizations from across the globe.

AWS Regions and Availability Zones

AWS serves more than a million dynamic customers in more than 190 nations. AWS continues to grow worldwide to enable its clients to accomplish lower latency and higher performance, and to guarantee that client data lives only in the AWS region the client designates. AWS helps organizations build their initial infrastructures and continually provides the scalable infrastructure that meets clients' requirements worldwide.

The AWS cloud infrastructure is connected globally and isolated as AWS regions and availability zones (AZs). An AWS region includes numerous AZs, each of which comprises one or more separate datacenters, each with redundant power, networking, and connectivity, and isolated in a separate location. As shown in Figure 1-2, AZs provide the infrastructure that enables organizations to create enterprise applications and databases that are more highly available, fault-tolerant, and scalable than what is possible with single, on-premises customer datacenters. As of June 2020, the AWS cloud covers 76 AZs in 24 geographically separate regions around the globe, with more regions and zones planned on the horizon. Please refer to https://aws.amazon.com/about-aws/global-infrastructure/?p=ngi&loc=0 for the latest information about regions and AZs.

Each Amazon region is totally separate from others, as demonstrated in Figure 1-3. This accomplishes the best options for dependability and to reduce critical failure issues. Although every AZ is segregated, AZs within a region are associated through low-latency links. This enables AWS to provide the flexibility for organizations to create instances and store data inside different geographic regions as well as over numerous AZs within a particular AWS region. Each AWS AZs are designed to prevent independent failure, which reduces the potential risk of a single point of failure.

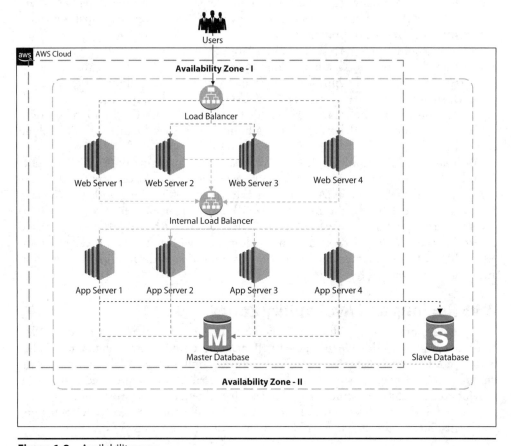

Figure 1-2 Availability zone

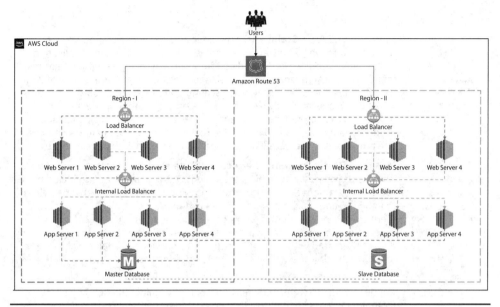

Figure 1-3 Availability zones within an AWS region can be associated with low-latency links

AWS Services

AWS offers a variety of global cloud-based products, as shown in the following table, that provide for compute, database, storage, networking, security, management tools, mobile, developer tools, analytics, and Internet of Things (IoT). Millions of customers, from large enterprises, to fast-growing startups, to leading government agencies, trust AWS to host their workloads and help them become more agile. AWS services help organizations to move to the cloud more quickly, at lower IT costs and scale.

	Description
Amazon EC2	**Amazon Elastic Compute Cloud (EC2)** is a secure and resizable virtual server provisioned in the cloud. It makes web-scale cloud computing simpler for developers. EC2 comes with a capacity called instance types, which comprises combinations of CPU, memory, storage, and networking that enable developers to choose the appropriate mix of resources to suit application needs. It also comes with different OS distributions, including Amazon Machine Images (AMI) products provided by vendors in the AWS Marketplace. EC2 is reliable, providing 99.99 percent availability for each Amazon region. AWS takes care of the physical infrastructure and provides tools to secure EC2 instances on the client side, such as Amazon Virtual Private Cloud (VPC), security groups, network access control lists (NACLs), and numerous other security services to manage and monitor EC2 instances.

	Description
Amazon EC2 Auto Scaling	**Amazon EC2 Auto Scaling** uses dynamic and predictive scaling features to add or remove EC2 instances automatically, and it maintains application availability based on predefined conditions. The fleet management features of EC2 Auto Scaling enable you to manage the health and availability of your EC2 fleet instances. It uses dynamic scaling and predictive scaling to scale up or down automatically to provide the correct number of EC2 instances to meet actual or predicted demand. EC2 instances can be scaled faster by using dynamic scaling and predictive scaling together. Unhealthy instances are automatically detected, terminated, and replaced with new instances.
Amazon Elastic Container Service	**Amazon Elastic Container Service (ECS)** is a container orchestration service that helps you easily build all types of containerized applications, including Docker containers, ranging from long-running applications, to microservices, batch jobs, and machine-learning applications. The granular access permissions in AWS Identity and Access Management (IAM) restrict access to each service and define what resources can be accessed by a container. ECS is integrated with other AWS services to provide a complete solution for building a wide variety of containerized applications.
Amazon EC2 Container Registry	**Amazon Elastic Container Registry (ECR)** is a managed service offering for developers to store, manage, and deploy container images. ECR hosts container images so that developers can deploy containers reliably in a highly available and scalable architecture. It is encrypted both at rest and in transit using HTTPS. ECR is integrated with Amazon ECS, which pulls container images into production from ECR. You pay only for the amount of data stored in the repository and for data transfers, with no commitment or upfront fees.
AWS Elastic Beanstalk	**AWS Elastic Beanstalk** enables developers to deploy and scale web applications and services on servers such as Apache, Nginx, and IIS. Web applications and services can be developed using Java, .NET, PHP, Node. js, Python, Ruby, Go, and Docker. Capacity provisioning, load balancing, auto-scaling, and application health monitoring are automatically managed by Elastic Beanstalk, enabling developers to upload code from the AWS Management Console, a GitHub repository, or an integrated development environment (IDE) such as Eclipse or Visual Studio. It frees developers from having to manage and configure servers, patches, databases, load balancers, firewalls, and network provisioning. You only pay for the resources needed to store and run your applications.
AWS Lambda	**AWS Lambda** lets you run code for virtually any type of application or backend service with zero administration. Simply upload your code, and Lambda takes care of everything required to run and scale it with high availability. Lambda can also trigger code automatically from other AWS services, or call it directly from any web or mobile app. You are charged based on the number of requests and the duration and the number of times your code is executed; you pay nothing when your code is not running.
Elastic Load Balancing	**Elastic Load Balancing (ELB)** handles all the incoming application traffic across multiple EC2 instances, Lambda functions, containers, and IP addresses. It supports traffic from a single AZ or across multiple zones. ELB offers three types of load balancers—Application Load Balancer, Network Load Balancer, and Classic Load Balancer—that offer features to make your applications fault-tolerant.

Description

Amazon Elastic
Container Service
for Kubernetes

Amazon Elastic Container Service for Kubernetes (Amazon EKS) is used to deploy, manage, and scale containerized applications using Kubernetes. It runs across multiple AWS AZs to eliminate a single point of failure. Any applications that are running on any standard Kubernetes environment can easily be migrated to Amazon EKS.

Amazon Lightsail

Amazon Lightsail provides a simple way to get started with AWS for developers, students, and small businesses that requires a simple virtual private server (VPS) solution. With Lightsail, developers can deploy and manage websites and web applications in the cloud. It has everything a developer needs to launch a project quickly, including a virtual machine, Domain Name System (DNS) management, a static IP, and solid-state drive (SSD)–based storage, for a predictable monthly price.

AWS Batch

AWS Batch enables developers, engineers, and scientists to run thousands of batch jobs on AWS. It dynamically provisions compute resources based on the volume and specific resource requirements. AWS Batch plans, schedules, and executes your batch workloads using Amazon EC2 and EC2 Spot Instances. It is free to use, but you must pay for the AWS resources you create to store and run your batch jobs.

AWS Fargate

AWS Fargate lets you to run containers without having to manage servers or clusters or provision, configure, and scale clusters to run containers. You don't need to choose server types, decide when to scale your clusters, or optimize cluster packing. Developers can focus on designing and building the applications instead of managing the infrastructure that runs them.

AWS Outposts

AWS Outposts brings native AWS services to your on-premises datacenter. Use the same tools on on-premises systems and the cloud to deliver a consistent hybrid experience. AWS Outposts supports workloads that need to remain on-premises due to low latency or compliance requirements. Developers can develop once and deploy code in the AWS cloud or on-premises without rewriting it.

AWS Serverless
Application
Repository

AWS Serverless Application Repository provides a managed repository for serverless applications to enable individual developers, teams, and organizations to store and share reusable applications. It removes the need to clone, build, package, or publish source code to AWS. Use prebuilt applications to reduce duplicated work and get to market faster. To share any application you've built, you can publish it to the AWS Serverless Application Repository.

Vmware Cloud
on AWS

VMware Cloud on AWS provides a highly scalable and secure service for organizations to migrate and extend their on-premises VMware vSphere–based environments to the AWS cloud using the EC2 bare metal infrastructure. It is ideal for enterprise IT infrastructure and operations organizations looking to migrate their on-premises vSphere-based workloads to the AWS cloud and modernize their disaster recovery solutions.

Amazon Simple
Storage Service
(S3)

Amazon Simple Storage Service (S3) is a highly available and secure object storage service. Organizations store data for a variety use cases, ranging from applications to IoT, to data lakes, analytics, and backup and disaster recovery. Amazon S3 offers 99.999999999 percent durability to protect data from zone-level failures, data corruption errors, and threats, so it is available at all times. Its finely tuned access policies for sensitive data restrict access requests to your S3 data and offer different encryption options for data in transit and data at rest.

	Description
Amazon Elastic Block Store (EBS)	**Amazon Elastic Block Store (EBS)** offers block storage to use with EC2 instances, and it's replicated automatically within its AZ to protect against failure. Amazon EBS volumes offer low latency and consistent performance needed to run your workloads. It is designed for application workloads including big data analytics engines, relational and NoSQL databases, stream and log processing applications, and data warehousing applications.
Amazon S3 Glacier	**Amazon S3 Glacier** is an extremely low-cost cloud archival storage service for long-term backup. It is designed for 99.999999999 percent durability to meet the most stringent regulatory requirements. It also provides a query-in-place function to run powerful analytics directly on your archival storage at rest. S3 Glacier provides three options to retrieve data depending on your needs, ranging from a few minutes to several hours.
Amazon Elastic File System	**Amazon Elastic File System (EFS)** offers elastic file system scalability for Linux-based workloads for use with on-premises resources and AWS cloud services. It can scale on demand to petabytes by growing and shrinking automatically as you add and remove files. It provides shared access to thousands of EC2 instances. EFS is a managed service that does not require any changes to your existing applications and tools.
AWS Snowball	**AWS Snowball** is a petabyte-scale data transfer service built as a secure, suitcase-sized device that enables you to move data in and out of the AWS cloud quickly from the AWS Management Console. The device is shipped to a designated site to store data. When data has been transferred, the device is shipped back to AWS, and the data is moved to your S3 bucket. Normally, it takes about a week from start to finish. Snowball can ship terabytes or petabytes of analytics data, video libraries, image repositories, health care, and life sciences data.
AWS Snowball Edge	**AWS Snowball Edge** devices offer petabyte-scale data transfer service along with a computing platform that helps you perform simple processing tasks. Devices can be clustered together or rack shelved to ease the collection and storage of data. These devices are in intermittent connectivity environments, such as manufacturing, transportation, and industrial environments, or in remote locations such as military or maritime operations. Snowball Edge delivers serverless computing using AWS IoT Greengrass and AWS Lambda functions. Common use cases include on-the-fly media transcoding, image compression, capturing IoT sensor streams, and industrial control signaling and metrics aggregation.
AWS Snowmobile	**AWS Snowmobile** can store up to 100PB of data and is ideal for exabyte-scale migrations and datacenter shutdowns. A Snowmobile—a 45-foot-long shipping container—is sent to the customer's datacenter; after data is transferred, it is driven to an AWS region, where the data is loaded into Amazon S3. The Snowmobile is waterproof, temperature controlled, tamper-resistant, and fire-safe. It has dedicated security personnel and offers physical security measures, including encryption, alarm monitoring, GPS tracking, 24/7 video surveillance, and an escort security vehicle during transit.

	Description
AWS Storage Gateway	**AWS Storage Gateway** offers hybrid storage by enabling on-premises applications to use AWS cloud storage. Common use cases include cloud data processing, migration, backup and archiving, storage tiering, and disaster recovery. It uses standard storage protocols such as Network File System (NFS), Server Message Block (SMB), and Internet Small Computer Systems Interface iSCSI. The gateway connects to other AWS storage services such as S3, S3 Glacier Deep Archive, EBS, S3 Glacier, and AWS Backup. The service has a highly optimized data transfer mechanism, a local cache for low-latency on-premises access, and automated network resilience.
AWS Backup	**AWS Backup** is a managed backup service used to centralize and automate data backup from on-premises datacenters using the AWS Storage Gateway and across AWS services. You can centrally configure backup policies and monitor backup activity for Amazon EBS, Amazon Relational Database Service (RDS), Amazon DynamoDB, EFS, and AWS Storage Gateway. It also automates and consolidates backup tasks performed service-by-service and removes the need to create custom scripts and manual processes. Create backup policies to automate backup schedules and retention management. AWS Backup provides a managed, policy-based backup solution, simplifying backup management and enabling you to meet your business and regulatory backup compliance requirements.
Amazon FSx for Lustre	**Amazon FSx for Lustre** offers a high-performance file system optimized for fast processing of workloads such as machine learning, video processing, financial modeling, high performance computing, and electronic design automation. These workloads are sent via a fast and scalable file system interface and are stored on S3. It enables you to run a file system in sub-milliseconds to your data with read and write capability up to hundreds of gigabytes per second of throughput and millions of IOPS (input/output operations per second).
Amazon FSx for Windows File Server	**Amazon FSx for Windows File Server** offers a managed native Microsoft Windows file system to move Windows-based applications. Amazon FSx provides compatibility and features for Windows-based applications, and it supports Active Directory integration, the SMB protocol, Distributed File System (DFS), and Windows NTFS. It uses SSD storage to provide fast performance with consistent sub-millisecond latencies and high levels of throughput and IOPS.
Amazon RDS	**Amazon Relational Database Service (RDS)** provides cost-efficient and resizable capacity and automates patching and backups. RDS is optimized for memory, I/O, and performance with popular database engines including Amazon Aurora, PostgreSQL, MySQL, MariaDB, Oracle Database, and SQL Server.
Amazon Aurora	**Amazon Aurora** is a MySQL- and PostgreSQL-compatible relational database built with enterprise-level performance and availability with open source cost-effectiveness. Aurora is five times faster than MySQL and three times faster than PostgreSQL. This distributed, self-healing storage system is fault-tolerant and auto-scales up to 64TB per database, delivering high performance and availability with replication across three AZs.

	Description
 Amazon DynamoDB	**Amazon DynamoDB** is a fully managed, key-value and document database with built-in security, single-digit millisecond performance, backup and restore, and in-memory caching. It can handle more than 10 trillion requests per day and supports peaks of more than 20 million requests per second. Many fast-growing businesses such as Lyft, Airbnb, and Redfin and enterprises such as Samsung, Toyota, and Capital One use DynamoDB for their mission-critical workloads.
 Amazon DocumentDB	**Amazon DocumentDB** is a fully managed document database service that supports MongoDB workloads and is used to store, manage, and retrieve semi-structured data. It is designed from the ground up to provide performance, scalability, and availability for mission-critical workloads. It uses a distributed, self-healing, fault-tolerant storage system that auto-scales up to 64TB per database cluster and replicates six copies of your data across three AWS AZs, with 99.99 percent availability.
 Amazon Redshift	**Amazon Redshift** makes it easy to analyze all your data across your data warehouse and data lake. It delivers faster performance by using massively parallel query execution, and by using machine learning and columnar storage on high-performance disks. You can deploy a data warehouse in minutes and run queries across petabytes of data in Redshift and exabytes of data in a data lake built on Amazon S3.
 Amazon ElastiCache	**Amazon ElastiCache** is a managed, Redis- and Memcached-compatible, in-memory data store for data-intensive apps. It also improves the performance of your existing apps. It is a popular choice for health care, gaming, financial services, advertising technology (ad tech), and IoT apps.
 Amazon Neptune	**Amazon Neptune** is a managed graph database service used to store billions of relationships. You can query the graph with milliseconds of latency. It powers graph use cases such as knowledge graphs, recommendation engines, drug discovery, fraud detection, and network security. It offers high availability, point-in-time recovery, and continuous backup to Amazon S3, with read replicas and replication across AZs. Neptune is secure with HTTPS-encrypted connections and encryption at rest.
 Amazon VPC	**Amazon Virtual Private Cloud (VPC)** is a logically isolated section in a cloud network that you define and where you can launch AWS resources. You have complete control over your virtual environment, including selecting your IP address range, configuration of route tables and network gateways, and creation of subnets. IPv4 and IPv6 can be used in your VPC to secure access to your applications. You can place backend systems, such as databases or application servers, in a private-facing subnet with no Internet access, and you can create a public-facing subnet for your web server that has access to the Internet.
 AWS VPN	**AWS Virtual Private Network (AWS VPN)** enables you to create a secure tunnel from your network to the AWS global network. AWS Site-to-Site VPN uses private sessions with IP Security (IPSec) and Transport Layer Security (TLS) tunnels to connect your on-premises network to your Amazon VPC. With AWS Client VPN, you can connect users to AWS or on-premises networks. To deliver uninterrupted access to cloud resources, AWS VPN provides two tunnels across multiple AZs. Primary traffic is streamed through the first tunnel, and the second tunnel used for redundancy.

	Description
AWS Direct Connect	**AWS Direct Connect** is a dedicated network connection from your on-premises datacenter to AWS. It uses private connectivity between AWS and your datacenter, which reduces your network costs, provides a more consistent network experience, and increases bandwidth throughput. AWS Direct Connect uses industry standard 802.1q VLANs and is further partitioned into multiple virtual interfaces. This enables you to access public resources such as Amazon S3 and private resources such as Amazon EC2 instances running within a VPC.
AWS Transit Gateway	**AWS Transit Gateway** enables you to connect your Amazon VPCs and on-premises networks to a single gateway. You create and manage a single connection from the central gateway into each Amazon VPC and on-premises data center. It acts as a hub that controls how traffic is routed among all the connected spokes. The hub-and-spoke model reduces operational costs and simplifies management. When you create a new VPC, it is connected to the Transit Gateway and is automatically ready to connect to very other network connected to the Transit Gateway.
Amazon Route 53	**Amazon Route 53** is a cloud DNS that provides a cost-effective way to route end users to Internet applications by translating names such as www.amazon.com into numeric IP addresses such as 197.180.4.2. It's fully compliant with IPv6. Route 53 is used to manage traffic globally through a variety of routing types, such as latency-based routing, Geo DNS, and Weighted Round Robin, which can be combined with DNS Failover to provide low-latency, fault-tolerant architectures. You can configure DNS health checks to route traffic to healthy endpoints or monitor application health. Use a simple visual editor to manage how end users are routed to application endpoints, whether they are in a single AWS region or distributed around the world. If you use domain name registration to purchase domain names, Route 53 will automatically configure the domains' DNS settings.
Amazon CloudFront	**Amazon CloudFront** is a fast CDN that securely delivers data and information to customers globally, with high transfer speeds and low latency. It works with services such as Amazon EC2 as origins for your applications, AWS Shield for Distributed Denial of Service (DDoS) mitigation, and Lambda@Edge to run custom code closer to a customer's users. You can use familiar tools, such as AWS CloudFormation, CLIs, SDKs, APIs, and the AWS Management Console to get started with the CDN within minutes.
Amazon API Gateway	**Amazon API Gateway** is a scalable managed service that lets you create, maintain, monitor, publish, and secure APIs. It handles all the tasks necessary to process and accept up to thousands of concurrent API calls, including monitoring, API version management, traffic management, and more. You pay only for the API calls you receive and the amount of data transferred out, with no minimum fees or startup costs.
AWS Identity and Access Management (IAM)	**AWS Identity and Access Management (IAM)** enables you to create and manage AWS users and groups to allow or deny access to AWS resources. This free AWS feature enables users to control access to AWS service APIs and to specific resources. You can also add specific conditions to control how a user can use AWS, the user's originating IP address, whether the user is using SSL, whether the user has authenticated with a multi-factor authentication device, and more.

	Description
 AWS CloudHSM	**AWS CloudHSM** enables you to generate and use your own encryption keys on the AWS cloud. FIPS 140-2 Level 3 validated hardware security modules (HSMs) are used to manage your own encryption keys. This cloud-based HSM offers you the flexibility to integrate with your applications using APIs such as Java Cryptography Extensions, Microsoft CryptoNG, and PKCS#11 libraries. It also enables you to export all of your keys to other commercially available HSMs and automates hardware provisioning, high availability, backups, and software patching. You can add and remove HSM capacity as needed, with no upfront costs.
 AWS Key Management Service	**AWS Key Management Service (KMS)** is used to create, manage, and control encryption keys. It uses FIPS 140-2 validated hardware security modules to protect your keys. Along with AWS CloudTrail, KMS provides logs of key usage to meet compliance and regulatory needs. Use KMS-protected data encryption keys to encrypt local applications and build encryption into your applications.
 Amazon Cognito	**Amazon Cognito** enables you to administer user sign-in and sign-up with social identity providers, such as Amazon, Facebook, and Google, via Security Assertion Markup Language (SAML) 2.0. It is HIPAA-eligible and complies with PCI DSS, ISO/IEC 27017, ISO/IEC 27018, SOC, ISO/IEC 27001, and ISO 9001. Cognito supports multifactor authentication and encryption of data at rest and in transit, and it supports IAM standards, such as SAML 2.0, OAuth 2.0, and OpenID Connect.
 Amazon GuardDuty	**Amazon GuardDuty** is a threat detection service that monitors for unauthorized behavior and malicious activity to protect your AWS accounts. Continuously collecting, aggregating, and analyzing log data are time-consuming activities for security teams and GuardDuty provides an intelligent and cost-effective option for continuous threat detection. It uses integrated threat intelligence, machine learning, and anomaly detection to identify and prioritize potential threats. It analyzes thousands of billions of events across multiple AWS data sources, such as Amazon VPC flow logs, AWS CloudTrail, and DNS logs. There is no software or hardware to deploy or maintain.
 Amazon Inspector	**Amazon Inspector** is an automated security assessment service that improves application security and compliance. It looks for vulnerabilities, deviation, and exposure based on best practices and produces a detailed list of security findings. It can be used to check for vulnerabilities or to look for any unintended network accessibility of your EC2 instances.
 AWS Shield	**AWS Shield** is a managed DDoS service that safeguards applications running on AWS. Its automatic inline mitigations and always-on detection minimize application downtime and latency. You can benefit from AWS Shield Standard at no additional charge. Shield Standard defends against most transport- and network-layer DDoS attacks against your applications or web site. When AWS Shield Standard is used with Amazon CloudFront and Amazon Route 53 you get comprehensive availability protection against all known infrastructure (layer 3 and 4) attacks.

	Description
AWS WAF	**AWS WAF** is a web application firewall that protects your web applications from common exploits, such as SQL injection and cross-site scripting, that could impact application availability, consume excessive resources, or compromise your security. It lets you control which traffic to block or allow to your web applications via customized web security rules that you create. New rules can be deployed within minutes when you need to respond quickly to changing traffic patterns. Use the WAF API to create, deploy, and maintain web security rules. Pricing is based on how many rules are deployed and how many requests are received, with no upfront commitments. WAF can be deployed on Amazon CloudFront, on your application load balancer or origin servers running on EC2, or on the Amazon API Gateway for your APIs.
AWS Security Hub	**AWS Security Hub** enables you to continuously monitor your compliance status and high-priority security alerts across your AWS accounts. Its powerful security tools include vulnerability and compliance scanners, firewalls, and endpoint protection. Use it to organize, aggregate, and prioritize your findings or security alerts from multiple AWS services, such as Amazon Inspector, Amazon GuardDuty, and Amazon Macie. Dashboards display findings with actionable graphs and tables. Its automated compliance checks are based on the AWS best practices and industry standards.
AWS Organizations	**AWS Organizations** enable you to govern your environment, control access and compliance, manage billing and security, and share resources across your AWS accounts. Centrally automate creation of accounts and groups of accounts and apply governance policies for them. Simplify billing by setting up a single payment method for all of your AWS accounts. The service is free for all AWS customers.
Amazon CloudWatch	**Amazon CloudWatch** is a monitoring service that offers actionable insights to help you understand and respond to performance changes, optimize resource utilization, and monitor and optimize your applications and ensure they are running smoothly. CloudWatch collects data using metrics, logs, and events, to provide a unified view of applications and services that run on AWS and on-premises servers. Use it to set high-resolution alarms, take automated actions, troubleshoot issues, and visualize logs and metrics such as memory and CPU utilization. You pay for what you use, with no upfront commitment or minimum fee.
AWS Management Console	**AWS Management Console** is a web-based portal where you can manage your AWS account, including setting up new IAM users, managing security credentials, monitoring monthly spending, and viewing and managing existing resources. Use the search functionality to locate and navigate available services, to select from recently visited services, or to create a list of all services. Personalize the Management Console by creating shortcuts to often visited services.
AWS CloudTrail	**AWS CloudTrail** offers operational auditing, compliance, governance, and risk auditing of your AWS account. You can continuously and automatically monitor, log, and retain account activity, and track and respond to unusual activity by defining workflows that are executed when security vulnerabilities and events are detected. CloudTrail provides an event history that includes actions taken through the AWS SDKs, command-line tools, and the AWS Management Console.

	Description
 AWS Config	**AWS Config** enables you to audit, assess, and evaluate your AWS resource configurations. It continuously records and monitors configurations and evaluates them against the configurations specified in your internal guidelines. You can review changes in configurations and configuration histories to determine your overall compliance to these guidelines. This simplifies security analysis, change management, compliance auditing, and operational troubleshooting. If a configuration change is detected, the Amazon Simple Notification Service (SNS) will notify you to review the change and take action if necessary.
 AWS CloudFormation	**AWS CloudFormation** provides infrastructure as code, which provisions all the infrastructure resources by using a simple text file to model and provision the resources across all regions and accounts automatically. This cloud formation template serves as the single source of truth and is available at no additional charge. It enables you to build and rebuild your infrastructure and applications, without requiring you to perform any manual actions. CloudFormation rolls back changes automatically if errors are detected during provisioning.
 AWS OpsWorks	**AWS OpsWorks** is a configuration management service that eliminates the need to operate your own configuration management systems and lets you use Chef and Puppet to automate how servers are configured, deployed, and managed across your environments. Chef Automate, Puppet Enterprise, and AWS OpsWorks Stacks are three offerings. OpsWorks maintains your Chef server by automatically updating, patching, and backing up your server. It gives access to all of the Chef Automate features including existing Chef cookbooks, Chef console, and command-line tools such as Knife.
 AWS Personal Health Dashboard	**AWS Personal Health Dashboard** displays the general status, alerts, proactive notification, and remediation guidance of the performance and availability of your AWS services. Alerts are triggered based on the health of AWS resources, to provide event visibility and guidance to help you quickly diagnose and resolve issues. You can set up timely alerts from multiple channels, including e-mail and mobile notifications, to help you plan for and deal with issues associated with upcoming changes.
 AWS Service Catalog	**AWS Service Catalog** enables you to create and manage IT services catalogs, including virtual machine images, software, databases, and servers, to complete multitier application architectures. It helps you achieve consistent governance and meet compliance requirements, while enabling you to deploy only the approved IT services that users need. You can define a catalog of AWS services to make them available for your end users to discover and deploy IT services quickly using a self-service portal.
 AWS Systems Manager	**AWS Systems Manager** provides the visibility to help you control and automate operational tasks across your AWS infrastructure. Group resources by application, view operational data for monitoring and troubleshooting, and take action quickly to resolve operational problems. Systems Manager offers a single interface that makes it easy to operate and manage your infrastructure securely at scale, providing automated maintenance and deployment tasks on Amazon EC2 and on-premises instances. You can apply configuration changes across any resource group and automatically apply patches and updates. Built-in safety controls enable you to roll out new changes incrementally, and when errors occur, they can be set up to halt a change roll-out automatically. Systems Manager also maintains security and compliance by scanning instances against your configuration, patch, and custom policies. You can maintain up-to-date antivirus definitions, define patch baselines, and enforce firewall policies without manually logging in to each server.

Description

AWS Trusted Advisor is an online tool that provides real-time guidance to help you optimize your entire AWS infrastructure, reduce your overall costs, increase security and performance, and monitor service limits. Use the provided alerts and recommendations to optimize your AWS solutions as part of ongoing improvement or new application development, and to establish new workflows. Integrate with CloudWatch to stay up to date with your AWS resource deployment, with weekly updates.

AWS Trusted Advisor

AWS Database Migration Service helps you speed up your databases migration securely. During migration, the source database remains fully operational with minimal downtime to applications that use the database. You can migrate your data to and from most open source and commercial databases. The service supports both homogeneous and heterogeneous migrations, such as Oracle-to-Oracle and Oracle-to-Amazon Aurora. It lets you continuously replicate your data and consolidate databases into a petabyte-scale data warehouse by streaming data to Amazon S3 and Amazon Redshift.

AWS Database Migration Service

Amazon Simple Queue Service (SQS) is a managed message queuing service that helps you decouple and scale distributed systems, microservices, and serverless applications. SQS makes it easier to operate and manage message-oriented middleware. You can send, receive, and store messages at any volume, without requiring other services to be available and without losing messages. Standard queues offer maximum throughput and at-least-once delivery, and FIFO queues are designed to ensure that messages are sent in the correct order and are processed exactly once.

Amazon Simple Queue Service

Amazon Simple Notification Service (SNS) is a secure, highly available, and durable fully managed pub/sub messaging service that enables you to decouple distributed systems, microservices, and serverless applications. It provides for push-based, many-to-many, and high-throughput messaging and can be used to fan out messages to subscriber endpoints for parallel processing, including AWS Lambda functions, HTTP/S webhooks, and Amazon SQS queues, in addition to using mobile push, e-mail, and SMS. SNS supports compliance programs, such as HIPAA, FIPS, SOC, PCI, ISO, and FedRAMP.

Amazon Simple Notification Service

AWS CodeBuild is a continuous integration service that compiles source code, runs tests, and produces software packages that are deployment ready. CodeBuild scales continuously and processes multiple builds concurrently. It offers prepackaged build environments, or you can create your own custom environments. AWS enables you to create complete, automated software release workflows for continuous integration and delivery (CI/CD). Integrate CodeBuild with your existing CI/CD workflow. It provides encryptions for your build artifacts, with keys managed by the AWS Key Management Service (KMS). User-specific permissions are managed by AWS IAM to control project access.

AWS CodeBuild

AWS CodeCommit is a managed source control service that hosts secure Git-based repositories and helps teams collaborate on code in a secure and highly scalable ecosystem. It eliminates the operational overhead of managing your own source control system and lets you securely store anything from source code to binaries. It automatically encrypts your files in transit and at rest and is integrated with AWS IAM to help you control access to your repositories. It works seamlessly with your existing Git tools and supports all Git commands.

AWS CodeCommit

	Description
AWS CodePipeline	**AWS CodePipeline** is a continuous delivery service that helps you automate the build, test, and deploy phases of your release process with every code change based on your release model. It can be easily integrated with third-party services such as GitHub. You can model the stages of your release process using the AWS CLI, AWS CloudFormation, the console interface, or AWS SDKs, and use prebuilt or custom plug-ins during the release process. With CodePipeline, you can test each code change and catch bugs while they are small and easily fixed. Verify the quality of your application or infrastructure code by running each change through your staging and release process. You pay only for what you use, with no upfront fees or long-term commitments.
AWS CodeDeploy	**AWS CodeDeploy** is a deployment service that helps you automate software deployments to a variety of services, including AWS Lambda, AWS Fargate, Amazon EC2, and on-premises servers. It helps you handle the complexity of updating your applications, rapidly release new features, and avoid downtime during application deployment. It frees you from error-prone manual operations by automating software deployments, so you can deploy reliably and rapidly. You can consistently deploy across environments and track the status of your deployments through the AWS Management Console or the AWS CLI. Reports provide an overview of when and to where each application was deployed, and you can choose to receive live updates about deployments.
AWS Budgets	**AWS Budgets** enables you to set up custom budgets that alert you when your costs or usage exceeds your budget. If you set up coverage targets, you can be alerted when your utilization drops below the threshold. Alerts are supported for Amazon RDS, Amazon Redshift, Amazon EC2, and Amazon ElastiCache. Create and track budgets at a yearly, quarterly, or monthly level, or use customized start and end dates. In addition, you can further refine cost tracking associated with a linked account, tag, or other AWS service.
AWS Cost Explorer	**AWS Cost Explorer** helps you visualize, understand, and manage your AWS costs and usage over time. Create custom reports as charts and tabular data to analyze cost and data usage and track usage across all accounts at a high level or at a highly granular instance level. Dive deeper to identify trends, detect anomalies, and pinpoint cost drivers. Set a custom time period to view your data at a daily level and filter and group functionality using a variety of dimensions.
Amazon EMR	**Amazon EMR** is a managed Hadoop framework for processing data across Amazon EC2 instances. It can interact with data in other AWS data stores, such as Amazon S3 and Amazon DynamoDB, and you can also run frameworks such as Apache HBase, Spark, and Flink in EMR. Launch a serverless Jupyter notebook to enable teams to collaborate and interactively explore process and data. EMR can securely handle many big data use cases, such as data transformations, machine learning, financial analysis, scientific simulation, log analysis, and more. It automatically configures EC2 firewall settings to control network access to instances and launches clusters in an Amazon VPC, a custom designed, logically isolated network.
Amazon Kinesis	**Amazon Kinesis** helps you process streaming data in real time to react quickly to new information. It helps you cost-effectively process streaming data by ingesting real-time data, including audio, application logs, website click streams, video, and IoT telemetry data for machine learning and analytics. Use it to process, analyze, and respond to data as it arrives, instead of storing it to a data warehouse database and waiting to begin the analysis process.

	Description
 AWS Glue	**AWS Glue** is a managed extract, transform, and load (ETL) service that you can create from the AWS Management Console. Then simply point Glue to your target data on AWS, where it discovers your data and stores the metadata in the Data Catalog. Data is immediately queryable, searchable, and available for ETL. This serverless service has no infrastructure to provision or manage. It handles the provisioning, configuration, and scaling of resources required to run your ETL jobs. It natively supports data stored in Aurora, RDS databases, S3, and Redshift, as well as database engines and databases in your VPC running on EC2. You pay only for the resources used while your jobs are running.
 Amazon Athena	**Amazon Athena** is a query service for analyzing data in Amazon S3 using ASCI SQL. Because it is serverless, no infrastructure management is required. Simply point to your data in S3, define the schema, and then start querying using SQL. Results are delivered within seconds and can be easily analyzed by anyone with SQL skills. Athena is integrated with the AWS Glue Data Catalog, which you can use to create metadata repository across various services. Populate the Data Catalog with modified and new tables. Use crawl data sources to discover schemas. Use Athena in conjunction with Glue to transform data into columnar formats to optimize cost and improve performance. You pay only for the queries that you run.
 Amazon Elasticsearch Service	**Amazon Elasticsearch Service** supports open-source Elasticsearch APIs, managed Kibana, and integrations with Logstash and other AWS services, enabling you to ingest data securely from any source and search, analyze, and visualize it in real time. It integrates with other AWS services such as AWS IoT, Amazon CloudWatch Logs for data ingestion, Amazon Kinesis Data Firehose, Amazon VPC, AWS KMS, AWS CloudTrail for auditing, AWS IAM for security, and Amazon Cognito. Encrypt data at rest and in-transit with keys you create and control through KMS, achieve network isolation with Amazon VPC, and manage authentication and access control with Amazon Cognito and AWS IAM policies. The service is HIPAA-eligible and compliant with ISO standards and PCI DSS regulations. You pay only for what you use, and there are no upfront costs or usage requirements.
 Amazon QuickSight	**Amazon QuickSight** lets you easily create and publish interactive, accessible dashboards that include machine learning insights. This serverless service scales automatically to tens of thousands of users, without requiring additional infrastructure or capacity planning. It easily integrates with your cloud and on-premises data sources, including native integration to AWS services such as S3, Athena, Aurora, RDS, IAM, Redshift, CloudTrail, and Cloud Directory by providing all you need to build an end-to-end business intelligence (BI) solution. With the Pay-per-Session pricing model, you can give everyone access to the data they need, and pay only for what you use.
 Alexa for Business	**Alexa for Business** enables organizations and employees to use the intelligent assistant to improve productivity at their desks, in meeting rooms, and even with the Alexa devices they have at home. The service helps IT administrators easily provision multiple Alexa devices at the same time and monitor device usage and status. CloudWatch alarms can alert personnel when devices are unplugged from a centralized console.

	Description
Amazon AppStream 2.0	**Amazon AppStream 2.0** is an application streaming service that lets you centrally manage your desktop applications and securely deliver them to any computer or to the cloud. You can easily scale to any number of users across the globe. AppStream is built with a network architecture that's designed for the most security-sensitive organizations. Each user can access applications with ease, because your applications run on virtual machines optimized to adjust automatically to network conditions. Software vendors can use AppStream 2.0 to deliver application demos, training, and trials, with no downloads or installations required.
Amazon WorkSpaces	**Amazon WorkSpaces** is a managed desktop solution that can be quickly provisioned and scaled to provide Windows or Linux desktops to workers across the globe. WorkSpaces helps you eliminate complexity in managing OS versions and patches and hardware inventory. It also eliminates the need to over-buy desktop and laptop resources by providing on-demand user access to cloud-based desktops. Users can access the desktop anywhere, anytime, from any supported device; data is stored in the cloud and not on the device. WorkSpaces is deployed within a VPC and uses encrypted storage volumes in the AWS cloud. It is integrated with AWS KMS. You pay either monthly or hourly for the service.
Amazon SageMaker	**Amazon SageMaker** offers developers and data scientist the ability to build, train, and deploy machine learning models. It covers the entire machine learning workflow to label and prepare your data, choose an algorithm, train the model, tune and optimize it for deployment, make predictions, and take action to train once, run anywhere by using the model optimization. Your models get to production faster with much less effort and lower cost with training and prebuilt notebooks for common problems.
AWS IoT Core	**AWS IoT Core** helps you connect and interact securely with cloud applications and devices. It can support billions of devices and trillions of messages with a lightweight communication protocol specifically designed to tolerate intermittent connections and reduce network bandwidth requirements, while minimizing the code footprint on devices. AWS IoT Core supports HTTP, WebSockets, and MQTT and makes it easy to use AWS services such as S3, SageMaker, DynamoDB, CloudWatch, CloudTrail, Lambda, Kinesis and QuickSight to build IoT applications that gather, process, analyze, and act without your having to manage any infrastructure. Your applications can keep track of and communicate with all your devices, all the time, even when they aren't connected and even if they are using different protocols.
AWS IoT Greengrass	**AWS IoT Greengrass** extends AWS to edge devices so they can locally execute predictions based on machine learning models, keep device data in sync, run AWS Lambda functions, and communicate with other devices securely, even when they're not connected to the Internet. It uses familiar languages to create, test, and deploy device software and filters device data, transmitting only necessary information back to the cloud. Connected devices operate even with intermittent connectivity to the cloud. Greengrass synchronizes data on the device with AWS IoT Core when it reconnects. Devices act on data locally to respond to local events, while also using the AWS cloud for management, analytics, and durable storage. You can develop code in the cloud and then deploy it seamlessly to your devices with AWS Lambda, and execute functions locally eliminating the complexity of developing embedded software.

	Description
 AWS IoT 1-Click	**AWS IoT 1-Click** empowers services to trigger Lambda functions that can execute an activity. Using supported devices, you can perform a variety of activities, such as tracking, notifications, and replenishment of goods. Supported devices are prepared for use directly out of the box, which means you don't have to write firmware or configure them for secure connectivity. IoT 1-Click devices are easily managed and can be grouped to associate them with a Lambda function to execute actions when triggered. You can also track device health and activity using prebuilt reports.
 AWS IoT Analytics	**AWS IoT Analytics** helps you run and operationalize sophisticated analytics on huge volumes of IoT information, without your having to build an IoT analytics platform from scratch. It makes it easy to run analytics on IoT data and get insights to make more accurate choices for IoT applications.
 AWS IoT Button	**AWS IoT Button**, based on the Amazon Dash Button hardware, is a programmable button that can be used by developers to get started with AWS IoT Core, AWS Lambda, and other AWS services without writing device-specific code. The button's logic can be coded to configure track items or button clicks to count, alert or call someone, stop or start a process, and more. Use the button to open a garage door, track the use of common chores, remotely control appliances, or order your favorite pizza for delivery.
 Amazon FreeRTOS	**Amazon FreeRTOS** is an open source OS for microcontrollers to make small, low-power edge devices easy to program, deploy, secure, manage, and connect to AWS cloud services such as AWS IoT Core or to local edge devices running AWS IoT Greengrass. It uses Transport Layer Security (TLS v1.2) to help devices connect securely to the cloud. Over-the-air (OTA) update lets you remotely update patches and load devices with feature enhancements.

AWS in Action

Let's now jump into action to showcase the capabilities of AWS. You will be building similar architectures on AWS in later chapters, where I will help you with step-by-step instructions. For this example, assume you have an e-commerce website in a traditional datacenter, as shown in Figure 1-4.

Your company has decided to migrate to AWS without making any modifications to the web application and database. If this e-commerce application is moved to AWS as lift and shift without any changes, your AWS e-commerce infrastructure will look similar to that shown in Figure 1-5. The traditional web server will be replaced by an AWS EC2 instance, and your traditional database will be replaced by Amazon RDS in an AWS AZ of your choice.

As your e-commerce website becomes more popular, you'll need to scale your infrastructure to accommodate the increased flow of traffic from all over the world, 24 hours a day, without any interruption. If you were still using a traditional on-premises infrastructure, it would take weeks to months to scale up. But because you've migrated the infrastructure to AWS, scaling up will be simple: you'll add a few more services manually via the AWS Management Console or use AWS CloudFormation to automate the infrastructure creation. Your scaled up infrastructure will look similar to Figure 1-6.

Figure 1-4
Traditional
e-commerce
infrastructure

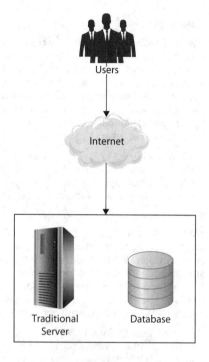

Figure 1-5
AWS e-commerce
infrastructure

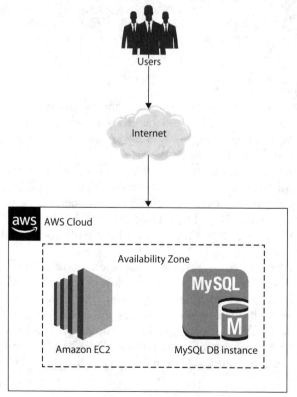

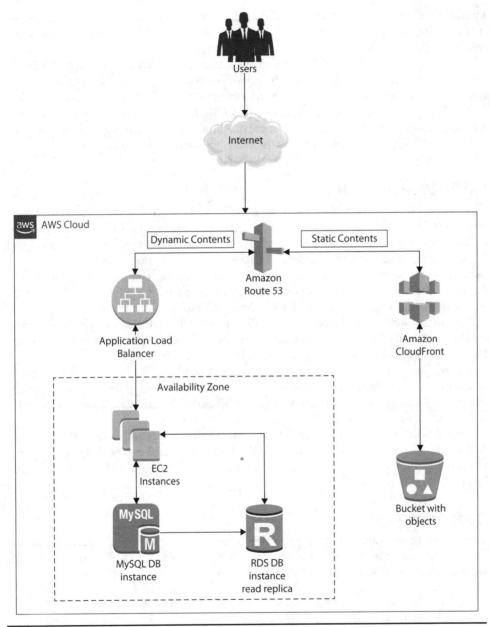

Figure 1-6   AWS e-commerce high-availability infrastructure

Now your e-commerce site has both dynamic content, such as products and price, and static content, such as images and videos. Separating the dynamic and static content will reduce the load and latency and improve performance by delivering the static contents from the AWS content delivery network, CloudFront. The workload will be shared by multiple smaller virtual machines behind an application load balancer. If one of the virtual machine fails, you'll use Amazon Elastic Load Balancing (ELB) to send the customer traffic to other running virtual machines, which improves reliability.

EC2 Auto Scaling will add a new instance to replace any failed instance and will add more instances automatically when traffic increases during a peak period. The RDS database instances will automatically failover to secondary instances if your primary database instance fails in a multi-AZ deployment. In addition, the Amazon RDS Read Replica will run all your read-only queries and reports. All of this can be configured and achieved in hours in AWS, versus weeks to months in a traditional datacenter environment.

Chapter Review

This chapter introduced and covered the benefits of cloud computing, along with various well-known cloud deployment models: Infrastructure as a Service (IaaS), Storage as a Service (STaaS), Platform as a Service (PaaS), Data as a Service (DaaS), Function as a Service (FaaS), and Software as a Service (SaaS). It also explained cloud services types—public, private, community, and hybrid—and offered a brief history of AWS, including how AWS started as an Amazon developer tool. I introduced you to various AWS regions and availability zones and discussed isolation techniques.

You were briefly introduced to each AWS service. It's crucial that you understand these—you should at least be familiar with what each service offers, to help you build highly available, highly scalable, and fault-tolerant applications in AWS.

Finally, you saw AWS in action. I demonstrated how easy it is to migrate your workload from an on-premises infrastructure to the AWS cloud and quickly scale that infrastructure. You may feel a bit overwhelmed at this point, but in subsequent chapters I'll provide practical and easy-to-follow information.

In addition to earning your AWS Certified Developer – Associate certification, you will be building secure, cloud-native applications on the AWS cloud. Let's begin the journey together. As the famous Chinese proverb says, "A journey of a thousand miles begins with a single step."

Questions

The following questions will help you gauge your understanding of the contents in this chapter. Read all the answers carefully because there might be more than one correct answer. Choose the best response for each question.

1. A traditional three-tier architecture comprises which of the following tiers? (Choose three.)

   A. Security tier

   B. Application tier

   C. Web tier

   D. Database tier

2. An AWS region comprises two or more physical locations that provide high availability and fault tolerance for your applications. Those physical locations are called what?

    A. Cloud datacenters

    B. Edge locations

    C. Availability zones

    D. DMZ zones

3. You want to deploy your applications and databases in a logically isolated section of the AWS cloud. Which AWS service provides you an isolated networking layer?

    A. Regions

    B. Amazon Route 53

    C. Amazon VPC

    D. Availability zones

4. You want to host a static website, and you don't want to manage any servers. Which of the following services will help you achieve this?

    A. AWS Lambda

    B. Amazon EC2

    C. Amazon OpsWorks

    D. Amazon S3

5. You want to monitor your EC2 instances for CPU utilization and memory and visualize the health of the server using a dashboard. Which of the following AWS services could be used for this case?

    A. Amazon OpsWorks

    B. Amazon CloudWatch

    C. AWS CloudTrial

    D. Amazon VPC Flowlogs

6. You want to scale your current EC2 servers and you do not want to manage the scaling manually. Which AWS service will detect when an instance is unhealthy, terminate it, and replace it with a new one?

    A. Amazon EC2 Auto Scaling

    B. Amazon Route 53

    C. Amazon CloudWatch

    D. Amazon Elastic Load Balancing

7. You have been storing your data in Amazon S3, and you are required to query the data without moving it to a database using ANSI SQL. Which AWS service enables you to quickly query the data stored in S3?

   A. Amazon EMR

   B. Amazon Simple Queue Service

   C. Amazon Athena

   D. Amazon Neptune

8. Your company needs a service that lets you run code without provisioning or managing servers. To save costs, the company doesn't want to pay for infrastructure in an idle state. Which of the following services could you use for this scenario?

   A. AWS Lambda

   B. Amazon EC2

   C. AWS Fargate

   D. Amazon Lightsail

9. You want to migrate your relational database to AWS, but you don't want to perform the time-consuming administration tasks such as database installation, patching, and backups. Which of the following will meet your needs?

   A. AWS Fargate

   B. Amazon RDS

   C. Amazon S3

   D. Amazon Athena

10. Your gaming application is a data-intensive application and requires high throughput and low latency for gamers who access your application. Which AWS service provides support for an in-memory database?

    A. Amazon EC2

    B. Amazon RDS

    C. Amazon S3

    D. Amazon ElastiCache

11. In your global enterprise, applications are running in different countries, and you want to route traffic to your applications based on a few criteria, such as the endpoint health of the server instance, the geographic location of the user, and latency. Which AWS service is most appropriate for this scenario?

    A. Amazon Route 53

    B. Application Load Balancer

    C. Network Load Balancer

    D. Classic Load Balancer

12. Your compliance team wants to audit your AWS environment to gain the event history of all your AWS account activity, including any actions taken using the AWS Management Console, AWS SDKs, or command-line tools. Which AWS service tracks user activity and API usage?

A. Amazon CloudWatch

B. AWS CloudTrail

C. Amazon VPC Flow Logs

D. Amazon Cognito

13. You have strict requirement to protect stored data against site-level failures, errors, and threats. Which AWS service provides unmatched durability by automatically storing data across multiple availability zones within an AWS region?

A. Amazon Neptune

B. Amazon RDS

C. Amazon S3

D. Amazon Timestream

14. You want to use a content delivery network (CDN) service to deliver data and videos securely to your global customers, with low latency and high transfer speeds. Which of the following AWS service will provide the CDN capability?

A. Amazon DynamoDB

B. Amazon S3

C. Amazon Route 53

D. Amazon CloudFront

15. You have large amount of data in tape storage in an on-premises datacenter, and you want to migrate it to AWS to save costs and to meet long-term backup compliance requirements. Which AWS service provides data archival at a low cost?

A. Amazon S3 Glacier

B. Amazon S3

C. Amazon CloudFront

D. Amazon RDS

16. You want to create and manage AWS users and groups to allow and deny access to AWS resources, but you do not want to pay for this service. Which of the following services provides this capability?

A. AWS IoT Core

B. Amazon Simple Notification Service (SNS)

C. AWS CloudFormation

D. AWS Identity and Access Management (IAM)

17. You have 75 terabytes of life sciences data in your datacenter and want to move to the AWS cloud quickly and efficiently. Which of the following services could quickly move the data to S3?

   A. AWS Snowball

   B. Amazon Redshift

   C. Amazon DynamoDB

   D. Amazon S3

18. Your company wants to use a dedicated network connection from on-premises to AWS to reduce network costs and increase bandwidth throughput without using the Internet. Which of the following services provides these capabilities?

   A. Amazon VPC

   B. AWS CloudFront

   C. AWS VPN

   D. AWS Direct Connect

19. Your new application needs a hybrid storage service that enables your on-premises applications to store data on AWS cloud storage. Which of the following provides the hybrid storage service?

   A. AWS Storage Gateway

   B. Amazon S3

   C. Amazon S3 Glacier

   D. Amazon EBS

20. You are developing an application that will be used by millions of users, and you want your users to sign-up and sign-in easily using social identity providers such as Facebook, Google, and Amazon. Which of the following services helps you to achieve this solution?

   A. Amazon Macie

   B. Amazon Inspector

   C. Amazon Cognito

   D. Amazon GuardDuty

21. You want use a managed distributed denial of service (DDoS) protection service to safeguard your applications that are running on AWS. Which AWS service provides always-on detection and automatic inline mitigations for DDoS protection?

   A. Amazon Macie

   B. AWS Shield

   C. Amazon GuardDuty

   D. AWS WAF

22. You want to use a web application firewall that helps protect your web applications from SQL injection and cross-site scripting. Which of the following services could be used to protect your web application?

    A. AWS WAF

    B. AWS Shield

    C. Amazon Inspector

    D. Amazon Macie

23. You want to automate the build, test, and deploy phases of your release cycle every time there is a code change. Which of the following developer tools services could you use?

    A. AWS CodeBuild

    B. AWS CodeCommit

    C. AWS CodeDeploy

    D. AWS CodePipeline

24. Your team wants to automate software deployments to eliminate the need for error-prone manual operations. Which of the following developer tools services automates software deployments?

    A. AWS CodeBuild

    B. AWS CodeCommit

    C. AWS CodeDeploy

    D. AWS CodePipeline

25. You want use an automated process to compile your source code, run tests, and produce software packages that are ready to deploy. Which of the following developer tools automates the compilation and tests your software packages?

    A. AWS CodePipeline

    B. AWS CodeDeploy

    C. AWS CodeCommit

    D. AWS CodeBuild

Answers

1. **B, C, D.** A traditional three-tier architecture consists of the Web tier, Application tier, and Database tier. In AWS, the Web tier will be in the public subnet, and the Application and Database tiers will be in a private subnet.

2. **C.** There will be at least two availability zones in each AWS region to provide high availability and fault tolerance to your applications.

3. **C.** Amazon Virtual Private Cloud (VPC) provides a logically isolated section of the AWS cloud and acts as a networking layer for your EC2 instances and database services.

4. D. Amazon S3 (Simple Storage Service) will help you host a static website without your having to provision and maintain any servers.

5. B. Amazon CloudWatch provides those metrics in one-minute and five-minute intervals. You can use a Personal Health Dashboard to monitor the EC2 instance's performance.

6. A. Amazon EC2 Auto Scaling will automatically detect when an instance is unhealthy, terminate it, and replace it with a new one.

7. C. With Amazon Athena, you can query data stored in Amazon S3 by defining the schema. You start querying using standard ANSI SQL.

8. A. Using AWS Lambda, you can run your code without provisioning or managing servers. Your company would pay only for the compute time that you consume, and there is no charge when your code is not running.

9. B. Amazon Relational Database Service (Amazon RDS) automates time-consuming database administration tasks, such as database installation, patching, and daily backups.

10. D. Amazon ElastiCache offers fully managed, in-memory data stores that can be used to build data-intensive gaming applications to provide high throughput and low latency for your users.

11. A. The Amazon Route 53 service routes your traffic based on the endpoint health of your instance, the geographic location of the user, and latency.

12. B. AWS CloudTrail helps you monitor continuously and provides event history of all AWS account activity.

13. C. Amazon S3 provides 99.99999999999 percent durability by storing data across multiple systems within an AWS region.

14. D. Amazon CloudFront is a CDN service that securely delivers videos, data, and applications to your customers.

15. A. Amazon S3 Glacier provides extremely low-cost cloud storage for long-term backup.

16. D. The AWS Identity and Access Management (IAM) service can be used to create and manage AWS users and groups to allow and deny access to AWS resources at no charge.

17. A. The AWS Snowball service could be used to transfer the data to the device, which is then shipped back to AWS, where the data is copied into your S3 bucket.

18. D. AWS Direct Connect provides private connectivity between AWS and your datacenter using a dedicated network connection to reduce network costs and increase bandwidth throughput without using the Internet.

19. A. The AWS Storage Gateway service provides hybrid storage service that enables your on-premises applications to store data on the AWS cloud.

20. C. Amazon Cognito scales to millions of users and supports sign-in with social identity providers via SAML 2.0.

21. **B.** AWS Shield provides a managed DDoS protection service that minimizes application downtime and latency.

22. **A.** The AWS WAF service acts as web application firewall and protects your web applications from common attack patterns such as SQL injection.

23. **D.** AWS CodePipeline is a fully managed continuous delivery service that helps you automate the build, test, and deploy phases of your release cycle every time there is a code change.

24. **C.** AWS CodeDeploy is a managed deployment service that automates software deployments and makes it easier to rapidly release new features, while avoiding error-prone manual operations.

25. **D.** AWS CodeBuild is a managed continuous integration service that compiles your source code, runs tests, and produces software packages that are ready for deployment.

Additional Resources

- **What is cloud computing?**   Visit this site for in-depth information about cloud computing, including types and benefits.
  `https://aws.amazon.com/what-is-cloud-computing/?nc1=f_cc`

- **Cloud Computing with AWS**   Consult this site to learn more about AWS and global network infrastructures, read customer stories, and so on.
  `https://aws.amazon.com/what-is-aws/`

- **AWS Blog**   This blog is organized by various categories, such as Compute, Database, DevOps, Storage, and Networking.
  `https://aws.amazon.com/blogs/`

- **AWS News Blog**   Read this blog periodically to learn what new AWS services and features are being launched.
  `https://aws.amazon.com/blogs/aws/category/news/launch/`

- **AWS Training and Certification**   Here you can find free digital training by AWS and AWS certification details. You can also register for the AWS Certification exam when you are ready.
  `https://aws.amazon.com/training/?nc2=h_ql_le_tc`

- **AWS FAQs**   This important resource for exam preparation lists the products and technical FAQs.
  `https://aws.amazon.com/faqs/`

- **Cloud Products**   Explore AWS products on this site.
  `https://aws.amazon.com/products/`

- **AWS Solutions**   Consult this site if you need help solving common problems and building faster. It offers solution details, a deployment guide, and instructions for automated deployment.
  `https://aws.amazon.com/solutions/`

- **AWS Documentation and News Blog**   On these two sites, you'll find user guides, developer guides, API references, tutorials, and more. There is no place like official AWS documentation to get the latest and correct information about all the AWS services. Always refer to the official AWS blogs to get the latest updates about new AWS services and updates to existing features. `https://docs.aws.amazon.com/index.html` and `https://aws.amazon.com/blogs/aws`

- **AWS Partner Network**   This site offers information about the global partner program for businesses that use AWS to build solutions and services for customers. It provides valuable business, technical, and marketing support. `https://aws.amazon.com/partners/`

S3 - static website hosting

Shield = DDoS

WAF = XSS/SQL Inj.

Interacting with AWS Using API, SDK, and CLI

In this chapter, you will learn
- Create new AWS account
- Explore AWS free services
- AWS Management Console
- AWS command line interface
- AWS Software Development Kit
- AWS tools for PowerShell
- AWS serverless application model
- AWS integrated development environment toolkits

I am excited to welcome you to this chapter, which will discuss how to create a new AWS account and various ways of connecting to your AWS services. As an AWS developer, you need to know and be familiar with various tools that are available to connect and interact securely with AWS services.

Create a New AWS Account

AWS accounts are available for free for 12 months to help you familiarize yourself with various AWS services. To create a new AWS account, go to `https://aws.amazon .com/free`, which is shown in Figure 2-1.

Click the Create a Free Account button to open the next screen, shown in Figure 2-2.

Enter your e-mail address and a password for your AWS root account. Enter a name for your AWS account (this can be changed later). Click Continue after you entered the required information to open the next screen, shown in Figure 2-3.

In this screen, select Professional if you intend to use this AWS account within your company, educational institution, or organization. Otherwise, select Personal and provide your contact details. Then read through the AWS Customer Agreement and click the check box to indicate that you've read it, before clicking Create Account and Continue. The next page is shown in Figure 2-4.

Figure 2-1 AWS Free Tier launch page

Enter your credit or debit card number, the card's expiration date, and cardholder's name and billing address. Click a button to indicate whether the billing address is the same or different from your contact address. Click Secure Submit to open the Select A Support Plan page, shown in Figure 2-5.

CAUTION Be aware that this is not a 100 percent free account, because you will be charged if you exceed the free limit quota. (The free quota available for each service is explained at https://aws.amazon.com/free/ explains.) It's always a best practice to delete any resources that you don't need. You can also set up a cost budget to monitor your costs against a specified dollar amount (for example, you can set up a budget for $50 and you can receive alerts when your user-defined thresholds are met) or usage budget. You can monitor your usage of one or more specified usage types or usage type groups (for example, monitor your monthly EC2 instance free usage hours and receive alerts when your user-defined thresholds are met) and receive an e-mail alert if you reach your predefined thresholds for the month.

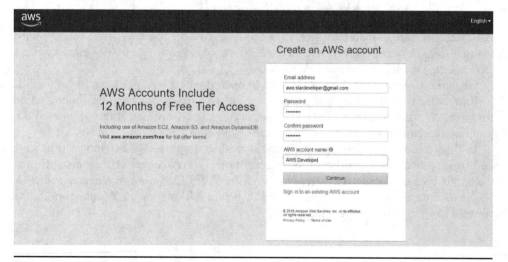

Figure 2-2 AWS free account creation page

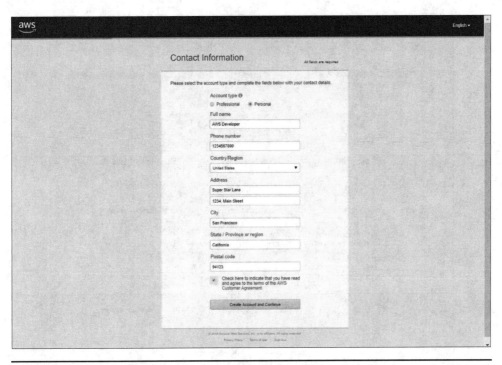

Figure 2-3   Contact information

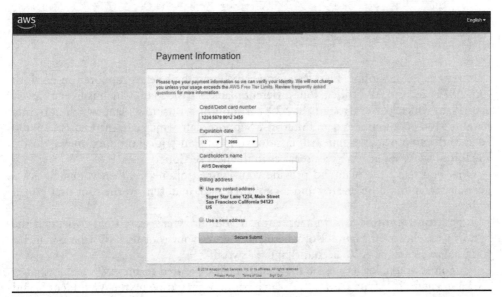

Figure 2-4   Payment information

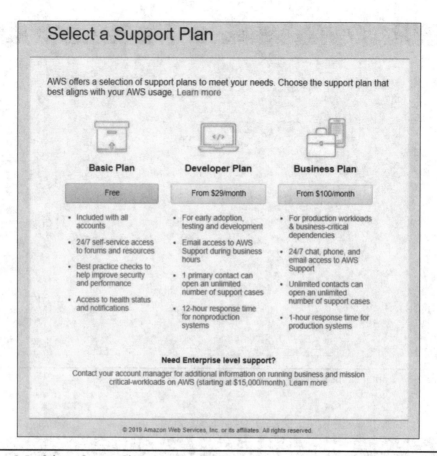

Figure 2-5   Select a Support Plan page

On the Select a Support Plan Page, you can choose the level of support you need for your AWS account. AWS offers four different plans: a Basic Plan, which is free; a Developer Plan, which currently starts at $29 per month; a Business Plan, which currently starts at $100 per month; and an Enterprise Support plan, which currently costs $15,000 per month and provides premier support for your mission-critical production workloads. You'll read more about AWS free services in the next section.

Once you select the plan and provide your contact phone number, your new AWS free tier account will be created and a confirmation e-mail sent to the root user e-mail address.

Type **https://console.aws.amazon.com** in your browser's search bar to launch the sign-in page shown in Figure 2-6, where you'll enter your root user ID (the e-mail ID you used to create the AWS account) and password.

As soon as you've logged in the first time, you'll be routed to the AWS Services page, shown in Figure 2-7. Type **IAM** in the search bar to begin setting up the AWS Identity and Access Management (IAM) service. Click IAM, from the search drop-down, to launch the IAM service console. Then you'll follow the IAM best practices to secure your account.

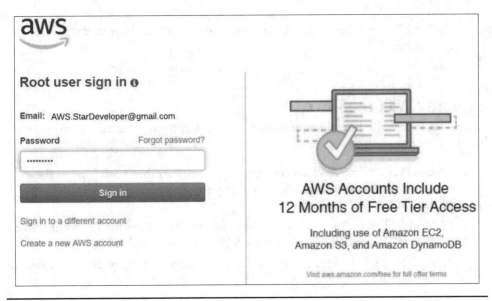

Figure 2-6 AWS sign-in page

CAUTION In IAM console, the best security practice is to delete your AWS root account access keys. Instead, use your IAM user access keys or temporary security credentials. You should never use your AWS root account for day-to-day interaction with AWS operations, because the root account provides unrestricted access to your AWS resources. You can also activate multifactor authentication (MFA) on your AWS root account to add another layer of protection. This will help to keep your account secure. For more information on IAM best practices, see https://docs.aws.amazon.com/IAM/latest/UserGuide/best-practices.html.

When you create IAM groups and users, you should always apply default access policies or custom access policies based on the least privilege access requirements of the users or groups who will be using IAM. This simplifies managing and auditing permissions in your account.

Figure 2-7 Type IAM in the search bar

NOTE   I will be discussing IAM and security practices in great detail in Chapter 10.

Explore AWS Free Tiers

When you choose the Basic Plan option, you can select from three tiers of free options based on the product you use:

- **Always Free**   Some AWS services are always free; in other words, use of these services does not expire even after your free use term ends. These services are available to all AWS customers.

- **12 Months Free**   AWS offers free usage for certain services for 12 months from your initial sign-up day. After 12 months, you pay standard service rates.

- **Trials**   These short-term free trial offers are available for many different software solutions. After the trial period expires, you pay standard service rates.

You can explore the following services during the free-trial period:

- **Amazon EC2**   750 hours per month, with 750 hours of Linux, RHEL, or SLES t2.micro instance usage and 750 hours of Windows t2.micro instance usage

- **Amazon S3**   5GB of free standard storage, 20,000 get requests, and 2000 put requests

- **Amazon RDS**   750 hours per month of db.t2.micro database usage for MySQL, PostgreSQL, MariaDB, Oracle BYOL, or SQL Server, including 20GB of General Purpose (SSD) database storage and 20GB of storage for DB Snapshots and database backups

- **Amazon DynamoDB**   25GB of storage, with 25 provisioned write capacity units (WCUs) and 25 provisioned read capacity units (RCUs); enough to handle up to 200 million requests per month.

- **Amazon SageMaker**   250 hours per month of t2.medium notebook usage for the first two months and 50 hours per month of m4.xlarge for training for the first two months, along with 125 hours per month of m4.xlarge for hosting for the first two months

- **AWS Lambda**   1 million free requests per month and up to 3.2 million seconds of compute time per month

- **Amazon Lightsail**   750 hours per month, with a trial of the $3.50 Lightsail plan free for one month when using Linux/Unix; also a trial of the $8 plan free for one month when using Lightsail for Microsoft Windows Server.

- **AWS Elastic Load Balancing**   750 hours per month shared between Classic and Application Load Balancers with 15GB of data processing for Classic Load Balancers and 15 LCUs for Application Load Balancers

- **AWS Key Management Service** 20,000 free requests per month
- **AWS Storage Gateway** First 100GB per account is free, and no data transfer charges into AWS
- **AWS Trusted Advisor** Four best-practice checks on performance and security (service limits, security groups, IAM, and MFA); notification and customization features
- **AWS CodeBuild** 100 build minutes per month of build.general1.small compute type usage
- **AWS CodeCommit** Five active users per month along with 50GB per month of storage and 10,000 Git requests per month
- **AWS CodePipeline** One active pipeline per month
- **AWS Data Pipeline** Three low frequency preconditions and five low frequency activities
- **AWS Database Migration Service** 750 hours of Amazon DMS single-AZ dms.t2.micro instance usage and 50GB of included General Purpose (SSD) storage
- **Amazon SWF** 10,000 activity tasks and 30,000 workflow-days along with 1000 initiated executions
- **Amazon Redshift** Two-month free trial of 750 DC2.Large hours per month
- **Amazon SES** 62,000 outbound messages per month to any recipient when you call Amazon SES from an Amazon EC2 instance directly or through AWS Elastic Beanstalk, and 1000 Inbound messages per month
- **Amazon EFS** 5GB of storage
- **Amazon Elastic Block Storage (EBS)** 30GiB of Amazon EBS with any combination of General Purpose (SSD) or Magnetic, and 2000,000 I/Os with EBS Magnetic storage along with 1GB of snapshot storage
- **Amazon Glacier** 10GB of Amazon Glacier data retrievals per month; can be used any time during the month and also applies to Standard retrievals
- **Amazon ElastiCache** 750 hours of cache.t2micro node usage along with enough hours to run continuously each month
- **Amazon Elasticsearch Service** t2.small.elasticsearch instance, 750 hours per month on a single AZ and 10GB per month of optional EBS storage, either Magnetic or General Purpose
- **Amazon CloudWatch** Ten custom metrics and ten alarms, along with 1 million API requests, plus 5GB of log data ingestion and 5GB of log data archive, and three dashboards with up to 50 metrics each per month
- **Amazon API Gateway** 1 million API calls received per month
- **Amazon CloudFront** 50GB of data transfer out and 2 million HTTP or HTTPS requests

- **Amazon Connect** 90 minutes per month of cloud-based contact center usage and a local direct inward dial (DID) number for the region; also 30 minutes per month of local inbound DID calls and 30 minutes per month of local outbound calls

- **Amazon SNS** 1 million publishes and 100,000 HTTP/S deliveries, along with 1000 e-mail deliveries

AWS Management Console

The AWS Management Console is an API-based web application that provides easy access to all the AWS services. It comprises and refers to a broad collection of service consoles for managing your Amazon Web Services. When you first sign in, you see the console home page, shown in Figure 2-8.

The home page provides access to all AWS services and corresponding documentation and tips. If you navigate the individual service consoles in the navigation pane, you'll see tools for working with EC2—for example, AMIs, Volumes, and Snapshots.

The AWS Management Console provides various ways for navigating to individual service consoles. In the search field at the top of the console, enter a service name—

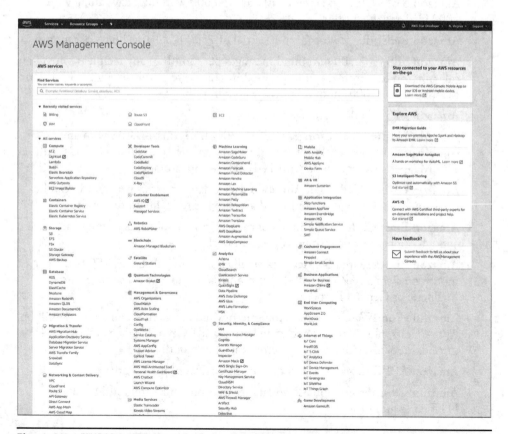

Figure 2-8 AWS Management Console home page

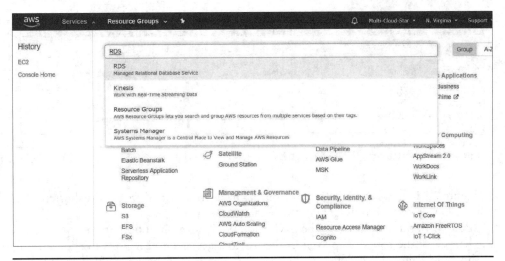

Figure 2-9 Searching for the RDS service

RDS was entered in Figure 2-9. Then choose the service that you need from the list of search results.

From the console you can add shortcuts for the service consoles that you use most frequently. To add a shortcut for the service consoles you use most, choose the pushpin icon on the navigation bar, which is shown in Figure 2-10. You can drag the service shortcut from the menu to the navigation bar.

Figure 2-10 Click the pushpin and drag a shortcut to the navigation bar

Figure 2-11   Shortcuts on the navigation bar

Figure 2-11 shows several shortcuts on the navigation bar. To remove a shortcut that you no longer need, simply drag it off the navigation bar.

Along with other options on the navigation bar is a region option on the right side of the bar. Click the region displayed in the bar to see a menu of regions to choose from, as shown in Figure 2-12. When you choose a region here, it becomes the default region used in the AWS Management Console.

TIP   Always make sure that you are working in the correct region—the one for which you intend to create or work on AWS services. I have experienced many people complaining that their resources are not available, only to realize that they are working in the wrong region. Also, beware of instances that use the same name in more than one region. When working in a secondary region, it's easy to inadvertently shut down an instance that uses the same name used in the primary region, for example.

Figure 2-12
Choosing a
region

Figure 2-13
Account
information

Even though you are able to choose a region that specifies where your resources are managed, you do not choose a region for the AWS Management Console or for some services, such as S3 and IAM.

In order to change the account settings, organization, billing dashboard, or security credential to change the password.

Click your account name on the navigation bar, which is to the left of the region menu. You'll see the options shown in Figure 2-13. Click My Account to access the following information about your user account:

- Account Settings
- Contact Information
- Payment Currency Preference
- Configure Security Challenge Questions
- AWS Regions
- IAM User and Role Access
- Reserved Instance Marketplace Settings
- Account Contract Information
- Communication Preferences
- Manage AWS Support Plans
- GovCloud (US)
- Close Account

If you are an account owner, you can change your AWS account password from the AWS Management Console. Click your account name on the navigation bar and select Security Credentials. Then follow the instructions to navigate to the page where you can change your password. You need to enter your current password and your new password two times. The new password must follow the minimum password standard (at least eight characters long and must include a symbol, a number, an uppercase letter, and a lowercase letter). Once you've filled out the password form, choose Change Password or Save Changes.

Figure 2-14
Support menu
options

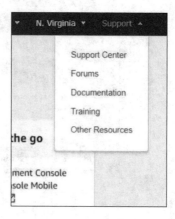

If you are a root user or have the necessary permissions, you can get information about your AWS charges from the console. Click your account name on the navigation bar and select My Billing Dashboard. The AWS Billing and Cost Management dashboard provides a summary a breakdown of your monthly spending.

Another important resource for all the AWS users is the Support menu, at the far-right side of the navigation bar, and shown in Figure 2-14. Use the Support menu to navigate to Support Center, Forums, Documentation, Training, and Other Resources. Visit the Support Center to create support tickets with AWS for any issues or to increase any soft limits. Forums are a treasure to AWS users and developers, because you'll quickly and easily find solutions to many real-world scenarios or issues that have already been resolved by another developer. This can help you avoid reinventing the wheel. Choose Documentation, Training, or Other Learning Resources to find more information about AWS, training options, and other sources of information.

The bell menu on the navigation bar offers a quick way to see any open issues or scheduled changes. In this menu, you'll see the options Open Issues, Scheduled Change, Other Notifications, and View All Alerts, as shown in Figure 2-15. Select an option to be directed to the CloudWatch dashboard, where you can quickly glance at all the open issues or scheduled changes.

The Resource Groups menu is located on the left side of the navigation pane, as shown in Figure 2-16. (You can also access a resource group by using the Resource

Figure 2-15
Alerts menu
options

Figure 2-16   Resource Groups menu

Groups API via the AWS CLI or by using AWS SDK programming languages, but you'll learn more about these options later.) You use resource groups to organize your AWS resources. Resource groups make it easier to manage and automate tasks on large numbers of resources at one time, instead of accessing them one at a time. From this menu, you can save or create a resource group.

An important and very useful option on this menu is the Tag Editor. A tag is a key-value pair that acts as metadata for organizing all your AWS resources. You can add tags for most AWS resources during resource creation, whether your working with an Amazon S3 bucket or an Amazon EC2 instance. You can then build a query for resources of various types, and add, remove, or replace tags for the resources from your search results.

AWS Command Line Interface

The AWS Command Line Interface (CLI) is an open source tool you can use to interact with AWS services using command-line shell. You can start using AWS functionality with minimal configuration from the command prompt by using following programs:

- **Linux shells**   Use common shell programs such as bash, zsh, and tsch to run commands in Linux, macOS, or Unix.

- **Windows command line**   Run commands in PowerShell or at the Windows command prompt.

- **Remote Access**   Run commands on Amazon EC2 instances through a remote terminal such as Secure Shell (SSH) or PuTTY.

All the functions available in the AWS Management Console are available in the AWS API and CLI immediately, or within 180 days of launch of any new service. Install the AWS CLI using pip3. You'll need Python 2 version 2.6.5 or later, or Python 3 version 3.3 or later. The CLI can be installed on Windows, Linux, macOS, or Unix.

As you will see, the AWS CLI uses a multipart structure on the command line that must be specified in this order:

```
$ aws <command><subcommand> [options and parameters]
```

EXAM TIP Be sure that you understand the structure of a CLI base command that calls to the AWS program. The top-level command typically corresponds to an AWS service supported by the AWS CLI. The subcommand specifies which operation to perform. Depending on the command and subcommand you specify, parameters can take various types of input values, such as numbers, strings, lists, maps, and JSON structures.

Installing and Setting Up a Profile in the AWS CLI

If you already have pip3 and Python v3 or later, you can install the AWS CLI by using the following command:

```
$ pip3 install awscli --upgrade –user
```

The --upgrade option instructs pip3 to upgrade any requirements that are already installed. The --user option instructs pip3 to install the program to a subdirectory of your user directory.

The bundled installer is for offline or automated installations on Linux, macOS, or Unix and includes the AWS CLI, its dependencies, and a shell script that performs the installation for you. You can also use the MSI installer on Windows.

After installing the AWS CLI, you need to add the path to the executable file to your PATH variable. For Linux, macOS, or Unix, add the AWS CLI executable to your command-line path like this:

```
export PATH=~/.local/bin:$PATH
```

This will add a path, ~/.local/bin, to your current PATH variable.

To load the updated profile into your current session, execute the following:

```
$ source ~/.bash_profile
```

In Windows, you can find where the AWS program is installed by running the following command. The /R path parameter tells it to search all folders.

```
C:\> where /R c:\ aws
c:\Program Files\Amazon\AWSCLI\bin\aws.exe
c:\Program Files\Amazon\AWSCLI\bincompat\aws.cmd
c:\Program Files\Amazon\AWSCLI\runtime\Scripts\aws
c:\Program Files\Amazon\AWSCLI\runtime\Scripts\aws.cmd
```

Press the WINDOWS key on your keyboard, type **cmd** in the search box, and press ENTER to open the Environment Variable. You can also find the command prompt in the Windows accessories. You need to choose Edit environment variables for your account. Here you can choose PATH, and then choose Edit. Then add the path to the end of the variable value field (such as C:\Program Files\Amazon\AWSCLI\bin\aws.exe). The following example shows the system PATH of aws.exe:

```
C:\> where aws
C:\Program Files\Amazon\AWSCLI\bin\aws.exe
```

The AWS CLI stores the credentials in a local file named credentials, in the .aws folder. For Windows, use the following command to show the contents of the .aws folder:

```
C:\> dir "%UserProfile%\.aws"
```

And for Linux, macOS, or Unix, use the following to list the contents of the .aws folder:

```
$ ls  ~/.aws
```

The AWS CLI provides low-level, API-equivalent commands. But several AWS services provide customizations and direct access to the public APIs of AWS services, and you can customize using higher-level commands that simplify using a service with a complex API. For example, the following example provides a shell-like copy command and automatically performs a multipart upload to transfer large files quickly to Amazon S3:

```
$ aws s3 cp newaudio.mp3 s3://yourbucket/
```

If you performed a similar task using the low-level commands, it would take a lot more effort.

Configuring Profiles

To configure a new profile, at the command line, enter **aws configure**, and then press ENTER. This command is interactive, so the AWS CLI outputs lines of texts, prompting you to enter additional information. Enter each of your access keys in turn, and then press ENTER. Then, enter an AWS region name in the format shown next, press ENTER, and then press ENTER a final time to skip the output format setting.

```
$ aws configure
AWS Access Key ID [None]: ABCDXYZEFGHI73SAMPLE
AWS Secret Access Key [None]: yMcedFDwqEFGH/M3EDCBA/aBcDefGHIJSAMPLEKEY
Default region name [None]: us-east-1
Default output format [None]: ENTER
```

This will result in a single profile named default.

You can create additional configurations by specifying the name of a profile using the --profile option to configure multiple users:

```
$ aws configure --profile myuserprofile
AWS Access Key ID [None]: ABCDXYZEFGHI73SAMPLE
AWS Secret Access Key [None]: yMcedFDwqEFGH/M3EDCBA/aBcDefGHIJSAMPLEKEY
Default region name [None]: us-west-1
Default output format [None]: text
```

When you run an AWS command, you can omit the --profile option to use the default profile:

```
$ aws s3 ls
```

And you can specify a profile name with --profile to create a profile stored under that name:

```
$ aws s3 ls --profile myuserprofile
```

To retrieve a value for any setting, use the get subcommand to view the current settings:

```
$ aws configure get region --profile myuserprofile
us-west-1
```

To modify the current setting, use the --profile option. For example, the following command updates the region setting in the profile named myuserprofile:

```
aws configure set region us-east-1 --profile myuserprofile
```

The following command updates the output setting in the profile named myuserprofile:

```
aws configure set outputtable --profile myuserprofile
```

Here is a simple noninteractive command to output from the service in the JSON format:

```
$ aws ec2 create-security-group --group-name my-secgrp --description
"My security group"
{
    "GroupId": "sg-123456f7"
}
```

To use this example, enter the full text of the command (the bold text after the prompt), and then press ENTER. (The name of the security group, my-secgrp, is replaceable. You could use the group name as shown, but you probably want to use a more descriptive name.) Note that the information within the curly braces is the JSON output of the command. JSON is the default output format, but if you configure your CLI to output in table or text format, the output will be formatted according to your choice.

To avoid specifying the profile in every command, you can set the AWS_DEFAULT_PROFILE environment variable at the command line. In Linux, macOS, or Unix, use the following:

```
$ export AWS_DEFAULT_PROFILE=myuserprofile
```

This changes the default profile until the end of your shell session, or until you set a different value. You can make an environment variable persistent across future sessions by adding the variable to the shell's startup script.

Here's how it looks in Windows:

```
C:\> setx AWS_DEFAULT_PROFILE myuserprofile
```

Using **setx** to set an environment variable affects the value used in both the current command shell and all command shells that you create after running the command.

Getting Help with CLI Commands

AWS offers a CLI command-completion feature: press TAB to complete a partially typed command. This feature is automatically configured and enabled by default on EC2 instances, but it isn't automatically installed on most systems, so you'll need to configure it manually if you want to use it. Here's an example: to see a list of available commands, enter a partial command, **s** in this case, and then press TAB:

```
$ aws sTAB
s3              ses            sqs              sts            swf
s3api           sns            storagegateway   support
```

You can always get help with any command when using the AWS CLI. Simply type **help** at the end of a command name:

```
$ aws help
```

Here's how to get help for Amazon EC2–specific commands.

```
$ aws ec2 help
$ aws ec2 describe-instances help
```

To view the help file one page at a time, you can add a pipe (|) to the output of the help command to add the more command. Press the SPACE BAR or PGDN to view more of the document, or press Q to quit.

```
E:\> aws ec2 describe-instances help | more
```

Working with EC2 Key Pairs Using the AWS CLI

When you create an EC2 instance, you need to provide a key pair that you'll use to authenticate when you try connecting to the instance.

To create a key pair on Linux, use the create-key-pair command with the --query and --output text options to pipe your private key directly into a file:

```
$ aws ec2 create-key-pair --key-name MyEC2KeyPair --query 'KeyMaterial'
--output text > MyEC2KeyPair.pem
```

Before you try connecting to your instance from a Linux computer, you need to change the permissions of your private key file so that only you can read it:

```
$ chmod 400 MyEC2KeyPair.pem
```

To display your key pairs, use the following command:

```
$ aws ec2 describe-key-pairs --key-name MyEC2KeyPair
{
    "KeyPairs": [
        {
            "KeyName": "MyEC2KeyPair",
```

```
            "KeyFingerprint": "2e:62:bd:37:ce:76:d8:e7:2e:34:4c:46:3e:6e:c7:d
b:8e:e4:e2:5b"
          }
      ]
}
```

To delete a key pair, use the following command:

```
$ aws ec2 delete-key-pair --key-name MyEC2KeyPair
```

Note that in Windows PowerShell, the > file redirection operator defaults to UTF-8 encoding, so you must convert the output by piping it to the out-file command by explicitly setting the -encoding option to ascii:

```
PS C:\>aws ec2 create-key-pair --key-name MyEC2KeyPair --query 'KeyMaterial'
--output text | out-file -encoding ascii -filepath MyEC2KeyPair.pem
```

Creating Security Groups Using the AWS CLI

You can create security groups associated for a specified Amazon Virtual Private Cloud (VPC) using the following command:

```
$ aws ec2 create-security-group --group-name my-sg-grp
--description "My security group" --vpc-id vpc-4q3w2e1r
{
    "GroupId": "sg-654321f7"
}
```

Use the describe-security-groups command to view initial information about your new security group. Notice that an EC2-VPC security group is referenced by its VPC ID (VcpID), not by its name:

```
$ aws ec2 describe-security-groups --group-ids sg-654321f7
{
    "SecurityGroups": [
        {
            "IpPermissionsEgress": [
                {
                    "IpProtocol": "-1",
                    "IpRanges": [
                        {
                            "CidrIp": "0.0.0.0/0"
                        }
                    ],
                    "UserIdGroupPairs": []
                }
            ],
            "Description": "My security group"
            "IpPermissions": [],
            "GroupName": "my-seg-grp",
            "VpcId": "vpc-1a2b3c4d",
            "OwnerId": "987654321098",
            "GroupId": "sg-654321f7"
        }
    ]
}
```

Confirm your public address using following command:

```
$ curl https://checkip.amazonaws.com
10.0.10.83
```

You can add a range to your security group to limit all the ingress traffic:

```
$ aws ec2 authorize-security-group-ingress --group-id sg-654321f7 --protocol
tcp --port 3389 --cidr 10.0.10.0/24
```

To enable SSH to instances in the my-sg-grp security group, add a rule by running the following command:

```
$ aws ec2 authorize-security-group-ingress --group-id sg-654321f7 --protocol
tcp --port 22 --cidr 10.0.10.0/24
```

To view changes to the security group, use the describe command, as follows:

```
$ aws ec2 describe-security-groups --group-ids sg-654321f7
{
    "SecurityGroups": [
        {
            "IpPermissionsEgress": [
                {
                    "IpProtocol": "-1",
                    "IpRanges": [
                        {
                            "CidrIp": "0.0.0.0/0"
                        }
                    ],
                    "UserIdGroupPairs": []
                }
            ],
            "Description": "My security group"
            "IpPermissions": [
                {
                    "ToPort": 22,
                    "IpProtocol": "tcp",
                    "IpRanges": [
                        {
                            "CidrIp": "10.0.10.0/24"
                        }
                    ]
                    "UserIdGroupPairs": [],
                    "FromPort": 22
                }
            ],
            "GroupName": "my-seg-grp",
            "OwnerId": "123456789012",
            "GroupId": "sg-654321f7"
        }
    ]
}
```

To delete a security group, use the delete-security-group command:

```
$ aws ec2 delete-security-group --group-id sg-654321f7
```

NOTE You will not be able to delete a security group if it's currently attached to an instance.

Launching an Instance Using the AWS CLI

You can launch an Amazon EC2 instance by using the run-instances command to launch a t2.micro instance in the specified subnet of a VPC:

```
$ aws ec2 run-instances --image-id ami-284c635b --count 1 --instance-type
t2.micro --key-name MyEC2KeyPair --security-group-ids sg-654321f7 --subnet-id
subnet-5d6e738d
```

To add metadata to your resources that you can use for a variety of purposes, add tags to your instance by using the create-tags command:

```
$ aws ec2 create-tags --resources i-4314533d --tags Key=Name,Value=MyFirstEC2
Instance
```

Using AWS CLI, you can list all your instances or filter the results based on the instances that you want to see:

```
$ aws ec2 describe-instances --filters "Name=tag:Name,Values=MyFirstEC2Instance"
```

You can list multiple instances that were launched using ami-i7654321, ami-j7654321, or ami-k7654321 using the following command:

```
$ aws ec2 describe-instances --filters "Name=image-id,Values=ami-
i7654321,ami-j7654321,ami-k7654321"
```

To terminate an instance you no longer need, use the terminate-instances command:

```
$ aws ec2 terminate-instances --instance-ids i-4314533d
{
    "TerminatingInstances": [
        {
            "InstanceId": "i-4314533d",
            "CurrentState": {
                "Code": 32,
                "Name": "shutting-down"
            },
            "PreviousState": {
                "Code": 16,
                "Name": "running"
            }
        }
    ]
}
```

NOTE If you think you may need to reconnect to this instance later, use stop-instances instead of terminate-instances, because as soon as the state of the instance changes to terminated, it can't be recovered unless you have a manual backup. You stop incurring charges for a terminated instance.

Creating an S3 Bucket Using the AWS CLI

Bucket names must be globally unique and should be DNS compliant. The names must start with a lowercase letter or number and can contain lowercase letters, dashes, periods, and numbers. They cannot contain underscores, have consecutive periods, end with a dash, or use dashes adjacent to a period.

To create an S3 bucket, use the s3 mb command:

```
$ aws s3 mb s3://my-s3-bucket-1
```

To list your S3 buckets, use the s3 ls command:

```
$ aws s3 ls

2019-05-22 16:12:23 my-s3-bucket-1
2019-05-23 12:45:32 my-s3-bucket-2
```

To list all the objects and folders in a bucket, use the following command:

```
$ aws s3 ls s3://my-s3-bucket-1

2019-05-21 17:12:35          2 My-Text-File.txt
2019-05-20 17:28:55          3 My-Image-File.jpg
```

To delete an S3 bucket, use the s3 rb command:

```
$ aws s3 rb s3://my-s3-bucket-2
```

TIP You must delete all the contents in the bucket before the bucket can be deleted; the s3 rb command will fail if the bucket is not empty. You can, however, remove a non-empty bucket by including the --force option.

To remove all the objects and subfolders in a bucket and then delete the bucket, use the following command:

```
$ aws s3 rb s3://my-s3-bucket-1 --force
```

NOTE If versioning is enabled for this bucket, this command does not allow you to remove the bucket.

AWS Software Development Kit

The AWS Software Development Kit (SDK) enables you to simplify the use of AWS services in your applications with an API tailored to your programming language or platform.

AWS SDK for Java 2.0

Before you can begin the AWS SDK for Java setup, you need to create an IAM user and access key. In the AWS Management Console, navigate to the IAM Console. From the side menu, click Users to view a list of IAM users. You can log in using an existing user account or create a new account. Assuming you have already set up an IAM user account, select an IAM user from the list and open the Security Credentials tab, and then click Create Access Key. Here you can either click the Download Credentials button to download the credential file to your computer, or click Show User Security Credentials to view the IAM user's access key ID and secret access key, which you can copy and paste, to use later.

Depending on your build system or integrated development environment (IDE), you can use the following build tools:

- **Gradle**   Import the Maven bill of materials (BOM) to your Gradle project to automatically manage SDK dependencies.
- **Apache Maven**   Specify only the SDK components you need as dependencies in your project. If you build the AWS SDK for Java using Maven, it downloads all the necessary dependencies, builds the SDK, and installs the SDK in one step.

If you're using Maven, your next step is to open the AWS SDK for Java 2.x and click the Clone or Download button to choose your download option. Then, from the terminal window, navigate to the directory where the downloaded the SDK source is located. Use the following command to build and install the SDK:

```
mvn clean install
```

A .jar file will be built in the target directory. You can optionally build the API reference documentation using the following command:

```
mvn javadoc:Javadoc
```

Java 8.0 or later is required for the AWS SDK, or you can use the Open Java Development Kit (OpenJDK), which is distributed by Amazon Corretto. AWS recommends that you use the 64-bit version of the Java Virtual Machine (JVM) for the best performance of server-based applications with the AWS SDK for Java.

You can set your credentials for use by the AWS SDK for Java in several ways. You can set credentials in the AWS credentials profile file on your local system at one of the following locations:

- **Linux, macOS, or Unix**   ~/.aws/credentials
- **Windows**   C:\Users\USERNAME\.aws\credentials

This profile file should contain the following format:

```
[default]
aws_access_key_id      = your_access_key_id
aws_secret_access_key  = your_secret_access_key
```

You'll substitute your AWS credentials values for the values your_access_key_id and your_secret_access_key.

To set these variables in Linux, macOS, or Unix, use the following:

```
export AWS_ACCESS_KEY_ID=your_access_key_id
export AWS_SECRET_ACCESS_KEY=your_secret_access_key
```

To set these variables in Windows, use this:

```
set AWS_ACCESS_KEY_ID=your_access_key_id
set AWS_SECRET_ACCESS_KEY=your_secret_access_key
```

By default, the credential provider chain loads credentials automatically as soon as you issue one of the preceding commands.

Similarly, you can set a default AWS region to use for accessing AWS services with the AWS SDK for Java. AWS recommends, for the best network performance, that you choose a region that's geographically close to you or to your customers. You need to update the AWS config file on your local system to set the AWS region:

- **Linux, macOS, or Unix** `~/.aws/config`
- **Windows** `C:\Users\USERNAME\.aws\config`

The config file uses the following format:

```
[default]
region = your_aws_region
```

> **NOTE** Substitute your AWS region (for example, us-east-1) for your_aws_region.

You can also use the AWS_REGION environment variable.

For Linux, macOS, or Unix, use the export command to set the region:

```
export AWS_REGION=your_aws_region
```

For Windows, use the set command to set the region:

```
set AWS_REGION=your_aws_region
```

AWS SDK for .NET

Before you can begin the AWS SDK for .NET setup, you need to create an IAM user and access key. In the AWS Management Console, navigate to the IAM Console. Click Users from the side menu to view your IAM users. You can either use an existing user or create a new user. Assuming you have already set up an IAM user account, select the IAM user from the list and open the Security Credentials tab, and then click Create Access Key. Then click the Download Credentials button to download the credential file to your computer, or click Show User Security Credentials to view the IAM user's access key ID and secret access key, which you can copy and paste to use later.

Creating a profile for each set of credentials in the SDK Store is the preferred approach for handling credentials. You can create and manage profiles with the AWS Toolkit for

PowerShell using cmdlets, Visual Studio, or programmatically with the AWS SDK for .NET. All the credentials are encrypted and stored separately from any of your projects. When you reference the profile using your application name, the credentials are inserted at build time. This ensures that your credentials are not unintentionally exposed with your project on any public site.

To install AWS SDK for .NET, you must have Microsoft .NET Framework 3.5 or later and Microsoft Visual Studio 2010 or later. The AWS SDK for .NET is installed with the AWS Toolkit for Visual Studio, along with a plug-in that provides a user interface for managing your AWS resources from Visual Studio. It also includes the AWS Tools for Windows PowerShell.

To install the AWS SDK for .NET from the AWS Management Console, navigate to AWS SDK for .NET. Then, in the Downloads section, choose Download MSI Installer to download the installer. Run the downloaded installer to start installation, and follow the on-screen instructions. You can install the AWSSDK assemblies, as well as the TraceListener and SessionProvider extensions, to your application by installing the AWS assemblies with NuGet or by installing AWS SDK for .NET, available on GitHub. You can choose a different installation directory to install AWS SDK for .NET as a non-administrator.

AWS Tools for PowerShell

The AWS Tools for PowerShell Core and AWS Tools for Windows PowerShell are PowerShell modules that are built on the functionality exposed by the AWS SDK for .NET. The AWS PowerShell tools enable you to script operations on your AWS resources from the PowerShell command line. The cmdlets provide an idiomatic experience for specifying parameters and handling results, even though the cmdlets are implemented using the service clients and methods from the SDK. For example, you can pipe PowerShell objects in and out of the cmdlets.

You can use the PowerShell tools with IAM user credentials, temporary security tokens, and IAM roles. These tools can be installed on Windows, Linux, or macOS operating systems.

In Windows

Depending on the release and edition, a Windows computer can run the AWS Tools for Windows PowerShell, the AWS Tools for PowerShell Core, or both. After you install Windows PowerShell 2.0 or later, you can either download and run the AWS Tools for Windows PowerShell MSI installer or start PowerShell.

The AWS Tools for Windows PowerShell is an optional component that you can install for Windows installer .msi. To download the installer, go to http://aws.amazon .com/powershell, and then choose AWS Tools for Windows.

The AWS Tools for Windows PowerShell is installed by default on all Windows-based Amazon Machine Images (AMIs). The AWS Tools for PowerShell Core can be installed for all users by running the Install-Module cmdlet as administrator:

```
PS E:\> Install-Module -Name AWSPowerShell.NetCore -AllowClobber
```

To install both AWS PowerShell and AWS PowerShell.NetCore on a Windows OS for the current user, run the following as administrator:

```
PS E:\> Install-Module -Scope CurrentUser -Name AWSPowerShell.NetCore -Force
-AllowClobber
```

You need to uninstall the existing module before you install a newer release of the AWS Tools for PowerShell Core. Close any open AWS tools for Windows or PowerShell sessions before you uninstall the existing Tools for PowerShell Core package. Then run the following command to uninstall the package:

```
PS E:\> Uninstall-Module -Name AWSPowerShell.NetCore -AllVersions
```

To install the updated module after the uninstall is completed, use the following command:

```
PS E:\> Install-Module -Name AWSPowerShell.NetCore
```

After you install the module, run

```
PS E:\> Import-Module AWSPowerShell.NetCore
```

to load the AWS Tools for PowerShell Core cmdlets into your PowerShell session.

On Linux and macOSX

To set up the AWS Tools for PowerShell Core on Linux machines, search for "Installing PowerShell on Linux" in your browser to see the latest instructions (the URL is https://docs.microsoft.com/en-us/powershell/scripting/install/installing-powershell-core-on-linux?view=powershell-6). For macOS X, search for "Installing PowerShell on macOS" in your browser (https://docs.microsoft.com/en-us/powershell/scripting/install/installing-powershell-core-on-macos?view=powershell-6).

AWS releases new versions of the AWS Tools for PowerShell Core and AWS Tools for PowerShell periodically to support new AWS services and features. To determine the version installed on your OS, run the following cmdlet:

```
PS> Get-AWSPowerShellVersion
```

Before you uninstall the existing Tools for PowerShell Core package or install a newer release, close any open PowerShell or AWS Tools for PowerShell Core sessions by pressing CTRL-D. Then run the following command to uninstall the package:

```
PS> Uninstall-Module -Name AWSPowerShell.NetCore -AllVersions
```

To install the updated module after uninstall is completed, use the following command:

```
PS> Install-Module -Name AWSPowerShell.NetCore
```

After you install the module, run

```
PS> Import-Module AWSPowerShell.NetCore
```

to load the AWS Tools for PowerShell Core cmdlets into your PowerShell session.

AWS Serverless Application Model

The AWS Serverless Application Model (SAM) is an open source framework you can use to make serverless applications on AWS. A *serverless application* is combination of event sources, Lambda functions, and other resources that work together to perform certain tasks. A serverless application is more than just a Lambda function, because it can include additional resources such as APIs, databases, and event source mappings.

You can use AWS SAM to outline your serverless applications and use the AWS SAM template specification to define your serverless applications. The template provides a simple and clean syntax you can use to describe the functions, APIs, permissions, configurations, and events that make up one, deployable, versioned serverless application.

Using the AWS SAM CLI

The SAM CLI is an open source framework you use to create serverless applications using a template. The CLI includes commands for invoking Lambda functions locally, stepping through Lambda function debugging, and verifying that AWS SAM template files are written according to specifications regarding packaging and deploying serverless applications to the AWS cloud.

Because SAM integrates with other AWS services in creating serverless applications, it offers the following benefits:

- SAM makes it easy to organize related resources and components and operate on a single stack. You can share timeouts and memory configurations between resources using AWS SAM, and all the related resources can be deployed together as a versioned entity.

- Because SAM is an extension of AWS CloudFormation, you'll benefit from the latter's reliable deployment capabilities. You can use AWS CloudFormation to define resources in your SAM template. You can also use the full suite of resources, intrinsic functions, and other template features that are available in CloudFormation.

- Use SAM to define and deploy your infrastructure as a configuration, which makes it possible for you to enforce best practices, such as code reviews. With a few lines of configuration, you can enable safe deployments thru CodeDeploy and can enable tracing by using AWS X-Ray.

- The SAM CLI enables you locally build, test, and debug serverless applications that are defined by SAM templates. The CLI provides a Lambda-like execution environment locally. You can catch issues proactively by providing parity with the actual Lambda execution environment.

- You can use SAM with AWS toolkits, such as the AWS Toolkit for PyCharm, AWS Toolkit for JetBrains, AWS Toolkit for Visual Studio Code, and AWS Toolkit for IntelliJ to step through and debug your code and to understand what the code is doing. This tightens the feedback loop by enabling you to find and troubleshoot issues in the cloud.

Use SAM along with a suite of AWS tools to build serverless applications. New applications can be discovered in the AWS Serverless Application Repository. Use the AWS Cloud9 IDE, for authoring, testing, and debugging SAM-based applications. Use CodeBuild, CodeDeploy, and CodePipeline to build a deployment pipeline for your serverless applications. A CI/CD pipeline is automatically configured for you, and you can also use AWS CodeStar to get started with a project structure, code repository. You can use the Jenkins plug-in to deploy your serverless application. To build production-ready applications, you can use the Stackery.io toolkit.

Before installing the SAM CLI on macOS, Windows, and Linux, you must do the following:

- Create an AWS account.
- Create an IAM user with administrator permissions.
- Install the AWS CLI.
- Install Docker.

For additional installation instructions, see https://docs.aws.amazon.com/serverless-application-model/latest/developerguide/serverless-sam-cli-install-mac.html.

Installing Docker on Linux

Assuming you've already created an AWS account and an IAM user, and installed the AWS CLI, you can next install Docker, which is a prerequisite for testing your applications locally. (For additional information, refer to https://docs.aws.amazon.com/cli/latest/userguide/install-cliv2-docker.html.) Before you can run serverless projects and functions locally with the SAM CLI, Docker must be installed and running. The SAM CLI uses the DOCKER_HOST environment variable to contact the Docker daemon.

To install Docker on Linux, in the left-hand column, choose Linux, and then choose your Linux distribution.

To verify that Docker is working, run the docker ps command. (See https://docs.aws.amazon.com/cli/latest/userguide/install-cliv2-docker.html for additional information.)

You don't need to install, fetch, or pull any containers because the SAM CLI does this automatically.

AWS IDE Toolkits

You can create, run, deploy, and debug applications using language-specific Integrated Development Environments (IDE), such as AWS Cloud9, Eclipse, IntelliJ, PyCharm, Visual Studio, Visual Studio Code, Visual Studio Team Services (VSTS), and Rider in Amazon Web Services.

The AWS Toolkit for Eclipse   *Eclipse = Java*

The AWS Toolkit for Eclipse (https://aws.amazon.com/eclipse/) is an open source plug-in for the Eclipse Java IDE that makes easier for developers to develop, debug, and deploy Java applications that use AWS services. The toolkit supports Windows, Linux, macOS, and Unix operating systems.

The Toolkit for Eclipse enhances the features of Eclipse IDE with the following:

- When you create a new AWS project using the Toolkit for Eclipse, the AWS SDK for Java is included and managed by Maven.
- AWS Explorer, an interface to AWS, lets you manage all your AWS resources from within the Eclipse environment.
- AWS SAM project and AWS Lambda Java project blueprint creation, deployment and debugging.
- AWS CodeCommit repository cloning
- Integration with AWS CodeStar
- AWS Elastic Beanstalk deployment and debugging
- An AWS CloudFormation template editor
- Support for multiple AWS accounts

The following are prerequisites for using the AWS Toolkit for Eclipse:

- Java 1.8 or higher
- Eclipse IDE for Java Developers 4.2 or later

NOTE   If you want AWS Toolkit for Eclipse support for the AWS Mobile SDK for Android, you must install Google Android Development Tools (ADT).

Installing the AWS Toolkit for Eclipse
Here's how to install the AWS Toolkit for Eclipse:

1. Open the Eclipse main console.
2. Within Eclipse, click on the Help and then click Install New Software option.
3. In the Work with box, type **https://aws.amazon.com/eclipse** and then press ENTER.
4. Now you can choose the components of the AWS Toolkit for Eclipse that you want to install. Click Select All to install all the components at once. Only the AWS Toolkit for Eclipse Core is mandatory and all other components are optional.
5. Click Next to complete installation, once you have made all your selections.
6. After you have set up the AWS Toolkit for Eclipse then you should configure your AWS Credentials.

It may take up to 30 minutes for the installation to complete, depending on the options selected, and on factors such as network speed, server latency, and system capabilities.

Upgrading the AWS Toolkit for Eclipse

You can use the same instructions for installing the toolkit for upgrading or reinstalling the AWS Toolkit for Eclipse. Due to a bug in old versions of the Oomph plug-in, some versions of Eclipse, (Mars and Neon), may fail to fetch the latest artifacts. But there is a work around for this issue:

1. The AWS Toolkit for Eclipse update site should point to https://aws.amazon.com/eclipse/site.xml

2. Then delete the ~/.eclipse/org.eclipse.oomph.p2/cache/ directory to remove any cached content.

3. Finally install the latest version of Oomph.

The Toolkit for Visual Studio

It is easier to develop, debug, and deploy .NET applications using AWS Toolkit for Visual Studio is a plug-in for the Visual Studio IDE that use Amazon Web Services. Visual Studio versions 2013 and later are supported.

In order to install and configure the Toolkit for Visual Studio, you must have the following prerequisites.

You should have Windows 10, Windows 8, or Windows 7 operating system. It is recommended to install the latest service packs and updates for the Windows version you're using.

You need to use Visual Studio 2013 or later including Community editions. It is recommended to install the latest service packs and updates.

The Toolkit for Visual Studio for Visual Studio 2019 and Visual Studio 2017 is distributed in the Visual Studio Marketplace. Also, you can install and update the toolkit using the Extensions and Updates dialog your existing Visual Studio.

The Toolkit for Visual Studio 2015 and 2013 versions are part of the AWS Tools for Windows.

Installing the Toolkit for Visual Studio in Windows

First, you need to download the installer for the AWS Toolkit for Visual Studio. The toolkit itself is installed automatically. Here's how to do this in Windows:

1. Go to the page AWS Toolkit for Visual Studio.

2. Choose Toolkit for Visual Studio 2013–2015 to download the installer, from the Download section.

3. Run the downloaded installer to start the installation, and follow the instructions.

The Toolkit for Visual Studio is installed by default in the Program Files directory, which requires administrator privileges. You can specify a different installation directory to install the Toolkit for Visual Studio as a non-administrator.

Uninstalling the Toolkit for Visual Studio in Windows

You must uninstall the AWS Tools for Windows before you can uninstall the AWS Toolkit for Visual Studio.

1. Open Programs and Features in the Control Panel.

2. You can run appwiz.cpl from a command prompt or the Windows Run dialog to open Programs and Features directly.

3. You need to choose AWS Tools for Windows, and then choose Uninstall to begin the installation.

4. You need to choose Yes to continue.

Samples directory doesn't get deleted after uninstalling the AWS Tools for Windows. This directory is saved for you in case you have modified the samples. You can manually remove this directory if you want to remove it.

AWS Tools for Visual Studio Team Services

Microsoft Visual Studio Team Services (VSTS) extension is AWS Tools for Microsoft Visual Studio Team Services. It contains tasks you can use in release and build definitions in VSTS and Microsoft Team Foundation Server (TFS) to interact with AWS services. The Visual Studio Marketplace has the AWS Tools for VSTS.

Installing AWS Tools for Visual Studio Team Services

You need to install the AWS Tools for VSTS to begin the setup and you also need to set up AWS credentials to use the tasks using either service endpoints, Amazon EC2 instance metadata or environment variables.

To use Visual Studio Team Services (VSTS), you will first need to sign up for a Visual Studio Team Services Account. Then you can install the AWS Tools for VSTS Extension.

The AWS Tools for VSTS can be installed from Visual Studio Marketplace. Do the following:

1. Sign in to your VSTS account, and then search for AWS Tools for Microsoft Visual Studio Team Services. You can choose Download to install into an on-premises Team Foundation Server or you can choose Install to download to VSTS. Download Team Services Extension and start setting up AWS Credentials for the AWS Tools for VSTS. You need to sign in to AWS and open IAM console to create an IAM user. Then choose Users in the sidebar to view your IAM users.

2. If you don't have any IAM users set up already then choose Create New Users to create new User. You then need to select the IAM user from the list that you want to use to access AWS. Now open the Security Credentials tab and then choose Create Access Key. AWS allows you to have a maximum of two active access keys for any IAM user. If this IAM user has two access keys already then you need to delete one before creating a new key.

3. From the pop-up dialog box that opens in a new window, you can either choose Download Credentials to download the file to your computer or choose Show User Security Credentials to view and can copy and paste. Once you close the dialog box, there is no way to obtain the secret access key. However, you can delete its associated access key ID and create a new key.

You can supply credentials to the tasks in the following ways:

- You can configure a service endpoint, of type AWS, and reference the endpoint when configuring tasks.

- You can create specific named variables in your build. The variable names for supplying credentials are AWS.SecretAccessKey, AWS.AccessKeyID, and AWS. SessionToken. In order to pass the region, you need to specify AWS.Region with the region code (eg us-east-1) of the region.

- You can use the standard AWS environment variables in the build agent process. These variables are AWS_SECRET_ACCESS_KEY, AWS_ACCESS_KEY_ID, and AWS_SESSION_TOKEN. In order to pass the region, you need to specify AWS.Region with the region code (eg us-east-1) of the region.

Chapter Review

This chapter began by explaining all the necessary steps that you need to create a new AWS free account. Because as a developer, it's crucial for you to have a free AWS account to practice everything. I then explained all the free services and limits that are available to you during the trial period and beyond. It's another important thing that you need to be aware while working with AWS because if you exceed the free limit then you will be charged by AWS. I then, introduced you the AWS management console where you learned how to search any AWS service using the search box, adding and removing shortcuts for the services that you use frequently. Then we explored on how to change a region, as well as account information where you can change the security credentials, see the support plans, GovCloud, and have an option to close the account. Then we delve into the Support Center, Alerts, Resource Group, and Tag Editor on the navigation pane. You also learned how to install, configure, and how to control multiple AWS services from the command line and automate them through scripts using the AWS Command Line Interface (CLI). We then introduced the AWS SDK, which removes the complexity of hard coding against a service interface and making it easier to code applications. By providing many of Java API for many of AWS Services, the AWS SDK for Java helps take the high complexities out of coding. It is the collection of all the developer's tools for the creation of .Net-based applications that run on AWS infrastructure, and it also helps to make AWS services and applications available through the web browser across many devices and operating systems in a reliable manner.

We also learned AWS PowerShell administration by installing and configuring the AWS PowerShell tools. The PowerShell helps administrators and developers to manage the AWS services using PowerShell scripting environment. We also explored how to run your serverless application locally for quick development and testing by using AWS Serverless Application Model (SAM). AWS SAM is open source and includes a template specification, which is an extension of CloudFormation template and a command-line interface (CLI) to invoke AWS Lambda functions and debug applications deployed on the AWS cloud. Finally, we have gone through the AWS Toolkit for Eclipse, which is an open source plug-in for the Eclipse Java IDE (Integrated Development Environment) that makes it easier for developers to develop, debug, and deploy Java applications that use AWS services. Also explored were the AWS Toolkit for Visual Studio, which is a plug-in for the Visual Studio IDE that makes it easier for developers to develop, debug, and deploy .NET applications that use AWS services. This chapter is the building block where we explored all the tools that you need to build the secure cloud native applications on the AWS cloud.

Exercises

The following exercises will help you practice to use the AWS CLI and the Console to perform various administrative tasks.

You need to create an AWS account as explained earlier in this chapter for performing the following exercises. You can use the Free Tier when launching AWS resources, but make sure to terminate them at the end.

Exercise 2-1: Create an IAM User Using the AWS Management Console

In this exercise, you create a new IAM User using the Console.

1. Sign in to the AWS Management Console and use search IAM in the console and go to https://console.aws.amazon.com/iam/.

2. Once you are in IAM navigation pane, choose Users and then choose Add User option.

3. You then need to type the user name for the new user. If you want to add more than one user at the same time, you can choose Add Another User for up to 10 users at one time.

4. Select the type of access for this user, either you can select programmatic access or access to the AWS Management Console, or both access.

5. On the Set permissions page, you can specify how you want to assign permissions from one of the following three options:

   - Add user to group

   - Copy permissions from existing user

   - Attach existing policies to user directly

6. Choose Next. Here you can enter Tags, which is the metadata to the user as key-value pairs.

7. Choose Next. Review all the options for the User.

8. You can choose Create User and then download access key IDs and secret access keys.

Exercise 2-2: Enable Multi-Factor Authentication MFA for an IAM User

In this exercise, you create an Enabling Multifactor authentication.

1. You need to first sign in to the AWS Management Console and open the IAM console at https://console.aws.amazon.com/iam/.

2. In the IAM navigation pane, choose Users.

3. In the User Name list, choose the name to which you want to enable MFA user.

4. Then you need to choose the Security credentials tab. Next to Assigned MFA device you need to choose the Manage option.

5. From the Manage MFA Device wizard, you need to choose Virtual MFA device and then select Continue.

6. Open your virtual MFA app.

7. Then you can do one of the following:

   - From the wizard, you need to choose Show QR code, and use the app to scan the QR code.

   —or—

   - From the Manage MFA Device wizard, you choose Show secret key, and then type the secret key into your MFA app.

   When it's finished, the virtual MFA device starts generating one-time passwords.

8. In the Manage MFA Device wizard, type the one-time password in MFA code 1 box that currently appears in the virtual MFA device. Then wait up to 30 seconds for the device to generate a new password. Now type the second password into the MFA code 2 box.

9. Choose Assign MFA option.

10. Now the virtual MFA device is ready for use with AWS.

Exercise 2-3: Use an AWS CLI to Create a Custom VPC and Subnets

In this exercise, you create a custom VPC and subnets.

1. You can create a custom VPC with a 192.168.0.0/16 CIDR block.
   ```
   aws ec2 create-vpc --cidr-block 192.168.0.0/16
   ```

2. Then create a subnet with a 192.168.1.0/24 CIDR block.
   ```
   aws ec2 create-subnet --vpc-id vpc-3e87b457 --cidr-block 192.168.1.0/24
   ```

3. Also create a second subnet in your VPC with a 192.168.2.0/24 CIDR block.
   ```
   aws ec2 create-subnet --vpc-id vpc-3e87b457 --cidr-block 192.168.2.0/24
   ```

4. In order to make your subnet public, you need to create an Internet gateway.
   ```
   aws ec2 create-internet-gateway
   ```

5. Then you need to attach the Internet gateway to your VPC.

```
aws ec2 attach-internet-gateway --vpc-id vpc-3e87b457 --internet-
gateway-id igw-2ee6b16c
```

6. Create a custom route table for your VPC to route the traffic.

```
aws ec2 create-route-table --vpc-id vpc-3e87b457
```

7. Now update the Route Table by creating a route that points all traffic (0.0.0.0/0) to the Internet gateway.

```
aws ec2 create-route --route-table-id rtb-d2d7ebb5 --destination-cidr-
block 0.0.0.0/0 --gateway-id igw-2ee6b16c
```

8. You then need to associate it with a subnet in your VPC, so that the traffic from that subnet is routed to the Internet gateway.

```
aws ec2 associate-route-table  --subnet-id subnet-c57143fd --route-
table-id rtb-d2d7ebb5
```

9. You need to modify the public IP addressing behavior of your subnet if you want the instances launched into the subnet to automatically receive a public IP address.

```
aws ec2 modify-subnet-attribute --subnet-id subnet-c57143fd --map-
public-ip-on-launch
```

Exercise 2-4: Use an AWS CLI to Create a Key Pair

In this exercise, you use an AWS CLI to create a key pair.

1. Now you need to create a key pair, to launch and connect to an instance in your public subnet.

```
aws ec2 create-key-pair --key-name MyEC2KeyPair --query 'KeyMaterial'
--output text > MyEC2KeyPair.pem
```

2. In order to use an SSH client on a Linux or Mac OS X operating system to connect to your EC2 instance, you need to use the following command to restrict the permissions of your private key file.

```
chmod 400 MyEC2KeyPair.pem
```

Exercise 2-5: Use an AWS CLI to Create a Security Group and EC2 Instance

In this exercise, you create an EC2 instance and security group using AWS CLI.

1. Create a security group in your VPC, and add a rule that allows SSH access from anywhere (it's not recommended for allowing SSH access from anywhere and you might need to restrict to known IP ranges).

```
aws ec2 create-security-group --group-name SSHAccess --description
"Security group for SSH access" --vpc-id vpc-3e87b457

aws ec2 authorize-security-group-ingress --protocol tcp --port
22--group-id sg-f2ec7d8b --cidr 0.0.0.0/0
```

2. You can now launch an EC2 instance into your public subnet, using the security group and key pair that we have created in previous steps.

```
aws ec2 run-instances --image-id ami-b5736ed8 --count 1 --instance-
type t2.micro --key-name MyEC2KeyPair --security-group-ids sg-f2ec7d8b
--subnet-id subnet-c57143fd
```

3. After your instance is in the running state, you can connect to it using an SSH client from a Linux or Mac OS X computer by using the following command:

```
ssh -i "MyEC2KeyPair.pem" ec2-user@63.176.157.124
```

Exercise 2-6: Use an AWS CLI to Delete the VPC and Subnets

In this exercise, you delete the VPC and subnets using AWS CLI.

1. Once you've verified that you can connect to your EC2 instance, and then you can terminate it if you no longer need it to save cost. So, we need to delete the dependencies before deleting the VPC. First, delete your security group:

```
aws ec2 delete-security-group --group-id f2ec7d8b
```

2. Then you can delete your subnets:

```
aws ec2 delete-subnet --subnet-id subnet-c57143fd
aws ec2 delete-subnet --subnet-id subnet-b57143ed
```

3. And then you can delete your custom route table:

```
aws ec2 delete-route-table --route-table-id rtb-d2d7ebb5
```

4. You need to detach your Internet gateway from your VPC before deleting it.

```
aws ec2 detach-internet-gateway --internet-gateway-id igw-2ee6b16c
--vpc-id vpc-3e87b457
```

5. Now you can delete your Internet gateway:

```
aws ec2 delete-internet-gateway --internet-gateway-id igw-2ee6b16c
```

6. Finally, you can delete your VPC:

```
aws ec2 delete-vpc --vpc-id vpc-3e87b457
```

Questions

The following questions will help you gauge your understanding of the contents in this chapter. Read all the answers carefully because there might be more than one correct answer. Choose the best response for each question.

1. What parameters do you need to set up an AWS CLI? (Choose all that apply.)

   A. AWS Access Key ID

   B. AWS Secret Access Key

   C. Default region name

   D. Default output format

2. What is the command to create EC2 key pair using an AWS CLI?

   A. `aws ec2 create-key-pair --key-name 'my key pair'`

   B. `aws ec2 modify-key-pair --key-name 'my key pair'`

   C. `aws ec2 delete-key-pair --key-name 'my key pair'`

   D. `aws ec2 stop-key-pair --key-name 'my key pair'`

3. Which of the following AWS CLI commands lists all your instances and view information about those EC2 instances?

A. `aws ec2 display-instances`

B. `aws ec2 describe-instances`

C. `aws ec2 discover-instances`

D. `aws ec2 show-instances`

4. Which of the following AWS PowerShell commands can be used to list your S3 bucket named my-s3-files?

A. `PS C:\> Read-S3Object -BucketName my-s3-files`

B. `PS C:\> Get-S3BucketPolicy -BucketName my-s3-files`

C. `PS C:\>Copy-S3Object -BucketName my-s3-files`

D. `PS C:\>Get-S3Bucket -BucketName my-s3-files`

5. You want to delete a S3 bucket named my-old-files. Which of the following AWS PowerShell commands can be used to delete it?

A. `PS C:\>Remove-S3Bucket -BucketName my-old-files`

B. `PS C:\>Delete-S3Bucket -BucketName my-old-files`

C. `PS C:\>Purge-S3Bucket -BucketName my-old-files`

D. `PS C:\>Drop-S3Bucket -BucketName my-old-files`

6. Which of the AWS PowerShell commands retrieves a collection of users in the current AWS account?

A. `PS C:\>Retrieve-IAMUserList`

B. `PS C:\>Pull-IAMUserList`

C. `PS C:\>Show-IAMUserList`

D. `PS C:\>Get-IAMUserList`

7. Mike left your team so you need to delete the IAM user named Mike using AWS PowerShell. Which of the following commands achieves this goal?

A. `PS C:\>Remove-IAMUser -UserName Mike`

B. `PS C:\>Delete-IAMUser -UserName Mike`

C. `PS C:\>Drop-IAMUser -UserName Mike`

D. `PS C:\>Purge-IAMUser -UserName Mike`

8. Which of the following is a CLI tool for local development and testing of Serverless applications?

A. `AWS PowerShell`

B. `AWS CLI`

C. `AWS SAM Local`

D. `AWS SDK`

9. Your networking team provided 192.172.0.0/22 CIDR block for creating AWS VPC. Which of the following AWS CLIs creates the VPC for you using the correct CIDR block?

   A. `aws ec2 initiate-vpc --cidr-block 192.172.0.0/22`

   B. `aws ec2 generate-vpc --cidr-block 192.172.0.0/22`

   C. `aws ec2 write-vpc --cidr-block 192.172.0.0/22`

   D. `aws ec2 create-vpc --cidr-block 192.172.0.0/22`

10. The following AWS CLI command attaches a volume (vol-9876543210fedcba0) to an instance (i-54321ab789c09876) as /dev/xvdh,

    ```
    aws ec2 attach-volume --volume-id vol-9876543210fedcba0
    --instance-id i-54321ab789c09876 --device /dev/xvdh
    ```

    A. True

    B. False

11. As part of your disaster recovery strategy, you need to copy the specified AMI from us-west-2 region to us-east-1 region using dry run option. The following AWS CLI command copies the AWS AMI from us-east1 to us-west-2.

    ```
    aws ec2 copy-image --dry-run --source-region us-west-2
    --region us-east-1 --source-image-id ami-6842234d --name
    "West server"
    ```

    A. False

    B. True

12. Your development team wants you to create an image of an existing EC2 instance. Which AWS CLI command will achieve the image creation?

    A. `aws ec2 create-image --instance-id i-9876543210fedcba0`

    B. `aws ec2 generate-image --instance-id i-9876543210fedcba0`

    C. `aws ec2 copy-image --instance-id i-9876543210fedcba0`

    D. `aws ec2 build-image --instance-id i-9876543210fedcba0`

13. As per best practice, you would like to add Tags to your AWS AMI to identify the environment. Which of the following AWS CLI commands creates a Tag for AMI?

    A. `aws ec2 generate-tags --resources ami-67b431221 --tags Key=ENV, Value=DEV`

    B. `aws ec2 copy-tags --resources ami-67b431221 --tags Key=ENV, Value=DEV`

    C. `aws ec2 create-tags --resources ami-67b431221 --tags Key=ENV, Value=DEV`

    D. `aws ec2 build-tags --resources ami-67b431221 --tags Key=ENV, Value=DEV`

14. You have created a custom VPC vpc-b12217d3 and want to create a route table for that VPC. Which of the following AWS CLI commands creates the route table?

   A. `aws ec2 build-route-table --vpc-id vpc-b12217d3`

   B. `aws ec2 generate-route-table --vpc-id vpc-b12217d3`

   C. `aws ec2 copy-route-table --vpc-id vpc-b12217d3`

   D. `aws ec2 create-route-table --vpc-id vpc-b12217d3`

15. You created an EC2 instance with IP 55.166.46.122 using MyEC2KeyPair. pem key-pair and you want to connect to it using an SSH client from a Linux machine. Which of the following commands helps you to successfully connect to your EC2 instance?

   A. `ssh -connect "MyEC2KeyPair.pem" ec2-user@55.166.46.122`

   B. `ssh -attach "MyEC2KeyPair.pem" ec2-user@55.166.46.122`

   C. `ssh -i "MyEC2KeyPair.pem" ec2-user@55.166.46.122`

   D. `ssh -link "MyEC2KeyPair.pem" ec2-user@55.166.46.122`

16. You Audit and Compliance team recommends using Least Privilege for IAM Users. How do you achieve it?

   A. By granting only the permissions required to perform a task

   B. By granting everyone root access to perform a task

   C. By revoking all the access from IAM Users

   D. By deleting the User from IAM console

17. You want to remove the complexity out of Java coding by using _____ for AWS services including Amazon S3, Amazon ECS, DynamoDB, and AWS Lambda.

   A. AWS SDK

   B. AWS CLI

   C. AWS PowerShell

   D. AWS SAM Local

18. The _____ is an open source plug-in for the Eclipse Java integrated development environment (IDE) and it makes it easier for developers to develop, debug, and deploy Java applications that use AWS.

   A. AWS CodeCommit

   B. AWS CodePipeline

   C. AWS CodeBuild

   D. AWS Toolkit for Eclipse

19. The _____ is a plug-in for the Visual Studio integrated development environment (IDE) and it makes it easier for developers to develop, debug, and deploy .NET applications that use AWS?

    A. AWS Toolkit for Visual Studio

    B. AWS CodeCommit

    C. AWS CodePipeline

    D. AWS CodeBuild

20. _____ contains tasks you can use in build and release definitions in VSTS to interact with AWS services, and it is available through the Visual Studio Marketplace.

    A. AWS CLI

    B. AWS SDK

    C. AWS PowerShell

    D. AWS Tools for Visual Studio Team Services (VSTS)

Answers

1. **A, B, C, D.** You need the AWS Access Key ID, AWS Secret Access Key, Default region name, and Default output format parameters to setup AWS CLI.

2. **A.** This is the correct AWS CLI command to create the EC2 key pair.

3. **B.** This AWS CLI command lists all your instances and let you view information about those EC2 instances.

4. **D.** This AWS PowerShell command lists your S3 bucket named my-s3-files.

5. **A.** It's the right AWS PowerShell command to delete a S3 bucket named my-old-files.

6. **D.** It is the correct AWS PowerShell command that lists collection of users in the current AWS account.

7. **A.** This AWS PowerShell command deletes the IAM user named Mike from your AWS account.

8. **C.** AWS SAM Local CLI tool is used for the local development and testing of Serverless applications (i.e., AWS Lambda functions).

9. **D.** This AWS CLI command creates a custom VPC using 192.172.0.0/22 CIDR block.

10. **A.** True. This AWS CLI command attaches the volume vol-9876543210fedcba0 to the instance i- i-54321ab789c09876 as /dev/xvdh.

11. **B.** True. It is the right AWS CLI command to copy the specified AMI from us-west-2 region to us-east-1 region.

12. A. The development team can use this AWS CLI command to create an image of an existing EC2 instance.

13. C. It is the correct AWS CLI command to add Tags to your AWS AMI to identify the environment.

14. D. It is the AWS CLI command to create a route table for your custom VPC vpc-b12217d3.

15. C. It is the correct way to connect to EC2 instance with IP 55.166.46.122 using MyEC2KeyPair.pem key-pair using an SSH client from a Linux machine.

16. A. By granting only the permissions required to perform a task, you need to find out what users need to do and then create access policies for them that let the users perform only those tasks.

17. A. AWS SDK will remove the complexity out of Java coding for AWS services including Amazon S3, Amazon ECS, DynamoDB, and AWS Lambda.

18. D. AWS Toolkit for Eclipse is the plug-in for the Eclipse Java IDE.

19. A. AWS Toolkit for Visual Studio is the plug-in for the Visual Studio IDE.

20. D. AWS Tools for Visual Studio Team Services contains tasks you can use in build and release definitions in VSTS to interact with AWS services.

Additional Resources

- **AWS Documentation**   There is no place like official AWS documentation to get the latest and correct information about all the AWS services. Always refer to the official AWS blogs to get the latest updates about new AWS services and update to existing features.
  `https://docs.aws.amazon.com` and `https://aws.amazon.com/blogs/aws`

- **AWS Command Line Interface**   This is a tool to control various AWS services from the command line and also to automate them through scripts.
  `https://docs.aws.amazon.com/cli/latest/reference/` and `https://github.com/aws/aws-cli`

- **Tools to Build on AWS**   List of tools for developing and managing applications on AWS using Go, Java, .Net, Node.js, Python, Ruby, etc.
  `https://aws.amazon.com/tools/` and `https://github.com/aws/aws-sdk-java`

- **AWS Tools for PowerShell**   This tool helps developers and administrators manage their AWS services and resources in Windows, Linux, and MacOS environments.
  `https://aws.amazon.com/powershell/` and `https://github.com/aws/aws-tools-for-powershell`

- **AWS Serverless Application Model**   is an open source framework, which provides functions, APIs, databases, and event source mappings for building serverless applications with a few lines of configuration.
  `https://aws.amazon.com/serverless/sam/` and `https://github.com/awslabs/serverless-application-model`

- **Developer Tools on AWS**   to code, build, test, and deploy your applications to AWS. It also help you to automate the provisioning and managing your infrastructure and by eliminating the need for manual updates to avoid any manual errors.
  `https://aws.amazon.com/products/developer-tools/`

PART I

Networking Using Amazon Virtual Private Cloud

In this chapter, you will learn
- Virtual Private Cloud (VPC)
- Subnets (public and private)
- Route tables
- Network access control lists (ACLs)
- Security groups
- Internet gateways
- Dynamic Host Configuration Protocol (DHCP) option sets
- Elastic Internet Protocols (IPs)
- Endpoints
- Network Address Translation (NAT) gateways
- Egress-only Internet gateways
- Peering connections
- Virtual private gateways
- Customer gateways
- Site-to-site virtual private network (VPN)
- Point-to-site VPN
- Direct connect
- Transit gateways

Welcome to the AWS networking chapter. In the last chapter we created an AWS free account and looked at various ways of connecting to AWS services. Then we saw how to enable multifactor authentication (MFA) for the root account and how to secure the root account against any unauthorized access (this will be explored in more depth in Chapter 10). The next thing we need is a logically isolated section of AWS that you can own and control, similar to separate networks in your on-premises datacenter. In this chapter, we will explore the core components of Amazon Virtual Private Cloud (VPC), and you will learn how to build your own VPC and VPN solution to securely connect using an Internet Protocol security (IPSec) tunnel. I highly recommend reading this chapter carefully and completing all the exercises, because a strong knowledge of Amazon VPC, connectivity, and troubleshooting will help you in both the real world and to pass the exam.

Amazon Virtual Private Cloud

Amazon VPC is the networking layer for Amazon Elastic Compute Cloud (EC2) instances and enables you to launch AWS resources into an isolated virtual network that you've provisioned. A VPC is a virtual network dedicated to your IP address range, subnets, network access control lists (NACLs), security groups, and route tables to your AWS account.

Assume you have a business with offices across the United States, Australia, and Europe and you need to set up datacenters, which will take a few weeks to months. You can create a VPC in each region within a few minutes, as shown in Figure 3-1, and secure it using NACLs and security groups.

Your AWS account comes with a default VPC that has a subnet in each availability zone that is ready for you to use. If you don't specify a subnet when you launch an instance, the instance will be launched into your default VPC. A VPC spans all the availability zones in a particular region, whereas a subnet must reside entirely within one availability zone and cannot span across zones.

You can also create your own VPC, which is called a nondefault VPC, and configure it as you need. Any subnets that you create in your default and nondefault VPCs are called nondefault subnets. You will not pay an additional charge for using the Amazon VPC; however, you will pay the standard rates for the EC2 instances and any site-to-site VPN connection and Network Address Translation (NAT) gateway.

Amazon VPC has been validated as being compliant with the Payment Card Industry (PCI) Data Security Standard (DSS) and supports the processing, storage, and transmission of credit card data by a merchant or service provider.

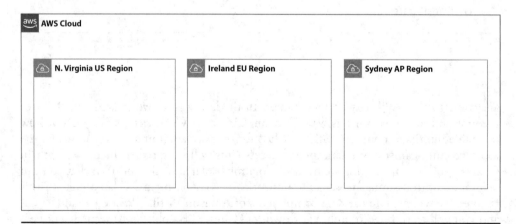

Figure 3-1 AWS accounts and regions

There are soft limits (which can be increased by submitting a request to AWS, e.g., on the Amazon VPC limit form) and hard limits (which can't be changed) to the number of Amazon VPCs and the components you can provision. You start with a default limit of five VPCs per region. There is a limit of 200 subnets per VPC. The limit for IPv4 is five IPv4 Classless Inter-Domain Routing (CIDR) blocks per VPC, and this comprises your primary CIDR block plus four secondary CIDR blocks. The limit for IPv6 is one IPv6 CIDR block per VPC, and this limit cannot be increased. These limits change over time so please refer to https://docs.aws.amazon.com/general/latest/gr/aws_service_limits .html for the latest AWS service limits.

Subnets

As mentioned, a VPC spans all the availability zones in a particular region, whereas a subnet must reside entirely within one availability zone and cannot span across them. You can add one or more subnets to each availability zone after creating the VPC. You can specify the CIDR block for the subnet when you create it, which should be a subset of the VPC CIDR block. You can protect your applications from failure by launching instances in separate availability zones, which are engineered to be isolated from failures in other availability zones.

You can assign IPv6 CIDR blocks to your subnets by assigning an IPv6 CIDR block to your VPC. A VPN connection enables you to communicate with your corporate network, and an Internet gateway enables communication over the Internet.

Public Subnet

A subnet is called public when its traffic is routed to an Internet gateway. Your instance must have a public IPv4 address or an elastic IP address (IPv4), which is a static public IPv4 address assigned by AWS, if it needs to communicate with the Internet over IPv4. Your instance must have an IPv6 address if it needs to communicate with the Internet over IPv6.

Private Subnet

A subnet is called private when it doesn't have a route to the Internet gateway. The internal IPv4 address range of the subnet is always private, regardless of the type of subnet, and AWS does not announce this address block to the Internet.

Route Tables

A route table has a set of rules that are used to determine where network traffic is directed. All your subnets in a VPC must be associated with a route table because this table controls the routing for the subnet. You can associate multiple subnets with the same route table; however, a single subnet can only be associated with one route table at any point in time.

A primary or main route table is created automatically with your VPC where you can add, remove, and modify routes based on your need. You can also create custom route tables for your VPC if required. Your subnet is implicitly associated with the primary route table if you don't explicitly associate a subnet with any particular custom route table.

The main route table controls the routing for all your subnets that are not explicitly associated with any other custom route table.

You cannot delete the main route table, and each route in a table specifies a destination CIDR and a target. AWS uses the most specific route that matches the traffic and determines how to route it. You must update the route table for any subnet that uses a virtual private gateway, an Internet gateway, an egress-only Internet gateway, a peering connection, a NAT device, or a VPC endpoint in your VPC. You can have 200 route tables per VPC, and this limit includes the main route table. You can add 50 nonpropagated routes per route table, and you can increase this limit up to a maximum of 1,000 if required. You can add 100 Border Gateway Protocol (BGP)–advertised propagated routes per route table, but this limit cannot be increased.

Network Access Control Lists

The VPC provides another layer of security by acting as a firewall for controlling traffic in and out of one or more subnets. The default VPC automatically comes with a modifiable default NACL, and it allows all inbound and outbound IPv4 and IPv6 traffic, if applicable. You can add or remove rules from the default NACL or create additional custom NACLs for your VPC. The changes are automatically applied to the subnets to which NACL is associated with when you add or remove rules from a network ACL.

All the subnets in your VPC must be associated with a NACL. Your subnet is automatically associated with the default NACL if you don't configure it otherwise. A subnet can be associated with only one NACL at a time, but you can associate a NACL with multiple subnets. The previous association is removed when you associate a new NACL with a subnet.

NACLs are stateless, so the inbound traffic allowed is subject to the rules for outbound traffic (and vice versa). A NACL contains a number of rules, and AWS evaluates them in an order from lowest to highest to decide whether traffic is allowed to and from the associated subnet. The highest number you can use for NACLs rules is 32766, and AWS recommends creating rules in increments to make it easy to add any new future rules that you may need later on.

Security Groups

A security group acts as another virtual firewall at the instance level that controls the inbound and outbound traffic. You can assign up to five security groups to the instance when you launch it in a VPC. NACLs act at the subnet level, and security groups act at the instance level. You can assign a different set of security groups to each instance in a subnet of your VPC. Your security group name must be unique within the VPC.

 EXAM TIP You don't have to add a rule to allow your instances to communicate with each other. If you use the default security group, it automatically allows communication; but you must add a rule to allow this if you use anything other than the security group.

You can add rules that control the inbound traffic to instances for each security group and add a separate set of rules that control the outbound traffic. The default number of security groups per region limit is 2,500 and the maximum limit is 10,000. The default security group rule limit is 60 for inbound and 60 for outbound per security group—for example, a security group can have 60 inbound rules for IPv4 traffic and 60 inbound rules for IPv6 traffic.

TIP   If you use ::/0 in your security group for IPv6, then you are enabling all IP addresses over the Internet to access your instance using Secure Shell (SSH) or Remote Desktop Protocol (RDP). This is acceptable only for your learning proof of concept (POC) or testing purpose, but it's unsafe and not a best practice in enterprise production environments. In a production environment, you'll authorize only a specific IP address or range of addresses to access your instance.

In a security group, you can only allow rules—you cannot not deny rules. You can specify separate rules for inbound traffic and another rule for outbound traffic. You can create a security group with no inbound rules, in which case the inbound traffic originating from another host to your instance will not be allowed until you explicitly add inbound rules to the security group. In the same way, if your security group has no outbound rules, no outbound traffic originating from your instance is allowed.

Security groups are stateful, which means that when you send a request from your instance, the return response traffic for that request is allowed to flow back to the instance, regardless of your inbound security group rules. In the same way, the responses to the inbound traffic are allowed to flow out, regardless of your outbound rules.

TIP   If you use 0.0.0.0/0 in your security group for IPv4, you are enabling all IP addresses over the Internet to access your instance using SSH or RDP. This is acceptable only for your learning POC or testing purpose; it's unsafe and not a best practice in enterprise production environments. In a production environment, you'll authorize only a specific IP address or range of addresses or a single IP address /32 to access your instance.

Internet Gateways

An Internet gateway is a highly available, redundant, and horizontally scaled VPC component that allows communication between the Internet and instances in your VPC. It doesn't impose bandwidth constraints or any availability risks on your network traffic. It serves two purposes: to perform NAT for instances that have not been assigned public IPv4 addresses and to provide a target in your VPC route tables for Internet-routable traffic, including IPv4 and IPv6 traffic.

You need to make sure that your NACL and security group rules allow the relevant traffic to flow to and from the Internet for instances in a VPC subnet. You need to attach an Internet gateway to a VPC and make sure that the subnet's route table points to it. Also make sure that instances in your subnet have a globally unique IP address (elastic IP address, public IPv4 address, or IPv6 address).

A subnet is called public when associated with a route table that has a route to an Internet gateway. Your instance must have a public IPv4 address or an elastic IP address that's associated with a private IPv4 address if you want to enable communication over the Internet for IPv4. Your VPC and subnet must have an associated IPv6 CIDR block, and your instance must be assigned an IPv6 address from the range of the subnet. IPv6 addresses are globally unique and are public by default if you want to enable communication over the Internet for IPv6.

Dynamic Host Configuration Protocol Option Sets

The options field of a Dynamic Host Configuration Protocol (DHCP) message contains configuration parameters like domain name, domain name server, and the NetBIOS node type, and it provides a standard for sending configuration details to hosts on the TCP/IP network.

The DHCP options sets can be configured for your VPC. The Amazon EC2 instances that you launch into a nondefault VPC are private by default. Unless you specifically assign a public IPv4 address during launch, they're not assigned, or you need to modify the subnet's public IPv4 address attribute. By default, AWS assigns an unresolvable host-name like ip-10-10-10-101 to all instances in any nondefault VPC. You can define your own domain name for your instances, and you must specify a special set of DHCP options to use with the VPC.

The IP addresses default to Amazon-provided DNS, or you can set up custom domain name servers, with the names separated by commas. You must set domain name servers to a custom DNS server if you want your instance to receive a custom DNS hostname, as specified in the domain name. After you attach the DHCP options with a VPC, both existing and new instances that you launch automatically pick up the changes within a few hours, depending on the current frequency with which the DHCP lease is renewed. You don't need to restart or relaunch the instances. If required, you can explicitly renew the lease using the operating system on that instance.

You can't modify the DHCP options after you create them. If required, you can set up your VPC to use no DHCP options at all. You can associate only one set of DHCP options with a VPC. The DHCP option is disassociated from the VPC when you delete it.

 NOTE Your default VPC automatically has a set of DHCP options with the Amazon-provided DNS server domain-nameservers=AmazonProvidedDNS that allows any public subnets in your VPC to communicate with the Internet over an Internet gateway.

Elastic Internet Protocols

can be moved to different VPCs

An elastic Internet Protocol (IP) address is a public static address that you can associate with an instance or network interface for any of your account VPCs. When you associate the elastic IP address with the network interface instead of directly associating it with an instance, you can move all the attributes of the network interface from one instance to another instance easily. AWS currently supports only IPv4 addresses and not IPv6 elastic IP addresses. Elastic IP address can be assigned to only one instance at a time. You can associate an elastic IP address with an instance, and it updates the network interface attached to it.

The elastic IP address can be moved from one instance to another either within the same VPC or another VPC. Until you explicitly release your elastic IP address, it remains associated with your AWS account. AWS charges for elastic IP addresses that are not associated with a running instance, that are stopped, or that are not attached to any network interface. You are not charged for an elastic IP address when the associated instance is running. As mentioned, you are limited to five elastic IP addresses, but you can increase this amount by creating a ticket with AWS. You can tag an elastic IP address; however, tags are not recovered when you recover an elastic IP address.

You are allowed to bring part or all of your public IPv4 address range from your on-premises network to your AWS account. Bring your own IP (BYOIP) enables you to move all or part of your existing publicly routable IPv4 address space to AWS. You will continue to own that IP range, but AWS will advertise it on the Internet. You can create elastic IPs from the IP space you bring to AWS and use them with your EC2 instances, network load balancers, and NAT gateways. You will continue to have access to AWS elastic IPs, so you can choose to use BYOIP elastic IPs, Amazon-supplied IPs, or both.

 EXAM TIP If you want your instance to be accessible via an IPv4 address over the Internet, SSH, or RDP, you must associate an elastic IP address (i.e., a static public IPv4 address) to your instance, and you must configure your security group rules to allow access over IPv4.

Endpoints

VPC endpoint services powered by the Private Link service do not require an Internet gateway, NAT device, VPN connection, or AWS Direct Connect connection, and they enable you to privately connect your VPC to supported AWS services. When you use the VPC endpoint, your instances do not require public IP addresses to communicate with other resources and the traffic does not leave the Amazon network.

Endpoints are virtual devices that are highly available, redundant, and horizontally scaled VPC components. Without imposing the availability risks or bandwidth constraints on your network traffic, they allow communication between instances in your VPC and various services. Interface endpoints and gateway endpoints are the two types of VPC endpoints that you can create.

Interface Endpoints

An interface endpoint is an elastic network interface that is powered by AWS Private Link with a private IP address that serves as an entry point for traffic destined to a supported service. The following services are supported interface endpoints:

- AWS CloudFormation
- Amazon API Gateway
- AWS CloudTrail
- Amazon CloudWatch
- Amazon CloudWatch Events
- Amazon CloudWatch Logs
- AWS CodePipeline
- AWS CodeBuild
- AWS Config
- AWS CodeCommit
- Amazon EC2 API
- Elastic Load Balancing
- Amazon Elastic Container Service
- Amazon Elastic Container Registry
- AWS Key Management Service
- Amazon Kinesis Data Streams
- Amazon Kinesis Data Firehose
- Amazon SageMaker and Amazon SageMaker Runtime
- Amazon SageMaker Notebook Instance
- AWS Secrets Manager
- AWS Security Token Service
- AWS Service Catalog
- Amazon SQS
- Amazon SNS
- AWS Systems Manager
- AWS Transfer for SFTP
- Endpoint services hosted by other AWS accounts
- Supported AWS Marketplace partner services

Gateway Endpoints

A gateway endpoint is the target of a specified route in your route table that is used for traffic destined to any supported AWS service. The following AWS services are supported:

- DynamoDB
- Amazon S3

Controlling the Use of VPC Endpoints

You need to create an AWS Identity and Access Management (IAM) user policy that grants users the required permissions to create, modify, describe, and delete endpoints because IAM users do not have permission to work with any endpoints by default. Here is an example of the IAM policy:

```
{
    "Version": "2012-10-17",
    "Statement":[{
    "Effect":"Allow",
    "Action":"ec2:*VpcEndpoint*",
    "Resource":"*"
    }
  ]
}
```

Network Address Translation Devices

If you want to enable instances in a private subnet to connect to the Internet but prevent the Internet from initiating connections with the instances, you need a NAT device. It forwards traffic from the instances in the private subnet to the Internet and then sends the response back to the instances. The source IPv4 address is replaced with the NAT device's address when traffic goes to the Internet, and the NAT device translates the address back to the instances' private IPv4 addresses when the response traffic is coming through.

You need to use an egress-only Internet gateway instead of NAT devices for IPv6 traffic because NAT devices are not configured for IPv6 traffic. AWS supports two kinds of NAT devices: NAT gateways and NAT instances. AWS recommends using NAT gateways over NAT instances, since the NAT gateway provides better availability and bandwidth. The NAT gateway service is offered as a managed service, so it does not require any administration efforts from you. You may need to choose a NAT instance for specific purposes, and it is launched from a NAT Amazon Machine Image (AMI).

NAT Gateways

A NAT gateway is charged in terms of hourly usage and data processing rates. You must specify the public subnet to create a NAT gateway and specify an elastic IP address to associate with it. You then need to update the route table, which is associated with one or more of your private subnets, to point Internet-bound traffic to the NAT gateway to enable the instances in your private subnets to communicate with the Internet.

If you attach a single NAT gateway to multiple private subnets, this will affect other subnets when the availability zone of the NAT gateway is down. So, if you want to create an availability zone–independent architecture, to avoid failure, you need to create a NAT gateway in each availability zone and configure the routing to ensure that your resources in private subnets use the NAT gateway in the same availability zone.

A NAT gateway bandwidth is 5 Gbps and automatically scales up to 45 Gbps as required. You can distribute the workload by splitting your resources into multiple subnets if you require more bandwidth and create a NAT gateway in each subnet. A NAT gateway supports Internet Control Message Protocol (ICMP), Transmission Control Protocol (TCP), and User Datagram Protocol (UDP) and uses ports from 1024 to 65535. A NAT gateway supports up to 55,000 simultaneous connections to each unique destination. You cannot associate a security group with a NAT gateway, but you can use a NACL to control the traffic to and from the subnet in which the NAT gateway is attached.

 CAUTION   You will be charged for creating and using a NAT gateway in your AWS account. It has hourly usage and data processing charges in addition to the Amazon EC2 charges for data transfer, so use caution when creating the NAT gateway and terminate it when you don't need it anymore.

NAT Instances

You need to create your NAT instance in a public subnet to enable instances in the private subnet to initiate outbound IPv4 traffic to the Internet but at the same time prevent the instances from receiving inbound traffic initiated by someone on the Internet. Amazon offers the Amazon Linux AMI, which is configured to run as a NAT instance. You can search for them in the Amazon EC2 console—they include the string amzn-ami-vpc-nat in their name.

Egress-Only Internet Gateways

An egress-only Internet gateway is a highly available, redundant, and horizontally scaled VPC component. It allows outbound communication over IPv6 from instances from your VPC to the Internet, and it prevents the Internet from initiating an IPv6 connection with your instances.

IPv6 addresses are public by default and globally unique. You need to add a route to your route table that points a specific range of IPv6 address or all IPv6 traffic (::/0) to the egress-only Internet gateway.

An egress-only Internet gateway is stateful, which means it forwards IPV6 traffic from the instances in the subnet to the Internet and then sends back the responses to the instances. NACL can be used to control the traffic to and from the subnet for which the egress-only Internet gateway routes the IPV6 traffic.

Peering Connections

A VPC peering connection routes the traffic between two VPCs privately, where instances in both VPCs can communicate with each other as if they are in the same network. You can create a VPC peering connection between your own VPCs or with a VPC in another

AWS account, or with a VPC in a different AWS region. AWS does not use a gateway or a site-to-site VPN connection and does not rely on a separate piece of physical hardware to create a VPC peering connection, so there is no bandwidth bottleneck or a single point of failure in terms of communication.

A VPC peering connection makes it easy to transfer data between your EC2 instances, Amazon Relational Database Service (RDS) databases, and AWS Lambda functions that run in different AWS regions using private IP addresses, without requiring a separate network appliance, gateway, or VPN connections. The peering connection traffic always stays on the global AWS backbone and never traverses the public Internet, which reduces threats such as DDoS attacks and other common exploits. The inter-region VPC peering connection provides a cost-effective and simple way to share resources between regions and makes it easy to replicate data in cases of geographic redundancy.

Virtual Private Gateways

A virtual private gateway is a VPN concentrator on the AWS side. If you want to configure a site-to-site VPN connection, you need create a virtual private gateway and attach it to your VPC. You also need to specify the private autonomous system number (ASN) for the gateway—the default ASN is 64512. The ASN cannot be changed after creating the virtual private gateway.

EXAM TIP   The instances that you created in the VPN-only subnet can't reach the Internet directly, so any Internet-bound traffic must first traverse the virtual private gateway to your network. From here, the traffic goes through your firewall using corporate security policies. The traffic from your network going to an elastic IP address for an instance in the public subnet goes over the Internet and not over your virtual private gateway. As a result, you need to set up the route table and security group rules to enable the traffic to come from your network over the virtual private gateway to the public subnet.

Customer Gateways

A customer gateway is a software application or physical device on your side of the site-to-site VPN connection, which you must create and which provides information to AWS about the customer gateway device. You'll need an Internet-routable IP address (the public IP address value must be static) and static or dynamic routing to create a customer gateway resource. You can use an existing ASN assigned to your network, or you can use a private ASN (in the 64512 to 65534 range). AWS automatically uses 65000 as the ASN if you use the VPC wizard in the console to set up your VPC.

The virtual private gateway is not the initiator, so the client customer gateway must initiate the traffic to the tunnels. The VPN tunnel comes up only when traffic is generated from the client side of the site-to-site VPN connection. The VPN tunnel may go down if your connection experiences idle time for a certain period (depending on your configuration), so you may need to use a network monitoring tool to generate keep-alive pings to prevent this.

Site-to-Site Virtual Private Network

The instances in your VPC by default can't communicate with your own (remote/on-premises) network. You need to attach a virtual private gateway, create a custom route table, update your security group rules, and create a site-to-site (S2S) VPN connection to enable access to your on-premises network from your VPC. The AWS site-to-site VPN currently does not support IPv6 traffic connection but does support IPSec VPN connections.

Point-to-Site Virtual Private Network

You need a point-to-site (P2S) VPN gateway connection if you want to securely access the instances in your VPC from either your laptop or from a client computer. You can establish a P2S connection by starting it from your computer. This solution is useful for anyone who has had to connect to the instances in the AWS VPC from a remote location, like from home or from a conference room or from another public location. When you have only a few clients that need to connect to a VPC, P2S VPN is a useful solution to use instead of S2S VPN.

 NOTE   The steps to create the point-to-site VPN connection are in the "Additional Resources" section.

Direct Connect

AWS Direct Connect uses a standard Ethernet fiber-optic cable to link your internal network to an AWS Direct Connect location. You will be connecting one end of the cable to your router and the other end to an AWS Direct Connect router. You can create a public virtual interface to access public services, like Amazon S3, and a private virtual interface to access your VPC, bypassing the Internet service providers (ISPs) in your network.

You will be using single-mode fiber with a 1000BASE-LX (1310 nm) transceiver for 1 gigabit Ethernet or a 10GBASE-LR (1310 nm) transceiver for 10 gigabit Ethernet and work with an AWS Direct Connect partner to create a dedicated 1 Gbps or 10 Gbps connection. Auto-negotiation for the port must be disabled, and the port speed, along with full-duplex mode, must be configured manually. Your connection, including intermediate devices, must support 802.1Q virtual area network (VLAN) encapsulation. Your device must support the Border Gateway Protocol (BGP) and BGP MD5 authentication. You can also get hosted connections of 50 Mbps, 100 Mbps, 200 Mbps, 300 Mbps, 400 Mbps, 500 Mbps, 1 Gbps, 2 Gbps, 5 Gbps, and 10 Gbps through working with an independent service provider who is an AWS Direct Connect partner. AWS Direct Connect supports both IPv4 and IPv6 communication protocols, and the IPv6 addresses are accessible through AWS Direct Connect public virtual interfaces.

Transit Gateways

In order to connect your VPC and on-premises networks, you need a transit gateway, which is a network transit hub. You can attach a VPN connection, an AWS Direct Connect gateway, or a VPC to a transit gateway. It has a default route table that includes dynamic and static routes, and it decides the next hop based on the destination IP address of the packet.

You must create static routes to peer two transit gateways and route traffic between them. The routes are propagated from the transit gateway to your on-premises router using BGP in the VPN connection. The following are some use cases of a transit gateway.

Centralized Router

The transit gateway can be configured as a centralized router that connects all of your VPCs and VPN connections. In this use case, all the attachments can route packets to each other, and the transit gateway serves as a simple layer 3 IP hub.

Isolated Routers

The transit gateway can be configured as multiple isolated routers, similar to using multiple transit gateways. This provides more flexibility in scenarios where the routes and attachments might change. In this use case, each isolated router has a single route table, so it cannot route packets to or receive packets from the attachments for another isolated router, but the attachments associated with one isolated router can route packets to each other.

Edge Consolidator

The transit gateway can be configured to route packets to one or more VPN connections but your VPCs cannot route packets to each other. In this use case, you can create a route table for the VPN connections and a route table for the VPCs.

Chapter Review

This chapter introduced the AWS Virtual Private Cloud (VPC) and its components. VPC is the networking layer that enables you to launch AWS resources into a logically isolated virtual network. A VPC subnet resides entirely within one availability zone and cannot span across zones. A subnet is called public when its traffic is routed to an Internet gateway, and it is called private when it doesn't have a route to the Internet gateway. A route table has a set of rules that are used to determine where network traffic is directed. The route table controls the routing for the subnet, so all your subnets in a VPC must be associated with a route table. You can add another layer of security using a network access control list to your VPC, which acts as a firewall controlling traffic in and out of one or more subnets by allowing all the inbound and outbound IPv4 traffic and, if applicable, IPv6 traffic. Security groups act at the instance level, and NACLs act at the subnet level. A different set of security groups can be assigned to each instance in a subnet of your VPC. An Internet gateway allows communication between the Internet and instances in your VPC. It performs network address translation (NAT) for instances that have not been assigned public IPv4 addresses and also provides a target in your VPC route tables for Internet-routable traffic. The options field of a Dynamic Host Configuration Protocol (DHCP) message contains the configuration parameters and provides a standard for sending configuration details to hosts on the TCP/IP network. An elastic IP address is a public static address that you will be able to associate with an instance or network interface for any of your account VPCs.

A VPC endpoint service is powered by Private Link, and it enables you to privately connect your VPC to supported AWS services using the Amazon network. A NAT device is used to enable instances in a private subnet to connect to the Internet but prevents the Internet from initiating connections with the instances. An egress-only Internet gateway allows outbound communication over IPv6 from instances from your VPC to the Internet, and it prevents the Internet from initiating an IPv6 connection with your instances. A VPC peering connection routes the traffic between your own VPCs or with a VPC in another AWS account, or with a VPC in a different AWS region privately, where instances in both VPCs can communicate with each other as if they are in the same network. A virtual private gateway is a VPN concentrator attached to your VPC on the AWS side. A customer gateway is a software application or physical device on the client side of the site-to-site VPN connection that provides information to AWS about your customer gateway device. A site-to-site VPN connection allows access to your on-premises network from your VPC using Internet Protocol security (IPSec). A point-to-site (P2S) VPN gateway connection allows access to the instances in your VPC from your individual laptop or from a client computer. AWS Direct Connect uses a standard Ethernet fiber-optic cable to link your internal network to an AWS Direct Connect location. You connect one end of the cable to your router and the other end to an AWS Direct Connect router. AWS Direct Connect allows you to use a dedicated private network connection between your on-premises network and one of the AWS Direct Connect locations. A transit gateway is a network transit hub that you can attach to a VPN connection, an AWS Direct Connect gateway, or a VPC.

Exercises

The following exercises will help you practice creating a VPC and related services. You need to create an AWS account, as explained earlier in this chapter, in order to perform the exercises. You can use the Free Tier when launching AWS resources, but make sure to terminate this at the end.

Exercise 3-1: Create a VPC Using the AWS Management Console

Let's jump into action and create a custom VPC with an IPv4 CIDR block. You can use the Amazon VPC wizard in the Amazon VPC console to create a VPC. The wizard creates a VPC with a /16 IPv4 CIDR block, which creates 65,536 private IP addresses with a /24 public subnet with 256 public IP addresses, as well as a /24 private subnet with 256 private IP addresses. It also attaches an Internet gateway to the VPC. It then creates a custom route table and associates it with your subnets so that traffic can flow between the subnet and the Internet gateway.

1. First log in to your AWS account by entering your AWS account username and password, and you will see the AWS Management Console page.

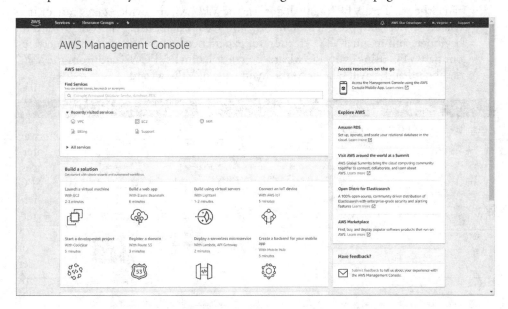

2. You can access all AWS services from this main AWS console page. You can search for a particular service below Find Services or select from Recently Visited Services if you used that service before, or you can go to All Services and select from the list of services. Use one of the methods to select VPC, and you will be directed to the VPC console page.

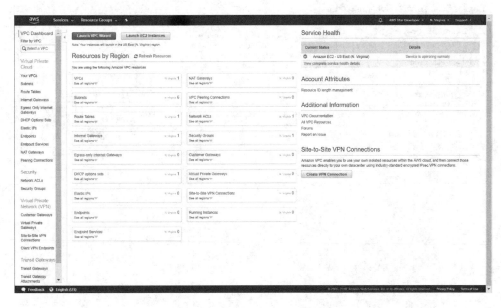

3. This VPC dashboard page will list all the VPC resources that you are currently using in this region, and you can navigate to them by selecting from the list. You can either create a VPC manually or use the VPC wizard, which takes care of the related services and provides them for you. I recommend using the VPC wizard for beginners and manual VPC creation for experienced users. We are going to create our first VPC using the VPC wizard, so select Launch VPC Wizard from the VPC dashboard and it will take us to the main page of VPC wizard.

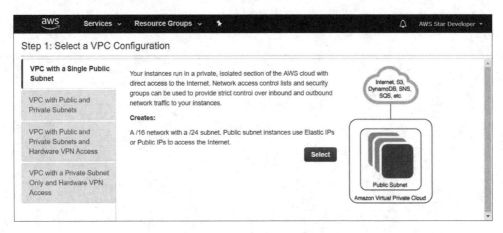

4. We are going to select the second option from the left pane, as you did in the first step, to create another VPC with one Public subnet and one Private subnet.

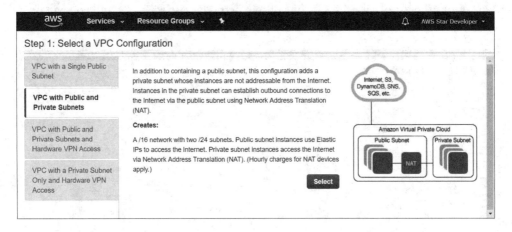

5. In the next step, you can provide the CIDR range for VPC, Name, Public and Private Subnet CIDR, and Availability Zone (if required) and attach an elastic IP.

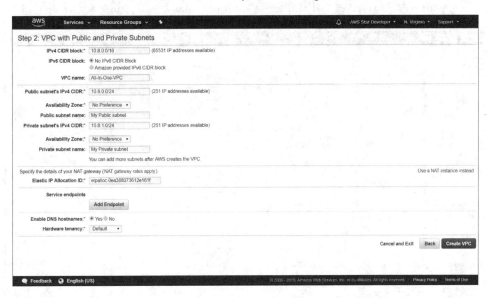

6. After verifying all the details, click the Create VPC button. All the related services that you need for a VPC are created.

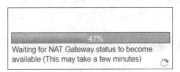

7. From the VPC console, select Your VPCs from the menu on the left, and here you can see all the details about the VPC in the Description tab.

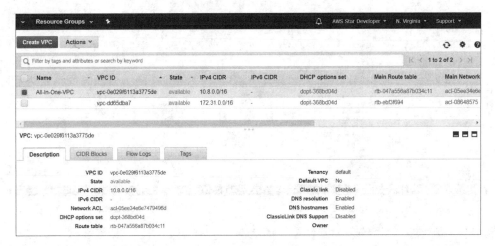

8. Select Subnets from the VPC console, and you will see the list of subnets in your AWS account. Select Private Subnet, and you can see 251 available IP addresses because AWS reserves 5 IP addresses from the total 256 IP addresses.

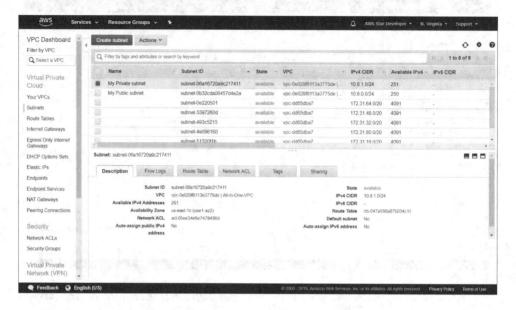

9. You can select My Public Subnet, as shown here, and you can see Subnet ID, Availability Zone, Network ACL, Route Table, and other details.

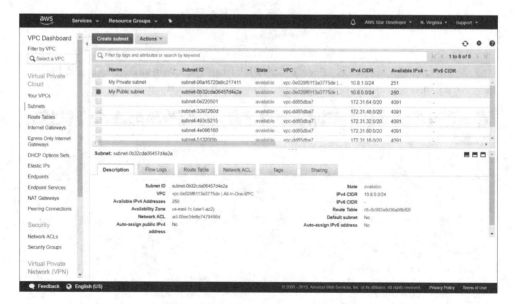

10. Now select Route Tables from the list and see the subnet's associated details.

11. Select the next route table in the list.

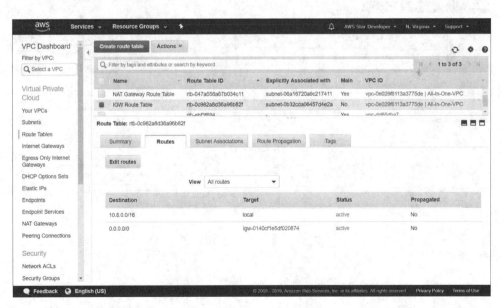

12. Select Internet Gateways from the list, which are attached to the VPC.

13. Select DHCP Option Sets from the list on the left side of your VPC console, and you will see the default option set provided by AWS.

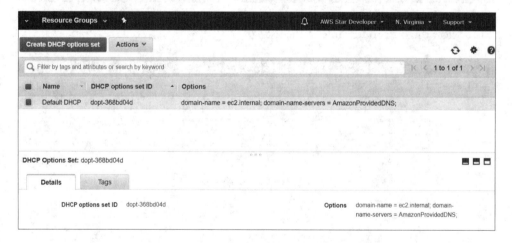

14. Select Elastic IPs.

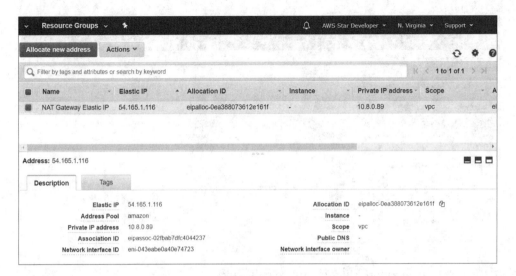

15. Select NAT Gateways from the list.

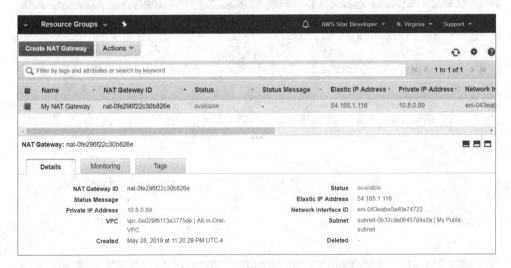

16. Select Network ACL from the list, and you can see the inbound and outbound rules.

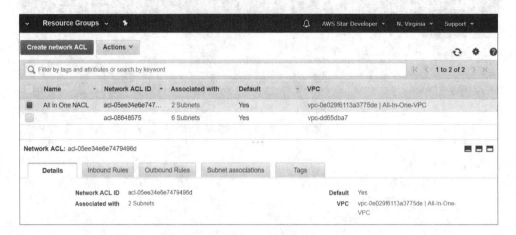

17. Select the Inbound Rules tab to see these rules.

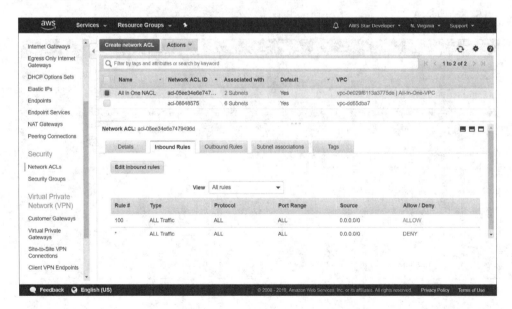

18. Select the Outbound Rules tab to see those rules.

19. Select the Subnet Associations tab in the Network ACL, as shown here:

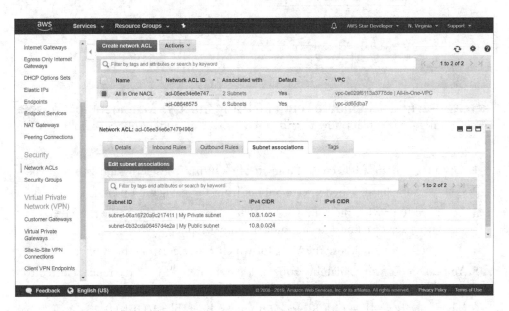

20. The VPC architecture diagram shows all the VPC and subnet details.

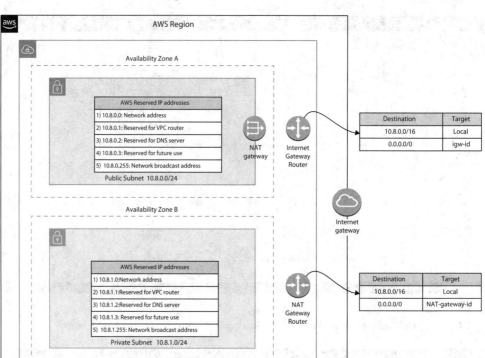

Exercise 3-2: Add a Subnet to Your VPC Using the AWS Management Console

The following steps explain how to add a new private or public subnet to your existing VPC.

1. Open the Amazon VPC console using the link https://console.aws.amazon.com/vpc/.

2. Choose Subnets and then Create Subnet from the navigation pane.

3. You need to provide the Name tag, which is a name for your subnet. It creates a tag with a key of name and the value of subnet-name.

4. Then you need to choose the VPC for which you're creating the subnet.

5. You can choose an availability zone or leave the default No Preference selected to let AWS choose it for you.

6. Then specify an IPv4 CIDR block for your subnet, like 10.0.10.0/23.

7. Verify all the input values and then choose Create Subnet.

8. This will be a private subnet if you don't attach an Internet gateway to it, and it will be a public subnet when you attach an Internet gateway to it.

Questions

The following questions will help you gauge your understanding of the VPC and the components explained in this chapter. Read all the answers carefully because there might be more than one correct answer. Choose the best responses for each question.

1. Your client decided to move to AWS and asked you define the logically isolated virtual network in AWS using the predefined IP address range. Which of the following will you need to create to accomplish this?

   A. Public subnet

   B. Private subnet

   C. Virtual private cloud

   D. NAT gateway

2. You created the VPC using the given range of the CIDR block by your network team. However, your application become so popular that you need to add new features, high availability, and redundancy; your AWS architect asked you to increase the size of VPC. Is it possible to resize it?

   A. Yes, it can be extended by adding four secondary IPV4 CIDR blocks.

   B. No, it is not possible to resize IPv4 CIDR blocks, but you can resize IPv6 CIDR blocks.

   C. No, it is not possible to resize the VPC.

   D. Yes, it is possible to increase the size of VPC, but you cannot reduce it.

3. You are designing your AWS network and need to create the largest VPC and smallest VPC based on your application requirements. What are the largest and smallest IPv4 VPCs that you are allowed to create in AWS?

   A. Largest /16 and smallest /30

   B. Largest /8 and smallest /32

   C. Largest /56 and smallest /64

   D. Largest /16 and smallest /28

4. A user has created a VPC with one public subnet and one private subnet. The user wants to run the patch updates for the instances in the private subnet, but the instances are not able to connect to the Internet. How can the instances from the user's private subnet connect to the Internet?

   A. Attach the Internet Gateway to the private subnet

   B. Allow inbound traffic for port 80 to allow Internet updates in the security group

   C. Use a NAT gateway or NAT instance with an elastic IP

   D. The instance on the private subnet can never connect to the Internet

5. You client asked you to automatically provision the VPC and all its related components quickly, so you decided to use the VPC wizard in the AWS Management VPC console. What options are provided for you by default in the VPC wizard? (Choose all that apply.)

   A. Amazon VPC with a single public subnet only

   B. Amazon VPC with public and private subnets

   C. Amazon VPC with public and private subnets and AWS site-to-site VPN access

   D. Amazon VPC with a private subnet only and AWS site-to-site VPN access

6. VPC endpoints allow you to privately connect to your services from those hosted on the AWS VPC without requiring an Internet gateway, a NAT device, or VPN connection. What two types of endpoints are available in Amazon VPC? (Choose two.)

   A. Site-to-site endpoints

   B. Gateway endpoints

   C. Interface endpoints

   D. Point-to-site endpoints

7. Security groups in a VPC operate at the instance level, where you specify which traffic is allowed to or from an Amazon EC2 instance. NACLs operate at the subnet level and evaluate all the traffic entering and exiting a subnet. Which of the following is not true?

   A. Security groups can be used to set both allow and deny rules.

   B. NACLs do not filter traffic between instances in the same subnet.

   C. NACLs perform stateless filtering, while security groups perform stateful filtering.

   D. NACLs can be used to set both allow and deny rules.

8. True or False: Transitive peering relationships are supported in Amazon VPC peering. For example, if I peer VPC X to VPC Y and I peer VPC Y to VPC Z, does that mean VPCs X and Z are peered?

   A. True

   B. False

9. Which of the following is false about elastic IP address pricing?

   A. You will not incur costs when the elastic IP address is associated with a running EC2 instance.

   B. You will not incur costs when the elastic IP address is associated with a stopped EC2 instance.

   C. You will not incur costs when the IP address is from a BYOIP address pool.

   D. You will not incur costs when the instance has only one elastic IP address attached to it.

10. A user has created a VPC with two public subnets and three security groups. The user has launched an instance in a public subnet and attached an elastic IP. He is still unable to connect to that EC2 instance. The Internet gateway has also been created. What could be the reason for the connection error?

A. The Internet gateway is not configured with the route table to route traffic

B. The private IP is not present for the instance

C. Outbound traffic is disabled on the security group

D. Traffic is denied on the security group

Answers

1. **C.** VPC logically isolates the virtual network in AWS using the predefined IP address range.

2. **A.** Yes, the VPC can be extended by adding four secondary IPV4 CIDR blocks, and you can decrease your VPC by deleting those secondary CIDR blocks. However, you cannot change the size of the IPv6 address range of your VPC.

3. **D.** AWS VPCs can vary in size from 16 addresses (/28 netmask), which is the smallest, to 65,536 addresses (/16 netmask), which is the largest.

4. **C.** You need to use a NAT device (NAT gateway or NAT instance) to enable instances in a private subnet to connect to the Internet to do patching and software updates but it prevents the incoming traffic initiated from Internet with these instances.

5. **A, B, C, D.** You can create four types of VPCs using the VPC wizard: Amazon VPC with a single public subnet only, Amazon VPC with public and private subnets, Amazon VPC with public and private subnets and AWS site-to-site VPN access, and Amazon VPC with a private subnet only and AWS site-to-site VPN access.

6. **B, C.** Amazon VPC offers two types of endpoints: gateway endpoints and interface endpoints. Endpoints allow you to privately connect your VPC to your services hosted on AWS without requiring an Internet gateway, NAT device, or VPN connection.

7. **A.** Security groups can be used to set only allow rules, not deny rules; however, network ACLs can be used to set both allow and deny rules.

8. **B.** No, transitive peering relationships are not supported in AWS.

9. **B.** False. You will incur costs when the elastic IP address is associated with a stopped EC2 instance.

10. **A.** You need to configure the Internet gateway with the route table to route traffic and then the user will be able to connect to the EC2 instance.

Additional Resources

- **AWS Documentation/Blogs**   There is no place like official AWS documentation to get the latest and most up-to-date information about all the AWS services and features.
  `https://docs.aws.amazon.com/vpc/index.html` and `https://aws.amazon.com/blogs/aws`

- **VPC Sharing**   Share subnets with other AWS accounts by decoupling accounts and networks within the same AWS organization. This blog explains in detail how to configure VPC sharing.
  `https://aws.amazon.com/blogs/networking-and-content-delivery/vpc-sharing-a-new-approach-to-multiple-accounts-and-vpc-management/`

- **AWS Transit Gateway Migration**   The AWS Transit Gateway is similar to a transit VPC where you can attach up to 5,000 VPCs and attach your AWS VPN connections. This blog explains transit gateway migration steps from your existing transit VPC solution to the AWS Transit Gateway service.
  `https://aws.amazon.com/blogs/networking-and-content-delivery/migrate-from-transit-vpc-to-aws-transit-gateway/`

- **AWS Client VPN Setup**   This is a fully managed service that provides the ability to securely access AWS and on-premises resources from any location using OpenVPN–based clients. This blog explains in detail how to configure client VPN setup.
  `https://aws.amazon.com/blogs/networking-and-content-delivery/introducing-aws-client-vpn-to-securely-access-aws-and-on-premises-resources/`

- **OpenVPN Setup**   This is a secure, open-source OpenVPN service, and this blog explains in detail how to deploy it using Amazon VPC and test some functionality.
  `https://aws.amazon.com/blogs/awsmarketplace/setting-up-openvpn-access-server-in-amazon-vpc/`

- **Debug Network Connectivity of Amazon VPC**   It is crucial to monitor the health and impact on performance, including latency and percentage of packet loss, across your network connectivity. This blog explains in detail how to configure AWSSupport-SetupIPMonitoringFromVPC to monitor these metrics.
  `https://aws.amazon.com/blogs/networking-and-content-delivery/debugging-tool-for-network-connectivity-from-amazon-vpc/`

Creating a Virtual Machine Using Amazon EC2

In this chapter, you will learn

- What is EC2?
- Amazon Machine Image (AMI)
- Tenancy options
- Instance types
- Pricing model for EC2
- EC2 instance virtualization types
- Storage options for Amazon EC2
- EC2 instance lifecycle
- Generating security keys
- Launching an Amazon EC2
- Security groups that protect instances
- Best practices for Amazon EC2

This chapter will explain how Amazon Elastic Compute Cloud (Amazon EC2) provides scalable, secure, and resizable elastic compute capacity in the cloud and how it is designed to make web-scale cloud computing easier for developers.

Elastic Compute Cloud

Amazon EC2 is a simple web service interface that allows you to obtain and boot new server instances in minutes. It allows you to quickly scale up and down to the required capacity whenever there is a spike or dip in your computing requirements, which reduces your need to forecast traffic. Amazon EC2 saves the cost of computing by allowing you to pay only for capacity that you actually use. You don't need to invest in hardware up-front, which allows you to develop and deploy applications faster. You can configure security, networking, and manage storage, and use EC2 to launch as many or as few virtual servers based on your need.

EXAM TIP You need to know the basics of launching an Amazon EC2 instance. In order to launch an instance, you must specify an AMI, which defines the software on the instance at launch, and an instance type, which defines the virtual hardware supporting the instance (memory, CPUs, storage, etc.).

Amazon Machine Image

An Amazon Machine Image (AMI) is a machine template that provides the information required to launch a new instance. You must specify an AMI when you launch an instance, and you can launch multiple instances from a single AMI. The AMI can be one or more Amazon Elastic Block Store (Amazon EBS) snapshots, instance store–backed AMIs, or a template for the root volume of the instance. AWS controls which account can use the AMI to launch instances based on permissions. When an AMI is launched, a block device mapping specifies the list of volumes that need to be attached to the instance.

As shown in Figure 4-1, you can launch instances from an AMI if either you created the AMI or the owner granted you launch permissions. You need to register an AMI after creating it before you can launch new instances. The AMI can be copied between regions or different AWS accounts. You can deregister the AMI when you no longer require it.

You can search for an AMI based on the criteria provided by AWS or from community AMIs or from the AWS Marketplace. As soon as you create an instance from an AMI, you can connect to it and use it just like you would any other server.

Bundle Tasks

A Windows instance can be bundled in order to create a Windows instance store–backed AMI. It can be used to create bundles of Amazon instances, and you need to register these bundles as AMIs before launching new instances.

Figure 4-1
AMI lifecycle

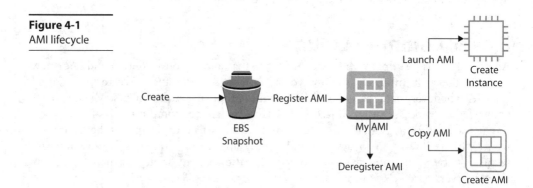

Root Device Types

The root device volume contains the image that will be used to boot when you launch an instance. When AWS introduced EC2, all AMIs were backed by the instance store. That means the root device is an instance store volume, which is typically created from a template stored in Amazon S3. When AWS introduced Amazon EBS, the AMIs were backed by it, which means that the root device for an instance was launched from the AMI, whereas the Amazon EBS volume was created from an Amazon EBS snapshot.

The AWS Marketplace

The AWS Marketplace is similar to any online store where you can buy products, and here you will buy software that runs on AWS, which includes the AMIs that you can use to launch your EC2 instance. In the AWS Marketplace, AMIs are organized into categories to allow you to find products that suit your requirements. Amazon EC2 is integrated with the AWS Marketplace to enable developers to charge other Amazon EC2 users for their use of AMIs or to provide support for the Marketplace instances.

No additional parameters are required when launching an instance from a paid AMI or launching it from any other AMI. The instance is charged the standard usage fees of the related web services, like any other instances, in addition to the rates set by the owner of the AMI, along with any additional taxes.

AMIs Generated from Existing Instances

You can generate an AMI from an existing instance that has been made available for other developers to use that has the components they need, although they can add custom content. Share AMIs at your own risk—Amazon won't vouch for their integrity or security. When you receive a shared AMI, you need to perform the appropriate due diligence and treat it as you would any unknown code that you might consider deploying in your own datacenter. AWS recommends getting shared AMIs from trusted sources. The owner of the AMI is not charged when it is launched by other AWS accounts, and only the accounts that are launching the shared AMI are billed for their use. Since AMIs are a regional resource, it is available only in the same region by default; if you want to make it available in a different region, you need to copy the AMI to that region and then share it. However, AMIs with encrypted volumes cannot be made public.

Tenancy Options

AWS provides a couple of options for tenancy, including the default type of shared and dedicated models. For example, assume you have a single family house—you could consider this a dedicated tenancy, since only one family lives there. However, if you have an apartment building, several families will be living in it, which would be a shared tenancy model.

Likewise, if multiple EC2 instances from different customers reside on the same physical hardware, it's called a shared tenancy model. If only your EC2 instances run on hardware and no other customers can use that hardware, it's called a dedicated model.

Shared Tenancy

The default tenancy model is the most commonly used, where multiple customers will share the same hardware even though they don't interact with each other. A hypervisor is running on the physical host to handle the virtualization of CPU, memory, storage, etc. When you choose to deploy an EC2 instance, AWS launches onto the appropriate physical host and isolates it from other customers, even if it's sharing the same physical resources. Unless you have regulatory compliance or licensing restrictions to use the dedicated model, you should be using shared tenancy, which is the cheaper option.

Dedicated Tenancy

A dedicated tenancy ensures that your EC2 instances are run on hardware dedicated to your account, but it is a costlier option. You might use it for exclusive scenarios, like if you're trying to use bring your own license (BYOL), which is based on the socket model, where the number of hosts sockets or cores are used for software licensing. In another scenario, regulatory compliance may dictate that you can't use the shared model. AWS offers two different options for dedicated tenancy: dedicated hosts and dedicated instances.

Dedicated Hosts

A dedicated host is a fully dedicated physical server that allows you to use your existing licenses, including Windows and Linux Enterprise Server. You're allowed to spin up as many EC2 instances as that host will allow for no additional charge, much like how you would manage an on-premises solution. You cannot mix EC2 instance types on the same dedicated host. You'll pay for the whole host, so you are responsible for the utilization. If you can manage that capacity well, this option may be cheaper than the shared tenancy model.

Dedicated Instances

Dedicated instances are for a single customer that runs on dedicated hardware, and even though it belongs to a different AWS account, it is physically isolated at the hardware level. The dedicated instances physically isolated at the hardware level are linked to a single-payer account. With a dedicated instance, you are not paying for the entire host all at once but you're still receiving the benefits of having separate hosts from the rest of the AWS customers. You are charged a higher rate for the instances, but you do not need to worry about the capacity of the hosts. This type of instance model ensures they're kept separate, which is similar to the default model where you don't worry about where the instances are. You don't want to manage the hosts, but you need a dedicated instance for compliance reasons that require that hosts are not shared between customers, and you can use the BYOL options for anything licensed by the user.

Instance Types

The instance type determines the hardware of the host computer, for example, different compute, storage, and memory, and it is grouped into families based on these capabilities. When you launch an instance, you can select an instance type based on your requirements in terms of application or software need.

The CPU, memory, and instance storage are dedicated to a particular instance and share the network and disk subsystem among other EC2 instances. Each instance on a host computer receives an equal share of those shared resources, so it tries to use as much of these shared resources as possible. However, an instance can consume a higher share of a resource when another resource is underused. The instance types will have a larger allocation of shared resources and provide higher or lower minimum performance from a shared resource, like the instance types with high I/O performance.

General Purpose

General-purpose instances can be used for a variety of workloads and provide a balance between compute, memory, and networking resources.

A1 Instances

The EC2 A1 instances offer significant cost savings and are ideally suited for scale-out workloads like web servers, containerized microservices, caching fleets, distributed data stores, and Arm-based workloads that are supported by the Arm ecosystem.

M5, M5a, M5ad, and M5d Instances

M5 instances offer a balance of compute, memory, and networking resources for a broad range of applications like web and application servers, small and medium databases, gaming servers, caching fleets, running SAP backend servers, SharePoint, and cluster computing.

NOTE m5.metal and m5d.metal instances provide your applications with direct access to the physical resources of the host server, such as processors and memory. They are suitable for workloads that require access to low-level hardware features that are not available or fully supported in virtualized environments. They are also suitable for applications that require a nonvirtualized environment for licensing or support.

T2, T3, and T3a Instances   = burst CPU performance

These instances provide the ability to burst to a higher level of CPU performance for any period of time when required by your workload. They are suitable for web applications; code repositories; development, build, test, and staging environments; and microservices.

Compute Optimized

Compute-optimized instances are ideal for compute-bound applications like media transcoding, high-performance web servers, high-performance computing (HPC), ad serving engines, scientific modeling, dedicated gaming servers, machine learning inference, batch processing workloads, and other compute-intensive applications that benefit from high-performance processors.

Memory Optimized

Memory-optimized R instances are designed to deliver fast performance for workloads that process large data sets in memory, like relational, NoSQL, and in-memory databases. They are also well suited for applications that perform real-time processing of big unstructured data.

 NOTE r5.metal and r5d.metal instances provide direct access to the physical resources of the host server, such as processors and memory. They are well suited for workloads that require access to low-level hardware features that are either not available or not fully supported in virtualized environments and for any applications that require a nonvirtualized environment for licensing or support.

High Memory Instances

High memory x1 and z1 instances offer 6TiB, 9TiB, or 12TiB of memory per instance and are designed to run large in-memory databases, like production installations of SAP HANA (an in-memory database), big data processing engines such as Apache Spark or Presto, and HPC applications and databases. These type of instances offer bare metal performance since it is directly attached to the host hardware.

 NOTE z1d.metal instances provide your applications with direct access to the physical resources of the host server, such as processors and memory. These instances are well suited for workloads that require access to low-level hardware and applications that require a nonvirtualized environment for licensing or support.

Storage Optimized

Storage-optimized instances are designed for workloads that require write access to very large data sets on local storage, as well as high workloads that perform sequential reads, like massive parallel processing (MPP) data warehouses, large log or data processing applications, MapReduce, and Hadoop distributed computing. They are optimized to deliver tens of thousands of low-latency, random I/O operations per second (IOPS) to applications like high-frequency online transaction processing (OLTP) systems, relational databases, NoSQL databases, caching for in-memory databases, data warehousing applications, and distributed file systems.

 NOTE i3.metal instances provide your applications with direct access to the physical resources of the host server, such as processors and memory. The workloads that require access to low-level hardware features are well suited for these instances because they are either not available or not fully supported in virtualized environments. They are also ideal for applications that require a nonvirtualized environment for licensing or support.

Accelerated Computing

Accelerated computing instances enable more parallelism for higher throughput on compute-intensive workloads, and they provide access to hardware-based compute accelerators such as graphics processing units (GPUs) or field programmable gate arrays (FPGAs).

GPU-based instances provide access to NVIDIA GPUs with thousands of compute cores, which can be used to accelerate scientific, engineering, and rendering applications by leveraging the Compute Unified Device Architecture (CUDA) or Open Computing Language (OpenCL) parallel computing frameworks. This can be used for graphics applications like game streaming and 3-D application streaming.

The elastic graphics accelerator is better suited for an instance type with different compute, memory, or storage specifications and can also be used when your application needs a small amount of additional graphics acceleration. The hardware acceleration code can either be purchased through the AWS Marketplace or you can develop it yourself.

NOTE   FPGA-based instances do not support Microsoft Windows.

Pricing Model for EC2

AWS offers 750 hours of Linux and Windows t2.micro instances each month for one year as part of the Free Tier option. As long as you use only EC2 micro instances, you will stay within the Free Tier amount. AWS offers four cost models to pay for Amazon EC2 instances: on-demand, savings plans, reserved instances, and spot instances. If you require EC2 instance capacity on physical servers for your dedicated use, you will have pay for dedicated hosts.

The EC2 instance lifecycle starts when it is newly launched and ends whenever you terminate that instance. The purchasing option and pricing affect the lifecycle as well. An on-demand instance runs from when you launch and ends when you terminate it. A spot instance runs until the capacity is available or until your maximum price is higher than the spot price. A scheduled instance is launched during its scheduled start time and is terminated three minutes before the scheduled time period ends.

EXAM TIP   You need to know what kinds of purchasing options are best suited for your requirements. Spot instances are well suited for workloads that are short lived or that can accommodate interruption. Reserved instances are best for consistent, long-term compute needs. On-demand instances provide flexible compute power to respond to scaling needs.

AWS also offers per-second billing, which takes the cost of unused instance minutes and seconds in an hour off of your bill, allowing you to focus on improving your applications instead of planning to maximize the usage to the hour. This especially benefits instances that run for irregular periods of time, like development, testing, analytics, data processing, gaming applications, and batch processing.

EC2 usage and provisioned storage for EBS volumes are billed in per-second increments, with a minimum of 60 seconds. Per-second billing is available for on-demand, reserved, and spot instances in all regions and availability zones for Amazon Linux and Ubuntu.

On-Demand

On-demand instances are billed either per second or per hour for compute capacity, depending on which instances you run. You don't need any up-front payments or any long-term commitments and only pay the specified hourly rates for the instance you use.

AWS recommends on-demand instances for first-time application development or proof of concepts (POCs) or for applications with short-term, spiky, or unpredictable workloads. They have the advantage of low cost and flexibility when launching EC2 without long-term commitments or up-front payments.

Spot Instances

EC2 spot instances provide spare or unused Amazon EC2 computing capacity for a price up to 90 percent less than the on-demand price. You can lower your Amazon EC2 costs significantly, since spot instances are available at steep discounts. Spot instance pricing is charged in hourly increments. AWS sets and adjusts the spot price gradually based on the long-term supply of and demand for spot instances in each availability zone. The spot instance will be available to you when the maximum price per hour for your request exceeds the spot price and the requested instance type capacity is available.

If your applications can be interrupted at any time or your application is flexible in terms of starting, then the spot instance is a cost-effective solution with, as mentioned, nearly 90 percent savings. Spot instances are well suited for applications that have flexible start and end times, optional tasks, background processing, data analysis, and batch jobs.

 EXAM TIP You need to know the properties of the Amazon EC2 pricing options to help your customers save on cost. On-demand instances require no up-front commitment, can be launched at any time, and are billed by the hour. Reserved instances require an up-front commitment and vary in cost, depending on whether they are paid entirely up-front, partially up-front, or not at all up-front. When your bid price exceeds the current spot price, spot instances are launched. Spot instances are terminated as soon as the spot price exceeds your bid price, although you will be given a two-minute warning before they terminate.

Reserved Instances

Reserved instances offer a significant discount—up to 72 percent in savings—compared to the on-demand instance pricing. Reserved instances provide a capacity reservation, since they are assigned to a specific availability zone, which gives you the ability to launch instances whenever you need them. The discount on reserved instances applies to on-demand instances or instances running in your AWS account. Reserved instances are not physical instances. In order to benefit from the billing discount, those on-demand instances must meet certain attributes.

If your applications have a steady state of predictable usage over a long period, reserved instances provide you with significant savings compared to using on-demand instances. Customers are allowed to purchase reserved instances over a one-year (31,536,000 seconds) or three-year (94,608,000 seconds) term to reduce total computing costs; the three-year plan offers a deeper discount compared to the one-year commitment.

Dedicated Hosts

An Amazon EC2 dedicated host is a physical server fully dedicated to your use with an EC2 instance capacity only allocated to you. Dedicated hosts allow you to reduce costs by using your existing per-socket, per-core, or per-VM software licenses, and can also help you meet compliance requirements. It can be purchased on-demand on an hourly basis or as a reservation for up to 70 percent off the on-demand price.

 EXAM TIP   You need to know how to combine multiple pricing options that result in cost optimization and scalability. When you need to scale up a web application that is running on reserved instances in response to a temporary traffic spike, you can use on-demand instances. For a workload with several reserved instances reading from a queue, it's possible to use spot instances to alleviate heavy traffic in a cost-effective way.

EC2 Instance Virtualization Types

Paravirtual (PV) and hardware virtual machine (HVM) are two types of virtualization that Linux Amazon Machine Images use. The way the AMIs boot and whether they use a special hardware extension for better performance determine whether it is a PV or HVM AMI. AWS recommends using the current-generation instance types and HVM AMIs when you launch your instances for the best performance.

HVM AMIs

HVM AMIs boot your image by executing the master boot record of the root block device and use a fully virtualized set of hardware. Without any modification, you have the ability to run an operating system directly on top of a virtual machine, as if it were run on the bare metal hardware. It emulates some or all of the underlying hardware to the guest.

The host's underlying hardware can be accessed quickly using HVM guest hardware extensions. AMIs built using HVM provide enhanced networking and GPU processing. The HVM virtualization provides native hardware platform access to the OS through instructions to the network and GPU devices.

PV AMIs

PV AMIs use PV-GRUB, a special boot loader, which starts the boot cycle and then chain-loads the kernel specified in the menu.lst file on your image. PV guests cannot take advantage of special hardware extensions, such as enhanced networking or GPU processing, but they can run on host hardware that does not have explicit support for virtualization. Current-generation instance types do not support PV AMIs, whereas the previous generation instance types, like C1, C3, HS1, M1, M3, M2, and T1, do support PV AMIs. Using the AWS console or the `describe-images` command, you can find a PV AMI and verify that the virtualization type is set to paravirtual.

Storage Options for Amazon EC2

You have the option to choose between AMIs backed by Amazon EBS and AMIs backed by the Amazon EC2 instance store, based on your requirements. However, AWS recommends using AMIs backed by Amazon EBS instead of instance store–backed AMIs, because the EBS-backed AMI launches faster and uses persistent storage.

Instance Store–Backed Instances

The root device has one or more instance store volumes available automatically for the instances that use instance stores, with at least one volume serving as the root device volume. The image that is used to boot the instance is copied to the root volume when you create the instance. You can also use additional instance store volumes, depending on the instance type.

 NOTE You cannot stop the instance store–backed instances because this action is not supported.

As long as the instance is running, the data on the instance store volumes persists. The instance store data is deleted when the instance is terminated or when the instance fails because of an underlying drive issue. These instances cannot be restored in this scenario, so AWS recommends you distribute the data on your instance stores across multiple availability zones. You need to have solid backup strategy for your critical data of your instance store volumes to persist the storage on a regular basis.

 EXAM TIP You need to know the lifetime of an instance store. When the instance is stopped or terminated, the data on an instance store is lost. However, the instance store data will survive an OS reboot.

Amazon EBS–Backed Instances

Root devices have an Amazon EBS volume attached automatically for instances that use Amazon EBS. AWS creates an EBS volume for each of the EBS snapshots referenced by the AMI that you use when you launch an EBS-backed instance. Depending on the instance type, you can either use other Amazon EBS volumes or instance store volumes for your EBS-backed instances.

The advantage of an Amazon EBS–backed instance is that it can be stopped and (re)started without affecting data that is stored in the attached volumes. When an

Amazon EBS–backed instance is in a stopped state, you can attach your root volume to a different running instance, update the kernel it is using, modify the properties of the instance, or change its size.

You can attach the volume to the new instance by creating a snapshot of the root volume and registering a new AMI. Based on your requirements, launch a new instance from this new AMI. Then detach the remaining EBS volumes from the old instance and reattach them to the new instance.

 EXAM TIP You need to know how Amazon EBS–optimized instances affect Amazon EBS performance. In addition to the IOPS that controls performance in and out of the Amazon EBS volume, use Amazon EBS–optimized instances to ensure additional dedicated capacity for Amazon EBS I/O.

The EC2 Instance Lifecycle

The EC2 instance lifecycle starts from the moment you launch, and it goes through various states until the instance terminates. This allows you to provide the best possible experience to your customers with the applications or sites that are hosted on the EC2. It is important to understand and know how the instance lifecycle affects the EC2 instance billing, as shown in Figure 4-2, both from the exam point of view and to support your enterprise environment.

When you launch an EC2 instance or when you restart an EC2 after being in the stopped state, it first enters into the pending state. The pending state is not billed for because the instance is preparing to enter the running state at this time. Billing starts when

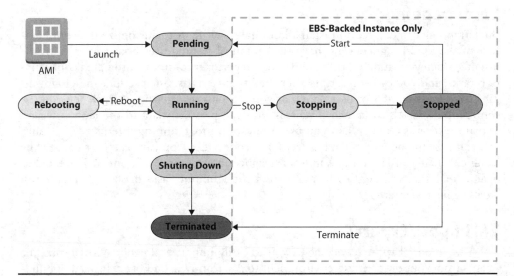

Figure 4-2 Instance lifecycle

the instance is in the running state and ready for use. The instance is not billed for when it is preparing to be stopped; however, billing does take place when the instance is preparing to hibernate. The instance is not billed for when it is shut down and cannot be used. During this state, the instance can be restarted at any time. It is not billed for when the instance is preparing to be terminated (i.e., permanently deleted and cannot be restarted).

Launching

As soon as you launch an instance, it goes to the pending state. AWS uses the instance type to determine the hardware of the host computer and uses the AMI to boot the instance. It enters into the running state once the instance is ready. You can connect to your running instance the same way that you'd connect to any computer to use it.

As soon as your instance transitions to the running state, even if the instance remains idle and you don't connect to it, you're billed for each hour or partial hour that you keep the instance running. An EC2 instance is a virtual server, and you launch it using an AMI, which provides the application server, operating system, and applications for your instance.

You can get started with Amazon EC2 for free when you sign up for AWS using the Free Tier. You can use a micro instance for free for 12 months, and Free Tier offers 750 hours per month of t2.micro or t3.micro instances, depending on the region. If you launch an instance, you incur the standard Amazon EC2 usage fees if it is not within the Free Tier.

You can connect to an instance after you launch it. However, there might be a short time before you can connect to it. The instance receives a public DNS name that you can use to contact the instance from the Internet. Other instances within the same Virtual Private Cloud (VPC) can use the instance's private DNS name to contact it.

Bootstrapping

Bootstrapping can be used to install additional software or to customize the configuration of the EC2 instances. You have the option of passing user bootstrap data to the instance when you launch it that can be used to perform common automated configuration tasks, and you can run scripts after the instance starts. Shell scripts and cloud-init directives are two types of user data that you can pass to Amazon EC2. When you use command-line tools to launch instances, you can pass this data to the launch wizard as plain text or as a file. When you use application programming interface (API) calls, you can pass the bootstrap data as base64-encoded text. You can pass user data to the instance when you launch a Windows instance in Amazon EC2, and it is treated as opaque data that will be used by automated configuration tasks or scripts that are run after the instance starts.

VM Import/Export

The VM Import/Export service helps you to easily import and export virtual machine images from your on-premises environment to Amazon EC2 and back. Instead of building the VMs from scratch to meet your IT security, configuration management, and compliance requirements, you can leverage your existing investments in the virtual machines and bring them into Amazon EC2 as ready-to-use instances. You can deploy workloads across your IT infrastructure by exporting the instances back to your on-premises virtualization infrastructure. Except for the standard usage charges of Amazon EC2 and Amazon S3, the VM Import/Export service is available at no additional charge to you.

You can use the AWS command-line interface (CLI) or other developer tools to import a virtual machine (VM) image from your on-premises VMware environment. You can use the AWS Management Portal for vCenter that converts your VM into an Amazon EC2 AMI as part of the import process that you can use to run Amazon EC2 instances.

You can export previously imported EC2 instances by specifying the target instance, virtual machine file format, and a destination S3 bucket, and VM Import/Export will automatically export the instance to the S3 bucket. You can then download from the S3 bucket and launch the exported VM into your on-premises virtualization infrastructure. Windows and Linux VMs can be imported that use Microsoft Hyper-V, Workstation, Citrix Xen, and VMware ESX virtualization formats. Also you can export the previously imported EC2 instances to Microsoft Hyper-V, Citrix Xen formats, or VMware ESX.

 EXAM TIP You need to know the capabilities of VM Import/Export. You can import your existing virtual machines as AMIs or Amazon EC2 instances to AWS using VM Import/Export. Amazon EC2 instances that were imported through VM Import/Export can also be exported back to a virtual environment.

Instance Recovery

You can create Amazon CloudWatch alarms that stop, terminate, reboot, or recover an instance. You can monitor the EC2 instances and automatically recover one when it becomes impaired due to any underlying hardware failure or a problem that requires repair by AWS. However, terminated instances cannot be recovered. The instance ID, private IP addresses, elastic IP addresses, and all instance metadata of the recovered instance will be identical to the original instance. The recovered instance runs in the placement group if the impaired instance was launched in one.

The recovery action is initiated when the StatusCheckFailed_System alarm is triggered, and you will be notified by the associated Amazon SNS topic. The instance is migrated during an instance reboot, and any data that is in memory is lost during instance recovery. The information is published to the SNS topic when the process is complete, and you will receive an e-mail notification that includes the status of the recovery attempt and any further instructions. If you log in to the AWS Management console and navigate to the EC2 main page, you will notice an instance reboot on the recovered instance. In addition, when AWS schedules stop or retire an instance due to the degradation of its underlying hardware, the recovery action can be triggered. The public IPv4 address of your instance will be retained after recovery. Common causes of system status check failures are loss of network connectivity, hardware issues on the physical host that affect network reachability, loss of system power, and software issues on the physical host.

Instance Metadata

Metadata is data about data, and EC2 instance metadata is data about the EC2 instances that you will be using to configure and manage your running instance. If you want to access user data that was specified when launching your instance, use instance metadata. You can either specify configuration parameters for your instance or attach it as a simple script. Instance metadata can be used to build more generic AMIs, and you can modify the configuration at launch time. For example, if you want to launch application servers for various medium-size businesses, you can use the same AMI and retrieve its content from your Amazon S3 bucket. If you want to add new small business customers at any time, simply create a new S3 bucket, add specific content to those new customers, and launch the new AMI. When an EC2 instance is launched, its dynamic data, like instance-identity/document, instance-identity/pkcs7, and instance-identity/signature, is generated.

NOTE   You will not be billed for HTTP requests used to retrieve instance metadata and user data.

You do not need to use the Amazon EC2 console or the AWS CLI to get your instance metadata. The instance metadata is available from your running instance, so you can write scripts to run from your instance like accessing the local IP address of your instance to manage a connection to an external application.

All categories of instance metadata can be retrieved from a running instance using the following command:

```
http://169.254.169.254/latest/meta-data/
```

The 169.254.169.254 IP address is a link-local address, and it is valid only if you run it from the instance. You can use PowerShell cmdlets for Windows to retrieve the details:

```
PS C:\> Invoke-RestMethod -uri http://169.254.169.254/latest/meta-data/
```

EXAM TIP   You need to know what instance metadata is and how it's obtained. Metadata is information like instance ID, instance type, and security groups about an Amazon EC2 instance, available from within the instance. It can be obtained through an HTTP call to a specific IP address.

You can also install a third-party tool such as GNU Wget or cURL and run the following from Linux machines:

```
[ec2-user ~]$ curl http://169.254.169.254/latest/meta-data/
```

```
[ec2-user ~]$ GET http://169.254.169.254/latest/meta-data/
```

CAUTION Instance metadata and user data are not protected by cryptographic methods. So anyone who has access to the instance can retrieve its metadata. Therefore, you should not store any sensitive data, such as usernames and passwords, as user data and should take suitable precautions to protect any sensitive data.

Instance Stop and Restart

If your instance root volume uses an Amazon EBS volume, it can be stopped and restarted. The instance changes the public IPv4 address unless you have assigned an elastic IP, and it retains its private IPv4 address and instance ID.

AWS shuts down the instance when you stop it, and you won't be charged for data transfer fees or usage charge for any stopped instances, but you incur a charge for any attached Amazon EBS volumes. Every time you stop and restart the instance, AWS charges a full instance hour, even if you stop and start multiple times within a single hour.

You can treat its root volume like any other volume while the instance is stopped and modify or repair any file system problems or update software. Once you stop the instance, you can just detach the volume and attach it to a running instance to make any required changes, detach the updated/repaired EBS volume from the running instance, and then reattach it to the original instance that was stopped. The storage device name should be the same as the root device in the block device mapping for the instance.

When you stop a running instance, the instance performs a normal shutdown and stops running. The status of the instance changes to "stopping." The data persists, and all the Amazon EBS volumes remain attached to the instance. The instance store volumes of the host computer or any data stored in the RAM of the host computer is deleted. The instance is migrated to a new underlying host computer when you restart the stopped instance. Whenever the instance is stopped and restarted, it retains its private IPv4 addresses and any IPv6 addresses. AWS assigns a new public IPv4 address when you restart the instance and releases the existing public IPv4 address but retains its associated elastic IP addresses. In this case, you will be charged for any elastic IP addresses associated with your stopped instance.

When you stop and start a Windows instance, the EC2Config service changes the drive letters for any attached Amazon EBS volume. Amazon EC2 returns the IncorrectInstanceState error when you try to modify instance type, user data, kernel, and RAM disk attributes while the instance is running, and you can modify them only when it is stopped.

Instance Hibernate

Instance Hibernate signals the operating system to perform hibernation, which saves the contents from the instance memory (RAM) to the Amazon EBS root volume. AWS preserves your instance's Amazon EBS root volume along with all other attached Amazon EBS data volumes during hibernation. When you restart your hibernated instance, the instance ID is retained, the EBS root volume is restored, the RAM contents are reloaded, and the processes are resumed in addition to reattaching the data volumes.

AWS won't charge when it is in the stopped state; however, it will charge for usage while the instance is in the stopped state during that time and the contents of the RAM are transferred to your EBS root volume. AWS won't charge usage for data transfer, but it will charge for the EBS volume storage.

Instance Reboot

It takes only a few minutes to reboot your instance, and it remains on the same physical host by keeping the same public DNS name (IPv4), IPv6 address, private IPv4 address, and any data on its instance store volumes. Rebooting is does not incur a charge and doesn't start a new instance billing period. You can schedule your instance for a reboot for necessary maintenance or any updates. You should use the Amazon EC2 console or a command-line tool or the Amazon EC2 API used to reboot your instance instead of using the operating system reboot command. AWS performs a hard reboot when you use the Amazon EC2 console, a command-line tool, or the Amazon EC2 API to reboot your instance but it does not cleanly shut down within four minutes.

Instance Retirement

AWS schedules an instance retirement when it detects an irreparable failure of the underlying hardware host. If your instance root device is an Amazon EBS volume, it is stopped; if your instance root device is an instance store volume, it is terminated by AWS as soon as it reaches its scheduled retirement date. Stopped instances migrate to a new hardware host, and the terminated instance cannot be used again.

Instance Termination

Terminating an instance refers to deleting your instance when you no longer need it. You stop incurring charges as soon as the state of an instance changes to shutting down or terminated. Once you have terminated the instance, you can't connect to it or restart it. However, it remains visible in the console for a short while, until resources such as tags and volumes are gradually disassociated from the instance, and then the entry is automatically deleted. When an instance gets terminated, the data on any associated instance store volumes, Amazon EBS root device volumes, and any additional EBS volumes is deleted unless you have set the DeleteOnTermination attribute to false for EBS volumes.

Generating Security Keys

Public key cryptography is used by Amazon EC2 to encrypt and then decrypt login information for EC2 instances. A public key will be used to encrypt a piece of data, and then a private key will be used by the recipient to decrypt the data. This pair of public and private keys is called a key pair.

You specify the key pair when you launch an instance. You can either specify a new key pair or an existing key pair that you create at the launch of an instance. The public key content is placed on the instance in an entry within ~/.ssh/authorized_keys at boot time. You must specify the private key to log in to your instance.

Amazon EC2 will be used to create the key pair, or you can use third-party solutions. You store the private key, and Amazon EC2 stores the public key with the name that you specify as the key name. It is your responsibility to store your private keys in a secure place because anyone who possesses your private key can decrypt your login information. The 2048-bit SSH-2 RSA keys are used by Amazon EC2, and you are allowed to have up to 5,000 key pairs per region.

You won't be able to connect to the instance if you don't specify a key pair when you launch it. You must specify the private key when you connect to the instance that corresponds to the key pair you specified when you launched it.

 NOTE AWS doesn't store a copy of your private key, so if the private key that you own is lost, there is no way to recover it.

You can add user accounts to your instance when several users require access. You need to add the public key information of each user key pair to the .ssh/authorized_keys file on your instance. You can distribute corresponding private key files to each user instead of distributing the root account private key file to multiple users.

Launching an Amazon EC2

You can launch a micro instance for free for 12 months when you use the Free Tier. You will be charged the standard Amazon EC2 usage fees if you launch an instance that is not within the Free Tier.

After you launch your instance, the state changes to pending. The instance will start booting before the state changes it to running. You can connect to the instance from the Internet using the public DNS name. You can also connect to the instance using its private DNS name.

Creating an Amazon EC2 Instance

The following are the steps to create your first Amazon EC2 instance:

1. Go to https://console.aws.amazon.com/ec2/ to open the Amazon EC2 console.
2. Select the region for the instance from the navigation bar at the top of the screen.
3. Choose Launch Instance from the Amazon EC2 console dashboard.
4. Choose an AMI on the Choose an Amazon Machine Image page:
   - Quick Start (this is the most popular option and lets you get started quickly)
   - My AMIs (private AMIs that either you own or are shared)
   - AWS Marketplace (an online store to buy AMIs that run on AWS)
   - Community AMIs (AWS community members share AMIs for others to use)

5. On the Choose An Instance Type page, choose the t2.micro instance type to remain in the Free Tier.

6. Then choose Next: Add Storage.

7. In the Network option, select the VPC where you want to create this instance.

8. In the Subnet option, select the subnet where you want to launch your instance.

9. Select Auto-Assign Public IP to receive a public IPv4 address, or select Auto-Assign IPv6 IP if your instance needs an IPv6 address.

10. Provide the AWS Identity and Access Management (IAM) role if you want to associate this with the Amazon EC2 instance that you are creating in this exercise.

11. Then choose the option to either stop or terminate the instance when it is shut down.

12. Select the check box to enable termination protection and prevent accidental termination.

13. Select the check box to enable detailed Amazon CloudWatch monitoring.

14. Choose Tenancy, Dedicated Hardware, or on a Dedicated Host, based on your requirements, for an additional cost.

15. Select the T2/T3 Unlimited check box to burst beyond the baseline for an additional charge.

16. Select an existing placement group if you want this instance to be placed in one.

17. Specify user data to run a configuration script or to configure an instance during launch, or to attach a configuration file.

18. On the Add Storage page, specify additional volumes to attach to the instance if required.

    - **Type** Select the instance store or Amazon EBS volumes based on your requirement.
    - **Device** Select the device name from the list for the volume.
    - **Snapshot** To restore a volume, enter the name or ID of the snapshot.
    - **Size** You can specify a storage size, but for the Free Tier, you must remain under 30GiB of total storage.
    - **Volume Type** For EBS volumes, select Magnetic Volume or Provisioned IOPS SSD or General Purpose SSD.
    - **IOPS** Enter the number of IOPS for the Provisioned IOPS SSD volume type.
    - **Delete On Termination** To delete the volume when the instance is terminated, select this check box.
    - **Encrypted** Select this option to encrypt the volume.

19. On the Add Tags page, specify tags for key and value pairs for the instance and volumes.

20. Choose Next to navigate to the Configure Security Group page.

21. Select an existing security group, or create new one to define the firewall rules for your instance.

22. Choose Review And Launch.

23. Check the details of your instance, and make changes if necessary.

24. Choose Launch when you are ready.

25. Now you will be prompted to select an existing key pair or create a new key pair.

26. The instance will be in a pending state until the boot configuration is complete.

27. You can connect to the instance as soon as its state changes to running.

Connecting to the Amazon EC2 Instance Using SSH

This exercise will help you connect to your Amazon EC2 instance using the SSH client.

1. You can connect to your instance and use it the way that you'd connect to any computer.

2. Verify that your instance passes the status checks.

3. Install an SSH client (openssh.com) on your local computer if it's not already installed (by typing **ssh** at the command line) by default.

4. Type **ssh -i /mypath/my-ins-key-pair.pemec2-user@ec2-197-38-200-6 .compute-1.amazonaws.com** (this gets your EC2 instance host name from the EC2 console). The text breaks down as follows:

   • ssh command connects to the instance.

   • my-ins-key-pair.pem is your private key file along with its path.

   • ec2-user is the user name for your AMI.

   • ec2-197-38-200-6.compute-1.amazonaws.com is the public DNS name for your instance.

5. You will be asked if you want to continue connecting.

6. When you type **yes**, you will see a response similar to "Warning: Permanently added 'ec2-198-51-100-1.compute-1.amazonaws.com' (RSA) to the list of known hosts." Now you are connected to your instance.

Connecting to an Amazon EC2 Instance Using a PuTTY Session

This exercise will show step-by-step details to connect to your Amazon EC2 instance using a PuTTy tool.

1. A few minutes after the instance is launched, the status checks will be passed and you are ready to connect.

2. Download and install PuTTY on your local computer.

3. Convert your private key format (.pem) to the PuTTYgeninto (.ppk) format.

4. Start PuTTY from your Start menu.

5. Choose Session in the Category pane.

6. Enter **user_name@public_dns_name** in the Host Name box (the username is ec2-user for Amazon Linux AMI and ubuntu for Ubuntu AMI).

7. Select SSH under Connection Type.

8. The Port Value is 22.

9. In the Category pane, expand Connection, SSH, and then Auth.

10. Choose Browse, select the .ppk file, and choose Open.

11. You can save the session under Category then Session, enter a name, and choose Save.

12. Choose Open.

13. PuTTY displays a security warning asking whether you trust the host.

14. Verify the fingerprint in the Security Alert dialog box to avoid a "man-in-the-middle" attack (this is an optional security feature).

15. If the fingerprint matches, choose Yes. Now you are connected to your instance.

 EXAM TIP You need to know the methods for accessing an instance over the Internet. You can access an Amazon EC2 instance over the Web via a public IP address, elastic IP address, or public DNS name. The private IP addresses and Elastic Network Interface (ENI) are additional ways to access an instance within an Amazon VPC.

Security Groups that Protect the Instances

A security group acts like a virtual firewall by controlling traffic to or from its associated instances, and you can add rules to allow traffic. When you launch an instance, you need to specify one or more security groups; otherwise, AWS uses the default security group. When you modify the security group, the new rules are automatically applied to all of its associated instances. AWS evaluates all the rules from all the security groups that are associated with the instance before deciding whether to allow traffic or not. You can maintain your own firewall on any of your instances in addition to using security groups when you have requirements that aren't met by security groups.

Security groups allow all outbound traffic by default, and the rules are always permissive, which means you can't create rules that deny access. Security groups are stateful, so the return response traffic for that request is allowed to flow in, regardless of inbound security group rules. Security Group rules can be added and removed at any time. Any changes you make to the security groups are automatically applied immediately to the associated instances.

The rules from each security group are effectively aggregated when you associate multiple security groups with an instance to create one set of rules. AWS uses this set of rules to determine whether to allow access to the instance. An instance can have hundreds of rules, since you can assign multiple security groups to an instance, but that might cause problems when accessing the instance. Thus AWS recommends that you condense your rules as much as possible.

EXAM TIP You need to know how security groups protect instances. Amazon EC2 instances use security groups as virtual firewalls, controlling traffic in and out of your instance. The inbound access of your custom security group is set to deny by default, and you can allow traffic by adding rules specifying traffic direction, port, protocol, and destination address via a Classless Inter-Domain Routing (CIDR) block. They are applied at the instance level, meaning that traffic between instances in the same security group must adhere to the rules of that security group. They are stateful, so if you send an outbound request from your instance, the return response inbound traffic is allowed, regardless of inbound security group rules, and vice versa.

The rule affects all instances associated with the security group when you specify a security group as the source or destination for a rule. Incoming traffic is allowed based on the private IP addresses, not the public IP or elastic IP addresses, of the instances that are associated with the source security group. AWS applies the most permissive rule if more than one rule is specified for a specific port.

The security group tracks information about traffic to and from the instance. Rules are applied to determine if the traffic is allowed or denied based on its connection state. The responses to inbound traffic are allowed to flow out, regardless of outbound security group rules and vice versa because security groups are stateful. The response traffic is not tracked.

EXAM TIP You need to know how to interpret the effect of security groups. When an instance is a member of multiple security groups, the effect is a union of all the rules in all the groups. Understand how AWS applies the most permissive rule if more than one rule is specified for a given port.

Best Practices for Amazon EC2

Follow these best practices to get the maximum benefit from Amazon EC2:

- It is very important to manage access to Amazon EC2 using identity federation, Identity and Access Management (IAM) users, and IAM roles.

- Credential management policies and procedures needs to be established for creating, distributing, rotating, and revoking AWS access credentials.

- The recommended approach is to implement the least permissive rules for your security group.

- You need to regularly patch, update, and secure the operating system and applications on your instance.

- Make sure you understand the implications of your instance root device type for data persistence, backup, and recovery.

- You need to use separate Amazon EBS volumes for the operating system versus your data.

- If required, you need to ensure that the volume with your data persists after instance termination and keep in mind that it's going to incur charges.

- Use the instance store for your instance to store temporary data.

- Always keep in mind that the data stored in an instance store is deleted when you stop or terminate your instance, so make sure you have a cluster with a replication factor that ensures fault tolerance when you use the instance store for database storage.

- You need to use instance metadata and custom resource tags to track and identify your AWS resources.

- Be aware of your current limits for Amazon EC2 and request any increases in advance if required.

- You need to regularly back up your EBS volumes using Amazon EBS snapshots and create an AMI to save the configuration of your instance as a template for launching future instances.

- AWS recommends deploying critical components of your application across multiple availability zones and replicating your data appropriately.

- If you are not using elastic IP addresses, then design your applications to handle dynamic IP addressing when your instance restarts.

- Use AWS CloudWatch Monitor to set up alerts and respond to events.

- To handle failover, you can either manually attach a network interface or elastic IP address to your replacement instance or use Amazon EC2 Auto Scaling.

- It is recommended that you regularly test the process of recovering your instances and Amazon EBS volumes if they fail as part of your business continuation plan.

Chapter Review

This chapter began by explaining all the necessary details that you need to know before creating your first EC2 instance. You learned what Amazon Elastic Compute Cloud (EC2) is. You explored the package with the bits that you need for your server, including the operating system and additional software, as preconfigured templates for your instances, also known as AMIs. PV and HVM are two types of virtualization that Linux AMIs use. The instance type relates to various configurations of CPU, memory, storage, and networking capacity. General-purpose instances can be used for a variety of workloads and provide a balance of compute, memory, and networking resources. Compute-optimized instances are ideal for compute-bound applications and other compute-intensive applications that benefit from high-performance processors. If you have workloads that process large data sets in memory, you need memory-optimized instances that are designed to deliver fast performance. If you have workloads that require high, sequential read and write access to very large data sets on local storage, you need storage-optimized instances. Accelerated computing instances enable more parallelism for higher throughput on compute-intensive workloads and provide access to hardware-based compute accelerators.

The chapter then explained how to secure login information for your instances using key pairs, where AWS stores the public key in the instance and you store your private key in a secure place. Amazon EC2 provides a web-based user interface called the Amazon EC2 console. You can access the Amazon EC2 console from the AWS Management Console and select the EC2 console page. You can launch Amazon EC2 resources, such as instances and volumes, directly from this console. The AWS CLI is supported on Windows, Mac, and Linux and provides commands for a broad set of AWS products. AWS also supports Windows PowerShell, which provides commands for a broad set of AWS products. Amazon EC2 provides a query API, and all these requests are HTTP or HTTPS requests that use the GET or POST and an Action parameter. AWS provides resources for software developers to build applications using language-specific APIs instead of submitting a request over HTTP or HTTPS. These libraries make it easier for you to get started by providing basic functions that automate tasks such as cryptographically signing your requests, handling error responses, and retrying requests.

Instance store volumes are used for temporary data that is deleted when you stop or terminate your instance. Amazon EBS volumes are persistent storage volumes for your instance data and root volume. Your instances and EBS volumes can be spread across multiple physical locations known as regions and availability zones. Security groups act as another firewall that enables you to specify inbound and outbound rules for the protocols, ports, and source IP ranges that can reach your instances. Elastic IP addresses are static IPv4 addresses that can be assigned to your EC2 instances and network interfaces. Tags are stored as key values on your Amazon EC2 resources. Metadata is data about data, and EC2 instance metadata is data about the EC2 instances that you will be using to configure and manage your running instance.

VM Import/Export is used to import VM images from your local on-premises environment into AWS and convert them into ready-to-use AMIs or instances. You can get started with Amazon EC2 for free using the Free Tier, and Amazon EC2 provides various purchasing options for additional instances. You can pay for the instances that you use and are charged per second, with no up-front payments or long-term commitments, by using on-demand instances. You can make a one-time, low, up-front payment for an instance and reserve it for a one- or three-year term, which allows you to pay a significantly lower hourly rate for your instances by using reserved instances. You can request unused EC2 instances, which can lower your costs significantly up to 90 percent by using spot instances.

Exercises

The following exercises will help you practice performing various tasks in Amazon EC2. You need to create an AWS account before you can perform these exercises. You can use the Free Tier when launching AWS resources, but make sure to terminate them at the end.

Exercise 4-1: Choosing an AMI by Root Device Type

The AMI that you specify when you launch your instance determines the type of root device volume that your instance has.

1. Open the Amazon EC2 console.

2. In the Navigation pane, choose AMIs.

3. From the filter lists, select the image type, and from the search bar choose Platform to select the operating system, like Amazon Linux, and Root Device Type to select EBS images.

4. Choose the Show/Hide Columns icon to see additional information, update the columns to display, and then choose Close.

5. Choose an AMI and write down its AMI ID.

Exercise 4-2: Selecting an Instance Store–Backed AMI

This exercise will show you the steps to select an instance store–backed AMI.

1. Open the Amazon EC2 console.

2. In the Navigation pane, choose AMIs.

3. From the filter lists, select the image type from the search bar, choose Platform to select the operating system, like Amazon Linux, and Root Device Type to select the Instance store.

4. Choose the Show/Hide Columns icon to get additional information to help you make your choice, update the columns to display, and then choose Close.

5. Choose an AMI and write down its AMI ID.

Exercise 4-3: Checking the Root Device Type of an Instance

This exercise will show you the steps to check whether the root device type of an instance is an instance store or EBS volume.

1. Open the Amazon EC2 console.

2. Choose Instances from the Navigation pane and select the instance you want.

3. You can then check the value of the Root device type in the Description tab.

4. This is an Amazon EBS–backed instance if the value is EBS. This is an instance store–backed instance if the value is instance store.

Exercise 4-4: Modifying the Root Device Volume to Persist at Launch

This exercise will show you the steps to modify the configuration of the root device volume at launch in order to persist this volume even after termination of its attached instance.

1. Open the Amazon EC2 console.

2. Choose Launch Instance from the Amazon EC2 console dashboard.

3. Select the AMI to use from the Choose an AMI page, and choose Select.

4. Choose an Instance Type and Configure Instance Details pages in the wizard.

5. Deselect Delete On Termination for the root volume on the Add Storage page.

6. After completing the remaining wizard pages, choose Launch.

7. You can verify the setting on the instance's Details pane by viewing details for the root device volume. Choose the entry for the root device volume next to Block Devices. Delete On Termination is True by default. Delete On Termination becomes False when you change the default behavior.

Questions

The following questions will help you gauge your understanding of Amazon EC2. Read all the answers carefully because there might be more than one correct answer. Choose the best responses for each question.

1. You have launched an EBS–backed EC2 instance in the us-west-2a region. To save on costs, you have stopped the instance and then tried to start it back after 35 days, but you are getting the "Insufficient Instance Capacity" error. What could be the reason for this error?

   A. AWS does not have sufficient on-demand capacity in that availability zone to service your request

   B. AWS availability zone mapping is changed for your user account

   C. There is an issue with the host machine capacity on which the instance is launched

   D. Your AWS account has reached the maximum EC2 instance limit

2. You are trying to connect to a running EC2 instance using SSH and are getting an "Unprotected Private Key File" error. Which of the following options can be a possible reason?

   A. Your private key file has the wrong file permission

   B. The .ppk file used for SSH has read-only permission

   C. The public key file has insufficient permission

   D. The username that you have provided is incorrect

3. You have launched an EC2 instance, but it was terminated. Is it possible to find the reason for termination and, if so, where can you find the details?

   A. It is not possible to find the details after the instance is terminated

   B. You can get the information by checking the instance description under the State Transition Reason label from the AWS console

   C. You can get the information by checking the instance description under the Status Change Reason label from the AWS console

   D. You can get the information by checking the instance description under the Instance Change Reason label from the AWS console

4. A user is trying to connect to a running EC2 instance using SSH, but the user gets a connection timeout error. Which is *not* a possible reason for rejection?

   A. You are connecting with the appropriate username for your instance AMI

   B. The security group is not configured properly to allow SSH

   C. The private key used to connect to the instance is not correct

   D. Your network ACL rules do not allow any inbound and outbound traffic

5. You are launching an EC2 instance in the US West region. Which option is recommended by AWS when selecting the availability zone?

   A. Always select us-west-1aavailability zone for high availability

   B. Do not select the availability zone; instead, let AWS choose it

   C. You cannot select the availability zone when launching an instance

   D. Always choose multiple availability zones when launching an instance

6. What are the two types of virtualization that Linux AMIs take advantage of in terms of special hardware extensions to boot the instance for better performance? (Choose two.)

   A. Amazon EC2 placement groups

   B. Amazon PV AMI

   C. Amazon HVM AMI

   D. Amazon VPC

7. Which of the following statements about Amazon instance store is correct?

   A. Instance store volume data persists only for the duration of the life of the Amazon EC2 instance

   B. When you update the security group rule, the data on the associated instance store volume will be lost

   C. Even after the associated Amazon EC2 instance is terminated, the data on an instance store volume persists until you manually delete it

   D. The instance store volume is recommended for the root volume of critical instances

8. You have launched an EC2 instance from an instance store–backed AMI and attached an additional instance store volume to it. Now you want to create an AMI from the running instance. Where will the additional instance store volume data be located?

   A. The additional instance store volume information will be on the block device mapping

   B. Only the root volume bundled on the instance uses instance store–backed AMIs

   C. It is not possible to add an instance store volume to the existing instance store

   D. It will not be a part of the AMI, since this is ephemeral storage

9. A user is using an EBS-backed instance. Which statement is true?

   A. Only when the instance is running will the user be charged for the volume and instance

   B. The user will be charged for the volume even if the instance is stopped

   C. Only the cost of the running instance will be charged to the user

   D. The user will not be charged for the volume if the instance is stopped

10. Status monitoring helps to quickly determine any problems that might prevent instances from running applications. EC2 automatically performs checks on every running EC2 instance to identify any hardware or software issues. Which of the following is true? (Choose two.)

   A. Status checks are performed every minute, and each returns a pass or a fail status

   B. If all checks pass, the overall status of the instance is OK

   C. If one or more checks fail, the overall status is Impaired

   D. Status checks cannot be disabled or deleted, since they are built into EC2

Answers

1. **A.** If you get an "Insufficient Instance Capacity" error when you try to launch an instance or restart a stopped instance, AWS does not currently have enough available on-demand capacity to service your request.

2. **A.** You need to set the 700 permission for the .ssh folder and set the 600 permission for the private key file. You need to grant the 644 permission to your public key file.

3. **B.** You can get the information by checking the instance description under the State Transition Reason label from the AWS console.

4. **A.** You are connecting with the appropriate username for your instance AMI. For the Amazon Linux AMI, the username is ec2-user; for an Ubuntu AMI, the username is ubuntu.

5. **B.** Do not select the availability zone; instead, let AWS choose it.

6. **B, C.** Amazon PV AMI and Amazon HVM AMI.

7. **A.** The data of instance store volume on your Amazon EC2 instance persists only during the life of the instance.

8. **A.** Yes, the additional instance store volume information will be on the block device mapping.

9. **B.** As long as there are attached EBS volumes to the EC2 instance, the user will be charged even if the instance is stopped.

10. **B, C.** If all checks pass, the overall status of the instance is OK. If one or more checks fail, the overall status is Impaired.

Additional Resources

- **AWS References** There is no place like official AWS documentation to get the most up-to-date information about all the AWS services. Always refer to the official AWS blogs to get the latest updates about new AWS services and updates to existing features.
  `https://docs.aws.amazon.com/ec2/index.html` and `https://aws.amazon.com/blogs/aws`

- **Amazon EC2 Instance Connect** This blog provides detailed steps to configure instance connections using a custom AuthorizedKeysCommand script.
  `https://aws.amazon.com/blogs/compute/new-using-amazon-ec2-instance-connect-for-ssh-access-to-your-ec2-instances/`

- **Hyper-V on Amazon EC2** This blog provides steps for launching, setting up, and configuring a Hyper-V–enabled host, launching a guest VM within Hyper-V running on i3.metal.
  `https://aws.amazon.com/blogs/compute/running-hyper-v-on-amazon-ec2-bare-metal-instances/`

- **Amazon EC2 Spot Instances** This blog explains how to use the spot instance interruption notices in CloudWatch events to automatically deregister spot instances.
  `https://aws.amazon.com/blogs/compute/taking-advantage-of-amazon-ec2-spot-instance-interruption-notices/`

- **Twelve-Factor App** This blog explains how to apply and compare the Twelve-Factor methodology to serverless application development for building modern, cloud-native applications.
  `https://aws.amazon.com/blogs/compute/applying-the-twelve-factor-app-methodology-to-serverless-applications/`

- **Lift-and-Shift EC2 Migration** This blog details the steps of automated migration using the CloudEndure tool to migrate a virtual machine from an on-premises environment to EC2 in AWS.
  `https://aws.amazon.com/blogs/compute/automating-your-lift-and-shift-migration-at-no-cost-with-cloudendure-migration/`

- **EC2 Predictive Scaling** This blog explains the steps to enable machine learning models to predict the EC2 usage and scale EC2 based on the prediction.
  `https://aws.amazon.com/blogs/aws/new-predictive-scaling-for-ec2-powered-by-machine-learning/`

PART II

AWS High Availability and Fault Tolerance

- **Chapter 5**   Elastic Load Balancing and Auto Scaling
- **Chapter 6**   Distributing the Contents via AWS CloudFront
- **Chapter 7**   Domain Name System and Amazon Route 53

Elastic Load Balancing and Auto Scaling

In this chapter, you will learn

- Introduction to elastic load balancers
- Types of elastic load balancers
- Listener configuration
- Target groups and targets
- Monitoring load balancers
- Elastic load balancer best practices
- Amazon EC2 Auto Scaling
- Auto Scaling lifecycle
- Launch templates and launch configurations
- Types of scaling
- Monitoring Auto Scaling

In this chapter you will see how Elastic Load Balancing and Auto Scaling help you to manage high availability and scaling of all your AWS services.

Elastic Load Balancing

The elastic load balancer acts as the single point of entry for your incoming application traffic and distributes it across multiple instances in multiple Availability Zones, which also increases the availability of your application. A listener checks for connection requests from clients and forwards requests to one or more target groups, using the protocol and port that you configure, based on the rules that you define, and you can add one or more listeners to your load balancer. You can add rules that specify different target groups to each listener based on the content of the request, which is called content-based routing.

Using the protocol and port number that you specified, each target group routes requests to one or more registered targets, such as EC2 instances. You can register a target (i.e., your EC2 instance) with multiple target groups. Health checks can be configured per target group basis, and these are performed on all registered targets of a target group. The diagram in Figure 5-1 illustrates the basic components of the Elastic Load Balancer.

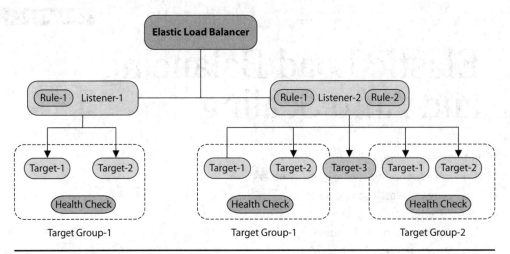

Figure 5-1 Elastic Load Balancer

As you can see, each listener contains a default rule, and a second listener contains an additional rule that routes requests to a different target group. The middle target, target-3, is registered with two target groups.

Types of Elastic Load Balancers

AWS provides three types of Elastic Load Balancing: Application Load Balancers, Network Load Balancers, and Classic Load Balancers.

Application Load Balancer

An Application Load Balancer functions at the seventh layer of the Open Systems Interconnection (OSI) model, which is also known as the application layer. When a request is received, the listener rules are evaluated by the Application Load Balancer in priority order to determine which rule to apply before selecting a target instance for the rule action from the target group. Even when a target is registered with multiple target groups, the routing is performed independently for each one.

As and when your application needs change, you can add or remove targets from your load balancer without disrupting your application's overall flow of requests. Based on your application changes over time, the Elastic Load Balancing scales in or scales out automatically for the majority of workloads. You can monitor the health of your registered targets (i.e., instances) so that the Load Balancer only sends requests to the healthy instance.

Network Load Balancer

A Network Load Balancer can handle millions of requests per second and it functions at the fourth layer of the OSI model, which is the network layer. The Load Balancer selects a target from the target group after it receives a connection request and opens a TCP connection to the selected target on the port specified in the listener configuration. Elastic Load Balancing creates a load balancer node in the Availability Zone when you enable it. Each load balancer node by default distributes the traffic across a single Availability Zone to its registered targets. Each load balancer node distributes traffic across the registered targets in all enabled Availability Zones only if you enable cross-zone load balancing.

The fault tolerance of your applications increases when you enable multiple Availability Zones for your load balancer and ensure that each target group has at least one target in each enabled Availability Zone. Elastic Load Balancing removes the IP address for the corresponding subnet from DNS when one or more target groups does not have a healthy target in an Availability Zone; however, the load balancer nodes in the other Availability Zones are still available to route traffic. If a client sends requests to the IP address after it is removed from DNS by not honoring time-to-live (TTL) settings, then the requests fail.

The load balancer selects a target for TCP traffic using a flow hash algorithm based on the protocol, destination IP address, source IP address, destination port, source port, and TCP sequence number. Different sequence numbers and source ports can be routed to different targets using TCP connections from your client. Each individual TCP connection is routed for the life of the connection to a single target. Using the flow hash algorithm based on the protocol, destination IP address, source IP address, destination port, and source port, the load balancer selects a target for User Datagram Protocol (UDP) traffic. A UDP flow is consistently routed to a single target throughout its lifetime, since it has the same source and destination. Different UDP flows can be routed to different targets because of different source IP addresses and ports.

A network interface is created in each Availability Zone that you enabled by Elastic Load Balancing. This network interface will be used to get a static IP address for each load balancer node in the Availability Zone. You can associate one Elastic IP address per subnet when you create an Internet-facing external load balancer. The target type determines whether you can register targets by instance ID or IP address when you create a target group. The source IP addresses of the clients are preserved and provided to your applications when you register targets by instance ID. The source IP addresses are the private IP addresses of the load balancer nodes when you register targets by IP address.

You can add and remove targets from your load balancer as your requirements change without disrupting your application's overall flow of requests. Based on your application usage requirements, the Elastic Load Balancing scales in or scales out the load balancer, and it can also scale to the majority of workloads automatically. You can configure health checks to monitor the health of the registered targets so that the load balancer can send requests only to healthy targets.

Classic Load Balancer

The Classic Load Balancer increases the fault tolerance of your applications by distributing the incoming application traffic across multiple EC2 instances in multiple Availability Zones and detects unhealthy instances and routes traffic only to healthy instances. Your load balancer increases the availability of your application and serves as a single point of contact for clients. You can add and remove instances without disrupting the overall flow of requests to your application from your load balancer as your needs change.

Elastic Load Balancing scales your load balancer to the vast majority of workloads automatically as application traffic changes. A listener checks the configured protocol and port for connection requests from clients and forwards the requests to one or more registered instances, and one or more listeners can be added to your load balancer. You can configure health checks and monitor the health of the registered instances so that your load balancer only sends requests to the healthy instances.

You need to enable cross-zone load balancing on your load balancer to distribute the traffic evenly across all registered instances in all enabled Availability Zones. It is important to keep approximately the same number of instances in each availability zone to ensure that your registered instances are able to handle the request load in each Availability Zone for better fault tolerance. The load balancer distributes the traffic evenly by default across the Availability Zones that you enable for your load balancer. The Classic Load Balancer supports EC2-Classic, TCP, and Secure Sockets Layer (SSL) listeners and also supports sticky sessions using application-generated cookies.

Elastic Load Balancing Concepts

The following are some of the important components of AWS Elastic Load Balancing concepts that you need to understand to create and manage an ELB.

Load Balancer Subnets

You must specify one public subnet from at least two Availability Zones when you create a load balancer, and you can specify only one public subnet per Availability Zone. You need to make sure each subnet for your load balancer has at least eight free IP addresses and has a minimum of /27 bitmask Classless Inter-Domain Routing (CIDR) block to make sure your load balancer can scale properly. Those IP addresses are used by your load balancer to establish connections with the targets.

Load Balancer Security Groups

The traffic to and from your load balancer is controlled by a security group, which acts as a firewall. The traffic is allowed for both inbound and outbound traffic using the ports and protocols that you configured. The rules for the security groups must allow traffic in both directions on both the listener and the health check ports associated with your load balancer. Whenever you update the health check port for a target group or add a listener to a load balancer, you must review and make sure your security group rules allow traffic on the new port in both inbound and outbound directions.

Load Balancer States

The states of a load balancer can be one of the following at any point in time:

- **Provisioning**   In this state, the load balancer is being set up.
- **Active**   In this state, the load balancer is fully set up and ready to route traffic.
- **Failed**   In this state, the load balancer cannot be set up.

Deletion Protection

You can enable deletion protection to prevent your load balancer from being deleted accidentally. Deletion protection is disabled by default for your load balancer. You must disable deletion protection if it is enabled already before you can delete the load balancer.

Connection Idle Timeout

The load balancer maintains two connections for each request that a client makes. A backend connection is between the load balancer and a target, and a frontend connection is between a client and the load balancer. When no data is sent or received over a frontend connection for a specified time period, then an idle timeout is triggered and the load balancer closes the connection.

Elastic Load Balancing by default sets the idle timeout value to 60 seconds. The load balancer can close the frontend connection if the target doesn't send some data at least every 60 seconds while the request is in flight. Increase the length of the idle timeout period as required; for example, to ensure that lengthy operations such as file uploads complete, send at least 1 byte of data before each idle timeout period elapses.

For backend connections, AWS recommends that you enable the HTTP keep-alive option for your EC2 instances. HTTP keep-alive can be enabled for your EC2 instances in the web server settings, so the load balancer can reuse backend connections until the keep-alive timeout expires. AWS also recommends that you configure the idle timeout of your application to be larger than the idle timeout configured for the load balancer.

Load Balancer Listeners

You must add one or more listeners before you start using your Load Balancer. A listener checks the protocol and port that you configured for connection requests. The listener rule defines how the load balancer routes requests to the targets in one or more target groups.

Listener Configuration

A listener supports HTTP and HTTPS protocols and 1 to 65,535 ports. Your applications can focus on their business logic, since the HTTPS listener is used to offload the encryption and decryption tasks to your load balancer. The HTTPS listener protocol requires at least one SSL certificate on the listener. Application Load Balancers provide native support for WebSockets, and WebSockets can be used with both HTTP and HTTPS listeners.

HTTP/2 with HTTPS listeners is natively supported by Application Load Balancers. An HTTP/2 connection can be used to send up to 128 requests in parallel. The load balancer converts these into individual HTTP/1.1 requests before distributing them across the healthy targets in your target group. Since HTTP/2 uses frontend connections more efficiently, you notice only fewer connections between the load balancer and clients, and you can't use the server-push feature of HTTP/2.

Listener Rules

Each listener will have a default rule, but you can add rules if required. Each rule consists of one or more conditions, a priority, and one or more actions. At any time, you can add or edit rules. You define actions for the default rule when you create a listener, and the default rules can't have conditions. When none of the listener's rules conditions are met, then the action defined in the default rule is performed.

- **Rule Priority**   Each rule will have a priority, and it is evaluated from the lowest value to the highest value in priority order. A nondefault priority can be changed at any time. The evaluation of the default rule is performed last, and the default priority cannot be changed.
- **Rule Actions**   Each rule has an order, a type, and the details required to perform an action.
- **Rule Conditions**   Each rule contains configuration details and type. An action is performed when the conditions of a rule are met.
- **Fixed-Response Actions**   Fixed-response actions can be used to return a custom HTTP response and to drop client requests. The action and the URL of the redirected target are recorded in the access logs when a fixed-response action is taken.
- **Forward Actions**   Forward actions are used to route requests to a particular target group.
- **Redirect Actions**   Redirect actions are used to redirect client requests from one URL to another.
- **Protocol**   You can redirect the HTTP to HTTP protocol, HTTP to HTTPS protocol, and HTTPS to HTTPS protocol, but you cannot redirect the HTTPS to HTTP protocol.
- **Hostname**   A hostname is case-insensitive and includes up to 128 alphanumeric characters.
- **Port**   Port numbers 1 to 65535 are allowed.
- **Path**   The absolute path starts with "/" as the leading character.
- **Query**   These are the query parameters.

Rule Condition Types

The AWS Elastic Load Balancer's listener rule supports the following condition types to configure rules that route requests based on the conditions set.

- **host-header**   Each route request is based on the hostname, which is also known as host-based routing. Multiple domains are supported using a single load balancer.
- **http-header**   Each route request is based on the HTTP headers, which can be standard or custom HTTP header fields.
- **http-request-method**   Each route request is based on the HTTP request and can specify standard or custom HTTP methods.

- **path-pattern**   Each route request is based on URL path patterns, which is also known as path-based routing. It is not applied to query parameters, only to the path of the URL.
- **query-string**   This is either key/value pair routing or a value in the query strings.
- **source-ip**   For source IP address routing of each request, the IP address should be in CIDR format. You can use IPv4 or IPv6 addresses; however, wildcard characters are not supported.

Each rule can contain either zero or one host-header, http-request-method, path-pattern, and source-ip conditions and include zero or more http-header and query-string conditions. Five match evaluations per rule can be specified, and wildcard characters can be included in the match evaluations for host-header, http-header, query-string, and path-pattern conditions, with a limit of five wildcard characters per rule.

Load Balancer Target Groups

A target group routes your requests to one or more registered targets. You specify a target group and conditions when you create each listener rule. Traffic is forwarded to the corresponding target group when a rule condition is met. Different target groups can be created for different types of requests.

Health check settings for your load balancer are defined on a per target group basis. Unless you override them when you create the target group or modify them later on, each target group uses the default health check settings. The load balancer continually monitors the health of all targets in an Availability Zone that are registered with the target group, based on the rules of the listeners. The load balancer routes requests to healthy registered targets.

Routing Configuration

A load balancer routes requests to its targets by default using the protocol and port number that you configured when you created the target group. When you register a target with the target group, you can also override the port used for routing traffic to a target. The protocols HTTP and HTTPS and ports 1 to 65535 are supported for target groups.

Target Type

The target type can be specified while creating a target group, which determines the type of targets that can be registered with this target group. You cannot change the type of target group after you create it. The following are the target types:

- **Instance**   The targets are specified by instance ID, and traffic is routed to instances using the primary private IP address specified in the primary network interface for the instance.
- **IP**   The targets are IP addresses, and you can specify IP addresses that are supported to enable you to register with a target group.
- **Lambda**   The target is a Lambda function, and you can register and invoke a Lambda function when the load balancer receives a request.

Registered Targets

Your load balancer distributes incoming traffic across its healthy registered targets and serves as a single point of contact for your clients. One or more target groups can be registered to each target. Each EC2 instance or IP address can be registered with the same target group multiple times using different ports, which enables the load balancer to route requests to microservices. You can register additional targets with one or more target groups to handle the increased demand of your application. The load balancer starts routing requests to a newly registered target as soon as the target passes the initial health checks and the registration process completes.

You can deregister targets or any additional targets you registered from your target groups when demand on your application decreases. Deregistering a target does not affect the target and just removes it from your target group. As soon as the target is deregistered, your load balancer stops routing requests to it. Until all the in-flight requests have completed, the target will be in the draining state. When you are ready to resume receiving requests again, reregister the target with a target group.

Deregistration Delay

Elastic Load Balancing stops sending requests to targets that are deregistering and waits 300 seconds by default before completing the deregistration process to allow the in-flight requests to complete. You can change the wait time by updating the deregistration delay value. The initial state of a deregistering target is called draining, and the target state becomes unused after the deregistration delay elapses to complete in-flight requests. If a deregistering target has no in-flight requests and no active connections, the deregistration process completes, without waiting for the deregistration delay to elapse.

Slow Start Mode

A target starts to receive its full share of requests by default, but using slow start mode gives targets time to warm up before the load balancer sends them their full share of requests. When in slow start mode, the load balancer linearly increases the number of requests that it sends to a target. After the slow start duration period elapses, a target exits slow start mode and the load balancer sends the full share of requests.

Sticky Sessions

Sticky sessions help you to route requests to the same target, and it is useful for servers that maintain state information using cookies in order to provide a continuous experience to clients. When a request is received from a client, it is routed to a target and generates a cookie to include in the response to the client. When the next request from the same client contains the cookie, the request goes to the same target group, and the load balancer routes the request to the same target of the cookie. Cookies are encrypted using a rotating key, and the load balancer–generated cookies cannot be decrypted or modified. The duration for the stickiness can be set in seconds, and it can be enabled at the target group level. The sticky session continues if the client sends a request before its duration period expires.

Load Balancer Monitoring

Load balancers need to be monitored continuously to alert on and troubleshoot issues, to target instances, and to analyze traffic patterns. This information can be kept in logs. Amazon CloudWatch can be used to retrieve statistics about data points for your load balancers and targets as an ordered set of time-series data, known as metrics. These metrics can be used to verify whether your system is performing as expected. The access logs contain detailed information about the requests you made to your load balancer, and access logs can be stored in your S3 bucket as log files.

You can track your HTTP requests using request tracing, and the load balancer adds a header with a trace identifier to each request it receives. Detailed information about application programming interface (API) calls made to the Elastic Load Balancer can be captured using AWS CloudTrail, which stores the log files in your S3 bucket. CloudTrail logs can be used to determine which calls were made, who made the call, when the call was made, and the source IP address where the call came from.

Elastic Load Balancer Best Practices

You need to use multiple Availability Zones in Elastic Load Balancing, as this provides high availability, fault tolerance, resiliency, and easy maintenance cycles because you can take an entire availability zone offline to perform your maintenance and still serve your customers. AWS recommends identifying the target Availability Zones and target group when provisioning the load balancer.

It is a best practice to configure health checks for the Elastic Load Balancer and monitor all the ports and protocols. Your security group for the Elastic Load Balancer must open only the required ports and protocols because security groups act as another firewall for your AWS resources. Create an Internet-facing Elastic Load Balancer only for external-facing workloads, and create an Internal Load Balancer for your internal needs.

If you create an Elastic Load Balancer for your web server application, you need to set up health checks for the HTTP/HTTPS protocol instead of creating health checks for the TCP/UDP protocols, which will be used for the Network Load Balancer. Use SSL security certificates to encrypt and decrypt HTTPS connections and terminate the SSL-based encrypted incoming traffic on the ELB instead of terminating the connection on your instances. This offloads SSL processing to AWS, saving you CPU time, costs, and administrative overhead.

Use connection draining while deleting Elastic Load Balancers and use slow start mode when starting Elastic Load Balancers for critical user applications. You can enable deletion protection to prevent your load balancer from being deleted accidentally, which is disabled by default. As mentioned earlier, load balancers need to be monitored continuously to detect and troubleshoot issues with your load balancers and target instances and to analyze traffic patterns.

Amazon EC2 Auto Scaling

Amazon EC2 Auto Scaling is a service that allows you to maintain the required number of Amazon EC2 instances available to handle the current load for your application. Auto Scaling groups are collections of EC2 instances where you can specify the minimum and maximum number of instances, so your Auto Scaling group never goes below or above these. You can also specify a desired capacity so your group maintains your desired number of instances. Amazon EC2 Auto Scaling can launch or terminate instances based on your application demand using scaling policies.

As shown in Figure 5-2, an Auto Scaling group has a minimum size of two instances, a desired capacity of three instances, and a maximum size of five instances. Based on your specified criteria, the scaling policy defines the number of instances and maintains this within your minimum and maximum numbers.

Advantages of Auto Scaling

Your application achieves better fault tolerance, availability, and cost savings when you add Amazon EC2 Auto Scaling; this also maximizes your benefits on the AWS Cloud. When one of your instances becomes unhealthy, Auto Scaling can detect it and terminate it, and also launch a new instance to replace the unhealthy instance. Amazon EC2 Auto Scaling supports multiple availability zones, so if you configure it to use multiple availability zones and one availability zone becomes unavailable, Auto Scaling can launch instances in another availability zone. This helps your application handle the current traffic demand and can dynamically increase and decrease capacity as needed. This also helps you save money by launching instances only when required and terminating them when the traffic is low.

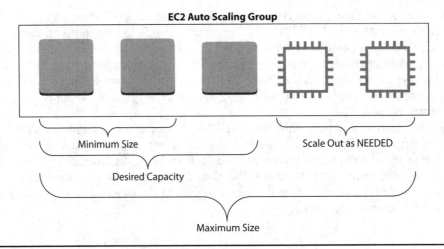

Figure 5-2 Auto Scaling group

Amazon EC2 Auto Scaling attempts to distribute instances evenly between the Availability Zones by launching new instances in the Availability Zone that has fewer instances when enabled. When you change the Availability Zones of your group, or explicitly terminate or detach instances, or an Availability Zone has insufficient capacity, or your spot bid price now has a market price below your bid price, then your Auto Scaling group will become unbalanced between Availability Zones. Amazon EC2 Auto Scaling compensates for all this by rebalancing the Availability Zones by launching new instances before terminating the old ones to avoid performance impact and to keep your application highly available.

The EC2 Auto Scaling Lifecycle

The lifecycle of EC2 instances in an Auto Scaling group starts when an instance is launched and it ends either when you terminate the instance or when the instance is taken out of service and terminated. You are billed for instances as soon as they are launched, including the time that they are not yet in service. Figure 5-3 shows different transitions between instance states during the lifecycle.

The Auto Scaling group launches new EC2 instances and attaches them to the group when you manually increase its size, or when you create a scaling policy to automatically increase based on an increase in demand, or when you set up scaling by schedule to increase the size of the group at a specific time.

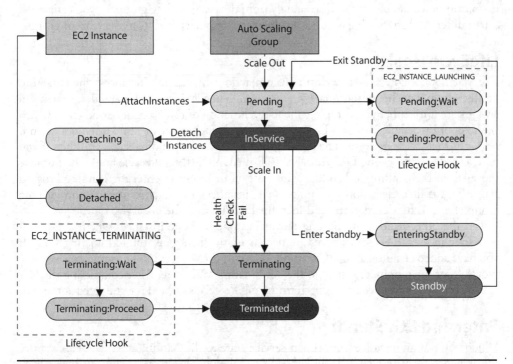

Figure 5-3   Auto Scaling lifecycle

Scale Out and In

When a scale-out event occurs, the Auto Scaling group launches the number of EC2 instances defined on the launch configuration. The instance state is initially "pending" until it is fully configured and passes the Amazon EC2 health checks. It is then attached to the Auto Scaling group and the state is changed to "in service" before it is counted toward the desired capacity of the Auto Scaling group. The instances remain in the in-service state until you put them into "standby" state, or you detach the instance from the Auto Scaling group, or the instance fails a required number of health checks, or a scale-in event occurs so it is removed from the Auto Scaling group and terminated.

A scale-in event occurs when you manually decrease the size of the group, or you create a scaling policy to automatically decrease the size when demand decreases, or you create a schedule to decrease the size of the group at a specific time. When a scale-in event occurs, the Auto Scaling group detaches one or more instances and uses the termination policy to determine which instances to terminate. Instances that are in the process of shutting down and enter the terminating state can't be put back into service. The instances are completely terminated before entering the terminated state.

Attach and Detach

You can attach or detach an EC2 instance that meets certain criteria from your Auto Scaling group. Your instance is managed as part of the Auto Scaling group after it is attached to it. Your instance can be managed separately from the Auto Scaling group, or you can attach it to a different Auto Scaling group after the instance is detached from the current group.

Lifecycle Hooks

Lifecycle hooks allow you to perform custom actions by pausing instances when an Auto Scaling group launches or terminates an instance. When an instance is paused, it remains in a wait state until either you complete the lifecycle action or the timeout period ends, which is one hour by default. Amazon EC2 Auto Scaling launches one or more instances when it responds to a scale-out event. The instance is initially in the pending state, and then if you have added an autoscaling:EC2_INSTANCE_LAUNCHING lifecycle hook, the instance moves from the pending to Pending:Wait state. Your instances enter the Pending:Proceed state after the lifecycle action is complete. The instances are attached to your Auto Scaling group after it is fully configured and then finally enter into the in-service state.

On the other hand, Auto Scaling terminates one or more instances when it responds to a scale-in event. These instances are detached and then enter the terminating state. If you have added an autoscaling:EC2_INSTANCE_TERMINATING lifecycle, the instance moves from the terminating state to the Terminating:Wait state. After completing the lifecycle action, your instance enters the Terminating:Proceed state and is terminated at the end.

Enter and Exit Standby

When you put an instance from the in-service state to the standby state, you can remove the instance from service or troubleshoot or make changes to it before putting it back into service. Instances are not an active part of your application when in the standby state; however, they are managed by the Auto Scaling group.

Launch Templates

A launch template, which is similar to a launch configuration, specifies the Amazon Machine Image (AMI) ID, security groups, a key pair, instance type, and other parameters that you need to launch EC2 instances. You can create multiple versions of a template using launch templates, and a subset of the full set of parameters can be created, which can be reused to create template versions or other templates. You can create a default template with the common configuration parameters and allow the other parameters to be specified as part of another version of the same template. AWS recommends using launch templates instead of launch configurations so that you can use the latest features of Amazon EC2. Launch templates allow you to provision both On-Demand instances and Spot instances across multiple instance types to achieve the desired cost, performance, and scale.

A launch template can be specified when you update an Auto Scaling group even if it was created using a launch configuration. You can create the template from scratch or create a new version of an existing template to use with an Auto Scaling group, or you can copy the parameters from a launch configuration, running instance, or another template.

Launch Configurations

A launch configuration is an instance configuration template that an Auto Scaling group uses to launch EC2 instances. You can specify instance information, including AMI ID, a key pair, security groups, instance type, and block device mapping when you create a launch configuration. A single launch configuration can be specified in multiple Auto Scaling groups, but only one launch configuration can be used with an Auto Scaling group at a time. Once you have created a launch configuration, it can't be modified, so you need to create a new launch configuration to update your Auto Scaling group with it.

You must specify a launch configuration, a launch template, or an EC2 instance whenever you create an Auto Scaling group. Amazon EC2 Auto Scaling automatically creates a launch configuration when you create an Auto Scaling group using an EC2 instance and associates it with the Auto Scaling group.

Auto Scaling Groups

An Auto Scaling group is a logical grouping of multiple Amazon EC2 instances that helps with automatic scaling and management. You can use features like health check replacements and scaling policies in an Auto Scaling group. Automatically scaling and maintaining the number of instances are the core functionalities of Auto Scaling groups.

You can adjust the size of an Auto Scaling group to meet demand either by using automatic scaling or manually. An Auto Scaling group begins with the desired capacity of instances and maintains it by performing periodic health checks on the instances in the group. Unhealthy instances are terminated by the Auto Scaling group, and Auto Scaling launches another new instance to replace the unhealthy instance. Auto Scaling policies or a schedule scale can be used to increase or decrease the number of instances in your group dynamically and to adjust the desired capacity of the group, as well as to launch or terminate instances as needed between the minimum and maximum capacity values that you specify.

An Auto Scaling group can launch On-Demand instances, Spot instances, or both when you configure the group to use a launch template. Amazon EC2 can terminate an individual Spot instance as the price or availability of Spot instances changes. The Auto Scaling group attempts to launch a replacement instance when a Spot instance is terminated to maintain the desired capacity for the group. The desired capacity is distributed automatically when you specify multiple Availability Zones, and Auto Scaling maintains the balance across all of your Availability Zones.

Scaling the Size

Scaling is a mechanism that helps you increase or decrease the capacity of the application instance that is serving your traffic. Scaling can be started with an event or an action, also known as scaling action, that triggers an Auto Scaling group to either launch or terminate Amazon EC2 instances. In order to best meet the needs of your applications, Amazon EC2 Auto Scaling provides a number of ways to adjust scaling.

Maintaining the Number of Instances

The Auto Scaling group starts by launching enough EC2 instances to meet the desired capacity, if specified, or the minimum capacity. Auto Scaling performs a periodic health check on running instances, and, as mentioned, when the instance is unhealthy, it terminates that instance and launches a new one. The instance is considered to be unhealthy if you stop or terminate it.

Manual Scaling

You can change the size of an existing Auto Scaling group manually at any time. You can either update the instances that are attached to the Auto Scaling group or update the desired capacity of the Auto Scaling group. Amazon EC2 Auto Scaling manages the process of launching or terminating instances when you change the size of your Auto Scaling group to maintain the new group size.

Scheduled Scaling

Scheduled scaling enables you to set your own schedule based on predictable workload changes, for example, if every week the traffic to your web application starts to increase on Friday, remains high on Saturday, and starts to decrease on Monday.

You need to create a scheduled action to configure your Auto Scaling group by defining the start and end time and the desired, minimum, and maximum number of instances for the scaling action. These scheduled actions can be either one time only or on a recurring schedule. You can temporarily disable scheduled scaling without deleting your scheduled actions, and you can create a maximum of 125 scheduled actions per Auto Scaling group. A scheduled action must have a unique time, otherwise, the call is rejected with an error message noting the conflict when you attempt to schedule an activity at a time when another scaling activity is already scheduled.

Dynamic Scaling

Dynamic Scaling allows you to scale based on a change in demand and supports target tracking scaling, step scaling, and simple scaling policies. In most cases, any one policy is sufficient to configure your Auto Scaling group to scale out or scale in automatically. You can also set up your Auto Scaling group to have more than one scaling policy, which provides greater flexibility to cover multiple scenarios. But it is possible that each policy could scale in or out at the same time when multiple policies are in force at the same time. In this case, Amazon EC2 Auto Scaling chooses the policy that provides the largest capacity for both scale out and scale in, even when the policies use different criteria for scaling in or out. The intention is to prevent Amazon EC2 Auto Scaling from removing or adding too many instances.

Target Tracking Scaling Policy

The target tracking scaling policy allows you to select a scaling metric and a target value. This works similar to the way you control the temperature of your home using a thermostat, where you select a temperature value and the thermostat automatically maintains this. CloudWatch alarms are used by Amazon EC2 Auto Scaling to create and manage the scaling policy, and Amazon EC2 Auto Scaling calculates the scaling adjustment based on the metric and the target value. The scaling policy removes or adds instances as required to keep the metric at the specified target value and adjusts to changes in the metric due to a changing workload pattern.

Step Scaling Policy

Step adjustments are used to increase or decrease the current capacity of your Auto Scaling group based on a set of scaling adjustments. These adjustments vary based on the size of the alarm breach. The policy continues to respond to additional alarms after a scaling activity is started, even while a scaling activity or health check replacement is in progress. Amazon EC2 Auto Scaling evaluates all the alarms that are breached as it receives the alarm messages, and it does not support cooldown periods for step scaling policies.

 TIP AWS recommends using step scaling policies instead of simple scaling policies, even if you have a single scaling adjustment.

Simple Scaling Policy

Simple scaling increases or decreases the current capacity of the group based on a single scaling adjustment value. Before responding to any additional alarms, the policy waits for the scaling activity or health check replacement to complete and waits until the cooldown period has expired. The cooldown period helps prevent the initiation of additional instances before the effects of previous activities are visible. Your policy is treated as a simple scaling policy if you created your scaling policy before target tracking and step policies were introduced.

Scaling Based on Amazon SQS

Dynamic Scaling allows you to scale based on the response to activity in an Amazon SQS queue, and it is useful for scaling in response to changing conditions, when you don't know when those conditions will change. An Auto Scaling group processes the messages from an SQS queue to manage the scaling of EC2 instances, and it measures the number of messages in the queue per EC2 instance. Dynamic Scaling uses a target tracking policy to scale based on the custom metric and a set target value, and the CloudWatch alarms invoke the scaling policy.

Deleting a Scaling Policy

You can delete a scaling policy when you no longer need it. When you delete a target tracking scaling policy, any associated CloudWatch alarms are deleted automatically. When you delete a step scaling policy or a simple scaling policy, the underlying alarm action is also deleted, but not the CloudWatch alarm associated with the scaling policy, so you need to delete this manually.

You can configure a termination policy for the Auto Scaling group to specify which instances to terminate first during a scale-in activity. You can also use Amazon EC2 termination protection to prevent specific instances from being accidentally terminated during automatic scale in.

Cooldown Period

When you define a cooldown period, the Auto Scaling group doesn't launch or terminate additional instances before the previous scaling activity completes. Only a simple scaling policy supports the cooldown period, not other scaling policies.

The default is not to wait for the cooldown period, when you manually scale your Auto Scaling group, but you can honor the cooldown period by overriding the default. The Auto Scaling group does not wait for the cooldown period to complete when an instance becomes unhealthy before replacing it.

Monitoring Auto Scaling Groups

Amazon EC2 Auto Scaling performs periodic health checks to identify the instances' health, but you can also configure Auto Scaling to determine the health status of an instance using Amazon EC2 status checks, Elastic Load Balancing health checks, or custom health checks. Amazon CloudWatch receives data points published by Amazon EC2 Auto Scaling about your Auto Scaling groups. These metrics are an ordered set of time-series data and can be used to verify that your system is performing as expected.

You can invoke a Lambda function based on the Amazon EC2 Auto Scaling event when your Auto Scaling groups launch or terminate instances or when a lifecycle action occurs. Amazon EC2 Auto Scaling can also send Amazon SNS notifications when your Auto Scaling groups launch or terminate instances. AWS CloudTrail tracks all the API calls made to the Amazon EC2 Auto Scaling and stores the information in log files in your Amazon S3 bucket. These log files can be monitored to verify the activity of your Auto Scaling groups. These logs include which requests were made, where the requests came from, who made the request, the source IP addresses, when the request was made, etc.

Chapter Review

This chapter explained the Elastic Load Balancer and Amazon EC2 Auto Scaling in detail, including all the details a developer needs to build high-performing AWS applications. There are three types of Elastic Load Balancers: Application Load Balancers, Network Load Balancers, and Classic Load Balancers. A load balancer acts as a single point of entry for your application traffic, and it distributes the incoming traffic across multiple targets in multiple availability zones, which increases the availability of your application. An Application Load Balancer functions at the seventh layer of the OSI model, which is the application layer. A Network Load Balancer can handle millions of requests per second and functions at the fourth layer of the OSI model, which is the network layer. You must specify one public subnet from at least two Availability Zones when you create a load balancer, and you can specify only one public subnet per Availability Zone.

The traffic to and from your load balancer is controlled by a security group, which acts as a firewall. The traffic is allowed for both inbound and outbound traffic using the ports and protocols that you configured. You can enable deletion protection to prevent your load balancer from being deleted accidentally. Elastic Load Balancing by default sets the idle timeout value to 60 seconds, and it closes the connection if no data has been sent or received by the time that the idle timeout period elapses. You must add one or more listeners before you start using your Load Balancer. A listener checks for connection requests, using the protocol and port that you configured. Target groups route your requests to one or more registered targets. You specify a target group and associated conditions when you create each listener rule. Your load balancer distributes incoming traffic across its healthy registered targets and serves as a single point of contact for your clients. Sticky sessions help you route requests to the same target and are useful for servers that maintain state information using cookies in order to provide a continuous experience to clients. Monitoring your load balancers helps you troubleshoot issues with your load balancers and target instances and analyze traffic patterns.

Amazon EC2 Auto Scaling is a service that allows you to maintain the required number of Amazon EC2 instances available to handle the current load for your application. Auto Scaling groups are collections of EC2 instances, where you can specify the minimum and maximum number of instances. The lifecycle of EC2 instances in an Auto Scaling group starts when an instance is launched and ends either when you terminate the instance or when the Auto Scaling group terminates the instance. When a scale-out event occurs, the Auto Scaling group launches the number of EC2 instances defined on the launch configuration. A scale-in event occurs when you manually decrease the size of the group, or you create a scaling policy to automatically decrease the size when demand decreases, or it can be scheduled to decrease the capacity of the group at a particular time. You can attach or detach an EC2 instance that meets certain criteria from your Auto Scaling group. Lifecycle hooks allow you to perform custom actions by pausing instances when an Auto Scaling group launches or terminates an instance.

Launch templates allow you to have multiple versions and create a subset of the full set of parameters that you can reuse to create other templates or template versions. A launch configuration is an instance configuration template that an Auto Scaling group uses to launch EC2 instances. AWS recommends using launch templates instead of launch configurations so that you can use the latest features of Amazon EC2. An Auto Scaling group is a logical grouping of multiple Amazon EC2 instances that helps with automatic scaling and management. Scheduled scaling enables you to set your own schedule based on predictable changes in workload. Dynamic Scaling allows you to scale based on changes in demand and supports target tracking scaling, step scaling, and simple scaling policies. When you define the cooldown period, the Auto Scaling group doesn't launch or terminate additional instances before the previous scaling activity completes. You can delete a scaling policy when you no longer need it. Amazon EC2 Auto Scaling periodically performs health checks to identify the instance's health, and you can also configure Auto Scaling to determine the health status of an instance using Amazon EC2 status checks, Elastic Load Balancing health checks, or custom health checks to identify any instances that are unhealthy.

Exercises

The following exercises will let you practice using the console to perform various administrative tasks. You need to create an AWS account, as explained earlier, to perform the following exercises. You can use the Free Tier when launching AWS resources, but make sure to terminate them at the end.

Exercise 5-1: Create an Application Load Balancer

This exercise will help you to gain practical experience creating an Application Load Balancer using the AWS Management Console.

1. Open the Amazon EC2 console at https://console.aws.amazon.com/ec2/.

2. You need to choose a region for your load balancer on top of the navigation bar and select the same region where your EC2 instances are.

3. Below LOAD BALANCING on the navigation pane, choose Load Balancers.

4. Then choose Create Load Balancer.

5. Since we are creating an Application Load balancer, select Application Load Balancer and choose Create.

Exercise 5-2: Configure Your Load Balancer and Listener

This exercise provides practical experience creating a listener using the AWS Management Console.

1. Under Name, type the appropriate name for your Application Load Balancer. Your Application Load Balancer name must be unique.

2. You can keep the default values for the Scheme and IP Address type.

3. By default, the listener accepts HTTP traffic on port 80, so keep this.

4. For Availability Zones, select the VPC that you used for your EC2 instances and then select the public subnet for that Availability Zone.

5. Choose Next: Configure Security Settings.

Exercise 5-3: Configure a Security Group for Your Load Balancer

This exercise provides practical experience configuring a security group using the AWS Management Console.

1. Choose Create A New Security Group.

2. Type a name and description for the security group, or you can keep the defaults.

3. When ready, choose Next to navigate to the Configure Routing page.

Exercise 5-4: Configure Your Target Group

This exercise provides practical experience configuring a target group using the AWS Management Console.

1. For Target Group, you can keep the default value, and then select New Target Group.

2. Provide an appropriate name for the new target group.

3. You can keep the default target type, which is an instance, HTTP as the protocol, and 80 for the port.

4. You can keep the default values for Health Checks.

5. When ready, choose Next to move to the Register Targets page.

Exercise 5-5: Register Targets with Your Target Group

This exercise provides practical experience registering targets using the AWS Management Console.

1. When you are on the Register Targets page, select one or more instances as required.

2. Here you can keep the default port as 80 and then choose Add To Registered Targets.

3. After you have finished selecting instances, choose Next to navigate to the Review page.

Exercise 5-6: Create and Test Your Load Balancer

This exercise provides practical experience creating and testing a load balancer using the AWS Management Console.

1. When you are on the Review page, if everything looks okay, choose Create.

2. Choose Close after you are notified that your load balancer was created successfully.

3. Below LOAD BALANCING on the navigation pane, you can choose Target Groups.

4. Select the newly created target group.

5. Verify that your instances are ready on the Targets tab.

6. After the status of at least one instance is healthy, you can test your load balancer.

7. Below LOAD BALANCING on the navigation pane, choose Load Balancers.

8. Select the newly created load balancer.

9. From the Description tab, copy the DNS name of the load balancer and paste it into an Internet-connected web browser.

10. If everything is working, the browser displays the default page of your server.

Exercise 5-7: Delete Your Load Balancer

As soon as your load balancer becomes available, you are billed for each hour or partial hour, so delete it if you no longer need it.

1. Open the Amazon EC2 console at https://console.aws.amazon.com/ec2/.

2. Below LOAD BALANCING on the navigation pane, choose Load Balancers.

3. Select the checkbox for the load balancer, and then choose Actions and select Delete from drop-down list to delete your load balancer.

4. When prompted for confirmation, choose Yes, Delete, which deletes your load balancer permanently.

Questions

The following questions will help you gauge your understanding of Elastic Load Balancing and Auto Scaling in this chapter. Read all the answers carefully because there might be more than one correct answer. Choose the best responses for each question.

1. What Load Balancers are available in AWS? (Choose three.)

   A. Application Load Balancer

   B. Network Load Balancer

   C. Global Load Balancer

   D. Classic Load Balancer

2. What are lifecycle hooks?

   A. It allows you to take actions before an instance goes into service or before it is terminated.

   B. It is a collection of EC2 instances used for Dynamic Scaling and fleet management.

   C. It is a template that your EC2 Auto Scaling group uses to launch EC2 instances based on the configuration.

   D. It is a failed user-configured ELB health check, or the hardware has become impaired.

3. Your customer wants to use a single Application Load Balancer to handle both HTTP and HTTPS requests. Is this possible?

   A. No, only HTTP port 80 listener can be added to any single Application Load Balancer.

   B. No, only HTTPS port 443 listener can be added to any single Application Load Balancer.

   C. No, both HTTP port 80 and HTTPS port 443 listeners cannot be added to a single Application Load Balancer.

   D. Yes, both HTTP port 80 and HTTPS port 443 listeners can be added to a single Application Load Balancer.

4. Your developer tries to use EC2 Auto Scaling groups to span multiple AWS regions for high availability but he is getting an error. Is it possible to configure an EC2 Auto Scaling Group to span across different AWS regions?

   A. Yes, EC2 Auto Scaling groups can span across multiple AWS regions.

   B. No, EC2 Auto Scaling cannot span across AWS regions; however, it can span across multiple availability zones.

   C. Yes, EC2 Auto Scaling groups can span across AWS regions only if this is defined in the launch configuration.

   D. Yes, EC2 Auto Scaling groups can span across AWS regions only if the lifecycle hooks are defined.

5. Which of the following about the Network Load Balancer are true? (Choose all that apply.)

   A. Network Load Balancer supports both TCP and UDP (layer 4) load balancing.

   B. Network Load Balancer can handle millions of requests per second and provides extremely low latency.

   C. Network Load Balancer supports TLS termination and preserves the source IP of the clients.

   D. Network Load Balancer supports long-running connections for WebSocket-type applications.

6. The instances in your application layer need to be load-balanced with your database layer without allowing any external Internet traffic. Can you use Network Load Balancer to set up internal load balancers?

A. No, the Network Load Balancer can only be set up as an Internet-facing external load balancer.

B. Yes, Network Load Balancer can be set up as either an Internet-facing external load balancer or an internal load balancer.

C. No, only Application Load Balancer can be set up as an internal load balancer.

D. No, only Classic Load Balancer can be set up as an internal load balancer.

7. Which of the following is supported in Application Load Balancer? (Choose three.)

A. WebSockets and Secure WebSockets are supported in Application Load Balancer.

B. Request tracing is supported and enabled by default in Application Load Balancer.

C. HTTP/2 support is enabled natively on an Application Load Balancer and can connect over TLS.

D. Application Load Balancer supports layer 4 load balancing.

8. Your development team is using Elastic Load Balancer, and before implementing it in production they want to know whether there is an SLA for load balancers. What do you tell them?

A. Elastic Load Balancing guarantees a monthly availability of at least 99.99 percent for Classic, Application, or Network Load Balancers.

B. Elastic Load Balancing does not guarantee any SLA for your Classic, Application, or Network Load Balancers.

C. Elastic Load Balancing guarantees a monthly availability of at least 98.99 percent for your Application and Network Load Balancers.

D. Elastic Load Balancing guarantees a monthly availability of at least 99.99 percent only for your Network Load Balancers.

9. You are configuring Amazon EC2 Auto Scaling and plan to use the health checks that work with your Application Load Balancers and Network Load Balancers. If any target group associated with it becomes unhealthy, will an instance be marked as unhealthy?

A. No, Amazon EC2 Auto Scaling does not work with the health check feature of Application Load Balancers and Network Load Balancers. You need to configure a different health check for EC2 Auto Scaling.

B. Yes, Amazon EC2 Auto Scaling works with the health check feature of Application Load Balancers, but not with Network Load Balancers.

C. Yes, Amazon EC2 Auto Scaling works with the health check feature of Network Load Balancers, but not with Application Load Balancers.

D. Yes, Amazon EC2 Auto Scaling works with the health check feature of both Application Load Balancers and Network Load Balancers.

10. Your manager asked you to set up an EC2 Auto Scaling group. Do you need to install CloudWatch agents manually or will the Amazon EC2 Auto Scaling group install the agents automatically?

    A. It is automatically installed on EC2 instances if your AMI contains a CloudWatch agent when you create an EC2 Auto Scaling group.

    B. You need to manually install this using the recommended yum command on each instance.

Answers

1. A, B, D. You can select Application Load Balancer when you need to load-balance HTTP requests, and for extreme performance/low latency applications, you can use Network Load Balancer. If your application needs HTTP, HTTPS (Secure HTTP), SSL (Secure TCP), or TCP, you can use Classic Load Balancer.

2. A. It allows you to perform custom actions by pausing instances when an Auto Scaling group launches or terminates the instance. When an instance is paused, it remains in a wait state until either you complete the lifecycle action or the timeout period ends, which is one hour by default.

3. D. Yes, both HTTP port 80 and HTTPS port 443 listeners can be added to a single Application Load Balancer.

4. B. No, EC2 Auto Scaling cannot span across AWS regions; however, it can span across multiple Availability Zones.

5. A, B, C, D. Network Load Balancer supports both TCP and UDP (layer 4) load balancing, and it can handle millions of requests per second and provides extremely low latency. Also, it supports TLS termination and preserves the source IP of the clients in addition to supporting long-running connections for WebSocket-type applications.

6. B. Yes, Network Load Balancer can be set up as either an Internet-facing external load balancer or an internal load balancer.

7. A, B, C. WebSockets and Secure WebSockets and request tracing are supported in addition to HTTP/2 support, which is enabled natively on an Application Load Balancer and can connect over TLS.

8. A. Yes, Amazon Elastic Load Balancing guarantees a monthly availability of at least 99.99 percent for your Classic, Application, or Network Load Balancers.

9. D. Yes, Amazon EC2 Auto Scaling works with the health check feature of both Application Load Balancers and Network Load Balancers.

10. A. Yes, it is automatically installed on EC2 instances if your AMI contains a CloudWatch agent when you create an EC2 Auto Scaling group.

Additional Resources

- **UDP Load Balancing** There is no place like the official AWS documentation to get the latest and most up-to-date information about all the AWS services and updates to existing features. The Network Load Balancer handles tens of millions of requests per second while maintaining high throughput and supports resource-based and tag-based permissions and the ability to load-balance UDP traffic. This blog explains in detail the steps to configure the same load balancer for both TCP and UDP traffic instead of maintaining a fleet of proxy servers to ingest UDP traffic.
  `https://aws.amazon.com/blogs/aws/new-udp-load-balancing-for-network-load-balancer/`
  `https://docs.aws.amazon.com` and `https://aws.amazon.com/blogs/aws`

- **Dynamic Scaling** This blog explains the detailed steps to launch and manage an entire fleet of EC2 Spot instances with one request using the RequestSpotFleet API, which helps achieve cost savings.
  `https://aws.amazon.com/blogs/compute/dynamic-scaling-with-ec2-spot-fleet/`

- **Advanced Request Routing** This blog explains the steps you need to write rules and route traffic based on standard and custom HTTP headers and methods, the query string, and the source IP address using AWS Application Load Balancers, which helps in eliminating the need for a proxy fleet for routing and to block unwanted traffic at the load balancer level.
  `https://aws.amazon.com/blogs/aws/new-advanced-request-routing-for-aws-application-load-balancers/`

- **Auto Scale Amazon EC2 Spot Instances** This blog explains how to architect the workload properly to handle the two-minute warning to avoid outages or disconnections by avoiding state or end-user stickiness to specific instances, fault tolerance, decoupling with queueing mechanisms, and keeping compute and storage decoupled.
  `https://aws.amazon.com/blogs/compute/running-high-scale-web-on-spot-instances/`

- **TLS Termination** This blog provides the steps for creating a Network Load Balancer and making use of TLS connections that terminate at a Network Load Balancer, as well as freeing your backend servers from the compute-intensive work of encrypting and decrypting all of your traffic.
  `https://aws.amazon.com/blogs/aws/new-tls-termination-for-network-load-balancers/`

Distributing the Contents via AWS CloudFront

In this chapter, you will learn
- Amazon CloudFront
- Origin servers
- Pricing
- Regional edge caches
- Securing content
- CloudFront distributions
- CNAME
- WebSocket support
- Optimizing content caching
- Content expiration
- Origin groups
- Lambda@Edge

In this chapter you will learn how Amazon CloudFront helps you distribute your content with low latency and high data transfer speeds in an easy and cost-effective way. You can access Amazon CloudFront using the AWS Management Console, AWS Software Development Kit (SDK), CloudFront application programming interface (API), AWS command-line interface, and AWS Tools for Windows PowerShell.

Amazon CloudFront

Amazon CloudFront is a content delivery service that speeds up distribution of your static and dynamic files to your end users using a global network of edge locations. It is offered to you as a self-service and is pay-per-use AWS offering, so you don't need to pay any minimum fees up-front or commit to using it long term. For example, when a user requests high-definition (HD) video content from CloudFront, the user is routed to the nearest edge location that provides the lowest time delay (i.e., latency) and provides the best possible performance. Figure 6-1 explains how the content is stored and delivered to users.

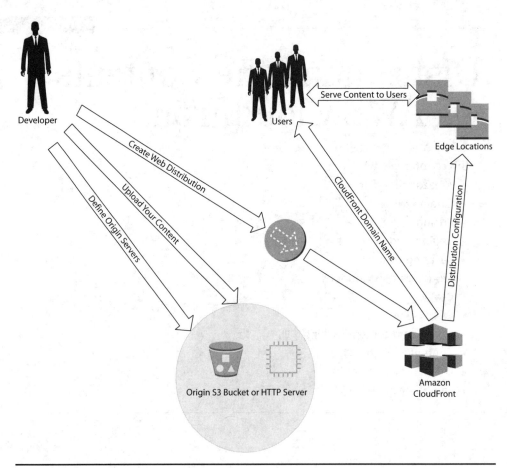

Figure 6-1 Configuring CloudFront

Amazon CloudFront delivers the requested content immediately to your user with the lowest latency if the content is already in the edge location. CloudFront retrieves the user-requested content from an Amazon S3 bucket, HTTP server, or MediaPackage channel if it is not in the edge location already. CloudFront uses the AWS backbone network, which speeds up the distribution, to best serve each user request through the nearest edge location.

CloudFront Origin Servers

Origin servers can be an Amazon S3 bucket or your web HTTP server that stores the original files—the definitive version of your objects. CloudFront retrieves your files from the origin server and then distributes it to CloudFront edge locations all over the world. Your origin server will always be an Amazon S3 bucket when you are using the Adobe Media Server Real-Time Messaging Protocol (RTMP) protocol to serve media files on demand.

You can upload your files, also known as objects, including media files, images, web pages, and anything that can be served over HTTP or Adobe RTMP, which is a protocol used by Adobe Flash Media Server. When using an Amazon S3 bucket as an origin server, if your bucket objects are publicly readable, they can be accessed using the CloudFront URL. However, you can keep the objects of your S3 bucket private and control access.

The CloudFront distribution instructs CloudFront which origin servers to contact to get the requested files. A domain name will be assigned to your new distribution, and you can add an alternative domain name if required. The distribution's configuration will be sent to all points of presence (POPs), which is a collection of servers in geographically dispersed datacenters, and to all the edge locations, where it caches copies of your files.

You can either use the domain name that CloudFront provides for your URL or you can set up CloudFront to use your own domain name with your distribution for your application. You can also indicate how long you want the files to stay in the cache in CloudFront edge locations by configuring headers to the file in your origin server. Files stay in an edge location for 24 hours by default, and 0 seconds is the minimum expiration time.

Assume you have a popular application and a user accesses it from a different region requesting one of your famous video files. Your domain name service routes the request to the nearest CloudFront edge location, which serves the content with low latency. If the requested file is not cached in the edge location, CloudFront forwards the request to your origin server and sends it to the nearest edge location. CloudFront begins to forward the files to the user as quickly as the first byte returns from the origin, in addition to saving it to the cache in the edge location for future requests.

CloudFront Pricing

It is very important to understand the pricing model of Amazon CloudFront—or any service to build a cost-effective AWS application, for that matter—and avoid unnecessary charges or surprises in the future. CloudFront doesn't require you to commit to how much content you'll have, and you don't have to pay any up-front fees. You only pay for what you use in a pay-as-you-go model.

You will be provided a billing report and summary report of CloudFront usage by AWS. The following are the typical charges that we will see for CloudFront:

- **Charges for storage**   You pay normal Amazon S3 storage charges to store objects in your bucket.

- **Charge for serving objects**   You will incur charges when CloudFront responds to requests for your objects that include data transfer for WebSocket data from your server to client. The CloudFront charges appear in the CloudFront portion of your AWS statement as "region– DataTransfer-Out-Bytes."

- **Charge for submitting data**   You incur charges when users transfer data to your origin, which includes DELETE, OPTIONS, PATCH, POST, and PUT requests and data transfers for WebSocket data from the client to your server. The CloudFront charges appear in the CloudFront portion of your AWS statement as "region – DataTransfer-Out-Bytes."

NOTE You also incur a surcharge for HTTPS requests and an additional surcharge for requests that have field-level encryption enabled.

Regional Edge Caches

CloudFront regional edge caches save popular content so it can be served to users quickly. Regional edge caches are deployed globally and are located between your origin server and the global edge locations. When new objects become more popular than older objects, the older objects will be removed from the cache.

Regional edge caches have a larger cache, so objects remain longer in these locations. This improves overall performance for users and reduces the need for CloudFront to go to your origin server to get the content. Instead, CloudFront keeps persistent connections with origin servers. Dynamic content requests and the proxy methods PUT, POST, PATCH, OPTIONS, or DELETE go directly to the origin from the edge cache locations and will not go to the regional edge caches.

Adding Content

You need to add files to the origins that were defined in the distribution, and then Cloud-Front distributes the content and exposes it as a CloudFront link. A CloudFront edge location fetches the new files from an origin only when it receives a user request for that object. The file must be added to the Amazon S3 buckets specified in your distribution or a custom origin to a directory in the specified domain for CloudFront to distribute.

You need to create the correct path pattern for the cache behavior to send requests to the correct origin. For example, when you have a cache whose behavior is *.html, CloudFront will only forward *.html files, not any other file format like .jpg files that you uploaded to the origin, since the corresponding cache behavior doesn't exist. AWS recommends setting the Content-Type header field when you upload a file to your origin.

Removing Content

When you no longer want your files to be included in your CloudFront distribution, you can delete them from your origin. However, the CloudFront still distributes files to users through the edge cache until the files expire. In order to remove the files right away, you must either invalidate the file or use file versioning, where different versions of a file have different names that can be used in the CloudFront distribution to return a different file to users.

Securing Content

You can configure HTTPS connections, use AWS Web Application Firewall (WAF), or set up field-level encryption to secure content in CloudFront distributions. You can use signed URLs or signed cookies to limit access to your private content by requiring access to CloudFront. For example, users from specific geographic locations can be prevented from accessing content distributed through CloudFront web distribution.

HTTPS with CloudFront

You can configure CloudFront to use HTTPS encrypted connections to request and deliver objects to your users.

Restrict Access in the Origin

You can restrict access to your files in the origin by either setting up an origin access identity (OAI) for your Amazon S3 bucket or configuring custom headers for a private HTTP server or configuring a S3 bucket as a website endpoint.

Restrict Access in Edge Caches

You can restrict access to your content in edge caches by configuring CloudFront to require users to use either signed URLs or signed cookies. Your application needs to distribute signed URLs or send Set-Cookie headers, which sets signed cookies for authenticated users. When users access the cached content, CloudFront compares the cookies and then serves the content only if it matches.

Signed URLs and Signed Cookies

If you want to distribute your content over the Internet but want to restrict access to business documents, sensitive data, media streams, or content that is intended for selected users like paid registered users, you can do so by using CloudFront signed URLs or signed cookies, not by accessing the origin server, which is either S3 bucket or HTTP server URLs.

Signed URLs

A signed URL contains a policy statement in JSON format that specifies the restrictions such as expiration date and time that gives you more control over who has access to your content. As mentioned, this is based on either a canned policy or a custom policy. Your CloudFront distribution contains one or more trusted signers who have permission to create signed URLs. The application creates signed URLs for the files or parts of the application that you want to restrict access to. When your user requests a file that requires signed URLs, your application verifies whether the user is entitled to this access—for example, they meet some access requirement or they've paid a fee or they've signed in. Your application then creates and returns a signed URL to the user, which immediately can be used to access the file from the CloudFront edge cache without any intervention from the user. Using the public key, CloudFront validates the signature and confirms that the URL hasn't been tampered with—the request is rejected if the signature is invalid. If the signature is valid, CloudFront looks at the policy statement to confirm that the request is still valid and that the user is accessing the content during the time period that you specified.

NOTE The same CloudFront distribution can have some signed URLs using canned policies and it can have some signed URLs using custom policies.

Lifetime of Signed URLs

A signed URL is valid for only a short time—possibly for as little as a few minutes—and they are good for distributing content on-the-fly to a user, like music downloads or distributing movie rentals. CloudFront compares the expiration time in the URL with the current time when the user starts to download a file or starts to play a media file to determine whether the URL is still valid.

Signed Cookies

CloudFront signed cookies allow you to control who can access your content using a policy statement in JSON format that specifies the restrictions when you don't want to change your current URLs or when you want to provide access to multiple restricted files. You can use canned policies or custom policies for this. You can define one or more trusted signers in your CloudFront distribution who have permission to create signed URLs and signed cookies.

Your application determines whether a user should have access to your content and sends three Set-Cookie headers to the user; a CloudFront signed cookie requires three Set-Cookies, each of which contains a name-value pair. The Set-Cookie headers must be sent to the users before your user can request your private content, and based on that it will have a minimum of two cache behaviors: one requiring authentication and another one without. When a registered user signs in to your website, your application returns the Set-Cookie headers in the response and the user stores the name-value pairs.

The user requests a file, and CloudFront uses the public key to validate the signature in the signed cookie to confirm that the cookie hasn't been tampered with. If the signature in the cookie is valid, CloudFront looks at the policy statement in the cookie to confirm that the request is still valid and confirms whether the user is accessing your content during the allowed time period. If the request satisfies the policy statement, then CloudFront determines whether the file is in the edge cache already; if not, the request is forwarded to the origin, which finally returns the content to the user.

Signed Cookie Lifetime

CloudFront checks the expiration date and time in the cookie at the time of the HTTP request to determine whether a signed cookie is still valid. If your user begins downloading a large file just before the expiration time, then the download completes successfully even if the expiration time has passed. However, if the TCP connection drops and the client tries to restart the download after the expiration time passes, the download will fail.

Choosing Between Signed URLs and Signed Cookies

Both signed URLs and signed cookies allow you to control who can access your content. You need to decide whether to use signed URLs or signed cookies when you want to serve private content using CloudFront.

Signed URLs are necessary when you want to use an RTMP distribution because signed cookies aren't supported. It is useful when you want to restrict access to individual files instead of your entire content. It can also be used for a client that doesn't support cookies.

The signed cookies can be used when you want to provide access to multiple restricted files. It is also useful when your application doesn't want to change the current URL.

Using Both Signed URLs and Signed Cookies

When your application uses both signed URLs and signed cookies to control access to the same set of files, then CloudFront determines whether to return the file to the requested user or not only based on the signed URL and ignores the signed cookie. When your application is not using a signed URL but the URL contains query string parameters like Expires, Policy, Signature, and Key-Pair-Id, then it is not possible to use either signed URLs or signed cookies because CloudFront thinks signed URLs are being used and will disregard signed cookies as well.

Origin Access Identity

You can prevent your users from directly accessing files using Amazon S3 URLs and bypassing CloudFront. OAI is a special CloudFront user that needs to be granted the identity permission to read the files in your bucket and remove any other permission to use the Amazon S3 URL.

You can create CloudFront signed URLs or signed cookies to limit access to files in your Amazon S3 bucket and create the OAI and associate it with your distribution. CloudFront uses OAI to access and serve files to your users and restrict direct URL access to the S3 bucket to access any file there.

AWS WAF to Control Access

You can configure WAF to monitor CloudFront's HTTP and HTTPS requests and control access to your content. Based on the request's IP address or query strings value, CloudFront responds either with the requested content or with an HTTP 403 status code for a forbidden request; you also can configure a custom error page when a request is blocked.

Restricting Geographic Distribution

Geoblocking is a feature that prevents users in specific geographic locations from accessing your content using the CloudFront distribution. The CloudFront geo restriction feature can be used to restrict access at the country level to all of the files in a distribution. If you need to restrict access at a finer granularity than the country level and restrict access to a subset of the files in a distribution, use a third-party geolocation service.

CloudFront Geo Restriction

CloudFront typically serves the requested content, regardless of where the user is located. However, you can use the CloudFront geo restriction feature to allow users to access your content only if they are from your approved whitelisted countries. You can prevent your users from accessing your content if they're in one of the countries on a blacklist of banned countries. For example, if you are not authorized to distribute your content to a country for copyright reasons, use CloudFront geo restriction to block the request.

Third-Party Geolocation

When you have geographic restrictions that are more granular than country boundaries or when you need to limit access to only few of the files, you need to combine Cloud-Front with a third-party geolocation service. You can control access to your content based on city, ZIP or postal code, or even latitude and longitude in addition to country. AWS recommends using CloudFront–signed URLs with an expiration date and time and the S3 bucket as your origin when you're using a third-party geolocation service because OAI can prevent users from accessing your content directly from the origin.

Field-Level Encryption

Field-level encryption adds another layer of security along with HTTPS, which enforces secure end-to-end connections to origin servers and lets you protect specific data by making sure only certain applications can see it. You can securely upload sensitive information like the credit card number of your payment processing system to your web servers securely using field-level encryption. The uploaded information is kept encrypted at the edge location closer to your user and remains encrypted throughout the entire application stack by making sure only applications that need the data that have the credentials to decrypt it can access it.

Field-level encryption can encrypt up to ten data fields in a request, and you can specify the set of fields in POST requests that needs be encrypted, along with the public key to encrypt them. When sensitive data forwarded to the origin by an HTTPS request that has field-level encryption is enabled, sensitive data will still be encrypted, thereby reducing the risk of accidental loss of the sensitive data or a data breach. Only the applications with the appropriate private key can decrypt and access the data. All sensitive data is encrypted by CloudFront automatically using your public key. Since the Cloud-Front field-level encryption uses asymmetric encryption, which is also called public-key encryption, it cannot be used to decrypt the encrypted values—your application needs to use your private key to decrypt it.

CloudFront Distributions

A CloudFront distribution defines where the contents are delivered from and when you want to distribute your content, as well as the details about how to track and manage content delivery. The content origin can be an Amazon S3 bucket, MediaPackage channel, or HTTP server, and a combination of up to 25 origins can be configured. You can allow the files to be available to everyone or restrict access to just some users. You can add more security by configuring CloudFront to require users to use HTTPS to access your content. CloudFront can be configured to forward cookies or query strings to your origin. You can prevent users in selected countries from accessing your content using geo restriction. You can also configure CloudFront to create access logs that show user activity.

Distribution Contents

You can configure and serve the content worldwide, as shown in Figure 6-2. You can serve contents over HTTP or HTTPS using distributions. Static and dynamic content can be

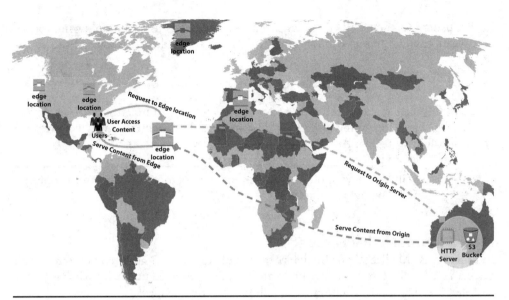

Figure 6-2   CloudFront content delivery

downloaded in .html, .css, .js, and image file formats. You can serve video on demand in Apple HTTP Live Streaming (HLS) and Microsoft Smooth Streaming formats. You can serve Adobe Flash multimedia content using a CloudFront RTMP distribution. You can also serve live streaming, like a meeting, conference, or concert, by creating the distribution automatically using an AWS CloudFormation stack.

Origins for Web Distributions

When creating a distribution, you can specify where CloudFront should send requests for your content. CloudFront supports using several AWS resources as origins. For example, you can specify an Amazon S3 bucket or a MediaStore container, a MediaPackage channel, or a custom origin, such as an Amazon EC2 instance or your own HTTP web server.

Amazon S3 Buckets

Amazon S3 can be used as an origin for your distribution, and you place any objects that you want CloudFront to deliver in it. You can use the S3 console, API, or a third-party tool to get your objects into Amazon S3. You can create a hierarchy in your bucket to store the objects and access Amazon S3 objects at the standard Amazon S3 price. AWS recommends the following format when you specify the Amazon S3 bucket using Cloud-Front to get objects:

```
Your-bucket-name.s3.region.amazonaws.com
```

Using this format allows you to configure CloudFront to communicate with your S3 bucket using SSL. It also allows you to use an OAI and update the contents of your bucket using POST and PUT requests. AWS recommends using the following format when you configure your CloudFront distribution using the S3 static website as the origin:

```
https://your-bucket-name.s3-website.region.amazonaws.com
```

Using this format allows you to use S3 redirects and S3 custom error documents. You will not be charged extra for using your S3 bucket as the CloudFront origin server, but you will still incur regular Amazon S3 charges.

 CAUTION For your bucket to work with CloudFront, the name must conform to DNS naming requirements.

MediaStore or MediaPackage

In order to use MediaStore or MediaPackage as the origin, you need to configure the S3 bucket as a MediaStore container or create endpoints or a channel with MediaPackage and then configure a distribution in CloudFront to stream videos.

Amazon EC2 Custom Origins

A custom origin is an HTTP server, and it can be an EC2 instance or your private HTTP server that you manage on-premises. A static website endpoint configured on S3 is also considered a custom origin. You need to specify the DNS name and HTTP and HTTPS ports, along with the protocol when using your own HTTP server as a custom origin. RTMP distribution is not supported as a custom origin content. Your private server content from a custom origin must remain publicly accessible for CloudFront to access it.

When using EC2 as your custom origin, AWS recommends using an AMI that automatically installs the software for a web server. Also put your EC2 instances behind an Elastic Load Balancing load balancer to handle traffic and specify the URL of the load balancer for the domain name of your origin server when creating your CloudFront distribution.

Alternate Domain Names

An alternate domain name, which is also called a CNAME, allows you to use your own domain name, like www.sample.com, instead of using the random domain name that CloudFront assigns to your distribution for your file links. CNAME is supported for both web and RTMP distributions. CloudFront returns a random domain name for the distribution, as shown, when you create a new distribution:

```
d666999fedxyz5.cloudfront.net
```

For your video file my-video.mpeg /videos/my-video.mpeg, the URL of the Cloud-Front domain name will look like this:

```
http://d666999fedxyz5.cloudfront.net/videos/my-video.mpeg
```

If you want to use your own or your company domain name instead of the cloudfront .net domain name, add an alternate domain name like www.sample.com to your distribution, and then the URL of your video file /videos/videos.mpeg will look like this:

```
http://www.sample.com/videos/my-video.mpeg
```

WebSocket Protocol

WebSocket, a TCP-based protocol, is used for long-lived bidirectional connections between clients and servers, and it is supported by CloudFront. It is used for real-time applications like online collaboration workspaces, social chat platforms, multiplayer gaming (which requires persistent connections), and financial trading platforms with real-time data feeds. When data is sent over a WebSocket connection, it can flow in both directions for full-duplex communication and with no additional configuration; CloudFront supports WebSocket connections on all regions worldwide. If both your client and server can support the WebSocket protocol, then CloudFront distributions can handle the long-lived real-time connections because it has built-in WebSocket protocol support. The WebSocket protocol uses port 80 for ordinary WebSocket connections and port 443 for TLS/SSL WebSocket connections, and the connection remains open for either the client or server to send data frames to each other without establishing new connections each time.

Optimizing Content Caching

You need to configure and manage caching of your contents wisely to improve performance and to meet your business obligations. One of the primary uses of CloudFront is to reduce the number of trips to your origin server to reduce the load on your origin server, which in turn reduces the latency because your contents are served from a CloudFront edge that is closer to your user. The majority of user requests are served from edge caches by CloudFront, and only a very few requests are forwarded to your origin to get the latest version of the content.

Cache Hit Ratio

Cache hit ratio refers whether content is served from CloudFront edge caches (cache hit) or your origin servers (cache miss). The CloudFront console can be used to view the percentage of user requests that are hits, misses, or errors. A number of factors affect the cache hit ratio, and you can improve performance by increasing the proportion of your user requests that are served from CloudFront edge caches.

Cache Lifetime

Your origin can be configured to add a Cache-Control max-age to your objects and specify the longest value for max-age to increase the cache hit ratio. If you configure a shorter cache duration, CloudFront forwards requests to your origin more frequently to find out whether the content has changed and to get the latest version.

Query String Parameters

CloudFront can be configured to cache based on query string parameters to improve caching. CloudFront forwards only the query string parameters for which your origin will return unique objects. It is case sensitive, so you need to pay attention to this so that separate requests are not forwarded to your origin. For example, if you use String1=Y and String2=y, then CloudFront sends two separate requests to the origin. Also you need to use the list parameters in the same order. As with differences in case, if one list request is list1=x&list2=y and another list request is list2=y&list1=x, CloudFront treats both of these requests separately and sends two requests to your origin and then separately caches them for future corresponding object requests even if they're identical.

Caching Based on Cookie Values

CloudFront can be configured to cache based on cookie values, and it can be improved by forwarding only to specific cookies instead of forwarding to all cookies. CloudFront forwards every combination of cookie name and value to your origin and separately caches the objects from your origin, even if they all are equal. For example, assume that a user included three cookies in every request and each cookie has four possible values. CloudFront forwards up to 12 different requests to your origin for each object. You can configure separate cache behaviors for static and dynamic content and set up CloudFront to forward cookies only for dynamic content to your origin.

Caching Based on Request Headers

CloudFront can be configured to forward and cache based only specified headers to improve caching instead of forwarding and caching based on all headers. CloudFront forwards every combination of header name and value by separately caching the objects from your origin even if they all are same. For example, when you want to serve different sizes of an image based on the user's device, you need to configure CloudFront to cache based on the CloudFront device-type headers CloudFront-Is-Desktop-User, Cloud-Front-Is-Tablet-User, CloudFront-Is-SmartTV-User, and CloudFront-Is-Mobile-User. When returning the identical version of the image for desktops and tablets, forward only the CloudFront-Is-Tablet-User header, not the CloudFront-Is-Desktop-User header.

Content Expiration at the Edge Cache

How long your files can stay in a CloudFront cache can be controlled before forwarding another request to your origin. Reducing and increasing the duration serve different purposes. When you reduce the duration, it allows you to serve dynamic content, and when you increase the duration your users get better performance because your files are most probably served directly from the edge cache. Your origin load can be reduced by setting a larger duration because CloudFront serves files from an edge location until the cache duration expires. Only after the expiration will CloudFront forward the request to the origin server to verify whether the cache contains the latest version of the file.

CloudFront Origin Groups

You can create an origin group by designating one as a primary origin and another as a secondary origin for CloudFront. The primary and secondary origin group can be any combination of different AWS origins, S3 buckets, Amazon EC2 instances, or HTTP web servers. You can define the cache behavior by defining the origin group as the primary origin, which can be used for origin failover scenarios and also provides high availability by automatically switching to the secondary origin when the primary origin returns HTTP 2xx or HTTP 3xx status code responses. When the primary origin returns a particular HTTP status code that was configured for failover or after a timeout occurs, CloudFront routes all the requests to the secondary backup origin in the origin group.

NOTE CloudFront issues a connection timeout error when it cannot connect to the origin after three consecutive attempts for a single request, and it waits up to ten seconds between connection attempts.

Domain Fronting

Domain fronting occurs when a client makes a TLS/SSL connection to a specific name but makes a HTTPS request for a different name, which occurs across different AWS accounts. For example, the TLS connection might connect to "www.sample.com" but then issue a request for "www.sample.edu." CloudFront includes protection against domain fronting by serving specific connections to the same AWS account that owns the request. If the two AWS account numbers do not match, then CloudFront responds with a 421 Misdirected Request response, which gives the client an option to connect using the correct domain.

Custom Error Pages

Custom error pages can be used with origin groups, and CloudFront can be configured to return a custom error page for the primary or secondary origin or both. Also you can return a custom error page for both primary and secondary origins. CloudFront returns the custom error page to users when the primary origin returns an HTTP status code error that you have not configured for failover or when the CloudFront fails over to the second origin.

Request and Response Behavior

CloudFront processes user requests and forwards them to your origin and then processes the responses from your origin and caches 4xx and 5xx HTTP status codes. CloudFront returns an HTTP 3xx status code when it requests an object from your origin server indicating that either the URL has changed, it was permanently moved (301 error), was redirected temporarily, the object hasn't changed since the last time it was requested (307 error), or was not modified (304 error). CloudFront caches 3xx responses for the duration specified by the settings in your CloudFront distribution and by the header fields that your origin returns along with an object.

When you request an object that is not in the edge cache, your origin returns an HTTP 5xx status code instead of returning a 304 (not modified) status code or an updated version of the object. Your origin returns an HTTP 4xx status code that is not restricted by a cache control header and is included in HTTP 4xx and 5xx status codes that CloudFront always caches.

Lambda@Edge

You can customize your content using Lambda@Edge, which you execute as Lambda functions before CloudFront delivers it to your users, without having to provision or manage your servers. Lambda@Edge can be created in the US-East-1 region using Node.js or Python and then it can be executed closer to your user. Lambda@Edge can scale automatically from a couple of requests per day to hundreds and thousands of requests per second, which significantly improves your user experience.

CloudFront intercepts user requests and responses at CloudFront edge locations when you associate the CloudFront distribution with a Lambda@Edge function. The Lambda@Edge functions can be executed when CloudFront receives a request from your user, or just before CloudFront forwards a request to the origin, or when it receives a response from your S3 bucket or HTTP web server, or just before CloudFront returns the response to your user. The Lambda@Edge function inspects cookies and modifies URLs so that users can see different versions of a site for A/B testing. Based on the user device, CloudFront returns different objects to users, like different images based on the screen size of the device, by checking the User-Agent header. For example, on a video library website that rents movies online, a Lambda@Edge function can change the request so that CloudFront returns the list of movies in the selected genre.

When CloudFront user request or origin request events occur, the Lambda@Edge function generates HTTP responses, inspects the headers or authorization tokens, and inserts a header to limit access to your content before forwarding the request to your origin. The Lambda@Edge function can make external network calls to verify user credentials or fetch additional content to customize your response. You choose the Cloud-Front distribution and cache behavior that specifies one or more CloudFront events, which are also called triggers, that execute the function. When you can create a trigger, it is replicated to AWS locations around the world and executes the function whenever CloudFront receives a request from a user.

Chapter Review

This chapter began by explaining how CloudFront helps to distribute your content and exposes it as a CloudFront link with low latency and high data transfer speeds in an easy and cost-effective way. An Amazon S3 bucket or your web HTTP EC2 server can be configured as origin servers that store the original contents. CloudFront retrieves your files from the origin server and then distributes them to CloudFront edge locations all over the world. CloudFront uses a pay-as-you-go model, and it doesn't require you to commit to how much content you'll have in your origin and you don't have to pay any up-front fees—you pay only for what you use. CloudFront regional edge caches save your popular content to serve users in different regions by bringing it closer to your users to improve performance. Regional edge caches are deployed globally and located between your origin server and the global edge locations to serve content directly to your users. You can secure your content by configuring HTTPS encrypted connections, or by using AWS WAF, or by setting up field-level encryption.

Users from specific geographic locations can be prevented from accessing content distributed through CloudFront web distributions. You can restrict access to your content in edge caches by configuring CloudFront to require users to use either signed URLs or signed cookies. A signed URL contains a policy statement in JSON format that specifies the restrictions, like an expiration date and time, that gives you more control over access to your content. You can prevent your users from directly accessing files using Amazon S3 URLs, bypassing CloudFront. OAI is a special CloudFront user that needs to be granted the identity permission to read the files in your bucket and remove any other permissions to use Amazon S3 URL. When you have geographic restrictions that are more granular than country boundaries or when you want to limit access to only few of the files, you need to combine CloudFront with a third-party geolocation service. Field-level encryption adds another layer of security along with HTTPS, which enforces secure end-to-end connections to origin servers and lets you protect specific data throughout system processing by making sure only certain applications can see it. A CloudFront distribution defines where content is delivered from and when you want to distribute your content and the details about how to track and manage content delivery. An alternate domain name, which is also called a CNAME, allows you to use your own domain name instead of using the random domain name that CloudFront assigns to your distribution for your file links. WebSocket, a TCP-based protocol, is used for long-lived bidirectional connections between clients and servers. Cache hit ratio refers to where the contents are served, whether from CloudFront edge caches (cache hit) or from your origin servers (cache miss). CloudFront processes user requests and forwards them to your origin and then processes the responses from your origin and caches 4xx and 5xx HTTP status codes. You can customize your content using Lambda@Edge, which you execute as Lambda functions before CloudFront delivers it to your users, without having to provision or manage servers.

Exercises

The following exercises will help you practice to using the console to perform various administrative tasks. You need to create an AWS account, as explained earlier, to perform these exercises. You can use the Free Tier when launching AWS resources, but make sure to terminate them at the end.

Exercise 6-1: Create an S3 Bucket for Your Content Origin
In this exercise, you will create a S3 bucket using the console.

1. Sign in to the AWS Management Console and open the Amazon S3 console at https://console.aws.amazon.com/s3/.

2. From the Amazon S3 console, choose Create Bucket.

3. In the Create Bucket dialog, on the Name And Region page, enter a bucket name and select an AWS region for your bucket.

4. Choose Next.

5. On the Configure Options page, choose options for versioning, tagging, and other features.

6. Choose Next.

7. On the Set Permissions page, uncheck the Block All Public Access checkbox.

8. Choose Next, and then choose Create Bucket.

9. Choose your bucket in the Buckets pane, and then choose Upload.

10. On the Select Files page, drag and drop your files to the bucket, or choose Add Files and choose the files that you want to upload.

11. Choose Next.

12. On the Set Permissions page, grant public read privileges for each file that you upload to your Amazon S3 bucket.

13. Choose Next to set permissions.

14. In the Manage Public Permissions drop-down list, choose Grant Public Read Access To This Object(s).

15. Choose Next.

16. Set any properties that you want for the object, such as encryption or tagging, and then choose Next.

17. Choose Upload.

18. After the upload completes, you can navigate to the item by using its URL. You can use the following URL to access the content:

```
http://s3-myregion.amazonaws.com/example-myawsbucket/filename
```

Exercise 6-2: Create CloudFront Distribution

In this exercise, you will gain practical experience of creating your first CloudFront distribution using the AWS Management Console.

1. Open the CloudFront console at https://console.aws.amazon.com/cloudfront/.

2. Choose Create Distribution.

3. On the Select A Delivery Method for your content page, in the Web section or the RTMP section, choose Get Started.

4. On the Create Distribution page, under Origin Settings, choose the Amazon S3 bucket that you created earlier. For the Origin ID, Path, Restrict Access, and Custom Headers, you can accept the default values.

5. Below the default Cache Behavior Settings, accept the default values.

6. Under Distribution Settings, choose the values for your distribution.

7. For the Price Class option, choose Use All Edge Locations (Best Performance), which is default, where CloudFront serves your objects from the edge locations in all CloudFront regions.

8. For the AWS WAF Web ACL option, choose None, unless you want to use the AWS WAF to allow or block HTTP and HTTPS requests.

9. For the Alternate Domain Names (CNAMEs) option, specify the domain name that you want to use for URLs for your objects instead of the CloudFront domain name when you create your distribution. The following video content:

   ```
   /videos/my-video.mpeg
   ```

   will look like this if you configure CNAME:

   ```
   http://www.sample.com/videos/my-video.mpeg
   ```

   and like this if you use the random generated URL:

   ```
   http://d666999xyzfed5.cloudfront.net/videos/my-video.mpeg
   ```

10. For the SSL Certificate, accept the default value: Default CloudFront Certificate.

11. Select Default Root Object, which is the object that you want CloudFront to request from your origin.

12. If you want CloudFront to log information about each request for an object and store the log files in an Amazon S3 bucket, select On.

13. Select Off for Cookie Logging.

14. Enter any comments that you want to save with the distribution.

15. Select Enabled for the Distribution States if you want CloudFront to begin processing requests as soon as the distribution is created.

16. Choose Create Distribution.

17. Once CloudFront finishes creating your distribution, the Status column value of your distribution will change from InProgress to Deployed, and it usually takes between 20 and 40 minutes.

18. Check the CloudFront.

19. Check the domain name for the distribution in the Domain Name column. You can see your domain name here.

20. Open your browser and type the domain name to access the domain.

21. You can use the dig command and look up the domain name of your distribution. You will see that your domain name returns several global IP addresses and their edge locations from all over the world. The IP addresses could be different when you search the record because CloudFront automatically routes requests for the content by using the following command:

   ```
   $ dig d666999xyzfed5.cloudfront
   ```

Exercise 6-3: Configure an Alias Record (CNAMEs) for the CloudFront Distribution

In this exercise, you will gain practical experience configuring an Alias record Cloud-Front distribution using the AWS Management Console.

1. Sign in to the AWS Management Console and move to the Route 53 console at `https://console.aws.amazon.com/route53`.

2. In the Dashboard section on the left-hand side, click on Hosted Zones.

3. Check the Domain Name box in which you want to create an alias record

4. Here click on Create Record Set.

5. Enter the following applicable values for each setting and click Create:

   - In the Name box, enter your record name.

   - In the Type box, use the default value: A – IPv4 address.

   - In the Alias box, choose Yes.

   - In the Alias Target box, enter the CloudFront domain name for your distribution.

6. Move to the CloudFront console, check the distribution, and click Distribution Settings.

7. In the General tab, click Edit.

8. In the Alternate Domain Names (CNAMEs) box, enter the alias record name, and click Yes, Edit.

9. Open your favorite browser and type the alias record to access the URL.

Questions

The following questions will help you gauge your understanding of the contents in this chapter. Read all the answers carefully because there might be more than one correct answer. Choose the best answers for each question.

1. Your company is building an application to distribute confidential business videos to its employees. Using CloudFront, which of the following methods could be used to serve the content that is stored in S3 but is not publicly accessible from S3 directly?

   A. Create an origin access identity (OAI) for CloudFront and grant access to the objects in your S3 bucket to that OAI and remove any other permission to use Amazon S3.

   B. Add the CloudFront account security group and add inbound/outbound rules.

   C. Create a standard IAM user for CloudFront and grant write access to the objects in your S3 bucket to that user.

   D. Create a S3 bucket policy to allow public access to all the objects.

2. Your company web application has added new product images on each page. The application is hosted in US-West, and your users from US-East are experiencing latency when these images are loading. What is the best way to speed up serving these images?

   A. Use Application Load Balancer to serve the images to US-West as well as US-East.

   B. Serve the images through CloudFront edge locations closer to your users in US-East.

   C. Serve the image using Amazon S3 instead of serving from your web application.

   D. Use an instance store instead of EBS volume to serve the images faster from your EC2 instances.

3. Your customer application has new requirements to support multiple devices such as iOS, Android, and Desktop to deliver the content. How this can be implemented efficiently?

   A. Store the video contents to Amazon S3 as an origin server and configure the Amazon CloudFront distribution with a streaming option.

   B. Store the video contents to Amazon S3 as an origin server and configure the Amazon CloudFront distribution to forward CloudFront-Is-Desktop-Viewer and CloudFront-Is-Mobile-Viewer headers from your custom origin.

   C. Launch a streaming server on EC2 and store the video contents as an origin server and configure the Amazon CloudFront distribution with a download option.

   D. Launch a streaming server on EC2 and store the video contents as an origin server and configure the required amount of streaming servers on Amazon EC2.

4. You are a developer for a video training application that can be accessed anywhere in the world, and your users can choose their own topic training videos. Since the application can also be used on a mobile phone, connection stability is required for streaming content, and delivery should be quick. What solution will optimize the user experience to view the content?

   A. Upload and store the content in a EBS volume, and use a CloudFront distribution for content delivery.

   B. Upload and store the content in an S3 bucket in the region closest to the user and share the S3 object URL with the users.

   C. Upload the content to an EC2 instance in the region closest to the user and use a CloudFront distribution for content delivery.

   D. Upload the content to a central S3 bucket and use CloudFront distribution for delivering the content by using the edge locations closest to the user.

5. Which of the following options do you need to enable end-to-end HTTPS connections from the user's browser to the origin via CloudFront?

   A. Use a self-signed certificate in the origin and CloudFront default certificate in CloudFront.

   B. You can use the CloudFront default certificate for both the origin and CloudFront.

   C. You need to use a third-party certificate authority (CA) certificate in the origin, and you need to use CloudFront's default certificate for CloudFront.

   D. Use a self-signed certificate in both the origin and CloudFront.

6. Your application serves all its requests through an ELB, which is in front of an EC2 Auto Scaling group. There are large traffic spikes during certain periods of the day because many people are requesting to read similar data at the same time. What is the easiest and cheapest way to fix this issue by reducing costs and scale only during a spike like this?

   A. Create an S3 bucket and asynchronously replicate common request responses into S3 objects and redirect the request to AWS S3.

   B. Create a new ELB and new Auto Scaling Group layer mounted on top of your system, adding a new tier to the system. Then you can serve most of your read requests using the top layer.

   C. Create a CloudFront distribution and direct ELB traffic to it. Use the ELB as an origin and specify cache behaviors to proxy cache requests.

   D. Create a Memcached cluster in AWS ElastiCache and create cache logic to serve requests, which can be served from the in-memory cache to increase performance.

7. You are developing a new application that aggregates a huge volume of data and delivers it on demand to your users. The requests are extremely spiky and geographically distributed and unpredictable. How you can make sure your users from all over the world experience a good response, low latency, and cost-effectiveness?

   A. Use a large RedShift cluster to perform the analysis and a fleet of Lambdas to perform record inserts into the RedShift tables, and it will scale rapidly enough for the traffic spikes.

   B. Use a CloudFront distribution with access to an S3 origin. Aggregated data should be sent to S3 periodically in the desired format.

   C. Invoke Lambda using an API gateway that puts records into Kinesis and an EMR running Spark to get records on Kinesis to scale with spikes.

   D. Use the AWS Elasticsearch service and EC2 Auto Scaling groups and to scale based on traffic throughput and stream into the Elasticsearch domain, which is scalable.

8. A website is serving on-demand videos. Users are distributed globally, are often on the move, and are using mobile devices and tablets to watch videos. This website requires you to pay for videos. How can you implement the most cost-efficient architecture with a high quality of video delivery?

   A. Use Amazon S3 to host videos and CloudFront to serve videos from S3.

   B. Use Amazon S3 to host videos with lifecycle management to archive all files to Glacier after a few days and then use CloudFront to serve videos from Glacier.

   C. Use an EC2 HTTP web server to host the videos, and use EFS to incrementally back up the original videos. Use CloudFront to serve the videos from EFS.

   D. Use EC2 and Auto Scaling to adjust the number of nodes depending on the demand. Use EBS volumes to host videos, and use CloudFront to serve videos from EC2.

9. You are developing an application that delivers high-quality HD videos to your users on demand globally. What type of server should be used to speed up the delivery of your HD video content by caching content closer to users?

   A. Edge server

   B. Origin server

   C. Base server

   D. Remote server

10. CloudFront uses a pay-as-you-go pricing model. Which of the following factors about CloudFront pricing are true? (Choose all that apply.)

    A. You need to pay for the standard Amazon S3 storage charges in your bucket.

    B. You incur charges when CloudFront responds to requests for your objects, which include the data transfer charges from server to client.

    C. You incur charges when users transfer data to your origin, including DELETE, OPTIONS, PATCH, POST, and PUT requests.

    D. You incur a surcharge for HTTPS requests and an additional surcharge for requests that use field-level encryption.

11. In CloudFront what happens when content is NOT present at an edge location and a request is made to it?

    A. A "404 not found" error is returned.

    B. CloudFront serves the content directly from the origin server and also stores it in the cache.

    C. The request is kept on hold till until origin content is stored on the edge location.

    D. The request is routed to the next nearby edge location for delivery.

12. Which of the following events can be triggered with Amazon CloudFront? (Choose all that apply.)

    A. A Viewer Request event occurs when an end user or a device on the Internet makes an HTTP(S) request to CloudFront and the request arrives at the edge location closest to that user.

    B. A Viewer Response event occurs when the CloudFront server at the edge is ready to respond to the end user or the device that made the request.

    C. An Origin Request event occurs when edge server does not already have the requested object ready to be sent to your backend origin.

    D. An Origin Response event occurs when the CloudFront server at the edge receives a response from your backend origin webserver.

Answers

1. **A.** You need to create an OAI for CloudFront and grant access to the objects in your S3 bucket to it and remove any other permission to use Amazon S3.

2. **B.** You need to use CloudFront and serve the images through edge locations closer to your users in US-East.

3. **B.** You need to store the video contents to Amazon S3 as an origin server and configure the Amazon CloudFront distribution to forward CloudFront-Is-Desktop-Viewer and CloudFront-Is-Mobile-Viewer headers to your custom origin.

4. **D.** You need to upload the content to a central S3 bucket and use CloudFront distribution to deliver the content by using the edge locations closest to the user, which reduces the latency.

5. **C.** You need to use a third-party CA certificate in the origin and a CloudFront default certificate in CloudFront. The origin cannot be self-signed and cannot use the CloudFront default certificate.

6. **C.** You need to create a CloudFront distribution and direct all your Elastic Load Balancer traffic to that. Also you can use the ELB as an origin for specifying cache behaviors to proxy cache requests.

7. **B.** You need to use a CloudFront distribution with access to the S3 origin. All your aggregated data should be sent to S3 periodically in the desired format that users access regularly.

8. **C.** The AWS SAM Local CLI tool is used for local development and testing of serverless applications (i.e., AWS Lambda functions).

9. **A.** An edge server is used to speed the delivery of content using a variety of techniques for caching content closer to users.

10. **A, B, C, D.** You need to pay for charges for storage, charges for serving objects. charges for submitting data, and additional surcharge for HTTPS requests.

11. B. This CloudFront delivers the content directly from the origin server and stores it in the cache of the edge location.

12. A, B, C, D. A Viewer Request event occurs when an end user or a device on the Internet makes an HTTP(S) request to CloudFront. A Viewer Response event occurs when the CloudFront server at the edge is ready to respond to the end user. An Origin Request event occurs when the CloudFront edge server does not already have the requested object in its cache. An Origin Response event occurs when the CloudFront server at the edge receives a response from your backend origin web server.

Additional Resources

- **Dynamic Application Content Delivery Using Amazon CloudFront** There is no place like official AWS documentation to get the latest and most up-to-date information about all the AWS services. Always refer to the official AWS blogs to get the latest about new AWS services and updates. This blog explains the steps, including a launch stack, to create an Amazon S3 bucket for static content, to create a web server on an Amazon EC2 for your dynamic content, and to create a CloudFront web distribution to deliver both dynamic and static content to users.
  https://aws.amazon.com/blogs/networking-and-content-delivery/deliver-your-apps-dynamic-content-using-amazon-cloudfront-getting-started-template/
  https://docs.aws.amazon.com and https://aws.amazon.com/blogs/aws

- **Debugging Your Content Delivery** This blog provides four steps to enable logging on CloudFront, setting up alarms using Amazon SNS and Amazon CloudWatch, and using the CloudFront Monitoring Dashboard to review errors and troubleshoot issues.
  https://aws.amazon.com/blogs/networking-and-content-delivery/four-steps-for-debugging-your-content-delivery-on-aws/

- **Aggregating Lambda@Edge Logs** This blog provides detailed steps to aggregate Lambda@Edge logs from different regions into a single region and use CloudWatch logs, Kinesis, and Amazon S3 for troubleshooting and analysis.
  https://aws.amazon.com/blogs/networking-and-content-delivery/aggregating-lambdaedge-logs/

- **Analyze Amazon CloudFront Access Logs** This blog describe the steps, including launch stacks, to store access logs with detailed information of every request to the Amazon Simple Storage Service (S3) and AWS Glue Data Catalog for this data and to query your data in S3 using Amazon Athena.
  https://aws.amazon.com/blogs/big-data/analyze-your-amazon-cloudfront-access-logs-at-scale/

- **Lambda@Edge and CloudFront Deployments Using a CI/CD Pipeline**
  This blog explains in detail how to use AWS CloudFormation to deploy and
  modify a Lambda@Edge function with a CloudFront and create a CI/CD pipeline
  to automate and validate your changes automatically by using a Lambda function.
  `https://aws.amazon.com/blogs/networking-and-content-`
  `delivery/managing-lambdaedge-and-cloudfront-deployments-`
  `by-using-a-ci-cd-pipeline/`

Domain Name System and Amazon Route 53

In this chapter, you will learn

- Domain name system (DNS)
- Name servers
- DNS records
- DNS resolution
- Amazon Route 53
- Domain registration
- Routing traffic
- Hosted zone
- Routing policy
- Health checks

In this chapter, we will start with an introduction to domain name servers (DNS) and then discuss Amazon Route 53 in detail, which is a scalable and highly available cloud domain name system (also abbreviated as DNS) service.

In general, DNS is the Internet's equivalent of a telephone directory or a smartphone contact list, where all the domain names can be thought of as Internet Protocol (IP) addresses that are maintained in a central registry. Web hosting companies and Internet service providers (ISPs) regularly interact with this central registry in order to get updated DNS information. When you type a web address, like www.sample.com, the ISP views the DNS associated with the domain name and translates it into a machine-friendly IP address like 10.20.30.40 before directing the Internet connection to the right website.

Amazon Route 53 is designed to give developers a reliable and cost-effective way to route end users to Internet applications by translating web addresses like www.sample .com into a numeric IP addresses like 10.20.30.40 that computers can use to connect to each other, and it supports IPv6 as well. Amazon Route 53 can also be used to configure DNS health checks to route traffic only to the healthy instances and to independently monitor the health of your applications. Route 53 uses different routing types, like weighted round robin, latency-based routing and geoproximity, etc., to manage global traffic effectively, including DNS failover, to support a variety of fault-tolerant architectures. In addition, Route 53 can be used to purchase and manage domain names, and it will automatically configure the DNS settings.

Domain Name System

DNS is the Internet's directory of names that match with IP addresses, which your instances use to communicate with each other. As mentioned, DNS directs web traffic by mapping memorable domain names like sample.com to IP addresses like 10.20.30.40. It is also possible to enter a particular IP address into your browser to reach the corresponding website.

How DNS Works

The hundreds of millions of domain names cannot be stored in a single directory in a single place, so the DNS directory that matches names to numbers is distributed around the world, stored on different domain name servers that communicate with each other consistently to provide updates and redundancies. Each domain name can be translated to more than one IP address because the server your instance reaches for www.amazon .com, for example, is most likely completely different from the server that someone else in a different country would reach by typing the same site into their browser. It is even possible that Amazon CloudFront edge locations are being used to distribute the traffic closer to members around the world.

Even though the DNS information is distributed and shared among many servers, it is also cached locally on user instances. When you first request www.sample.com, for example, it goes to a recursive resolver, a server operated by an ISP, and it identifies which DNS servers it needs to probe to resolve the name of a site with its IP address. Then the request goes to a root server, which stores top-level domains, such as .com, .net, and .org, along with country-level domains like .us (United States) and .ca (Canada), so it directs the user to the closest geographic location. Then the request goes to a top-level domain name server, which stores the corresponding second-level domain, like "amazon" in the amazon.com. Finally, the request goes to the Domain Name Server, which has the corresponding IP address. As soon as the IP address is determined, the response is sent back to the user to visit the correct website: www.amazon.com. Even though it looks like a very lengthy process, everything is done in milliseconds. Now, let us take a look at the different components of DNS.

Domain Names

The website you enter normally uses either the Hypertext Transfer Protocol (HTTP) or Hypertext Transfer Protocol Secure (HTTPS) protocol followed by subdomain(s), which is the name before the broad domain categorization like .com or .org, as shown in Figure 7-1.

Figure 7-1
Domain Name
System

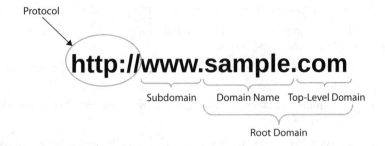

Each name to the left of the top-level domain, which is separated by a period, is considered a more specific subdomain. The first-level subdomain (sample) plus its top-level domain (.com) are referred to as root domains or just domains.

```
support.help.sample.com
```

Referring to the left of the string, "help" and "support" are the second- and third-level subdomains, respectively. The subdomains are typically used to uniquely identify specific services or pages defined by the domain owner.

Name Servers

Name servers are used to point your domain name to the hosting company that controls your domain's DNS records. Normally, you will point your name servers to the company that hosts your website. The connecting user devices will know where to find your DNS information so your domain can resolve. The domain's DNS information is stored in a text file called a zone file on the name servers. You'll need to specify name servers on your domain registrar's website, and they publish that information to the higher-level name servers. You need to specify at least two name servers so when one of the servers is down, the other server can continue to provide your DNS information.

Sample name servers include the following:

```
NS1.SAMPLE.COM
NS2.SAMPLE.COM
NS3.SAMPLE.COM
```

DNS Resolution

Now let us see how DNS resolution actually works. First the domain name is translated into your IP address. Then DNS verifies the zone file, which is a special text file that contains the human-friendly domain names with their corresponding computer-friendly IP addresses. A zone file is like a phone directory that matches names with phone numbers.

The DNS lookup process works in the following way:

1. First your user types in a domain name like sample.com in the browser's address bar.

2. The user's computer is then connected to the Internet through their ISP. The root name server will be queried by the ISP's DNS resolver to get the correct top-level domain (TLD) name server.

3. The root name server returns the IP address for the .com name server.

4. The .com name server will be queried by the ISP's DNS resolver, using the IP address from the root name server.

5. Then the .com name server returns the IP address of the requested sample.com name server.

6. The zone file of the domain (sample.com) name server will be read by the ISP's DNS resolver.

7. The zone file shows the mapping of which IP address corresponds to the domain.

8. The domain name server returns the IP address of the website requested to the ISP.

9. Finally, the ISP has the IP address 44.34.24.14 for sample.com, which will be returned to your browser.

10. Using the IP address, the sample.com site will be accessed from the web server.

Figure 7-2 shows what will happen only if your user's computer or ISP has no current information about the requested domain. In reality, either your computer locally or your ISP caches the DNS information after it is resolved the first time, which results in faster lookups and avoid the trip to DNS servers each time.

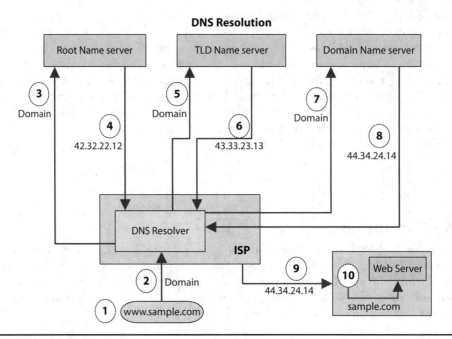

Figure 7-2 DNS resolution

DNS Records and Zone Files

The DNS record resolves domain names to IP addresses, and it automatically bundles it into a zone file, which allows connecting devices to look up the correct IP address for the domain. The default zone file contains records similar to the following:

```
; sample.com [775696]
$TTL 95311
@   IN  SOA ns1.sample.com. admin.sample.com. 2020010529 14400 14400 2318511 75311
@       NS  ns1.sample.com.
@       NS  ns2.sample.com.
@       NS  ns3.sample.com.
@       NS  ns4.sample.com.
@       NS  ns5.sample.com.
@       MX  10  mail.sample.com.
@       A   10.20.30.40
mail    A   10.20.30.40
www  A   10.20.30.40
```

Each zone file contains the DNS records, the name servers, and domain administrator's e-mail address, and you can create a variety of DNS records for as many different subdomains as you wish.

Types of DNS Records

DNS records provide important information about a domain or hostname, and they are an essential part of getting domains to operate correctly by serving as a map that tells the DNS server which domain the IP address is associated with and how the access requests should be handled. The most common DNS record types are discussed in the following sections.

A Record

An A record points your domain or subdomain to your sample.com IP address, which permits the web traffic to reach your sample.com domain, and it is the core function of DNS. The normal A record definition looks like the following:

```
sample.com      A       10.20.30.40
help.sample.com     A       10.20.30.40
```

You are allowed to point different subdomains to different IP addresses, and if you want to point all your subdomains of sample.com to your 10.20.30.40 IP address, then you can use an asterisk (*) as your subdomain:

```
*.sample.com   A       10.20.30.40
```

AAAA Record

An AAAA record is similar to an A record, but it is used for 128-bit Internet address that represents the IPv6 IP addresses. You can use multiple AAAA records for the same domain in order to provide redundancy, and you can use `dig` to determine the AAAA record associated with a domain name:

```
$ dig AAAA ns1.sample.com
```

A typical AAAA record looks like this:

```
sample.com         AAAA        4321:8765:98xy:mnop:4321:8765:98rs:tuvw
help.sample.com      AAAA        4321:8765:98xy:mnop:4321:8765:98rs:tuvw
support.sample.com      AAAA        4321:8765:98xy:mnop:4321:8765:98rs:tuvw
```

AXFR

An AXFR record is used for DNS replication and is also used on a slave DNS server to replicate the zone file from a master DNS server. For example, the sample.com administrator has two DNS servers, ns1.sample.com and ns2.sample.com. You can edit the sample.com data on ns1.sample.com and rely on AXFR to pull the same data to ns2.sample.com. However, there are more modern and secure ways to perform DNS replication. When a DNS server receives an AXFR request, it sends all known data to the requested domain by assuming the request has come from the replicating DNS server of the zone transfer. But if the DNS server is not configured correctly, then any user can access this data, resulting in security issue.

CAA

The DNS Certification Authority Authorization (CAA) record is used to specify which certificate authorities (CAs) are allowed to issue certificates for a domain. Any CA is allowed to issue a certificate for your domain when you have no CAA record, but when a CAA record is defined, then only the CAs listed are allowed to issue certificates. You can use the CAA record to set a policy for the entire domain or just specific hostnames. Since CAA records are inherited by subdomains, a CAA record set on sample.com also applies to any subdomain, like help.sample.com. You can control the issuance of certificate types, like single-name certificates or wildcard certificates or both, using CAA records.

CNAME

A CNAME record, or canonical name record, maps a domain or subdomain to a different domain. DNS lookups use the target domain's DNS resolution as the alias's resolution for the CNAME record. Here's an example:

```
sample.com      A      10.20.30.40
specimen.com         CNAME      sample.com
```

Using this configuration, when you request specimen.com, the initial DNS lookup will find the CNAME entry with the target of sample.com, and a new DNS lookup will be initiated for sample.com, which will return the IP address 10.20.30.40. At the end, users directed to specimen.com will be directed to 10.20.30.40.

Domains can have aliases using CNAME records, and the target domain should have a normal A-record resolution. Chaining or looping CNAME records is not a recommended practice.

```
sample.com      A      10.20.30.40
www.sample.com         CNAME      sample.com
```

As a result of this configuration, sample.com points to the server IP address 10.20.30.40, and www.sample.com points to the same address via sample.com. When the IP address changes in the future, you only need to update it in one place by editing the A record for sample.com, and www.sample.com automatically inherits the changes.

 NOTE A CNAME record must always point to another domain name, never directly to an IP address.

DKIM

A Domain Keys Identified Mail (DKIM) record displays the public key for authenticating messages that have been signed with the DKIM protocol. This practice increases the capability to check mail authenticity, and it provides a way to validate that an organization delivering an e-mail has the right to do so by using a public key. The key is generally provided to you by the organization that is sending your e-mail, and it will either be inserted directly into your zone as a TXT record or CNAME pointing to the key of the DNS provider.

```
amazon.domainkey.sample.com        TXT      k=rsa;p=K9dUCv335j197jL
```

In the previous example the DKIM selector is Amazon.

MX

The Mail eXchange (MX) record defines the mail delivery destination for a domain or subdomain. You can have many MX records for a domain, which provides redundancy to ensure e-mail will always be delivered. A classic MX record looks like this:

```
sample.com          MX      20  mail.sample.com
mail.sample.com     A           10.30.40.50
```

This record configuration will direct mail for sample.com to the mail.sample.com server. The target domain should have its own A record that resolves to your mail server's IP address. An MX record should ultimately point to a domain that is also the hostname for its server.

Another component of MX records is priority. This is the number (20 in the previous example) written between the record type and the target server. You can designate fallback servers based on the priority for a particular domain, and the higher numbers have a lower priority, whereas the lower numbers have a higher priority. Here's an example configuration of a domain that has two fallback mail servers:

```
sample.com          MX      20  mail_1.sample.com
sample.com          MX      40  mail_2.sample.com
sample.com          MX      60  mail_3.sample.com
```

Here when mail_1.sample.com is down, then mail will be delivered to mail_2.sample.com. The mail will be delivered to mail_3.sample.com when both mail_1.sample.com and mail_2.sample.com are down.

NS

Name Server (NS) records are used to set the name servers for a domain or subdomain. The primary Name Server records for your domain are set both at your domain registrar and in your zone file. For example, the entries delegating sample.com to the name servers in the .com name servers is as shown here:

```
sample.com      NS      ns1.sample.com
sample.com      NS      ns2.sample.com
sample.com      NS      ns3.sample.com
sample.com      NS      ns4.sample.com
sample.com      NS      ns5.sample.com
```

The name servers you designate at your domain registrar then carry the zone file for your domain. Different name servers can be set up for any of your subdomains. The primary domain's zone file will be used to configure subdomain NS records. You can configure separate NS records in your zone file for the subdomain mail.sample.com, as shown here:

```
mail.sample.com     NS      ns1.nameserver.com
mail.sample.com     NS      ns2.nameserver.com
```

Primary name servers are configured at your domain registrar, and secondary subdomain name servers are configured in the primary domain's zone file. The order of NS records does not matter. The servers randomly receive DNS requests and respond accordingly. If any one of the server hosts fail to respond, another one will be queried.

PTR

A Pointer (PTR) record matches up an IP address to a domain or subdomain. It is the opposite of the A record, and it will give you the domain associated with a particular IP address, instead of vice versa. For reverse DNS searches in the reverse-lookup zones, you can use the PTR record. A valid A or AAAA record along with the IP address is the prerequisite for adding a PTR record. If you want an IPv4 PTR record, point the domain or subdomain to your IPv4 address. If you want an IPv6 PTR record, point the domain to your IPv6 address. IPv4 and IPv6 PTR records work similarly with the corresponding A or AAAA record.

SOA

A Start of Authority (SOA) record stores a zone file with the name of the host where it was originally created and then it lists the contact e-mail address for the person responsible for the domain. Normally the SOA record looks like this:

```
ns1.sample.com. admin.sample.com. 2020011536 13300 3322 1108500 75300
```

- **Primary name server**   ns1.sample.com. is the primary name server for the domain sample.com.
- **Responsible party**   admin.sample.com. is the responsible party for the domain sample.com.

- **Serial number**   2020011536 is the revision number for this domain's zone file, and it changes when the file is updated.

- **Refresh time**   13300 is the amount of time in seconds until the secondary DNS server will keep the zone file before it checks for changes.

- **Retry time**   3322 is the amount of time the secondary DNS server will wait before retrying a failed zone file transfer.

- **Expire time**   1108500 is the amount of time the secondary DNS server will wait before expiring its current zone file copy if it cannot update itself.

- **Minimum TTL**   75300 is the minimum amount of time other servers should keep data cached from this zone file.

 NOTE   The administrative e-mail address is written with a period (.) instead of an @ symbol.

SPF

The Sender Policy Framework (SPF) record lists the designated mail servers for a domain or subdomain. The legitimacy of your mail server is established by reducing the chances of spoofing, which normally occurs when some hacker fakes the headers on an e-mail to make it look like it's coming from your domain, even though it is not.

An SPF record for your domain notifies the other receiving mail servers which outgoing server(s) are valid sources of e-mail so they can reject spoofed mail from your domain that has originated from unauthorized servers. A common SPF record looks like this:

```
sample.com    TXT     "v=spf1 a ~all"
```

You can list all the mail servers in your SPF record from which you send mail, and all the other servers are excluded. Your SPF record will have a domain or subdomain; a type, which is TXT or SPF based on your name server support; and text that starts with v=spf1.

SRV

A Service (SRV) record matches up a specific service that runs on your domain or subdomain to a target domain and directs and controls the traffic of specific services to another server. A typical SRV record looks like the following:

```
service._protocol.sample.com  SRV   5    0   5357   service.sample.com
```

- **Protocol**   service._protocol.sample.com is the name of the protocol must be preceded by an underscore (_) and followed by a period (.). The protocol could be something like _tcp.

- **Domain**   SRV is the domain name that receives the original traffic.

- **Priority**   5 is the first number that allows you to set the priority for the target server. Higher numbers have a lower priority.
- **Weight**   When the two records have same priority, then weight is used. 0 is the weight in this example.
- **Port**   The TCP or UDP port on which the service runs. 5357 is the port number in this example.
- **Target**   service.sample.com is the target domain or subdomain.

TXT

The Text (TXT) record provides information about the domain in question to other resources on the Internet. The TXT record serves different kinds of purposes, depending on the contents, and it's a flexible DNS record. One common use of the TXT record is to create an SPF record on name servers that don't natively support SPF. Another use is ownership validation—to prove you own the domain, and a provider may require you to add a TXT record with a particular value to your domain. Another use is to create a DKIM record for mail signing.

Amazon Route 53

Amazon Route 53 is a highly available and scalable Domain Name System (DNS) that can be used to perform three main functions in any combination: domain registration, DNS routing, and health checking. When you want to create a new website you can use Route 53 to register the name of your website or web application (also called the domain name). When a user goes to a web browser and enters your domain name—for example, sample.com—or a subdomain name—for example, help.sample.com—in the address bar, then Route 53 supports the user browser connection with your website or web application. Also Route 53 sends automated requests to your resource, like a web server, to verify that it's reachable, available, and functional. If you prefer, you can receive notifications when any of your instances becomes unavailable and route the traffic to healthy instances instead of unhealthy instances. Amazon Route 53 can be accessed in the following ways:

- AWS Management Console
- AWS SDKs
- Route 53 application programming interface (API)
- AWS command-line interface
- AWS tools for Windows PowerShell

Route 53 Concepts

Let us discuss some of the key concepts of Amazon Route 53 DNS:

- **Domain name**   The domain name is what any user types in the address bar of a web browser to access your website domain, like www.sample.com.

- **Domain registrar** An Internet Corporation for Assigned Names and Numbers (ICANN)–accredited company that processes domain registrations for particular top-level domains.

- **Domain registry** A company that has the right to sell domains for a particular top-level domain. It defines the rules for registering and maintains the authoritative database for all domains that have the same TLD.

- **Domain reseller** Amazon Route 53 is a domain reseller that sells domain names on behalf of registrars.

- **Top-level domain** The TLD is the end part of domain, like .com, or .org, and there are two types of top-level domains: (1) generic TLDs like .com or .bike or .hockey and (2) geographic TLDs like .us or .ca or au.

- **Alias record** A type of Route 53 record that is used to route traffic to AWS resources.

- **Authoritative name server** This has definitive information about the name servers for every registered .com domain, so when it receives a request for www.sample.com from a DNS resolver, it responds with the names of the name servers for the DNS service for the domain. Route 53 name servers are the authoritative name servers and store the hosted zones for the domains that use Route 53 as the DNS service.

- **DNS query** When a user opens a browser and types a domain name into the address bar, and the response to the DNS query typically is the IP address associated with a web server. The device that initiated the request uses the IP address to communicate with the web page from a web server.

- **DNS resolver** A DNS resolver managed by an ISP communicates with DNS name servers to get the IP address for the corresponding resource, such as a web server.

- **Domain Name System** This is a global network of servers that facilitate computers, smartphones, tablets, and other IP-enabled devices to communicate with each other by translating the easily understood names like sample.com into IP addresses to allow computers to find each other on the Internet.

- **Hosted zone** This contains information about how to route traffic for a domain and all of its subdomains.

- **IP address** All laptops, smartphones, and web servers are assigned an IP address (either IPv4 or IPv6) on the Internet to allow those devices to communicate with each other.

- **Name servers** This is a DNS resolver, also called a recursive name server or authoritative name server, that translates domain names into the IP addresses that computers use to communicate with one another.

- **Private DNS** A private DNS allows you to route traffic for a domain and its subdomains within one or more Amazon VPCs.

PART II

- **Record**   A record, or DNS record, defines how you want to route traffic for your domain or subdomain. You can create records for sample.com and www.sample.com to route traffic to a web server that has an IP address of 10.30.50.70, for example.

- **Recursive name server**   This translates domain names into the IP addresses that computers use to communicate with one another; this is also known as a DNS resolver.

- **Reusable delegation set**   This is a set of authoritative name servers, where you can create a reusable delegation set and associate it with new hosted zones.

- **Routing policy**   This determines how Route 53 responds to DNS queries and supports the following routing policies:

  - **Simple routing policy**   This is used to route Internet traffic to a single resource to perform a given function for your domain.

  - **Failover routing policy**   This is used to configure active-passive failover.

  - **Geolocation routing policy**   This used when you want to route Internet traffic to your resources based on your user's location.

  - **Geoproximity routing policy**   This is used when you want to route traffic based on the location of your resources.

  - **Latency routing policy**   This is used when you want to route traffic to the resource that provides the best latency.

  - **Multivalue answer routing policy**   This is used when you want to respond to DNS queries with up to eight healthy records selected at random.

  - **Weighted routing policy**   This is used to route traffic to multiple resources in percentages that you specify.

- **Subdomain**   This is a domain name that has one or more labels prefixed to the registered domain name. For example, if your domain name is sample.com, then help.sample.com is a subdomain.

- **Time to live (TTL)**   This is the amount of time the DNS resolver caches the values of a record before submitting another request to Route 53 to get the current values.

- **A**   The value of an A record is an IPv4 address in dotted decimal notation.

- **AAAA**   The value of an AAAA record is an IPv6 address in colon-separated hexadecimal format.

- **CAA**   This specifies which CAs are allowed to issue certificates for a domain or subdomain, and it helps to prevent the wrong CAs from issuing certificates for your domains.

- **CNAME**   This is used to create CNAME records.

- **MX**   This is an integer that represents the priority for an e-mail server and the domain name of the e-mail server.
- **NAPTR**   This is used to convert one value to another or to replace one value with another.
- **NS**   This is the domain name of a name server for the hosted zone.
- **PTR**   This has the same format as a domain name.
- **SOA**   This provides details about a domain and the corresponding Route 53 hosted zone.
- **SPF**   This was used to verify the identity of the sender of e-mail messages. However, AWS no longer recommends creating SPF records; instead, you can create a TXT record that contains the applicable value.
- **SRV**   This consists of four space-separated values representing priority, weight, domain name, and port.
- **TXT**   This provides information about the domain and serves different kinds of purposes, depending on its content.

Domain Registration

To begin creating a website or a web application, you start by registering the name of the website, also known as a domain name, like sample.com, that your users enter in a browser to display your website. After choosing your domain name, Route 53 confirms whether it's available to make sure that no one else has registered the domain name that you are requesting. If the domain name you want is already in use, then either you can try other names or try changing only the top-level domain, such as .com, to another top-level domain, such as .net or .org. If your new domain is available and you register the domain name with Route 53, you need to provide names and contact information for the domain owner and other contact information.

During the domain registration, Route 53 automatically creates the DNS service by creating a hosted zone that has the same name as your new domain. It then assigns a set of four name servers to the hosted zone so when someone uses a browser to access your website, those name servers instruct the user browser where to find your resources. You can also add the name servers from the hosted zone to the domain. At the end of the registration process, AWS sends your information to the registrar for the domain, which is either Amazon Registrar, Inc. (for .com, .net, and .org) or their registrar associate Gandi (for .apartments, .boutique, and .camera). The registrar sends your information to the registry, which, as mentioned, sells domain registrations for one or more top-level domains. The registry stores your domain information in their database in addition to storing some information in the public WHOIS database. You can choose to transfer the domain registration to Route 53 if you already registered your domain name with another registrar, even though this isn't mandatory to use other Route 53 features.

Routing Traffic

All devices on the Internet, whether it is a smartphone, laptop, or enterprise server, that serves video content for websites need to communicate with one another by using IP addresses in one of the following formats:

- Internet Protocol version 4 (IPv4) format, such as 10.20.30.40, which is the most common
- Internet Protocol version 6 (IPv6) format, such as 3112:1ec7:74b2:1111:2222:mnop:2223:7654

You don't have to remember and enter a long number for either IPv4 or IPv6 when you open a browser to visit a website. You can enter a domain name such as sample.com instead. The Amazon Route 53 DNS service handles the connection between domain names and IP addresses. You need to create the Name, Value, and Type resource record in your hosted zone, as noted next:

- **Name** The name of the record can be either a domain name or subdomain name, but you need to make sure the name of every record (www.sample.com, help.sample.com) ends with the name of the hosted zone (sample.com).
- **Type** The resource (A = Web server or MX = e-mail server) type is specified in the record type.
- **Value** The value of the Type. So for the MX type, specify the e-mail server and for the A type specify an IP address.

Let's discuss what happens in just a few milliseconds when your user requests content from www.sample.com in AWS.

1. As shown in Figure 7-3, the user enters **www.sample.com** in a web browser's address bar.
2. The domain request for www.sample.com is first routed to a DNS resolver that is managed by your user's Internet service provider.
3. The DNS resolver forwards the request to a DNS root name server.
4. The DNS resolver forwards the request again to one of the TLD name servers for .com domains.
5. The DNS resolver chooses Route 53 as the name server and forwards the request.
6. The Route 53 name server verifies the hosted zone record and gets the associated IP address for a web server and returns the IP address to the DNS resolver.
7. The DNS resolver now has the IP address that the user requested and returns it to your user's web browser.
8. The web browser sends the request to the IP address 10.20.30.40 to the web server that's configured as a website endpoint.
9. The web server then returns the web page for www.sample.com to the web browser, and the web browser displays the page.

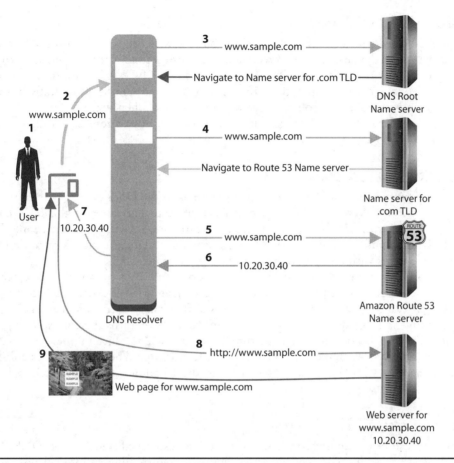

PART II

Figure 7-3 Domain name resolution in AWS

NOTE The DNS resolver caches the IP address of your domain for a specified time in order to respond quickly the next time someone browses your domain.

Hosted Zones

A hosted zone is a container for records, which contains information about how you want to route traffic for a specific domain, such as sample.com, and its subdomains (help.sample.com, support.sample.com, etc.). There are two types of hosted zones: (1) public hosted zones contain records that specify how you want to route traffic on the Internet and (2) private hosted zones contain records that specify how you want to route traffic in an Amazon Virtual Private Cloud (VPC).

Public Hosted Zone

A public hosted zone contains information about how traffic is routed on the Internet for a particular domain. You can create a public hosted zone when you want to route Internet traffic to your resources that you have hosted on EC2 instances. After creating a hosted zone, you can create records that specify how you want to route traffic for the domain and subdomains. You can delete a hosted zone when you no longer need it; however, this prevents you from accidentally deleting a hosted zone that still contains records.

Private Hosted Zone

A private hosted zone can be configured to respond to the DNS queries within one or more VPCs for a domain and its subdomains. You create a private hosted zone, such as sample.com, and specify the VPCs that you want to associate with the hosted zone. The hosted zone record determines how Route 53 responds to DNS queries for your domain and subdomains within or among your VPCs.

For example, suppose you have a database server that runs on an EC2 instance in one of the VPCs in your private hosted zone. You create an A or AAAA record, such as db.sample.com, and you specify the IP address of the database server. When an application submits a DNS query for db.sample.com, Route 53 returns the corresponding IP address. The application must also be running on an EC2 instance in one of the VPCs that you associated with the sample.com private hosted zone. The application establishes the connection with the database server using the IP address that was received from Route 53.

Split-View DNS

Route 53 can be configured to use split-view DNS, also called split-horizon DNS. The public and private hosted zones can be configured to return different internal and external IP addresses for the same domain name if you want to maintain internal and external versions of the same website or if you are testing changes to your application before you make them public. You need to create a public and private hosted zone with the same domain name and create the same subdomains in both hosted zones.

Routing Traffic for Subdomains

When you want to route traffic to your resources for a subdomain, such as help.sample.com or support.sample.com, you have two options: (1) You can create a record in the hosted zone with the same domain name. For example, to route Internet traffic for help.sample.com to a web server, you need to create a record help.sample .com in the sample.com hosted zone. (2) You can create a hosted zone for the subdomain, like help.sample.com, and then you create records in the new hosted zone that define how you want to route traffic for the subdomain and its subdomains, such as backend.help.sample.com.

Choosing a Routing Policy

You can choose a routing policy when you create a record that determines how Amazon Route 53 responds to queries.

Simple Routing

Simple routing lets you configure standard DNS records to route traffic to a single resource. You can't create multiple records that have the same name and type when you choose the simple routing policy in the Route 53 console. Route 53 returns all values to the recursive resolver in random order when you specify multiple values in a record, and the resolver returns the values to the client web browser that submitted the DNS query. The client then chooses a value and resubmits the query.

Failover Routing

Failover routing allows you to route traffic to healthy resources when any resource becomes unhealthy. The primary and secondary records can route traffic to healthy endpoints based on the configuration to a complex tree of records.

Geolocation Routing

Geolocation routing allows you to serve your traffic based on your user's geographic location. It can be used to localize your content and present some of or your entire website in the language of your local users. It can also be used to restrict distribution of content to only the locations in which you have distribution rights. It can also be used to balance the load across endpoints, so that both locations are consistently routed to the same endpoint instance. You can specify geographic locations by continent, by country, or by state in the country.

Geoproximity Routing

Geoproximity routing allows you to route traffic based on the geographic location of your users and your resources. You can use bias to route more or less traffic to a given resource based on a value.

Latency-Based Routing

You can improve performance for your users by serving their requests from the AWS region that provides the lowest latency if your application is hosted in multiple AWS regions. You need to create latency records for your resources in multiple AWS regions to use latency-based routing. When Route 53 receives a DNS query for your domain or subdomain, it determines which AWS regions you've created latency records for, determines the lowest latency regions, and selects the latency record of that region. Then Route 53 responds with the IP address for a web server.

Multivalue Answer Routing

Amazon Route 53 can be configured for multivalue answer routing to return multiple values, such as IP addresses for your web servers, in response to DNS queries. You can specify multiple values for almost any record, but multivalue answer routing also lets you check the health of each resource, so Route 53 returns only values for healthy resources.

You need to create one multivalue answer record for each resource to route traffic more or less randomly to multiple resources, such as web servers, and associate a Route 53 health check with each record. Route 53 responds to DNS queries with up to eight healthy records and gives different answers to different DNS resolvers.

Weighted Routing

You can associate multiple resources with a single domain name (sample.com) or subdomain name (help.sample.com) using weighted routing and choose how much traffic is routed to each resource. This is used for a variety of purposes, including load balancing and testing new versions of the application. You need to create records that have the same name and type for each of your resources to configure weighted routing. You can then assign each record a relative weight that corresponds with how much traffic you want to send to each resource, for example, 20 percent to instance A and 80 percent to instance B.

Amazon Route 53 Health Checks

The health of your resources such as web servers and e-mail servers can be monitored by Amazon Route 53 health checks. Amazon CloudWatch alarms can be configured to receive a notification when a resource becomes unavailable. In Route 53, you can monitor whether a specified endpoint, such as a web server, is healthy and receive a notification when an endpoint becomes unhealthy. The resource endpoint, like a web server, can be configured to monitor the health check by specifying an endpoint by IPv4 address, by IPv6 address, or by domain name. Also you can configure the DNS failover to reroute the traffic from an unhealthy resource to a healthy resource. When you have more than one resource performing the same function, then Route 53 health checks can be configured to route traffic only to healthy resources.

Figure 7-4 shows the overview of how health checking works in Amazon Route 53 when you want to be notified when a resource becomes unavailable.

1. You create a health check and specify values that define how you want the health check to work, such as the following:

   - Route 53 can monitor the IP address or domain name of your endpoint web server in addition to monitoring the status of other health checks and the state of a CloudWatch alarm.

   - Route 53 can check the HTTP, HTTPS, or TCP protocols.

Figure 7-4
Route 53 health
check

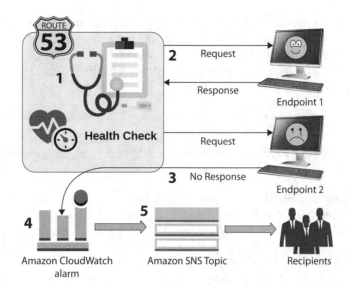

- You can define the request interval in Route 53 to send a request to your endpoints.
- The failure threshold can be set in Route 53 to verify how many consecutive times the endpoint must fail to respond to requests before considering it unhealthy.
- You can use CloudWatch, which uses Amazon SNS, to notify users when Route 53 detects that the endpoint is unhealthy.

2. Route 53 starts to send a request to the endpoint at a specified interval, and it considers an endpoint healthy when it responds and continues to serve traffic.

3. Route 53 starts the count of consecutive requests when the endpoint doesn't respond:

- If the count reaches the failure threshold value, then Route 53 considers the endpoint to be unhealthy.
- If the endpoint starts responding again before the failure threshold, then the count resets to 0.

4. Route 53 notifies CloudWatch when the endpoint is unhealthy, and if you didn't configure a notification, the status can be checked from the Route 53 console.

5. CloudWatch triggers an alarm if you configured a notification for the health check and uses Amazon SNS to send the notification to the specified recipients.

If you have multiple web servers or database servers that perform the same function and you want Route 53 to route traffic only to the healthy resources, then you can configure DNS failover by associating it with a health check. Route 53 has health checkers around the world, and it determines whether the underlying resource is unhealthy. When you create a health check that monitors an endpoint, health checkers start to send requests to the endpoint that you specify. You can choose the locations and time intervals (10 or 30 seconds) for Route 53. Each health checker evaluates the health of the endpoint based on two values:

- **Response time** A resource can either fail or be slow to respond to a health check request for different reasons.
- **Failure threshold** Whether the endpoint responds to a number of consecutive health checks that you specify.

Route 53 determines whether the endpoint is healthy by aggregating the data from the health checkers. When more than 18 percent of health checkers report that an endpoint is healthy, Route 53 considers it healthy; otherwise, it considers it unhealthy. Route 53 must be able to establish a TCP connection with the endpoint within four seconds for HTTP and HTTPS health checks. After connecting, the endpoint must respond with a 2xx or 3xx HTTP status code within two seconds. Route 53 must be able to establish a TCP connection with the endpoint within ten seconds for TCP health checks.

Route 53 health checks can also be used to monitor the status of other health checks, which is called a calculated health check. Parent health checks do the monitoring, and child health checks get monitored. Up to 255 child health checks can be monitored by one parent health check. When you create a health check based on a CloudWatch alarm, Route 53 monitors the data stream—the OK state is considered healthy and the Alarm state is considered unhealthy. Route 53 considers a new health check healthy until it has enough data to determine the actual status. You also can choose to invert the health check status, so a new health check is considered unhealthy until there is enough data.

Chapter Review

The chapter began by explaining DNS and then discussed Route 53, which is Amazon's DNS service. It's crucial to understand the Domain Name Service and how it works in AWS before implementing a cloud solution. The DNS is the Internet's directory of names that match with IP addresses, which your instances use to communicate with each other. DNS directs web traffic by mapping memorable domain names to IP addresses. Name servers are used to point your domain name to the hosting company that controls your domain's DNS records. The DNS record resolves domain names to IP addresses and automatically bundles them into a zone file, which allows connecting devices to look up the correct IP address for the domain. An A record points your domain or subdomain to your IP address, which permits the web traffic to reach your domain, and it is the core function of DNS. An AAAA record is similar to an A record, as explained, but it is used for 128-bit Internet addresses, which represent IPv6 IP addresses. An AXFR record is used for DNS replication, and they are used on a slave DNS server to replicate the zone

PART II

file from a master DNS server. A CAA record specifies which CAs are allowed to issue certificates for a particular domain. A CNAME record maps a domain or subdomain to a different domain. A DKIM record displays the public key for authenticating messages that have been signed with the DKIM protocol. An MX record defines the mail delivery destination for a domain or subdomain. NS records are used to set the name servers for a domain or subdomain. A PTR record matches up an IP address to a domain or subdomain. An SOA record stores a zone file with the name of the host where it was originally created and then it lists the contact e-mail address for the person responsible for the domain. The SPF record lists the designated mail servers for a domain or subdomain. An SRV record matches up a specific service that runs on your domain or subdomain to a target domain. A TXT record provides information about the domain in question to other resources on the Internet.

The chapter then looked in detail at Amazon Route 53, which is a highly available and scalable DNS that can be used to perform three main functions in any combination: domain registration, DNS routing, and health checking. If you want to create a website or a web application, you need to register the name of the website. All devices on the Internet need to communicate with one another by using IP addresses. The health of your resources, such as web servers and e-mail servers, can be monitored by Amazon Route 53 health checks. The domain registrar is an ICANN-accredited company that processes domain registrations for particular top-level domains. The domain registry is a company that has the right to sell domains for a particular top-level domain. The top-level domain is the end part of the domain, like .com or .org, and there are two types of top-level domains: generic and geographic. The routing policy determines how Route 53 responds to DNS queries. A simple routing policy is used to route Internet traffic to a single resource to perform a given function for your domain. A failover routing policy is used to configure active-passive failover. A geolocation routing policy is used when you want to route Internet traffic to your resources based on your user's location. A geoproximity routing policy is used when you want to route traffic based on the location of your resources. A latency routing policy is used when you want to route traffic to the resource that provides the best latency. A multivalue answer routing policy is used when you want to respond to DNS queries with up to eight healthy records selected at random. A weighted routing policy is used to route traffic to multiple resources in percentages that you specify. A hosted zone is a container for records, which contains information about how you want to route traffic for a specific domain and its subdomains. There are two types of hosted zones: public hosted zones and private hosted zones.

Exercises

The following exercises will help you practice using Amazon Route 53. You need to create an AWS account, as explained in earlier, before you can do these exercises. You can use the Free Tier when launching AWS resources, but make sure to terminate them at the end.

Exercise 7-1: Register a New Domain Using freenom.com

In this exercise, you will register a new domain.

1. Start by going to https://www.freenom.com/en/index.html?lang=en.

2. Enter the domain name, for example, **awsdeveloper**, that you want to register, and choose Check Availability to find out whether the domain name is available.

3. If the domain is available, click Get It Now.

4. Select the top-level domain that you like—I selected .ml—and click the Checkout button.

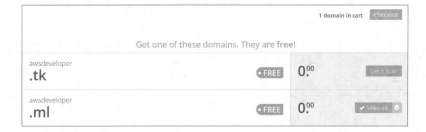

5. The domain is free for 12 months. Click Continue.

6. In the shopping cart, provide the e-mail address that you want to register the domain for.

7. To register, enter the address, accept the terms and conditions, and click Complete Order. Choose Services and then My Domains to list your domains.

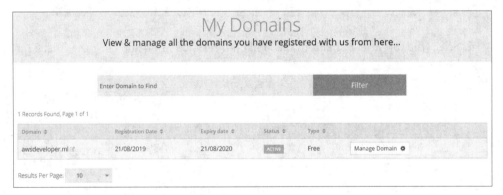

Exercise 7-2: Create Two S3 Buckets for Static Website Hosting

In this exercise, you will be creating two Amazon S3 buckets using AWS management console.

1. Log in to the AWS Management Console and select the Amazon S3 console at https://console.aws.amazon.com/s3/.

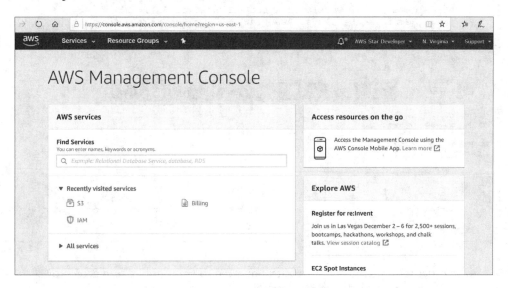

2. Create two buckets that match your domain name and subdomain, for example, awsdeveloper.ml and www.awsdeveloper.ml.

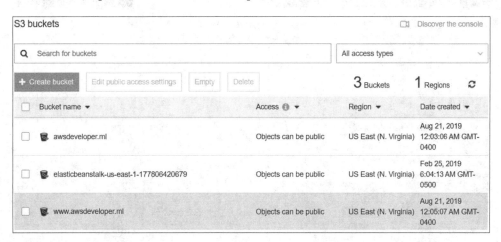

3. Upload your static website data to the awsdeveloper.ml bucket as index.html and an image if you want one. Here is a sample index.html page:

```
<html xmlns="http://www.w3.org/1999/xhtml" >
<head>
<title>McGraw Hill building S3 static Website Home Page</title>
</head>
<body>
<h1>Welcome to AWS Developer website hosted on S3 !</h1>
<p>AWS Certified Developer Associate All-in-One Exam Guide</p>
</body>
<img src="McGrawHill.jpg" width=400/>
</html>
```

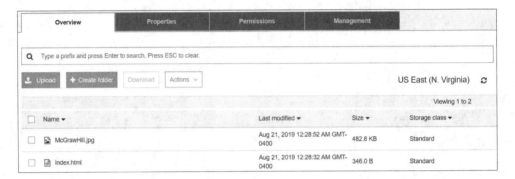

4. In order to host your static website, you need to grant public read access for awsdeveloper.ml. Select the relevant checkbox.

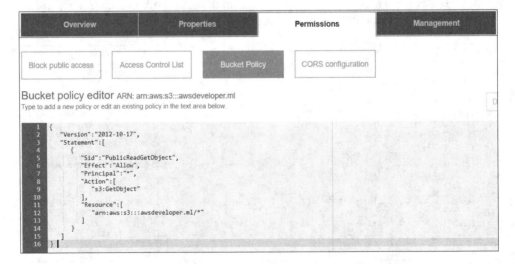

Exercise 7-3: Configure Buckets for Website Hosting and Redirecting

In this exercise, you will be configuring the Amazon S3 buckets for website hosting using AWS management console.

1. From the S3 console, in the Buckets list, choose your bucket: www.awsdeveloper.ml.

2. Choose Properties and then Static Website Hosting. Below the Use This Bucket To Host A Website option, type **index.html** and choose Save.

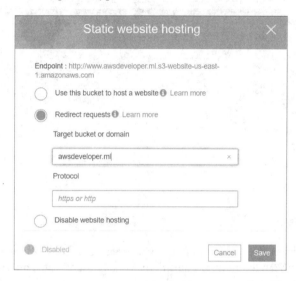

3. Choose Properties and then Static Website Hosting. Choose Redirect Requests. In the Target Bucket Or Domain field, type **awsdeveloper.ml** and choose Save.

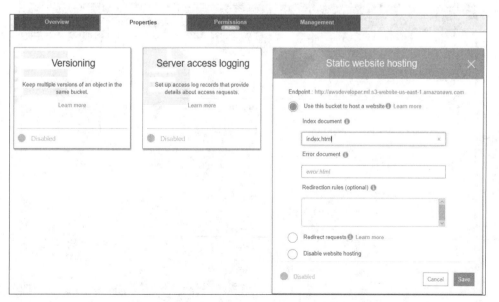

Exercise 7-4: Create a Route 53 Hosted Zone and Add Alias Records for awsdeveloper.ml and www.awsdeveloper.ml

In this exercise, you will be creating Amazon Route 53 hosted zone and create alias records using AWS management console.

    1. Log in to AWS, go to the Route 53 console, and select Create Public Hosted Zone.

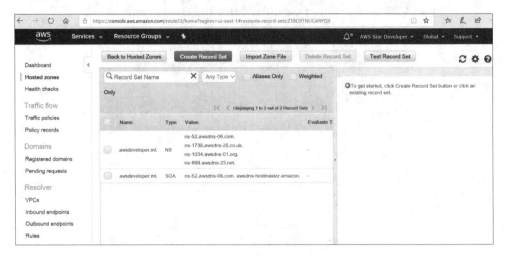

    2. Now go to freenom.com and log in. Select Services. You will see your domain listed. Select Manage Domain and then Management Tools and then select Nameservers from the drop-down list.

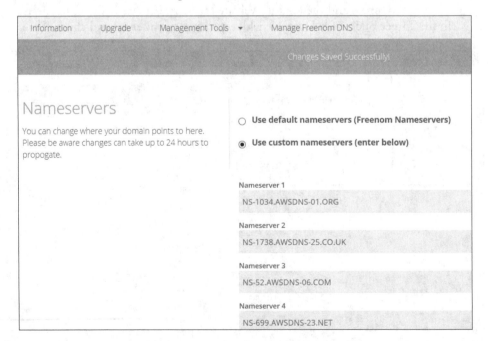

3. Choose Create Record Set. Leave Type as **A – IPv4 address**. Then for Alias, choose Yes, and for Alias Target select awsdeveloper.ml. For the Routing Policy, choose Simple and then choose Create.

4. Again, choose Record Set. Leave Type as **A – IPv4 address**. Then for Alias, choose Yes and for Alias Target select www.awsdeveloper.ml. Set the Routing Policy as Simple and choose Create.

5. Now you will see four records in your hosted zone.

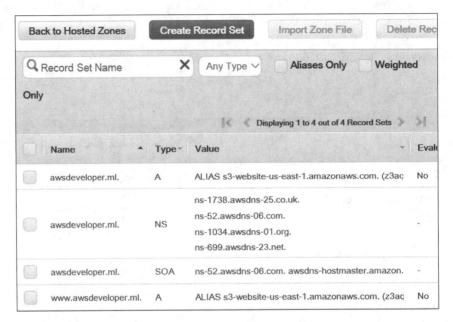

6. Now it is time to test your domain. Go to your browser and type **awsdeveloper.ml**.

7. This was successful, so now let's test your domains. Go to your browser and type **www.awsdeveloper.ml**. You are redirected to awsdeveloper.ml, so you see the same domain awsdeveloper.ml.

Questions

The following questions will help you gauge your understanding of the contents in this chapter. Read all the answers carefully because there might be more than one correct answer. Choose the best responses for each question.

1. What is the Domain Name Systems (DNS)?

    A. It is similar to a phone book of the Internet, which translates domain names to IP addresses so browsers can load websites.

    B. It is a virtual server on AWS Cloud that can be accessed by IP address.

    C. It is a special type of record that allows you to map your domain name to your Amazon S3 website bucket.

    D. It lets you to assign weights to resource record sets to specify the frequency for different responses.

2. Which DNS record types are valid? (Choose three.)

    A. A record – IPv4 address record

    B. AAAA record – IPv6 address record

    C. CNAME – Canonical name record

    D. BAA record – Board Authority Approval record

3. Which of the following statements are true regarding CNAME and Alias records in Amazon Route 53? (Choose three.)

    A. There are no differences, and you can use CNAME and Alias records interchangeably.

    B. An Alias record can be created for both the root domain and subdomains, whereas CNAME records can be used only for subdomains.

    C. Route 53 charges for CNAME queries, but it doesn't charge for Alias queries to AWS resources.

    D. A CNAME record can redirect DNS queries to any DNS record, whereas an Alias record can only redirect queries to selected AWS resources.

4. Which hosted zones are supported in AWS? (Choose two.)

    A. Hybrid hosted zone

    B. Public hosted zone

    C. Private hosted zone

    D. Community hosted zone

5. What routing policy lets you choose resources closer to your users and lets you localize content in the language of your local users?

   A. Simple routing policy

   B. Failover routing policy

   C. Geolocation routing policy

   D. Latency routing policy

6. What routing policy is used when you want to route traffic to a healthy resource or to a different resource when the original resource becomes unhealthy?

   A. Simple routing policy

   B. Failover routing policy

   C. Geolocation routing policy

   D. Latency routing policy

7. Your application team wants to point the domain's zone apex example.com to an Elastic Load Balancer for a new application. Which of the following DNS records could be used to make it work?

   A. You need to configure an Amazon Route 53 CNAME record

   B. You need to configure an A record

   C. You need to configure an AAAA record

   D. You need to configure an Amazon Route 53 Alias record

8. Your company wants to do A/B testing by sending 25 percent of traffic to a new server on which they have made new changes and the remaining 75 percent traffic to the old server. They want to increase new server traffic to 50 percent and then 75 percent and finally 100 percent to the new server and decommission the old server without any disruption to users. How can you achieve this in Route 53?

   A. You can use a latency routing policy

   B. This cannot be achieved in Route 53

   C. This can be achieved by using a weighted routing policy

   D. This can be achieved by using a geoproximity routing policy

9. You want to configure Route 53 to use split-view DNS (split-horizon DNS) in order to maintain internal and external versions of the same website when testing changes to your application before making them public. How this can be achieved?

   A. You need to set up a multivalue answer routing policy.

   B. You need to create a local version of the CNAME record to route traffic for a domain and its subdomains.

   C. You need to create a remote version of the Alias record to route traffic for a domain and its subdomains.

   D. You need to configure public and private hosted zones to return different internal and external IP addresses for the same domain name.

10. You have an application server located on-premises in your datacenter and you want to use it as failover server. Is it possible to create a Route 53 DNS record to point to your on-premises server and set up health checks and failover during a disaster scenario?

    A. Yes

    B. No

Answers

1. **A.** It is similar to phone book of the Internet, which translates domain names to IP addresses so browsers can load websites.

2. **A, B, C.** A record for IPv4 addresses, AAAA record for IPv6 addresses, and CNAME for Canonical Name record.

3. **B, C, D.** An Alias record can be created for both the root domain and subdomains, whereas CNAME records can be used only for subdomains. Route 53 charges for CNAME queries, but it doesn't charge for Alias queries to AWS resources. A CNAME record can redirect DNS queries to any DNS record, whereas an Alias record can only redirect queries to selected AWS resources.

4. **B, C.** You can use a public hosted zone to route Internet traffic to your resources and a private hosted zone to route traffic within your VPC.

5. **C.** You need to configure a geolocation routing policy to route the traffic based on the user location.

6. **B.** You need to configure a failover routing policy in order to configure active-passive failover.

7. **D.** You need to configure an Amazon Route 53 Alias record for the domain's zone apex (example.com).

8. **C.** This can be achieved by using a weighted routing policy to route traffic to more than one resource in percentages that you specify.

9. **D.** You need to configure public and private hosted zones to return different internal and external IP addresses for the same domain name to maintain two different versions of the same application.

10. **A.** Yes. You can create a DNS record and set up health checks of your legacy application residing in your datacenter, and when the application running in AWS fails the health checks, it will fail over automatically to your instance.

Additional Resources

- **AWS Docs** There is no place like official AWS documentation to get the latest and most up-to-date information about all the AWS services. Always refer to the official AWS blogs to get the latest about new AWS services and updates to existing features. `https://docs.aws.amazon.com` and `https://aws.amazon.com/blogs/aws`

- **Integrating Amazon Route 53 with AWS Transit Gateway and AWS PrivateLink**
  This blogs details the steps for using the AWS Transit Gateway, along with Amazon
  Route 53 Resolver, to share AWS PrivateLink interface endpoints between multiple
  connected Amazon Virtual Private Clouds (VPCs) and an on-premises environment
  to reduce the number of VPC endpoints, simplify VPC endpoint deployment, and
  help optimize costs when deploying at scale.
  ```
  https://aws.amazon.com/blogs/networking-and-content-
  delivery/integrating-aws-transit-gateway-with-aws-
  privatelink-and-amazon-route-53-resolver/
  ```

- **Connectivity Between On-Premises Network to AWS**   This blog explains
  the details to configure the connectivity between your on-premises network and
  AWS VPC that uses Amazon Route 53 and AWS Directory Service to provide
  DNS resolution between on-premises networks and AWS VPC environments.
  ```
  https://aws.amazon.com/blogs/security/how-to-set-up-dns-
  resolution-between-on-premises-networks-and-aws-using-
  aws-directory-service-and-amazon-route-53/
  ```

- **Protect Your Web Application Against DDoS Attacks**   A distributed denial
  of service (DDoS) attacks is when a malicious actor floods your network, system,
  or application with more traffic than it can handle. This blog details the steps
  needed to protect the root domain of your web application by using Route 53.
  ```
  https://aws.amazon.com/blogs/security/how-to-protect-
  your-web-application-against-ddos-attacks-by-using-
  amazon-route-53-and-a-content-delivery-network/
  ```

- **DNS Management in a Multiaccount Environment**   This blog explains the
  details to centralize DNS management in a multiaccount environment by using
  Route 53 Resolver without the need to run a domain controller in AWS.
  ```
  https://aws.amazon.com/blogs/security/simplify-dns-
  management-in-a-multiaccount-environment-with-route-53-
  resolver/
  ```

- **Centralized DNS Management of a Hybrid Cloud**   This blog explains the
  best practices while architecting centrally managed DNS and the recommended
  approach for managing DNS across multiple interconnected Amazon VPCs.
  ```
  https://aws.amazon.com/blogs/networking-and-content-
  delivery/centralized-dns-management-of-hybrid-cloud-with-
  amazon-route-53-and-aws-transit-gateway/
  ```

- **DNS Introduction**   You can find a detailed introduction to DNS and additional
  networking tutorials in the following guide.
  ```
  https://www.linode.com/docs/networking/dns/
  ```

PART III

Working with Cloud Storage

■ **Chapter 8**   Working with Simple Storage Service
■ **Chapter 9**   Amazon EBS, Amazon EFS, and Amazon S3 Glacier

Working with Simple Storage Service

In this chapter, you will learn

- Simple Storage Service (S3)
- Buckets
- Cross-origin resource sharing (CORS)
- Cross-region replication (CRR)
- Event notifications
- Transfer acceleration
- Billing and reporting
- Hosting a static website
- Server access logging
- Folders and objects
- Storage classes
- Object lifecycle management
- Object versioning
- Bucket and user policies
- Operations on objects
- Data protection
- Access control lists (ACLs)
- Best practices

The Simple Storage Service (S3) enables you to easily create a new S3 bucket and securely store your objects. You can also enable versioning to protect against accidental updates or deletion of objects.

Amazon Simple Storage Service

Amazon Simple Storage Service (Amazon S3) is a simple way to store and retrieve any amount of data from anywhere around the world at any time. Amazon S3 is designed for mission-critical, primary data storage and is highly durable. Objects are stored on multiple devices across multiple facilities in an Amazon S3 region. An Amazon S3 PUT operation synchronously stores the data across multiple Availability Zones (AZs) to ensure data durability. The object's durability is maintained by Amazon S3 by quickly detecting and repairing any lost redundancy. Buckets are the fundamental container of S3 for data storage, where you can store as many objects as you like. The objects are stored and retrieved using a unique key that allows you to store up to 5TB of data. You can download your data and enable others to download your data at any time. You need to grant access to others who want to upload or download data to and from your Amazon S3 bucket. You can also deny access to objects from your S3 bucket. A strong authentication mechanism helps keep your data secure from unauthorized access.

Buckets

A bucket is a logical container for objects that you store in Amazon S3. All your files are stored as objects in a bucket, which organizes the Amazon S3 namespace at the highest level and helps distinguish the account liable for storage and data transfer charges. Buckets can be created in a specific region and you can create a role using access control. A unique version ID is generated each time an object is added if versioning is enabled. The Amazon S3 basic structure is shown in Figure 8-1.

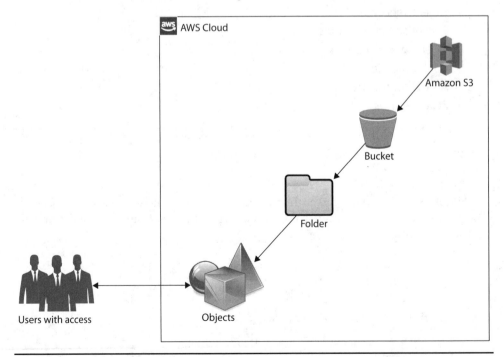

Figure 8-1 Amazon Simple Storage Service (S3)

Creating a Bucket

Amazon S3 buckets can be created using either the console or programmatically. By default, you can create up to 100 buckets, but the limit can be increased to a maximum of 1,000 buckets by submitting a service request. You need to provide a unique name and the AWS region where you want to create the S3 bucket. Once you create the bucket, you can store any number of objects in it.

Accessing Your Bucket

The Amazon S3 console can be used to perform almost all bucket operations without writing any code. Amazon S3 supports two types of URLs to access a bucket:

- The bucket name is part of the domain name in the virtual-hosted–style URL, as shown here:

```
http://my-first-bucket.s3-aws-region.amazonaws.com
http://my-first-bucket.s3.amazonaws.com
```

- The bucket name is not part of the domain in the path-style URL, as shown here for a region-specific endpoint:

```
http://s3-aws-region.amazonaws.com/my-first-bucket
```

And for the US East region endpoint, the URL is as follows:

```
http://s3.amazonaws.com/my-first-bucket
```

TIP AWS recommends you create buckets with DNS-compliant bucket names, since the bucket can be accessed using virtual-hosted–style and path-style URLs.

Bucket Configuration Options

Amazon S3 supports configuring your bucket for website hosting and managing the object lifecycle in the bucket in addition to configuring the bucket for log access. Amazon S3 supports sub-resources—for example, cross-origin resource sharing (CORS), cross-region replication (CRR), object locking, transfer acceleration, and versioning—to manage the bucket configuration information. You can use the AWS Management Console, the AWS software development kits (SDKs), or the Amazon S3 application programming interface (API) to create and manage these sub-resources.

Cross-Origin Resource Sharing

CORS specifies a way for web applications loaded in one domain to interact with resources in a different domain. Using CORS, you will be able to build rich customer web applications with Amazon S3 and allow cross-origin access to your Amazon S3 resources. CORS can be enabled using the Amazon S3 console, the Amazon S3 REST API, or the AWS SDKs.

Cross-Region Replication

CRR enables automatic and asynchronous replication of objects between buckets across different AWS regions owned by the same or a different AWS account. It is enabled at the bucket level, and you need give a destination bucket an AWS Identity and Access Management (IAM) role to replicate the objects. All your objects, or a subset of objects, in the source bucket can be replicated by adding a replication configuration to your source bucket. The subset can be identified by providing a key name prefix and one or more object tags, or both, in the configuration. The replicated objects will have the same key names and metadata information like creation time, user-defined metadata, and version ID as the original object. Secure Sockets Layer (SSL) is used to encrypt all data in transit across AWS regions.

The storage class is the same in both source and destination objects by default in addition to replicating the corresponding object access control list (ACL) by assuming that the replicated object is owned by the same owner as the source object. However, you can specify a different storage class for the destination objects, and the destination bucket owner can be changed by configuring CRR.

Amazon S3 Event Notifications

You can receive notifications when a specific event happens in your bucket by enabling the Amazon S3 event notification feature. You need to add a notification configuration defining the events and destinations. When a new object is created or deleted, Amazon S3 publishes notifications, regardless of the API used. Notifications can be requested for initiation of a restore or object restoration completion. Notification messages also can be sent by Amazon S3 when the object of the RRS storage class has been lost.

Amazon S3 event notifications can be published to an Amazon Simple Notification Service (SNS) topic, and the recipients can dynamically subscribe to receive them. Amazon S3 notification configuration can be used to request events to be published in an Amazon Simple Queue Service (SQS) queue. You can run custom code using AWS Lambda in response to Amazon S3 bucket events. You can upload your custom code to create an AWS Lambda function so when Amazon S3 detects a specific event, it publishes the event to AWS Lambda, which invokes and executes your Lambda function.

Amazon S3 Transfer Acceleration

The transfer acceleration feature enables high-speed transfer of files between your customer and an S3 bucket by using Amazon CloudFront's globally distributed edge locations. When the feature is enabled, data is routed to Amazon S3 as soon as it arrives at an edge location, although for an additional data transfer charge. Transfer acceleration can be used when you upload to a centralized bucket from around the world or when transferring terabytes of data across continents, or if you are unable to utilize all of your available bandwidth when uploading to Amazon S3.

You can use the Amazon S3 Transfer Acceleration Speed Comparison tool to compare accelerated and nonaccelerated upload speeds across different Amazon S3 regions. This uses multipart uploads to transfer a file from your browser to various Amazon S3 regions with and without using transfer acceleration.

Billing and Usage Reporting for S3 Buckets

You pay only for what you use, and you don't have to commit to how much content you'll store when using Amazon S3, and you don't have to pay any up-front fees. AWS provides two kinds of reports for Amazon S3:

- Billing reports provide high-level views of all of the activity of Amazon S3. The owner of the S3 bucket is billed for Amazon S3 fees, unless you created the bucket as a Requester Pays bucket.

- Usage reports provide a summary of activity for a specific service, aggregated by hour, day, or month, and it allows you to choose which usage type and operation to include and how the data is aggregated.

Requester Pays Buckets

By default, the bucket owner pays for the storage and data transfer costs of Amazon S3. However, buckets can be configured to be a Requester Pays bucket so the requester pays for the request and data download costs. The bucket owner still pays the cost of storing data, but the requester pays the charges associated with accessing it.

 EXAM TIP   If you enable Requester Pays on a bucket, anonymous access to that bucket is not allowed.

Static Website on Amazon S3

As you saw in the Chapter 7 exercises, you can host a static website on Amazon S3. You need to configure an Amazon S3 bucket for website hosting and then upload your website content to the bucket. This bucket must have public read access, since the intention is that everyone in the world will have read access. The website will be available in one of the following formats:

```
<your-bucket-name>.s3-website-<AWS-region>.amazonaws.com
<your-bucket-name>.s3-website.<AWS-region>.amazonaws.com
```

You can use your own domain, like sample.com, instead of using an Amazon S3 website endpoint to serve your content. This website can be hosted using Amazon S3 and Amazon Route 53, as we did in the exercises in Chapter 6.

 EXAM TIP   The Amazon S3 website endpoints do not support HTTPS.

Amazon S3 Server Access Logging

Amazon S3 server access logging provides details of the requests that are made to a bucket. Security and access audits help you learn about your customer base, as well as to understand your Amazon S3 bill. The server access log record provides details about each access request, like the bucket name, request time, request action, response status, requester, and an error code.

Most log records are delivered within a few hours of the time that they are recorded, but they can be delivered more frequently. Logging is disabled by default, and when it is enabled, the logs are saved to a bucket in the same AWS region as the source bucket. You need to turn on the log delivery by adding logging configuration on the source bucket for which you want Amazon S3 to deliver access logs. Also, you need to grant the Amazon S3 Log Delivery group write permission on the target bucket where you want the access logs saved.

 EXAM TIP There is no extra charge for enabling server access logging; however, you accrue the usual storage charges, and access to the delivered log files is charged the same as any other data transfer.

Folders

Amazon S3 lets you group objects in folders before storing them. You cannot create buckets within buckets; however, you can create folders within folders, and you can upload and copy objects directly into the folder. Folders cannot be renamed but can be created, deleted, and even made public. Objects can be copied from one folder to another. When you make a folder public, it will be available for viewing or downloading for anyone on the Internet. You cannot make a folder private after making it public, and you must set permissions on each individual object.

Objects

Amazon S3 is designed to store as many objects you want, and it is stored as a simple key/value store. You can store these objects in one or more buckets. The key is the name that you can assign to your object. You will use the key to retrieve the object later. If you enable versioning, Amazon S3 generates a string called Version ID when you add an object to a bucket, and the bucket key and version ID combination uniquely identify your object. The size of an object is measured in the value, and it can range in size from 0 to 5TB. You can store information regarding your object, which is a set of name/value pairs called metadata. Also Amazon S3 assigns system metadata to your objects to manage them. Sub-resources are associated with some other entity, such as an object or a bucket, and are used to store additional object-specific information. Both the resource-based access control, such as an ACL and bucket policies, and user-based access control are supported by Amazon S3, which will be used to control access to all the objects that you store in Amazon S3.

Object Key and Metadata

Every Amazon S3 object has a key, data, and metadata. The key name or object key uniquely identifies the object in a bucket. Object metadata is a set of name/value pairs, which can be set at the time of uploading the object. You cannot modify object metadata after you upload the object; the only way to modify object metadata is to make a copy of the object and set the metadata.

When you create an object, you give the bucket a unique key name. This name is the object key, which is a sequence of Unicode characters whose UTF-8 encoding is, at most, 1,024 bytes long. Every object stored in a bucket contains two kinds of metadata: system metadata and user-defined metadata. Amazon S3 maintains a set of system metadata like object creation date, size and storage class, and whether the object has server-side encryption enabled. You can assign user metadata when you upload an object as a name/value (key/value) pair. The user-defined metadata names must begin with "x-amz-meta-" when using the REST API.

Storage Classes

Amazon S3 offers a variety of storage classes designed for various use cases. These include

- For the general-purpose frequently accessed data, you can use the S3 Standard class.
- For changing access patterns or unknown data, you can use the S3 Intelligent-Tiering class.
- For the infrequently accessed data, you can use the S3 Standard-Infrequent Access (S3 Standard-IA).
- For long-lived but less frequently accessed data, you can use the S3 One Zone-Infrequent Access (S3 One Zone-IA).
- For archival storage, you can use Amazon S3 Glacier (S3 Glacier).
- For long-term archive and digital preservation, you can use the Amazon S3 Glacier Deep Archive (S3 Glacier Deep Archive).

Your data can be managed throughout its lifecycle, and once the S3 lifecycle policy is enabled, without any changes to your application, your data be will automatically transferred to a different storage class.

General-Purpose Amazon S3 Standard

S3 Standard offers 99.99 percent availability, 99.999999999 percent durability, and high-performance object storage for frequently accessed data. Amazon S3 supports encryption of your data at rest, and SSL is used for the data in transit. S3 Standard is appropriate for a wide variety of use cases, since it delivers low latency and high throughput, including cloud applications, gaming applications, mobile and big data analytics, content distribution, and dynamic websites. A single bucket can contain objects that are stored across the S3 Standard class, S3 One Zone-IA class, S3 Standard-IA class, and S3 Intelligent-Tiering class, since S3 storage classes are configured at the object level.

Unknown or Changing Access: Amazon S3 Intelligent-Tiering

By automatically moving data to the most cost-effective access tier, you benefit from the cost optimization without performance impact or operational overhead. The objects are stored in two access tiers: a low-cost tier for infrequent access and another tier for frequent access. It has 99.9 percent availability and 99.999999999 percent durability. It also supports SSL for the data in transit and encryption of your data at rest. The access patterns of objects are monitored by Amazon S3 for a monthly monitoring and automation fee per object, and the objects are moved to the infrequent access tier if not accessed for the last 30 consecutive days. The object is automatically moved back to the frequent access tier if an object is accessed. There are no additional tiering fees when objects are moved between access tiers and no retrieval fees when using the S3 Intelligent-Tiering storage class. When the access patterns are unknown or unpredictable and data is long-lived, this is the ideal storage class.

Infrequent Access: Amazon S3 Standard-Infrequent Access

Amazon S3 Standard-Infrequent Access is accessed less frequently and is for data that requires rapid access when needed. S3 Standard-IA offers 99.9 percent availability, high throughput, low latency, and 99.999999999 percent of durability, with a low per-gigabyte storage price and low per-gigabyte retrieval fee. Both the low cost and high performance make the S3 Standard-IA ideal for the backups and as a data store for disaster recovery files, and also for long-term storage. Amazon S3 Standard-IA supports SSL for your data that is in transit and encryption of your data at rest.

Amazon S3 One Zone-Infrequent Access

Amazon S3 One Zone-Infrequent Access is for data that requires rapid access when needed but is accessed less frequently. S3 One Zone-IA stores data in a single AZ not in a minimum of three AZs, like other S3 storage classes, and it costs 20 percent less than S3 Standard-IA. It has durability of 99.999999999 percent of objects in a single AZ and 99.5 percent availability along with SSL for your data in transit and encryption of your data at rest. S3 One Zone-IA is ideal for customers who do not require the availability and resilience of S3 Standard or S3 Standard-IA but want a lower-cost option for infrequently accessed data. It's a good choice for storing easily re-creatable data or secondary backup copies of on-premises data. You can also use it for S3 CRR where the data is replicated from another AWS region.

Archive: Amazon S3 Glacier

Amazon S3 Glacier (S3 Glacier) is a low-cost, durable, and secure storage class for data archiving. This storage class allows you to reliably store any amount of data at costs that are cheaper than on-premises solutions. S3 Glacier provides three retrieval options that range from a few minutes to hours to keep costs low yet suitable for varying needs. It has 99.999999999 percent durability and SSL for your data in transit and encryption of your data at rest.

Amazon S3 Glacier Deep Archive

Amazon S3 Glacier Deep Archive is the lowest-cost storage class and supports long-term retention for data that may be accessed once a year. It is designed for financial services, healthcare, and public sector customers and highly regulated industries that retain data sets for seven to ten years or longer to meet regulatory requirements. S3 Glacier Deep Archive is a cost-effective and easy-to-manage alternative to magnetic tape systems used for backup and disaster recovery use-cases. S3 Glacier Deep Archive complements Amazon S3 Glacier, which is ideal for archives where data is regularly retrieved and when some of the data may be needed in minutes. All objects stored in S3 Glacier Deep Archive are protected by 99.999999999 percent durability and are replicated and stored across at least three geographically dispersed Availability Zones, and data can be restored within 12 hours.

Object Lifecycle Management

Your objects can be stored cost-effectively throughout their lifecycle using a lifecycle configuration, which is a set of rules that define actions applied to a group of objects. A lifecycle configuration uses the XML format, which comprises a set of rules with predefined actions to perform on objects during their lifetime. You can use PUT bucket lifecycle, GET bucket lifecycle, and DELETE bucket lifecycle operations for managing lifecycle configuration. The two types of actions are

- Transition actions defines when to transition to another storage class objects, such as transitioning objects to the Standard-IA storage class after 30 days or archive the objects to Glacier after one year, but costs are associated with the lifecycle transition requests.

- Expiration actions define when objects will expire. Amazon S3 deletes expired objects, and the cost depends on when the object expires.

Lifecycle Transitions

Lifecycle transitions allow you to move between storage classes during an object's lifecycle, as shown in Figure 8-2. Based on the lifecycle policy, objects can be transitioned automatically to another storage class after a certain number of days. In this example, 30-day-old objects are moved from S3 Standard to S3 Infrequent-Access; after 90 days, they are moved to Glacier; they are deleted after 365 days.

The Standard storage class can be transitioned to any other storage class. The Standard-IA storage class can be transitioned to either Intelligent-Tiering or One Zone-IA storage classes, and the Intelligent-Tiering storage class can be transitioned to the One Zone-IA storage class. The Glacier storage class can be transitioned to the Deep-Archive storage class.

Configuring Object Expiration

You can expire objects to delete them permanently, and when an object reaches the end of its lifetime, it is removed asynchronously. You may see some delay between the expiration date and the actual date the object will be removed, but you will not be

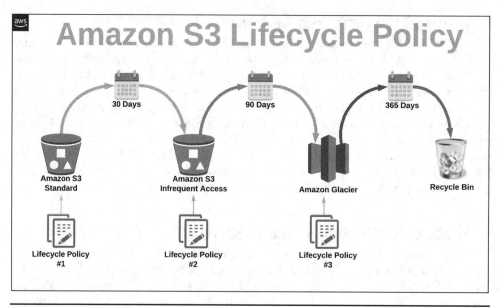

Figure 8-2   Amazon S3 lifecycle policy

charged for storage time associated with an object that has expired. You can find the objects that are scheduled to expire by using the HEAD Object or the GET Object API operations.

Object Versioning

Object versioning allows you to keep multiple variants of an object in the same bucket in order to prevent the accidental deletion and restoration of every version of every object stored in your Amazon S3 bucket. It is easy to recover objects from both unintended user actions like accidental deletion or overwrite and application failures. When you enable versioning, you will have two objects with the same key (name) but different version IDs, such as my-video.mpeg (version 333444) and my-video.mpeg (version 444555). You must explicitly enable versioning on your bucket; versioning is disabled by default, and the version ID is null. The versioning state applies to all the objects in a bucket, not to any subset of objects. You can enable and suspend versioning at the bucket level.

 TIP   If you observe a huge increase in the number of HTTP 503-slow down responses for Amazon S3 PUT or DELETE object requests, one or more objects in the bucket might have millions of versions.

Buckets may be in one of three states. The first state is unversioned (the default), the second state is versioning-enabled, and the third state is versioning-suspended. When enabled, all the objects are protected from accidental deletion, so when you try to delete an object, Amazon S3 inserts a delete marker instead of removing it permanently, which becomes the current object version. When you overwrite an object, it results in a new object version in the bucket. In both cases you can always restore the previous version.

 EXAM TIP Once you version-enable a bucket, it can never return to an unversioned state. You can, however, suspend versioning on that bucket.

When you put an object in a versioning-enabled bucket that already contains an object with the same name, the original object remains in the bucket, but Amazon S3 adds a newer version ID to the bucket, as you can see in Figure 8-3.

If you accidentally overwrite or delete an object, you can retrieve a previous version of the same object. During the delete operation Amazon S3 inserts a delete marker and leaves all other versions intact, as shown in Figure 8-4.

Since the delete marker becomes the current version of the object, the GET Object request returns a 403 Forbidden error, as seen in Figure 8-5.

However, you can retrieve an old version of a deleted object by specifying its version ID, as shown in Figure 8-6 shows. Amazon S3 allows you to retrieve an object's older version even though it's not the current version.

If you are the owner of an Amazon S3 bucket, you can permanently delete an object by specifying its version number. As Figure 8-7 shows, the DELETE version ID permanently deletes an object from a bucket and no delete marker is inserted.

You can add another layer of security by configuring a bucket to enable multifactor authentication (MFA) deletions. In order to MFA-delete a version or change the versioning state of the bucket, the bucket owner must include two forms of authentication in any request. MFA deletions require additional authentication to change the versioning state of your bucket and to permanently delete an object version.

Figure 8-3
Putting an object in a version-enabled bucket

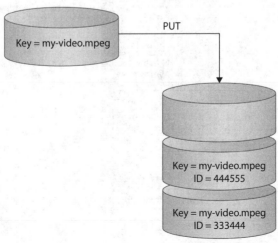

Version-Enabled Object

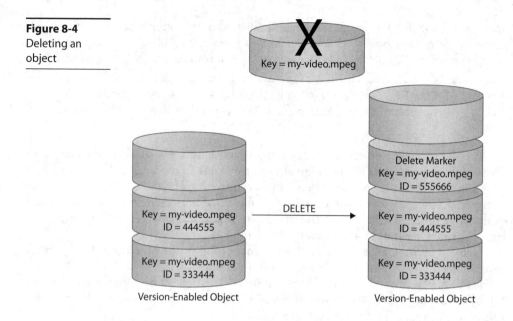

Figure 8-4
Deleting an object

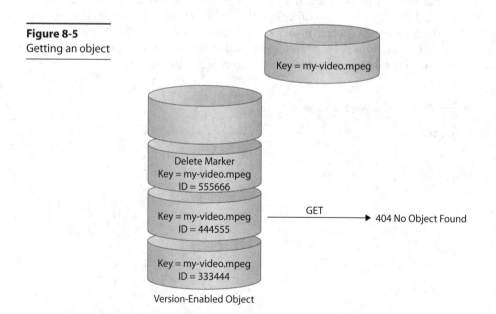

Figure 8-5
Getting an object

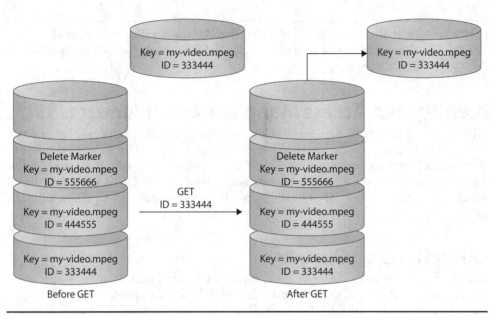

Figure 8-6   Getting an older object

Figure 8-7
Deleting an old
object

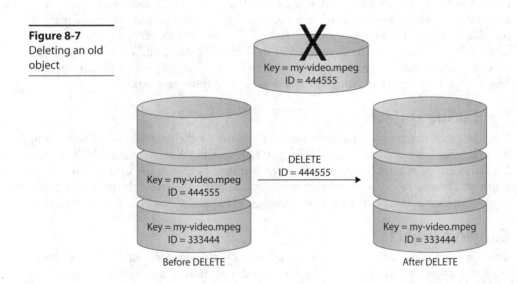

EXAM TIP Even though all authorized IAM users, including the bucket owner, can enable versioning, only the bucket owner can enable an MFA-delete operation.

Identity and Access Management in Amazon S3

All Amazon S3 resources, including buckets, objects, and related sub-resources, are private by default and only the resource owner can access them. The resource owner can grant access permissions to others by using either resource-based policies or user policies. Access policies that are attached to buckets and objects are referred to as resource-based policies, including bucket policies and ACLs. When you attach access policies to users, they are called user policies.

Operations on Objects

Amazon S3 enables you to store, retrieve, copy, and delete objects. In a single operation, you can upload objects of up to 5GB in size; to upload objects greater than 5GB, you can use the multipart upload API, which allows you to upload objects up to 5TB each.

Getting Objects

You can retrieve objects directly from Amazon S3. You can use a single GET operation to retrieve the entire object, or you can use the Range HTTP header in a GET request to retrieve a specific range of bytes in an object. You can resume fetching other parts of the object whenever your application is ready. This resumable download feature is useful when you only need portions of your object data, and it is also useful when network connectivity is poor and you need to react to failures. You need to provide the appropriate request headers when retrieving objects that are stored using server-side encryption.

Uploading Objects

You can use different options, depending on the size of the data you are uploading to Amazon S3. You can use a single PUT operation to upload objects up to 5GB in size, and you can use the multipart upload API to upload large objects, up to 5TB, which improves the upload experience for larger objects. When you upload the objects in parts, they are uploaded independently, in any order, and in parallel from 5MB to 5TB in size.

Copying Objects

The copy operation creates a copy of an object that is already stored in Amazon S3 up to 5GB in a single atomic operation. As mentioned, you need to use the multipart upload API to copy an object that is greater than 5GB. The copy operation creates additional copies of objects and renames them by copying and deleting the original ones. The copy operation is also used to move objects across Amazon S3 locations, like from us-east-1 to us-west-1, and to change object metadata. If you try to copy the object to another bucket and the source objects are archived in Glacier or Deep-Archive then you must first restore a temporary copy. When copying encrypted objects, you need to provide encryption information in your request so Amazon S3 can decrypt the object.

 EXAM TIP Copying objects across locations incurs bandwidth charges.

Listing Object Keys

You can use the list operation to select and browse object keys, which is similar to how files are stored in directories within a file system. Amazon S3 exposes a list operation that lets you catalog the keys contained in a bucket and list the keys by bucket and prefix.

Deleting Objects

You can delete one or more objects directly from Amazon S3 using a single HTTP request. You can use the Delete API to delete one object and the Multi-Object Delete API to delete up to 1,000 objects in a single HTTP request. It is enough to provide only the object key name when deleting objects from a bucket that is not version-enabled and provide the version ID of the object to delete a specific version of it.

If your bucket is version-enabled and you specify the object key, then Amazon S3 creates a delete marker, and the return response will be its version ID. If you specify both the key and a version ID, Amazon S3 deletes the specific version of the object if the version ID maps to a specific object version. If the version ID maps to the delete marker of that object, Amazon S3 deletes the delete marker, making the object reappear in your bucket.

A versioned delete request will always fail if you provide an invalid MFA token or no token at all when deleting objects from an MFA-enabled bucket. When you have an MFA-enabled bucket and make a normal delete request without an MFA token, the delete operation succeeds. If you make a multi-object delete request and specify only non-versioned objects to delete from an MFA-enabled bucket, the deletion is successful even if you don't provide an MFA token.

Selecting Content from Objects

You can use Structured Query Language (SQL) statements to retrieve the contents or just the subset of data that you need using Amazon S3 Select. You can filter the result set to reduce the amount of data that Amazon S3 transfers, which in turn reduces the cost and latency to retrieve the data. The objects are stored in CSV, JSON, or Apache Parquet format and compressed with GZIP or BZIP2, and server-side encrypted objects are supported using Amazon S3 Select. You can perform SQL queries using the Select Object Content REST API, AWS SDKs, or the AWS command-line interface (CLI) or the Amazon S3 console. The amount of data returned is limited to 40MB if you use the Amazon S3 console, so use the AWS CLI or the API to retrieve more data.

Restoring Archived Objects

You cannot access objects in real time that you archived to the Glacier or Deep-Archive storage classes. You need to wait until a temporary copy of the object is available after initiating the restore request for the number of days that you specify. The temporary copy of the object is available only for the specified duration. The restored object copy is deleted after the duration period.

Data Protection in Amazon S3

You can protect your data while it travels to and from Amazon S3 (in transit) and while it is stored on disks in Amazon S3 datacenters (at rest). By using SSL or client-side encryption, you can protect data in transit. Data at rest is protected in Amazon S3 by using both server-side encryption and client-side encryption. When you request Amazon S3 to encrypt your object before saving it on disks and then decrypt it when you retrieve the objects, this is known as server-side encryption. When you encrypt data at the client side before uploading it to Amazon S3 and manage the encryption process, encryption keys, and related tools, it is called client-side encryption.

 TIP You can't apply different types of server-side encryption to the same object simultaneously.

There are three mutually exclusive options available, depending on how you want to manage the encryption keys:

- **Server-Side Encryption with Amazon S3-Managed Keys (SSE-S3)**, where each object is encrypted with a unique key. The key is encrypted with a master key that is regularly rotated as an additional safeguard. Amazon S3 server-side encryption uses the 256-bit Advanced Encryption Standard (AES-256), which is one of the strongest block ciphers available, to encrypt your data.

- **Server-Side Encryption with Keys Stored in AWS Key Management Service (KMS) (SSE-KMS)** is similar to SSE-S3 and protects the encryption key, which provides additional protection against unauthorized access. It also provides an audit trail of when your key was used and by whom, in addition to allowing you to have the option to create or manage encryption keys or use a unique default key.

- **Server-Side Encryption with Customer-Provided Keys (SSE-C)** where the client manages the encryption key and other related tools and Amazon S3 manages the encryption when writing to disks and decrypts it when you access your objects.

Access Control Lists

ACLs are the resource-level access policy options available to manage access to your buckets and objects. ACLs can be used to grant basic read/write permissions to other AWS accounts. ACLs can only be used to grant permissions to other AWS accounts and cannot grant permissions to users in your account. Also, you cannot grant conditional permissions and you cannot explicitly deny permissions. ACLs are suitable when the bucket owner allows other AWS accounts to upload objects, and permissions to these objects can only be managed using an object ACL by the AWS account that owns the object.

 TIP An ACL can have up to 100 grants.

Amazon S3 Object Lock

Amazon S3 Object Lock is used to prevent objects from being deleted or overwritten for either a specific period of time or permanently. It provides two retention modes:

- **Governance mode** You can control the deletion of an object version and overwrites by altering the lock settings. You need to explicitly grant users to alter the retention settings or delete the object if necessary.
- **Compliance mode** The object version can't be overwritten or deleted by any user, including the root user in your AWS account. The object's retention mode can't be changed or shortened when it is locked in compliance mode.

Retention Periods

A retention period protects an object version for a fixed amount of time, and Amazon S3 stores a timestamp in the object version's metadata—noted in the Retain Until Date setting—to indicate when the retention period expires. The object version can be overwritten or deleted only after the retention period expires, unless you also place a legal hold on the object version.

 EXAM TIP If your request to place an object version in a bucket contains an explicit retention mode and period, those settings override any bucket default settings for that object version.

Legal Holds

Amazon S3 Object Lock enables you to place a legal hold on an object version to protect it from being overwritten or deleted. The Amazon S3 object doesn't have an associated retention period and remains in effect until removed, and it can be placed and removed by any user who has the required permission. It is independent from retention periods because, regardless of whether the specified object version has a retention period set or not, you can place and remove legal holds. Similarly, the object version remains protected until the retention period expires even if you remove a legal hold.

 EXAM TIP You can only enable Amazon S3 Object Lock for new buckets. If you want to turn on Amazon S3 Object Lock for an existing bucket, you need to contact AWS Support.

Best Practices for Amazon S3

Amazon S3 provides a variety of features to implement security, and following these best practices can help prevent security incidents in Amazon S3.

- **Protect Amazon S3 buckets from public access**   Unless you explicitly require anyone on the Internet to read or write to your S3 bucket, you should ensure that your Amazon S3 blocks public access.

- **Use AWS CloudTrail**   This provides a record of actions taken by a user, role, or AWS service in Amazon S3, which helps you determine the request that was made to Amazon S3, the IP address from where the request was initiated, by whom, when, and other additional details.

- **Enable AWS Config**   This enables you to assess, audit, and evaluate the configurations of your AWS resources and allows you to evaluate the recorded configurations against the desired secure configurations. You can review configuration changes and AWS resource relationships, investigate configuration histories, and examine the compliance configurations specified in your internal guidelines.

- **Enable encryption of data at rest**   You can protect the data at rest in Amazon S3 by using the following tools:

  - **Server-side encryption** helps reduce the risk to your data in the AWS Cloud by encrypting the data with a key that is stored in a different mechanism from the mechanism that stores the data itself.

  - **Client-side encryption** can help reduce risk to a customer or consumer by encrypting data with a key that is stored in a different mechanism from the mechanism that stores the data itself.

- **Enable encryption of data in transit**   HTTPS (TLS) is used to help prevent potential attackers from manipulating network traffic using man-in-the-middle or similar attacks.

- **Least privilege access**   You can control what permissions users have and grant only the fewest permissions required to perform a task to reduce the security risk by using IAM user policies, Amazon S3 ACLs, Amazon S3 bucket policies, or service control policies.

- **Use IAM roles for Amazon S3 access**   You should not store AWS credentials directly in the application or Amazon EC2 instance or other AWS services. Instead, use an IAM role to manage temporary credentials so you don't have to distribute credentials like a username, password, or access keys.

- **Consider enabling versioning**   This will allow you to keep multiple variants of an object to preserve, retrieve, and restore every version of every object stored in your Amazon S3 bucket and to easily recover from application failures or unintentional user actions.

- **Use MFA Delete**   MFA Delete can help prevent accidental bucket deletions, and it requires additional authentication to change the versioning state of your bucket and to permanently delete an object version.

- **Consider using Amazon S3 Object Lock**   This enables you to store objects using a "Write Once Read Many" (WORM) model and helps prevent accidental or inappropriate deletion of data.

- **Use Amazon S3 cross-region replication**   Use this to automatically replicate data between different AWS regions to asynchronously copy the objects across buckets.

- **Consider VPC endpoints for Amazon S3 access**   This will allow connectivity only to Amazon S3 and lets you use policies to control access to buckets from specific Amazon VPC endpoints or specific Virtual Private Clouds (VPCs). A VPC endpoint can help prevent traffic from potentially traversing the open Internet.

- **Use AWS Trusted Advisor/ListBuckets API to inspect your Amazon S3**   Implement ongoing detective controls using managed AWS Config rules. Regularly scan all of your Amazon S3 buckets to determine whether the bucket has compliant access controls and configuration.

- **Identify and audit all your Amazon S3 buckets**   It is a crucial aspect of governance and security to have all of your Amazon S3 resources visible to assess their security posture and act on potential areas of weakness. Use Amazon S3 inventory to audit and report on the replication and encryption status of your objects for business, compliance, and regulatory needs.

- **Apply monitoring**   Monitoring is an important of maintaining the security, reliability, performance, and availability of Amazon S3 and your other AWS solutions. AWS provides a variety of tools and services to monitor Amazon S3 resources.

- **Implement Amazon S3 server access logging**   This assists in access audits and security to help you learn more about your customers and to understand your Amazon S3 bill.

- **Consider using Amazon Macie with Amazon S3**   Amazon Macie uses machine learning to automatically discover, classify, and protect sensitive data in AWS, and it recognizes sensitive data such as personally identifiable information (PII) or intellectual property.

- **Monitor AWS security advisories**   Regularly check security advisories posted in Trusted Advisor and note warnings about Amazon S3 buckets with "open access permissions." Also actively monitor the primary e-mail addresses registered to each of your AWS accounts. The AWS operational issues with broad impact are posted on the AWS Service Health Dashboard and are posted to individual accounts via the Personal Health Dashboard.

 EXAM TIP   CRR requires that both source and destination S3 buckets have versioning enabled.

Chapter Review

Amazon S3 allows you to store and retrieve any amount of data from anywhere around the world at any time. A bucket is a logical container for objects that you store in Amazon S3. All objects are stored in a bucket. CORS specifies a way for web applications loaded in one domain to interact with resources in a different domain. Using CORS, you can build rich customer web applications with Amazon S3 and allow cross-origin access to your Amazon S3 resources. CRR enables automatic and asynchronous replication of objects between buckets across different AWS regions owned by either the same or a different AWS account. You can receive notifications when a specific event happens in your bucket by enabling the Amazon S3 event notification feature. Amazon S3 Transfer Acceleration enables fast and secure transfers of files over long distances between your client and an S3 bucket. You don't have to pay any up-front fees or commit to how much content you'll store when using Amazon S3—you pay only for what you use. Amazon S3 server access logging provides details of the requests that are made to a bucket. Amazon S3 supports creating folders to group objects in before storing them. You cannot create buckets within buckets; however, you can create folders within folders and you can upload and copy objects directly into folders. Amazon S3 is designed to store as many objects as you want, and objects are stored as a simple key/value store. You can store these objects in one or more buckets. Every Amazon S3 object has a key, data, and metadata. The key name or object key uniquely identifies the object in a bucket. Object metadata is a set of name/value pairs that can be set when you upload the object.

For the general-purpose frequently accessed data, you can use the S3 Standard class. For changing access patterns or unknown data, you can use the S3 Intelligent-Tiering class. For infrequently accessed data, you can use the S3 Standard-Infrequent Access class. For long-lived but less frequently accessed data, you can use the S3 One Zone-Infrequent Access class. For archival storage, you can use the Amazon S3 Glacier class. For long-term archive and digital preservation, you can use the Amazon S3 Glacier Deep Archive class.

Your objects can be stored cost-effectively throughout their lifecycle using a lifecycle configuration, which is a set of rules that define actions applied to a group of objects. The lifecycle transitions allow you to move between storage classes. Objects can be set to expire in order to delete them permanently, and when an object reaches the end of its lifetime, it is removed asynchronously. Object versioning allows you to keep multiple variants of an object in the same bucket in order to prevent accidental deletion and restoration of every version of every object stored in your Amazon S3 bucket. It is easy to recover objects from both unintended user actions, like accidental deletions, or overwrite and application failures. You can grant permissions to your Amazon S3 resources using a bucket policy and user policy, and both use JSON-based access policy language. You can use SQL statements to retrieve the contents of objects or just the subset of data that you need using Amazon S3 Select. You can protect your data both in transit and at rest. ACLs are resource-level access policy options available to manage access to your buckets and objects. Amazon S3 Object Lock can be used to store objects using a WORM model, which prevents objects from being deleted or overwritten either for a fixed amount of time or indefinitely. A retention period protects an object version for a fixed amount of time, and Amazon S3 stores a timestamp in the object version's metadata to indicate when the retention period expires. Amazon S3 Object Lock allows you to place a legal hold on an object version to protect it from being overwritten or deleted.

Exercises

The following exercises will help you practice creating Amazon S3 buckets and perform some related tasks to get familiar with this service.

You need to create an AWS account, as explained earlier, to perform these exercises. You can use the Free Tier when launching AWS resources, but make sure to delete the buckets at the end if they are not required.

Exercise 8-1: Create Your First S3 Bucket Using the AWS Management Console

In this exercise, you create an S3 bucket using the Management Console.

1. Sign in to the AWS Management Console and use Search IAM to go to https:// console.aws.amazon.com/s3/.

2. Choose Create Bucket.

3. On the Name And Region page, provide the name for your bucket and region where it resides.

4. Type **my-first-bucket-01012020** for the name, which is unique among all existing bucket names in Amazon S3.

5. Choose an AWS region that is close to you to minimize latency and costs, and click Next.

6. On the Configure Options page, configure versioning, server access logging, tags, object-level logging, default encryption, Object Lock, and CloudWatch request metrics.

7. Select Versioning to keep all versions of an object in the same bucket.

8. Select Server Access Logging, which enables you to retrieve detailed records of your bucket.

9. Select Tags. Tags are a key/value pair so enter **key** for the Name field and **My first S3 bucket** for the Value field.

10. Select Object-Level Logging to enable this feature with CloudTrail.

 CAUTION   You will incur additional costs for enabling object-level logging with CloudTrail.

11. Select Default Encryption to automatically encrypt objects when they are stored in S3.

12. Select Object Lock for any objects in the bucket, which requires that you enable versioning in step 7.

13. Select CloudWatch Request Metrics and click Next.

 CAUTION You will incur additional costs for enabling monitoring using CloudWatch.

14. On the Set Permissions page, uncheck Block Public Access—it is not recommended, but is just for testing purpose. Change the permissions if you want, and select Next.

15. On the Review page, verify that everything is correct and choose Create Bucket.

Exercise 8-2: Upload Folders and Files to an Amazon S3 Bucket

This exercise will show the step-by-step details to upload your files and folders into an Amazon S3 bucket using the AWS Management Console.

1. Sign in to the AWS Management Console and open the IAM console at https://console.aws.amazon.com/s3/.

2. From the Bucket Name list, choose the bucket icon next to the my-first-bucket-01012020 bucket where you want to upload the file.

3. Choose Upload.

4. From Upload dialog box choose Add Files.

5. Choose a file (cars.jpg) to upload, and then choose Open and then choose Upload.

6. To set permissions or properties for the files that you are uploading, choose Next.

7. On the Set Permissions page, under Manage Users, you can change the permissions for the AWS account owner. Select Read and Write.

8. Choose Add Account to grant access to another AWS account (you can skip this step unless you have another AWS account you want to grant access to).

9. Under Manage Public Permissions, grant read access to your objects to the general public. It is not recommended practice, but it is just for testing purpose, and you can update the permission or delete the object later.

10. Click Next to set properties.

11. Choose a storage class, select Standard, and explore the other storage classes.

12. For the type of encryption, choose Amazon S3 Master-Key.

13. For the metadata header choose x-amz-meta-my-first-metadata1 and for the value choose MyUserDefinedMetadata.

14. Tags are key/value pairs, so select image for the key and car for the value, and click Save.

15. Choose Next.

16. On the Upload Review page, verify everything is correct and choose Upload.

17. You can see the progress of the upload at the bottom of the browser window, as well as a successful or failed states.

Exercise 8-3: Copy or Move an Object to Another Folder

This exercise will demonstrate the details to copy or move a file or object in an Amazon S3 bucket to another Amazon S3 folder using the AWS Management Console.

1. Sign in to the AWS Management Console and open the IAM console at https:// console.aws.amazon.com/s3/.

2. From the Bucket Name list, choose the bucket icon next to the my-first-bucket-01012020 bucket from where you want to copy.

3. Choose Create Folder, type **my-favorite-cars** for the folder name, choose None for the encryption setting (for testing purposes), and then choose Save.

4. In the Name list, select the check box next to the object (cars.jpg) that you want to copy, choose More, and then choose Copy from the dropdown list.

5. In the Name list, choose the name of the folder: my-favorite-cars.

6. Now Choose More, and then choose Paste from the dropdown list.

7. You will see a message like "All affected objects will be pasted." Choose Paste.

Exercise 8-4: Delete an Object from a Bucket

This exercise will show the details to delete an object or file from Amazon S3 bucket using the AWS Management Console.

1. Sign in to the AWS Management Console and open the IAM console at https:// console.aws.amazon.com/s3/.

2. From the Bucket Name list, choose the bucket icon next to the my-first-bucket-01012020 bucket that you want to delete an object from (cars.jpg).

3. In the Name list, select the check box next to the object (cars.jpg), choose More, and then choose Delete from the dropdown list.

4. In the Delete Objects dialog box, verify that the name of the object (cars.jpg) is listed, and then choose Delete.

Exercise 8-5: Delete the S3 Bucket that You Created Before

This exercise will present the step-by-step details to delete an Amazon S3 bucket using the AWS Management Console.

1. Sign in to the AWS Management Console and open the IAM console at https:// console.aws.amazon.com/s3/.

2. From the Bucket Name list, choose the bucket icon next to the my-second-bucket-01012020 bucket that you want to delete.

PART III

3. Choose Delete Bucket. The Delete bucket dialog box appears.

4. Type **my-second-bucket-01012020** as the bucket name to confirm the action and to avoid accidental deletion.

5. Choose Confirm. The bucket will be deleted, including any contents.

Questions

The following questions will help you gauge your understanding of the contents in this chapter. Read all the answers carefully because there might be more than one correct answer. Choose the best responses for each question.

1. Your application team needs a simple storage solution to store and retrieve data from anywhere around the world at any time and needs a highly durable storage infrastructure. Which of the following service securely stores your objects?

    A. Amazon S3

    B. Amazon EC2

    C. AWS Snowball

    D. AWS Lambda

2. Your development team is building web applications that make requests to domains other than the one that supplied the primary content, and they want to use JavaScript and HTML5 to directly interact with Amazon S3. Which S3 feature do you need to enable to achieve this?

    A. Cross-region replication (CRR)

    B. Cross-origin resource sharing (CORS)

    C. Amazon S3 Transfer Acceleration

    D. AWS Identity and Access Management (IAM)

3. You are storing multiple files in your S3 bucket daily in the US East region, and you have a requirement to replicate the newly created files and file updates from your source bucket to your destination bucket in the US West Region. Which of the following S3 features needs to be enabled to achieve this?

    A. AWS Identity and Access Management (IAM)

    B. Cross-origin resource sharing (CORS)

    C. Amazon S3 Transfer Acceleration

    D. Cross-region replication (CRR)

4. A startup company stores hundreds of image and videos in Amazon S3. The company is planning to save costs by archiving one-year-old files. What should you do in this scenario to automatically archive storage after one year?

    A. Create a VPC endpoint for Amazon S3 and move the files to Glacier

    B. Create an AWS Lambda function to move files to Glacier

C. Enable a lifecycle policy rule and choose to transition to Glacier after one year

D. Enable cross-region replication to move the files to Glacier

5. You are working in a Windows environment and want to delete an S3 bucket named my-expired-bucket. You don't want to be prompted for confirmation before the command executes. Which of the following AWS PowerShell command can be used to delete it?

A. `PS C:\>Remove-S3Bucket -BucketName my-expired-bucket -Force`

B. `PS C:\>Delete-S3Bucket -BucketName my-expired-bucket -Force`

C. `PS C:\>Purge-S3Bucket -BucketName my-expired-bucket -Force`

D. `PS C:\>Drop-S3Bucket -BucketName my-expired-bucket -Force`

6. Your company produces files every day 200GB in size that you are uploading to Amazon S3. The upload time takes more than four hours. What you can do to reduce the upload time?

A. Upload the file to multiple S3 buckets

B. Compress the files and upload them to Glacier

C. Use cross-region replication to update the files

D. Use multipart upload to upload the files in parallel to S3

7. Which of the following storage classes are supported by Amazon S3 for different storage use cases? (Choose all that apply.)

A. S3 Standard class

B. S3 Intelligent-Tiering class

C. S3 Standard-Infrequent Access

D. S3 One Zone-Infrequent Access

E. Amazon S3 Glacier

F. Amazon S3 Glacier Deep Archive

8. You are designing an application that stores files in an Amazon S3 bucket. You can't predict the access pattern of these files, so you want to store them in a storage class that is designed to optimize costs by automatically moving data to the most cost-effective access tier, without performance impact or operational overhead. Which of the following storage classes provide this feature?

A. S3 Standard class

B. S3 Intelligent-Tiering class

C. S3 Standard-Infrequent Access

D. S3 One Zone-Infrequent Access

PART III

9. You want to permanently delete a version-enabled object without inserting any delete marker. How can you achieve this?

   A. Log in as the owner of the Amazon S3 bucket and delete the object by specifying the version ID you want to delete

   B. Log in as the owner of the Amazon S3 bucket and use the GET command to delete the object.

   C. Log in as the owner of the Amazon S3 bucket and use the PUT command to delete the object.

   D. You cannot delete a version-enabled object.

10. You want to enable server-side encryption to protect the data at rest in Amazon S3. Which three mutually exclusive options should you use, based on how you choose to manage the encryption keys? (Choose three.)

    A. Server-side encryption with Amazon S3 managed keys (SSE-S3)

    B. Server-side encryption with Amazon EC2 key pairs (SSE-EC2)

    C. Server-side encryption with keys stored in AWS KMS (SSE-KMS)

    D. Server-side encryption with customer-provided keys (SSE-C)

Answers

1. **A.** Amazon S3 is a simple storage solution that allows you to store and retrieve data from anywhere around the world at any time, and it is a highly durable storage infrastructure.

2. **B.** Cross-origin resource sharing (CORS) allows you to build web applications that make requests to domains other than the one that supplied the primary content.

3. **D.** Cross-region replication (CRR) replicates your newly created objects and object updates from a source bucket in one region to your destination bucket in a different region.

4. **C.** You need to enable a lifecycle policy rule and then choose to transition to Glacier after one year.

5. **A.** This is the correct AWS PowerShell command to delete an S3 bucket named my-expired-bucket with the –Force option.

6. **D.** You need to use a multipart upload to upload the files in parallel to S3.

7. **A, B, C, D, E, F.** Amazon S3 offers the S3 Standard class, S3 Intelligent-Tiering class, S3 Standard-Infrequent Access, S3 One Zone-Infrequent Access, Amazon S3 Glacier, and Amazon S3 Glacier Deep Archive storage classes.

8. **B.** The S3 Intelligent-Tiering class can automatically move objects to the infrequently accessed storage class.

9. **A.** You need to log in as the owner of the Amazon S3 bucket and provide the version ID to delete the version-enabled object.

10. **A, C, D.** Amazon S3 supports server-side encryption with Amazon S3 managed keys (SSE-S3), server-side encryption with keys stored in AWS KMS (SSE-KMS), and server-side encryption with customer-provided keys (SSE-C) encryptions for data at rest.

Additional Resources

- **AWS Blogs**   There is no place like official AWS documentation to get the latest and most up-to-date information about all the AWS services. Always refer to the official AWS blogs to get the latest updates about new AWS services and updates to existing features.
  ```
  https://docs.aws.amazon.com and https://aws.amazon.com/
  blogs/aws
  ```

- **Protecting Data Using Amazon S3 Object Lock**   This blog explains the steps to protect your data using Amazon S3 object locking features such as retention period and legal hold.
  ```
  https://aws.amazon.com/blogs/storage/protecting-data-
  with-amazon-s3-object-lock/
  ```

- **S3 Batches for Transcoding Files**   This blog explains the steps to configure S3 batch operations to invoke a video transcoding job using AWS Lambda from the video stored in Amazon S3.
  ```
  https://aws.amazon.com/blogs/storage/transcoding-video-
  files-with-s3-batch-operations/
  ```

- **Encrypting Objects Using Amazon S3 Batch Operations**   This blog explains the detailed steps to configure an S3 batch operations job and list objects using Amazon Athena to encrypt your objects.
  ```
  https://aws.amazon.com/blogs/storage/encrypting-objects-
  with-amazon-s3-batch-operations/
  ```

- **Build Messages Using Amazon S3 and AWS Lambda**   This blog details the steps necessary to configure building a dynamic personalized message and deliver it using Amazon S3 and AWS Lambda.
  ```
  https://aws.amazon.com/blogs/gametech/how-to-build-a-
  dynamic-message-of-the-day-with-aws-lambda/
  ```

- **Data Migration to AWS Snowball Edge**   This blog detailed the steps and best practices to cost-effectively migrate to Snowball Edge.
  ```
  https://aws.amazon.com/blogs/storage/data-migration-best-
  practices-with-snowball-edge/
  ```

PART III

Amazon EBS, Amazon EFS, and Amazon S3 Glacier

In this chapter, you will learn
- Amazon Elastic Block Store
- Working with EBS volume
- Amazon EBS snapshots
- Amazon EBS encryption
- Amazon EBS best practices
- Amazon Elastic File System
- EFS encryption
- Lifecycle policy
- Amazon EFS best practices
- Amazon S3 Glacier
- Vault, archives, and jobs
- Notification configuration
- Logging and monitoring

This chapter will show how Amazon EBS, Amazon EFS, and Glacier help you with a variety of storage requirements.

Amazon Elastic Block Store

Amazon Elastic Block Store (Amazon EBS) provides block-level storage volumes, which behave like raw, unformatted block devices and are used for EC2 instances. You pay only for what you use, and you can mount a single volume as a device or mount multiple volumes on the same instance; however, each volume can be attached to only one instance at a time. A file system can be created on top of the EBS volume, or it can be used like a hard drive. The volume configuration, which can be changed dynamically, is attached to an instance. EBS volumes can be attached to any running instance in the same Availability Zone, which persists independently from the life of that instance. AWS recommends using Amazon EBS when you need to access data quickly and store it long term and for

249

file systems; databases; or raw, unformatted, block-level storage. Amazon EBS is well suited for random reads and writes and for long, continuous reads and writes.

EBS volumes are specific to an Availability Zone, and you can attach them to an instance in the same Availability Zone. If you need to make an EBS volume available to another Availability Zone in the same region or to another Availability Zone in different region, you need to create a snapshot from the existing Availability Zone, copy the snapshot to the target location, and restore the snapshot to a new volume in the target Availability Zone. EBS volumes support live configuration changes, like modifying the volume type, volume size, and input/output operations per second (IOPS) capacity without service interruption. Amazon EBS provides solid-state drive (SSD)–backed volumes, which are optimized for transactional workloads with frequent read/write operations using small input/output (I/O) size. Hard disk drive (HDD)–backed volumes are optimized for large streaming workloads where throughput is a better performance measure than IOPS. Amazon EBS offers following volume types:

- **General-purpose SSD (gp2)** offers performance from IOPS/GiB and burst performance up to 3,000 IOPS and is ideal for a wide range of use cases like small- and medium-size databases, boot volumes, and development and test environments. A gp2 volume size ranges from 1GiB to 16TiB and delivers 90 percent of the provisioned performance 99 percent of the time.

- **Provisioned IOPS SSD (io1)** volumes offer up to 64,000 IOPS and a throughput of 1,000 MiB/s and scale to tens of thousands of IOPS per EC2 instance. They are designed to meet the needs of I/O-intensive workloads, particularly database workloads, which need strong consistency and storage performance. An io1 volume size ranges from 4GiB to 16TiB and delivers the provisioned IOPS performance 99.9 percent of the time.

- **Throughput-optimized HDD (st1)** volumes offers low-cost magnetic storage that is ideal for sequential, large workloads such as Extract, Transform, Load (ETL), Amazon Elastic MapReduce (EMR), log processing, and data warehouses. The st1 volumes use a burst-bucket model for performance and are designed to support frequently accessed data involving large, sequential I/O.

- **Cold HDD (sc1)** volumes offer low-cost magnetic storage that is ideal for sequential, cold-data workloads when you require infrequent access and want to save costs. The sc1 uses a burst-bucket model for performance.

- **Magnetic (standard)** volumes are backed by magnetic drives and are suited for infrequently accessed workloads and low-cost storage. It delivers 100 IOPS on average, and the size ranges from 1GiB to 1TiB.

The burst-bucket level for gp2, st1, and sc1 volumes can be monitored using the EBS BurstBalance metric available in Amazon CloudWatch, and it shows the percentage of I/O credits for gp2 volumes or throughput credits for st1 and sc1 volumes remaining in the burst bucket. An alarm can be set up in CloudWatch to notify you when the BurstBalance value falls to a specific level. You need to create EBS volumes as encrypted volumes for compliance, regulatory, and audit requirements. When you attach an encrypted EBS volume to an instance, the data stored on the volume, and snapshots are encrypted at rest and the disk I/O is encrypted in transit. The encryption occurs on the servers that provide encryption of data-in-transit from EC2 instances to EBS storage. Point-in-time snapshots of EBS volumes can be created and stored on Amazon S3. Snapshots protect data and can be used to create as many EBS volumes as you like. These snapshots can be copied across AWS Availability Zones and regions. Amazon CloudWatch provides metrics like latency, bandwidth, average queue length, and throughput to monitor the volume performance.

EBS volumes are automatically replicated within the zone to prevent any data loss due to failure of any single hardware component. When you attach it to an EC2 instance, it appears as a native block device, same as a hard drive or any other physical device. The instance can format the EBS volume like a local drive with a file system, such as ext3, before installing the applications. You can attach multiple EBS volumes to a single instance; however, a single EBS volume can be attached to only one instance at a time. You can stripe data across the volumes when you have multiple volumes attached to a device for increased I/O and throughput performance. An EBS volume can persist independently from the life of an instance, and you incur volume usage charges as long as the data persists. Based on the Delete On Termination flag, either the EBS volume is deleted automatically when the instance is terminated or the EBS volumes persists by detaching automatically when the instance is terminated. The detached volume can then be reattached to a new instance to enable quick recovery. You can stop and restart an instance without affecting the data when you are using an EBS-backed instance, and the volume remains attached during the stop-and-start cycle. The data persists on the volume until the volume is deleted explicitly, and the deleted EBS volumes are overwritten with zeroes.

Create an Amazon EBS Volume

You can create an Amazon EBS volume in the same Availability Zone where you want to attach to an EC2 instance as an encrypted EBS volume, but it can only be attached to selected instance types. An Amazon EBS volume can be restored using snapshot ID, which is stored in Amazon S3, and you should have snapshot access permissions. The preferred backup tool on Amazon EC2 is EBS snapshots because of their speed, cost, and convenience. You can re-create the volume state at a specific point in the past with all data intact when restoring it from a snapshot. You can restore a volume to copy data across regions, to retrieve specific files, to create test environments, and to transfer them to another attached volume or to replace a damaged or corrupted volume. After a volume is created from a snapshot, you don't need to wait for all of the data to transfer from Amazon S3 to your EBS volume before accessing the volume and all its data because it loads in the background. The volume immediately downloads the requested data from Amazon S3 when your instance accesses data that hasn't yet been loaded and then continues loading the rest of the volume data in the background.

Working with Amazon EBS Volume

An Amazon EBS volume is exposed as a block device after you attach it to your instance. The volume can be formatted with any file system and then mounted. When you make the EBS volume available for use, it can be accessed as you access any other volume. The data is written directly to the EBS volume and is transparent to applications using the device. Snapshots can be taken from your EBS volume for backup purposes or to use as a baseline. The descriptive information, including its size, volume type, whether the volume is encrypted, which master key was used to encrypt the volume, and the specific instance to which the volume is attached, can be viewed. The available disk space for the EBS volume from the Linux operating system can be viewed using the following:

```
[ec2-user ~]$ df -hT /dev/xvdb1
Filesystem     Type      Size  Used Avail Use% Mounted on
/dev/xvcb1     xfs       9.0G  3.2G  5.8G  20% /
```

Detach an Amazon EBS Volume

An Amazon EBS volume can be detached from an instance explicitly or when you terminate it. You need to unmount the volume from the instance if it is running. Before you can detach the volume, you need to stop the instance if an EBS volume is the root device. The volume might not get the same mount point when you reattach a volume that you detached without unmounting it. If there were writes to the volume in progress when it was detached, then the data on the volume might be out of sync.

 EXAM TIP   If the storage amount exceeds the limit of the AWS Free Tier, then you will be charged for volume storage even after detaching the volume. If you no longer need it, you can delete the volume to avoid incurring further charges.

Delete an Amazon EBS Volume

You can delete an Amazon EBS volume if you no longer need it. After deleting the volume, its data is not available, nor can it be attached to any instance. You can take a snapshot of the volume before deletion, which can be used to re-create the volume later.

Monitor Amazon EBS Volumes

You can use volume status checks to better understand, manage, and track potential inconsistencies in the data on an Amazon EBS volume, which provides you with the information you need to determine whether the volumes are impaired. These checks automatically run every five minutes and return a pass or fail status. The status of the volume is OK if all checks pass. The status of the volume is impaired if a check fails. If the status reports insufficient data, the checks may still be in progress on the volume.

Volume Status	I/O Enabled Status	I/O Performance Status
OK	Enabled (I/O Enabled or Auto-Enabled)	Normal (as expected)
Warning	Enabled (I/O Enabled or Auto-Enabled)	Degraded (below expectations) –Or– Severely Degraded (well below expectations)
Impaired	Enabled (I/O Enabled or Auto-Enabled) –Or– Disabled (volume is offline and waiting for the user to enable I/O)	Stalled (severely affected) –Or– Not Available (I/O is disabled)
Insufficient-data	Enabled (I/O Enabled or Auto-Enabled)	Insufficient Data

By default the I/O is disabled from the attached EC2 instance when the Amazon EBS determines that a volume's data is potentially inconsistent to prevent data corruption. The next volume status check fails once I/O is disabled, and the volume status is impaired. An event is generated so you can resolve the impaired status of the volume by enabling I/O for the volume. AWS allows you to enable I/O to let your instances use the volume, and you can run a consistency check using the `fsck` command before enabling I/O. If the consistency of a volume is not a concern, you can override the default behavior by configuring the volume to automatically enable I/O, which causes the volume status checks to continue to pass. In addition, an event is generated to let you know that the volume was determined to be potentially inconsistent so you can check the volume's consistency or replace it at a later time. The I/O performance status check is not valid for Throughput-Optimized HDD (st1), General-Purpose SSD (gp2), Magnetic (standard), or Cold HDD (sc1) volumes and is only available for io1 volumes that are attached to an instance. CloudWatch collects this data every five minutes even though the I/O performance status check is performed once a minute.

Amazon EBS Snapshots

You can create backups of your Amazon EBS volumes using snapshots, which are stored in Amazon S3 in multiple Availability Zones. You can take snapshots even when the volume does not need to be attached to a running instance. You can create a snapshot of a volume to use it as a baseline, and it can be used to create multiple new EBS volumes or moved across Availability Zones. The snapshots you create from an encrypted EBS volume are automatically encrypted. A new EBS volume that is created from a snapshot is an exact copy of its original volume at the time the snapshot was taken. When you restore EBS volumes from an encrypted snapshot, it is automatically encrypted. You can create a duplicate volume in another Availability Zone by specifying it. You can share your snapshots with specific AWS accounts or even make them public. You incur Amazon S3 charges based on the volume's total size while creating the snapshots. The successive incremental snapshots are charged only for any additional data stored beyond the volume's original size. A snapshot uses an incremental backup, in that only the blocks on the volume that have changed after your most recent snapshot are stored. For example, if you have a volume with 215GiB of data but only 3.6GiB of data have changed from the time of the last snapshot, only the 3.6GiB of the modified data are written to Amazon S3. Even though snapshots are incremental, the snapshot deletion process retains only the most recent snapshot in order to restore the volume. To help categorize and manage your volumes and snapshots, tag them with metadata.

An Amazon EBS volume allows you to take point-in-time snapshots to back up the data to Amazon S3. Snapshots are incremental because only the blocks that have changed since your most recent snapshot are backed up to minimize the time and save storage costs by avoiding duplicate data. Only the data that is unique to that snapshot is removed when you delete a snapshot. Each snapshot contains all of the information that was captured from the moment when the snapshot was taken, and the snapshot information is required to restore your data to a new EBS volume. When you restore a snapshot to create an EBS volume, the new volume begins as an exact replica of the original volume that was used to create that snapshot. You can begin using the replicated volume immediately while it loads data in the background. If you try to access data that hasn't been loaded yet, it is downloaded immediately from Amazon S3 and then the rest of the volume's data is loaded in the background.

Multivolume Snapshots

You can create snapshot backups of critical workloads like a large database or a file system that spans across multiple EBS volumes. Multivolume snapshots can be taken across multiple EBS volumes attached to an EC2 instance, which allows you to take exact point-in-time, crash-consistent, and data-coordinated snapshots. Snapshots are automatically taken across multiple EBS volumes without requiring you to stop your instance or coordinate between volumes to ensure crash consistency. CloudWatch events can be used to track the status of your EBS snapshots.

Delete an Amazon EBS Snapshot

Only the data referenced exclusively by a snapshot is deleted when you delete a snapshot. Deleting previous snapshots of a volume does not affect your ability to restore volumes from later snapshots. The original volume is not affected when you delete a snapshot of that volume. When you delete a volume, it will not have any impact on the snapshots made from the deleted volume. The snapshots are incremental when you create periodic snapshots of a volume for backup. You just need to retain only the most recent snapshot in order to restore the volume even though snapshots are saved incrementally. You need to retrieve all of the snapshots for your multivolume group to delete multivolume snapshots, using the tag you applied to the group when you created the snapshots. You are allowed to delete individual snapshots in the multivolume snapshots group.

Copy an Amazon EBS Snapshot

You can copy an Amazon EBS snapshot from one AWS region to another or within the same region, and the data in transit uses Amazon S3 server-side encryption (256-bit AES). The snapshot copy receives a different snapshot ID than the original snapshot ID. You need to individually copy the snapshots when copying multivolume snapshots to another region. You need to either modify the snapshot permissions or make the snapshot public for someone from another account to be able to copy your snapshot. As long as the encryption status of a snapshot copy does not change and it happens in the same region and in the same AWS account, then the copy operation does not copy any actual data, so you will not incur any data transfer charges.

 EXAM TIP When you copy a snapshot to a new region or use a new CMK to encrypt, a full copy of the data is created, which results in an additional delay and additional storage costs.

The following are some of the snapshot copy use cases and scenarios:

- You are expanding your company to serve different geographic locations and want to launch your applications in a new AWS region.

- You plan to perform migration of your application from the US East region to US West region, where you have the majority of your customers, to enable better availability and to minimize cost.

- You need to back up your application and database, including logs, across different geographical locations at regular intervals for disaster recovery. You should be able to restore your applications using point-in-time backups stored in the secondary region to minimize data loss and recovery time.

- You need to encrypt a previously unencrypted snapshot or change the key with which the snapshot is encrypted, or you need to create a copy that you own from the shared encrypted copy in order to restore a volume from it.

- You need to copy your encrypted EBS snapshots from one AWS account to another for data retention and auditing requirements, which requires preserving data logs. A different AWS account protects you even if your main account is compromised and helps prevent accidental snapshot deletions.

 EXAM TIP You need to apply user-defined tags to the new snapshot after the copy operation is complete, since the user-defined tags are not copied from the source snapshot to the new snapshot.

Amazon EBS Snapshot Lifecycle

Amazon Data Lifecycle Manager (Amazon DLM) can be used to automate the creation, retention, and deletion of snapshots taken to back up your Amazon EBS volumes. DLM allows you to protect valuable data by enforcing a regular backup schedule and retain backups based on the duration required by auditors or internal compliance. It also saves costs by deleting outdated backups. Amazon DLM can be combined with Amazon CloudWatch events and AWS CloudTrail to provide a complete backup solution for EBS volumes at no additional cost.

Amazon EBS Elastic Volumes

Amazon EBS Elastic Volumes can be used to increase the volume size, change the volume type, or adjust the performance of your EBS volumes. You can change the configuration of Elastic Volumes without detaching the volume or restarting the instance, which enables you to continue using your application while the changes take effect.

Amazon EBS Encryption

You can create encrypted EBS volumes to meet a wide range of data-at-rest encryption requirements for regulation and audit compliance data and applications. The encryption of data in transit from the EC2 instance to Amazon EBS storage uses 256-bit Advanced Encryption Standard algorithms (AES-256) and an Amazon-managed key infrastructure. When creating encrypted volumes and encrypted volume snapshots, Amazon EBS encryption uses AWS Key Management Service (AWS KMS) master keys. A default master key is created for you automatically, and it is used for Amazon EBS encryption unless you select a customer master key (CMK). When using CMK, you can create, disable, rotate, audit the encryption keys, and define access controls to protect your data. The EBS volumes are automatically encrypted when restored from an encrypted snapshot. The volume can be encrypted on the fly when restoring from an unencrypted snapshot. You can attach encrypted volumes only to the instance types that support EBS encryption. In order to restore an EBS volume from a shared encrypted snapshot, you need to create a copy of the snapshot and then it can be restored from that copy.

Amazon EBS encryption uses AWS KMS CMKs when creating encrypted volumes, which means you don't need to build, maintain, and secure your own key management infrastructure. When you create an encrypted EBS volume and attach it to a supported instance type, the data at rest inside the volume, all the data moving between the volume and the instance, all the snapshots created from the volume, all volumes created from those snapshots, and both the boot and data volumes of an EC2 instance are encrypted. Encryption operations happen on the servers where EC2 instances are hosted to ensure the security of both data at rest and data in transit between an instance and its EBS storage. Encryption is supported by all EBS volume types, and with a minimal impact on latency, you can expect similar IOPS performance on both encrypted and unencrypted volumes. Both the encrypted and unencrypted volumes can be accessed the same way. Encryption and decryption require no additional action from you or your applications and are handled transparently.

Key Management

A unique AWS-managed CMK is created automatically in each region, and you can specify a customer-managed CMK that you create to use as the default key for encryption.

The CMK associated with an existing snapshot or encrypted volume cannot be changed, but during a snapshot copy operation you can associate a different CMK so the resulting copied snapshot is encrypted using your new CMK. The industry-standard AES-256 algorithm is used to encrypt your volume and is stored on disk with your encrypted data. Any subsequent volumes created from those snapshots use the same key and are shared by snapshots of the volume.

 NOTE   You will have more flexibility and security and satisfy compliance requirements when creating your own CMK, in addition to the ability to create, rotate, and disable keys to define access controls.

Restoring and Copying Snapshots

In this section, you will see the step-by-step instructions to restore an unencrypted snapshot, restore an unencrypted snapshot with a key, copy an unencrypted snapshot, copy a snapshot with a new key, and copy an unencrypted snapshot with a key.

A volume restored from an unencrypted snapshot is unencrypted by default when the encryption is not enabled (which is also the default). However, by setting the encrypted parameter and the KmsKeyId parameter, the resulting volume can be encrypted. Figure 9-1 illustrates the process.

The resulting volume is encrypted using your default CMK when you leave out the KmsKeyId parameter, and you must supply a key ID to encrypt the volume to a different CMK. When you try to restore unencrypted volumes that have encryption enabled by default, then encryption is mandatory for volumes restored from unencrypted snapshots, and no other encryption parameters are required to use your default CMK. Figure 9-2 shows this simple default case.

You need to provide both the Encrypted and KmsKeyId parameters when you want to encrypt the restored volume to a customer-managed CMK. A copy of an unencrypted snapshot is unencrypted by default when encryption is not enabled by default.

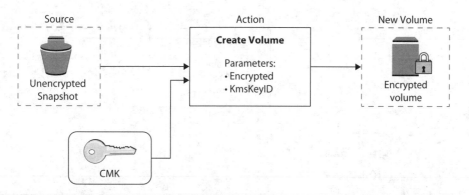

Figure 9-1   Restoring an unencrypted snapshot

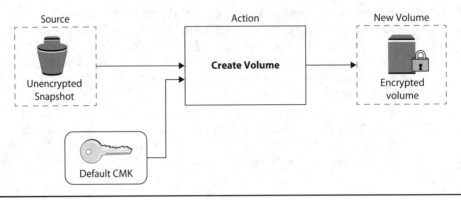

Figure 9-2 Restoring an unencrypted snapshot with a key

The resulting snapshot can be encrypted by setting the Encrypted parameter and the KmsKeyId parameter. When KmsKeyId is omitted, then the resulting snapshot is encrypted using your default CMK. In order to encrypt the volume to a different CMK, you must specify the key ID. Figure 9-3 illustrates the process.

You can create an encrypted snapshot from an unencrypted snapshot by copying an unencrypted snapshot to an encrypted snapshot and then creating a volume. When you have encryption enabled by default, then encryption is mandatory for copies of unencrypted snapshots and you don't need to provide any encryption parameters to use your default CMK. Figure 9-4 illustrates this default case.

 EXAM TIP There will be an additional delay and storage costs when you copy a snapshot and encrypt it to a new CMK where a complete nonincremental copy is created always.

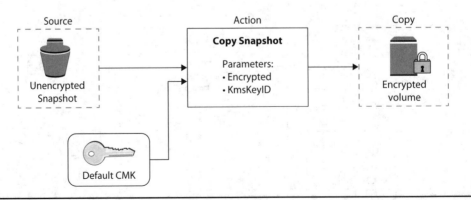

Figure 9-3 Copying an unencrypted snapshot

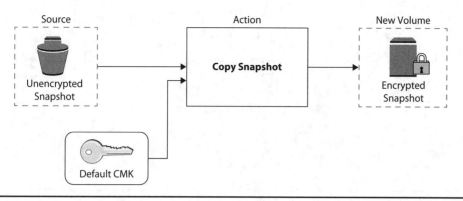

Figure 9-4 Copying an unencrypted snapshot with a key

You have the option of re-encrypting it with a different CMK when the CreateVolume action operates on an encrypted snapshot. For example, let's say own two CMKs, CMK X and CMK Y, and the source snapshots are encrypted by CMK X, as shown in Figure 9-5. The key ID of CMK Y is supplied as a parameter during the volume creation, and then the source data is automatically decrypted and then re-encrypted by CMK Y.

You can encrypt a snapshot during copying and apply a new CMK to an already-encrypted snapshot that you own. The restored volumes are only accessible using the new CMK. For example, let's say you own two CMKs, CMK X and CMK Y, and the source snapshots are encrypted using CMK X, as shown in Figure 9-6. During the copy, if you provide the key ID as CMK Y as a parameter, then the source data is automatically re-encrypted by CMK Y.

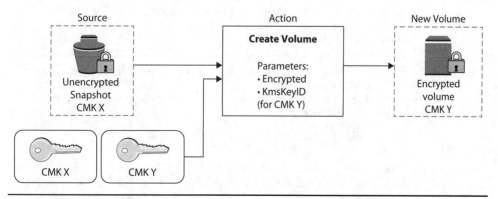

Figure 9-5 Creating a volume with a new key

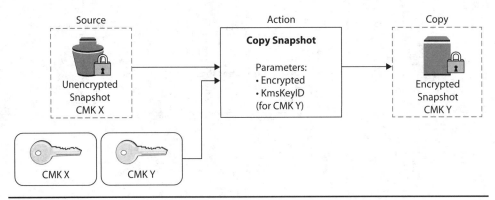

Figure 9-6 Copying a snapshot with a new key

EXAM TIP When someone shares a snapshot with you, AWS recommends creating a copy of it using a different CMK that you control to protect your access to the volume because either the original CMK can be compromised or the owner might revoke the CMK for some reason.

RAID Configuration on Linux

Amazon EBS can be used to create any standard RAID configurations that you can use with a traditional bare-metal server, as long as it is supported by the operating system for your instance, since RAID is accomplished at the software level. RAID 0 stripes multiple volumes together and provides greater I/O performance than you can achieve with a single volume, and RAID 1 mirrors two volumes together to offer on-instance redundancy.

Configuration	Use	Advantages	Disadvantages
RAID 0	Used for heavily used databases where I/O performance is more important than fault tolerance.	I/O is distributed across the volumes in a stripe, and adding a volume increases the throughput.	The stripe performance is based on the lowest-performing volume in the set, and losing a single volume results in a complete data loss for the array.
RAID 1	Used for critical applications where fault tolerance is more important than I/O performance.	Provides more data durability.	Since the data is written to multiple volumes simultaneously, it requires more Amazon EC2 to Amazon EBS bandwidth than non-RAID configurations.

NOTE Because of the parity write operations of RAID 5 and RAID 6 modes, it is not recommended for Amazon EBS, and these RAID modes consume some of the IOPS available to your volumes.

You need to use EBS multivolume snapshots to create a consistent set of snapshots for your RAID array because it allows you to take data-coordinated, point-in-time snapshots. It also gives crash-consistent snapshots across multiple EBS volumes attached to an EC2 instance. The snapshots are automatically taken across multiple EBS volumes, and you do not have to stop your instance to coordinate between volumes to ensure consistency.

Amazon EBS Metrics

CloudWatch provides metrics that can be used to view, analyze, and set alarms on the operational behavior of your volumes. There are two types of monitoring data available for your Amazon EBS volumes, as mentioned in the following table.

Type	Description
Basic	Metrics are available automatically in five-minute intervals at no charge, which includes data for the root device volumes for EBS-backed instances.
Detailed	The one-minute metrics are automatically sent to CloudWatch by the provisioned IOPS SSD (io1) volumes.

Amazon EBS emits notifications based on Amazon CloudWatch events for a different volume, encryption, and snapshot status changes. You can trigger programmatic actions in response to a change in volume, snapshot, or encryption key state by establishing rules to use CloudWatch Events as JSON objects. For example, you can trigger an AWS Lambda function when a snapshot is created to share the completed snapshot with a different account or copy it to a different region for disaster-recovery purposes.

Amazon EBS Best Practices

The following tips represent the best practices for getting optimal performance from your EBS volumes in different user scenarios:

- You need to use an EBS-optimized instance because the network traffic will not be competing with the traffic between your instance and your EBS volumes, since the two types of traffic are kept separate on EBS-optimized instances.

- You need to be aware of the relationship between the maximum performance of your EBS volumes, the size and number of I/O operations, and the time it takes for each action to complete. The performance, I/O, and latency factors affect each other, and different applications are more sensitive to one factor or another.

- You need to perform initialization, also called prewarming, after restoring a new EBS volume from a snapshot because there will be a significant increase in latency when you first access each block of data. You need to access each block prior to placing the volume into production to avoid the performance hit.

- Performance may be dropped while the snapshot is in progress for throughput-optimized HDD (st1) or cold HDD (sc1) volumes and excessive amounts of small, random I/O on the volume.

- HDD-backed volumes must maintain a queue length of four or more when performing 1MiB sequential I/O to achieve maximum consistency because the performance is affected when your application isn't sending enough I/O requests, which is monitored by the queue length (the number of pending I/O requests from your application to your volume) and I/O size.

- For HDD volumes, AWS recommends configuring the read-ahead per-block-device setting to 1MiB for workloads that are read-heavy and access the block device through the operating system page cache. This setting can only be used when your workload consists of large, sequential I/Os; otherwise, this setting will degrade the performance.

- You should use a general-purpose SSD (gp2) volume instead of st1 or sc1 volumes when your workload consists mostly of small or random I/Os.

- Consider using a modern Linux kernel with support for indirect descriptors. Linux kernels 3.8 and above or any current-generation EC2 instance has this support.

- You can join multiple gp2, io1, st1, or sc1 volumes together in a RAID 0 configuration to use the available bandwidth for the instance types that will help delivering more I/O throughput than what a single EBS volume can deliver.

- You can analyze and view performance metrics of Amazon EBS and status checks that you can use to monitor the health of your volumes using Amazon CloudWatch.

Amazon Elastic File System

The Amazon Elastic File System (Amazon EFS) provides elastic storage capacity so as you add and remove files, it grows and shrinks automatically, so your applications have the storage when they need it by providing simple, scalable file storage for use with Amazon EC2. EFS manages the entire storage infrastructure by avoiding the complexity of patching, deploying, and maintaining complex file system configurations. The applications and tools that use the Network File System (NFS) version 4 protocol work seamlessly with Amazon EFS. An Amazon EFS file system can be accessed by multiple Amazon EC2 instances at the same time by providing a common data source for workloads and applications running on more than one instance or server.

You pay only for the storage used by your file system with no minimum fee, up-front costs, or setup costs for Amazon EFS, and it offers Standard and Infrequent Access (IA) storage classes. You can store frequently accessed files in the Standard storage class and long-lived, infrequently accessed files in the IA storage class, which is designed for cost-effective storage. EFS stores the data across multiple Availability Zones in an AWS region and can grow to the petabyte scale, drive high levels of throughput, and allow massively parallel access from Amazon EC2 instances to your data. Amazon EFS provides strong data consistency and file locking and uses Portable Operating System Interface (POSIX) permissions. Amazon EFS supports both encryption in transit and encryption at rest, which can be enabled when creating an Amazon EFS file system or when you mount the file system. Amazon EFS is designed to provide two performance modes and two throughput modes:

- The general-purpose performance mode is ideal for the content management systems, home directories, web-serving environments, and general file serving.
- The bursting throughput mode is ideal to scale as your file system grows.

 EXAM TIP   You can mount an Amazon EFS file system on instances in only one VPC at a time.

You need to create one or more mount targets in the Virtual Private Cloud (VPC), which provides an IP address for an NFSv4 endpoint where you can mount an Amazon EFS file system. The file system can be mounted using its Domain Name Service (DNS) name, which resolves to the IP address of the EFS mount target in the same Availability Zone of your EC2 instance. Mount targets need to be created in each Availability Zone of your AWS region. Mount targets are highly available and will fail over to other Availability Zones when the primary Availability Zone is not available. You can use EFS like any other file system after mounting the file system using the mount target. When you connect to your Amazon VPC using AWS Direct Connect, you can mount your Amazon EFS file systems on your on-premises datacenter servers as well. You can migrate your data sets to EFS or back up your on-premises data to EFS.

 EXAM TIP   The IP addresses and DNS for your mount targets in each AZ are static.

Amazon EFS with Amazon EC2

Figure 9-7 shows an example VPC accessing an Amazon EFS file system. Here, EC2 instances in the VPC have file systems mounted.

In the figure, the VPC has three Availability Zones and each has at least one mount target created in it. AWS recommends accessing the file system from a single mount target within the same Availability Zone. As shown in the diagram, one of the Availability Zones has two subnets but with only one mount target in one of the subnets. This setup is created as follows:

- You create your Amazon VPC resources and launch your Amazon EC2 instance.
- You create your Amazon EFS file system.
- You then connect to your Amazon EC2 instance and mount the Amazon EFS file system.

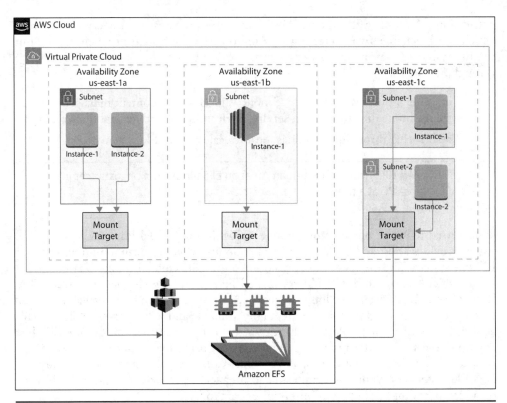

Figure 9-7 VPC access to Amazon EFS file system

Amazon EFS with AWS Direct Connect and VPN

You can mount an Amazon EFS file system on an on-premises server to migrate on-premises data into the AWS cloud hosted in an Amazon EFS file system. You can move data from your on-premises servers into Amazon EFS and analyze it on a fleet of Amazon EC2 instances in your Amazon VPC by taking advantage of bursting. The results can be stored permanently in your file system or can be moved back to your on-premises server. AWS recommends that the on-premises server have a Linux-based operating system and have Linux kernel version 4.0 or later. Also, AWS recommends mounting an Amazon EFS file system on an on-premises server using a mount target IP address instead of a DNS name. There is no extra charge for on-premises access to your Amazon EFS file systems; however, you are charged for the AWS Direct Connect connection to your Amazon VPC. Figure 9-8 shows how to access an Amazon EFS file system from on-premises servers with mounted file systems.

Any mount target can be used from your VPC to reach the mount target's subnet by using an AWS Direct Connect connection between your on-premises server and VPC. To access Amazon EFS from an on-premises server, add a rule to your mount

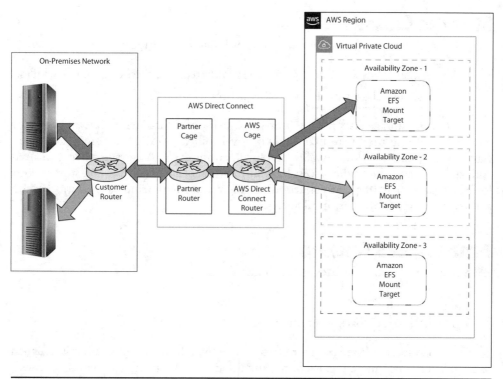

Figure 9-8   Connecting to Amazon EFS with AWS Direct Connect

target security group to allow inbound traffic to the NFS port (2049) from your on-premises server.

Perform the following steps to create this setup:

1. The AWS Direct Connect connection needs to be established between your on-premises datacenter and your Amazon VPC.

2. Create your Amazon EFS file system.

3. Mount the Amazon EFS file system on your on-premises server.

Data Consistency

Amazon EFS provides the close-to-open consistency semantics that applications expect from NFS. When an application performs synchronous write operations, they are durably stored across Availability Zones. Your application closes a file and, depending on the access pattern, Amazon EFS can provide stronger consistency guarantees than close-to-open semantics. Applications that perform synchronous data access and nonappending writes have read-after-write consistency for data access.

Storage Classes

As mentioned, Amazon EFS offers two storage classes for your file systems:

- The IA class is lower-cost storage designed for infrequently accessed, long-lived files.
- The Standard class is used to store frequently accessed files.

The EFS IA storage class reduces storage costs for files that aren't accessed every day without sacrificing the high-durability, high-availability, POSIX file system access and elasticity that EFS provides. AWS recommends using EFS IA storage when you need your full data set to be readily accessible and want to automatically save on storage costs for files that are less frequently accessed to satisfy audit requirements, perform backup and recovery, or perform historical analysis.

Amazon EFS Backup

AWS offers two options for backing up your EFS file systems:

- AWS Backup service
- The EFS-to-EFS backup solution

AWS Backup can be used as a cost-effective way to perform backups, and it is designed to simplify creating, migrating, restoring, and deleting the backups, in addition to providing improved reporting and auditing. The EFS-to-EFS backup solution includes an AWS CloudFormation template that launches, configures, and runs the AWS services required to deploy this solution in all AWS regions. You can perform file system management tasks such as creating and deleting file systems, managing tags, and managing network accessibility like creating and managing mount targets using the Amazon EFS console, the AWS Command Line Interface (AWS CLI), or programmatically. You incur charges for the amount of data in each storage class and are also charged for data access when files in IA storage are read and when files are transitioned to IA storage from Standard storage.

 NOTE You don't incur data access charges when using AWS Backup to back up lifecycle management–enabled EFS file systems.

Amazon EFS Encryption

Amazon EFS supports two forms of encryption for file systems: encryption in transit and encryption at rest. You may need to perform key management for encryption at rest, and Amazon EFS automatically manages the keys for encryption in transit. The data and metadata are encrypted when you create a file system that uses encryption at rest using AWS KMS and a CMK. The CMK can be managed either by AWS or by you directly. The contents of your files are encrypted at rest using the CMK that you specified when you created your file system, and the metadata such as filenames, directory names, and directory contents are encrypted by a key that is managed by Amazon EFS. You can manage your CMKs and the contents of the encrypted file systems using AWS Identity and Access Management (IAM) policies and AWS KMS.

Lifecycle Policy

Amazon EFS Lifecycle Management automatically manages cost-effective file storage for your file systems, and it migrates files that haven't been accessed for a specified period of time to the IA storage class. Using lifecycle policy, you have control to define when EFS transitions files to the IA storage class. A lifecycle policy applies to the entire file system, and you can specify one of four lifecycle policies: AFTER_14_DAYS, AFTER_30_DAYS, AFTER_60_DAYS, or AFTER_90_DAYS

Monitoring Amazon EFS

For any of your AWS solutions, including Amazon EFS, monitoring plays an important role in maintaining the availability, reliability, and performance by collecting the monitoring data from all of the parts of your AWS solution to make debugging a multipoint failure easier when it occurs. As soon as the monitoring is in place, you need to establish a baseline for normal Amazon EFS performance in your environment by measuring performance at various times and under different load conditions. The historical monitoring data will give you a baseline to compare against with current performance data to identify performance anomalies and normal performance patterns and to devise methods to address issues. You can monitor Amazon EFS network throughput, metadata operations, client connections, I/O for read and write, and burst credit balances of your file systems.

You can monitor a single metric over a period that is specified in your Amazon Cloud-Watch alarm, and you can perform actions based on this threshold. AWS CloudTrail logs can be monitored and stored using Amazon CloudWatch logs. You can match events using Amazon CloudWatch events and route them to one or more target functions or streams to make changes, capture state information, and take corrective action. You can share CloudTrail log files between accounts, write log processing applications, and validate that your log files have not changed after delivery, and you can monitor them in real time while sending them to CloudWatch logs.

Amazon EFS Performance

Amazon EFS file systems are distributed across storage servers to grow elastically to a petabyte scale to support massively parallel access from Amazon EC2 instances to your data. The Amazon EFS data is distributed across multiple Availability Zones, providing a high level of durability and availability and to meet the performance needs of the following use cases:

- Amazon EFS provides the high throughput to compute nodes of big data applications coupled with read-after-write consistency and low-latency file operations.

- The video editing, broadcast processing, studio production, rendering, and sound design depend on shared storage to cut the time it takes to perform and consolidate multiple file repositories into one location for all media workflow users.

- The Amazon EFS high-throughput file system is used for content management systems that store and serve information for websites, online publications, archives and access to people across an organization.

Amazon EFS Best Practices

The following are some of the recommended best practices to increase throughput and performance, to reduce latency, and to secure your EFS file system.

- The distributed nature of Amazon EFS results in a small latency overhead for each file operation, so you need to increase the average I/O size to increase the overall throughput.

- You can deliver higher throughput levels on your file system when you aggregate across instances by parallelizing your application across more instances.

- Every operation goes through a round trip between the client and Amazon EFS, and enabling asynchronous writes reduces the latency because the pending write operations are buffered on the Amazon EC2 instance before they are written to Amazon EFS asynchronously.

- Amazon EFS supports the Network File System versions 4.0 and 4.1 (NFSv4) protocols when mounting your file systems on Amazon EC2 instances, and NFSv4.1 provides better performance.

- Choose instance types that have the amount of resources that your application needs when it performs a large number of read and write operations, since it needs more memory or computing capacity.

- Amazon EFS supports two forms of encryption, so choose to enable either or both types so your file system has a minimal effect on I/O latency and throughput.

- You can enable encryption of data at rest when creating an Amazon EFS file system and enable encryption of data in transit when you mount the file system by enabling Transport Layer Security (TLS).

- You need to enforce data encryption policies for Amazon EFS file systems by using Amazon CloudWatch and AWS CloudTrail to detect the creation of a file system and verify that encryption is enabled.

Amazon S3 Glacier

Amazon Simple Storage Service Glacier (S3 Glacier) is a storage service optimized for infrequently used cold data, and it is a very low-cost storage service that provides durable storage with security features for data archiving and backup. Glacier enables customers to store their data cost-effectively for months, years, or even decades. You can offload the administrative burdens like operations and scaling of storage to AWS, which saves you from hardware provisioning, capacity planning, data replication, time-consuming hardware migrations, or hardware failure detection and recovery. In Amazon S3 Glacier, a vault is a container for storing any object like photos, videos, or documents. You can use Amazon S3 lifecycle configuration to transition objects to the Amazon S3 Glacier storage class for archival. Amazon S3 uses Glacier internally for durable storage at a lower cost. Objects remain Amazon S3 objects even when stored in Glacier, but you cannot access them directly through Glacier. Glacier is a REST-based web service, and its data model includes vaults, archives, jobs, and notification configuration resources.

 EXAM TIP You can use the Glacier console to create and delete vaults, but all other interactions with Glacier require that you use the AWS CLI or write code.

Vault

In Glacier, a vault is a container for storing archives. You need to specify a name and AWS region when you create a vault, and each vault resource will have a unique address. The general form is:

```
https://<region-specific endpoint>/<account-id>/vaults/<vaultname>
```

For example, suppose that you create a vault (samplevault) in the US East (N. Virginia) Region, and it can then be addressed as shown:

```
https://glacier.us-east-1.amazonaws.com/444466668888/vaults/samplevault
```

In the URI, glacier.us-east-1.amazonaws.com identifies the US East (N. Virginia) region. The AWS account ID vault is 444466668888, and "vaults" refers to the collection of vaults owned by that AWS account. The specific vault in the vaults collection is "samplevault." Vaults can be created in any supported AWS region, and the vault name must be unique in a particular region, although you can create vaults with the same name in different regions. Based on business or application needs, an unlimited number of archives can be stored in a vault or multiple vaults. Many vault operations, such as creating a vault or listing the vaults, are region specific and you cannot perform those operations from a different region.

Archives

An archive is a base unit of storage in Glacier, which can be any data item such as a photo, video, or document. Glacier assigns the archive an ID and description, which you can specify only during the upload of an archive. Each archive has a unique address. The general form is as follows:

```
https://<region-specific endpoint>/<account-id>/vaults/<vault-name>/
archives/<archive-id>
```

Following is an example URI of an archive stored in the samplevault vault in the US East (N. Virginia) region:

```
https://glacier.us-east-1.amazonaws.com/444466668888/vaults/samplevault/
archives/NkeSAMPLEArchiveId
```

Jobs

You can use Glacier jobs to retrieve an archive, perform a select query on an archive, or get an inventory of a vault. When performing a query on an archive, you initiate a job providing a SQL query and a list of Glacier archive objects. You can use Glacier Select to run the query in place and can write the output results to Amazon S3. Retrieving an archive and vault inventory (list of archives) are asynchronous operations in Glacier in which you first initiate a job and then download the job output after Glacier completes it. You need to provide a vault name to initiate a vault inventory job. Select and archive retrieval jobs require the vault name, archive ID, and job description to help identify the jobs. You can run multiple jobs in a vault at any point in time, and each job is uniquely identified as follows:

```
https://<region-specific endpoint>/<account-id>/vaults/<vault-name>/
jobs/<job-id>
```

The following is an example of a job associated with the samplevault vault:

```
https://glacier.us-east-1.amazonaws.com/444466668888/vaults/samplevault/jobs/
QVyh7vSAMPLEjobID
```

Glacier maintains information such as job type, description, creation date, completion date, and job status for each job. The information about a particular job or list of jobs can be obtained from a vault. The list of jobs that Glacier returns includes all the in-progress and recently finished jobs.

 EXAM TIP Glacier is a cold storage system that you can use as a data archival solution at a very low cost. If you need a storage system that requires real-time data retrieval, you should use Amazon S3.

Notification Configuration

Glacier uses the Amazon Simple Notification Service (Amazon SNS) to send a notification when a job is complete. An SNS topic can be specified for each vault in the notification configuration, and it is stored as a JSON document. The following is an example vault notification configuration:

```
{
    "Topic": "arn:aws:sns:us-east-1:444466668888:mytopic",
    "Events": ["ArchiveRetrievalCompleted", "InventoryRetrievalCompleted"]
}
```

The vault notification configuration resource is uniquely identified by a URI in the form:

```
https://<region-specific endpoint>/<account-id>/
vaults/<vault-name>/notification-configuration
```

You can use notification configurations for set, get, and delete operations.

Glacier Operations

The following asynchronous operations can be used to work with vaults and archives:

- Retrieving an archive
- Retrieving a vault inventory (list of archives)

You need to first initiate a job and then download the job output. A Glacier job can be initiated to perform a select query on an archive, retrieve an archive, or get an inventory of a vault. The following are the types of Glacier jobs:

- **Select** Performs a select query on any archive.
- **archive-retrieval** Retrieves an item from an archive.
- **inventory-retrieval** Retrieves the inventory from a vault.

Vaults can be created in a specific AWS region and send your requests to a region-specific endpoint.

 EXAM TIP Glacier provides a management console, and you can use it to create and delete vaults. However, you need to use the AWS CLI or write the code to make requests, using either the REST API directly or by using the AWS SDKs for all other interactions with Glacier.

Creating and Deleting Vaults

You can create up to 1,000 vaults per region, and you can delete a vault only if there are no archives in it and no writes to the vault since the last inventory.

 CAUTION Glacier prepares an inventory for each vault periodically every 24 hours, so the inventory might not reflect the latest information. Glacier ensures the vault is empty by checking whether there have been any write operations from the time of the last vault inventory.

You can use application programming interface (API) calls to retrieve vault information such as the vault creation date, number of archives in the vault, and the total size of all the archives in the Glacier vault in a specific region in your account. You can download a vault inventory that provides archive information such as the archive ID, creation date, and size. Glacier updates the vault inventory approximately once a day, and the vault inventory must exist for you to be able to download it. You need to initiate a job (POST jobs) to retrieve anything from Glacier, and then you can download the output (GET output) when the job completes using Glacier notifications.

 TIP If you have a restricted retrieval policy, your retrieval job request may fail with a PolicyEnforcedException exception.

The status of the job can be determined by job completion notification, or you can explicitly request a describe job operation (Describe Job (GET JobID)). As mentioned, an Amazon S3 Glacier vault can be deleted only when there are no archives in the vault since the last inventory and no writes to the vault from the time of the last inventory.

Archive Operations

You can use Glacier to upload, download, and delete archives. Archives can be uploaded in a single operation, or you can upload them in parts using API calls. When you initiate a job to download a specific archive, Glacier prepares the archive for download; after the job completes, you can download your archive data, which is an asynchronous operation. You can use API calls to delete archives. You cannot update the archive content or its description after the upload. The only way to update is by deleting the archive and uploading another archive. Glacier returns a unique archive ID each time you upload an archive.

You can make an Expedited, Standard, or Bulk retrieval by setting the Tier parameter in the Initiate Job (POST jobs) REST API request, or in the AWS CLI or AWS SDKs Choose from the following options when initiating a job to retrieve an archive based on your access time and cost requirements:

- **Expedited** Allows you to quickly access your data typically within one to five minutes. The retrieval capacity is based on the provisioned capacity for Expedited retrievals.

- **Standard** Allows you to access any of your archives within 3 to 5 hours, which is the default option for retrieval requests that do not specify any retrieval option.

- **Bulk** Allows you to retrieve large amounts of data inexpensively in a day and takes 5 to12 hours to complete.

You need to have Provisioned capacity to ensure the retrieval capacity for expedited retrievals is available when you need it, and each unit of capacity provides up to 150 MB/s of retrieval throughput. You can specify a range or portion of the archive to retrieve when you retrieve an archive from Glacier; the default is to retrieve the entire archive. You can use Glacier Select to perform filtering operations using simple Structured Query Language (SQL) statements directly on your data in Glacier. Glacier Select runs the SQL query in place and writes the output results to Amazon S3.

Data Retrieval Policy

There are three types of Glacier data retrieval policies: No Retrieval Limit, Free Tier Only, and Max Retrieval Rate. No Retrieval Limit is the default policy, and when used, no retrieval limit is set and all valid data retrieval requests are accepted. The Free Tier Only policy can be used to keep your retrievals within your daily Free Tier allowance and not incur any additional cost. The Max Retrieval Rate policy enables the peak retrieval rate from all retrieval jobs across your account in a region, and it will not exceed the bytes-per-hour limit you set. The data retrieval policy can be viewed by using the Glacier REST API or by using the AWS software development kits (SDKs).

Vault Lock

The compliance controls can be enforced by using a Glacier Vault Lock policy, such as write once read many (WORM), and lock the policy against future edits. The policy can no longer be changed once it is locked. A vault access policy is different from a vault lock policy, and both govern access controls to your vault. The vault lock policy is used to prevent future changes by providing strong enforcement for your compliance controls. The vault lock policy is used to deploy regulatory and compliance controls, and the vault access policy is used to implement access controls that are not temporary or compliance related and are subject to frequent modification. Both policies can be used together, for example, to implement time-based data retention rules in the vault lock policy to deny deletes and grant read access to third parties or your business partners. The lock is initiated when attaching a vault lock policy to your vault that sets the lock to an in-progress state and returns a lock ID, and you can validate your vault lock policy within 24 hours before the lock ID expires. The lock ID is used to complete the lock process. You can abort the lock and restart from the beginning if the vault lock policy doesn't work as expected.

Data Protection

Amazon S3 Glacier delivers 99.999999999 percent durability and provides comprehensive security and compliance capabilities to help you meet stringent regulatory requirements by synchronously storing your data across multiple Availability Zones. You can protect your data using Secure Sockets Layer (SSL) or client-side encryption while in transit while traveling to and from Amazon S3 Glacier and at rest when it is stored in AWS datacenters. You can use Amazon S3 lifecycle configuration on an Amazon S3 bucket to transition objects to the Amazon S3 Glacier storage class for archival. The data in transit between Amazon S3 and Glacier via lifecycle policies is encrypted using SSL, and the data stored at rest in Glacier is automatically encrypted using either server-side encryption or client-side encryption. AWS recommends TLS 1.2 or later. You must sign requests using an access key ID and a secret access key, or use the AWS Security Token Service (AWS STS) to generate temporary security credentials to sign requests.

Logging and Monitoring

Monitoring is an important part of maintaining the reliability, availability, and performance of Amazon S3 Glacier, and you should collect monitoring data to easily identify and debug the source of a failure when it occurs. Amazon CloudWatch alarms can be used to watch a single metric over a time period that you specify. A notification is sent to an Amazon SNS topic or AWS Auto Scaling policy when the metric exceeds a given threshold. CloudTrail captures the API calls from the Glacier console and code calls to the Glacier APIs as events. You can use Trusted Advisor to get the best practices learned from many AWS customers, and it inspects your AWS environment and makes appropriate recommendations to improve system availability and performance, to save money, and to help close security gaps. The third-party auditors, as part of multiple AWS compliance programs, access the security and compliance of Amazon S3 Glacier, including

- Health Insurance Portability and Accountability Act (HIPAA)
- System and Organization Controls (SOC)
- Federal Risk and Authorization Management Program (FedRAMP)
- Payment Card Industry (PCI) Data Security Standard

The third-party audit reports are available in AWS Artifact for download. You can use AWS Config to assess how well your resource configurations comply with industry guidelines, internal practices, and regulations. You can use AWS Security Hub to get a comprehensive view of your security state within AWS, which can help you comply with the security, industry standards, and best practices.

Chapter Review

This chapter explained Amazon Elastic Block Store, Amazon Elastic File System, and Amazon S3 Glacier in detail. Amazon EBS provides block level storage volumes, which behave like raw, unformatted block devices and are used for EC2 instances, and you pay only for what you use. You can create an Amazon EBS volume in the same Availability Zone where you want to attach it to an EC2 instance as an encrypted EBS volume, but it can only be attached to selected instance types. An Amazon EBS volume can be detached from an instance explicitly or when you terminate the instance. You need to unmount the volume from the instance if the instance is running. Before you can detach the volume, you need to stop the instance if an EBS volume is the root device of an instance. You can delete an Amazon EBS volume if you no longer need it. After deleting the volume, its data is not available, nor can it be attached to any instance. You can create backups of your Amazon EBS volumes using snapshots, which are redundantly stored in multiple Availability Zones in Amazon S3. You can take snapshots even when the volume does not need to be attached to a running instance. Multivolume snapshots can be taken across multiple EBS volumes attached to an EC2 instance, which allows you to take exact point-in-time, crash-consistent, and data-coordinated snapshots. You can copy Amazon EBS snapshots from one AWS region to another or within the same region, and the data in transit uses Amazon S3 server-side encryption (256-bit AES). Amazon DLM can be used to automate the creation, retention, and deletion of snapshots taken to back up your Amazon EBS volumes. You can analyze and view performance metrics for Amazon EBS and status checks that you can use to monitor the health of your volumes using Amazon CloudWatch.

Amazon EFS provides elastic storage capacity, so as you add and remove files, it grows and shrinks automatically—thus, your applications have the storage when they need it by providing simple, scalable file storage for use with Amazon EC2. You can mount an Amazon EFS file system on an on-premises server to migrate on-premises data into the AWS cloud. Amazon EFS provides close-to-open consistency semantics that applications expect from NFS. When an application performs a synchronous write operation, these operations are durably stored across Availability Zones. Amazon EFS offers two storage classes for your file systems. The IA class is a lower-cost storage system designed for infrequently accessed, long-lived files, and the Standard class is used to store frequently accessed files. Amazon EFS supports two forms of encryption for file systems: encryption in transit and encryption at rest. You may need to perform key management for encryption at rest, and Amazon EFS automatically manages the keys for encryption in transit. Amazon EFS file systems are distributed across storage servers to grow elastically to the petabyte scale to allow massively parallel access from Amazon EC2 instances to your data.

Amazon Simple Storage Service Glacier is a storage service optimized for infrequently used cold data, and it is a very low-cost storage service that provides durable storage with security features for data archiving and backup. Glacier enables customers to store their data cost-effectively for months, years, or even decades. In Glacier, a vault is a container for storing archives. You need to specify a name and AWS region when you create the vault, and each vault resource will have a unique address. An archive is a base unit of storage in Glacier, which can be any data such as a photo, video, or document. You can use Glacier jobs to retrieve an archive, perform a select query on an archive, or get an inventory of a vault. When performing a query on an archive, you initiate a job providing a SQL query and list of Glacier archive objects. Glacier uses Amazon SNS to send a notification when a job is complete. The SNS topic can be specified for each vault in the notification configuration, and it is stored as a JSON document. There are three types of Glacier data retrieval policies: No Retrieval Limit, Free Tier Only, and Max Retrieval Rate. The compliance controls can be enforced by using a Glacier Vault Lock policy such as WORM and lock the policy from future edits. Monitoring is an important part of maintaining the reliability, availability, and performance of Amazon S3 Glacier, and you should collect monitoring data to easily identify and debug the source of a failure when it occurs.

Exercises

The following exercises will help you practice using Amazon EBS, EFS, and Glacier to perform various tasks.

You need to create an AWS account, as explained earlier, to perform the following exercises. You can use the Free Tier when launching AWS resources, but make sure to terminate them when you are done.

Exercise 9-1: Create a New EBS Volume Using the Console

In this exercise, the step-by-step instructions will help you create a new EBS volume using the AWS Management Console.

1. Log in to your AWS account and open the Amazon EC2 console at https://console .aws.amazon.com/ec2/.

2. From the top right side of the navigation bar, select the region where you would like to create your volume.

3. In the navigation pane on the left, choose Amazon Elastic Block Store and then Volumes.

4. Choose Create Volume From Here.

5. Choose a volume type.

6. For the Size (GiB) field, type **5** GiB for the volume

7. Choose the Provisioned IOPS SSD volume, and type **250** for the maximum number of IOPS.

8. Choose us-east-1a for the Availability Zone.

9. Select the Encrypted box and choose aws/ebs (the default) for the Master Key.

10. Choose Tag, type **key** for the Name and **My first EBS volume** for the Volume.

11. Choose Create Volume.

Exercise 9-2: Create an EBS Volume from a Snapshot Using the Console

1. In this exercise, the step-by-step instructions will assist you in creating an EBS volume from the backup snapshot using the AWS Management Console. Log in to your AWS account and open the Amazon EC2 console at https://console.aws .amazon.com/ec2/.

2. From the top right side of navigation bar, select the region where you would like to create your volume.

3. In the left navigation pane, choose Elastic Block Store and then Volumes.

4. Choose Create Volume.

5. Choose a volume type.

6. Start typing the ID or description of the snapshot from which you are restoring the volume, and choose it from the dropdown list of suggestions.

7. Select Encrypt This Volume to change the encryption of your new volume.

8. For the Size (GiB) field, type **5**.

9. Choose us-east-1a for the Availability Zone.

10. Choose Add Tags and type **Name** for the Key and **My second EBS volume** for the Value.

11. Choose Create Volume.

Exercise 9-3: Attach an EBS Volume to an Instance Using the Console

In this exercise, the step-by-step instructions will assist you in attaching the new EBS volume to your existing Amazon EC2 instance using the AWS Management Console.

1. Log in to your AWS account and open the Amazon EC2 console at https://console .aws.amazon.com/ec2/.

2. From the top right side of navigation bar, select the region where you would like to create your volume.

3. In the left navigation pane, choose Elastic Block Store and then Volumes.

4. Select a volume from the list of available volumes and choose Actions and then Attach Volume.

5. Start typing the name or ID of the instance and select it from the dropdown list.

6. For Device, type **/dev/sdf1**.

7. Choose Attach.

8. Now you can connect to your instance and mount the volume.

Exercise 9-4: Detach an EBS Volume Using the Console

In this exercise, the step-by-step instructions will help you detach the EBS volume from your existing Amazon EC2 instance using the AWS Management Console.

1. You can use the following command to unmount the /dev/sdf1 device:

```
[ec2-user ~]$ umount -d /dev/sdf1
```

2. Log in to your AWS account and open the Amazon EC2 console at https://console .aws.amazon.com/ec2/.

3. From the top right side of navigation bar, select the region where you would like to create your volume.

4. From the left navigation pane, choose Elastic Block Store and then Volumes.

5. Select a volume you want to detach and choose Actions, and then Detach Volume.

6. In the confirmation dialog box, choose Yes.

Exercise 9-5: Delete an EBS Volume Using the Console

In this exercise, the step-by-step instructions will assist you in deleting your EBS volume using the AWS Management Console.

1. Log in to your AWS account and open the Amazon EC2 console at https://console .aws.amazon.com/ec2/.

2. From the top right side of navigation bar, select the region where you would like to delete your volume.

3. In the left navigation pane, choose Elastic Block Store and then Volumes.

4. Select a volume from the list of available volumes and choose Actions and then Delete Volume.

5. In the confirmation dialog box, choose Yes, Delete.

Exercise 9-6: Create a Snapshot Using the Console

In this exercise, the step-by-step instructions will show you how to take an EBS volume backup snapshot using the AWS Management Console.

1. Log in to your AWS account and open the Amazon EC2 console at https://console .aws.amazon.com/ec2/.

2. From the top right side of navigation bar, select the region where you would like to create your snapshot.

3. In the left navigation pane, choose Elastic Block Store and then Snapshots.

4. Choose Create Snapshot.

5. From Select Resource Type, choose Volume and enter a description of the snapshot.

6. Choose Add Tags and type **Name** for the key and **My EBS snapshot** for the value.

7. Choose Create Snapshot.

Exercise 9-7: Delete a Snapshot Using the Console

In this exercise, the step-by-step instructions will help you delete your EBS volume snapshot using the AWS Management Console.

1. Log in to your AWS account and open the Amazon EC2 console at https://console .aws.amazon.com/ec2/.

2. From the top right side of navigation bar, select the region where you would like to delete your volume.

3. From the left navigation pane, choose Elastic Block Store and then Snapshots.

4. Select a snapshot from the list of available snapshots and then choose Delete from the Actions list.

5. Choose Yes, Delete.

Questions

The following questions will help you gauge your understanding of the material in this chapter. Read all the answers carefully because there might be more than one correct answer. Choose the best response for each question.

1. Which of the following Amazon EBS volume types provide single-digit milliseconds latency between EC2 instances and EBS?

   A. Provisioned IOPS SSD (io1)

   B. General-Purpose SSD (gp2)

   C. Throughput-Optimized HDD (st1)

   D. Cold HDD (sc1)

2. You need to keep EBS volumes intact even if the EC2 instance where your EBS volume is attached is terminated. How can you prevent the deletion of the EBS volume during EC2 instance termination?

A. Change the DeleteOnTermination flag to false

B. Change the RemoveOnTermination flag to false

C. Change the DeleteOnTermination flag to true

D. Change the TerminateOnDeletion flag to false

3. You are working with the development team to migrate the application and database to the cloud. The application team needs a secure encrypted database storage option to migrate the database to an EC2 instance. What AWS storage option would you recommend?

A. Amazon S3 with client-side encryption

B. Amazon EBS with encryption

C. Amazon EFS

D. AWS Snowball

4. Your DevOps team stopped all their sandbox Amazon EC2 instances to save costs, but they are still incurring charges for Amazon EBS storage. They want to know how to stop EBS charges accruing for stopped instances that they are not using. Which statement about EBS volumes is true?

A. The DevOps team will be charged for the EBS volume and instance only when the instance is running.

B. The DevOps team will be charged for the EBS volume even if the instance is stopped since it's measured in gigabyte-months.

C. The DevOps team will be charged only for the instance's running cost.

D. The DevOps team will not be charged for the EBS volume if the instance is stopped.

5. Your performance testing team is complaining about inadequate storage, and they want an additional EBS volume attached to instance-B. The DevOps team tries to attach an underutilized volume, which is attached to another running instance-A in the same Availability Zone to instance-B but is getting an error. How can the underutilized EBS volume attached to a running instance (instance-A) be attached to a new running instance (instance-B)?

A. You need to terminate the instance-A, and only then it can be attached to the instance-B.

B. You can attach the volume as read only to instance-B.

C. You need to detach the volume from instance-A and then attach it to instance-B.

D. You don't need to detach from instance-A. You can just select the volume and attach it to the instance-B, because mapping will be done internally.

6. An EC2 instance uses an EBS-backed root volume and an instance store (i.e., ephemeral store) volume for temporary processes. Can you stop this EC2 instance and, if so, what happens to the data on any ephemeral store volumes when it is started?

   A. The instance can't be stopped, and the ephemeral data is automatically saved in an EBS volume.

   B. The instance can be stopped, and the ephemeral data is unavailable until the instance is restarted.

   C. The instance can be stopped, and the ephemeral data will be deleted and will no longer be accessible.

   D. The instance can't be stopped, and the ephemeral data is automatically saved as an EBS snapshot.

7. Your application team is looking for file storage for use with Amazon EC2 that provides strong consistency, file locking, and is concurrently accessible by thousands of other Amazon EC2 instances. Which cloud storage service supports the required storage workload?

   A. Amazon EBS, which is block-level storage and can be used with Amazon EC2

   B. Amazon S3, which provides object storage and can be accessed anywhere

   C. Amazon EFS, which provides a file system interface that can be used with Amazon EC2

   D. Amazon S3 Glacier, which provides extremely low-cost storage for data archival and backup

8. Your management team has asked to you to find a strategy that saves costs on backing up files that are not accessed every day. Your cloud architect informed you that the EFS IA storage class could save up to 85 percent of the EFS Standard class. What can you do to move infrequently accessed files to another storage class and save costs?

   A. Enable the S3 Lifecycle Management policy to move the infrequently accessed files to Amazon S3 Glacier.

   B. Enable EFS Lifecycle Management and choose an age-off policy to move the files to EFS IA, which automatically moves your data to the EFS IA storage class based on the lifecycle policy.

   C. Set up a daily job to move infrequently accessed files to the EFS IA storage class.

   D. Delete the old files that are no longer required and move the infrequently accessed files to EBS storage to save costs.

9. As part of cost optimization, you have identified huge chunks of old files in tapes and other old storage media that may not be required in the future unless there is a compliance issue. You want to save those files in a cost-effective way. What is the best possible solution that saves costs for the archival storage?

   A. Amazon EFS

   B. Amazon S3

   C. Amazon EBS

   D. Amazon S3 Glacier

10. You are planning an archival strategy for your company to store all infrequently accessed data in Amazon S3 Glacier. You want to know the maximum limit, minimum limit, and size of an individual archival file to plan this efficiently. Which of the following statements is true?

   A. Maximum 5 terabytes, no minimum, individual archive 1 byte to 4 terabytes.

   B. No maximum, minimum 5 terabytes, individual archive 1 byte to 14 terabytes

   C. No maximum, no minimum, individual archive 1 byte to 40 terabytes

   D. Maximum 999 terabytes, minimum 1 byte, individual archive 1 byte to 44 terabytes

Answers

1. **A.** The Provisioned IOPS SSD (io1) helps you achieve an average of single-digit millisecond latency between EC2 instances and EBS.

2. **A.** By changing the DeleteOnTermination flag to false, you can prevent the deletion of the EBS volume during EC2 instance termination.

3. **B.** Amazon EBS with encryption will help the application team secure database storage in the cloud.

4. **B.** The DevOps team will be charged for the EBS volume even if the instance is stopped, since it's measured in gigabyte-months.

5. **C.** You need to detach the volume from instance-A and then attach it to instance-B.

6. **C.** The instance can be stopped, and the ephemeral data will be deleted and will no longer be accessible.

7. **C.** Use Amazon EFS, which provides a file system interface that can be used with Amazon EC2.

8. **B.** Enable EFS Lifecycle Management and choose an age-off policy to move the files to EFS IA, which automatically moves your data to the EFS IA storage class based on the lifecycle policy.

9. **D.** Amazon S3 Glacier is the best possible solution for the archival storage to save those files in a cost-effective way.

10. **C.** There is no maximum or minimum limit, and the individual archive is from 1 byte to 40 terabytes.

Additional Resources

- **AWS Reference** There is no place like official AWS documentation to get the latest and most up-to-date information about all the AWS services. Always refer to the official AWS blogs to get the latest updates about new AWS services and updates to existing features.
  Amazon EBS- `https://docs.aws.amazon.com/AWSEC2/latest/UserGuide/AmazonEBS.html`, Amazon EFS- `https://docs.aws.amazon.com/AWSEC2/latest/UserGuide/AmazonEFS.html`, Amazon S3 Glacier- `https://docs.aws.amazon.com/glacier/` and `https://aws.amazon.com/blogs/aws`

- **Data Archival Using PowerShell** This blog explains detailed steps to migrate large amounts of data to Amazon S3 Glacier using the AWS PowerShell.
  `https://aws.amazon.com/blogs/developer/archiving-data-to-amazon-s3-glacier-using-powershell/`

- **Automating Amazon EBS Snapshots** This blog explains the detailed steps to automate Amazon EBS snapshots with Amazon CloudWatch events, Amazon Lambda, and AWS Step Functions using AWS CLI.
  `https://aws.amazon.com/blogs/compute/automating-amazon-ebs-snapshot-management-with-aws-step-functions-and-amazon-cloudwatch-events/`

- **Recovering Files from an Amazon EBS** This blog shows how to restore an EBS snapshot volume, attach an EBS volume to an EC2 instance, and copy the files to be recovered.
  `https://aws.amazon.com/blogs/compute/recovering-files-from-an-amazon-ebs-volume-backup/`

- **Consistent Snapshots of Your Multiple Amazon EBS Volumes** This blog explains how to create crash-consistent snapshots across all the EBS volumes attached to an EC2 instance using the AWS Command Line Interface and console and automate snapshot management using Amazon DLM.
  `https://aws.amazon.com/blogs/storage/taking-crash-consistent-snapshots-across-multiple-amazon-ebs-volumes-on-an-amazon-ec2-instance/`

- **Data Protection Using AWS Backup** This blog explains the steps to create and maintain backup schedules and monitor AWS Backup jobs.
  `https://aws.amazon.com/blogs/storage/protecting-your-data-with-aws-backup/`

PART IV

Authentication and Authorization

- **Chapter 10**   Securing AWS Resources with Identity and Access Management
- **Chapter 11**   Web Identity Federation and Amazon Cognito for User Authentication
- **Chapter 12**   Protecting Your Data Using Server-Side and Client-Side Encryption

Securing AWS Resources with Identity and Access Management

In this chapter, you will learn
- Identity Access Management
- Create individual users
- Manage permissions with groups
- IAM roles for users and AWS services
- Configure a strong password policy
- Enable MFA for privileged users
- Policies and permissions
- IAM best practices

AWS Identity and Access Management (IAM) helps you manage access to all of your AWS services and resources securely. Also with IAM, you can create and manage AWS users and groups, and use permissions to allow and deny their access to AWS resources.

Identity and Access Management

AWS IAM is used to control who is signed in (i.e., authenticated) and has permissions (i.e., authorized) to use resources. You normally use single sign-in in an enterprise environment that has complete access to all services and resources in order to avoid multiple sign-in. AWS recommends not using the root user for your everyday tasks, even for administrative tasks. The best practice of using the root user is only to create your first IAM user. You then need to securely lock away the root user credentials and use them only to perform a few account and service management tasks.

Access can be granted to others to administer and use resources in your AWS account without having to share your password or access key. Various permissions can be granted to different people for different resources. You will be able to allow your admin users complete access to Amazon EC2, Amazon S3, Amazon DynamoDB, Amazon Redshift, and other AWS services. You will be able to allow read-only access to your audit users to just some of your S3 buckets, or grant permission to administer just some EC2 instances, or to access your billing information. IAM features can be used to securely provide credentials for applications that run on EC2 instances, and it provide permissions for your application to access other AWS resources like S3 buckets and DynamoDB tables. Multifactor authentication (MFA) can be added to individual users for extra security and to your account. You must provide both a code from a configured device and a password or access key to make MFA work. Users who already have passwords in their corporate network or with an Internet identity provider to get temporary access to your AWS account can be allowed. AWS CloudTrail can be used to receive log records that include information about everyone who made requests for all the resources in your account. Figure 10-1 illustrates an overview of User, Group, Role, and Permissions.

IAM is eventual consistent, like many other AWS services, and you can use the AWS command-line tools to issue commands at your system's command line to perform IAM and AWS tasks. The command-line tools are useful for building scripts and performing

Figure 10-1
User, Group, Role, and Permissions

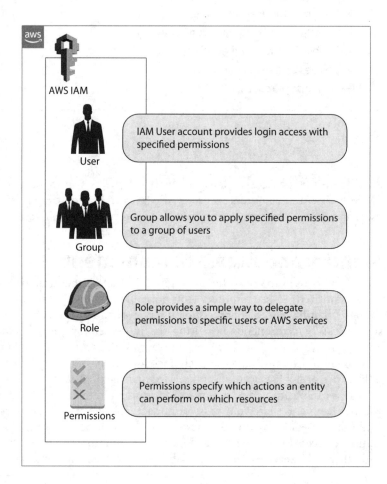

various AWS tasks, and using the command line is faster and more convenient than using the console. AWS provides AWS CLI, PowerShell, and SDKs that consist of libraries and sample code for various programming languages (Java, Python, Ruby, .NET, etc.) and platforms (iOS, Android, etc.). You can access IAM and AWS programmatically by using the IAM HTTPS API, which lets you issue HTTPS requests directly to the service.

- **Identities** are users, groups, and roles that allow you to attach a policy and are used to identify and group resource objects.
- **Entities** are IAM resource objects, such as users and roles, that are used by AWS for authentication. IAM users or users federated through a web identity or Security Assertion Markup Language (SAML) can assume roles from your account or another account.
- **Principal** is an IAM entity or a root user that makes requests to AWS.

EXAM TIP As a best practice, you should create users and roles, and you can create federated users or programmatic access to allow an application to access your account.

- **Requests** These are used by AWS to evaluate and authorize and can be carried out from the AWS Management Console, the AWS API, or the AWS CLI when the principal is sending a request to AWS.
- **Authentication** A principal (root user) or any other IAM user must use their e-mail address and password to sign in to AWS to get authenticated; in addition, the IAM user needs to provide the account ID or its alias. An access key and secret key must be provided for API or AWS CLI authentication.

EXAM TIP As a best practice and for additional security, AWS recommends enabling MFA in order to increase the security of your account.

- **Authorization** In order to allow your request, AWS checks the authorization policies to determine whether to allow or deny the request. The policies are in JSON format and contain allowed permissions for the users or roles. You need to use resource-based policies to grant cross-account access.
- **Operations** These define what you can do to any AWS resource, for example, view or list, create, update, and delete an AWS resource after it has been authenticated and authorized.
- **Resources** This is an object that exists within a service and determines a set of operations that can be performed on the resource.

Users

An AWS user is an entity consists of names and credentials that you create in AWS to represent a person or an application that uses it to interact with AWS. An IAM User in AWS consists of a username and credentials. An AWS root user and IAM user with administrator permissions are not the same as the AWS account root user. An Amazon Resource Name (ARN) (e.g., arn:aws:iam::123456789876:user/Mike) is assigned to the user and is used to uniquely identify him or her. An ARN is used to specify the user as a principal in an IAM policy. When you create a user, IAM uses the name that you specified for it. ARN can uniquely identify users across all of AWS, and a unique identifier is used only when you use the API, PowerShell, or AWS CLI, which will not be visible in the console.

Users and Credentials

AWS can be accessed in various ways, depending on the user credentials:

- **User ID and password**   You need a user-id and password to sign in to the AWS Management Console and an account number or alias if you are not the root user.

- **Access keys**   These can be assigned to a user for programmatic access, which consists of an access key ID and a secret access key.

- **SSH keys**   These can be used to authenticate with CodeCommit, which is in the OpenSSH format.

- **Server certificates**   You can use SSL/TLS certificates to authenticate with some AWS services.

 EXAM TIP   AWS recommends using the AWS Certificate Manager (ACM) to provision, manage, and deploy your server certificates. IAM can be used only when you must support HTTPS connections in a region that is not supported by ACM.

When you create a new IAM user using the AWS CLI or AWS API, the user will not have any credentials, and you must create these based on your user's needs. You need to set a policy to enforce a minimum password complexity. You can create and update access keys for programmatic access to the resources in your account. You can enable MFA to enhance the security of the user's credentials. Users must provide what they know (a password or access key) and what they have (a code from a hardware or software device like a smartphone or tablet).

You need to remove passwords and access keys when users no longer need them as a security best practice. Credential reports can be generated and downloaded to your account that list all IAM users with the status of their various credentials, including passwords, access keys, and MFA devices. You assign permissions individually to each IAM user to limit permissions to just the tasks and resources required for the job. You can use a permissions boundary to limit the maximum permissions that can be granted to a user or role. An IAM user can only be associated with only one AWS account, and any AWS activity performed by users is billed to your account. You can create up to 5,000 IAM users in an AWS account. An IAM user can be a person or an application that uses its credentials to make AWS requests, which is called a service account.

Password: Configure a Strong Password Policy

You need a password to access the AWS Management Console, but the AWS CLI or PowerShell or the AWS SDKs or APIs do not need passwords. The complexity requirements and mandatory rotation periods can be specified as a password policy on your AWS account. A password policy can be used to do the following:

- Set a minimum password length.
- Request specific character types like lowercase letters, uppercase letters, numbers, and non-alphanumeric characters.

 TIP   Passwords are case sensitive.

- Allow all IAM users to change their own passwords after a specified period of time by enabling password expiration.
- Prevent IAM users from reusing previous passwords.

The password policy settings force users to change their passwords when logging in for the first time. However, some of the settings are enforced immediately.

Multifactor Authentication

AWS recommends configuring MFA for increased security to protect your AWS resources. MFA can be enabled for IAM users or the root user. You can use any of the following methods to configure MFA:

- **Virtual MFA**   This is a software application that runs on a phone or tablet device and emulates a physical device. A six-digit numeric code is generated by the device based on a time-synchronized, one-time password algorithm. The user must type a valid code from the device on a second web page during sign-in, and every user must have unique virtual MFA device.

- **U2F security key**   This is a device that can be plugged to your USB port and uses the open authentication standard hosted by the FIDO (Fast Identity Online) Alliance. Instead of manually entering a code, you can sign in by entering your credentials and then tapping the device when you enable the U2F security key.

- **Hardware MFA device** This device will generate a six-digit numeric code based on a time-synchronized, one-time password algorithm. The user must type a valid code from the device on a second web page during sign-in. Each MFA device assigned to a user must be unique, and you cannot type a code from another user's device to be authenticated.

- **SMS-based MFA** AWS sends a six-digit code using a SMS text message to your mobile device when you try to sign in. The user is required to type that code on a second web page during sign-in. SMS-based MFA is not available for the AWS account root user and is enabled only for other IAM users.

CAUTION AWS will soon end support for SMS MFA. So AWS recommends you switch to a virtual (software-based) MFA device, hardware MFA device, or U2F security key.

Groups

Groups is a collection of IAM users that lets you specify permissions for multiple users. Any users who are assigned to a group automatically inherit the group permissions, which makes it easier to manage the permissions from one place. When any new user joins your organization, you can assign the appropriate permissions by adding the user to an existing group, and when a user leaves your organization, you can just remove the user from that group. Similarly, when a person changes job roles in your organization, instead of editing that user's permissions, you can remove the user from the old groups and add the user to the appropriate new groups. A group consists of many users, and a user can be part of multiple groups. Nesting is now allowed in Groups so they can include only users, but not other groups. AWS does not provide a default group that all users are automatically a part of. You need to create a group explicitly and assign appropriate users to it.

EXAM TIP IAM Groups is not truly an identity because it cannot be identified as a Principal in a permission policy. This helps you attach policies to multiple users at one time and manage them easily.

Figure 10-2 shows a simple example of a small company. The company owner creates an Administrator group (Lisa, John, and Zoey) for users to create and manage other users as the company grows. The Administrator group creates a Developers group (James, Emily, DevApp1, and so on) and a Test group (George, Claire, TestApp1, and so on). Each of these groups consists of users that interact with AWS. Each user will have their own individual security credentials, and they belong to a single group. However, the users can belong to multiple groups as well.

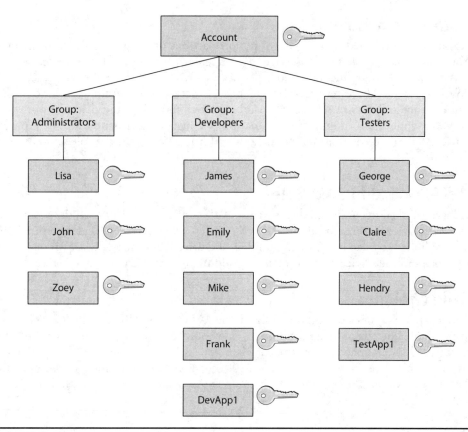

Figure 10-2 Groups

IAM Roles

You can create an IAM role in your account, similar to an IAM user that has specific permissions that define what the identity (role) can and cannot do in AWS. You can assume a role if required, and it's not associated with one person. A role provides you with temporary security credentials for your session, but it does not have a password or access keys associated with it. Roles can be used to delegate access to services, applications, or users that do not have access to your AWS resources. You can grant users in your AWS account access to resources, or grant users from one AWS account access to resources in another account. You can use roles when you want to allow a mobile application to use AWS resources without embedding AWS keys or credentials within the application because it will be difficult to rotate keys, and also it has the potential risk of extracting them from the code. IAM Role can also be used to give access to AWS resources to your corporate users or to third parties.

AWS Service Role

A role can be assumed by a service to perform actions on your behalf in your account. You must define a role for the service to assume when you set up the AWS service, and this service role must include all the permissions required for the service to access the AWS resources. These service roles can provide access only within your account and not to other accounts. A service role can be created, modified, and deleted from within IAM. An application running on an Amazon EC2 instance can assume a service role and retrieve security credentials temporarily to perform actions that the role allows in your account.

AWS Service-Linked Role

A service-linked role is linked directly to an AWS service and includes all the permissions that the service requires to call other AWS services. The linked service determines how a service-linked role can be created, modified, and deleted automatically as part of a wizard or process in the service without manually adding the necessary permissions.

Role Chaining

When a role assumes a second role through the AWS CLI or API, it's called role chaining, which limits the session to a maximum of one hour. You can specify the session duration using the DurationSeconds parameter when you use the AssumeRole API operation to assume a role. The value can be up to 43,200 seconds (12 hours); however, the operation fails if you assume a role using role chaining and provide a DurationSeconds parameter value greater than one hour.

Delegation

You can delegate by granting permissions to someone so they have access to resources that you control. This involves setting up a trust between the account that owns the resource and the account that contains the users who need to access the resource.

Federation

A federation is the trust relationship between AWS and an external identity provider, where users can log in to a web identity provider, Amazon, Facebook, Google, or an enterprise identity system. When you use a trust relationship between AWS and these external identity providers, the user is assigned to an IAM role and receives temporary credentials, which allow them to access your AWS resources.

Role for Cross-Account Access

A role can be used to grant access to resources in one account to a trusted user in another account. Some of the AWS services, such as Amazon S3, Glacier, Amazon SNS, and Amazon SQS, allow you to attach a policy directly to a resource instead of using a role as a proxy. This is known as a resource-based policy.

Policies and Permissions

You can define what any user or role is allowed to do in an AWS account using permissions or access management. A person or application is known as an IAM entity and is authenticated using a user or role. AWS permissions can be managed by creating access policies and attaching them to IAM identities like users, groups of users, or roles or AWS resources. An access policy is an object that defines permissions in AWS that can be associated with an identity or resource. When a user or role makes a request, AWS evaluates the policies, which are stored in AWS as JSON documents, before determining whether the request should be allowed or denied. It is difficult to manage permissions across multiple accounts using IAM roles, resource-based policies, or access control lists (ACLs) for cross-account permissions, so AWS recommends using the AWS Organizations service to manage permissions across multiple accounts.

New IAM users, which are identities in your account, can't access anything until you give them permission by creating an identity-based policy that is attached to the user or a group to which the user belongs. The following sample JSON policy show what is allowed for a user to perform all Amazon S3 actions (S3:*) on the samplebucket:

```
{
  "Version": "2012-10-17",
  "Statement": {
    "Effect": "Allow",
"Principal":{"AWS":"1111111111"},
    "Action": "S3:*",
    "Resource": "arn:aws:s3:::samplebucket/*"
  }
}
```

After you attach this policy to your IAM user, the user only has those S3 permissions and is not allowed to perform any actions in Amazon EC2, DynamoDB, or any other AWS service, since those services are not included in the policy. You can organize IAM users into IAM groups and attach a policy to a group for easier permissions management and to follow AWS IAM best practices. Individual users in the group will still have their own credentials, but all the users in a group have the permissions that are attached to the group.

Even if users or groups have multiple policies attached without an explicit permission for an action of a resource, the user does not have those permissions. Like IAM users, federated users don't have permanent identities in your AWS account. You need to create a role and define permissions for it. The federated user will be associated with the role and will be granted permissions temporarily that are defined ahead of time.

IAM Policy Types

You can attach identity-based policies to an IAM identity, such as an IAM user, group, or role. You can attach resource-based policies to a resource such as an Amazon S3 bucket or an IAM role trust policy. You can control what actions the identity can perform on

PART IV

which resources and under what conditions using identity-based policies. Policies can be further categorized as follows:

- Managed policies are standalone identity-based policies that can be attached to multiple users, groups, and roles in your AWS account. There are two types of managed policies:
  - AWS-managed policies are created and managed by AWS. If you are new to using access policies, AWS recommends using this form.
  - Customer-managed policies that you create and manage in your AWS account. This provides more precise control over your policies compared to AWS-managed policies. You can either create or edit an IAM policy using the visual editor or by creating the JSON policy document directly.

- Inline policies that you create and manage and that are embedded directly into a single user, group, or role. In most cases, AWS doesn't recommend using inline policies, since they are complex to maintain.

- Resource-based policies control what actions can be performed on a resource and under what conditions. These are inline policies, and to enable cross-account access, you can specify an entire account or IAM entities in another account as the principal.

The IAM service only supports trust policies that can be attached to an IAM role. Trust policies define which principal entities (accounts, users, roles, and federated users) can assume the role, and you must attach both a trust policy and an identity-based policy to an IAM role.

Permissions Boundaries

You can set the maximum permissions that an identity-based policy can grant to an IAM entity using an advanced feature called permissions boundary. The entity can perform only allowed actions by both its identity-based policies and its permissions boundaries. The principal, such as a user or role, is not limited by the permissions boundary using resource-based policies. An explicit deny in any of these policies overrides the allow rule. You can group and centrally manage your AWS accounts and apply service control policies (SCPs) to any or all of your accounts. The maximum permissions for an organization or organizational unit (OU) are specified in SCP using the JSON format. The permission boundary limits permissions for entities, including each AWS account root user.

IAM Policy

AWS identity-based policies are JSON policy documents used to set permissions boundaries that you attach to a user or role. Resource-based policies can be attached to a resource and AWS organization OU. ACLs can be attached to a resource using different syntax. You can use session policies to assume a role or federated user session. The visual editor can be used in the AWS Management Console to create and edit customer-managed policies without using JSON. However, you still need to use a JSON editor to create and edit the inline policies for groups and for complex policies.

IAM Policy Structure

A JSON policy document includes optional policy-wide information at the top of the document and one or more individual statements, as shown in Figure 10-3. Each statement contains information about a single permission, and AWS applies a logical OR across the statements when evaluating them if a policy includes multiple statements. When AWS evaluates multiple policies, it applies a logical OR across all of those policies.

As illustrated in Figure 10-3, the information in a statement is contained within a series of elements:

- Version specifies the version of the policy language; as a best practice, use the latest 2012-10-17 version.

- Statement is the container for the other main policy elements. You can include more than one statement in a policy.

- The statement ID is used to differentiate between your statements.

- The effect is to either allow or deny access.

- Principal indicates the account, user, role, or federated user to which you would like to allow or deny access.

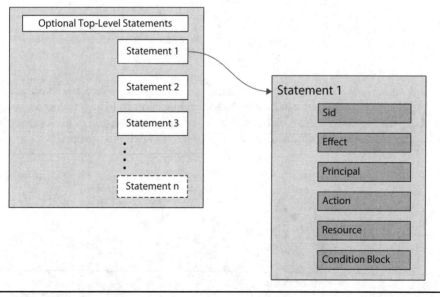

Figure 10-3　IAM policy structure

- Action includes a list of actions that the policy allows or denies.

- Resource specifies a list of resources to which the actions apply; if not included, it applies to the resource to which the policy is attached.

- Condition specifies the circumstances under which the policy grants permission.

IAM Policy Versioning

Versioning helps you multiple versions of access policies. Whether you make changes to your managed policy or AWS changes an AWS-managed policy, the changed policy doesn't overwrite the existing policy. IAM creates a new version of the managed policy instead of updating the existing policy. You can use IAM to store up to five versions of your customer-managed policies, but it does not support versioning for inline policies. Figure 10-4 illustrates versioning for a customer-managed policy.

The Version policy element defines the version of the policy language, and it can be used to track changes to a managed policy version. When you discover that the policy change you made had unintended effects, you can roll back to a previous version of the managed policy by setting the previous version as the default version. The following policy can be used to deny a user access to change an existing customer-managed policy:

```
{
    "Version": "2012-10-17",
    "Statement": [
        {
            "Effect": "Deny",
            "Action": [
                "iam:CreatePolicyVersion",
                "iam:SetDefaultPolicyVersion"
            ],
            "Resource": "arn:aws:iam::*:policy/POLICY-NAME"
        }
    ]
}
```

The default version of a customer-managed policy can be set to roll back your changes. The JSON policy document can be viewed for each version to help you decide. Any version of the managed policy can be deleted except the default version. The version identifiers for the remaining versions do not change when you delete a version.

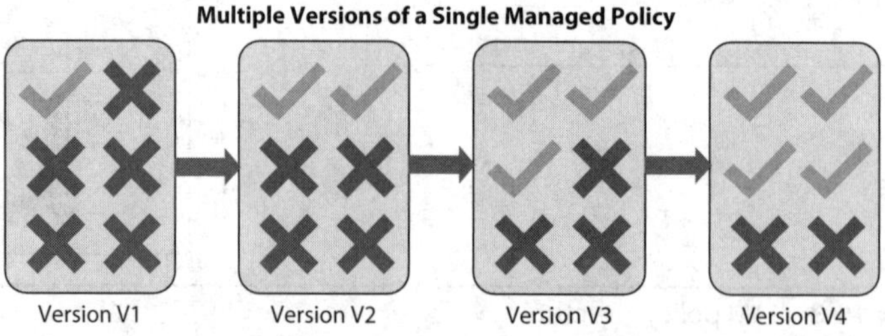

Figure 10-4
IAM policy
versioning

Multiple Versions of a Single Managed Policy

Version V1   Version V2   Version V3   Version V4

IAM Best Practices

Keep the following AWS IAM best practices in mind to secure all your AWS resources and users.

- *AWS account root user access keys should be locked away.* The access key for your AWS account root user gives full access to all your resources for all AWS services, including your billing information, and you cannot reduce the permissions associated with your AWS account root user access key. You shouldn't create an access key for your AWS account root user unless you absolutely need it. Instead, create an IAM user for yourself that has administrative permissions and use this. Unless you can rotate the access key regularly and keep it safe, you need to delete the access key of your AWS account root user. AWS account root user password or access keys should never be shared with anyone, and a strong password needs to be used to help protect account-level access to your AWS Management Console. You need to enable AWS MFA on your AWS account root user account as well.

- *Create individual IAM users.* You should not use your AWS account root user credentials to access AWS. Instead, create individual users for anyone who needs access to your AWS account.

- *Use groups to assign permissions to IAM users.* You need to create groups based on the job functions (administrators, developers, accounting, etc.) instead of defining permissions for individual IAM users. When people move around different lines of business within your company or change positions, you can easily change the IAM group to which they belong.

- *Grant least privilege.* Always follow the standard security advice of granting least privilege, or granting only the permissions required to perform a task.

- *Start with AWS-managed policies.* You can use AWS-managed policies to give your employees the permissions they need to get started, and these policies are already available for many common use cases in your account and are maintained and updated by AWS.

- *Use customer-managed policies instead of inline policies.* AWS recommends using managed policies instead of inline policies because inline policies exist only on an IAM identity (user, group, or role), and managed policies are separate IAM resources that you can attach to multiple identities.

- *Review IAM permissions regularly.* You should regularly review and monitor each of your IAM policies and access levels of all your users. You need to use the access-level column of the policy summary to understand the level of access that the policy provides, and you can take action to make your AWS account more secure.

- *Always configure a strong password policy for your users.* You need to require that your users create strong passwords and that they rotate their passwords periodically.

- *Enable MFA for your root user and IAM users.* AWS recommends that you require MFA for all users in your account. When using MFA, the user's device generates a response to an authentication challenge. Both the user's credentials and the device-generated response are required to complete the sign-in process.

- *Use roles for applications that run on Amazon EC2 instances.* IAM dynamically provides temporary credentials to the EC2 instance, and these credentials are automatically rotated.

- *Use roles to delegate permissions.* You need to use a role that specifies what permissions the IAM users in the other account are allowed. This defines which access is to be designated to IAM users in other AWS accounts who are allowed to assume the role.

- *Do not share access keys since they provide programmatic access to AWS.* You must not embed access keys within unencrypted code or share the security credentials between users in your AWS account.

- *Rotate your credentials regularly.* You need to change your own passwords and access keys regularly to make sure that all IAM users in your account do as well. A password policy can be applied to your account to require all of your IAM users to rotate their passwords regularly, and you can choose how often they must do so.

- *Remove unnecessary credentials.* You must remove IAM user credentials, like passwords and access keys, that are not needed. Remove the access keys of any user if they only use the console.

- *Use policy conditions for extra security.* You need to define the IAM policy conditions to allow access to a resource. You can define which request is allowed within a specified range of allowable IP addresses or a date range or a time range, or require the use of Secure Sockets Layer (SSL) or MFA.

- *Closely monitor your AWS account activity.* Enable logging features in AWS and determine the actions users have taken in your account and the resources that were used. The time and date of actions, the source IP, failed actions due to inadequate permissions, and more can be found in the log files.

- *Turn on AWS CloudTrail auditing.* Since IAM is integrated with the AWS CloudTrail service, it provides an audit of all the actions taken by any IAM user or role. CloudTrail captures all API calls for IAM as events, and you need to create a trail before you can enable continuous delivery of CloudTrail events that will be stored in your Amazon S3 bucket. CloudTrail events can be viewed in the CloudTrail console in Event history even if you don't configure a trail.

Chapter Review

This chapter began by explaining AWS Identity and Access Management (IAM). It is crucial for you to understand who is signed in (i.e., authenticated) and has permissions (i.e., authorized to use resources). Normally, anyone who uses single sign-on in an enterprise environment has complete access to all services and resources and can avoid multiple sign-ins. An AWS user is an entity that consists of names and credentials that you create in AWS to represent a person or an application that uses it to interact with AWS.

PART IV

An IAM user in AWS consists of a username and credentials. An AWS root user and IAM user with administrator permissions are not the same as the AWS account root user. You need a password to access the AWS Management Console, but AWS CLI or PowerShell or the AWS SDKs or APIs do not need passwords.

AWS recommends configuring multifactor authentication (MFA) for increased security to protect your AWS resources. MFA can be enabled for IAM users or the root user. You can use any of the following methods to configure MFA. Use a collection of IAM users to specify permissions for multiple users. Any users who are assigned to a group automatically inherit the group permissions, and this makes it easier to manage the permissions from one place. You can create an IAM role in your account similar to an IAM user that has specific permissions that define what the identity (role) can and cannot do in AWS. You can assume a role if required, and it's not associated with one person. A role provides you with temporary security credentials for your session, but it does not have a password or access keys associated with it. AWS identity-based policies are JSON policy documents used to set permissions boundaries that you attach to a user or role. AWS-managed policies are managed by AWS, and you can create inline policies and manage them directly for a single user, group, or role. Resource-based policies control what actions can be performed on a resource under what conditions.

Exercises

The following exercises will help you practice performing various tasks in AWS IAM. You need to create an AWS account, as explained earlier, in order to perform the exercises. You can use the Free Tier when launching AWS resources, but make sure to terminate them at the end.

Exercise 10-1: Create an Administrator User Instead of Using the Root User to Perform Admin Tasks

The following step-by-step instructions will show you how to create an IAM Administrator user to perform regular administration tasks using the AWS Management Console.

1. Sign in to the AWS account using your account e-mail address and password as the root user to the IAM console at https://console.aws.amazon.com/iam/.

2. Choose your account name on the navigation bar and then choose My Account.

3. Next to IAM User and Role Access to Billing Information, choose Edit.

4. Now select the checkbox to activate IAM Access and choose Update.

5. Return to the IAM dashboard by choosing Services and then IAM on the navigation bar.

6. Choose Users from the left navigation pane and then choose Add User.

7. Type **Account-Administrator** for User Name.

8. Select the checkbox for Programmatic Access only if you plan to log in using AWS CLI or use API or SDK, and next to AWS Management Console access, select Custom Password and type a new password in the text box.

9. Choose Next: Permissions to navigate to the permissions page.

10. Choose Add User To Group on the Set permissions page.

11. Choose Create Group.

12. In the Create Group dialog box that appears, for Group Name type **Account-Administrators**.

13. Choose the search in Filter policies and choose the AWS managed - job function to filter the table contents.

14. Select the checkbox for Administrator Access from the policy list and choose Create Group.

15. From the list of groups, select the checkbox for your new group.

16. Now choose Next Tags to navigate to the Add Tags page.

17. Type **Name** for the key and **Account-Administrators** for the value.

18. Choose Next: Review to navigate to the next page for a review summary that lists the group memberships to be added to the new user.

19. After reviewing carefully and when you are ready to proceed, choose Create User.

20. You will see a success page where you can download the credentials as a CSV file and an option to send an e-mail along with URL, as shown:

```
https://123456789098.signin.aws.amazon.com/console
```

Exercise 10-2: Create an IAM User Using the IAM Console

The following step-by-step instructions will help you create an IAM user using the AWS Management Console.

1. Sign in to your AWS account using the AWS Management Console and then open the IAM console at https://console.aws.amazon.com/iam/.

2. Choose Users from the navigation pane on the left and then choose Add User.

3. Type **Developer** for the new user; you are allowed to add up to ten users at one time if required.

4. Select the type of access for this user from the two options available:

   • Select Programmatic Access only if the user requires access to the AWS CLI, API, or PowerShell.

   • Select AWS Management Console Access only if the user requires access to the console.

5. For our exercise, we select both login options. Choose either Auto Generated Password or Custom Password. If you select Custom Password, type the password.

6. AWS recommends selecting the Require Password Reset checkbox to make sure that users are forced to change their password when they sign in for the first time.

7. Choose Next: Permissions to navigate to the permissions page.

8. On the Set Permissions page, you can choose Add User To Group or Copy Permissions From Existing User or Attach Existing Policies To User Directly. For this exercise, select Attach Existing Policies Directly and choose ReadOnlyAccess.

9. Here you can also set the permissions boundary to control the maximum user permissions. For this exercise, leave it at the default.

10. Choose Next: Tags to navigate to the Tags page.

11. For the metadata key-value pair, type Name for the key and Developer for the value.

12. Choose Next: Review to navigate to the summary page where you can see all of the choices you made.

13. When you are ready to proceed, choose Create User.

14. You will see a success page where you can download the credentials as a CSV file and an option to send an e-mail along with URL, as shown:

    ```
    https://123456789098.signin.aws.amazon.com/console
    ```

Exercise 10-3: Create an IAM Group Using the IAM Console

The following step-by-step instructions will assist you in creating IAM Groups using the AWS Management Console.

1. Sign in to the AWS account using the AWS Management Console and open the IAM console at https://console.aws.amazon.com/iam/.

2. Select Groups from the navigation pane on the left.

3. Click Create New Group.

4. In the Set Group Name box, type **DevOps** for the name of the group and then click Next Step.

5. Select the checkbox for ReadOnlyAccess from the list of policies that would be applied to all members of the group.

6. Click Next Step to see a summary of all the choices you made.

7. Click Create Group.

Exercise 10-4: Add a User to an IAM Group Using the IAM Console

The following step-by-step instructions will show you how to add an IAM user to your IAM Group using the AWS Management Console.

1. Sign in to your AWS account using the AWS Management Console and open the IAM console at https://console.aws.amazon.com/iam/.

2. Choose Groups from the left navigation pane and then click on the name of the group.

3. Choose the Users tab and then choose Add Users To Group.

4. Select the checkbox next to the Developer user.

5. Choose Add Users to add the user to the group.

Exercise 10-5: Attach a Policy to a Group Using the IAM Console

The following step-by-step instructions will help you attach an IAM policy to your IAM Group using the AWS Management Console.

1. Sign in to the AWS account using the AWS Management Console and open the IAM console at https://console.aws.amazon.com/iam/.
2. Select Policies from the left navigation pane.
3. From the list of policies, select the checkbox next to ViewOnlyAccess policy.
4. Select the Policy Actions dropdown and select Attach.
5. Click Type to sort.
6. Select the checkbox next to the DevOps group to attach the policy.
7. Now click Attach Policy.

Exercise 10-6: Remove a User from an IAM Group Using the IAM Console

The following step-by-step instructions will show you how to delete an IAM user from your IAM Group using the AWS Management Console.

1. Sign in to the AWS account using the AWS Management Console and open the IAM console at https://console.aws.amazon.com/iam/.
2. Choose Groups from the left navigation pane and then choose the DevOps group.
3. Choose the Users tab.
4. Choose Remove Users From Group under Actions.
5. Select the checkbox next to the Developer user.
6. Choose Remove Users From Group.

Exercise 10-7: Delete an IAM Group Using the IAM Console

The following step-by-step instructions will show you how to delete your IAM Group using the AWS Management Console.

1. Sign in to the AWS account using the AWS Management Console and open the IAM console at https://console.aws.amazon.com/iam/.
2. Choose Groups from the left navigation pane.
3. From the list of groups, select the checkbox next to the DevOps group.
4. Click on the Group Actions dropdown list and select Delete Group.
5. From the popup confirmation box, click Yes, Delete to delete the group.

Questions

The following questions will help you gauge your understanding of the contents in this chapter. Read all the answers carefully because there might be more than one correct answer. Choose the best responses for each question.

1. A company has created 950 IAM users and has introduced a new policy that will change the access of a few IAM users. How can the company implement this effectively so that there is no need to apply the policy for every individual at the user level?

   A. Use the IAM groups and add the users based on their role to different groups and apply a policy to the group.

   B. Create a new policy and apply it to multiple users in a single go with the AWS CLI.

   C. Add each user to the IAM role based on their role to achieve effective policy setup.

   D. Use the IAM role to implement the required access at the role level.

2. Your company's compliance team requires that all privileged users use one-time access credentials in addition to a username/password combination. Which two of the following options enforces the policy for AWS users? (Choose two.)

   A. You need to configure multifactor authentication for your privileged IAM users.

   B. You need to create IAM users for your privileged accounts.

   C. You need to implement identity federation between your company's identity provider and the IAM Security Token Service.

   D. You must enable the IAM one-time-use password policy option for your privileged users.

3. Your company is preparing for a security audit of your AWS environment. Which two IAM best practices should you consider implementing before the audit begins? (Choose two.)

   A. You need to create individual IAM users for everyone in your organization.

   B. You need to configure MFA on the root account and for all your privileged IAM users.

   C. You need to assign IAM users to a group that is configured with policies granting least privilege access.

   D. You must ensure all users have been assigned a username, password, access ID, and secret key.

PART IV

4. Your organization currently has created an AWS IAM role for an Amazon EC2 instance, which permits the instance to have access to Amazon DynamoDB. Now the organization wants their EC2 instances created in the new region with the same privileges. How can this be achieved?

   A. You must create a new IAM role with associated policies in the new region.

   B. You can assign the existing IAM role to the new Amazon EC2 instance in the new region.

   C. You need to copy the IAM role and the associated policies to the new region and attach it to the new instance.

   D. You need to create an AMI of the original instance and copy it to the desired region using the AMI Copy feature.

5. Your company created multiple IAM users and enabled MFA. As a security best practice, your company wants every IAM user to access the IAM console only within the company network and not from outside the network. How can you achieve this?

   A. Create an IAM policy with the security group and use it to log in to the AWS console.

   B. Create an IAM policy with a condition to deny access when the IP address range is not within the company network range.

   C. Configure the EC2 instance security group and allow traffic only from the company's IP range.

   D. Create an IAM policy with your Virtual Private Cloud (VPC) and allow a secure gateway between the company network and AWS Management Console.

6. AWS IAM evaluates policies depending on the request context. Which of the following are correct statements with regard to policy evaluation logic? (Choose two.)

   A. All the requests are denied by default.

   B. The explicit allow policy overrides an explicit deny policy.

   C. The explicit allow policy overrides the default deny policy.

   D. All the requests are allowed by default.

7. You have an application deployed on an EC2 instance that is writing data to a DynamoDB table and the security keys should not be allowed to be stored on the EC2 instance. How can you achieve this? (Choose two.)

   A. Create an IAM role that allows write access to the DynamoDB table.

   B. Add an IAM role to the running EC2 instance.

   C. Create an IAM user and give it write access to the DynamoDB table.

   D. Add an IAM user to a running EC2 instance.

8. When should you use an IAM user, IAM group, or IAM role? (Choose three.)

   A. An IAM user has permanent long-term credentials and is used to directly interact with AWS services.

   B. An IAM group is primarily a management convenience to manage the same set of permissions for a set of IAM users.

   C. An IAM role has permanent long-term credentials and is used to directly interact with AWS services.

   D. IAM roles cannot make direct requests to AWS services and can only be assumed by IAM users, applications, or AWS services, and IAM roles are used to delegate access within or between AWS accounts.

9. Your company wants to deploy Amazon EC2 instances and allow them to have access to Amazon DynamoDB. You don't want to embed the credentials in EC2 and want to rotate the security credentials automatically. What features of IAM allow you to achieve this?

   A. Use IAM group for the EC2 instance to assign the same set of permissions to multiple IAM users.

   B. Use IAM roles for the EC2 instance, which uses the AWS temporary security credentials when making requests from running EC2 instances to AWS services.

   C. Use IAM roles for the EC2 instance to automaticlly rotate the AWS temporary security credentials.

   D. Use IAM roles for the EC2 instance to grant granular AWS service permissions for applications running on EC2 instances.

10. What is the difference between an IAM role and an IAM user? (Choose three.)

   A. An IAM user can be used to directly interact with AWS services, and it has permanent long-term credentials.

   B. An IAM role cannot make direct requests to AWS services, and it doesn't have any credentials.

   C. IAM roles can be assumed by entities like IAM users, applications, or an AWS service such as EC2.

   D. IAM groups can be assumed to assign the same set of permissions to multiple IAM users.

Answers

1. **A.** You can use the IAM groups and add users based on their role to different groups and apply a policy to a group.

2. **A, B.** You need to create IAM users for your privileged accounts and configure multifactor authentication for your privileged IAM users.

3. B, C. You need to assign IAM users to a group that is configured with policies granting least privilege access, and you need to configure MFA on the root account and for all your privileged IAM users.

4. B. You can assign the existing IAM role to the new Amazon EC2 instances in the new region.

5. B. You can create an IAM policy with a condition to deny access when the IP address range is not within the company network range.

6. A, C. All the requests are denied by default, and the explicit allow policy overrides the default deny policy.

7. A, B. You need to create an IAM role that allows write access to the DynamoDB table, and you need add an IAM role to the running EC2 instance.

8. A, B, D. An IAM user has long-term credentials and interacts directly with AWS services. An IAM group is used to manage a set of IAM users. IAM roles can be assumed by IAM users, applications, or AWS services and are used to delegate access within or between AWS accounts.

9. B, C, D. Use IAM roles for the EC2 instance in order to use AWS temporary security credentials, to automatically rotate the AWS temporary security credentials, and to grant granular AWS service permissions for applications running on EC2 instances.

10. A, B, C. An IAM user can be used to directly interact with AWS services, whereas an IAM role cannot make direct requests to AWS services. An IAM user has permanent long-term credentials, whereas the IAM role doesn't have any credentials. In addition, IAM roles can be assumed by entities like IAM users, applications, or an AWS service such as EC2.

Additional Resources

- **AWS Document Reference**   There is no place like official AWS documentation to get the latest and most up-to-date information about all the AWS services. Always refer to the official AWS blogs to get the latest updates about new AWS services and updates to existing features.
  `https://docs.aws.amazon.com/iam/index.html` and `https://aws.amazon.com/blogs/aws`

- **Sign In as an IAM User**   Use the following link to sign into the AWS Management Console as an IAM user. You need to provide your account ID or account alias in addition to your username and password.
  `https://docs.aws.amazon.com/IAM/latest/UserGuide/id_users_sign-in.html`

- **Changing the AWS Account Root User Password**   You need to have an administrator password in order to access the AWS Management Console, but you can change the AWS account root user password by using the following link.
  `https://docs.aws.amazon.com/IAM/latest/UserGuide/id_`
  `credentials_passwords_change-root.html`

- **Create, Change, or Delete an IAM User Password**   Use the Management Console, CLI, or API to create, change, or delete an IAM user using the following link.
  `https://docs.aws.amazon.com/IAM/latest/UserGuide/id_`
  `credentials_passwords_admin-change-user.html`

- **Manage IAM Policies**   Use the following link to create, validate, test, apply versioning, edit, and delete IAM policies.
  `https://docs.aws.amazon.com/IAM/latest/UserGuide/access_`
  `policies_manage.html`

- **Add Multifactor Authentication (MFA)**   You can add a virtual MFA device for your AWS account root user using the following link.
  `https://docs.aws.amazon.com/IAM/latest/UserGuide/id_`
  `credentials_mfa_enable_virtual.html#enable-virt-mfa-for-`
  `root`

  You can use the following link to enable a virtual MFA device for an IAM user.
  `https://docs.aws.amazon.com/IAM/latest/UserGuide/id_`
  `credentials_mfa_enable_virtual.html#enable-virt-mfa-for-`
  `iam-user`

- **Tag a User or Role**   Use the following link to tag an IAM user or role using the IAM console, the AWS CLI, or the API through one of the AWS SDKs.
  `https://docs.aws.amazon.com/IAM/latest/UserGuide/id_tags`
  `.html#id_tags_procs-console`

- **Troubleshoot IAM Policies**   Use the following link to diagnose and fix common issues that you might encounter when working with IAM policies.
  `https://docs.aws.amazon.com/IAM/latest/UserGuide/`
  `troubleshoot_policies.html`

- **Troubleshooting IAM Roles**   Use the details found in the following link to help diagnose and fix common issues that you might encounter when working with IAM roles.
  `https://docs.aws.amazon.com/IAM/latest/UserGuide/`
  `troubleshoot_roles.html`

CHAPTER 11

Web Identity Federation and Amazon Cognito for User Authentication

In this chapter, you will learn
- Identity federation and providers
- Web Identity Federation
- Amazon Cognito
- SAML 2.0
- Session policies

In this chapter, we will see how Identity Federation works with AWS identity services and how to use Amazon Cognito for user management of your web and mobile apps using a username and password or through a third party such as Amazon, Google, or Facebook.

Identity Federation and Providers

Identity federation is based on the trust between two or more domains, which can be another business unit or your partner organization, to allow users of those domains to access your applications and services using the same identity. An identity broker is any Identity and Access Management (IAM) service provider who specializes in mediating the access control between multiple service providers, based on trust relationships. The trusted connection between two or more such identity brokers across organizations is known as identity federation. An identity provider can be any identity broker who is responsible for affirming digital identities with claims for service providers to consume. A resident identity provider is the identity provider responsible for affirming the digital identities within its trust domain—also known as a local identity provider. A federated identity provider is based on a trust domain and is responsible for affirming digital identities that belong to another specific trusted domain, and a trust relationship can be established between the two identity providers.

Identity federation provides a seamless user experience by requiring users to remember only one set of credentials by using single sign-on and avoiding the administrative overhead by delegating account and password management responsibilities to the local identity provider, in place of having multiple identity silos to manage. It simplifies data management and storage costs and also avoids privacy and compliance burdens. The federated identity management is used to provide access to users from supplier, distributor, and partner networks and acts as a temporary arrangement for supporting transitioning between IAM and Social Login such as Amazon, Facebook, Google, etc. Identify federation allows you to manage your access to AWS Cloud resources centrally using single sign-on (SSO) from your corporate directory. Federation exchanges the identity and security information between an identity provider (IdP) and an application using open standards like Security Assertion Markup Language 2.0 (SAML).

AWS IAM can be used to sign in to your AWS accounts using your existing corporate credentials. AWS SSO can be used to manage SSO access to multiple AWS accounts and applications. Amazon Cognito can be used to add federation to your own web and mobile applications. Users can sign in to the AWS Management Console using AWS Microsoft Active Directory (AD), AWS Command Line Interface (CLI), and Windows applications running on the AWS Cloud using Microsoft AD credentials. When you manage user identities such as a corporate user directory outside of AWS, IAM identity providers can be used instead of creating IAM users in your AWS account. You can manage your user identities outside of AWS using an IdP, and it is useful if you are creating a mobile app or web application that requires access to AWS resources.

You don't have to create custom sign-in or manage user identities when using an IAM identity provider. Your external users sign in through a well-known IdP, such as Amazon, Google, or Facebook, and the permissions can be given to those external identities to use your AWS resources in your account. Since you don't have to distribute or embed long-term security credentials like access keys to your application, the IAM identity providers help you to keep your AWS account secure. You need to create an IAM identity provider entity to establish a trust relationship between your AWS account and the IdP. Compatible IdPs like OpenID Connect (OIDC) or SAML 2.0 are supported by AWS IAM.

Web Identity Federation

Let's say you are creating a mobile game application that stores player and score information in Amazon S3 and DynamoDB. Your mobile application makes requests to AWS using an AWS access key, but it is not a best practice to embed or distribute long-term AWS credentials with applications that a user can download to a device, or even in an encrypted store. Instead, your mobile application should be using the temporary AWS security credentials dynamically using web identity federation. An AWS role should be mapped to that temporary credential, which has only the permissions needed to perform the tasks required by the mobile application.

You don't need to create a custom sign-in or manage user identities when using an external IdP that receives an authentication token and then exchange the token for temporary security credentials that can be mapped to an IAM role with only required permissions to use the resources in your AWS account. AWS recommends using Amazon Cognito, since it acts as an identity broker and does the majority of the federation work for you. You need to write code to interact with a web IdP, like Amazon or Google, if you aren't using Amazon Cognito, which calls the AssumeRoleWithWebIdentity application programming interface (API) to trade the authentication token for temporary AWS security credentials.

Amazon Cognito

Amazon Cognito provides user management in addition to authentication and authorization for your web and mobile applications by allowing you to sign in directly with your username and password or through a third party such as Amazon or Google. The user pools and identity pools are the two main components of Amazon Cognito. The user directories that provide sign-up and sign-in options for your application users are called user pools. Identity pools allow you to grant users the required access to other AWS services. Both identity pools and user pools can be used together or separately.

Figure 11-1 shows a common Amazon Cognito scenario where both the user pool and identity pool are used. The scenario involves authenticating a user and granting access to other AWS service(s).

- Your mobile application user signs in through the Cognito user pool and receives user pool tokens after a successful authentication.

- Then the mobile application trades in the user pool tokens for AWS credentials through the Cognito identity pool.

- Those AWS credentials can be used by your mobile application to access other AWS services such as DynamoDB or Amazon S3.

- In turn, Cognito keeps your AWS account secure, since long-term security credentials are not distributed or embedded in your application.

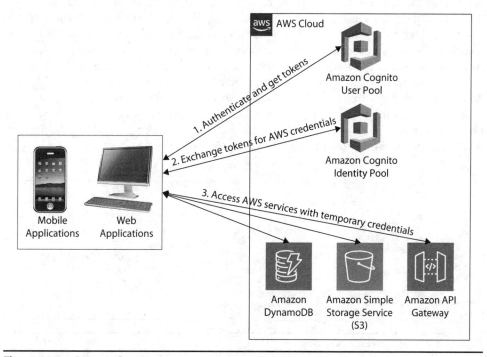

Figure 11-1 Amazon Cognito

Cognito User Pools

A user pool is a user directory where users can sign in through Amazon Cognito or federate through a third-party IdP to a directory profile that can be accessed through an SDK. User pools can be used for sign-up and sign-in services. They can be used for signing in with Amazon or Google, as well as SAML identity providers, from your user pool. Cognito also has a customizable built-in web user interface (UI) to sign in users along with multifactor authentication (MFA) and customized workflows. Amazon Cognito issues JSON web tokens (JWTs) after successful authentication that can be used to secure and authorize access to your own APIs, or exchange them for AWS credentials, as shown in Figure 11-2.

You can configure an identity pool to exchange user pool tokens for AWS credentials to enable users in your user pool to access AWS resources. Token handling takes place through the Amazon Cognito user pool identity SDKs for JavaScript, Android, and iOS.

Identity Pools

You can create unique identities for your users and authenticate them with identity providers using Amazon Cognito identity pools. You can obtain temporary, limited-privilege AWS credentials to access other AWS services using identity federation, and Cognito Identity Pool supports public identity providers such as Amazon, Google, and developer-authenticated identities.

Mobile or web-based applications that need accesses to AWS resources need security credentials in order to make programmatic requests to AWS. AWS recommends using Amazon Cognito for most mobile and web-based application scenarios. Amazon Cognito can be used with the AWS Mobile SDK for iOS, Android, and Fire OS to create unique identities for users and can authenticate secure access to your specific AWS resources. Amazon Cognito supports developer-authenticated identities and guest (unauthenticated) access and also provides API operations for synchronizing and preserving user data as users move between devices. It works with the third-party services and supports anonymous sign-ins by doing most of the behind-the-scenes work with public identity provider services. You can also work directly with a third-party service like Login with Amazon, Google, Facebook, or any OIDC-compatible IdP.

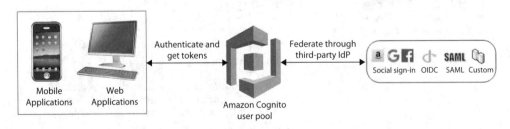

Figure 11-2   Amazon Cognito user pool

Amazon Cognito Sync

Amazon Cognito Sync is a client library that enables cross-device syncing of application-related user data. It can be used to synchronize user profile data across mobile devices and web applications. It caches the data locally in order for your application to read and write data, regardless if the device is online or offline. When the device is back online, the data will be synchronized, and if you configure push sync, then other devices are notified immediately about the available update.

Amazon Cognito for Mobile Apps

Let's say you are a developer building a soccer game for a mobile device and your users' data is stored in Amazon S3 and Amazon DynamoDB. You are using Amazon Cognito to keep your local data synchronized across devices. Since the long-term AWS security credentials should not be distributed with the game for security and maintenance reasons and the game will have a large number of users, you don't want to create new user identities in IAM for each player. So, you create your mobile application to use external IdPs, such as Login with Amazon, Google, Facebook, or any IdP that is compatible with OIDC. Your mobile application will take advantage of the authentication mechanism from one of those providers to validate your users' identity. You register the developer ID with your IdP to enable the mobile app to access their AWS resources, and you also configure the application with each of those providers. You can use Amazon Cognito to create IAM roles that precisely define permissions that the game needs from your AWS account that contains the Amazon S3 bucket and DynamoDB table for your soccer game mobile application.

In the mobile application code, you can call the sign-in interface for the IdP that you configured, where the IdP handles all the details of letting the user sign in. The application gets an OAuth access token or OIDC ID token from the provider, and your application can trade this authentication information for a set of temporary security credentials that consist of a session token, a secret access key, and an AWS access key ID. Then the application uses those temporary credentials to access web services offered by AWS. The application is limited to those permissions that are defined in the role that it assumes. Figure 11-3 shows a flowchart for how using Login with Amazon as the IdP will work. The steps are as follows:

1. A user starts your game application on a mobile device, and the application asks the user to sign in.

2. The application redirects the user to Login with Amazon to accept the user's credentials.

3. The application uses the Cognito API to exchange the Login with Amazon ID token for a Cognito token.

4. The application then passes the Cognito token and requests temporary security credentials from AWS Security Token Service (STS).

5. The temporary security credentials can then be used by your mobile application to access any AWS resources required, like Amazon S3 and Amazon DynamoDB. The associated role of the temporary security credentials determines what can be accessed from those AWS services.

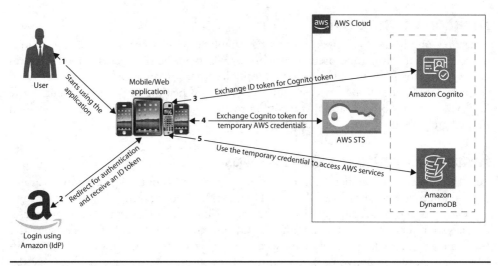

Figure 11-3 Login with Amazon IdP

Authenticating with User Pool

Figure 11-4 shows how to enable your users to authenticate with a user pool in this sample scenario.

1. First your application users need to sign in either directly through a user pool or through a third-party IdP.

2. The Cognito user pool handles the tokens that are returned from a social sign-in service like Google, Amazon, and SAML IdPs, or from OIDC.

3. After the authentication is successful, Amazon Cognito will send the user pool tokens to your application.

4. The user pool tokens can be used to retrieve AWS credentials to allow users to access other AWS services.

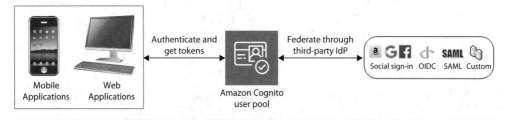

Figure 11-4 Authenticate with the user pool

Accessing Server-Side Resources Using the User Pool

In this sample scenario, we will see how to access server-side resources using the user pool, as shown in Figure 11-5.

1. Your application users sign in through a user pool.

2. If the authentication is successful, Amazon Cognito will send the user pool tokens to your web or mobile application.

3. The user pool tokens will then be used to control access to your server-side resources.

4. User pool groups can be created to manage permissions and to specify different types of users.

5. You can use the hosted web UI provided by Amazon Cognito to add sign-up and sign-in pages to your app.

6. You can create your own resource server to access protected resources for your users using this OAuth 2.0 foundation.

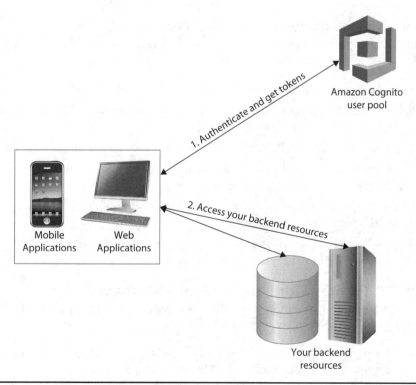

Figure 11-5 Backend resource authentications

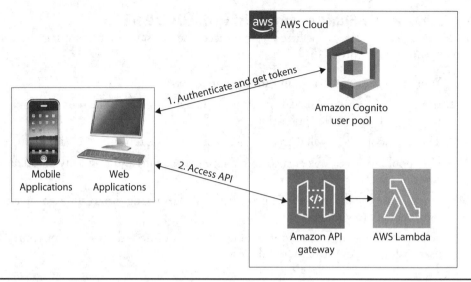

Figure 11-6   Accessing API Gateway

Accessing the API Gateway with a User Pool

We will see how to access your API through the API Gateway and Lambda using a user pool. Figure 11-6 provides a diagram of the steps.

1. Your application users sign in to the Cognito user pool.

2. When the authentication is successful, Amazon Cognito will send the user pool tokens back to your application.

3. The user pool tokens will then be used to access your API through API Gateway.

4. API Gateway validates the user pool tokens and uses them to grant your users access to resources like Lambda functions or your API.

5. User pool groups can be created to control permissions with API Gateway by mapping group membership to IAM roles.

6. The user pool tokens can be submitted to request an API Gateway be verified by an Amazon Cognito authorizer Lambda function.

Access AWS Services with a User Pool and an Identity Pool

Your application users can sign in either directly through a user pool or federate through a third-party IdP, as you can see in Figure 11-7.

1. The Cognito user pool handles the tokens that are returned from social sign-in services like Google, Amazon, and SAML IdPs or from OIDC.

2. After the authentication is successful, Amazon Cognito will send the user pool tokens to your application.

3. The user pool tokens can be exchanged for temporary access to other AWS services with an identity pool.

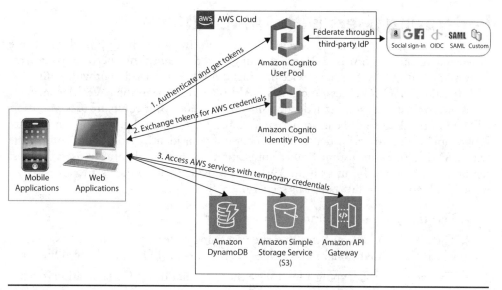

Figure 11-7   Authentication with Amazon Cognito user and identity pools

Authenticating with a Third-Party Identity Provider

Your application users can federate through a third-party IdP, as you see in Figure 11-8.

1. Your application gets the IdP token from social sign-in like Google, Amazon, and SAML IdPs or from OpenID Connect (OIDC).

2. The IdP tokens can be exchanged for temporary access to other AWS services with an identity pool.

Figure 11-8
Authentication
with an identity
pool

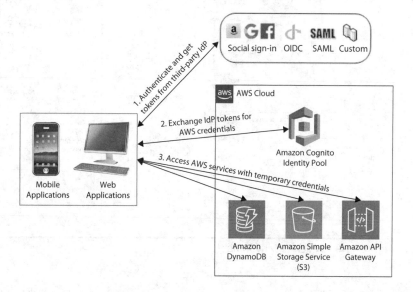

PART IV

Federating Users with SAML 2.0

In most cases, your organization might already be using an identity provider software package that supports SAML 2.0, and you may need to create a trust between your company as the IdP and AWS as the service provider. SAML can be used to provide your users with federated SSO for access to call AWS API operations or to the AWS Management Console. For instance, you can federate using SAML 2.0 if your company uses Microsoft AD and Active Directory Federation Services. You may need to build a custom identity broker application to perform a similar function if your identity store is not compatible with SAML 2.0. Your custom broker application needs to authenticate users, request temporary credentials for users from AWS, and provide them to the user to access AWS resources. Figure 11-9 illustrates this scenario.

1. The user accesses your custom identity broker.

2. The identity broker authenticates the user using your corporate identity system, which can be Lightweight Directory Access Protocol (LDAP) or Active Directory.

3. The identity broker application calls either AssumeRole or GetFederationToken to obtain temporary security credentials.

4. The call returns credentials consisting of an AWS access key ID, a secret access key, and a session token.

5. The application uses the temporary credentials to call AWS API operations or the AWS Management Console.

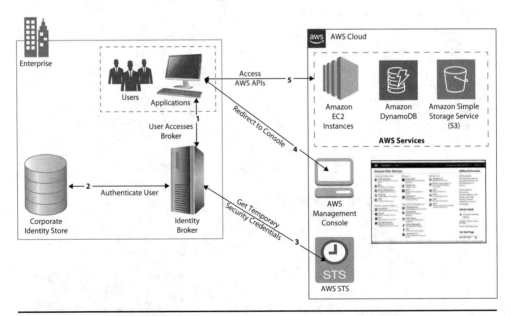

Figure 11-9   Federate with SAML

The identity broker application stores these temporary security credentials to other internal company applications by caching the credentials until they expire and then requests a new set of temporary credentials.

Session Policies

An advanced policy that can be passed in a parameter when you programmatically create a temporary session for a role or federated user is known as a session policy. The intersection of the identity-based policies and resource-based policy for the IAM entity is used to create the session policies, where an explicit deny overrides allow. By using the AssumeRoleWithSAML, AssumeRole, or AssumeRoleWithWebIdentity API, the role session and pass session policies can be created programmatically. A single JSON inline session policy document can be passed using the Policy parameter, and the PolicyArns parameter can be used to specify up to ten managed session policies.

You can use an IAM user's access keys to create a federated user session by programmatically calling the GetFederationToken API operation and also pass session policies. This scenario results in session permissions that are the intersection of the IAM user's identity-based policy and the session policy. A resource-based policy specifies the Amazon Resource Name (ARN) of the user or role as a principal, where the permissions from the resource-based policy are added to the role or user's identity-based policy before the session is created. The session policy can be used to limit the total permissions granted by the resource-based policy and the identity-based policy. This scenario results in session permissions that are the intersection of the session policies and either the identity-based policy or the resource-based policy, as shown in Figure 11-10.

Figure 11-10
Effective
policies I

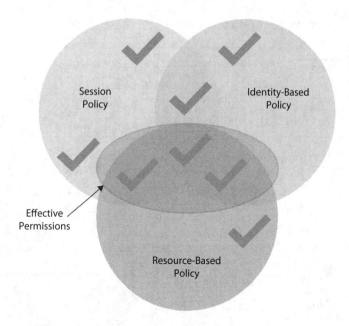

Session
Policy

Identity-Based
Policy

Effective
Permissions

Resource-Based
Policy

Figure 11-11
Effective
policies II

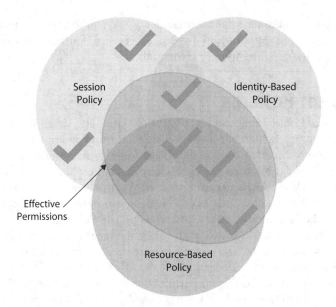

A resource-based policy can be specified by the ARN of the session as a principal, and the resource-based policy permissions are added after the session is created. The resource-based policy permissions are not limited by the session policy, which results in the permissions of the resource-based policy plus the intersection of the identity-based policy and the session policy, as shown in Figure 11-11.

The maximum permissions for a user or role can be set using a permissions boundary to create a session. The resulting session's permissions are the intersection of the identity-based policy, the permissions boundary, and the session policy, as shown in Figure 11-12.

Figure 11-12
Effective
policies III

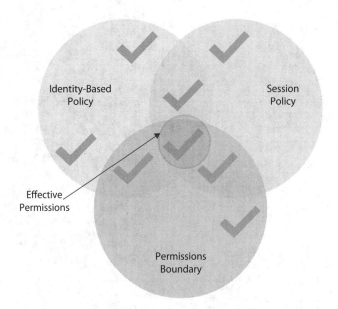

The AWS account root user cannot be attached to identity-based policies, and the permissions boundary cannot be set for the root user. But you can specify the root user as the principal in a resource-based policy.

Chapter Review

This chapter began by explaining identity federation and identity providers. It then explained Amazon Cognito, which provides user management using user pools and identity pools. Identity federation is based on the trust between two or more domains, which can be another business unit or your partner organization, to allow users of those domains to access your applications and services using the same identity. An identity broker is any IAM service provider who specializes in mediating the access control between multiple service providers, based on trust relationships. The trusted connection between two or more such identity brokers across organizations is known as identity federation. Federated identity management is used to provide access to users from supplier, distributor, and partner networks and acts as a temporary arrangement for supporting transitioning between IAM and social login services such as Amazon, Facebook, Google, etc. Identify federation allows you to manage your access to AWS Cloud resources centrally using SSO from your corporate directory. Federation exchanges the identity and security information between an IdP and an application using open standards like SAML.

Amazon Cognito provides user management in addition to authentication and authorization for your web and mobile applications by allowing you to sign in directly with your username and password or through a third party such as Amazon or Google. User pools and identity pools are the two main components of Amazon Cognito. The user directories that provide sign-up and sign-in options for your application users are called user pools. Identity pools allow you to grant users the required access to other AWS services. Both identity pools and user pools can be used together or separately. SAML can be used to provide your users with federated SSO for access to call AWS API operations or to the AWS Management Console. For instance, you can federate using SAML 2.0 if your company uses Microsoft AD and Active Directory Federation Services. An advanced policy that can be passed in a parameter when you programmatically create a temporary session for a role or federated user is known as a session policy. The intersection of the identity-based policies and resource-based policy for the IAM entity is used to create the session policies, where an explicit deny overrides an allow.

Exercises

The following exercises will help you practice using Amazon Cognito user pools and identity pools. You need to create an AWS account, as explained earlier, to perform these exercises. You can use the Free Tier when launching AWS resources, but make sure to terminate them at the end.

Exercise 11-1: Create an Amazon Cognito User Pool

In this exercise, you will find the step-by-step guidelines to create an Amazon Cognito user pool using the AWS Management Console.

1. Log in to your AWS console and provide your credentials to go to the Amazon Cognito console at https://console.aws.amazon.com/cognito/.

2. Click on the Manage Your User Pools button. The Your User Pools page appears.

3. Click the Create A User Pool button in the upper-right corner.

4. Enter my-dev-pool for your user pool name.

5. Now you have two options: either choose Review Defaults to accept all the default values to save the name or choose Step Through Settings to choose attributes, policies, MFA, message, tags, devices, app clients, and triggers.

6. On the Review page, click the Create Pool button to create the user pool.

Exercise 11-2: Create an Amazon Cognito Identity Pool

This exercise will help you with the step-by-step guidelines to create an Amazon Cognito identity pool using the AWS Management Console.

1. Log in to your AWS console and provide your credentials to go to the Amazon Cognito console at https://console.aws.amazon.com/cognito/.

2. Click Manage Identity Pools to open the Getting Started Wizard page.

3. Choose Step-1 Create New Identity Pool.

4. Type **my_dev_identity_pool** for your identity pool name.

5. Choose to enable unauthenticated identities for guest access without login.

6. Choose the authentication providers Cognito, Amazon, Facebook, Google+, Twitter/Digits, OpenID, SAML, or Custom based on your need. Leave the defaults for this example.

7. Click on Create Pool.

8. Now you will be prompted for access to your AWS resources. Choose Allow to create the two default roles (Cognito_my_dev_identity_poolAuth_Role and Cognito_my_dev_identity_poolUnauth_Role) associated with your identity pool.

9. Store your identity pool ID number: us-west-1:321ab7c3-12d3-123e-f123-1f23456g7h89, // Identity pool ID. You will see different platforms like Android, iOS, JavaScript, Unity, Xamarin, and .NET.

10. Click on Go To Dashboard to see the list of identity pools.

Exercise 11-3: Delete an Amazon Cognito Identity Pool

In this exercise, you will find the step-by-step instructions to delete your Amazon Cognito identity pool using the AWS Management Console.

1. Log in to your AWS console and provide your credentials to go to the Amazon Cognito console at https://console.aws.amazon.com/cognito/.

2. Click on the Manage Identity Pools button.

3. From the list of identity pools, select my_dev_identity_pool. The Dashboard page will appear.

4. Choose Edit Identity Pool, which is in the top-right corner of the dashboard.

5. Scroll through the available options and choose the last option: Delete Identity Pool to expand it.

6. Click on the Delete Identity Pool button.

7. The popup window will ask you for confirmation. Choose Delete Pool.

Exercise 11-4: Delete an Amazon Cognito User Pool

In this exercise, you will find the step-by-step guidelines to delete your Amazon Cognito user pool using the AWS Management Console.

1. Log in to your AWS console and provide your credentials to go to the Amazon Cognito console at https://console.aws.amazon.com/cognito/.

2. Click on the Manage Your User Pools button. The Your User Pools page will appear.

3. Choose the user pool my-dev-pool that you created in Exercise 11-1.

4. On the General Settings page, click on the Delete Pool button, which is in the upper-right corner of the page.

5. Enter **delete** in the popup prompt to confirm and click Delete Pool.

Questions

The following questions will help you gauge your understanding of the contents in this chapter. Read all the answers carefully because there might be more than one correct answer. Choose the best responses for each question.

1. What is an Amazon Cognito user pool?
   A. It is a user directory that can be configured for your web and mobile applications where you can securely store your users' profile attributes.
   B. It allows you to stream large volume of data to Kinesis in real time.
   C. It enables developers to run multiple AWS Lambda functions.
   D. It allows customers to encrypt their data using the Cognito key.

2. What is an Amazon Cognito identity pool?
   A. It enables developers to run multiple AWS Lambda functions.
   B. It allows customers to encrypt their data using the Cognito key.
   C. It can be configured for your web and mobile applications where you can securely store your users' profile attributes.
   D. It allows you to create unique identities for users and authenticate them with third-party identity providers.

3. Which AWS service supports SAML or OpenID Connect, social identity providers like Amazon, Twitter, and Facebook, and also allows you to integrate with your own identity provider?

   A. AWS Lambda

   B. Amazon EC2

   C. Amazon Cognito

   D. Amazon S3

4. Can you customize sign-up and sign-in by adding your application-specific logic to the user sign-up and sign-in flows in workflows?

   A. No, it is not possible to customize the workflow.

   B. Yes, it is possible to customize the workflow by using Amazon Route 53.

   C. Yes, it is possible to customize the workflow by using Amazon EBS.

   D. Yes, it is possible using Lambda functions to customize the workflow.

5. Is it possible to migrate your existing users to the Amazon Cognito user pool?

   A. Yes, the import tool can be used to migrate the existing users to the user pool.

   B. No, it is not possible to import the existing users other than manually adding them to the user pool.

   C. Yes, it is possible using Amazon Polly.

   D. Yes, you can use the AWS Database Migration Service to import the users to the user pool.

6. Where do you store data associated with a Cognito identity?

   A. Data can be stored on the Amazon Aurora database and on Amazon S3.

   B. Data can be stored both locally on the device and in the Cognito sync store as key/value pairs.

   C. Data can be stored on the Amazon Redshift database and on Amazon Glacier.

   D. Data can be stored on Amazon EBS volumes and on Amazon EFS.

7. You want to enable federated single sign-on (SSO) for your users to log in to the AWS Management Console or call the AWS API operations without creating an IAM user for everyone in your organization. Which of the following you can use as the solution for this scenario?

   A. You can use an open standard such as SAML 2.0

   B. Amazon Virtual Private Cloud (VPC)

   C. Amazon Elastic Compute Cloud (EC2)

   D. Amazon Route 53

8. You don't want your application to manage the overhead of handling the tokens returned from social sign-in through Amazon, Google, and Facebook. What feature of Amazon Cognito handles this for you?

   A. Amazon Cognito sync

   B. Amazon Cognito identity pool

   C. Amazon Cognito user pool

   D. AWS Identity and Access Management (IAM)

9. Your customer wants to add a second level of authentication instead of solely relying on a username and password combination to access your Amazon Cognito user pool. How can you achieve this?

   A. You can add multifactor authentication (MFA) to a user pool.

   B. You can add MFA to an identity pool.

   C. You can add MFA to a sync.

   D. It is not possible to add a second level of authentication.

10. You can create an AWS Lambda function and then trigger that function during which of the following user pool operations with a Lambda trigger? (Choose three.)

    A. User sign-up

    B. Confirmation

    C. Sign-in

    D. Multiple Availability Zones (AZs)

Answers

1. **A.** It is a user directory that can be configured for your web and mobile applications where you can securely store your users' profile attributes.

2. **D.** It allows you to create unique identities for users and authenticate them with third-party identity providers.

3. **C.** Amazon Cognito supports SAML or OpenID Connect, social identity providers, and also allows your own identity provider.

4. **D.** Yes, it is possible using Lambda functions to customize the workflow.

5. **A.** Yes, the import tool can be used to migrate the existing users to the user pool.

6. **B.** Data can be stored both locally on the device and in the Cognito sync store as key/value pairs.

7. **A.** You can use an open standard such as SAML 2.0 to enable federated SSO.

8. **C.** An Amazon Cognito user pool manages the overhead of handling the tokens returned from social sign-in.

9. **A.** You can add multifactor authentication (MFA) to a user pool for a second level of authentication.

10. **A, B, C.** The AWS Lambda function can be triggered during user sign-up, confirmation, and sign-in user pool operations.

Additional Resources

- **AWS Blogs**   There is no place like official AWS documentation to get the latest and most up-to-date information about all the AWS services. Always refer to the official AWS blogs to get the latest updates about new AWS services and updates to existing features.
  `https://docs.aws.amazon.com/cognito` and `https://aws.amazon.com/blogs/aws`

- **User Sign-in and Sign-up with Amazon Cognito**   This blog explains how AWS Mobile Hub and Amazon Cognito enable user sign-up and sign-in.
  `https://aws.amazon.com/blogs/mobile/user-sign-in-and-sign-up-for-ionic-mobile-apps-with-amazon-cognito/`

- **Fine-Grained Authorization with Amazon Cognito**   This blog explains how to integrate authentication and authorization by using Amazon Cognito to control permissions for different user groups in your application to ensure users have appropriate access to backend resources.
  `https://aws.amazon.com/blogs/mobile/building-fine-grained-authorization-using-amazon-cognito-user-pools-groups/`

- **Migrating Users to Amazon Cognito**   This blog explains the options and provides step-by-step instructions on how to use Amazon Cognito User Pools.
  `https://aws.amazon.com/blogs/mobile/migrating-users-to-amazon-cognito-user-pools/`

- **Use Amazon Cognito with AWS Lambda to Detect Cheating**   This blog explains how to prevent an exploit using Amazon Cognito and AWS Lambda.
  `https://aws.amazon.com/blogs/mobile/using-amazon-cognito-and-aws-lambda-to-detect-cheating/`

- **Passwordless E-mail Authentication Using Amazon Cognito**   This blog explains how to implement passwordless authentication by sending a one-time login code to the user's e-mail address.
  `https://aws.amazon.com/blogs/mobile/implementing-passwordless-email-authentication-with-amazon-cognito/`

CHAPTER 12

Protecting Your Data Using Server-Side and Client-Side Encryption

In this chapter, you will learn

- Data protection
- Server-side encryption
- Client-side encryption

In this chapter, we will explore how to protect your data using both server-side encryption and client-side encryption.

Data Protection

AWS offers many services to protect your data at rest or in transit. First let's look at some of the cryptographic concepts and then explore the services provided by AWS. Cryptography uses coded algorithms, signatures, and hashes to protect your data, which can be at rest, such as in a file on a hard drive, or in transit, such as electronic communication exchanged between two or more parties. The primary goals of cryptography are

- **Confidentiality**   To make sure the data is available only to authorized users and no one else.
- **Data Integrity**   To ensure the data has not been manipulated during transit or at rest.
- **Authentication**   To confirm the authenticity of the data or the identity of a user who has access to the data.
- **Nonrepudiation**   To provide assurance to the sender and recipient of the data so neither can deny sending or receiving it.

Cryptography uses a primitive, which is a cryptographic algorithm, including encryption algorithms, digital signature algorithms, hashes, and other functions to provide information security, and AWS uses well-established primitives.

- **Plaintext**   This is any data that is in human-readable or unprotected form, which needs to be encrypted for security or compliance reasons.

- **Encryption**   This is the process of converting readable plaintext data into ciphertext, an unreadable form using an encryption algorithm that is nearly impossible to reverse without an encryption key. AWS supports and transparently encrypts the data that you store and decrypts it for you.

- **Encryption Algorithm**   This is a defined set of instructions that lists exactly how plaintext data is converted into ciphertext by using an encryption key as input and the ciphertext as output. The AWS Key Management Service (KMS) uses the Advanced Encryption Standard (AES) symmetric algorithm.

- **Decryption**   This is the process of transforming the ciphertext back to the original plaintext using an encryption key and any additional authenticated data (AAD).

- **Data Key**   A data encryption key is used to protect data by encrypting data or other data keys. You can use the AWS Key Management Service to generate a data key, which returns a plaintext key, and to encrypt your customer master key.

- **Master Key**   This is used to encrypt data keys and key encryption keys, and it must be kept in plaintext in order to decrypt the encrypted keys. The AWS Key Management Service generates and protects master keys, and the customer master keys (CMKs) are managed entirely within AWS KMS.

- **Private Key**   This is one part of a pair of keys used to protect data in asymmetric encryption, where the public key is distributed to multiple entities and the private key is distributed to a single entity so only the private key holder can decrypt it.

- **Public Key**   This is one part of a pair of keys used to protect data in an asymmetric encryption, where the public key is distributed to multiple entities and it can be authenticated, since the public key signature proves that a trusted entity encrypted and sent it.

- **Asymmetric and Symmetric Encryption**   When both encryption and decryption use the same secret key, it's called symmetric encryption. When a public key is used for encryption and its corresponding private key is used for decryption, it's called asymmetric encryption.

- **AAD**   This is additional data provided for encryption and decryption purposes that serves as an additional authenticity check and verifies integrity of the encrypted data. The data decryption will fail if the AAD supplied for encryption does not match the AAD supplied during the encryption process, and both the AWS Encryption software development kit (SDK) and AWS Key KMS support AAD.

- **Encryption Context** This is a type of AAD that consists of nonsecret name-value pairs that KMS uses to encrypt and decrypt data.

- **Stream Cipher** This is an algorithm that encrypts data one bit at a time.

- **Block Cipher** This is an algorithm that encrypts data one block at a time.

- **Ciphertext** This is encrypted data in an unreadable format.

- **Key Encryption Key** This encryption key is used to encrypt a data key or another key encryption key, and it is encrypted and protected with a master key.

- **Envelope Encryption** This is a strategy for protecting the encryption keys that were used to encrypt your data. Plaintext data is encrypted with a data key, which in turn is encrypted with the key encryption key. The data encryption key is encrypted with another encryption key, and finally, the master key is used to encrypt the key encryption key. The master key is the top-level plaintext key encryption key, as shown in Figure 12-1.

Figure 12-1
Envelope
encryption

Master Key

Encrypt

Key Encryption Key

Encrypt

Key Encryption Key

Encrypt

Data Key

Encrypt

Data

Figure 12-2
Symmetric key
encryption

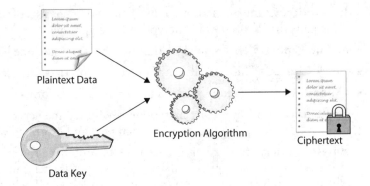

The AWS Key Management Service protects the master key that must remain in plaintext, and it will never allow the master key to leave the service unencrypted.

- **Cryptographic Algorithms**   An encryption algorithm is set of instructions that transform readable plaintext into unreadable ciphertext. Algorithms use advanced mathematics to make it relatively easy to encrypt but virtually impossible to decrypt without the necessary keys. The AWS Key Management Service uses the AES algorithm with 256-bit secret keys.

- **Symmetric Algorithms**   Encryption is symmetric if it uses the same key to both encrypt and decrypt your plaintext. AES with 128-, 192-, or 256-bit keys and Triple DES (3DES) with three 56-bit keys are two widely used symmetric algorithms.

 EXAM TIP   Symmetric encryption is known as shared key, shared secret, and secret key encryption.

An algorithm and a symmetric key are used to convert a plaintext message into ciphertext, as shown in Figure 12-2.

Figure 12-3 shows the same secret key and symmetric algorithm being used to turn ciphertext back into plaintext.

Figure 12-3
Symmetric key
decryption

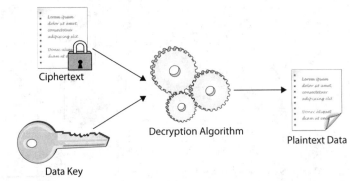

Block ciphers and stream ciphers are the two types of symmetric key ciphers. When the plaintext is divided into fixed-length blocks and encrypts one block at a time, it is called a block cipher. It is more powerful and practical primitives but slower. When the plaintext is encrypted one unit at a time, it's called a stream cipher.

- **Asymmetric Algorithms** Encryption is asymmetric when it uses one key for encryption and another mathematically related key for decryption. One key is distributed publicly (a public key), while its other related key is kept private and secure (a private key). Public key cryptography is based on mathematical problems that cannot be easily reversed.

 EXAM TIP AWS Signature Version 4 should be used for uploading or accessing objects encrypted by SSE-KMS for added security.

Data protection refers to both protecting your data while in transit as it travels to and from Amazon S3 and at rest while it is stored on disks in Amazon S3 datacenters. The data can be protected in transit using Secure Sockets Layer (SSL) or client-side encryption. You can use AWS CloudHSM to create and manage the hardware security modules that store your encryption keys. You can use AWS Key Management Service to protect your encryption keys. You can use AWS Encryption SDK, the DynamoDB Encryption Client, or the Amazon S3 Encryption Client to protect your data before sending it to AWS for client-side encryption.

- **Server-Side Encryption** Amazon S3 encrypts your object before saving it to disks and then decrypts it when you want to download the object.
- **Client-Side Encryption** You encrypt your data on the client side and upload the encrypted data to Amazon S3. Here, the customer (you) manages the encryption keys, encryption process, and its related tools.

 EXAM TIP When you list objects in your bucket, the API returns a list of all objects, regardless of whether they are encrypted.

Server-Side Encryption

When a service or application encrypts the data at its destination, it's known as server-side encryption. Amazon S3 supports server-side encryption and encrypts your data before writing it to disks in its datacenters and then decrypts it when accessing the object. There is no difference in the way encrypted or unencrypted objects are accessed. Server-side encryption has three mutually exclusive options, as described next, depending on how you manage the encryption keys:

- **Amazon S3–Managed Keys (SSE-S3)** Here each object is encrypted with a unique key in addition to encrypting the key itself with a master key, which is rotated regularly. Amazon S3 server-side encryption uses the 256-bit Advanced Encryption Standard to encrypt your data.

- **CMKs Using KMS**   Here each object is encrypted with a unique key in addition to encrypting the key itself with a master key, which is rotated regularly. This requires separate permissions and provides an audit trail of when your CMK was used and by whom. You are allowed to create and manage customer-managed CMKs, or you can use AWS-managed CMKs that are unique to your region.
- **Customer-Provided Keys (SSE-C)**   Here Amazon S3 uses a customer-provided encryption key to encrypt the data before writing it to the disks, and Amazon S3 decrypts the data when you access your objects by using the customer-provided key.

 EXAM TIP   You can't apply different types of server-side encryption to the same object simultaneously.

Server-Side Encryption with Customer-Managed Keys in KMS

When the data is encrypted at the destination by a service or application, it is known as server-side encryption. Amazon S3 uses AWS KMS CMKs to encrypt the objects in your Amazon S3 bucket if you choose. It encrypts only the object data, not its metadata, using the AWS Management Console or AWS KMS application programming interfaces (APIs). Amazon S3 creates an AWS-managed CMK when you add an SSE-KMS–encrypted object to a bucket and uses the same CMK for SSE-KMS encryption, unless you select a separate customer-managed CMK to add flexibility.

 EXAM TIP   AWS KMS CMK should be in the same region when you use SSE-KMS encryption with an S3 bucket.

You can create and manage a customer-managed key or use an Amazon S3 key that AWS manages for you. Both the AWS CMK– and customer-managed CMK are unique to your region and AWS account, where only Amazon S3 has permission to use this CMK on your behalf. The data key that was used to encrypt your data is encrypted and stored with the data it protects. You can use the AWS KMS console to create, disable, and rotate CMKs, and its security controls help you meet your encryption-related compliance requirements. The bucket policy can be used for server-side encryption of all objects in a particular Amazon S3 bucket. As shown next, the bucket policy allows the upload object (s3:PutObject) permission to apply to everyone only if the request includes the x-amz-server-side-encryption header, which is used with SSE-KMS.

```
{
    "Version":"2012-10-17",
    "Id":"PutObjPolicy",
    "Statement":[{
        "Sid":"AllowUnEncryptedObjectUploads",
        "Effect":"Allow",
        "Principal":"*",
        "Action":"s3:PutObject",
        "Resource":"arn:aws:s3:::YourBucket/*",
```

```
      "Condition":{
        "StringEquals":{
          "s3:x-amz-server-side-encryption":"aws:kms"
        }
      }
    }
  ]
}
```

 EXAM TIP   All GET and PUT requests should be made via either SSL or SigV4 for an object protected by AWS KMS; otherwise, the requests will fail.

You need to use the x-amz-server-side-encryption request header to request SSE-KMS in the object creation REST APIs. You need to use x-amz-server-side-encryption-aws-kms-key-id to specify the ID of the AWS KMS CMK that was used for the object. Amazon S3 APIs support the PUT operation to upload data and specify request headers. You can initiate a multipart upload for large objects using the multipart upload API. You can use the POST operation to upload an object instead of the request headers. The COPY operation can be used to copy an object from a source object to a target object. You can apply SSE-KMS headers to the target objects using the COPY operation, and the AWS SDK provides wrapper APIs to request SSE-KMS with Amazon S3.

Server-Side Encryption with Amazon S3–Managed Encryption Keys

You can protect your data at rest using server-side encryption, and Amazon S3 uses a unique key to encrypt each object; in addition, it encrypts the key itself with a master key that gets rotated regularly. Amazon S3 server-side encryption uses the 256-bit Advanced Encryption Standard to encrypt your data, and a bucket policy can be used to encrypt all the objects in a bucket. As shown here, the bucket policy allows permissions to upload an object when the request includes the x-amz-server-side-encryption header to request server-side encryption:

```
{
  "Version": "2012-10-17",
  "Id": "PutObjPolicy",
  "Statement": [
    {
      "Sid": "AllowCorrectEncryptionHeader",
      "Effect": "Allow",
      "Principal": "*",
      "Action": "s3:PutObject",
      "Resource": "arn:aws:s3:::YourBucket/*",
      "Condition": {
        "StringNotEquals": {
          "s3:x-amz-server-side-encryption": "AES256"
        }
      }
    },
```

```
{
  "Sid": "AllowEncryptedObjectUploads",
  "Effect": "Allow",
  "Principal": "*",
  "Action": "s3:PutObject",
  "Resource": "arn:aws:s3:::YourBucket/*",
  "Condition": {
    "Null": {
      "s3:x-amz-server-side-encryption": "true"
    }
  }
}
        }
    ]
}
```

 NOTE In addition to kms:ReEncrypt, kms:GenerateDataKey, and kms:DescribeKey, you need the kms:Decrypt permission to upload or download an Amazon S3 object encrypted with an AWS KMS CMK.

You need to use the x-amz-server-side-encryption request header to request server-side encryption using the object creation REST APIs. The Amazon S3 APIs support PUT operations to specify the request header when uploading data. You can initiate multipart upload to upload large objects. COPY operations can be used to copy an object from a source object to a target object. You can use the AWS Management Console to upload objects and request server-side encryption, or use the AWS SDKs, which provide wrapper APIs, to request server-side encryption.

Server-Side Encryption with Customer-Provided Encryption Keys

You can protect your data at rest using server-side encryption with customer-provided encryption keys (SSE-C), where Amazon S3 manages both the encryption when it writes to disks and decryption as you access your objects. You don't need to maintain any code to perform data encryption or decryption, except managing the encryption keys that you provided. Amazon S3 uses the encryption key when you upload an object to apply AES-256 encryption to your data. You must provide the same encryption key when you retrieve an object, and Amazon S3 first verifies the encryption key before decrypting the object data.

 EXAM TIP If you lose encryption key, you lose the object because Amazon S3 does not store the encryption key and stores a randomly salted hash based message authentication code (HMAC) value instead, which cannot be used either to obtain the encryption key or to decrypt the contents of the encrypted object.

You must use HTTPS because Amazon S3 rejects any requests made over HTTP when using SSE-C. You need to manage a mapping of which object is using which encryption key, since Amazon S3 does not store or manage the encryption keys. You are responsible for tracking each object's encryption key, and each object version can have its own encryption key when you upload using this feature with versioning enabled. In addition to managing the encryption keys on the client side, you need to perform key rotation on the client side.

CAUTION   Any GET request without an encryption key fails if you lose the encryption key, and in turn you lose the object.

You must provide encryption key information when using server-side encryption with customer-provided encryption keys (SSE-C) for the x-amz-server-side-encryption-customer-algorithm to specify the encryption algorithm with the header value AES256. The x-amz-server-side-encryption-customer-key can be used to provide the 256-bit, base64-encoded encryption key for encrypting or decrypting your data. The x-amz-server-side-encryption-customer-key-MD5 can be used to provide the 128-bit MD5, base64-encoded encryption key for a message integrity check to make sure it was transmitted without error. AWS SDK wrapper libraries can be used to add the headers to your request, and you can make the Amazon S3 REST API calls directly in your application.

Amazon S3 APIs support the GET operation when retrieving objects and the HEAD operation to retrieve object metadata by specifying the request headers. The PUT operation is used when uploading data, and the multipart upload is used to upload large objects. The POST operation can be used to upload an object, instead of the request headers, and the COPY operation to copy an object from a source object to a target object.

EXAM TIP   The Amazon S3 console cannot be used to update an existing object or to upload an object and request SSE-C.

Client-Side Encryption

When you encrypt data before sending it to Amazon S3, it is known as client-side encryption, and it can use either a CMK stored in AWS KMS or use a master key stored within your application.

CMK Stored in AWS KMS

When you use the CMK ID to upload an object, the client sends the request to AWS KMS for a CMK to encrypt your object data. AWS KMS returns two versions of a randomly generated data key, a plaintext version of the data key, and a cipher blob of the same data key. The client downloads the encrypted object from Amazon S3 along with object metadata when downloading an object. The client then sends the cipher blob to decrypt the object data using AWS KMS to get the plaintext version of the data key.

EXAM TIP The client receives a unique data key for every uploaded object.

Master Key Stored in the Application

You can use the master key stored within your application for client-side data encryption. It's important to safely manage your encryption keys because neither client-side master keys nor your unencrypted data are sent to AWS, so you can't decrypt your data if you lose it. You provide a client-side master key to the Amazon S3 encryption client when uploading an object. The master key is used by the client to encrypt the data; the encryption key is generated randomly. The Amazon S3 encryption client generates a one-time-use data encryption key, or data key, locally. It uses the data key to encrypt the data of a single Amazon S3 object, and the client generates a separate data key for each object. The client encrypts the data encryption key using the master key, and then the client uploads the encrypted data key as part of the object metadata. The client determines which client-side master key is used for decryption based on the material description. The client uploads the encrypted data and saves the encrypted data key in Amazon S3 as metadata. The client downloads the encrypted object when you download an object from Amazon S3. The client determines which master key from the object's metadata to use it for decrypting the data key. The master key is used by the client to decrypt the data key, and then it uses the data key to decrypt the object. The symmetric key or a public/private key pair can be your client-side master key.

Command-Line Encryption and Decryption

Data is encrypted and decrypted at the command line using the AWS Encryption CLI, which has advanced data protection built into it. The AWS Encryption CLI is built for Python and supported on Linux, macOS, and Windows platforms. Data can be encrypted and decrypted in a shell on Linux and macOS, in a Command (CMD) Prompt window on Windows, or in a PowerShell console on any system.

Encrypt a File

We are going to encrypt the mask.txt file using the AWS Encryption CLI. The mask.txt file contains an AWS Developer string that is stored in your current directory, and the encrypted output will be stored to the same directory.

```
$ ls
mask.txt

$ cat mask.txt
AWS Developer
```

This example is using macOS shell, which is similar to Linux shell, a CMD Prompt, or a PowerShell.

As shown in Figure 12-4, you specify a data key when you encrypt data. We can use an AWS KMS CMK as the master key, and your credentials are available to the AWS Encryption CLI, which has permission to call Decrypt APIs and AWS KMS Generate-DataKey on the CMK. You need to save the AWS KMS CMK ID in the $keyID variable, as shown in the first line. Then you can use the -- encrypt parameter to encrypt the data in the mask.txt file, as shown in the second line.

```
1. $ keyID = "432112344321"
2. $ aws-encryption-cli --encrypt --input mask.txt \
                --master-keys key=$keyID \
                --encryption-context purpose=enc-test \
                --metadata-output ~/metadata \
                --output .
```

The --encrypt parameter specifies the encryption action, the --master-keys parameter specifies the AWS KMS CMK ID, and the --encryption-context parameter specifies an encryption context, a key-value pair, and purpose=enc-test—it is also a recommended best practice. The --metadata-output parameter specifies the location to write the metadata, which includes the full paths to the input and output files. The --input parameter is mask.txt, and the --output parameter mask.txt. encrypted (which gets created when the -- encrypt command is successful) and (.) represent the output location, which is the current directory. Now use ls to view directory listing, as shown here.

```
$ ls
mask.txt  mask.txt.encrypted
```

The output file of the --encrypt command will be same as the input filename and will have the .encrypted suffix by default, but it can be changed by using --suffix. The mask.txt.encrypted file contains the secure encrypted message, including metadata, encryption context, and encrypted copy of the data key, in addition to the encrypted data.

Figure 12-4
Encryption

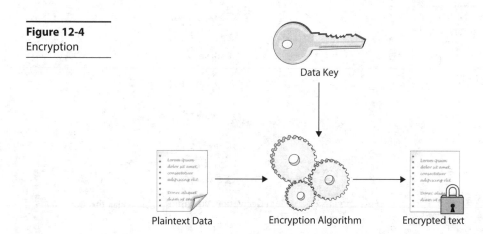

Data Key

Plaintext Data   Encryption Algorithm   Encrypted text

Decrypt a File

Now, let us decrypt the mask.txt.encrypted file that we created in the previous section. Use the following command to decrypt the contents of the mask.txt.encrypted file:

```
$ aws-encryption-cli --decrypt --input mask.txt.encrypted \
                     --encryption-context purpose=enc-test \
                     --metadata-output ~/metadata \
                     --output .
```

The --decrypt command requires the --input parameter as mask.txt.encrypted file and the --output parameter mask.txt.encrypted.decrypted (which is created when the -- decrypt command is successful), and (.) represents the output location, which is the current directory. We need to supply the same --encryption-context parameter that was used in the encrypt command as a best practice. The --metatdata-output parameter defines the location of the metadata for the decrypt command.

As shown in Figure 12-5, the decrypt command generates the file of decrypted (plaintext) data when it is successful; use the ls command to list the files in the current location and then the cat command to display the contents of the file.

```
$ ls
mask.txt  mask.txt.encrypted mask.txt.encrypted.decrypted

$ cat mask.txt.encrypted.decrypted
AWS Developer
```

As you can see, the decrypt output file has the same name as the input file with the .decrypted suffix, and we can use the --suffix parameter to create a custom suffix. We have gone through the steps to encrypt and decrypt a single file, and you can use the AWS Encryption CLI to encrypt and decrypt all or just selected files in a directory and its subdirectories.

Figure 12-5
Decryption

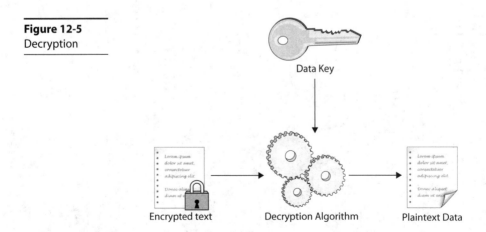

Data Key

Encrypted text   Decryption Algorithm   Plaintext Data

Data Protection Best Practices

The following best practices describe the steps that you need to take to secure your data using encryption.

- **Identify data protection requirements**   Plan and identify your data protection requirements, like encryption for data in transit, at rest, and data retention, that meet your compliance, legal, and organizational requirements.

- **Secure key administration**   Define strict controls to store and rotate your encryption keys, and use different keys based on data classification and retention requirements.

- **Encryption at rest**   It is mandatory to encrypt all your data at rest as a best practice to help protect it.

- **Strict access control**   Enforce least privileges and provide only the access required. Monitor the access list regularly, and remove users who no longer need access.

- **Protect sensitive data**   Expose as an API or create an Amazon QuickSight dashboard instead of providing direct access to your sensitive data.

- **Identify compliance requirements**   Discover the organizational, legal, and compliance requirements your workload needs to comply with.

- **Data retention**   Identify your data retention requirements, including the length of time and number of previous versions or copies.

- **AWS Secrets Manager**   You can manage secrets like database credentials, passwords, third-party API keys, and any arbitrary text using AWS Secrets Manager.

- **Split data by classification**   You can use different AWS accounts for production and nonproduction environments.

- **Amazon S3 encryption**   Take advantage of Amazon S3 encryption and encrypt your objects using either client-side or server-side techniques.

- **Encrypt Amazon Machine Images (AMIs)**   You can use Copy to encrypt an existing AMI with encryption enabled to automatically encrypt root volumes and snapshots.

- **Enable Amazon RDS encryption**   Enable encryption for the Amazon RDS database and snapshots at rest.

- **Amazon DynamoDB encryption**   Use the AWS KMS–managed encryption key to encrypt DynamoDB data at rest.

- **AWS Encryption SDK**   Use AWS KMS with AWS Encryption SDK to encrypt data on the client side based on your application requirements.

PART IV

Chapter Review

This chapter began by explaining data protection while the data is in transit and at rest. It then introduced server-side encryption, where your object is encrypted before being saved to disks. The object is then decrypted when you download it. Client-side encryption is used to encrypt your data on the client side and upload the encrypted data to Amazon S3. Amazon S3–managed keys were discussed next, where each object is encrypted with a unique key in addition to encrypting the key itself with a master key, which is rotated regularly. Amazon S3 server-side encryption uses the 256-bit Advanced Encryption Standard to encrypt your data. CMKs using KMS is used to encrypt objects with a unique key, in addition to encrypting the key itself with a master key, which is rotated regularly. Customer-provided keys are used by Amazon S3 to encrypt the data before writing it to the disks, and Amazon S3 decrypts the data when you access your objects using the customer-provided key. You can use client-side encryption to encrypt your objects before sending them to Amazon S3 by using either a CMK stored in AWS KMS or using a master key stored in your application. The chapter then showed the steps to encrypt and decrypt the data at the command line using AWS Encryption CLI and finally listed best practices to help protect your data.

Exercises

The following exercises will help you practice creating and managing CMKs. You need to create an AWS account, as explained earlier, to perform these exercises. You can use the Free Tier when launching AWS resources, but make sure to terminate them at the end.

Exercise 12-1: Create CMKs Using the AWS Management Console

The step-by-step instructions will help you create a customer-managed key using the AWS Management Console.

1. Use your AWS account e-mail address and password to sign in and then navigate to the AWS KMS console at https://console.aws.amazon.com/kms/.
2. Verify the AWS region by using the selector in the upper-right corner of the page.
3. From the navigation pane on the left, choose Customer Managed Keys.
4. Click the Create Key button.
5. Type **my-custom-key** for the alias.
6. Type **This is my first customer managed key my-custom-key** for the description.
7. In Advanced Options choose KMS, which is the default.
8. Choose Next to navigate to the next page.
9. Type **Name** for the tag key and **My First Custom Key** for the tag value.
10. Choose Next to navigate to the next page.
11. Select the IAM users and roles from the list that can administer this CMK.
12. From the Key Deletion section at the bottom of the page, leave the default checkbox Allow Key Administrators To Delete This Key selected.

13. Choose Next.

14. Select the IAM users and roles from the list that can use the CMK for cryptographic operations.

15. You can also allow other AWS accounts to use this CMK for cryptographic operations by choosing Add Another AWS Account or leave this at the default.

16. Choose Next to navigate to the next screen.

17. Review the key policy JSON document that was created based on your previous choices. You can edit it from here as well.

18. Click on the Finish button to create the CMK.

19. You will see a success message with the alias name, key ID, status, and creation date.

Exercise 12-2: Create a List of Your Customer-Managed Keys in the AWS Management Console

The step-by-step instructions will assist you in listing all your customer-managed keys using AWS Management Console.

1. Use your AWS account e-mail address and password to sign in and then navigate to the AWS KMS console at https://console.aws.amazon.com/kms/.

2. Verify the AWS region by using the Region selector in the upper-right corner of the page.

3. You can choose to view the customer-managed keys or AWS-managed keys by selecting from the left navigation menu.

4. From the Customer Managed Keys page, in the top-center filter box, enter all or part of the alias name or the key ID **my-custom-key** of a CMK.

Exercise 12-3: Enable Key Rotations Using the AWS Management Console

The following step-by-step instructions will help you enable key rotations using the AWS Management Console.

1. Use your AWS account e-mail address and password to sign in and then navigate to the AWS KMS console at https://console.aws.amazon.com/kms/.

2. Verify the AWS region by using the Region selector in the upper-right corner of the page.

3. From the left navigation pane, choose Customer Managed Keys.

4. Choose the alias my-custom-key that you want to enable key rotation for.

5. Select the Key Rotation tab below the General Configuration area.

6. Select the Automatically Rotate This CMK Every Year checkbox.

7. Click Save to save your updates.

Exercise 12-4: Update the CMK Tag in the AWS Management Console

The following step-by-step instructions will help you update the customer-managed key tags using the AWS Management Console.

1. Use your AWS account e-mail address and password to sign in and then navigate to the AWS KMS console at https://console.aws.amazon.com/kms/.

2. Verify the AWS region by using the Region selector in the upper-right corner of the page.

3. From the left navigation pane, choose Customer Managed Keys.

4. Choose the alias my-custom-key to edit its description.

5. From the upper-right corner, choose Edit, which is next to Key Actions.

6. For Description, type **This is my updated customer managed key my-custom-key**.

7. Click Save to save your changes.

Exercise 12-5: Disable CMK Using the AWS Management Console

The following step-by-step instructions will assist you in disabling the customer-managed key using the AWS Management Console.

1. Use your AWS account e-mail address and password to sign in and then navigate to the AWS KMS console at https://console.aws.amazon.com/kms/.

2. Verify the AWS region by using the Region selector in the upper-right corner of the page.

3. From the left navigation pane, choose Customer Managed Keys.

4. Select the check box next to my-custom-key.

5. To disable the my-custom-key CMK, choose Key Actions, Disable.

6. From the pop-up menu, select Confirm and click on Disable Key.

Questions

The following questions will help you gauge your understanding of the contents in this chapter. Read all the answers carefully because there might be more than one correct answer. Choose the best responses for each question.

1. You are storing sensitive data on Amazon Simple Storage Service (S3) that must be encrypted at rest per your company's compliance requirements. Which of the following methods can achieve this? (Choose three.)

   A. You can use Amazon S3 server-side encryption with AWS Key Management Service–managed keys.

   B. You can use Amazon S3 server-side encryption with customer-provided keys.

    C. You can encrypt the data on the client side before writing to Amazon S3 using your own master key.

    D. You can use Amazon S3 bucket policies to restrict access to the data at rest.

2. Your company security policy mandates that you encrypt data before ingesting it to Amazon S3. What are the options to enable client-side encryption? (Choose two.)

    A. You can use a customer master key stored in AWS Key Management Service.

    B. You can use a master key you store within your application.

    C. You can use server-side encryption with Amazon S3–managed keys.

    D. You can use server-side encryption with keys stored in AWS Key Management Service.

3. Which of the following request headers are supported in Amazon S3 APIs? (Choose three.)

    A. Use the PUT operation to upload your data using the PUT API.

    B. Use the MULTIPLY operation to upload large objects using the multipart upload API.

    C. Use the POST operation to upload an object.

    D. Use the COPY operation to copy an object from the source to the target.

4. What request header can be explicitly specified when you are uploading an object to Amazon S3 to request server-side encryption using the REST API?

    A. x-amz-storage-class

    B. Content-MD5

    C. x-amz-security-token

    D. x-amz-server-side-encryption

5. You are downloading an encrypted object from Amazon S3, which was encrypted using server-side encryption. How you can decrypt the object after downloading it from the S3 bucket?

    A. Amazon S3 does not support server-side decryption.

    B. Amazon S3 provides a separate server-side key to encrypt and decrypt the object.

    C. You need to decrypt each object using your own private key.

    D. Amazon S3 manages encryption and decryption automatically.

6. A company stores static web content in Amazon S3 in us-west-1 that is encrypted using SSE-KMS encryption. Where must the AWS KMS CMK reside?

    A. AWS KMS CMK must be in the eu-central-1 region.

    B. AWS KMS CMK must be in the us-east-1 region.

    C. AWS KMS CMK must be in us-west-1 region.

    D. AWS KMS CMK must be in the eu-west-1 region.

7. Your company is planning to encrypt all objects uploaded to Amazon S3 from an application. They don't want to implement their own encryption algorithm; instead, they are planning to use server-side encryption by supplying their own key. Which of the following parameters is not required while making a call for SSE-C?

   A. x-amz-server-side-encryption-customer-algorithm

   B. x-amz-server-side-encryption-customer-key-AES256(Ans)

   C. x-amz-server-side-encryption-customer-key-MD5

   D. x-amz-server-side-encryption-customer-key

8. You have enabled versioning on an Amazon S3 bucket with server-side encryption for data at rest. What is the recommended best practice in terms of security when you supply your own keys for encryption (SSE-C)?

   A. You should always use Amazon S3 encryption key for increased security.

   B. You should not use your own security key, as it is not entirely secure.

   C. You need to configure Amazon S3 to use SSL for more security.

   D. You need to keep rotating the encryption key manually at the client side.

9. A company wants to encrypt all their objects stored in Amazon S3 using server-side encryption. But your company does not want to use the AES 256 encryption key provided by Amazon S3. What is the solution?

   A. The company should upload its secret key for Amazon S3 to decrypt the objects.

   B. The company should upload the encryption key to each S3 bucket.

   C. Amazon S3 does not support client-supplied encryption keys.

   D. The company should send the keys and encryption algorithm with each API call.

10. A company has enabled versioning on all their Amazon S3 buckets and is using server-side encryption for data at rest. If the company is supplying its own keys for encryption (SSE-C), which of the following statements is true?

   A. The company should use just one encryption key for all versions of the same object.

   B. Different encryption keys will be used for different versions of the same object.

   C. Amazon S3 does not allow user keys for server-side encryption.

   D. You cannot use SSE-C when versioning is enabled.

Answers

1. **A, B, C.** You can use Amazon S3 server-side encryption with AWS Key Management Service–managed keys, use Amazon S3 server-side encryption with customer-provided keys, or encrypt the data on the client side before writing to Amazon S3 using your own master key.

2. **A, B.** You can use a customer master key stored in AWS Key Management Service, or use a master key you store within your application.

3. **A, C, D.** Use the PUT operation to upload your data using the PUT API, the POST operation is used to upload an object, and the COPY operation is used to copy an object from the source to target.

4. **D.** You need to use the x-amz-server-side-encryption request header explicitly in a request when you are uploading an object to Amazon S3 to request server-side encryption using the REST API.

5. **D.** Amazon S3 manages encryption and decryption automatically.

6. **C.** AWS KMS CMK must be in the us-west-1 region.

7. **B.** The x-amz-server-side-encryption-customer-key-AES256 parameter is not required while making a call for SSE-C.

8. **D.** When you supply your own keys for encryption (SSE-C), you need to keep rotating the encryption key manually on the client side.

9. **D.** The company should send the keys and encryption algorithm with each API call.

10. **B.** Different encryption keys will be used for different versions of the same object.

Additional Resources

- **AWS Docs**   There is no place like official AWS documentation to get the latest and most up-to-date information about all the AWS services. Always refer to the official AWS blogs to get the latest updates about new AWS services and updates to existing features.
  `https://docs.aws.amazon.com` and `https://aws.amazon.com/blogs/security/tag/encryption/`

- **Securing Data with AWS KMS Encryption**   This blog explains key management, creating keys and encrypted databases, and how to rotate keys and control key access.
  `https://aws.amazon.com/blogs/database/securing-data-in-amazon-rds-using-aws-kms-encryption/`

- **Create EBS-Backed EC2 Instances**   This blog demonstrates how to use an unencrypted AMI and launch an encrypted EBS-backed Amazon EC2 instance using the AWS Management Console.
  `https://aws.amazon.com/blogs/security/how-to-quickly-launch-encrypted-ebs-backed-ec2-instances-from-unencrypted-amis/`

- **SQL Database Client-Side Encryption**   This blog explains the approach to client-side encryption with SQL databases using AWS KMS.
  `https://aws.amazon.com/blogs/database/performing-sql-database-client-side-encryption-for-multi-region-high-availability/`

PART V

Creating SQL and NoSQL Database in AWS Cloud

■ **Chapter 13**   AWS Relational Database Services
■ **Chapter 14**   AWS NoSQL Database Service: Amazon DynamoDB

AWS Relational Database Services

In this chapter, you will learn

- Amazon RDS
- Read replicas
- Option groups
- DB parameter groups
- Backups
- Snapshots
- Security
- Monitoring
- Best practices

This chapter will explain in detail the Amazon Relational Database Service (RDS) and its features.

Amazon Relational Database Service

The Amazon RDS offers different database options to choose from, like MySQL, MariaDB, PostgreSQL, Oracle, Microsoft SQL Server, and Amazon Aurora. RDS scales up the database based on CPU, memory, storage, and input\output operations per second (IOPS), and it manages software patching, backups, recovery, and automatic failure detection. The automated backups can be configured based on your need, or you can create manual backup snapshots. When you enable Multi-AZ, the primary DB instance offers high availability, and you can easily fail over to a synchronous secondary instance when required. The RDS database can be protected by creating it within a Virtual Private Cloud (VPC); in addition, you can control who can access your RDS databases by using AWS Identity and Access Management (IAM) that defines users and permissions.

Amazon RDS creates a DB instance as an isolated database environment, where you can contain multiple user-created databases. You can use the same tools and applications that you use with an on-premise database instance to access your DB instance. The RDS DB instances can be created or modified by using the AWS Command Line Interface

(CLI), Amazon RDS application programming interface (API), or the AWS Management Console. You can choose on-demand DB instances or reserved DB instances for your Amazon RDS database instance.

Based on the DB Engine, the RDS databases have specific features and a set of parameters in a DB parameter group, which controls the behavior of the databases. The DB instance class determines the computation and memory capacity of a DB instance. Although you select the DB instance depending on your needs, it can be changed over time when your need changes. Magnetic, General Purpose (SSD), and Provisioned IOPS (PIOPS) are the three types of DB instance storage types that differ in performance characteristics and price. The database engine and storage type determine the minimum and maximum storage requirements of the DB instance. It's important to have enough storage to write the database content or logs in addition to have room to grow.

Amazon RDS can be used either within a VPC or outside it without any additional cost. Amazon RDS uses the Network Time Protocol (NTP) to synchronize the time, and it manages software patching, automatic failure detection, backups, and recovery. The DB instance can be run in multiple Availability Zones, which is called a Multi-AZ deployment. Amazon automatically creates and manages the secondary standby database instance in a different Availability Zone. In Multi-AZ, the primary DB instance is synchronously replicated to the secondary instance across another Availability Zone. This helps eliminate I/O freezes and provides data redundancy and failover support, in addition to minimizing the latency spikes during system backups.

There are many ways to connect with your Amazon RDS instance. You can use the web-based user interface to manage your DB instances from the AWS Management Console by navigating to https://console.aws.amazon.com/rds/. The AWS CLI can be used to access the Amazon RDS API interactively. You can access the Amazon RDS programmatically using AWS software development kits (SDKs) for application development that handles low-level details such as authentication, error handling, and retry logic. By default, you can create up to 40 Amazon RDS DB instances, including 10 for SQL Server (Enterprise, Standard, Web, and Express editions) and 40 for MySQL, Oracle, MariaDB, or PostgreSQL; if you need any additional DB instances, use the form at

```
https://console.aws.amazon.com/support/home#/case/create?issueType=service-
limit-increase&limitType=service-code-rds-instances.
```

The Amazon RDS API and AWS CLI use the DB instance identifier, which uniquely identifies the DB instance, and the RDS-supplied DNS hostname includes the identifier. You can create PostgreSQL, MySQL, Oracle, MariaDB, Microsoft SQL Server, and Amazon Aurora DB instances. The DB name should be unique within the DB instance. A master user account is created, which has permissions to create other databases and to perform Data Manipulation Language (DML) and Data Definition Language (DDL) operations on tables. When you create a DB instance, you need to configure the master user password, which can be changed any time using the AWS CLI, Amazon RDS API operations, or the AWS Management Console, in addition to using standard SQL commands. The compute and memory capacity of an Amazon RDS DB instance is determined by the DB instance class, and RDS supports the Burstable Performance instance class, Memory Optimized instance class, and Standard instance class. The following are DB Instance Class hardware specifications:

- **vCPU** Specifies the number of virtual central processing units (CPUs) and is a unit of capacity that you can use to compare DB instance classes when renting capacity by the hour.
- **ECU** Specifies the relative measure of the integer processing power expressed in terms of these EC2 compute units.
- **Memory (GiB)** Specifies the RAM, in gibibytes, allocated to the DB instance and mostly is a consistent ratio between memory and vCPU.
- **VPC Only** Specifies that the instance class is supported only for DB instances that are in a VPC based on the Amazon VPC service.
- **EBS-Optimized** Uses an optimized Elastic Block Store (EBS) storage, which provides additional dedicated capacity for I/O for best performance for your instance.
- **Max. Bandwidth (Mbps)** Specifies the maximum bandwidth in megabits per second.
- **Network Performance** Specifies the network speed relative to other DB instance classes.

Amazon RDS instance performance metrics are on the summary page for your instance, and you can also use Amazon CloudWatch to monitor those metrics. The following are some of the useful metrics for your DB instance:

- **IOPS** The number of I/O operations per second; the total IOPS is calculated from the sum of the read and write IOPS.
- **Latency** The elapsed time between I/O request submission and completion and is reported as the average latency for a given time interval in milliseconds (ms).
- **Throughput** The number of bytes per second transferred; the average throughput ranges from zero to the maximum bandwidth.
- **Queue Depth** The number of I/O requests waiting to be serviced but not sent to the device, since the device is servicing other I/O requests.

 EXAM TIP You can use any standard SQL client application to access the Amazon RDS database because you are not allowed to directly access the database host.

High Availability (Multi-AZ)

Amazon RDS offers high availability and failover support using Multi-AZ deployments. When you create a Multi-AZ database, Amazon RDS creates a synchronous standby replica in another Availability Zone to eliminate I/O freezes and to provide data redundancy. A DB instance with high availability enabled can enhance availability by protecting your databases against DB instance failure and Availability Zone disruption during planned system maintenance.

You can create a Multi-AZ deployment from the RDS console by choosing Multi-AZ when creating a DB instance. You can also convert existing DB instances to Multi-AZ deployments from the console by modifying the DB instance and choosing the Multi-AZ option. The Availability Zone of the standby replica can be viewed in the RDS console or from the AWS CLI by using the `describe-db-instances` command or by using the Amazon RDS API DescribeDBInstances operation. Due to the nature of synchronous data replication, the Multi-AZ deployments may have write and commit latency compared to a Single-AZ deployment. AWS recommends using Provisioned IOPS for your production workloads to ensure consistent performance. When you convert your DB instance from a Single-AZ deployment to a Multi-AZ deployment, Amazon RDS takes a snapshot of the primary DB instance from your deployment, and then restores it into another Availability Zone.

EXAM TIP The Multi-AZ feature is not a scaling solution, so it cannot be used for read-only scenarios; instead, you should use a read replica for read-only traffic.

Multi-AZ Failover Process

An Amazon RDS Multi-AZ instance automatically switches to a standby replica in another Availability Zone in the event of either a planned or unplanned outage. The failover time depends on the database's current activity, size, and other constraints when the primary DB becomes unavailable. It may take additional time for the RDS console user interface (UI) to reflect the new Availability Zone after the failover is complete. The failover automatically changes the DNS record of the DB instance to point to the standby DB instance. The database operations can be resumed quickly without DBA intervention, since failovers are handled automatically. The primary DB instance of Multi-AZ switches over automatically to its standby replica instance when any of the following events occur:

- Whenever there is an outage of an Availability Zone
- The primary DB instance of your Multi-AZ DB instance fails
- The server type of the DB instance is changed
- During patching at the operating system level
- You have initiated a manual failover using reboot with failover

EXAM TIP You can force a Multi-AZ failover manually when you reboot a DB instance.

The Amazon RDS Lifecycle

The Amazon RDS lifecycle includes create, modify, maintain, and upgrade; backups, restore; reboot; and delete.

Modify

Most DB instance changes can be applied immediately or delayed until an upcoming maintenance window. Rebooting is necessary before parameter group changes can take effect. The modify instructions can be applied by selecting the Apply Immediately option in the AWS Management Console, or use the `--apply-immediately` parameter in AWS CLI, or use the ApplyImmediately parameter in Amazon RDS API. The changes are put into the pending modifications queue if you don't choose to apply changes immediately.

 CAUTION Any pending modifications require downtime, so if you choose Apply Immediately, then it can cause unexpected downtime.

Maintain

Amazon RDS performs maintenance on Amazon RDS resources, including updates to the hardware, operating system, or DB engine version. Normally the operating system updates often occurs for security issues and should be implemented as soon as possible. The operating system or database patching might require taking your DB instance offline for a short time. The security and instance reliability patching is automatically scheduled during your maintenance window.

Maintenance Window

During the weekly maintenance window, all the system changes are applied, and some of the larger maintenance events may take more than 30 minutes to complete if you don't explicitly specify a preferred maintenance window.

 EXAM TIP Upgrade can be deferred to the next maintenance window and delay the DB instance update.

Upgrade

Amazon RDS releases the latest versions of database engines periodically based on the security enhancements, bug fixes, and other improvements. You can choose when and how to upgrade your database DB instances whenever Amazon RDS releases a new version of a database engine. Amazon RDS provides two categories of upgrades: major and minor. A major engine version upgrade introduces changes that may not be compatible with existing applications; in contrast, the minor version upgrade changes are backward-compatible with existing applications or can be a minor engine version update to a DB engine version within a major engine version. You can enable auto minor version upgrades for the database if you want Amazon RDS to upgrade the DB engine version of a database automatically.

Rename

A DB instance can be renamed by using the AWS Management Console, using the `modify-db-instance` command in AWS CLI, or using the ModifyDBInstance action in Amazon RDS API. Renaming a DB instance changes the endpoint for the DB instance, since the URL includes the DB instance name. The common reason for renaming a DB instance is to promote a read replica or DB snapshot restore or point-in-time recovery. You can replace the DB instance without changing any application code by renaming the database. You need to do the following:

- Stop all traffic going to the master DB instance by redirecting or preventing traffic from accessing the databases on the DB instance.
- Rename the DB instance to a required new name.
- You can create a new DB instance by restoring from a DB snapshot or by promoting a read replica.
- You can now associate any read replicas.
- It is your responsibility to delete any unwanted DB snapshots of the old database instance.

Reboot

You normally reboot your DB instance for maintenance reasons, such as making certain modifications or changing the associated DB parameter group. You can perform the reboot with a failover if it is an Amazon RDS Multi-AZ instance. After a successful Amazon RDS reboot, an event is created. When you reboot, you can force a failover from one Availability Zone to another in a Multi-AZ deployment, and Amazon RDS automatically switches to a standby replica, and the DNS record is updated to point to the standby DB instance. After this, you need to re-establish and clean up any existing connections to your DB instance.

 CAUTION When forcing a failover from one Availability Zone to another, the change might not be reflected immediately in the AWS Management Console.

Stop

Your Amazon RDS DB instance can be stopped temporarily to save money; during that time, you are charged only for provisioned storage and backup storage but not for DB instance hours. The MariaDB, Microsoft SQL Server, MySQL, Oracle, and PostgreSQL DB instances can be stopped and started based on your need in all AWS regions, including Multi-AZ deployments. Because of the replica configuration, you can't stop a SQL

Server DB instance in Multi-AZ. The DB instance performs a normal shutdown and stops running, and the DB instance status changes to stopping and then stopped. All the storage volumes remain attached to the DB instance, and their data is kept intact, but the data stored in the RAM is deleted. The stopped DB instance is started automatically if it is not started manually after seven days. The DB instance retains its ID, Domain Name Server (DNS) endpoint, parameter group, security group, and option group, including the transaction logs, so you can do a point-in-time restore if required. The DB instance with a read replica cannot be stopped, nor can the SQL Server DB instance in a Multi-AZ configuration. You cannot modify stopped DB instances, and you cannot delete a DB instance if an option group or DB parameter group is associated with it.

 EXAM TIP Stopping and starting the DB instances might take more time in some cases compared to rebooting the DB instance.

Start

You can temporarily stop an Amazon RDS DB instance to save costs; restart it to begin using it. Your stopped DB instance retains the ID, DNS endpoint, parameter group, security group, and option group when restarted. You will be charged a full instance hour when you start a stopped instance. The DB instances can be started from the Amazon RDS console at https://console.aws.amazon.com/rds/. Then choose the DB instance that you want to start. You can call the start-db-instance command with the --db-instance-identifier to start a DB instance using the AWS CLI.

Delete

You can delete a DB instance that is no longer required by providing the instance name. You can choose to take the final DB snapshot of the instance that doesn't have delete protection enabled. You will normally have the option to enable delete protection during the creation or modification of a DB instance so that others can't delete it. When you use the AWS CLI and API commands, by default the delete protection is disabled, and it is enabled when you use the AWS Management Console. However, when deleting the DB instance, Amazon RDS enforces delete protection whether you use the console, the CLI, or the API. You first need to modify the instance and disable delete protection before deleting a DB instance that has deletion protection enabled. As with a read replica–enabled DB instance, you should either promote the read replica or delete it before you delete the DB instance.

Read Replicas

Amazon RDS uses a built-in replication functionality to create a read replica from a source DB instance by asynchronously copying the updates to it. The workload of your source DB instance can be reduced by routing read queries from your applications to the read replica. The read replica can elastically scale beyond the capacity constraints of a single DB instance for read-heavy database workloads. You can use an existing DB instance as the source when creating a read replica, and when you take a snapshot, it creates a read-only instance based on it. The read replica is updated using asynchronous replication whenever there is a change to the source DB instance, and it allows only read-only connections. Your applications can connect to a read replica the same way they can connect to any DB instance. The read replica can reside in a different Availability Zone and even a different AWS region than its source DB instance. The read replica can be used for your business or data warehousing reporting, where you can run the queries against the read replica instead of your primary DB instance. The read replica can be used for disaster recovery, where you can promote your read replica to a stand-alone DB instance when your primary DB instance fails. Normally the read replica is created with the same storage type as its primary DB instance, but you can change it to a different storage type based on need.

Create a Read Replica

A read replica can be created from an existing DB instance from the AWS Management Console, AWS CLI, or AWS API. Amazon RDS creates a snapshot at the start when you create multiple read replicas in parallel, and the automatic backups should be enabled by configuring the backup retention period to more than 0.

Promote a Read Replica

You can promote a read replica into a stand-alone DB instance; during that time, your DB instance is rebooted before it becomes available for use. DDL operations, like creating or rebuilding indexes, can be performed on a read replica and then the read replica can be promoted to direct your application traffic to the promoted instance. Your read replica can be used for sharding, where a large database is split into many small databases. RDS provides synchronous replication, automatic failure detection, and failover so you can promote a read replica when the source DB instance fails.

Monitor Read Replication

Your read replica can be monitored in several ways: by using the Amazon RDS console, the AWS CLI, or the Amazon RDS API. The status of a read replica can be replicating, which means it is replicating successfully; error, which means an error has occurred; terminated, which means replication is terminated; and stopped, which means replication has stopped.

Option Groups

Amazon RDS option groups are used to provide security and management of your data and databases based on the features that are enabled for a DB instance. You can create, copy, or modify an option group before associating it with your DB instance. Option groups are associated with the DB instance and snapshots. When you restore a DB instance from a DB snapshot or point-in-time restore, the new DB instance will have the option group that was originally associated with the snapshot. You can associate a different option group with the new restored DB instance as long as it contains any persistent or permanent options from the original option group. Options normally require additional memory, so you might need to launch a larger instance, depending on your current use of the DB instance.

You are not allowed to remove a persistent option group when it is associated with DB instances—for example, if your DB instance has the TDE option for Microsoft SQL Server transparent data encryption (TDE) associated, then this option group cannot be removed before disassociating all DB instances from it.

You cannot remove the permanent options, such as the TDE option for Oracle Advanced Security, from an option group. You are allowed to change the option group of an associated DB instance, but it must include the same permanent option.

DB Parameter Groups

DB parameter groups are used to apply different configurations to customize one or more DB instances by using built-in formulas, functions, and variables. The default DB parameter group is applied and cannot be modified, but you can create a new parameter group by choosing the relevant settings. The dynamic changes are applied immediately, regardless of the Apply Immediately setting, and the static parameter changes are applied after rebooting the DB instance.

 EXAM TIP The default DB parameter group cannot be modified, since it contains the preferred parameter settings, so you need create a custom parameter group to update any parameter.

Storage

Some DB instance classes have a combination of memory and vCPUs for common workloads, and you can also manually optimize your DB instance for specific workloads or business needs. The processor settings for a DB instance are associated with snapshots of the DB instance; when you restore a snapshot, the feature settings used when the snapshot was taken are applied. Amazon RDS uses Amazon EBS volumes for database instances and log storage. Amazon RDS automatically stripes across multiple Amazon EBS volumes to enhance performance based on the amount of storage requested. Amazon RDS offers General Purpose SSD (gp2), Provisioned IOPS SSD (io1), and Magnetic, which differ in terms of performance characteristics and price.

- **General Purpose SSD**   Offers cost-effective storage that is ideal for a broad range of workloads, and it can burst to 3,000 IOPS.

- **Provisioned IOPS**   Ideal for I/O-intensive workloads, specifically database workloads, which require consistent I/O throughput and low I/O latency.

- **Magnetic**   Ideal for backward compatibility; AWS recommends using General Purpose SSD or Provisioned IOPS for any new storage needs.

PART V

When you create or modify your Amazon RDS DB instance, you have the option to choose the storage type and size by using the Amazon RDS Management Console or Amazon RDS API or AWS CLI. AWS recommends creating an Amazon CloudWatch alarm to monitor the DB instance free storage and increase it if necessary. If you have a DB instance that has an unpredictable workload, you have the option to enable the Amazon RDS storage autoscaling feature that scales up automatically based on need. You can set the maximum storage threshold, which can be equal to or less than the maximum allocated storage, by using the Amazon RDS console, AWS CLI, or Amazon RDS API.

 EXAM TIP   Only the IOPS provisioned to your DB instance can be scaled down; the General Purpose SSD and Magnetic storage cannot be reduced.

Billing

Amazon RDS On-Demand instances can be used to pay by the hour based on the usage, which is calculated on per-second basis with a minimum of 10 minutes. Amazon RDS reserved instances can be purchased at a significant discount for a one-year or three-year term, where the billing discount is applied to certain instance types and AWS regions. There are three types of reserved DB instances: No Upfront, where you get a discounted hourly rate and no up-front payment is required; Partial Upfront, where you pay part up-front and the remainder at a discounted hourly rate; and All Upfront, where full payment is made at the start with no other costs, regardless of the hours used. Amazon RDS is billed for data transfer to and from the Internet.

 EXAM TIP   You can save the cost of DB instance hours by stopping the Amazon RDS database instance; however, you are charged for provisioned storage, including manual snapshots and automated backups.

Backups

You can enable automated backups as a snapshot with a backup retention period, and your database can be recovered to any point in time based on this period. Automated backups will not occur when the DB instance is in a stopped state. A manual backup can be taken anytime or before you make any major update to the data or database. Both the automatic and manual DB snapshots can be copied, shared, and stored in the same region. You cannot recover your database without an automated or manual backup. You may need to temporarily disable backups when loading large amounts of data to your database. Before you delete your DB instance, Amazon RDS offers the option to take a final snapshot that can be used to recover the DB instance. You need to make sure that your backup window does not overlap with the weekly maintenance window, and the storage I/O might be suspended briefly while the backup process initializes for a few seconds. The default backup retention period is 1 day, but it can be set to up to 35 days. Remember that a backup retention period of 0 disables automated backups and your automated backups do not have any limit; however, the manual snapshot has a limit of 100 per region. The stored backups can be restored or removed using the AWS Management Console, RDS API, and AWS CLI.

Snapshots

Amazon RDS takes a snapshot of your DB instance, and the backup time varies based on the size of your database, storage volume, and size of temporary files. The storage volume of the database is backed up as the DB snapshot, which you can restore using a new name and also using a different storage type than the original snapshot.

After copying the snapshot, it becomes manual, and you are allowed to copy across AWS regions. You can even copy snapshots across AWS accounts by creating a manual snapshot first and then manually copying it to the other account; however, you can copy only within the same AWS region if the snapshot is encrypted. Automated snapshots are deleted after the retention period is up, but you can take a manual snapshot if you want to keep them until you delete them. The DB instance can be restored to a specific point in time by using the DB snapshot, and it applies the default DB security group to the new DB instance. The DB snapshots can be deleted when you no longer need them by using the AWS Management Console, the AWS CLI, or the RDS API. Automated DB snapshots can be deleted by changing the backup retention period of your DB instance to 0 and re-enabled by changing the backup retention period to a number greater than 0.

 EXAM TIP The shared encrypted DB snapshot cannot be restored directly; however, you can restore the DB instance from the copy of its snapshot.

Security

Security is the highest priority for every organization, especially if you are moving to the cloud. The AWS datacenters and network architecture are built securely to meet your compliance and security requirements. Cloud providers, including AWS, provide a shared security responsibility with their customers—that is, AWS takes the responsibility of protecting their infrastructure, and you as the customer should take the responsibility of securing your data based on sensitivity, compliance, and regulations. Amazon VPC provides total network access control to run your RDS DB instance. Amazon RDS resources can be managed using AWS IAM policies to assign permissions based on the least privilege role.

You can use DB security groups to set and control required IP addresses or ranges, like your company network range, to connect to your RDS databases or Amazon EC2 instances. DB security groups, EC2 security groups, and VPC security groups are supported in Amazon RDS. You can control access to a DB instance that is not in a VPC using a DB security group. You can control access to a DB instance that is inside a VPC using a VPC security group. You can control access to an EC2 instance using EC2 security group; these can also be used with a DB instance. The performance and health of a

DB instance can be tracked in many ways, such as an Amazon CloudWatch service or subscribing to Amazon RDS events to be notified about changes to your DB instance, parameter groups, security groups, or snapshots. Amazon RDS uses the AES-256 encryption algorithm, and both the Secure Sockets Layer (SSL) and Transport Layer Security (TLS) connections can be used. In addition, you can enable the standard security features of your RDS database engine using DB parameter groups.

Encryption

In Amazon RDS you can encrypt the underlying storage—all logs, backups, and snapshots, including its read replica—to provide an additional layer of data protection from any unauthorized access and meet your data-at-rest compliance requirements. You can enable TDE in your RDS database instance for Oracle or SQL Server DB instances, but keep in mind that this might affect the performance because of the additional encryption/decryption steps. You can use either AWS server-side encryption, where the key management is handled by AWS, or your own key using AWS Key Management Service (KMS), where you can enable CloudTrail to audit your key usage. When you copy your encrypted snapshot to other regions, you need to use a different KMS encryption key in the target region because KMS keys are bound to a region. The default AWS KMS encryption key cannot be used when you want to copy a snapshot to another region in the same AWS account. Your database client applications do not need to be changed when using Amazon RDS because encryption and decryption of your data happen transparently with negligible impact on DB instance performance.

Monitoring

You need to monitor your Amazon RDS database regularly using Amazon RDS events, enhanced monitoring; Amazon CloudWatch logs, metrics, alarms; and database logs to make sure it performs well and is available. Amazon CloudWatch receives the database metrics and dimensions every minute from Amazon RDS. The monitoring logs data can be used to debug any database issues like performance, network throughput, I/O for read and write, and connection issues of your DB instances. You might need to change the DB instance size or add more read replicas when your database is not performing up to the standard baseline defined already. You need to look for high CPU, RAM, IOPS, or disk space consumption based on your threshold value. Monitoring the network traffic and database connections is significant to keep your database performing at the expected level and investigate immediately if it is consistently lower than your baseline. The Amazon RDS console provides the number of DB connections, read and write operations, memory, CPU, and storage utilization in addition to the amount of network traffic to and from your DB instance. The AWS Trusted Advisor dashboard provides the number of idle DB instances, security group access risk, and Amazon RDS backups information. Amazon CloudWatch provides the current status, alarms, resources, and service health status. You can also create a CloudWatch dashboard to monitor the services, discover trends, and view AWS resource metrics.

Amazon Resource Names

All the resources that you create in AWS will have a uniquely identifiable Amazon Resource Name (ARN). You may need to uniquely identify an Amazon RDS resource for some specific operations, such as creating a read replica, where you need to specify the source DB instance ARN. The ARN is constructed using the following format for your Amazon RDS resource:

```
arn:aws:rds:<region>:<account number>:<resourcetype>:<name>
```

Tagging

Amazon RDS tags contain a name-value pair that is used to add metadata to DB instances, to manage access to Amazon RDS resources, to control what actions can be applied, and to track costs by grouping similar resources. All Amazon RDS resources can be tagged, including DB instances, DB snapshots, DB clusters, DB cluster snapshots, DB cluster parameter groups, read replicas, reserved DB instances, DB option groups, event subscriptions, DB security groups, DB parameter groups, and DB subnet groups. You can copy tags from the DB instance to snapshots of the DB instance when you create or restore a DB instance—it is not copied by default. Tags can be copied when creating a DB instance, restoring a DB instance, creating a read replica, and copying a DB snapshot. Tags are used to organize the AWS bill to reflect the cost structure and to see the cost of combined resources and organize your billing information according to resources with the same tag key values. A tag set can contain as many as 50 tags, and when you add a tag that already exists, the new value overwrites the old value.

Best Practices

The following are basic operational best practices to follow when working with Amazon RDS:

- Monitor your memory, CPU, and storage using Amazon CloudWatch and set up alerts to notify you when usage patterns change or are approaching the defined capacity.

- You can scale up your DB instance based on storage capacity and memory limits to accommodate unforeseen increases in demand from your applications.

- You need to enable automatic backups and set up an appropriate backup window based on the daily low in write IOPS.

- You can convert from standard storage to either provisioned IOPS or general-purpose storage based on your requirement and workload.

- You need to periodically test the failover for your DB instance to know how long the process takes for your use case and to make sure that your application can automatically connect to the failover DB instance.

- AWS recommends allocating enough RAM so that your entire working set of data resides completely in memory, which can be verified using the ReadIOPS metric in Amazon CloudWatch.

- You can monitor the real-time metrics of the operating system (OS) where your DB instance runs from the console, or consume the Enhanced Monitoring JSON output from Amazon CloudWatch logs.

- You can set Amazon CloudWatch alarms for important metric thresholds like CPU utilization (i.e., percentage of computer processing capacity), free memory (i.e., RAM available), free storage space, read IOPS, write IOPS, read latency, write latency, read throughput, write throughput, queue depth, network receive throughput, network transmit throughput, swap usage, and DB connections used.

- Monitor high CPU, RAM consumption, throughput, or concurrency, which might be appropriate based on your goals for your application and are expected.

- The disk space consumption must be monitored closely to check whether the space used is consistently at or above 85 percent; then you may delete old data that is no longer required or you archive data to a cold storage service like Amazon Glacier.

- Monitor and take appropriate action when the network traffic throughput is consistently lower than expected.

- Continuously monitor database connections so you can see if high numbers of user connections appear in conjunction with decreases in instance performance and response time.

- Closely monitor IOPS metrics and compare them with the expected values, which depend on disk specification and server configuration, and make sure your typical working set will fit into memory to minimize read and write operations.

- Tune your most commonly used and most resource-intensive queries to make them less expensive to run and lower the pressure on system resources, which in turn will improve DB instance performance.

- If the DB issue persists after tuning your queries, consider upgrading your DB instance class to one with more of the resource (RAM, CPU, network bandwidth, disk space, and I/O capacity) based on the issue.

- AWS recommends properly testing the DB instance before applying any parameter group changes to your production DB instances because it can have unintended adverse effects, including degraded performance and system instability.

- Always exercise caution when modifying any DB engine parameters, and make sure to back up your DB instance before modifying and applying a DB parameter group change.

Chapter Review

The chapter began by explaining Amazon RDS. It then introduced the Multi-AZ database, which offers availability and failover. The chapter then explained the read replica, which replicates from a source DB instance by asynchronously copying the updates, and how the workload can be reduced by copying read-only traffic to the read replica. We then saw how the Amazon RDS option groups are used to secure and manage your databases based on the features that are enabled for a DB instance. The DB parameter groups are used to customize your DB instances by using built-in functions and variables. There are DB instance classes that have a combination of memory and number of vCPUs for common workloads, and you can also specify these manually to optimize your DB instance for specific workloads or business needs. The processor settings for a DB instance are associated with snapshots of the DB instance; when you restore a snapshot, the feature settings are those used when the snapshot was taken. Amazon RDS On-Demand instances can be used to pay by the hour based on the usage, which is calculated on a per-second basis with a minimum of ten minutes. Amazon RDS reserved instances can be purchased at a significant discount for a one-year or three-year term, where the billing discount is applied to a certain instance type and AWS region. You can enable automated backups as a snapshot with a backup retention period, and your database can be recovered to any point in time based on this. The automated backups will not occur when the DB instance is in a stopped state. Amazon RDS takes a snapshot of your DB instance, and the backup time varies based on the size of your database, storage volume, and size of temporary files by using the AWS Management Console, AWS CLI, or the RDS API.

Security is the highest priority for every organization, especially if you are moving to the cloud. The AWS datacenters and its network architecture are built securely to meet your compliance and security requirements. You need to monitor your Amazon RDS database regularly using Amazon RDS events; enhanced monitoring; Amazon CloudWatch logs, metrics, alarms; and Database logs to make sure it performs well and is available. Amazon CloudWatch receives the database metrics and dimensions every minute from Amazon RDS. The monitoring log data can be used to debug any database issues like performance, network throughput, I/O for read and write, and connection issues.

Exercise

The following exercise will help you practice creating an Amazon RDS database. You need to create an AWS account, as explained earlier, in order to perform these exercises. You can use the Free Tier when launching AWS resources, but make sure to terminate them at the end.

Exercise 13-1: Create an Amazon RDS Using the AWS Management Console

The following step-by-step instructions help you create Amazon RDS PostgreSQL database using the AWS Management Console.

1. Use your AWS account e-mail address and password to sign in to the AWS account and then navigate to the Amazon RDS console at https://console.aws.amazon .com/rds/.

2. Verify the AWS region by using the Region selector in the upper-right corner of the page.

3. From the navigation pane, choose Databases.

4. Click on the Create Database button.

5. On the Create Database page, choose Standard Create.

6. For the Engine Type choose PostgreSQL.

7. For the Version choose 11.5-R1, although at the time of this writing you have the option to choose from version 9.3 to 11.5.

8. For Templates choose Free Tier.

9. In the DB Instance Identifier field type **My-RDS-DB1**.

10. For the Master Username type **postgres** and for the Master Password type **MyP@ssw0rd**.

11. For the DB instance size, select db.t2.micro.

12. Choose General Purpose (SSD) or Provisioned IOPS (SSD) for the Storage Type.

13. For Allocated Storage select 20 GiB.

14. Check Enable Storage Auto-Scaling, which increases your storage automatically when the threshold is reached.

15. Leave the default of 1000 GiB for the Maximum Storage Threshold selected.

16. Choose a Multi-AZ deployment or standby instance.

17. Select the VPC where you want to create your DB instance.

18. In the Additional Connectivity Configuration area, select the Subnet Group. For Publicly Accessible, select Yes but select No with regard to the enterprise environment.

19. Either choose an existing VPN security group or select the option to create a new one.

20. Now select the Availability Zone or leave No Preference selected to let AWS choose the Availability Zone for you.

21. Then select the database port. PostgreSQL's default port is 5432, but you can change it to any custom TCP/IP port.

22. Choose the authentication method from the three available options: Password Authentication, Password and IAM Database Authentication, or Password and Kerberos Authentication.

23. In the Additional Configuration area, type **mydatabase1** for the initial database name.

24. For the DB Parameter Group choose default.postgress11 and for the Option Group choose default.postgress-11.

25. Select Enable Automatic Backups and choose 3 days for the retention period.

26. You can select the backup window you desire, or leave no preference selected, where the time is in UTC.

27. Choose Copy Tags To Snapshots.

28. You can enable performance insights for advance database performance monitoring for a default of seven days or a long-term duration of two years.

29. Choose the default AWS key or provide your own key from KMS.

30. You can enable enhanced monitoring from 1 second to 60 seconds and use the RDS-monitoring-role or leave as the default, which will create a role for you.

31. Check both Postgresql Log and Upgrade Log to send the data to CloudWatch logs.

32. In the Maintenance section, check Enable Auto Minor Version Upgrade and select the maintenance window in UTC or leave No Preference selected to let AWS determine the window for you.

33. Finally check the Enable Deletion Protection option to prevent the accidental deletion of your database.

34. Before clicking on the Create Database button, you will see the estimated monthly costs for DB instance, Storage, Multi-AZ standby instance, and Provisioned IOPS.

35. Once you have reviewed everything, click on the Create Database button.

36. From the Amazon RDS screen, go to RDS | Databases | my-rds-db1 and click on Connectivity & Security, where you will see the endpoint database hostname, post number, networking, and security details.

37. From the Amazon RDS screen, go to RDS | Databases | my-rds-db1 and click on Monitoring to see CPU utilization percentage, DB connections count, free storage space in MB, free memory in MB, write IOPS, and read IOPS.

38. From the Amazon RDS screen, go to RDS | Databases | my-rds-db1 and click on Logs & Events, where you can see the list of CloudWatch alarms, create alarms, and see recent events and logs that can be viewed or downloaded.

39. From the Amazon RDS screen, go to RDS | Databases | my-rds-db1 and click on Configuration, where you can see instance configuration, instance class, storage information and performance insight details.

40. From the Amazon RDS screen, go to RDS | Databases | my-rds-db1 and click on Maintenance & Backups, where you can view the maintenance details, pending maintenance details, backup, and DB Snapshots from where you can take additional snapshot or restore the DB instance from the snapshot.

41. From the Amazon RDS screen, go to RDS | Databases | my-rds-db1 and click on Tags to add, edit, and delete tags for your DB instance.

42. From the Amazon RDS screen, go to RDS | Databases | my-rds-db1 and click on Modify on the top-right side to update any of the instance specifications, settings, network and security, database options, Kerberos authentication, backup, monitoring, log exports, performance insights, maintenance, and deletion protection options.

43. From the Amazon RDS screen, go to RDS | Databases | my-rds-db1 and click on Actions on the top right side to stop, reboot, delete, upgrade now, defer the upgrade, create a read replica, promote, take a snapshot, and restore to a point in time from your backup snapshots.

Questions

The following questions will help you gauge your understanding of the contents in this chapter. Read all the answers carefully because there might be more than one correct answer. Choose the best responses for each question.

1. Your manager has asked you to provision a Redshift data warehousing database for reporting using Amazon RDS service. Which of the following database engines are supported in Amazon RDS?

A. Amazon Aurora, MySQL, MariaDB, Oracle, SQL Server, and PostgreSQL database engines

B. Amazon DynamoDB, MongoDB, SQL Server, and MySQL database engines

C. Amazon Redshift, Cassandra, MariaDB, Oracle, and MySQL database engines

D. MongoDB, MySQL, Oracle, SQL Server, and PostgreSQL database engines

2. You are migrating on-premise applications and databases to the AWS Cloud and would like to choose a database service that provides automated administrative tasks, including daily backups, patching, and automated minor upgrades. Which of the following Amazon services offers that database automation?

A. Amazon EC2

B. Amazon RDS

C. Amazon S3

D. Amazon Route 53

3. Your application team is running hundreds of reports in addition to performing lots of read, write, update, and delete operations on the Amazon RDS database instance. They are complaining about how slowly the database is running and report a running longer time occasionally. What you could do to help the application team run reports and perform I/O at the same time?

A. Enable Multi-AZ

B. Create two RDS DB instances

C. Create a replica for running reports

D. Increase the DB instance size

4. You have successfully migrated your on-premises database to Amazon RDS. Your manager wants to understand the RDS billing and asked you how RDS is charged. Which of the following are correct charges? (Choose all that apply.)

A. DB instance hours

B. Storage (per GB per month) and backup storage

C. I/O requests per month and data transfer

D. Provisioned IOPS per month

5. You are asked to help your company save costs by stopping the RDS database after working hours and on weekends. You configured an automated script to stop the RDS instances. What are the following charges incurred on the stopped RDS instances? (Choose three.)

A. Storage (per GB per month)

B. Backup storage

C. Provisioned IOPS per month

D. DB instance hours

6. Your company has planned to implement Amazon RDS and use it for a long time, so you suggest reserved instances (RIs), which gives a significant discount compared to On-Demand instance pricing. What three RI payment options available? (Choose three.)

A. On-Demand

B. No Upfront

C. Partial Upfront

D. All Upfront

7. Your company has bought reserved instances for us-east-1a availability in US-EAST region for three years. Now they realize the instances need to be provisioned in us-east-1d instead. Can you move the reserved instances between Availability Zones?

A. Yes, you can move the reserved instances between Availability Zones.

B. Yes, you can move the reserved instances between regions.

C. No, you cannot move the reserved instances between Availability Zones.

D. No, reserved instances cannot be moved at all.

8. You have created a read replica with the DB instance class and the same region. Your manager wants to know whether the DB instance reservation can be applied to your read replica. Is it possible to apply reserved instances to your read replica?

A. Yes, only if the read replica's region is different.

B. No, even if the DB instance class and region are the same.

C. No, you cannot use reserved instances for a read replica.

D. Yes, but only if the DB instance class and region are the same.

9. A company created an Amazon RDS DB instance and enabled automatic backup with a retention period of 7 days. After a few weeks they realized that the retention period should be changed to 35 days. How can this be achieved?

   A. Modify your DB instance to change the retention period to 35 days.

   B. The retention period cannot be changed after the DB creation.

   C. The maximum retention period is 30 days.

   D. The DB instance needs to be terminated and created with correct retention period.

10. Your team created a DB instance in a single Availability Zone and the company decides to make the database highly available. What happens when you try to convert your RDS instance from a Single Availability Zone to a Multi-AZ database? (Choose three.)

   A. You need to stop your RDS DB instance before converting it.

   B. The primary instance snapshot should be taken.

   C. Using that snapshot, another standby instance is created in a different Availability Zone.

   D. The synchronous replication is set up between your primary instance and standby instance.

Answers

1. **A.** Amazon offers the Amazon Aurora, MySQL, MariaDB, Oracle, SQL Server, and PostgreSQL database engines.

2. **B.** Amazon RDS automates common database administration tasks.

3. **C.** Create a replica for running reports and use the primary database for I/O operations.

4. **A, B, C, D.** DB instance hours, storage (per GB per month), backup storage, I/O requests per month, data transfer and provisioned IOPS per month.

5. **A, B, C.** Storage, backup storage, and provisioned IOPS.

6. **B, C, D.** No Upfront, Partial Upfront, and All Upfront.

7. **A.** Yes, you can move the reserved instances between Availability Zones.

8. **D.** Yes, but only if the DB instance class and region are the same.

9. **A.** You can modify your DB instance to change the retention period to 35 days.

10. **B, C, D.** First the primary instance snapshot is taken and then a new standby instance is created in a different Availability Zone using the snapshot. Finally, synchronous replication is configured between your primary instance and standby instance.

Additional Resources

- **AWS Documentation**   There is no other place to get all the latest information than AWS documentation because it's always up to date. Always refer to the official AWS blogs to get the latest updates about new AWS services and updates to existing features. The RDS User Guide can be accessed using the following link.
  `https://docs.aws.amazon.com/AmazonRDS/latest/UserGuide/Welcome.html`
  The Amazon RDS CLI reference guide can be accessed using the following link.
  `https://docs.aws.amazon.com/cli/latest/reference/rds/`
  The Amazon RDS API reference guide can be accessed from the following link.
  `https://docs.aws.amazon.com/AmazonRDS/latest/APIReference/Welcome.html`

- **Guide to AWS re:Invent 2019 Amazon RDS Sessions**   This is an important blog that has some very interesting Amazon RDS sessions and workshops.
  `https://aws.amazon.com/blogs/database/your-guide-to-amazon-rds-sessions-workshops-and-chalk-talks-at-aws-reinvent-2019/`

- **AWS CloudFormation to Perform Point-in-Time Recovery of Amazon RDS**   This blog explains the steps in detail to perform the point-in-time recovery of your Amazon RDS database using the AWS CloudFormation template.
  `https://aws.amazon.com/blogs/database/building-an-aws-cloudformation-custom-resource-to-manage-amazon-rds-point-in-time-recovery/`

- **Client-Side Encryption for a Multiregional Amazon RDS**   This blog shows you the steps to perform client-side encryption using the customer master key and data encryption key stored in KMS.
  `https://aws.amazon.com/blogs/database/performing-sql-database-client-side-encryption-for-multi-region-high-availability/`

- **Amazon RDS Multi-AZ**   This is another very interesting blog that explains how the Amazon Multi-AZ works under the hood.
  `https://aws.amazon.com/blogs/database/amazon-rds-under-the-hood-multi-az/`

PART V

CHAPTER 14

AWS NoSQL Database Service: Amazon DynamoDB

In this chapter, you will learn
- DynamoDB components
- NoSQL vs. SQL comparison
- DynamoDB Accelerator (DAX)
- DynamoDB Local and Web
- Logging and monitoring
- Data protection

This chapter will discuss how the AWS NoSQL database service, DynamoDB, works and its configuration and access.

Amazon DynamoDB

Amazon DynamoDB is a managed NoSQL database offering low latency, high performance, and seamless scalability. DynamoDB handles the cluster setup, configuration, replication, backup, hardware provisioning, and software patching. Since DynamoDB handles the encryption of your data at rest, you don't need to encrypt the data manually and manage the encryption/decryption process. DynamoDB allows you to create database tables where you can store huge volumes of data and retrieve it easily. It can quickly scale up and down and serve massive traffic requests without any performance issue or downtime.

The DynamoDB table performance metrics, in addition to resource utilization monitoring, can be viewed in the AWS Management Console. You can create a full backup of your DynamoDB tables using on-demand backup for short-term or long-term retention. You can protect your DynamoDB tables from accidental deletion and incorrect write operations by enabling point-in-time recovery up to 35 days.

When you store a very large volume of session data, event logs, usage patterns, and other temporary data in DynamoDB tables, you can enable Time to Live (TTL) with the Expiration Time set to automatically delete the obsolete data. Amazon DynamoDB uses solid-state disks (SSD) for high performance while automatically replicating the data across multiple Availability Zones to provide high availability. The data is automatically spread across multiple servers to handle high throughput, and global tables are replicated and spread over multiple AWS regions. The core components of DynamoDB are as follows:

- **Tables**   A collection of data that stores data in tables and is schema-less, so you do not need to define attributes or its data types beforehand.

- **Items**   A group of unique attributes, and every table can have zero or more items. An item can have a nested attribute up to 32 levels deep.

- **Attributes**   A basic data element that cannot be broken down further, and one or more attributes are contained in each item. An attribute can have only one value, which can be strings, binary, or numbers.

- **Primary key**   Uniquely identifies every item, and no two items can have the same key in a table.

- **Partition key**   Contains a single attribute, which is used as input to an internal hash function, and the output determines the physical partition of the item. When a table has only a partition key, then no two items can have the same key value.

- **Composite primary key**   A combination of partition key and sort key, where the two items can have the same partition key but with different sort key values.

- **Hash attribute**   The partition key item used for internal hash functions to evenly distribute data items across partitions.

- **Range attribute**   The sort key item used to store items with the same partition key physically close together in sorted order.

- **Secondary index**   Allows you query using an alternative key in addition to the primary key, and you can have one or more secondary indexes on a table.

- **Global secondary index**   Contains a partition key and a sort key that can be different from the indexes on the table.

- **Local secondary index**   Contains the same partition key as in the table, but can have a different sort key.

- **DynamoDB streams**   Capture all data modification events, like when a new item is added, updated, or deleted in DynamoDB tables in near-real time. Streams are represented by a system record, and DynamoDB writes it in the order in which the events occurred. The DynamoDB stream contains a table name and timestamp with a lifetime of 24 hours.

Data Types

DynamoDB is a schema-less NoSQL database where you do not have to define any attributes or data types when you create tables. DynamoDB offers the following data types:

- **Scalar Types**   Binary, Boolean, string, null, and number.
- **Document Types**   It is a nested structure in JSON format represented as a list, which is an ordered collection of values enclosed in [ ], and maps, which is an unordered collection of name value pairs enclosed in { }.
- **Set Types**   It is represented as sets of numbers, strings, and binary.

Control Plane Operations

Control plane operations are similar to Data Definition Language (DDL) in SQL that allow you to create and manage DynamoDB tables, indexes, and streams.

- **CreateTable**   Creates tables, indexes, and enable streams.
- **DescribeTable**   Fetches primary key schema, throughput settings, and index information.
- **ListTables**   Fetches the names of all DynamoDB tables, and an array of the table names of the current account and endpoint is returned.
- **UpdateTable**   Creates, updates, and removes indexes in addition to modifying DynamoDB streams.
- **DeleteTable**   Deletes the DynamoDB table and its dependent objects.

Data Plane Operations

Data plane operations, also called CRUD (create, read, update, delete), is similar to the Data Manipulation Language (DML) in terms of create, read, update, and delete operations on data from a DynamoDB table.

- **Create**
  PutItem and BatchWriteItem   You can write a single item to your DynamoDB table using PutItem and write up to 25 items using BatchWriteItem, which is more efficient because it uses only a single network round trip to write the items.
- **Read**
  GetItem and BatchGetItem   You can retrieve a single item from your DynamoDB table using GetItem and retrieve up to 100 items using BatchGetItem, which is more efficient because it uses only a single network round trip to read the items.

  Query and Scan   You can retrieve all items or subsets based on your partition key using Query, and you can retrieve all items or subsets from your table or index using Scan.

PART V

- **Update**
  UpdateItem You can modify one or more attributes based on the primary key for the item in addition to performing conditional updates when a condition is met.

- **Delete**
  DeleteItem and BatchWriteItem You can delete a single item from your DynamoDB table using DeleteItem and delete up to 25 items using BatchWriteItem from one or more tables.

- **Streams**
  ListStreams You can list streams of a particular table or list all your streams using ListStreams.

  DescribeStream You can get information (i.e., metadata) about your stream using DescribeStream.

  GetShardIterator This returns the data structure (i.e., shard iterator) from the stream.

  GetRecords Using shard iterator, it retrieves one or more stream records.

SQL vs. NoSQL

Structured Query Language (SQL) is used by the traditional relational database management system (RDBMS) to store structured data. Not Only SQL (NoSQL) is used in a nonrelational database to store unstructured data. The following table compares how they each perform common database tasks.

	SQL	NoSQL

Create Table	`CREATE TABLE Employee (`
	`    EMP_ID          INT    NOT NULL,`
	`    EMP_Name        CHAR(50),`
	`    EMP_Sal         FLOAT,`
	`    PRIMARY KEY(EMP_ID)`
	`);`
		`{ TableName : "Employee",`
		`    KeySchema: [`
		`            { AttributeName: "EMP_ID",`
		`                    KeyType: "HASH", // key  }`
		`        ],`
		`        AttributeDefinitions: [`
		`            { AttributeName: "EMP_ID",`
		`                    AttributeType: "I"    },`
		`            { AttributeName: "EMP_Name",`
		`                    AttributeType: "S"    },`
		`            { AttributeName: "EMP_Sal",`
		`                    AttributeType: "F"    }`
		`        ]`
		`    }`

	SQL	NoSQL

Insert Data	INSERT INTO Employee
	    (EMP_ID, EMP_Name, EMP_Sal)
	VALUES(123, 'Kamesh Ganesan',
	900,000.00);
		{ TableName: "Employee",
		   Item: { "EMP_ID": 123,
		       "EMP_Name":
		"Kamesh Ganesan",
		       "EMP_Sal":
		900,000.00 }
		}

Select Data	SELECT EMP_ID, EMP_Name, EMP_Sal FROM Employee WHERE EMP_ID = 123;	{ TableName: "Employee", Key: { "EMP_ID": 123 } }

Update Data	UPDATE Employee
	SET EMP_Sal = 1,200,000.00
	WHERE EMP_ID = 123;
		{ TableName: "Employee",
		   Key: { "EMP_ID":123 },
		   UpdateExpression: "SET
		EMP_Sal = :label",
		
		   ExpressionAttributeValues:
		{ ":label": 1,200,000.00 }
		}

Delete Data	DELETE FROM Employee WHERE EMP_ID = 123;	{ TableName: "Employee", Key: { EMP_ID: 123 } }

DynamoDB Transactions

DynamoDB transactions offer atomicity, consistency, isolation, and durability (ACID) properties to maintain integrity of your data.

- **TransactWriteItems**   DynamoDB offers Put, Update, and Delete batch operations.
- **TransactGetItems**   DynamoDB offers Get batch operations.

Amazon DynamoDB transactions can be enabled for adding, updating, or deleting multiple complex items as a single or all-or-nothing transaction with no additional cost, and you pay only for the reads or writes of your transaction. There will be two reads or writes of every record in the transaction; the first one is to prepare, and the second is to commit the transaction, which can be viewed in the Amazon CloudWatch metrics. You can group up to 25 write actions in a single all-or-nothing transaction atomically, so either all succeed or all are rolled back (do not succeed). You can use Put that initiates a PutItem to either create a new item or replace an old item. You can use Update to initiate an UpdateItem to edit an existing item or add a new item if it is not available. You can use Delete to initiate a DeleteItem to delete a single transaction. As soon as the transaction is completed, all the transaction changes are replicated to global secondary indexes (GSIs), streams, and backups. You can use Get to initiate a GetItem to fetch the data item based on the primary key.

PART V

Read Consistency

DynamoDB provides strong read consistency and eventual read consistency. The DynamoDB sends the HTTP 200 response (OK) when the write is completed to your application. When you read data from a DynamoDB table and the response contains some stale data, it is known as eventual read consistency. When your request returns only the committed data, it is known as strong consistency. Strongly consistent reads might have higher latency, since they are read from the physical table.

Read/Write Capacity Mode

Amazon DynamoDB offers on-demand and provisioned read and write capacity modes. When using the on-demand mode, DynamoDB quickly scales up or down based on the workload, which can be used for both new and existing tables without changing code. When using the provisioned mode, you can specify the number of reads and writes per second for your application and use auto-scaling to respond to any future traffic changes.

 EXAM TIP Eventually consistent read is preferred by DynamoDB, unless you update the configuration. When you use the ConsistentRead parameter with GetItem, Query, and Scan read operations, DynamoDB uses strongly consistent reads.

Isolation Levels

Isolation levels are an important concept to understand before configuring your transactions in DynamoDB or on any other database. DynamoDB provides a serializable isolation level to make sure the output of your multiple concurrent operations display the same results as if this is the only transaction taking place. No other transactions take place until this finishes. DynamoDB provides a read-committed isolation level to make sure the read always returns committed data and will not prevent changes to the data after the read. Whenever there is a concurrent item-level request on the same item within a transaction, then a transactional conflict will happen. For example, a PutItem for a data item can conflict with another TransactWriteItems on the same data item. The transactional conflict can be captured with CloudWatch as a TransactionConflict metric of the failed item-level requests.

DynamoDB Accelerator

Amazon DynamoDB Accelerator (DAX) is designed for read-intensive applications that require responses from single-digit milliseconds to microseconds that run within your Amazon Virtual Private Cloud (VPC) environment. DAX clusters can be launched in your VPC using the AWS Management Console, and you can use security groups to control access to your DAX clusters. You just need to deploy your application that needs access to DAX in an EC2 instance with a DAX client in the same Amazon VPC. The DAX client sends all requests to the DAX cluster (called a cache hit when the items are available in DAX), and it sends the request to DynamoDB only if the items are not available in the DAX cluster (called a cache miss when the items are not available in DAX, so the response from DynamoDB is written to the DAX primary node and DAX returns the response to the application).

DAX Components

A DAX cluster may consist of one or more nodes, and each node runs its own cashing DAX instance. The nodes can be a primary node or read replica node of the cluster. DAX can be accessed using its endpoint, and it performs load balancing and routing to evenly distribute the incoming requests across all of the nodes in the cluster.

DAX Read

When your application requests items with strong consistent reads, DAX sends it to DynamoDB and returns the results to the application without saving it on DAX. Any write requests from your application are sent to DynamoDB directly, and the DAX cluster is updated only after a successful write on DynamoDB. When your application tries to create or update a table, it is performed directly on the DynamoDB, not on the DAX. All the results from GetItem and BatchGetItem are stored in a cache for a duration based on its TTL value using its primary key in DAX. When your application sends the request, the items are read directly from the cache and return the result to your application. A timestamp is assigned to each item in the cache and items expire based on the TTL value. If the incoming application request is on any expired item, DAX sends it to DynamoDB because it's considered a cache miss.

DAX LRU

By default, the well-known least recently used (LRU) algorithm is also used in the DAX cache so when the cache becomes full, DAX evicts older LRU items even if they have not yet expired in order to make space for new items; this feature is not configurable. DAX also maintains a cache that stores the result sets from queries and scans based on their parameter values. The query or scan request from an application uses this cache to return the results based on its parameter values. DAX returns the results to your application immediately when a cache hit occurs (i.e., the result set is found in the query cache). DAX sends the request to DynamoDB when a cache miss occurs (i.e., the result set is not found in the query cache). The return query result from DynamoDB is stored in DAX and a return response is sent back to your application. The LRU algorithm is applied to the query cache as well by default, and this is not configurable.

DAX Cluster and Nodes

A DAX cluster is a logical group of more than one node, where one node is assigned as the primary node. A node is the building block that runs an instance of the DAX along with a single replica. You can add one or more nodes to your DAX cluster to increase the overall read throughput, or you can use a larger node with more capacity that increases throughput in a different DAX cluster because each DAX cluster can contain only nodes of the same type. The primary node responds to application requests for cached data, handles the write operations, and evicts data from the cache based on the LRU or TTL in addition to replicating the data changes to all of the replica nodes. The replica provides read-scaling and automatically fails over to become the new primary node. AWS recommends using at least three nodes by placing each node in different Availability Zones to make your DAX cluster fault-tolerant. The DAX cluster is completely isolated from other AWS regions, and it can interact with the DynamoDB tables that are in the same region, so you need to provision a new DAX cluster in another region if you have DynamoDB tables in more than one region.

DAX Control

Similar to Amazon RDS parameter groups, you can use parameter groups to optimize performance using set of parameters applied to a cluster. All the nodes in the cluster share the same parameter group and are configured in the same way. A DAX cluster uses a security group as its virtual firewall to control inbound network traffic, and since security groups are stateful, the same ingress rule that you add to your security group to allow incoming network traffic applies to outgoing network traffic by default. The DAX cluster has an Amazon Resource Name (ARN)—arn:aws:dax:us-east-1:1234567890:cache/my-dax-cluster—that can be used in an Identity and Access Management (IAM) policy to grant fine-grained access permissions for your DAX cluster. Both the DAX cluster and node have an endpoint—for example, my-dax-cluster.cache.amazonaws.com:8111—to use in your application; however, AWS recommends using a DAX cluster endpoint instead of a node endpoint because your application does not need to keep track of adding or removing nodes from the cluster. You need to monitor DAX events like success or failure when you add a node or make changes to any configurations (e.g., security groups). An Amazon Simple Notification Service (SNS) topic can be configured to immediately notify you when any event occurs in your DAX cluster.

DAX Write

DAX can be used for TransactWriteItems and TransactGetItems in DynamoDB. When you use TransactWriteItems through DAX, the return response using TransactGetItems is populated after the write. When using DAX, you use two read capacity units (RCUs) for every item in the TransactWriteItems transaction. As a best practice, you can either enable automatic scaling or provision enough throughput capacity for two read or write operations for each item in your transaction. AWS recommends splitting up meaningful simple transactions to improve throughput instead of grouping multiple distinct transactions. Follow data-modeling best practices to avoid multiple transactions updating the same data concurrently, which leads to cancelled transactions. You can use DAX caching, which provides fast in-memory performance to your applications from single-digit milliseconds to microsecond response times and requires very minimal changes to your application.

DAX Encryption

DAX provides encryption at rest using server-side encryption. In addition, DAX provides microsecond latency by allowing access to eventually consistent data from DynamoDB tables. DAX is ideal for applications that need quick response times for reads, applications that read more frequently, read-intensive applications, and applications that read large sets of data repeatedly. DAX may not be ideal for applications that expect strong consistent reads, applications that are write-intensive, and applications that are not read-intensive.

Auto-Scaling

DynamoDB offers auto-scaling where you define the upper and lower limits for your read and write capacity needs. When you enable auto-scaling, DynamoDB increases or decrease its provisioned read and write capacity to handle a sudden increase or decrease in traffic. Similar to reserved EC2 instances, you can purchase the DynamoDB reserved capacity in advance, where you need to commit to and pay up-front for your read and write capacity units, which offers you a huge cost savings instead of using on-demand provisioned mode.

Data Distribution

When you create an Amazon DynamoDB table, the data is stored in partitions in SSDs and replicated across multiple Availability Zones in a single AWS region. Amazon DynamoDB handles the partition management automatically and takes care of your applications' provisioned throughput requirements. The global secondary indexes in your DynamoDB are stored separately from the data in partitions. The data is stored in DynamoDB based on the key—if your table contains only a simple primary key, it stores and retrieves the data using the partition key value; if your table contains a composite primary key, DynamoDB uses both the partition key and sort key to store and retrieve your data.

DynamoDB Local

AWS also offers a downloadable version of DynamoDB to save on provisioned through-put, data storage, and data transfer fees, which allows you to write and test applications without accessing the DynamoDB web service or using an Internet connection. You can access DynamoDB running locally by using --endpoint-url as shown:

```
aws dynamodb describe-table --table-name Employee --endpoint-url
http://localhost:8000
```

You can either use the -sharedDb option or -inMemory option while creating the DynamoDB database locally. When you use the -sharedDb option, the data is stored in the shared-local-instance.db file, and when you use the -inMemory option, all data is written to memory and is not stored locally. You can use the downloadable version of

DynamoDB for development and testing purposes, and you should use the DynamoDB web service for production, which provides availability, durability, and scalability in addition to Amazon managing the DynamoDB for you.

The CreateTable table requires provisioned throughput settings, but it is ignored in downloadable DynamoDB. Scan operations are performed sequentially instead of parallel scans. The speed of read and write operations on table data is limited only by the speed of your machine. Read operations are eventually consistent, but might appear to be strongly consistent. Item collection metrics and sizes are not tracked in downloadable DynamoDB.

DynamoDB Web

Amazon DynamoDB can be accessed through the AWS Management Console or AWS Command Line Interface (CLI). From the console, you can create, update, or delete tables; manage streams; monitor alerts; and monitor the capacity and health of the DynamoDB database. You can add, view, scan, query, update, or delete items from the DynamoDB table. Amazon DynamoDB table names are case sensitive in the DynamoDB web service. For example, a table named KAMESH and another one named kamesh can both coexist as separate tables in the DynamoDB web service. However, with the downloadable Amazon DynamoDB, table names are case insensitive, so you will get an error if you try creating a table name of JACK and another table name of jack.

Secondary Indexes

Secondary indexes support your query operations when performing an index scan to retrieve the data instead of a table scan (i.e., querying the entire table). You can create multiple secondary indexes, but they are associated with a single table called a base table. You can also create an alternative key using a partition key and sort key for the index. The following are the two types of secondary indexes allowed in DynamoDB:

- **Global secondary index (GSI)**   Where the partition key and a sort key can be different from the base table and the index spans across all partitions. The read and write capacity must be specified separately.
- **Local secondary index (LSI)**   Where the partition key must be the same as the base table, but with a different sort key, and the index has the same partition key value. The read and write capacity of the base table is used.

DynamoDB Stream

The DynamoDB stream provides a stream of information about all the changes to your data in a DynamoDB table. Similar to triggers in the traditional relational database, the DynamoDB stream captures data whenever you create, update, or delete data items from the table. A stream can capture the before or after images of your data items. DynamoDB streams appear in the same sequence as the actual modifications and appear only once in near-real time. DynamoDB streams have separate endpoints, and you can use streams .dynamodb.us-east-1.amazonaws.com to access DynamoDB streams. DynamoDB streams can be enabled while creating a new table or added to an existing table without any performance impact and receive a unique ARN. A stream consists of modification records that are organized into shards, which contain multiple stream records, and they are removed automatically after 24 hours.

Backup and Recovery

You can perform an on-demand backup of your DynamoDB database without any performance impact or additional cost; however, you pay for the backup storage cost. You can perform a point-in-time recovery from the backup using EarliestRestorableDate-Time (35 days) or LatestRestorableDateTime (5 minutes), which protects you from accidental delete or write operations and can be stored for a long time to satisfy your audit or compliance requirements. The backups can be kept even after the original table in the same region is deleted, and it will not consume the provisioned throughput of your table. You can use either AWS Lambda or AWS Backup to schedule your backup, but don't forget to periodically delete the old backups. When you restore a table, the provisioned read and write capacity of original table is set to the new restored table in addition to any LSIs and GSIs. If you have enabled AWS CloudTrail then all your backup and recovery actions will be captured for monitoring and auditing.

DynamoDB Global Tables

This is a fully managed multiregion solution, and you just need to specify the AWS regions where you want the DynamoDB table, and the identical tables are created in those regions, and all your data changes are replicated to them. DynamoDB global tables use the TTL feature to replicate the TTL deletes to all replica tables. However, ACID is guaranteed only within the region and is not supported across regions in global tables because the data changes will be replicated to other regions only after they are committed in the original region.

NoSQL Workbench

The NoSQL Workbench is in preview at this time, and AWS recommends using the preview release tools or services for nonproduction environments, not in your production environments. NoSQL Workbench is a cross-platform client-side application available for Windows and macOS. It can be used for data modeling, data visualization, creating, querying, and managing your DynamoDB tables. NoSQL Workbench for DynamoDB can be used to build new data models using your existing data models, and you can also import and export the data model. NoSQL Workbench can be used as a data model visualizer to see the access patterns of your query mapping without writing code. You can manually add data or import data to your data model. You can use the graphical user interface to view and query your DynamoDB tables.

Data Protection

Your data is stored on multiple nodes across multiple Availability Zones in an Amazon region. The user data stored at rest and data in transit are protected with encryption because often the company policies, industry or government regulations, and compliance or audit requirements require this. All user data that is stored in durable media, including primary key, local and global secondary indexes, streams, global tables, backups, and DAX clusters, is encrypted at rest using encryption keys stored in AWS Key Management Service (KMS). During the creation of a new table, you can choose the AWS-owned customer master key (CMK), which is the default encryption type where the key is owned by DynamoDB with no additional charge. Or you can choose the AWS-managed CMK, where the key is stored in your account and managed by AWS KMS, so the charges apply for this type of encryption. Or you can choose a customer-managed CMK, where the key is stored in your account and owned, created, and managed by you and AWS KMS charges still apply. DynamoDB decrypts data when you access an encrypted table. The encryption key can be switched from the AWS-owned CMK to AWS-managed CMK to customer-managed CMK without changing your application code. Amazon DynamoDB uses the 256-bit Advanced Encryption Standard (AES-256) to secure your data from any unauthorized access, and you can encrypt only the entire table, not a subset of items in a table.

When you use AWS-owned CMKs, the key is not stored in your AWS account. AWS owns and manages the CMKs to protect your data, so you don't have the ability to view or audit key use. You don't need to create, manage, and rotate the key regularly to protect the keys, and you are not charged a monthly fee or a usage fee with AWS-owned CMKs.

You can use AWS-managed CMKs where the CMKs are in your account but they are created and managed on your behalf by AWS. AWS-managed CMKs can be viewed, including key policies, and you can audit the key usage from AWS CloudTrail logs. Even though you own the AWS account and KMS key, you cannot manage or change CMKs permissions because AWS creates and manages the key for you. You will incur AWS KMS charges, since it uses your key.

You can also use customer-managed CMKs where you create, own, and manage the CMKs in your AWS account. You have full responsibility and control over these CMKs and you need to establish and maintain the key policies, IAM policies, and rotating cryptographic material. When you delete or update the encryption key, any read or write operations are prevented on the table, the table status is changed to Inaccessible, and you receive an email notification. You must provide a new encryption key with DynamoDB access within seven days. You incur AWS KMS charges for using your own KMS key.

- **Data in transit**   All data in transit is encrypted, except DAX data, and the to-and-from communication uses the HTTPS protocol with Secure Sockets Layer (SSL)/Transport Layer Security (TLS) encryption to protect your data in transit.
- **Data in use**   You can use your existing client-side encryption to encrypt your data before sending it to DynamoDB.

The DynamoDB streams and backups are encrypted, and the LSIs and GSIs are encrypted using a base table encryption key. You can use the AWS-owned CMK or AWS-managed CMK to encrypt global tables.

Maintenance Window

The DAX cluster has a weekly maintenance window to apply system changes, and DAX assigns a 60-minute window randomly if the preferred window is not assigned during the creation or modification of your cluster. AWS recommends selecting a maintenance window during the lowest usage of your DAX cluster and its nodes.

Logging and Monitoring

Monitoring is an important part of any solution that you build, and you should collect monitoring data from DynamoDB so that you can debug any failure. You need to establish a baseline for normal DynamoDB performance based on various times and load conditions. This will be compared with the current performance to find any anomalies. The baseline should contain the number of read or write capacity units consumed over the specified time period. It also should contain the requests that exceeded a table's provisioned write or read capacity during the specified time period.

Here's a list of the monitoring tools:

- **Amazon CloudWatch**   DynamoDB can be monitored using CloudWatch, which collects the near-real-time metrics automatically. You can retain these statistics for a certain duration based on your requirements for comparing application performance. You can keep track of the TTL deletions by monitoring TimeToLiveDeletedItemCount for a certain period. You can track provisioned throughput by monitoring ConsumedReadCapacityUnits or ConsumedWriteCapacityUnits for a certain period. You can find which event is throttling your request by comparing ThrottledRequests with ReadThrottleEvents and WriteThrottleEvents metrics. Normally, the SystemErrors should return zero, and it can be monitored to find any request returns server error (i.e., HTTP 500) to investigate further. AWS CloudTrail captures all DynamoDB application programming interface (API) calls as events, which can be continuously delivered to an Amazon S3 bucket to help you find who made the request and when the request was made.

- **Amazon CloudWatch Alarms**   You can create alarms based on metrics and monitor them over a time to perform an action based on the threshold value. The action can be an Amazon SNS notification or auto-scaling. CloudWatch alarms are triggered when the state is changed and during a specified time period.

- **Amazon CloudWatch Logs**   Monitor, store, and access your log files.

- **Amazon CloudWatch Events** When an event occurs, route it to one or more target streams or functions and take the appropriate corrective action.
- **AWS CloudTrail Log Monitoring** You can share log files, monitor CloudTrail log files, and validate whether log files have changed after delivery.

Infrastructure Security

All DynamoDB API calls are captured in AWS CloudTrail. AWS recommends using TLS 1.2 and clients that support the Ephemeral Diffie-Hellman (DHE) or Elliptic Curve Diffie-Hellman Ephemeral (ECDHE) cipher. All requests must be authenticated using an IAM access key ID and a secret access key, or use AWS Security Token Service (STS) to generate temporary sign-in security credentials. It is a good practice to use a Virtual Private Cloud (VPC) endpoint for DynamoDB to enable Amazon EC2 instances in your VPC to use their private IP addresses to access DynamoDB with no exposure to the public Internet.

When you use Amazon VPC to launch the DAX cluster and your application, it offers full control over the IP range, subnets, and security groups. The to-and-from network communication to your DynamoDB uses HTTPS, which uses SSL/TLS encryption protection. You can avoid privacy and security concerns by using an IPSec virtual private network (VPN) tunnel to route your network traffic instead of using the Internet. In addition, you can use VPC endpoints for DynamoDB so the traffic between your VPC endpoint and DynamoDB service does not leave the Amazon network and is not exposed to the public Internet.

Security Best Practices

- **Encryption at rest** DynamoDB data is stored in tables, indexes, and streams, and is encrypted using AWS-owned or AWS-managed KMS key to protect the data from unauthorized access.
- **Use IAM roles** Use an IAM role for your users and applications to obtain temporary access keys to access DynamoDB instead of storing AWS credentials directly in the application.
- **Use IAM policies** Implement the least access privilege policy that reduces security risk and impact, where users get only the absolutely required permissions to perform their operations on DynamoDB by using AWS- or customer-managed policies.
- **Fine-grained access** DynamoDB allows you to control fine-grained access by granting only read-only or write-only access to certain items and attributes in a table or a secondary index based on the role of the user.
- **VPC endpoint** This prevents traffic from traversing the public Internet and allows you to control and limit access to the DynamoDB table.

- **Client-side encryption**   Use the Amazon DynamoDB Encryption Client software library to encrypt your data before sending it to DynamoDB.

- **Use AWS CloudTrail**   Use CloudTrail logs to audit all AWS KMS requests for when and what operation used the CMK, who requested it from which IP address, and so on.

- **Control-plane operations**   You can use CloudTrail to obtain important information about who and when a DynamoDB was created, updated, or deleted to track table changes made to your tables, indexes, and streams.

- **Data-plane operations**   Use the Amazon DynamoDB stream to log and monitor data-plane operations, like GetItem and PutItem, and trigger a Lambda function to send a notification.

- **DynamoDB configuration**   Use AWS Config to continuously monitor any DynamoDB configuration changes and trigger an Amazon SNS notification.

Chapter Review

This chapter began with an introduction to Amazon DynamoDB, which is the NoSQL offering from AWS. It then introduced all the Amazon DynamoDB core components and how the cluster setup, configuration, replication, backup, hardware provisioning, and software patching are handled in Amazon DynamoDB. It discussed the control-plane operations that allow you to create and manage DynamoDB tables, indexes, and streams and data-plane operations that create, read, update, and delete data from a DynamoDB table. Since most of us are familiar with SQL, the chapter explained in detail with code the differences between SQL and NoSQL databases. DynamoDB transactions offer ACID properties to maintain integrity of your data. Isolation levels are an important concept to understand before configuring your transactions in DynamoDB or on any other database. DynamoDB provides a serializable isolation level to make sure the output of your multiple concurrent operations displays the same results as if this were the only transaction taking place and no other transactions occur until this finishes.

Amazon DAX is designed for read-intensive applications that require responses from single-digit milliseconds to microseconds that run within your Amazon VPC environment. DAX clusters can be launched in your VPC using the AWS Management Console, and you can use security groups to control access to your DAX clusters. You just need to deploy your application that needs access to DAX in an EC2 instance with the DAX client in the same Amazon VPC. The DAX client sends all requests to the DAX cluster (called a cache hit when the items are available in DAX), and it sends the request to DynamoDB only if the items are not available in the DAX cluster (called a cache miss), so the response from DynamoDB is written to the DAX primary node and DAX returns the response to the application. AWS also offers a downloadable version of DynamoDB to save on provisioned throughput, data storage, and data transfer fees, which allows you to write and test applications without accessing the DynamoDB web service or using an Internet connection.

A secondary index is designed to support your query operations to perform an index scan to retrieve the data instead of a table scan (i.e., querying the entire table). The GSI has the partition key and a sort key that can be different from the base table and the index span across all partitions. The LSI has the partition key that is similar to the base table, but it can have a different sort key and the index has the same partition key value. DynamoDB stream provides a stream of information about all the changes to your data in a DynamoDB table. Similar to triggers in the traditional relational database, the DynamoDB stream captures data whenever you create, update, or delete data items from the table. A stream can capture the before or after images of your data items. DynamoDB streams appear in the same sequence as the actual modifications and they appear only once in near-real time. The NoSQL Workbench for DynamoDB can be used to build new data models based on your existing data models, and you can also import and export the data model. NoSQL Workbench can be used as data model visualizer, where you visualize the access patterns of your query mapping without writing code. You can also manually add data or import data to your data model. You can use the graphical user interface to view and query your DynamoDB tables.

AWS-owned CMKs are used but are not stored in your AWS account. AWS owns and manages the CMKs to protect your data, so you don't have the ability to view or audit key use. You don't need to create, manage, and rotate the key regularly to protect the keys, and you are not charged a monthly fee or a usage fee for AWS-owned CMKs. You can use AWS-managed CMKs, where the CMKs are in your account but they are created and managed on your behalf by AWS. You can also use customer-managed CMKs, where you create, own, and manage the CMKs in your AWS account. You have full responsibility and control over these CMKs if you need to establish and maintain the key policies, IAM policies, and rotating cryptographic material. You incur AWS KMS charges for using your own KMS key.

Exercises

The following exercises will help you practice creating and managing DynamoDB tables. You need to create an AWS account, as explained earlier, before performing these exercises. You can use the Free Tier when launching AWS resources, but make sure to terminate them at the end.

Exercise 14-1: Create a DynamoDB Table Using the AWS Management Console

1. Use your AWS account e-mail address and password to sign in and then navigate to the AWS DynamoDB console at https://console.aws.amazon.com/dynamodb/.
2. Verify the AWS region by using the Region selector in the upper-right corner of the page.
3. From the navigation pane on the left, choose DynamoDB.
4. From the navigation pane, choose Dashboard.
5. From the center of the page, choose Create Table.

6. For the table name, enter your new table name as **Employee**.

7. For the partition key, enter the key as **EMP_ID** and select the data type as Number from the dropdown.

8. Select the checkbox to choose Add Sort Key.

9. Enter **EMP_Name** as the sort key and select the data type as String from the dropdown menu.

10. Select the checkbox for Use Default Settings

11. Add a tag for the key/value pair, with **name** as the key and **Employee** as the value.

12. Click Create to create the table.

Exercise 14-2: Write to the DynamoDB Table Using the AWS Management Console

1. Use your AWS account e-mail address and password to sign in and then navigate to the AWS DynamoDB console at https://console.aws.amazon.com/dynamodb/.

2. Verify the AWS region by using the Region selector in the upper-right corner of the page.

3. From the navigation pane on the left, choose DynamoDB Tables.

4. From the list of tables, choose the Employee table.

5. Then choose the Items tab for the Employee table.

6. Click on the Items tab and choose Create Item.

7. Click the + symbol next to EMP_Name.

8. Choose Append, and then choose String and name the field **Job_Name**.

9. Repeat this process to create a string with the name **Department**.

10. For EMP_ID, enter **10001** as the value.

11. For EMP_Name, enter **Jack Ryan**.

12. For Job_Name, enter **Developer**.

13. For Department, enter **Cloud**.

14. Click Save.

Exercise 14-3: Read from the DynamoDB Table Using the AWS Management Console

1. Use your AWS account e-mail address and password to sign in and then navigate to the AWS DynamoDB console at https://console.aws.amazon.com/dynamodb/.

2. Verify the AWS region by using the Region selector in the upper-right corner of the page.

3. From the navigation pane on the left, choose DynamoDB tables.

4. From the list of tables, choose the Employee table.

5. Choose the Items tab for the Employee table.

6. On the Items tab, you can view the list of items stored in the table, sorted by EMP_ID and EMP_Name. The first item in the list is sorted ascending by EMP_ID.

Exercise 14-4: Update Data in the DynamoDB Table Using the AWS Management Console

1. Use your AWS account e-mail address and password to sign in and then navigate to the AWS DynamoDB console at https://console.aws.amazon.com/dynamodb/.

2. Verify the AWS region by using the Region selector in the upper-right corner of the page.

3. From the navigation pane on the left, choose DynamoDB tables.

4. From the list of tables, choose the Employee table.

5. Choose the Items tab for the Employee table.

6. Choose the item whose EMP_ID is 10001 and EMP_Name value is Jack Ryan.

7. Update the Job_Name value to **Senior Developer**, and then choose Save.

Exercise 14-5: Query the DynamoDB Table Using the AWS Management Console

1. Use your AWS account e-mail address and password to sign in and then navigate to the AWS DynamoDB console at https://console.aws.amazon.com/dynamodb/.

2. Verify the AWS region by using the Region selector in the upper-right corner of the page.

3. From the navigation pane on the left, choose DynamoDB tables.

4. From the list of tables, choose the Employee table.

5. Choose the Items tab for the Employee table.

6. Choose Query from the dropdown list.

Exercise 14-6: Scan the DynamoDB Table Using the AWS Management Console

1. Use your AWS account e-mail address and password to sign in and then navigate to the AWS DynamoDB console at https://console.aws.amazon.com/dynamodb/.

2. Verify the AWS region by using the Region selector in the upper-right corner of the page.

3. From the navigation pane on the left, choose DynamoDB tables.

4. From the list of tables, choose the Employee table.

5. Choose the Items tab for the Employee table.

6. Choose Scan from the dropdown list.

Questions

The following questions will help you gauge your understanding of the contents in this chapter. Read all the answers carefully because there might be more than one correct answer. Choose the best response for each question.

1. Your application needs to store large volumes of semi-structured data and retrieve it with single-digit millisecond to microsecond latency. Which of the following NoSQL databases is suitable for your application?

   A. Amazon DynamoDB

   B. Amazon RDS

   C. Amazon S3

   D. Amazon EBS

2. Which of the following keys uniquely identifies each item in an Amazon DynamoDB table to make sure no two items can have the same key?

   A. Sort key

   B. Foreign key

   C. Primary key

   D. Composite key

3. Which of the following secondary indexes are supported in Amazon DynamoDB? (Choose two.)

   A. Regional secondary index has the same partition and sort key

   B. Global secondary index has a partition key and sort key that can be different from the base table

   C. Local secondary index has the same partition key as the table, but a different sort key

   D. State secondary index has the same sort key, but a different partition key

4. Your application writes nearly 25 items in a transaction by using PutItem multiple times, consuming many network round trips. How can you reduce the latency and network round trips for multiple items?

   A. Use DynamoDB Accelerator (DAX)

   B. Use BatchGetItem to write multiple items

   C. Use GetItem to write items

   D. Use BatchWriteItem instead of PutItem to write bulk records

5. Your company's compliance policy requires that all data modifications are captured for audit purposes in your Amazon DynamoDB database. How can you capture the events that are happening in near real-time during any add, update, and delete operation?

   A. Enable Amazon DynamoDB Accelerator (DAX)

   B. Create a global table to capture the events

   C. Enable Amazon DynamoDB streams to capture before and after images of your data

   D. Enable Amazon DynamoDB transactions to capture the events automatically

6. Which of the following are control-plane operations that can be used to create and manage Amazon DynamoDB tables? (Choose three.)

   A. CreateTable can be used to create a new table and indexes and to enable Amazon DynamoDB streams of a table

   B. UpdateTable can be used to modify the table and indexes and to modify Amazon DynamoDB streams of a table

   C. DeleteTable can be used to remove a table and its objects from the Amazon DynamoDB table

   D. PutItem can be used to write a single item to an Amazon DynamoDB table

7. A developer accidently ran a test script in a production database and deleted 12 tables and updated data from 46 tables at 2 P.M. today from the Amazon DynamoDB database that has point-in-time recovery enabled for 35 days. How can you fix this quickly and restore those 58 tables in production?

   A. You can restore all the tables using LatestRestorableDateTime to just before 2 P.M. today.

   B. You can restore only the 12 tables but not those 46 tables that were updated.

   C. You can restore only 46 tables but not those 12 tables that were deleted.

   D. It is not possible to restore any tables; you need to use yesterday's manual backup to restore the entire database.

8. You have a large online shopping website, and your customers are spread across US East/West Coast, Europe, and Asia Pacific regions. At the moment you have eight identical DynamoDB tables for your products in eight different AWS regions that are entirely separate from each other. You have managed a replication solution to keep all the data changes in sync, but it's time-consuming and requires a lot of labor. Now you need to add four more regions and want to avoid this time-consuming and labor-intensive replication effort. Which feature of Amazon DynamoDB solves this issue?

   A. Amazon DynamoDB Accelerator (DAX)

   B. Amazon DynamoDB global tables

   C. Amazon DynamoDB streams

   D. Amazon DynamoDB transactions

9. Amazon DynamoDB supports different isolation levels to ensure that the results of multiple concurrent operations are the same, as if only one operation in the transaction is occurring and ensures the read operations always return committed values for an item. Which of the following isolations are supported in Amazon DynamoDB? (Choose two.)

   A. Parallelable

   B. Write-committed

   C. Serializable

   D. Read-committed

10. You want to enable encryption when creating a new Amazon DynamoDB table. Which of the following encryption options are available? (Choose three.)

   A. Server-managed SMK, where the EC2 server owns and manages the key

   B. AWS-owned CMK, where the key is owned by DynamoDB

   C. AWS-managed CMK, where the key is stored in your account and is managed by AWS KMS

   D. Customer-managed CMK, where the key is stored in your account and is created, owned, and managed by you.

Answers

1. **A.** You can use Amazon DynamoDB to retrieve the data with single-digit millisecond to microsecond latency.

2. **C.** Amazon DynamoDB uses a primary key to uniquely store and identify the items in a table.

3. **B, C.** Amazon DynamoDB supports a global secondary index and local secondary index.

4. **D.** You need to use BatchWriteItem instead of PutItem for writing bulk records.

5. **C.** You can enable Amazon DynamoDB streams to capture before and after images of your data.

6. **A, B, C.** CreateTable, UpdateTable, and DeleteTable are the control-plane operations available in Amazon DynamoDB.

7. **A.** You can restore all the tables using LatestRestorableDateTime to just before 2 P.M. today.

8. **B.** Amazon DynamoDB global tables can manage the replication across regions for you.

9. **C, D.** Amazon DynamoDB supports serializable and read-committed isolation levels.

10. **B, C, D.** Amazon DynamoDB supports AWS-owned CMKs, AWS-managed CMKs, and customer-managed CMKs.

Additional Resources

- **Amazon DynamoDB Documentation**   There is no place like official AWS documentation to get the latest and most up-to-date information about Amazon DynamoDB database.
  `https://docs.aws.amazon.com/dynamodb/index.html`

- **Amazon DynamoDB AWS re:Invent videos**   This blog lists all useful videos and slide decks from AWS re:Invent 2019.
  `https://aws.amazon.com/blogs/database/amazon-dynamodb-related-videos-and-slide-decks-from-aws-reinvent-2019/`

- **Getting Started with Amazon DynamoDB**   This blog is the one-stop shop to get you quickly get started with Amazon DynamoDB by creating a table, adding items, and querying.
  `https://aws.amazon.com/blogs/database/getting-started-with-amazon-dynamodb/`

- **Amazon DynamoDB in 2019**   This is another interesting blog that lists all the major updates for Amazon DynamoDB in 2019.
  `https://aws.amazon.com/blogs/database/2019-the-year-in-review-for-amazon-dynamodb/`

- **Secure Your Data in Amazon DynamoDB**   This blog explains step by step the procedures and best practices to secure your sensitive data in Amazon DynamoDB.
  `https://aws.amazon.com/blogs/database/applying-best-practices-for-securing-sensitive-data-in-amazon-dynamodb/`

PART VI

AWS Application Integration and Management

■ **Chapter 15**   Amazon Simple Queue Service
                   and Simple Notification Service
■ **Chapter 16**   Amazon Simple Workflow Service, Amazon API
                   Gateway, and AWS Step Functions
■ **Chapter 17**   Monitoring Using Amazon CloudWatch,
                   AWS CloudTrail, and AWS Config
■ **Chapter 18**   Infrastructure as Code Using AWS CloudFormation

Amazon Simple Queue Service and Simple Notification Service

In this chapter, you will learn
- Amazon Simple Queue Service
- Amazon SQS architecture
- Standard queues
- First in/first out (FIFO) queues
- Amazon Simple Notification Service
- Amazon SNS architecture
- Delivery policy
- Dead-letter queues
- Data encryption
- Logging
- Monitoring

This chapter discusses in detail how Amazon Simple Queue Service and Amazon Simple Notification service work.

Amazon Simple Queue Service

Amazon Simple Queue Service (Amazon SQS) is a hosted queue used to integrate and decouple distributed applications with features like dead-letter queues and cost allocation tags. You have control over who can receive or send messages from and to your queue. The contents of your message queue are encrypted using server-side encryption, using the AWS Key Management Service (KMS) key. Amazon SQS stores your message queues to multiple servers to provide durability. There are two types of queues:

- Standard queues that support at-least-once message delivery
- First in/first out (FIFO) queues that support just-once message processing

You can concurrently access Amazon SQS messages, and you can produce and consume messages without any interruption, since Amazon SQS handles the high availability. Amazon SQS handles any amount of load increase or spikes without you manually provisioning any additional resources. Amazon SQS message locking allows multiple producers and consumers to send and receive messages at the same time. You are allowed to set a delay on your queue and store the message contents in Amazon S3 or Amazon DynamoDB.

Amazon SQS Architecture

The main parts of a distributed messaging system are

- Your distributed system services (S1, S2, and S3)
- Your Amazon SQS queues (Q1 and Q2)
- The messages in the queue (M1, M2, M3, M4, and M5)

Your system S1 needs to send messages M1, M2, and M3 to another distributed system, S2, using the Q1 queue, and system S1 needs to send messages M4 and M5 to system S3 using the Q2 queue. Queues Q1 and Q2 redundantly store the messages M1, M2, M3, M4, and M5 across multiple Amazon SQS servers.

Queue Lifecycle

The Amazon SQS message lifecycle begins with its creation and ends with its deletion from the queue. Your distributed system S1 sends messages M1, M2, and M3 to queue Q1, and those messages are distributed across multiple Amazon SQS servers to provide redundancy. When consumer system S2 is ready to process messages M1, M2, and M3, it consumes all those messages from queue Q1. The messages remain in the queue until it's processed and for the duration of visibility timeout. The consumer system S2 deletes the messages from queue Q1 to prevent messages M1, M2, and M3 from processing again.

Similarly, your system S1 sends messages M4 and M5 using the Q2 queue to another distributed system, S3. As soon as the consumer system S3 is ready to process messages M4 and M5, it starts consuming from queue Q2. Once messages M4 and M5 are processed by system S3, messages M4 and M5 are deleted from queue Q2 to prevent them from processing again.

 NOTE The message retention period is from 60 seconds to 14 days, and the default message retention period is 4 days.

Standard Queues

The standard queue is the Amazon SQS default queue type that supports an unlimited number of transactions per second (TPS) per SendMessage or ReceiveMessage or DeleteMessage application programming interface (API) actions. It supports at-least-once message delivery, and occasionally it is possible that more than one copy of the same message gets delivered out of order. Standard queues deliver messages in the same order as they are sent. These queues are suitable for applications that can process messages that arrive out of order and that do so more than once. You can use the standard message queue to decouple your user requests from another complex task that allows your users to perform multiple tasks in your application. As mentioned, the standard queue might deliver more than one copy of the same message out of order, so you need to design your application to be idempotent so that it will not be affected negatively when same message is processed more than once.

First In/First Out Queues

FIFO queues deliver messages in exactly the same order as they are received. This queue is designed for applications where the order of messages is critical and duplicate messages cannot be tolerated. It's ideally suited for applications that need to execute critical commands in exactly the same order—for example, a modified product price needs to appear in the correct order or a user needs to be prevented from selling or buying a product before registering for an account. The FIFO queue provides just-once processing for up to 300 messages per second, per SendMessage, ReceiveMessage, or DeleteMessage API action, and with batching, it supports up to 3,000 messages per second. You can increase this default limit by submitting a support request. FIFO makes sure that no duplicates are introduced into your queue. The names of a FIFO queue are limited to 80 characters in length, including the .fifo suffix. The order is strictly preserved and available until a consumer processes and deletes it. You can send multiple ordered message groups within a single queue using FIFO queues.

- **Message Deduplication ID**   This is a token used for deduplication of sent messages. When a message with a particular message deduplication ID is sent again, it will not be delivered during the five-minute deduplication interval.

- **Message Group ID**   When a message is part of a particular message group, it is processed one by one, in a strict order, relative to the message group.

- **Receive Request Attempt ID**   The ReceiveMessage calls token is used for deduplication.

- **Sequence Number**   Amazon SQS assigns a large, nonconsecutive number to every message.

Sending Messages

When multiple messages are sent to the Amazon SQS FIFO queue, a distinct deduplication ID is assigned to each message and returns an acknowledgment. Then, messages are ordered based on a unique message group ID that each producer uses when sending the messages. Each message in the FIFO queue is sent and received in a strict order based on its message group ID value. This allows you to resend as many times as necessary using the same deduplication ID until the producer receives at least one acknowledgment without introducing any duplicates.

Receiving Messages

The FIFO queue processes messages with the same message group ID when receiving messages, and it allows you to retry the same receive request attempt ID as many times as necessary until you receive at least one acknowledgment without affecting the ordering of messages. FIFO queues don't introduce duplicates. You can enable content-based deduplication by using a SHA-256 hash to generate the deduplication ID using the message body.

Migrate a Standard Queue to a FIFO Queue

In order to migrate from a standard queue to a FIFO queue, your application and queue need to be configured differently. FIFO queues support only per-queue delays, not per-message delays, so if your application assigns DelaySeconds for each message, then it needs to be modified to assign on the queue instead. Each message in a FIFO queue needs a message group ID, so either you need multiple message groups IDs or the same message group ID for all your messages.

- **Queue Name** The Amazon SQS queue name is limited to 80 characters and must be unique for your AWS account region; if the name ends with .fifo, it is a FIFO queue.

- **Queue URL** Amazon SQS assigns each queue a URL with your AWS account number and queue name; for example:

  https://sqs.us-west-1.amazonaws.com/120987654321/my-first-queue

- **Message ID** Amazon SQS returns a system-assigned message ID for every message in the SendMessage response, with a maximum length of 100 characters.

- **Receipt Handle** You receive a receipt handle each time you receive a message from a queue that is associated with the receive action, not the message itself. Messages have a maximum length of 1,024 characters.

- **Message Deduplication ID** This is the sent messages token, so if a message is sent successfully, any subsequent message request with same message deduplication ID is not delivered until the five-minute deduplication interval has passed.

- **Message Group ID** This is the tag of the particular message group that is always processed one by one in a strict order.

- **Sequence Number** This is the large, nonconsecutive number that Amazon SQS assigns to each message.

- **Message Metadata** This is custom metadata of message attributes to your Amazon SQS messages used by your applications or other AWS services.

- **Message Attributes** You can have ten message attributes, like identifiers, signatures, timestamps, and geospatial data, that are separate from the message body.

- **Message Attribute Components** The message attribute components are Name, Type, and Value, and the message body cannot be null or empty.

- **Message Attribute Data Types** Amazon SQS supports the logical data types String, Number, and Binary with optional custom data type labels.

- **Message System Attributes**   The message system attribute is AWSTraceHeader, which is a string data type, and its size doesn't count toward the total size of a message.
- **Cost Allocation Tags**   These help you organize and identify your Amazon SQS queues and organize your AWS bill to reflect your cost based on key-value pairs.

Short Polling

Amazon SQS queries only a set of its servers rather than all servers for short polling, which is the default, based on a weighted random distribution and returns messages from only those servers. So, your ReceiveMessage request may return fewer messages as opposed to all of them. When the WaitTimeSeconds is set to 0 for ReceiveMessage call or the queue attribute ReceiveMessageWaitTimeSeconds is set to 0, it is called short polling.

Long Polling

Amazon SQS eliminates the number of empty responses and false-empty responses by querying all servers instead of a subset of servers for long polling when the wait time is greater than 0 for the ReceiveMessage call by waiting until a message is available in the queue before sending a response.

Dead-Letter Queues

Amazon SQS writes failed messages with its original message ID and en-queue time-stamp to a dead-letter queue for debugging, which helps to quickly isolate the problematic messages. If the message retention period is two days, for example, then the message is deleted after two days, so AWS recommends setting a longer retention period for the dead-letter queue than your original queue retention period. If your application is able to keep retrying a message indefinitely, then you don't need to use a dead-letter queue with standard queues. If your application requires an exact order of messages or operations, then you don't need to use a dead-letter queue with a FIFO queue.

Visibility Timeout

Amazon SQS doesn't delete the message automatically; it remains in the queue until the consumer deletes it. The visibility timeout prevents the message from being received and processed again. The minimum visibility timeout is 0 seconds, the maximum is 12 hours, and the default is 30 seconds.

Inflight Messages

An Amazon SQS message has the following three basic states:

- Message sent to a queue by a producer.
- Message is received from the queue by a consumer.
- Message is deleted from the queue.

Any message can be considered stored after it is sent to a queue but not yet received, and there is no quota for stored messages. Any message can be considered as in flight after it is received but not yet deleted, and there is a quota to in-flight messages.

Standard queues have 120,000 in-flight messages, and Amazon SQS returns an OverLimit error message if you reach this quota. So, you can either delete messages from the queue after processing or request a quota increase by submitting a support request. A maximum of 20,000 in-flight messages can be received by a consumer from FIFO queues.

Delay Queues

Delay queues let you postpone the delivery of new messages (which remain invisible) for a number of seconds, with a minimum of 0 seconds to a maximum of 15 minutes. Changing the per-queue delay in the FIFO queue affects the messages that are already in the queue. A message is hidden when it is first added to the delay queue and is hidden again after it is consumed for visibility timeouts from the queue.

Temporary Queues

You can use temporary queues to save development time and deployment costs for common message patterns that allow your application to make fewer API calls and clean up the temporary queue automatically when no longer in use. The temporary queries can be created and deleted without incurring any additional cost.

Virtual Queues

Virtual queues are local data structures that let you combine multiple low-traffic destinations into a single Amazon SQS queue. They are created by the temporary queue using the HostQueueURL attribute.

Message Timers

You can use message timers to specify an initial invisibility period for a message, with a minimum delay of 0 seconds and a maximum of 15 minutes, so if your message has a 12-second timer, for example, then the message will not be visible for the first 12 seconds. The delay period is for the entire queue, and the message timer is for individual messages; in addition, the message timer overrides the DelaySeconds on an Amazon SQS delay queue.

Large Messages

You can use Amazon S3 for storing and consuming messages up to 2GB in size. You can send a message that references a single message object stored in your Amazon S3 bucket. You can also get the corresponding message or delete the corresponding message object from an Amazon S3 bucket.

Data Encryption

You can protect messages in transit using Secure Sockets Layer (SSL) and protect messages at rest by enabling encryption before saving them to disk and decrypting them when received. Server-side encryption (SSE) can be used to transmit sensitive data in encrypted queues using keys managed in AWS KMS. The messages are encrypted using SSE as soon as Amazon SQS receives it, and the messages are stored in encrypted form in Amazon SQS. You can either manage the customer master key (CMK) yourself or use the AWS-managed CMK for your Amazon SQS queues. SSE encrypts the message body where your sensitive data is stored but it does not encrypt the queue or message metadata.

Virtual Private Cloud Endpoints

You can use a Virtual Private Cloud (VPC) endpoint to connect your Amazon SQS without using the public Internet and instead use the Amazon network for your communication between your VPC endpoint to Amazon SQS.

Logging

You can use AWS CloudTrail to record all of the Amazon SQS API calls that a user, role, or AWS service makes. You can identify a specific request, the IP address, the requester's identity, and the date and time from the AWS CloudTrail logs. You can enable continuous delivery of CloudTrail events to an Amazon S3 bucket, or you can view the events in the CloudTrail console.

Monitoring

CloudWatch can be used to view and analyze metrics of your Amazon SQS queues in addition to setting up CloudWatch alarms for Amazon SQS metrics. All metrics of active Amazon SQS queues are collected and pushed to CloudWatch every five minutes. A queue is active for up to six hours or if any action accesses it, and you can collect CloudWatch metrics from both standard and FIFO queues.

Amazon Simple Notification Service

Amazon Simple Notification Service (Amazon SNS) sends messages to subscribing endpoints and clients, called publishers and subscribers, respectively, which are also known as producers and consumers. A publisher can communicate asynchronously with subscribers by producing and sending a message to a topic communication channel. A subscriber like a web server, e-mail address, Amazon SQS queue, and AWS Lambda function can receive the message over one of the supported protocols when subscribed to the topic. You can create a topic using Amazon SNS and grant access to publishers and subscribers. A publisher creates topics to send messages and then Amazon SNS matches the topic to its list of subscribers and delivers the message.

Amazon SNS Architecture

An Amazon SNS topic has a unique name and endpoint for publishers and subscribers for both posting and receiving messages. An Amazon SNS topic is a logical access point that lets you group multiple endpoints to broadcast messages to services that require them. You can start publishing messages as soon as you create a topic. You need to subscribe to an endpoint like AWS Lambda, Amazon SQS, HTTP, or e-mail ID of the topic to receive relevant. As soon as you confirm your subscription, the subscribed endpoint begins to receive messages from Amazon SNS. Metadata tags are used to track your Amazon SNS resources for cost allocation and distribution. When a message cannot be delivered to its subscribers, it is moved to an Amazon SQS dead-letter queue for further analysis or resending. Consumers can unsubscribe from a topic if they no longer need to receive messages from it.

SSE can be enabled for a topic to protect its data. You can secure messages by using the AWS private network when publishing messages from an Amazon EC2 instance that's hosted on your Amazon VPC. Sensitive messages that contain either personally identifiable information (PII) or market regulations applications data will stay within the AWS network without traveling the public Internet. An interface VPC endpoint powered by AWS PrivateLink is useful for message data that needs to be in compliance with the Payment Card Industry (PCI) Data Security Standard (DSS) or the Health Insurance Portability and Accountability Act (HIPAA).

Fanout

The Amazon SNS message from a topic fans out to multiple subscribed endpoints, like HTTP endpoints, e-mail addresses, and Amazon SQS queues, using parallel asynchronous processing. An application can send a message to a topic whenever a request is for an address change. A Lambda function that is subscribed to that topic handles the process by updating the address, while the other Lambda updates the data warehouse for analysis and reporting. Another way to use "fanout" is to send e-mail in addition to responding to an event. You have a Lambda function and e-mail subscribed to an event topic, and when a particular event happens, the Lambda function spins up more instances in addition to sending an e-mail.

Alerts

You can receive application and system alerts based on predefined thresholds either by Short Message Service (SMS) or e-mail. For example, when a threshold is reached in your Amazon EC2 Auto Scaling group from 12 instances to 8 instances or one of the instances fails, it can trigger an e-mail or SMS message based on your preference.

Push Message

Push e-mails and text messaging are used to transmit messages to individuals or groups. For example, if you are stopping and starting your nonproduction EC2 instances after working hours, you can send an e-mail or SMS message to your manager or to your entire team either after or before stopping and starting the EC2 instances. Individuals receive a notification to subscribe to the topic, or they can unsubscribe from the topic when they no longer need updates.

Push Notifications

Mobile push notifications can be used to send messages directly to your mobile applications, similar to the operating system notifications that you get on your smartphone. You can use Amazon SNS to send notifications when an update is available for the mobile application by including a link to download and install the update.

Message Durability

All messages received by Amazon SNS are stored as multiple copies to disk in different isolated AWS Availability Zones for durability. As soon as Amazon SNS receives a publish request, it stores multiple copies to disk before sending the confirmation back to the sender.

Message Delivery Status

The delivery status of application, HTTP, Lambda, and SQS log entries are sent to CloudWatch logs for the topic subscribed to an Amazon SNS endpoint. Logging helps you determine whether a message was delivered, to find the response sent from the Amazon SNS endpoint to Amazon SNS, and to determine the dwell time, which is the time between the publish timestamp and handing off-timestamp to an Amazon SNS endpoint.

You can grant Amazon SNS write access to use CloudWatch logs by using the <Application, HTTP, Lambda or SQS> SuccessFeedbackRoleArn and <Application, HTTP, Lambda or SQS> FailureFeedbackRoleArn attributes. You can get the sample rate percentage (0 to 100 percent) of the successfully delivered messages by using the <Application, HTTP, Lambda or SQS> SuccessFeedbackSampleRate attribute. All failed message deliveries can be generated in CloudWatch logs by configuring the <Application, HTTP, Lambda or SQS> FailureFeedbackRoleArn attribute.

Message Delivery Retries

A delivery policy can be defined in Amazon SNS for all delivery protocols, which determine how Amazon SNS retries the delivery of messages. Amazon SNS stops the delivery retry when the policy is exhausted and deletes the messages if it is not attached to a dead-letter queue.

Delivery Policies

A delivery policy contains the following four phases:

- **Immediate Retry (No Delay) Phase**   Occurs immediately without any delay after the initial delivery attempt, and there is no delay between retries.
- **Pre-Backoff Phase**   This follows the previous no-delay phase and is used to attempt a set of retries before applying a backoff by specifying the number of retries and the amount of delay between them.

PART VI

- **Backoff Phase**   Delays between retries are controlled by using the retry-backoff function by setting a minimum delay and a maximum delay. The retry-backoff function defines how quickly the delay increases from the minimum to the maximum delay, and the backoff function can be arithmetic, exponential, geometric, or linear in nature.

- **Post-Backoff Phase**   This follows the previous backoff phase and specifies a number of retries and the amount of delay between them, which is the final phase.

Creating a Delivery Policy

The delivery policy and its four phases can be used to define how Amazon SNS retries the delivery of messages to HTTP/S endpoints by overriding the default retry policy when required. The HTTP/S delivery policy can be set up at the subscription or topic level, and the policy applies to all HTTP/S subscriptions associated with the policy at the topic level. The delivery policy can be customized based on your HTTP/S server's capacity. AWS recommends setting the delivery policy at the topic level so that it remains valid for all HTTP/S subscriptions of that topic instead of composing a delivery policy for each HTTP/S subscription. You can calculate the number of retries using the following formula:

```
numRetries - numNoDelayRetries - numMinDelayRetries - numMaxDelayRetries
```

- **minDelayTarget**   Delay of first retry attempt in backoff phase
- **maxDelayTarget**   Delay of final retry attempt in backoff phase
- **backoffFunction**   Algorithm to calculate the delays with retry attempts between retries

Dead-Letter Queues

As mentioned earlier, a dead-letter queue is an Amazon SQS queue that an Amazon SNS subscription uses for messages that can't be successfully delivered to its subscribers. Messages with client errors or server errors that can't be successfully delivered are held in the dead-letter queue for further analysis or reprocessing. Message delivery fails when Amazon SNS can't access a subscribed endpoint due to a client-side or server-side error. When Amazon SNS receives a client-side error or server-side error beyond the number of retries configured in its retry policy, Amazon SNS either discards the message or sends it to the dead-letter queue.

Client-Side Errors

A client-side error occurs when Amazon SNS has stale metadata because the owner deleted the subscribed endpoint or changed the subscribed endpoint policy, which prevents Amazon SNS from delivering messages. If the message delivery fails because of a client-side error, Amazon SNS doesn't retry to deliver it.

Server-Side Errors

Server-side errors can happen when the system responsible for the subscribed endpoint becomes unavailable or returns an exception that indicates it can't process a valid request from Amazon SNS. When server-side errors occur, Amazon SNS retries the failed deliveries using either a linear or exponential backoff function.

Message Attributes

Amazon SNS supports delivery of message attributes like timestamps, identifiers, signatures, and geospatial data for the message. Message attributes are separate from the message body but are sent together. The receiver can use the message, which can contain up to ten attributes, and decide how the message will be handled before processing it. Message attributes make your messages filterable using filter policies:

- **Name** Contains A–Z, a–z, 0–9, underscore (_), hyphen (-), and period (.) characters
- **Type** Data types are String, Number, and Binary; they are case sensitive, and have a length up to 256 bytes
- **Value** User-specified message attribute value, and the message body cannot be null or empty
- **String** UTF-8 binary encoding
- **Number** Positive or negative integers or floating-point numbers
- **Binary** Can store any binary data like encrypted data, compressed data, or images

Message Filtering

A topic subscriber receives all the messages published to a topic by default. However, the subscriber can use a filter policy to receive just a subset of the messages. A filter policy is a JSON object that contains attributes that define which messages can be received by the subscriber. Amazon SNS uses filter policy attributes before sending messages to the subscriber and can skip it without sending the message.

Tags

Tags can be used to organize Amazon SNS resources and to find related tagged topics. Tags are metadata about your topics to identify its purpose, environment, or owner with a key-value pair, and it is case-sensitive.

Data Encryption

Your data will be protected using SSL or client-side encryption while in transit traveling to and from Amazon SNS and at rest when it is stored on disks in Amazon datacenters. You can protect data at rest by requesting Amazon SNS to encrypt your messages before saving them to disk in its datacenters and then decrypt them when the messages are received.

Encryption at Rest

SSE can be used to encrypt sensitive data in topics using AWS KMS. Amazon SNS encrypts your messages as soon as it receives them and stores the messages in encrypted form. Amazon SNS decrypts messages only when requested by an authorized receiver. SSE encrypts the message body of an Amazon SNS topic, but not the topic or message metadata, and any encrypted messages remain encrypted even if the encryption of the topic is disabled.

Logging

All Amazon SNS–supported events are recorded in a CloudTrail that can be used to view, search, and download information. You can create a "path" to enable CloudTrail to deliver log files to your Amazon S3 bucket where the path applies to all AWS regions. The path logs events from all regions, which are delivered to your Amazon S3 bucket for further analysis to determine who made the request, the IP address of the request, and when it was made.

Monitoring

You can collect, monitor, and analyze Amazon SNS metrics using the CloudWatch console, programmatically using the CloudWatch API, or using CloudWatch's own Command Line Interface (CLI). There are no additional charges for monitoring CloudWatch metrics, since it is provided as part of the Amazon SNS service. The performance metrics of your Amazon SNS topics, SMS deliveries, or push notifications are automatically collected and pushed to CloudWatch every five minutes.

Infrastructure Security

You can securely access Amazon SNS using the AWS API through the AWS network. AWS recommends using Transport Layer Security (TLS) 1.2 or later with clients that support cipher suites with perfect forward secrecy (PFS), like Elliptic Curve Ephemeral Diffie-Hellman (ECDHE) or Ephemeral Diffie-Hellman (DHE). You need to use Identity and Access Management (IAM) credentials or use the AWS Security Token Service (STS) to generate temporary security credentials.

Internetwork Traffic

You can create an Amazon SNS endpoint in your VPC, which is a logical entity that allows connectivity only to Amazon SNS. The VPC routes requests to Amazon SNS endpoints and routes responses back to the VPC using the AWS private network connection without traversing through the public Internet. The endpoint provides secure connectivity to Amazon SNS without any Internet gateway, Network Address Translation (NAT) gateway, or virtual private network (VPN) connection.

Publicly Accessible

Your Amazon SNS topic should not be accessible by everyone in the world from the public Internet or by any AWS unauthenticated user. Never create policies with the principal set to "" or use wildcard (*) instead of providing a particular username.

Least-Privilege Access

Least-privilege access is important to reduce the negative effect of errors or malicious intent and to reduce security risks. You always need to grant only the permissions required to perform a particular task. In the Amazon SNS publisher-subscriber model, administrators are able to create, modify, and delete topics and policies. Publishers are able to send messages to topics, and subscribers are able to subscribe to topics.

Server-Side Encryption

You can use encryption at rest to encrypt your messages to mitigate data leakage issues using a key stored in a different location from the location that stores your messages. Data encryption at rest is provided by SSE using the AWS KMS key. Encryption of your data happens at the message level, and the message is decrypted for you when you access it. You can access the messages without any difference between accessing encrypted and unencrypted topics as long as you authenticate your request and have access permissions.

Data in Transit Encryption

You can prevent a network-based attacker from eavesdropping on network traffic or manipulate it using an attack such as man-in-the-middle by using HTTPS (TLS). You can use the aws:SecureTransport condition in the topic policy to allow only encrypted connections over HTTPS (TLS) that forces requests to use SSL.

Using VPC Endpoints

If you do not want to expose your topics through the Internet, you can use VPC endpoints to limit access to hosts within a particular VPC. You can control access to topics from specific Amazon VPCs or from specific VPC endpoints. This provides you with full control over the requests and users that are allowed to access your VPC endpoint.

Chapter Review

This chapter began by exploring Amazon SQS and Amazon SNS. It then explored both messaging services. The chapter explained that Amazon SQS is a hosted queue that can be used to integrate and decouple your distributed applications. You have control over who can receive or send messages from and to your queue. All the contents of your message queue are encrypted using server-side encryption, using the AWS KMS key. Amazon SQS offers standard queues that support at-least-once message delivery, and FIFO queues that supports just-once message processing. Amazon SQS stores your message queues on multiple servers to provide durability. For short polling, Amazon SQS queries only a set of its servers rather than all servers by default. For long polling, Amazon SQS queries all servers instead of a subset of servers to eliminate empty responses and false-empty responses.

Amazon SQS writes failed messages with the original message ID to a dead-letter queue for debugging and to help you quickly isolate problematic messages. A visibility timeout prevents messages from being received and processed again. Delay queues let you postpone delivery and keep new messages invisible for a certain number of seconds. Temporary queues are used to save development time and costs for common message patterns. Virtual queues are local data structures that let you combine multiple low-traffic destinations into a single Amazon SQS queue. Messages in transit use SSL, and messages at rest are protected by enabling encryption before saving them to disk and decrypting them when received. AWS CloudTrail can be used to record all of the Amazon SQS API calls that a user, role, or AWS service makes. You can identify a specific request, the IP address, the requester's identity, and the date and time from the AWS CloudTrail logs.

CloudWatch can be used to view and analyze metrics of your Amazon SQS queues in addition to setting up CloudWatch alarms for Amazon SQS metrics. All the metrics of active Amazon SQS queues are collected and pushed to CloudWatch every five minutes.

Amazon SNS is a managed publication-subscription service that lets you group multiple endpoints to broadcast messages to services that require them. You can start publishing messages once you create a topic. Consumers can subscribe a topic endpoint like AWS Lambda, Amazon SQS, HTTP, or e-mail ID and receive relevant messages. The Amazon SNS message from a topic fans out to multiple subscribed endpoints using parallel asynchronous processing.

Delivery policies have four phases—immediate retry (no delay), pre-backoff, backoff phase, and post-backoff—and can be used to define how Amazon SNS retries the delivery of messages to HTTP/S endpoints by overriding the default retry policy when required. A dead-letter queue is an Amazon SQS queue that an Amazon SNS subscription uses for messages that can't be successfully delivered to subscribers. Messages with client errors or server errors that can't be successfully delivered are held in the dead-letter queue for further analysis or reprocessing. A topic subscriber receives the entire message published to a topic by default. However, the subscriber can use a filter policy to receive just a subset of the messages. A filter policy is a JSON object that contains attributes to define which messages can be received by the subscriber.

Your data will be protected using SSL or client-side encryption while in transit traveling to and from Amazon SNS and at rest when it is stored on disks in Amazon datacenters. All Amazon SNS–supported events are recorded in a CloudTrail that can be used to view, search, and download information about those events. You can create a "path" to enable CloudTrail to deliver log files to your Amazon S3 bucket, where the path applies to all AWS regions. You can collect, monitor, and analyze Amazon SNS metrics using the CloudWatch console, programmatically using the CloudWatch API, or using CloudWatch's own CLI.

Exercises

The following exercises will help you practice working with Amazon SQS and Amazon SNS. You need to create an AWS account, as explained earlier, in order to perform these exercises. You can use the Free Tier when launching AWS resources, but make sure to terminate them at the end.

Exercise 15-1: Create a Standard Amazon SQS Queue Using the AWS Management Console

1. Use your AWS account e-mail address and password to sign in and then navigate to the Amazon SQS console at https://console.aws.amazon.com/sqs/.

2. Verify the AWS region by using the Region selector in the upper-right corner of the page.

3. From the center of page, choose Get Started Now.

4. For the queue name, enter **my-std-queue**.

5. Choose Standard Queue and click on Configure Queue.

6. Configure the Default Visibility Timeout to 10 minutes.

7. Configure the Message Retention Period to 3 days.

8. Configure the Maximum Message Size to 256KB.

9. Configure the Delivery Delay to 5 seconds.

10. Configure the Receive Message Wait Time to 10 seconds.

11. For the Dead Letter Queue settings, check Use Redrive Policy.

12. For the Dead Letter Queue name, enter **my-dead-letter-queue** (it should be an existing queue).

13. Configure the Maximum Receives to 100.

14. For Server-Side Encryption (SSE) Settings, check Use SSE.

15. For AWS KMS Customer Master Key (CMK), use either (Default) aws/sqs or select your CMK from the dropdown.

16. Configure the Data Key Reuse Period to 10 minutes.

17. Click on Create Queue.

Exercise 15-2: Create a FIFO Amazon SQS Queue Using the AWS Management Console

1. Use your AWS account e-mail address and password to sign in and then navigate to the Amazon SQS console at https://console.aws.amazon.com/sqs/.

2. Verify the AWS region by using the Region selector in the upper-right corner of the page.

3. From the top left navigation pane, click on Create New Queue.

4. For the queue name, enter **my-fifo-queue.fifo**.

5. Choose FIFO Queue and click on Configure Queue.

6. Configure the Default Visibility Timeout to 10 minutes.

7. Configure the Message Retention Period to 3 days.

8. Configure the Maximum Message Size to 256KB.

9. Configure the Delivery Delay to 5 seconds.

10. Configure the Receive Message Wait Time to 10 seconds.

11. For Dead Letter Queue settings, check Use Redrive Policy.

12. For the Dead Letter Queue name, enter **my-dead-letter-queue** (it should be an existing queue).

13. Configure the Maximum Receives to 100.

14. For the Server-Side Encryption (SSE) Settings, check Use SSE.

15. For the AWS KMS Customer Master Key (CMK), use either (Default) aws/sqs or select your CMK from the dropdown.

16. Configure the Data Key Reuse Period to 10 minutes.

17. Click on Create Queue.

Exercise 15-3: Create an Amazon SNS Topic Using the AWS Management Console

1. Use your AWS account e-mail address and password to sign in and then navigate to the Amazon SNS console at https://console.aws.amazon.com/sns/.

2. Verify the AWS region by using the Region selector in the upper-right corner of the page.

3. From the top-left navigation pane, click on Create Topic.

4. For the Topic Name enter **my-first-topic**.

5. For the Display Name enter **my-topic**.

6. Click on Encryption and choose Enable Encryption.

7. Click on Access Policy and choose Basic for the method.

8. Choose who can publish messages to the topic: only the topic owner, everyone, or choose specified AWS accounts (include the AWS account numbers).

9. Choose who can subscribe to this topic: only the topic owner, everyone, specified AWS accounts (include AWS account numbers), or only requesters with certain endpoints.

10. Next click on Delivery Retry Policy (HTTP/S) and uncheck Use The Default Delivery Retry Policy.

11. For the Number Of Retries, enter **5**.

12. For Retries Without Delay, enter **2**.

13. For Minimum Delay, enter **5 seconds**.

14. For Minimum Delay Retries, enter **2**.

15. For Maximum Delay Retries, enter **4**.

16. For the Maximum Receive Rate, enter **3 per second**.

17. For the Retry-Backoff Function, make your choice from the dropdown menu.

18. Check Override Subscription Policy.

19. Next click on Delivery Status Logging and for the log delivery status for these protocols, choose AWS Lambda, Amazon SQS, HTTP/S, and Platform Application Endpoint.

20. For the Success Sample Rate, choose 100%.

21. For IAM roles, choose Existing Roles (or choose Create New Service Role if a role does not already exist)

22. For the IAM role for successful deliveries, enter **my-sns-success-role**.

23. For the IAM role for failed deliveries, enter **my-sns-limited-role**.

24. Next click on Tags, enter **name** for the key, and enter **my-first-topic** for the value.

25. Click on Create Topic.

Questions

The following questions will help you gauge your understanding of the content in this chapter. Read all the answers carefully because there might be more than one correct answer. Choose the best response for each question.

1. Your company is building a new application that needs to process billions of messages and they do not want to build or manage the queue. Which AWS service provides this kind of massive scale without administration overhead from customers?

   A. Amazon S3

   B. AWS CodePipeline

   C. AWS Glue

   D. Amazon SQS

2. What two types of queues are available in Amazon SQS based on the ordering of messages, throughput, and delivery? (Choose two.)

   A. Standard queue

   B. General queue

   C. First in/first out (FIFO) queue

   D. First in/last out (FILO) queue

3. You want to eliminate the number of empty responses and false-empty responses. How can you achieve this in your Amazon SQS queue?

   A. Use short polling

   B. Use long polling

   C. Use loose polling

   D. Use batch polling

4. You want to handle Amazon SQS message failure by isolating failed messages that can't be processed correctly and want to find out why those message processing didn't succeed by examining logs. How can you achieve this in Amazon SQS?

   A. Use dead-letter queues

   B. Use short polling

   C. Use server-side encryption (SSE)

   D. Use long polling

5. One of your consumers received and processed message MSG-1 from your Amazon SQS queue Q1; since Amazon SQS doesn't automatically delete the message MSG-1 from queue Q1, the message remains in your queue Q1. You want to prevent other consumers from processing the message MSG-1 again for a period of 2 hours. How can you achieve this in Amazon SQS?

   A. Use long polling

   B. Use dead-letter queues

   C. Use temporary queues

   D. Use visibility timeout

6. A new application that you are developing needs a publish and subscribe messaging system. You do not want to build or manage a solution and want to take advantage of an existing solution. Which of the following AWS services provides a publishing/ subscription model messaging system?

   A. Amazon SNS

   B. Amazon SQS

   C. Amazon RDS

   D. Amazon SWF

7. What operations are available to Amazon SNS subscribers? (Choose all that apply.)

   A. Subscribe

   B. Unsubscribe

   C. ListSubscriptions

   D. ConfirmSubscription

8. As an Amazon SNS consumer, you can use various transport protocols as part of subscription requests. What flexible delivery transport protocols are available for receiving notifications for customers? (Choose all that apply.)

   A. HTTP and HTTPS

   B. SMS

   C. SQS

   D. E-mail and e-mail-JSON

9. All your subscribers are receiving every message that you publish to a topic. Some of the subscribers are complaining about receiving irrelevant messages and want to receive only messages that they are interested in processing. How can you send only a subset of the entire message and skipping all irrelevant messages?

   A. Use subscription filter policies

   B. Use dead-letter queues

   C. Use visibility timeout

   D. Use short polling

10. Messages that you are publishing from your application through Amazon SNS are relevant only for 30 minutes. So, you want a way to delete messages that were not delivered and read by your users in a 30-minute time frame. How can you achieve this in Amazon SNS?

   A. Set Time to Live (TTL) to 1800 seconds

   B. Set Visibility Timeout to 30 minutes

   C. Set Short Polling for 30 minutes

   D. Set Delay Queue to 1800 seconds

Answers

1. **D.** Amazon SQS can be used to process billions of messages without administration overhead from customers.

2. **A, C.** Standard and FIFO are the two types of queues based on ordering of messages, throughput, and delivery.

3. **B.** Use long polling to eliminate the number of empty responses and false-empty responses.

4. **A.** Use dead-letter queues to handle Amazon SQS message failure by isolating failed messages that can't be processed correctly and determine why this didn't succeed by examining the logs.

5. **D.** Set Visibility Timeout to 2 hours to prevent other consumers from processing message MSG-1 again for this period.

6. **A.** Amazon SNS is a publishing/subscription model for messaging.

7. **A, B, C, D.** Subscribe, Unsubscribe, ListSubscriptions, and ConfirmSubscription are the operations available for Amazon SNS subscribers.

8. **A, B, C, D.** HTTP, HTTPS, SMS, SQS, e-mail, and e-mail-JSON are the available transport protocols as part of Amazon SNS subscription requests.

9. **A.** Use subscription filter policies to send only a subset of the entire message and skip all other irrelevant messages.

10. **A.** Set Time to Live (TTL) to 1800 seconds to delete the messages that were not delivered and read by your users in 30 minutes.

Additional Resources

- **Amazon SQS Documentation**   There is no place like official AWS documentation to get the latest and most up-to-date information about the Amazon SQS service. `https://docs.aws.amazon.com/sqs/index.html`

- **Amazon SNS Documentation**   Always refer to the official AWS documentation to get the latest and most up-to-date information about the Amazon SNS service. `https://docs.aws.amazon.com/sns/index.html`

PART VI

- **Build a Cost-Effective Solution for Spot Instances**   This blog explains the approach to maximize cost savings using Amazon SQS and spot instances. `https://aws.amazon.com/blogs/compute/running-cost-effective-queue-workers-with-amazon-sqs-and-amazon-ec2-spot-instances/`

- **Build a Durable Serverless Application**   This blog details the steps necessary to create a durable serverless application using dead-letter queues for Amazon SNS, Amazon SQS, and AWS Lambda. `https://aws.amazon.com/blogs/compute/designing-durable-serverless-apps-with-dlqs-for-amazon-sns-amazon-sqs-aws-lambda/`

CHAPTER 16

Amazon Simple Workflow Service, Amazon API Gateway, and AWS Step Functions

In this chapter, you will learn

- Amazon Simple Workflow Service
- Amazon API Gateway
- AWS Step Functions

In this chapter, you will learn how Amazon Simple Workflow Service, Amazon API Gateway, and AWS Step Functions services help you develop and manage distributed applications and services.

Amazon Simple Workflow Service

Amazon Simple Workflow Service (Amazon SWF) helps you build applications that coordinate tasks across distributed components featuring both sequential and parallel processing. A task is the logical unit of work performed by a single component of your application, and you need to coordinate multiple tasks across your application in addition to managing the interdependencies based on the logical flow of the application. Amazon SWF offers full control over implementing and coordinating the tasks without worrying about the complexities of concurrency, scheduling, or tracking the progress. The following are the list of basic steps to develop and run a workflow:

- First, you need to develop activity workers that provide the processing steps in your workflow.

- Second, you need to develop a decider that provides coordination logic for your workflow.

- Then you need to register your activities and workflow with Amazon SWF either by using the AWS Management Console or programmatically.

- You can then start your activity workers and deciders. Once started, both will start polling Amazon SWF for the next tasks to perform.

- Then start one or more executions either from the AWS Management Console or programmatically. Each execution runs independently and with its input data, and Amazon SWF schedules the initial decision task. Then your decider begins initiating the next activity tasks until it decides to close the execution.

- You can filter and view the complete details of running and completed workflow executions using the AWS Management Console.

The Amazon SWF workers perform those tasks that can be run from your on-premises location or from the cloud using Amazon EC2. Distributed application tasks can be long-running—some require restarts, and some may fail or time out—and Amazon SWF tracks each task's progress using workers and maintains the task's state until completion. You can deploy, modify, and scale application components independently using Amazon SWF different scenarios that require task coordination, such as business process workflows, web application backends, analytics pipelines, and media processing. There are different ways to implement your workflow solutions using Amazon SWF:

- **AWS Software Development Kits (SDKs)**   You can develop your workflow starters, activities, or deciders using the Amazon SWF HTTP application programming interface (API) in any of the supported programming language such as Java, .NET, Node.js, PHP, PHP version 2, Python, or Ruby and expose those libraries. You can also create your own Amazon SWF monitoring and reporting tools by using the access visibility operations through these libraries.

- **AWS Flow Framework**   This provides simple classes for complex distributed and asynchronous programs that run as workflows on Amazon SWF by using Ruby or Java programming languages. With the support of standard object-oriented exception-based error handling, it allows you to use predefined types to map the methods of your program in your workflow directly and allows you to create, debug, and execute using your integrated development environment (IDE) or preferred editor.

- **HTTP Service API**   You can access service operations through HTTP requests, which can be used to communicate with Amazon SWF directly. You can use the HTTP Service API to develop libraries in any programming language that communicates with Amazon SWF using the Hypertext Transfer Protocol (HTTP) protocol.

Development Environment

First you need to set up a development environment based on the programming language that you plan to use. For example, if you intend to use Java to develop for Amazon SWF, then you need to install the AWS Toolkit for Eclipse in addition to installing the Eclipse IDE. For scalability and flexibility, applications are relying on autonomous distributed components and asynchronous processing. Also, application developers can take advantage of cloud computing and have the ability to combine existing on-premises assets with cloud-based assets.

Developing and executing multiple distributed components involving message queues and databases with the complex logic to synchronize require coordination and might increase latency and unreliability in terms of communication. Amazon SWF provides a programming model and infrastructure to develop asynchronous and distributed applications and let you focus on building applications that your business and clients need.

- **Domain**   Amazon SWF provides the structure and components for a workflow, which is a set of activities, and a logic that coordinates all the activities, which runs in an AWS resource called a domain. Domains provide a way of scoping all your Amazon SWF resources. Your AWS account can have multiple domains, and each domain can contain multiple workflows.

- **Actors**   Actors can be workflow starters, deciders, or activity workers that can be developed in any programming language, and Amazon SWF interacts with a number of different types of programmatic actors and communicates its API.

- **Activity**   When you design an Amazon SWF workflow, you can register each activity as an Amazon SWF activity type with name, version, and timeout values. In a workflow some activities may be performed multiple times with different inputs, similar to a customer buying multiple items, and your activity needs to run multiple times.

- **Activity worker**   This can be a program or person that receives activity tasks and provides results after performing those tasks, which can be written in different programming languages and can run on different operating systems.

- **Activity task**   This contains all the information that the activity worker needs to perform its function, either asynchronously or synchronously, and instructs an activity worker to perform its function, like an address change. Activity tasks can be on a single server or distributed across multiple servers in different regions.

- **Activity task lists**   Each activity task list contains multiple activity types, where the tasks are scheduled in order on a best-effort basis, so for some scenarios, the tasks may not come off the list in order.

- **Lambda task**   This is similar to an activity task described earlier and executes a Lambda function instead of an Amazon SWF activity.

- **Decision task**   This contains the current workflow history and notifies the decider when the state of the workflow execution is changed so the decider can determine the next activity to perform. Each activity task is assigned to only one activity worker by Amazon SWF, so no other activity worker can claim or perform that specific task.

- **Decision task lists**   Specific decision task lists are assigned to each workflow execution, and you can specify a default task list when the workflow starter initiates the workflow execution.

- **Coordination logic**   The decider schedules activity tasks by providing input to the activity workers, processes events, and closes the workflow when it is completed. Amazon SWF acts as a central hub through which data is exchanged between the decider and the activity workers in addition to maintaining the state of each workflow execution.

- **Workflow starters**   These can be any application that initiates workflow execution.

- **Deciders**   These contain the workflow's coordination logic that controls the flow of activity tasks in a workflow execution. Whenever a change occurs, like task completion, a task decision with the workflow history will be sent to a decider. The decider analyzes the workflow execution history and determines the next step in the workflow execution and communicates these steps back to Amazon SWF using decisions. The default task list is used when the decider doesn't specify a task list.

- **Decision**   This is either an action or set of actions in the workflow, like scheduling an activity task. It is used to delay the execution of an activity, to request cancellation of an activity, and to complete or close the workflow.

- **Polling**   This is a method by which activity workers receive activity tasks and the decider receives decision tasks from the Amazon SWF service. Amazon SWF returns the state of the workflow along with the current workflow execution history that has a list of workflow execution events using long polling. If a task is available, Amazon SWF returns the response; if not, it holds the TCP connection open for up to 60 seconds to use the same connection for an upcoming task.

- **Events**   These describe the important changes in the state of the workflow execution, like task completion, timeout, or the expiration of a timer.

- **Workflow type**   This is specified in the call to RegisterWorkflowType and is identified by its name, version, and domain.

- **Activity type**   This is specified in the call to RegisterActivityType and is identified by its name, version, and domain.

- **Workflow execution**   This is specified in the call to StartWorkflowExecution, which then returns run ID, and is identified by the run ID, workflow ID, and domain.

- **Workflow history**   This provides a reliable, complete, and consistent record of the workflow's progress and every event that occurred since the workflow execution started, which enables applications to be stateless. The workflow execution uses information such as scheduled activities, its current status, and their results to determine the next steps, in addition to providing a detailed audit trail to monitor running workflow executions and validate completed workflow executions.

- **Task routing**   This involves assigning an activity task list to an activity worker. If a task list isn't specified, the default task list is used.

- **Versioning**   This enables you to have multiple variations of the same workflow or activity running simultaneously, like one for basic users and another version for your premium users, based on your requirements.

- **Signals**   These allow you to insert information into a running workflow execution since something has changed or to inform it of an external event.

- **Child workflows**   Use these to break your complicated workflows into smaller, more manageable, and reusable components. A child workflow is initiated by a parent workflow when the decider of the parent workflow uses the StartChildWorkflowExecution decision.

- **Markers**   These enable you to record information that can be used for any custom or application-specific purposes to help implement decider logic.

- **Timers**   These are to delay the execution of an activity task and enable you to notify a decider after a specific time and the decider responds with a StartTimer decision.

Tags

Tags are used for workflow execution when you have many resources. Cost allocation tags are used to organize your AWS bill. You need to assign tags when you start workflow execution because you can't add, edit, or remove tags after it starts.

Manage Access

You can control access to Amazon SWF using the following two types of permissions:

- **Resource permissions**   These determine which Amazon SWF resources a user can access, where the resource permissions apply only to domains.

- **API permissions**   These determine which Amazon SWF actions a user can call, where a user is allowed to call an Amazon SWF action in any domain or deny access to it.

Tag-Based Policies

You can control access based on tags by providing them in the Identity and Access Management (IAM) policy condition. You can create IAM access policies based on tags for Amazon SWF to restrict domains by including a tag with the key and the value to allow or deny access.

Monitoring

You can use CloudWatch to track your workflows and activities and set alarms for the threshold values you choose. Amazon SWF metrics can be viewed using the AWS Management Console, which is measured in milliseconds, or as a count, or as a count per second. You can view graphs for metrics, and you can change the graph parameters using the Time Range controls. You can configure alarm notifications when a particular threshold is reached, like sending notifications to a Simple Notification Service (SNS) topic or sending an e-mail when a certain threshold is reached.

PART VI

Logging

AWS CloudTrail captures a record of all actions taken by any user, role, or AWS service in Amazon SWF. It captures all API calls for Amazon SWF as events, including calls from the Amazon SWF console and code calls to Amazon SWF API operations. After creating a trail, you can enable continuous delivery of AWS CloudTrail events to an Amazon S3 bucket and find out who made a request to Amazon SWF, from which IP address, and when it was made. You can view the most recent events in the AWS CloudTrail console in Event History.

Amazon API Gateway

The Amazon API Gateway can be used for creating, maintaining, securing, and monitoring WebSocket and REST APIs on a large scale. You can create APIs to access AWS services or for use in your own applications or to create third-party app developers. You can use API Gateway to create HTTP-based REST APIs that adhere to the REST protocol by enabling stateless client-server communication and implement HTTP methods like GET, PUT, DELETE, POST, and PATCH. You can use API Gateway to create WebSocket APIs that adhere to the WebSocket protocol by enabling stateful, full-duplex communication between the client and server and route incoming messages based on message content. API Gateway handles thousands of concurrent API calls in addition to managing access control, authorization, API version management and monitoring, and traffic management. API Gateway is the entry point for your application to any functionality or business logic or to access data from your backend servers or databases. Take advantage of canary release deployments to safely roll out changes in production environments. AWS CloudTrail can be used for logging and monitoring API usage. Amazon CloudWatch can be used for monitoring, access logging, and execution logging, in addition to setting alarms. AWS CloudFormation templates can be used to automate API creation, and you can integrate this with AWS Web Application Firewall (WAF) to protect your API traffic against common web exploits. Amazon API Gateway can be accessed from the AWS Management Console, AWS SDKs, API Gateway APIs, AWS Command Line Interface, and AWS Tools for Windows PowerShell.

The following is a list of concepts, along with components and use cases, for the Amazon API Gateway:

- **Serverless Infrastructure**   You can use AWS Lambda along with the API Gateway to build a serverless application by taking advantage of AWS Lambda that runs your code on a highly available computing infrastructure. AWS Lambda manages the necessary execution and administration of computing resources, and API Gateway supports proxy integrations with HTTP endpoints.

- **REST API**   REpresentational State Transfer (REST) is stateless because it does not store the client session on the server side. It is a collection of HTTP methods integrated with backend HTTP endpoints and Lambda functions. API resources are organized as per the application logic, where each API resource can be exposed as one or more API methods.

- **WebSocket API**   This is stateful and is integrated with backend HTTP endpoints and Lambda functions. API methods use the frontend WebSocket connections that are associated with the domain name.

- **API endpoint**   This is a hostname for your API that is deployed in a specific region in the format api-id.execute-api.us-west-1.amazonaws.com. The API endpoints can be edge-optimized, private, or regional.

- **API key**   API Gateway uses an alphanumeric string to identify someone who uses your REST or WebSocket API. You can either import it as CSV file, or API Gateway can generate API keys for you that can be used to control access to your APIs or Lambda authorizers.

- **API stage**   This can be identified by the API ID and name refers to a stage in the lifecycle of your REST or WebSocket API, like development, stage, or production.

- **Callback URL**   When your client uses a WebSocket connection, API Gateway stores the client's callback uniform resource locator (URL). The callback URL is used to send messages to the client from the backend system.

- **Edge-optimized API endpoint**   This is an API Gateway hostname that uses a CloudFront distribution for client access across regions. All API requests are routed to the nearest CloudFront point of presence (POP), which improves connection time for your customers.

- **Integration request**   This is the mapping of a route request of a WebSocket API or the parameters and body of a method request required by the backend REST API method in API Gateway.

- **Integration response**   This is the mapping of the status codes, headers, and payload of the route response of a WebSocket API or REST API method API Gateway returned to a client application.

- **Mapping template**   Velocity Template Language (VTL) helps you transform a request body or response body from the frontend data format to the backend data format, and vice versa, and is used in the integration request or integration response.

- **Method request**   This defines the parameters and body that you send through requests to access the backend using the public interface of a REST API method in API Gateway.

- **Method response**   This defines the headers, body models, and status codes that you receive as responses from the public interface of a REST API.

- **Mock integration**   As a developer, you want to verify API responses that are generated from API Gateway directly before you develop an integration backend code. Based on the mock integration results, you can configure the method's integration request and response.

- **Model**   This is a data schema defining and validating the structure of a request or response payload and is used for generating a strongly typed SDK of an API. You can generate a sample mapping template by initiating the creation of another mapping template for another environment, like production.

- **Private API endpoint**   An API endpoint allows a client to securely access private API resources inside a Virtual Private Cloud (VPC) through interface VPC endpoints. It is isolated from the public Internet and can only be accessed if you have required access through VPC endpoints for API Gateway.

- **Private integration**   The resources are inside a customer's VPC and can only be accessed through a private REST API endpoint without exposure to the public Internet.

- **Proxy integration**   You can set up API Gateway proxy integration configuration for a REST or WebSocket API as either HTTP proxy integration or Lambda proxy integration. The API Gateway passes the entire request and response between the frontend and an HTTP backend for the HTTP proxy integration and sends the entire request as input to a backend Lambda function for the Lambda proxy integration, where API Gateway transforms the Lambda function output to a frontend HTTP response.

- **Regional API endpoint**   You can deploy the hostname of an API in a specific AWS region to serve its clients. You can direct your API request target directly to the region-specific API Gateway without going through any CloudFront distribution. A regional endpoint bypasses the unnecessary round trip to a CloudFront distribution of your in-region requests.

- **Route**   In API Gateway, WebSocket routes the incoming messages to a specific integration based on the message content. You need to specify a route key, which is a message body attribute, and an integration backend. The integration backend is invoked when the route key is matched in the incoming message.

- **Route request**   This is a request body that access the backend through the public interface of a WebSocket API method in API Gateway.

- **Route response**   The response status codes and headers received through the public interface of a WebSocket API from API Gateway.

- **Usage plan**   You can enforce throttling and quota limits on individual client API keys through a usage plan when accessing REST or WebSocket APIs.

- **WebSocket connection**   This is a persistent connection that API Gateway maintains between clients and API Gateway based on the message content received from clients.

- **Pricing**   You are not charged for authorization and authentication failures for calls to methods with the authorization type of CUSTOM, COGNITO_USER_POOLS, and AWS_IAM. You are not charged when API keys are missing or invalid for calling methods that require API keys. You are not charged when the request rate or burst rate exceeds the preconfigured limits in API Gateway—throttled requests.

You are not charged when rate limits or quotas exceed the preconfigured limits for usage plan–throttled requests.

- **PCI DSS**   API Gateway is compliant with the Payment Card Industry (PCI) Data Security Standard (DSS).
- **HIPAA**   API Gateway is a Health Insurance Portability and Accountability Act (HIPAA)–eligible service.

REST API

The REST API contains resources and methods, where resource is a logical entity that is accessed by an application through a resource path, the method represents the REST API request submitted by the user, and the response is returned to the user. A combination of a resource path and operations like GET, PUT, DELETE, and POST identify a method of the API. For example, a POST /address method could add an address of the user and GET /address method could query the current address of the user. Your application does not need to know where the data requested is stored and fetched from on the backend— it can be on the Amazon RDS or DynamoDB database. The frontend is encapsulated by method requests and method responses in the API Gateway REST APIs, and similarly the backend is encapsulated by integration requests and integration responses.

API Gateway provides REST API management functionality for generating SDKs and creating API documentation using API Gateway extensions to OpenAPI. You can use API Gateway to create WebSocket APIs and throttle HTTP requests. The client and the server can send messages at any time to each other using WebSocket API. You can avoid implementing complex polling mechanisms for connecting users and devices with your backend servers. You can build a serverless application to send and receive messages to and from individual users or groups of users in a chat room using an API Gateway WebSocket API and AWS Lambda. You also can use API Gateway WebSocket APIs to build real-time communication applications without having to provision or manage any servers to control connections or large-scale data exchanges.

An API developer requires IAM permissions to create and deploy an API and to enable the required functionality in API Gateway. The application developer is the customer of the API developer, who takes advantage of WebSocket or REST API developed in API Gateway for building application functions. An API developer uses the API Gateway service to create and deploy an API that includes a set of resources and methods by using the API Gateway console, using API Gateway V1/V2 API, using AWS CLI, or by using an AWS SDK in addition to using AWS CloudFormation templates. An application developer uses execute-api to invoke an API that was created or deployed in API Gateway where the underlying programming entities are exposed.

API with Lambda Integration

You can use either Lambda proxy integration or nonproxy integration to build an API with Lambda integrations. The input for the Lambda function can be request headers, query string parameters, path variables, and the body in addition to using API configuration to influence the execution logic in the proxy. The integration request and integration response are configured by API Gateway for you without modifying the existing settings. You must ensure that input to the Lambda function is supplied as the integration request payload in the nonproxy integration. Here you need to map any input data the client supplied as request parameters into the proper integration request body in addition to translating the client-supplied request body into a format recognized by the Lambda function.

Create a REST API

You can build a REST API, which is a collection of programmable entities, by using Amazon API Gateway resources. The Resource entity can have one or more Method resources represented in the request parameters and body, where a Method defines the API for the client to access any incoming requests submitted. You can forward the incoming request to a specified integration endpoint uniform resource identifier (URI) and create an integration resource to integrate the Method with a backend integration endpoint. The request parameters or body can be transferred to meet the backend requirements. You then create a MethodResponse resource to represent the request response received by the client, and you create an IntegrationResponse resource representing the request response returned by the backend. You can either transform the backend response data or pass the backend response as-is to the client.

You can also provide documentation for the API to help your customers understand it by adding a DocumentationPart resource. IAM permissions, Amazon Cognito, or a Lambda authorizer can be used to control how clients call an API. You can set up usage plans to throttle API requests to meter the use of your API when creating or updating it. All these tasks can be performed using the API Gateway console, the AWS CLI, the API Gateway REST API, or one of the AWS SDKs. You can manage an API by viewing, updating, and deleting the existing setups. You can update an API by modifying resource properties or configuration settings. You need to redeploy the API when you update resource properties, but you don't need to redeploy APIs for configuration updates.

You can call the API by submitting requests to the URL for the API Gateway using execute-api. The REST APIs base URL format is

```
https://{restapi_id}.execute-api.us-west-1.amazonaws.com/{stage_name}/
```

The {restapi_id} represents the API identifier, and {stage_name} represents the stage name of the API deployment. You can publish your deployed APIs using a developer portal or sell your APIs as Software as a Service (SaaS) through the AWS Marketplace. AWS Config can be used to record all the configuration changes made to your API Gateway API resources and send you or your team notifications based on these changes. It is very useful to maintain the history of configuration changes for operational audit, troubleshooting, and compliance use cases. You can also use the AWS Config Rules feature to define configuration rules that automatically detect, alert, and track rule violations. You can use tags, which is metadata consisting of a key and value, and both are case-sensitive. You can control access to your API resources based on the tags specified in AWS IAM policy conditions. Also, tags are used to track your AWS costs by categorizing them and delivering a monthly allocation report.

AWS Step Functions

AWS Step Functions help you coordinate multiple components of distributed applications and microservices using visual workflows. You can build an application that performs an isolated function and you can scale applications quickly. You can coordinate components and step through the functions using a graphical console to visualize the components as a series of steps. Step Function logs the state of each step and automatically tracks errors so your application execute as expected each time. As a result, you can diagnose and debug problems quickly if things go wrong. In order to ensure that your application is available at any scale, Step Functions manages the operations and underlying infrastructure for you. You can access and use Step Functions by using the Step Functions console, the AWS SDKs, or an HTTP API. Step Functions is based on the tasks and state machines that you define using the JSON language. The console of Step Functions displays a graphical view of your state machine's structure and provides a way to visually check your state machine's logic and monitor executions. Step Functions integrates with other AWS services, so you can use API actions and coordinate executions directly.

Standard Workflows

You need to select a type of workflow—either Standard or Express—during the creation of a new state machine using the Amazon States Language. Based on the type, your state machine executions will behave differently, and the type cannot be changed after the state machine is created. Standard workflows are ideal for durable, long-running, and auditable workflows. They run for up to a year and allow you to retrieve the full execution history for up to 90 days using the Step Functions API. Standard workflows have just-once workflow execution, whereas Express workflows have at-least-once workflow execution. Standard workflows always run from beginning to end, and the execution state is internally persisted on every state transition, and every execution will be run exactly once. Only one execution will start even if you attempt to start a Standard workflow with the same name more than once.

Express Workflows

Express workflows are suitable for high-volume event processing workloads and enable cost-effective processing for short-duration, high-event-rate workloads. When logging is enabled for an express workflow, it can be monitored and analyzed using Amazon CloudWatch logs. Express workflows have no internally persistent state to monitor the progress of executions and cannot guarantee that one execution will run only once. You can attempt to start executions concurrently when you start an express workflow with the same name more than once, and each runs at least once. You need to make sure your state machine logic is idempotent and will not be affected adversely by multiple concurrent executions of the same input when using express workflows.

Standard vs. Express Workflows

Standard workflows use an at-most-once model, where your tasks and states are never executed more than once, which makes it suited to orchestrating nonidempotent actions. The executions are billed according to the number of state transitions processed. Both standard and express workflows can start automatically in response to events.

Express workflows are used for high-volume workloads, which run for up to five minutes and store the execution history in Amazon CloudWatch logs. Express workflows use the at-least-once model, where an execution might be run more than once, which makes express workflows ideal for orchestrating idempotent actions, and it is billed based on the duration of execution, memory consumed, and total number of executions.

Step Functions Local

AWS Step Functions state machines can be implemented in several ways, including the Management Console and the SDKs. You can also install and run Step Functions on your local machine for testing and development purposes. You can start an execution on any machine using Step Functions Local. The local version of Step Functions can invoke AWS Lambda functions running both on AWS and locally. You can also coordinate other supported AWS services. You can use the downloadable version of AWS Step Functions that runs on Windows, Linux, and macOS, and you need to install the AWS CLI. Download and install Step Functions and then open a command prompt window, navigate to the directory where you extracted StepFunctionsLocal.jar, and enter the following command:

```
java -jar StepFunctionsLocal.jar
```

You can access Step Functions running locally using the following command:

```
aws stepfunctions --endpoint-url http://localhost:8083 command
```

First you need to create a simple state machine using two Pass states, which means an instruction with no operation, by using the predefined state machine Hello World template.

Amazon States Language

Amazon States Language is a structured JSON-based language that defines the state machine, a collection of states, task states, choice states, and fail states.

Step Functions Console

A state machine can be defined using the Step Functions console. Complex state machines can be developed in the cloud by using AWS Lambda and the Step Functions console to define your state machine.

AWS SDKs

You can develop Step Functions state machines, activities, or starters using the AWS SDKs for Java, PHP, .NET, Python, Ruby, Go, C++, and JavaScript. These SDKs offer a convenient way to develop the Step Functions in various programming languages and access visibility operations to develop your own Step Functions reporting tools and monitoring.

HTTPS Service API

Step Functions offers service operations through HTTPS requests to communicate directly with Step Functions to develop libraries in any language. The service API actions can be used to develop state machines, state machine starters, and workers in addition to accessing visibility operations to develop your own reporting and monitoring tools.

Templates in Step Functions

You can choose state machine templates from the Step Functions console to automatically fill the Code pane. You can use any of following blueprints as the template, and every template is fully functional:

- **Hello world**   A state machine with a Pass state.
- **Wait state**   A state machine that shows different methods of injecting a Wait state.
- **Retry failure**   A state machine that retries a task after the task fails.
- **Parallel**   A state machine that shows how to run two branches at the same time.
- **Catch failure**   A state machine that shows how to call different tasks depending on the failure type of its primary task.
- **Choice state**   A state machine that makes a choice to run either a Task state or a Fail state.
- **Map state**   A state machine that uses a map state to dynamically process the data in an array.

States

Individual states can be used to make decisions, perform actions, and pass output to other states. States are elements referred to be name, which must be unique within the scope of the entire state machine. In AWS Step Functions the workflows are defined in the JSON Amazon States Language. The Step Functions console helps you visualize your application logic by using the graphical representation of the state machine. A variety of functions can be performed in your state machine by using states:

- **Task state**   Does some work in your state machine
- **Choice state**   Makes a choice between branches of execution
- **Fail or Succeed state**   Stops an execution with a success or failure
- **Pass state**   Passes its input to its output or injects some data
- **Wait state**   Provides a delay for a certain amount of time
- **Parallel state**   Begins parallel branches of execution
- **Map state**   Dynamically iterates steps

These are the state fields:

- **Type**   The state's type
- **Next**   The name of the next state that is run when the current state finishes
- **End**   Ends the execution when set to true
- **Comment**   Contains a description of the state
- **InputPath**   A path that selects a portion of the state's input to be passed for processing
- **OutputPath**   A path that selects a portion of the state's input to be passed to the output

Tagging

You can tag state machines of both standard and express workflows and activities to track and manage the costs associated with the resources. When defining cost allocation tags, you can add metadata that identifies the purpose of a state machine or activity to organize your AWS bill and reflect the cost structure. You can control access to resources based on tags by providing the tags in the condition of an IAM policy.

Monitoring

You can use AWS CloudWatch to monitor the availability and performance of AWS Step Functions by collecting monitoring data to debug any multipoint failures. As a first step to monitor Step Functions, you need to store historical monitoring data for a baseline to compare against current performance data, to identify performance anomalies. The metrics represent the stages of your execution, activity, and Lambda function timeouts, with descriptive names. You can configure CloudWatch events for status changes in Step Functions execution to monitor your workflows without having to constantly poll.

Logging

AWS CloudTrail provides data about the actions taken by a user, role, or AWS service in Step Functions by capturing all API calls of Step Functions as events. You can enable continuous delivery of Step Functions CloudTrail events to an Amazon S3 bucket using a trail. However, you can view the events in the console if you didn't configure a trail. CloudTrail logs are used to find the requests made to Step Functions, the IP address of the request, who made the request, and when. CloudTrail logs are not an ordered trace of API calls, so they may not appear in any specific order. You need to configure Amazon CloudWatch logs to see the execution history and results of your express workflow, and logs don't block or slow down executions.

Security

AWS recommends protecting AWS account credentials and setting up individual user accounts with AWS IAM, so that each user is given only the permissions necessary to fulfill their job duties. You need to enable multifactor authentication (MFA) for each account and use Secure Sockets Layer/Transport Layer Security (SSL/TLS) to communicate with your AWS resources. Configure API and user activity logging with AWS CloudTrail, and use AWS encryption solutions. AWS strongly recommends you never put sensitive identifying information, such as your customers' personal information, into free-form fields. Any data that you enter into Step Functions might get picked up for inclusion in diagnostic logs, so never include credentials information in the URL to validate your request to that server.

Encryption at Rest

Your data at rest in Step Functions is always encrypted using server-side encryption, which reduces the operational burden and complexity involved in protecting sensitive data because AWS manages it for you. You can build security-sensitive applications that meet encryption compliance and regulatory requirements with encryption at rest.

Encryption in Transit

The data in transit between Step Functions and integrated services is encrypted in Step Functions using TLS.

Amazon VPC Endpoints

Amazon VPC endpoints enable you to establish a private connection between your Amazon VPC and AWS Step Functions workflows without crossing the public Internet. Amazon VPC controls network settings like the IP address range, subnets, and route tables.

Chapter Review

This chapter began by explaining Amazon Simple Workflow Service concepts. It then explained how to build applications that coordinate tasks across distributed components featuring both sequential and parallel processing. Then the chapter described tasks, which are the logical units of work of your application, and explained how to coordinate multiple tasks across applications. Amazon SWF workers can run either from your on-premises setup or from the cloud using Amazon EC2. Distributed application tasks can be long-running—some require restarts and some tasks may fail or time out. Amazon SWF tracks each task's progress using workers and maintains the task's state until it is complete.

The Amazon API Gateway can be used for creating, maintaining, securing, and monitoring WebSocket and REST APIs. Use API Gateway to create HTTP-based REST APIs that adhere to the REST protocol by enabling stateless client-server communication and implement HTTP methods like GET, PUT, DELETE, POST, and PATCH. You can use API Gateway to create WebSocket APIs that adhere to the WebSocket protocol by enabling stateful, full-duplex communication between the client and server and route the incoming messages based on content. API Gateway is the entry point for your application to any functionality, business logic, or to access data from your backend servers or databases. Take advantage of canary release deployments to safely roll out changes in production environments.

PART VI

AWS Step Functions is used to coordinate multiple components of distributed applications using visual workflows. You can build an application that performs an isolated function and allows you to scale applications quickly. You can coordinate components and step through the functions using a graphical console to visualize the components as a series of steps. Step Functions logs the state of each step and automatically tracks errors so your application executes as expected each time. However, you can diagnose and debug problems quickly if things go wrong. The console of Step Functions displays a graphical view of your state machine's structure and provides a way to visually check your logic and monitor executions. Step Functions integrates with other AWS services, so you can use API actions and coordinate executions directly.

Exercises

The following exercises will help you practice working with Amazon Simple Workflow Service, Amazon API Gateway, and AWS Step Functions. You need to create an AWS account, as explained earlier, to perform these exercises. You can use the Free Tier when launching AWS resources, but make sure to terminate them at the end.

Exercise 16-1: Create Amazon SWF Domain
Using AWS Management Console

1. Use your AWS account e-mail address and password to sign in and then navigate to the Amazon Simple Workflow Service console at https://console.aws.amazon .com/swf/.

2. Verify the AWS region by using the Region selector in the upper-right corner of the page.

3. From the Welcome To AWF page, choose Create A New Domain.

4. In the popup window, for Name enter **my-swf-domain**, for Workflow Execution Retention Period, enter **3 days**, and for description, enter **this is my swf domain used for testing with an expiration of 3 days**.

5. Click the Register button.

6. Once successful, you will receive a message that the domain was successfully registered.

Exercise 16-2: Register a Workflow Type
Using the AWS Management Console

1. Use your AWS account e-mail address and password to sign in and then navigate to the Amazon Simple Workflow Service console at https://console.aws.amazon .com/swf/.

2. Verify the AWS region by using the Region selector in the upper-right corner of the page.

3. From the Amazon Simple Workflow Service Dashboard, click on Workflow Type from the pane on the left.

4. From the My Workflow Types page, select the domain from the dropdown.

5. Click on Register New to register a new workflow type.

6. From the popup menu, make sure the domain is selected and enter **my-workflow-type** for the Workflow Type Name.

7. For the Workflow Type Version, enter **0.1**.

8. For the Default Task List, enter **TL1**.

9. For the Default Execution Start To Close Timeout, enter **10 minutes**.

10. For the Default Task Start To Close Timeout enter **5 minutes**.

11. Click on the Continue button.

12. In the next popup window, for the Default Task Priority, enter **100**.

13. For the Description enter **this is my workflow type with version 0.1 and priority 100**.

14. For the Default Child Policy enter **Terminate**.

15. Choose Default Lambda Role or enter the role if you have one available.

16. Click on Review.

17. Review all the values and click on Register Workflow.

Exercise 16-3: Register an Activity Type Using the AWS Management Console

1. Use your AWS account e-mail address and password to sign in and then navigate to the Amazon Simple Workflow Service console at https://console.aws.amazon.com/swf/.

2. Verify the AWS region by using the Region selector in the upper-right corner of the page.

3. From the Amazon Simple Workflow Service Dashboard, click on Activity Type from the pane on the left.

4. From the My Activity Types page, select the domain from the dropdown.

5. Click on Register New to register a new activity type.

6. From the popup menu, make sure the domain is selected and for the Activity Type Name, enter **my-activity-type**.

7. For the Activity Type Version, enter **0.1**.

8. For the Task List, enter **TL1**.

9. For the Task Priority, enter **100**.

10. For the Task Schedule To Start Timeout, enter **10 minutes**.

11. For the Task Start To Close Timeout, enter **5 minutes**.

12. Click on the Continue button.

13. In the next popup window, for the Description, enter **this is my activity type with version 0.1 and priority 100**.

14. For the Heartbeat Timeout, enter **30 seconds**.

15. For the Task Schedule To Close Timeout, enter **60 minutes**.

16. Click on Review.

17. Review all the values and click on Register Activity.

Questions

The following questions will help you gauge your understanding of the contents in this chapter. Read all the answers carefully because there might be more than one correct answer. Choose the best response for each question.

1. Your application team plans to develop an asynchronous program using simple programming constructs for initiating tasks to run remotely and track the program's runtime state. They also want to maintain the application execution state without using databases or ad hoc solutions. Which AWS service is suitable for this use case?

   A. Amazon S3

   B. AWS CodeStar

   C. Amazon SWF

   D. AWS Snowball

2. Amazon allows developers to access the Amazon Simple Workflow Service in different ways to make it easy for development and management. Which of the following ways are possible to access Amazon SWF? (Choose all that apply.)

   A. AWS Management Console

   B. AWS SDK for Java, .NET, PHP, and Ruby

   C. Amazon SWF web service APIs

   D. AWS Flow Framework for Java

3. You want your developers to be able to quickly create APIs and reduce development effort and time-to-market for your applications. You want to automatically meter the API traffic and extract utilization data for each API key. Your developers should be able to build and test new versions of APIs to add new functionality, allowing multiple API versions to operate simultaneously. Which Amazon service is suitable in this scenario?

   A. Amazon API Gateway

   B. AWS Storage Gateway

    C. AWS Elastic Beanstalk

    D. Amazon Polly

4. You want to create an API by taking advantage of Amazon API Gateway, which offers a few options to create APIs. What the types of APIs are supported by Amazon API Gateway? (Choose three.)

    A. REST API

    B. HTTP API

    C. WebSocket API

    D. SOAP API

5. You interact with a number of different types of programmatic actors that communicate with Amazon SWF through its API, which can be developed in any programming language. Which of the following are actors in Amazon SWF?

    A. Domains

    B. Deciders

    C. Activity workers

    D. Workflow starters

6. Your development team wants to adopt a strategy where both the new version of an API and a base API version are deployed in a production environment to support normal operations. After completing enough testing, the new API can be promoted to the production environment, which makes the new features available in the production stage without much impact to your end users. Which of the following release strategies should your application adopt for the production release?

    A. Rolling deployment

    B. Blue green deployment

    C. Red black deployment

    D. Canary development

7. You want to use a managed service that coordinates distributed application components by using visual workflows that let you scale easily and change applications quickly. You need to step through the functions of your application and visualize the components as a series of steps. You should be able to change or add steps without writing code. Which of the following AWS services is suitable for your use case?

    A. AWS Step Functions

    B. AWS SageMaker

    C. AWS OpsWorks

    D. AWS Glue

8. Which of the following workflows are available in AWS Step Function? (Choose two.)

   A. Standard workflows

   B. Small workflows

   C. Large workflows

   D. Express workflows

9. Which component provides a way of scoping Amazon SWF resources like workflow type and activity types within your AWS account?

   A. Domain

   B. Actors

   C. Tasks

   D. Polling

10. In AWS Step Functions, states can make decisions based on the input and perform certain actions, which are unique within the scope of the entire state machine. Which of the following are valid states that can be performed in your state machine? (Choose all that apply.)

   A. Succeed

   B. Task

   C. Wait

   D. Pass

Answers

1. **C.** Amazon SWF allows you to develop asynchronous programs for initiating tasks to run remotely and track the program's runtime state.

2. **A, B, C, D.** You can use the AWS Management Console, AWS SDK, Web Service APIs, and AWS Flow Framework.

3. **A.** Amazon API Gateway allows you to quickly create APIs by reducing development effort and time-to-market for your applications.

4. **A, B, C.** Amazon API Gateway supports REST API, HTTP API, and WebSocket API.

5. **B, C, D.** Deciders, activity workers, and workflow starters are programmatic actors in Amazon SWF.

6. **D.** The canary development strategy can be used to promote a new API to production without much impact to your end users.

7. **A.** AWS Step Functions can be used to manage and coordinate distributed applications by using visual workflows.

8. **A, D.** Standard workflows and express workflows are available in AWS Step Functions.

9. **A.** A domain provides a way of scoping Amazon SWF resources like workflow type and activity types within your AWS account.

10. **A, B, C, D.** Succeed, task, wait, and pass are the states available in AWS Step Functions.

Additional Resources

- **Amazon SWF**   The recommended documentation for any AWS services, including Amazon Simple Workflow Service, is the official AWS documentation where you always get the latest and most up-to-date information.
  `https://docs.aws.amazon.com/swf/index.html` and `https://aws.amazon.com/blogs/aws/tag/amazon-simple-workflow-service/`

- **Amazon API Gateway**   The one-stop shop to find up-to-date details about all the new features of any AWS services, including Amazon API Gateway, is the official AWS documentation.
  `https://docs.aws.amazon.com/apigateway/index.html` and `https://aws.amazon.com/blogs/compute/tag/amazon-api-gateway/`

- **AWS Step Functions**   There is no other place to get the latest information about any AWS services, including AWS Step Functions, other than the official AWS documentation.
  `https://docs.aws.amazon.com/step-functions/index.html` and `https://aws.amazon.com/blogs/compute/category/application-services/aws-step-functions/`

CHAPTER 17

Monitoring Using Amazon CloudWatch, AWS CloudTrail, and AWS Config

In this chapter, you will learn
- Amazon CloudWatch
- AWS CloudTrail
- AWS Config

This chapter explains in depth how Amazon CloudWatch, AWS CloudTrail, and AWS Config services work.

Amazon CloudWatch

You can monitor all your AWS resources, collect and track metrics, and create alarms and dashboards to display all metrics in real time using Amazon CloudWatch. You can also monitor running applications, and you can configure notifications to be sent when a threshold is reached. You can also automatically make changes to the resources that you are monitoring based on threshold changes. For example, you can launch additional EC2 instances based on CPU usage to handle increased traffic. You can see AWS resource utilization, health, and performance, and you can use this data to scale down under-used instances—for example, you can change to a smaller instance to save money. You can access Amazon CloudWatch using the AWS console, AWS Command Line Interface (CLI), AWS software development kit (SDKs), and Amazon CloudWatch application programming interface (API). You can use Amazon Simple Notification Service (SNS) along with Amazon CloudWatch to send messages to subscribed clients when an alarm threshold is reached. You can use Amazon EC2 Auto Scaling along with Amazon CloudWatch to automatically launch new Amazon EC2 instances based on user-defined policies or to terminate existing Amazon EC2 instances based on health status checks, or scale up your Amazon EC2 instances based on demand. You can use AWS CloudTrail with Amazon CloudWatch to monitor all API calls made to your account and write the log files to your Amazon S3 bucket.

Amazon CloudWatch is a repository where all AWS services send their metrics continuously, in addition to the custom metrics that you configured, and you can use metrics to calculate statistics and present them graphically in your CloudWatch dashboard. Amazon EC2 instances can be stopped, started, or terminated based on alarm thresholds. All Amazon CloudWatch metrics are stored in specific regions separately, and you can aggregate statistics from different regions by using Amazon CloudWatch's cross-region functionality.

Metrics

Metrics are time series data that are published to CloudWatch. It is similar to a data point variable representing the values from an application or business activities that are sent to CloudWatch in addition to your custom metrics. The data points can be in any order and at any rate, but you can retrieve them as an ordered set of time-series data. Metrics automatically expire after 15 months, and as new data points arrive, the older data is dropped. Each data point in a metric has a unique name, namespace, timestamp, and dimension. The resolution of data points is based on the period—more granular metrics are available for shorter periods. The metrics are available based on the granularity, so if a metrics granularity is less than 60 seconds, they are only available for 3 hours, 1-minute granular metrics are available for 15 days, 5-minute granular metrics are available for 63 days, and 1-hour granular metrics are available for 15 months.

Many of the AWS services provide metrics, which is data about your system performance. Free monitoring is enabled by default that provides metrics in five-minute intervals, but you can enable detailed monitoring that provides metrics in one-minute intervals for an additional charge. All the AWS resource metrics and custom application metrics are stored in Amazon CloudWatch from where you can perform a search, create graphs, and set up alarms. Metrics are grouped by namespace and then by dimensions within each namespace, and you can search for metrics that have a matching namespace, metric name, or dimensions.

Custom Metrics

AWS CLI or an API can be used to publish your own metrics to CloudWatch, and you can use the AWS Management Console to view statistical graphs of your published custom metrics. The custom metrics are stored in CloudWatch as a series of data points along with a timestamp. A custom metrics statistic set, which is an aggregated set of data points, can be published as well.

High-Resolution Metrics

Amazon CloudWatch metrics can be either standard resolution, with one-minute granularity data points, or high resolution, with a granularity of one second. By default, all the metrics produced by your AWS services are standard resolution. You can use either standard resolution or high resolution for your custom metrics. If you want to publish high-resolution custom metrics, you need to use the PutMetricData call, which incurs additional charges. So, higher resolution can lead to higher charges, since you need to call PutMetricData multiple times.

Namespaces   A namespace acts as a container, where metrics in different namespaces are isolated from each other. For example, Amazon EC2 uses AWS/EC2 as the namespace and Amazon S3 uses AWS/S3 as the namespace to avoid metrics from different services being mistakenly aggregated into the same statistics. You need to specify a custom namespace for each data point you publish from your application to CloudWatch that can be used when you create a metric.

Timestamps   For time-series data, all metric data points contain a timestamp that can be provided by you, or CloudWatch can create it when the data point arrives in UTC (Coordinated Universal Time) format.

Sum   This is the combination of all the metrics and is used to determine the total volume of a metric.

SampleCount   This is the number of data points used in a calculation.

Dimensions   This is a name and value pair used to identify a metric part, and each metric can have up to ten dimensions. Dimensions are part of the unique identifier for a metric, and you can create a new variation of a metric by adding a unique name and value pair, which can be used to filter the CloudWatch results. For example, you can use EC2 InstanceID to get statistics for a particular EC2 instance while searching for metrics, and CloudWatch can aggregate data based on the dimension. Even if the metrics have the same name, each unique combination of dimensions is treated as a separate metric by CloudWatch.

Statistics   This is the aggregation of metrics over a period of time using the namespace, metric name, dimensions, and data point unit of measure. The statistics are provided by CloudWatch based on the custom metric data points or by other AWS services. You can aggregate the metrics across multiple resources within the same region but not across regions. EC2 instances statistics have detailed monitoring enabled for an additional charge, so you can monitor total bytes written to disk or average CPU utilization for all instances over 60-second time intervals for a one-day period.

Average   This is the value of Sum / SampleCount that can be used to find the full scope of a metric and to find how close this is to the average use so you can determine when to increase or decrease your resources as needed.

Units   This is a unit of measure in bytes, seconds, count, and percent used by statistics that provides a meaning to your metrics data and is aggregated separately. When you create a custom metric, you need specify a unit; otherwise, the unit will be updated as None by CloudWatch.

Periods   This is the length of time associated with a particular statistic defined in numbers of seconds, varying from 1 second to 86,400 seconds (one day). The custom metrics support sub-minute periods, and you can specify a period, with a start time and

PART VI

end time, when you retrieve statistics. CloudWatch compares the metric with the threshold value when an alarm is created to monitor a particular metric. For example, CloudWatch doesn't notify you until five failures are found when you specify five evaluation periods.

Aggregation   Statistics are aggregated based on the period when they are retrieved. The data points can be published with the same timestamps or namespace and dimensions. Multiple data points can be published with any timestamp for the same or different metrics. You can insert a pre-aggregated statistic set with Min, Max, and Sum for data points when collecting data many times in a minute. Amazon CloudWatch treats these as a single metric when you publish a metric with the same namespace and dimensions from different sources that is used for service metrics of a distributed and scaled system, which in turn allows you to get the statistics for Min, Max, Avg, and Sum of all requests across your application.

Percentiles   This is the relative value in a data set used to isolate anomalies. For example, the 75th percentile indicates that 25 percent of data is higher than 75 percent of the data based on the distribution of your metric data. When monitoring the CPU utilization of your EC2 instances, for example, you need to monitor the Max to find a single anomaly from the results. Percentile statistics are available for custom metrics but are not available for negative number values.

Alarms   Alarms are used to automatically initiate actions after watching a single metric over a specified period, based on the threshold value over time. The action can be a notification e-mail or creating or terminating an instance using the Auto Scaling policy. CloudWatch alarms invoke actions only when the state is changed and are maintained for a particular number of periods. You need to select a frequency for the metric to be monitored when creating an alarm—for basic monitoring, metrics are available every five minutes, and for detailed monitoring, metrics are available every one minute. You can create a high-resolution metric alarm with a period of five seconds, which is free, or for ten seconds, which incurs an additional charge.

Alarm States   An alarm has the following possible states:

- **OK**   Specifies the metric is within the threshold.
- **ALARM**   Specifies the metric is outside of the threshold.
- **INSUFFICIENT_DATA**   Specifies the alarm has just started, not enough data is available, or the metric is not available to determine the alarm state.

Dashboards   Amazon CloudWatch dashboards are used to monitor in a single view resources that are spread across different regions, and you can create customized views of the metrics and alarms to help assess the health of your applications and resources across one or more regions. You can easily track the same metric across multiple graphs by using different colors on each graph. Dashboards can be created by using the console, AWS CLI, or API, which provide a common view of critical resource and application measurements that can be shared for faster communication during any operational event. You can use a cross-account, cross-region dashboard to summarize data from multiple AWS accounts and multiple regions. You can drill down for more specific details in addition to getting an overview of your application without switching regions or accounts. Graphs that represent one or more metrics can be added, resized, edited, removed, or temporarily hidden from your dashboard for resource monitoring.

Graphs   You can use graphs to see the metric activity of your services, and these are created using the CloudWatch console by selecting metrics data as Min, Max, Avg, and Sum. Graphs can display different levels of detail, ranging from a one-minute view, which can be useful when troubleshooting, to a one-hour view, which can be useful when seeing trends over time.

Dynamic Labels   Dynamic labels can be added for the selected metrics in graphs. The values are derived from the time range, including minimum, maximum, average, and sum, which is updated automatically when either the graph or dashboard is refreshed. Dynamic labels are attached to every metric in the search expression. You can easily add, edit, and change the position or include other customization of a dynamic label using the CloudWatch console.

Dimensions   You can have up to ten dimensions for each custom metric, which defines what the metric is and what data it stores by using a name and value pair. You can use the `list-metrics` command to list what dimensions are defined for each metric. For example, the following is the command for two dimensions:

```
--dimensions InstanceId=E-987654321, InstanceType=m4.large
```

The following command can be used to retrieve statistics for multiple dimensions:

```
--dimensions Name=InstanceId, Value=E-987654321, Name=InstanceType,

Value=m4.large --start-time 2020-01-12T06:00:00Z
--end-time 2020-01-12T09:00:00Z
```

Single Data Points   You can use the `put-metric-data` command to publish a single data point for a new or existing metric using one value and timestamp. The data points with timestamps are aggregated to a granularity of one second by CloudWatch, which records the average for each period. The `get-metric-statistics` command is used to retrieve statistics based on the data points, and you can aggregate your data or aggregate as statistic set using the `--statistic-values` parameter before publishing it to CloudWatch. You can't retrieve percentile statistics if you publish data using a statistic set, and you can publish zeros by including data points with the value 0.

Metric Math   Metric math uses math expressions to create new time-series data based on the metrics and enables you to query multiple CloudWatch metrics. You can add the time series to dashboards and visualize them on the CloudWatch console or programmatically using the GetMetricData API call.

Anomaly Detection   You can use CloudWatch to create an alarm that mines past metric data and creates an anomaly detection model of expected values. CloudWatch uses an anomaly detection threshold with the model to determine the abnormal value from the metric and trigger a notification e-mail when the metric value is either above or below the expected value.

CloudWatch Agent

The CloudWatch agent collects system-level metrics from Amazon EC2 instances across operating systems including on-premises servers not managed by AWS. You can use the CloudWatch agent to retrieve custom metrics from your applications or from the StatsD protocol, which supports both Windows and Linux server statistics, and the collected protocol, which only supports Linux servers. The CloudWatch agent metrics can be stored in CloudWatch, and by default, it uses CWAgent as the namespace for metrics, but you can define another namespace during CloudWatch agent configuration. The logs from the CloudWatch agents are processed and stored in Amazon CloudWatch logs, and they are billed as custom metrics. You need to create a CloudWatch agent configuration JSON file that specifies the custom metrics and logs before installing the Cloud-Watch agent on any servers. CloudWatch agents can be installed on both Amazon EC2 instances and on-premises servers with either the Linux or Windows operating system.

Data Protection

AWS recommends that you secure your data by using multifactor authentication (MFA), Transport Layer Security (TLS) for communication, AWS CloudTrail for API and user activity logging, AWS encryption solutions, and Amazon Macie to discover and secure any personal data stored in your Amazon S3 bucket. AWS strongly recommends never using any sensitive user-identifying information in the logs or metadata and never including credentials in the URL to validate your request to an external server. Grafana 6.5.0 or later can be configured and used to query a dynamic list of metrics by using wildcards. You can create multiple dashboards using prebuilt dashboards and graphs to monitor metrics for AWS resources.

Logging

AWS CloudTrail records all actions by API calls, including calls from the CloudWatch console and code calls in CloudWatch. You can enable continuous delivery of your CloudTrail events and CloudWatch events to an Amazon S3 bucket when you create a trail. You can find the request, the IP address, who made the request, and when it was made. The trail log events from all your regions are delivered to your Amazon S3 bucket, and you can analyze and trigger an event from the data collected in CloudTrail logs.

AWS CloudTrail

AWS CloudTrail records all API calls to provide compliance, operational governance, and risk auditing to your AWS account. All actions, including every event in the AWS Management Console, AWS CLI, AWS SDKs, and API calls to an AWS service, are recorded in CloudTrail as events. When you create your AWS account, AWS CloudTrail is enabled automatically and starts recording activities in a CloudTrail event that can be viewed in the CloudTrail console in Event History. You can create a trail to record the ongoing activities and any events in your AWS account. This helps provide visibility of all the activities in your AWS account for security best practices. It enables you to view, search, download, archive, analyze, and respond to account activity across your AWS infrastructure. You can identify who or what service took a particular action on what resources, in addition to identifying when the event occurred in order, to analyze and respond to activity in your AWS account. AWS CloudTrail Insights can be enabled on a trail for an additional cost to identify and respond to any unusual activity. CloudTrail can be integrated into your applications to automate trail creation for your entire organization and to check the status of trails, in addition to controlling how users view CloudTrail events.

When you create your AWS account and AWS CloudTrail is enabled, all activity is recorded in a CloudTrail event, which as mentioned, can be viewed in the Event History of the CloudTrail console page. You can view, search, and download up to 90 days of activity from Event History, and you can archive, analyze, and respond to changes in your AWS resources by creating a CloudTrail trail, which enables you to store the events to your Amazon S3 bucket. You can use Amazon CloudWatch logs and Amazon CloudWatch events to analyze events in your trail. You can create two types of trails: trails for all regions or trails for one region using the CloudTrail console, CloudTrail API, or AWS CLI. AWS CloudTrail records and stores every event from all regions or for just a single region to your S3 bucket. You can create an organization trail if your AWS account is part of an AWS organization, where all events of all AWS accounts will be logged in that organization for all AWS regions or for a single region, based on the configuration. Since an organization trail is created on the master account, it is automatically applied to all member accounts. This provides an additional security benefit, since the member accounts will only able to see, but cannot modify or delete, the organization trail.

The configuration of a trail can be changed later as to whether it logs events in one region or all regions, which affects what events are logged. CloudTrail event log files use Amazon S3 server-side encryption (SSE) for encryption, and AWS Key Management Service (AWS KMS) key can also be used to encrypt the log files. You can set up Amazon SNS notifications if you want notifications about log file delivery and validation, and log files are delivered within 15 minutes of account activity. In addition, CloudTrail publishes log files multiple times an hour—about every five minutes. These log files contain API calls from services in the account that support CloudTrail.

The CloudTrail Lifecycle

An activity is an action taken by any user, role, or service that is monitored and captured by AWS CloudTrail. All activities of your AWS account are stored as events in CloudTrail, which provides a history of both API and non-API account activity made through the AWS CLI, AWS, and AWS SDKs. The events are logged as management events and data events in CloudTrail using the JSON log format. The data-plane operations are events that provide information about the resource operations, which is often a high-volume activity like GetObject, DeleteObject, and PutObject Amazon S3 API operations.

You can capture unusual activity events in your AWS account using CloudTrail Insights, which detects unusual activity, and the Insights events are stored in the S3 bucket of your trail. Insights events are captured and stored only when a change is detected that significantly differs from the account's typical usage patterns. An Insights event is logged at the start of the unusual activity, along with its relevant API, statics, and incident time to help you understand and act on the identified unusual activity. Another Insights event is logged at the end of the unusual activity, along with its relevant API, statics, and incident time. You must explicitly enable AWS CloudTrail Insights event collection on a new or existing trail, since it is disabled by default. You can view, search, and download CloudTrail event history for up to 90 days to gain visibility of all the actions taken in your AWS account using the AWS CLI, AWS SDK, and AWS Management Console and other AWS services.

Control Access

AWS Identity and Access Management (IAM) can be used to control access to AWS CloudTrail by giving the least amount of privileges needed to do work. You can create multiple individual IAM users and give each IAM user a unique set of security credentials. You can grant different levels of permissions to each IAM user based on their role. Amazon CloudWatch monitors, collects, and tracks metrics of your applications and other resources on your AWS account. You can use Amazon CloudWatch logs to monitor log data.

Since CloudTrail is integrated with CloudWatch logs, it can send API activity events of your AWS account to the CloudWatch logs group, and it can trigger alarms based on the predefined metric filters, in addition to sending notifications or making changes to your resources. Your application, operating system events, and other AWS services events can be tracked using CloudWatch logs in near real time. Rules can be created to trigger any event recorded by CloudTrail. You need to have at least one trail to send the log data to CloudWatch logs or CloudWatch events. You can create a trail for a single region or all regions—the best practice is to create a trail that applies to all regions. When you create a CloudTrail for all regions, you can easily control the configurations across all AWS regions and use a single S3 bucket. Monitoring log activity across all regions is simple, and any new AWS region is automatically added to your trail. SNS notifications can be delivered to all regions, and log integrity validation can be enabled for the trail. Multiple trails can be created—up to five trails per region—for different line-of-business or user groups.

As mentioned, all API activity and events will be available for 90 days in the Event History of the CloudTrail console. You can programmatically look up all events related to AWS resource creation, modification, and deletion by using the AWS SDK or AWS CLI. Events cannot be manually deleted from Event History. An AWS IAM user can be used to control the creation, modification, and deletion of AWS CloudTrail trails. You can create an audit user with permission to only view trail activity and restrict them from starting or stopping logging of a trail, which provides granular control over your trails and user access. You can configure CloudTrail to evaluate the events and deliver them to your Amazon S3 bucket or Amazon CloudWatch Logs log group only when the event matches your trail settings. When you have multiple trails, you have the option to designate a trail for data events, another trail for management operation events, and another one for Insights events to capture unusual activities that can be delivered to separate S3 buckets. CloudTrail logs all management events by default, but not data or Insights events, since you incur additional charges for these. You can share your CloudTrail log files between multiple AWS accounts and grant read-only access to the accounts that generated the log files, and you can grant access to all of the log files to a centralized log account that can analyze the log files for your organization. You can validate whether your log file was deleted or modified by using CloudTrail log file integrity validation, which uses the SHA-256 algorithm for hashing and SHA-256 with RSA for digital signing. This feature makes sure that your CloudTrail log files cannot be forged, deleted, or modified without detection and helps with your audit and compliance requirements, in addition to helping with security and forensic investigations.

AWS CloudTrail Security

As a best practice, always use MFA for your accounts and communicate with all your AWS resources only using SSL/TLS. Log all your API and user activities to AWS CloudTrail, but never put any sensitive information, like personally identifiable information, on it because diagnostic logs might be shared with an external user. Use Amazon S3 lifecycle policies to archive or delete old CloudTrail log files automatically after a certain period. Encrypt your CloudTrail log files with AWS KMS keys (SSE-KMS) and enable an Amazon S3 bucket policy for your CloudTrail destination S3 buckets. Always validate CloudTrail log file integrity, especially if you are sharing CloudTrail log files between multiple AWS accounts.

You need to use centralized logging using a separate AWS account with restricted access to only administrative users and a dedicated Amazon S3 bucket with MFA delete enabled to ensure the integrity, completeness, and availability of CloudTrail logs for auditing and forensic purposes. This allows you to strictly enforce security controls, segregation of duties, and access controls. Limit and restrict the users with the AWSCloudTrailFullAccess, since it gives you the ability to disable or reconfigure important auditing functions. Implement detective controls to make sure all trails are encrypted with SSE-KMS, and configure the lifecycle policy of your Amazon S3 bucket that was used to store CloudTrail log files. Always use the principle of least privilege, and remove any unnecessary access.

AWS Config

AWS Config offers a comprehensive view to quickly determine any configuration or relationship changes over time. It evaluates the desired configurations against the current configurations using a snapshot. You can retrieve either all AWS resources or only few AWS resources for your audit requirements using AWS Config, in addition to retrieving historical configurations and relationships between your AWS resources. It is important to identify all the AWS resources in your AWS account and how they are related to each other, in addition to identifying how each AWS resource is configured both in the present and in the past. You can receive a notification whenever a resource configuration is changed, like create, modify, or delete. AWS Config help you oversee your application resource configurations and detect any misconfigurations. It continuously evaluates and notifies you whenever resources are created, modified, or deleted by polling the calls made to each resource without explicitly monitoring these changes. AWS Config evaluates the configuration settings and sends a notification when it detects any resource violation and flags the resource as noncompliant. AWS Config can be used when your internal policies and best practices require the data to be audited frequently to make sure it complies with the historical configurations.

AWS Config can monitor all your AWS resources that depend on one another and notify you when a misconfiguration of one resource might have unintended consequences on its other related resources and help you to assess the impact of the configuration change. When you troubleshoot configuration issues for your AWS services, the historical configurations of those AWS services from AWS Config can help you access the last known correct working configuration to resolve the problem.

Security Analysis

When your audit and compliance team analyzes potential security weaknesses in your AWS account, they need detailed historical information about your AWS resource configurations, like EC2 security groups with inbound and outbound port rules that were open at a particular time to determine whether a specific security group is blocking the incoming or allowing the outgoing TCP traffic to and from a specific port, or IAM permissions that are granted to users, groups, or roles to modify certain AWS resources at a specific time to determine whether correct permissions are granted to a user. AWS Config helps you track resource inventory and changes and evaluate configurations of your AWS resources, like Amazon EC2 instances, security groups, Amazon Elastic Block Store (EBS) volumes, and Amazon Virtual Private Cloud (VPCs), and it uses the unique resource identifier known as Amazon Resource Name (ARN).

Resource Configuration

The audit team uses AWS Configs configuration history, which is a collection of the configuration items of all your resources from the beginning of their creation. It is available in multiple formats and can be automatically delivered to your Amazon S3 bucket. You can either use the AWS Config console or use the API to view all previous configurations of any resource using its timeline. A point-in-time view of different attributes, like metadata, current configuration, related events, and relationships, will be available in a AWS Config configuration item. The configuration history is populated as soon as it detects a change to a resource type, like when it is created, updated, or deleted. The configurations of your AWS resources in your account are stored as configuration items by a configuration recorder, which is automatically created and started by AWS Config. You can create, start, stop, and restart the configuration recorder at any time. You can either record all the resources or a set of customized configurations by using the AWS CLI or AWS Management Console.

Configuration Snapshot

You can get a collection of the complete view of your resources from a configuration snapshot, and it will be useful for validating the configuration regularly for resources that potentially should not exist or were incorrectly configured. All configuration items are added to the configuration stream each time your AWS resource is created, modified, or deleted. You can integrate the configuration stream with an Amazon SNS topic based on your requirements. You can use the configuration stream to observe, monitor potential issues, and receive notifications on configuration changes to your AWS resources.

You can use AWS Config to discover AWS resources from your AWS account and also create a map of relationships between AWS resources. You can create an AWS Config rule with the desired configuration settings of your entire AWS account or a specific AWS resource. AWS Config allows you to create custom rules to track configuration changes by continually monitoring and sending the configuration item a change notification using Amazon SNS. You can aggregate data for multiple AWS accounts and multiple regions using AWS Config to aggregate compliance data and AWS Config configuration and store it in a single account, which will be used to monitor compliance of all your multiple AWS accounts. A source account is the AWS account that you use to aggregate, and the source region is where you want to aggregate all your AWS Config resource configurations and compliance data. You can use the AWS Config aggregator to collect compliance and configuration data from multiple regions and multiple source accounts. A conformance pack, which is a combination of AWS Config rules and remediation actions in YAML (YAML Ain't Markup Language, which used to be called Yet Another Markup Language) format, can be implemented for a single account or the entire AWS organization using the AWS Config console or the AWS CLI.

Managing AWS Config

The AWS Config console can be used to configure resources, choose an Amazon S3 bucket, and choose an Amazon SNS topic. You can create AWS Config managed rules and custom rules and configuration aggregators, in addition to viewing configuration snapshots and relationships between AWS resources. You can use AWS Config REST-ful APIs and AWS CLI to program AWS Config directly. In addition, you can use one of the AWS SDKs to manage errors, retry requests automatically, and sign requests cryptographically.

AWS Config integrates with AWS IAM to create and manage users and user permissions, including anyone who needs access to AWS Config. AWS IAM allows you to create permission policies to attach to your IAM role, Amazon S3 buckets, and Amazon SNS topics. AWS IAM can be used to create AWS Config permission policies, which is a set of statements that grant AWS Config permissions to attach to the IAM roles. You can also set up read-only permissions using AWS IAM, where users can search for resources by tags or only view the configurations of resources. Resource-level permissions can be used to control when users are allowed to use those actions for specific resources in AWS Config. AWS Config can be used to continuously track configuration changes to check whether they violate any of the conditions and flag it as noncompliant. This helps you ensure that your resource configurations comply with regulations, industry guidelines, and internal practices.

AWS Config Managed and Custom Rules

You can use custom or AWS managed rules to make sure that all your AWS resources comply with industry best practices. These can be customized based on your needs, and they start by comparing your resources and running an evaluation each time they are triggered. You can use the AWS Lambda function along with an AWS Config rule to evaluate whether all your AWS resources are in compliance. You can correct noncompliant resources using AWS Systems Manager Automation by using the AWS Management Console or by using APIs.

Monitoring AWS Config

Amazon CloudWatch events can be used to detect and correct changes based on AWS Config events, and Amazon SNS can be used to send notifications whenever an AWS resource is created, deleted, or updated based on user API activity. When you use Amazon VPC to host your AWS resources, you can create VPC endpoints to establish a private connection between your VPC and other AWS services, including AWS Config, without going through the Internet. The VPC endpoints use AWS PrivateLink, which enables private communication between your AWS services, and it also provides scalable and reliable connectivity to AWS Config without an Internet gateway, Network Address Translation (NAT) gateway, or virtual private network (VPN) connection.

You can capture all the API calls to AWS Config as events in CloudTrail. This will help you determine who made the request, from where, and when it was made. You can enable CloudTrail on your AWS account to record activity that occurs in AWS Config, along with other AWS services events, in Event History. CloudTrail records all the ongoing events, including events for AWS Config, in your AWS account and stores the log files in an Amazon S3 bucket. You can log events from all regions and configure them using other AWS services, and you can analyze and resolve the events from your CloudTrail logs.

Chapter Review

This chapter began by explaining how to monitor all your AWS services using Amazon CloudWatch. It then discussed how to record all API calls using AWS CloudTrail and explained how to track configuration changes to your AWS resources using AWS Config. You can monitor, collect, and track metrics; create alarms; and use dashboards to display all the metrics using Amazon CloudWatch in real time. You can create thresholds for your applications and monitor them using Amazon CloudWatch and send notifications when a threshold is reached. AWS resource utilization, health, and performance data can be used to scale down underused instances or scale up overutilized instances automatically and save money. The AWS console, AWS CLI, AWS SDKs, or Amazon CloudWatch API can be used to access Amazon CloudWatch. You can send alert messages using Amazon SNS to all subscribed clients when an alarm threshold is reached. Amazon EC2 Auto Scaling can utilize Amazon CloudWatch to automatically launch new instances based on user-defined policies, to terminate existing Amazon EC2 instances based on health status checks, or to scale up your Amazon EC2 instances based on demand.

AWS CloudTrail is used to record all API calls, which provides operational governance, compliance, and help auditing the risks to your AWS account. All actions and events in the AWS Management Console, AWS CLI, AWS SDKs, and API calls to any of your AWS services are recorded in CloudTrail. AWS CloudTrail is enabled automatically when you create your AWS account and starts recording activities in an event that can be viewed in Event History. CloudTrail records all ongoing activities and events in your AWS account in your specified S3 bucket. Complete visibility of all the activities into your AWS account for security best practices can be achieved using AWS CloudTrail as well. You can view, search, download, archive, analyze, and respond to all activities across your AWS infrastructure. This helps you determine who or what service took a particular action on what resources, in addition to identifying when the event occurred, in order to help you analyze and respond to activity in your AWS account. AWS CloudTrail Insights can be enabled on a trail for an additional cost to identify and respond to any unusual activity.

All configuration changes or relationship changes to your AWS services over time can be captured and tracked using AWS Config. Your desired configurations can be evaluated against the current configurations using a snapshot. All AWS resources of your account or only few can be retrieved, based on your audit requirements, using AWS Config, in addition to retrieving historical configurations and relationships between your AWS resources. Identifying the configuration of all AWS resources in your AWS account is important, in addition to determining how they are related to each other and identifying how each AWS resource is configured both in the present and in the past. You can receive a notification whenever a resource configuration is changed, like create, modify, or delete. AWS Config helps you oversee your application resource configurations and detect any misconfigurations. AWS Config enables you to continuously evaluate and notify whenever resources are created, modified, or deleted by polling the calls made to each resource without explicitly monitoring these changes. AWS Config also evaluates the configuration settings and sends a notification when it detects any resource violation and flags the resource as noncompliant. AWS Config can be used to audit your AWS environment frequently to make sure it complies with the historical configurations based on your internal policies and best practices.

Exercises

The following exercises will help you practice using Amazon CloudWatch alarms, AWS CloudTrail, and AWS Config. You need to create an AWS account, as explained earlier, to perform these exercises. You can use the Free Tier when launching AWS resources, but make sure to terminate them at the end.

Exercise 17-1: Create a CloudWatch Alarm Using the AWS Management Console

1. Use your AWS account e-mail address and password to sign in and then navigate to the Amazon CloudWatch console at https://console.aws.amazon.com/cloudwatch.

2. Verify the AWS region by using the Region selector in the upper-right corner of the page.

3. From the navigation pane on the left, choose Alarms, and select Create Alarm.

4. Choose Select Metric and choose the service namespace based on the metric that you want.

5. Continue drilling down to narrow your choices and select the checkbox next to the metric that you want.

6. From the search box, enter the name of a metric, resource ID, or dimension and press ENTER.

7. Choose one of the results and continue until a list of metrics appears.

8. Select the checkbox next to the metric that you want.

9. Choose the Graphed Metrics tab.

10. Choose one of the statistics under Statistic.

11. Choose the evaluation period for the alarm under Period.

12. When creating the alarm, select whether the y-axis legend appears on the left or right.

13. Choose Select metric. Specify the Metric And Conditions page.

14. Under Conditions, enter a name and description for the alarm and specify the threshold value.

15. Choose Additional Configuration and specify how many evaluation periods.

16. Choose how to have the alarm behave when some data points are missing for the Missing Data Treatment field.

17. Choose Next.

18. Select an SNS topic under Notification to notify when the alarm is in ALARM state, OK state, or INSUFFICIENT_DATA state.

19. Choose Add Notification and choose Next.

20. Enter a name and description for the alarm and choose Next.

21. Preview all the details and then choose Create Alarm.

Exercise 17-2: Create a CloudTrail Trail Using the AWS Management Console

1. Use your AWS account e-mail address and password to sign in and then navigate to the AWS CloudTrail console at https://console.aws.amazon.com/cloudtrail/.

2. Verify the AWS region by using the Region selector in the upper-right corner of the page.

3. In the left navigation pane, choose Trails.

4. From the Trails page, choose Get Started Now or Create Trail.

5. Give your new trail a name, like **My-First-Trail**.

6. From the Management Events, set Read/Write Events to All.

7. Leave the default Yes selected for Log AWS KMS Events.

8. Do not make any changes in Data Events so that your new trail will not log any data events.

9. At the Storage Location section of Create A New S3 Bucket, choose Yes and give it a name like **s3-cloudtrail-logs**.

10. In the Tags section, enter **name** for the key and **trail** for the value.

11. Choose Create.

Exercise 17-3: Set Up AWS Config Using the AWS Management Console

1. Use your AWS account e-mail address and password to sign in and then navigate to the AWS Config console at https://console.aws.amazon.com/config/.

2. Verify the AWS region by using the Region selector in the upper-right corner of the page.

3. Click on the Get Started Now button.

4. From the Settings page, for Resource Types To Record, specify All Resources so that AWS Config automatically starts recording resources. Optionally, you can include global resources like IAM resources.

5. Select Specific Types only if you need to record configuration changes for specific AWS resource types.

6. Then you can either create a new bucket or choose an existing bucket from your account or from another account.

7. Choose Stream Configuration Changes And Notifications To An Amazon SNS Topic and choose the target topic by either creating new topic or choosing a topic from your account by providing the ARN.

8. For AWS Config Role, you need to choose the IAM role by either creating a new role or choosing a role from your account.

9. Choose Next And Save. Verify that AWS Config displays on the Resource Inventory page.

Questions

The following questions will help you gauge your understanding of the contents in this chapter. Read all the answers carefully because there might be more than one correct answer. Choose the best response for each question.

1. A customer needs to monitor the CPU utilization percentage of their AWS EC2 instance and send real-time alerts to their on-call support team. Which two AWS services can accomplish this? (Choose two.)

   A. Amazon CloudWatch

   B. Amazon Simple Queue Service

   C. Amazon Route 53

   D. Amazon Simple Notification Service

2. Your company wants you to analyze traffic patterns for your application. You need to capture all connection information from your load balancer every 15 minutes. Which solution will enable you to do this?

   A. Enable access logs on the load balancer

   B. Create a detailed custom metric CloudWatch on your load balancer

   C. Use a CloudWatch logs agent

   D. Use AWS CloudTrail with your load balancer

3. Your client wants you to automatically launch or terminate Amazon EC2 instances based on health status checks. What tool can you use with Amazon EC2 Auto Scaling to scale your EC2 instances based on demand?

   A. CloudWatch alarm

   B. CloudTrail

   C. CloudFormation

   D. CloudFront

4. Which of the following could be scheduled and monitored only by using a custom CloudWatch metric?

   A. EC2 network IO

   B. EC2 disk IO

   C. EC2 CPU utilization

   D. EC2 memory utilization

5. What is the minimum time interval that Amazon CloudWatch receives and aggregates data?

   A. 15 seconds

   B. 1 minute

   C. 3 minutes

   D. 5 minutes

6. Your company wants to understand, improve, and debug the applications by viewing and searching their logs. Which of the following provides an interactive, pay-as-you-go, and integrated log analytics capability?

   A. CloudWatch Logs Insights

   B. Direct Connect

   C. Virtual Private Cloud (VPC)

   D. CloudTrail

7. True or False: You can find the root cause of an issue by accessing the metrics data for a terminated Amazon EC2 instance and its deleted Elastic Load Balancer.

   A. True

   B. False

8. What resolution granularities can you get from a custom metric? (Choose two.)

   A. Standard resolution with one-minute data granularity

   B. High resolution with one-second granularity

   C. Medium resolution with three-minute data granularity

   D. Default resolution with five-minute data granularity

9. True or False: You can set up Amazon CloudWatch metric filters to use regular expressions with the log data.

   A. True

   B. False

10. Your audit team wants to have access to logs insights. Which two IAM policies must be included to access this? (Choose two.)

    A. logs:DescribeLogGroups

    B. logs:FilterLogEvents

    C. logs:GrantAccess

    D. logs:FullAccess

11. Your development team is configuring the Amazon CloudWatch logs to monitor, store, and access your log files from Amazon EC2 instances. What is the default retention period for the logs?

    A. Never expire

    B. 1 day

    C. 10 years

    D. 455 days

12. Your company needs to track all API calls made to Amazon CloudWatch. Which service will help you to monitor and track this?

    A. CloudTrail

    B. IAM

    C. S3

    D. Route 53

13. Which two services provide detailed monitoring metrics without incurring extra charges? (Choose two.)

    A. RDS

    B. Route 53

    C. CloudFront

    D. VPC

14. True or False: When using CloudWatch logs to monitor applications running in the EC2 instance, the log data is encrypted while in transit and while at rest.

    A. True

    B. False

15. You team wants to build a system that sends data to Amazon CloudWatch every six minutes for tracking and monitoring. Which of the following is required as part of the put-metric-data request?

    A. Key

    B. Namespace

    C. Metric name

    D. Timestamp

16. You configured a custom metric in Amazon S3 with CloudWatch and granted permission to your team members to upload data using CLI. Is it possible to track your team members' activities?

    A. Yes, you need to enable logging in CloudWatch to capture the activities

    B. No, the S3 bucket uploads cannot be captured

    C. Yes, but you need to enable detailed monitoring of Amazon CloudWatch

    D. Yes, you can use CloudTrail to monitor the API calls

17. You are using CloudTrail to record details about each action like who made a request, from where, what services are used, which actions are performed, and the response elements returned by the AWS service. When troubleshooting an issue, what search filters can you use along with time range to view account activity? (Choose all that apply.)

    A. Event name

    B. Username

    C. Resource name

    D. Event source

    E. Event ID

    F. Resource type

18. Which of the following contains the AWS CloudTrail configuration item (CI) that refers to the resource configuration at a given point in time? (Choose all that apply.)

    A. Basic information like ARNs and tags

    B. Configuration data like EC2 instance type

    C. Mapping relationships

    D. AWS CloudTrail event ID

    E. Metadata like version of the CI and when it was captured

19. You can use the AWS Config dashboard to evaluate which of the following against your configuration?

    A. Assess your overall compliance

    B. Risk status from a configuration perspective

    C. View compliance trends over time

    D. Use a rule to identify compliance drift that is caused by configuration change

20. Your central IT administrators team needs to monitor compliance for all AWS accounts in the enterprise. How can you aggregate AWS Config data from multiple accounts and regions into a single account?

    A. Use multiaccount, multiregion data aggregation

    B. Create multiple S3 buckets

    C. Create multiple IAM roles

    D. Use single-account data aggregation

Answers

1. **A, D.** Amazon CloudWatch will be used to monitor the CPU utilization percentage of the AWS EC2 instance, and SNS will be used send real-time alerts to the on-call support team.

2. **A.** Since the requirement is to get the information every 15 minutes, the basic CloudWatch metric will provide this.

3. **A.** A CloudWatch alarm along with Amazon EC2 Auto Scaling will be used to scale your EC2 instances based on demand.

4. **D.** Memory utilization will be provided by using the custom CloudWatch metrics. The metrics are available with basic monitoring.

5. **B.** One minute is the minimum amount of time the Amazon CloudWatch receives and aggregates the data.

6. **A.** Using CloudWatch Logs Insights, you can understand, improve, and debug applications using an interactive, pay-as-you-go, and integrated log analytics capability.

7. **A.** True, the data will be available for 15 months.

8. **A, B.** The standard resolution with one-minute data granularity and high resolution with one-second granularity.

9. **B.** False, it's not supported. Amazon Kinesis could be used to connect the stream with a regular expression processing engine.

10. **A, B.** The logs:DescribeLogGroups and logs:FilterLogEvents are valid IAM policies that can be used to gain access.

11. **A.** The logs never expire, but you can change the retention period from one day to ten years.

12. **A.** CloudTrail will help monitor and track the API calls.

13. **A, B.** The Relational Database Service (RDS) and Route 53 send the detailed monitoring metrics without incurring extra charges.

14. **A.** True, the log data is encrypted while in transit and while it is at rest.

15. **B.** put-metric-data publishes metric data points to Amazon CloudWatch, which associates the data points with the specified metric namespace

16. **D.** Yes, you just need to enable CloudTrail to monitor the API calls.

17. **A, B, C, D, E, F.** You can use all these attributes along with the time range.

18. **A, B, C, D, E.** These are the CI sections.

19. **A, B, C, D.** You can assess, view, and find the status from dashboard.

20. **A.** You need to use multiaccount, multiregion data aggregation.

Additional Resources

- **Amazon CloudWatch**   The recommended documentation for any AWS services, including Amazon CloudWatch, is the official AWS documentation, where you always can get the most up-to-date information.
  `https://docs.aws.amazon.com/cloudwatch/index.html` and
  `https://aws.amazon.com/blogs/aws/tag/amazon-cloud-watch/`

- **AWS CloudTrail**   The one-stop shop to find up-to-date details about all the new features of any AWS services, including AWS CloudTrail, is the official AWS documentation.
  `https://docs.aws.amazon.com/cloudtrail/` and `https://aws.amazon.com/blogs/mt/category/management-tools/aws-cloudtrail/`

- **AWS Config**   There is no other place to get the latest information about any AWS services, including AWS Config, other than the official AWS documentation.
  `https://docs.aws.amazon.com/config/` and `https://aws.amazon.com/blogs/mt/category/management-tools/aws-config/`

Infrastructure as Code Using AWS CloudFormation

In this chapter, you will learn
- Templates
- Stacks
- Change sets

In this chapter, we will discuss what AWS CloudFormation is and how templates, stacks, and change sets work to automate your infrastructure using code.

AWS CloudFormation

The AWS CloudFormation service enables you to design and create your AWS resources in an automated and secure manner. It helps reduce the time for creating and managing your AWS resources and allows you to focus on your applications that run in AWS. The AWS CloudFormation template describes all the AWS resources and takes care of provisioning the resources for you. It handles the dependencies when you create and configure your AWS resources and third-party application resources in your AWS cloud environment across all regions and accounts. It acts as a single source for your AWS and third-party resources and helps you to standardize infrastructure components used across your organization, enabling configuration compliance and faster troubleshooting. Your application resources can be provisioned in a secure, reusable fashion, allowing you to build and re-create your infrastructure and applications without having to perform manual actions or write custom scripts. You don't need to determine the right operations to perform when managing your stack or worry about orchestrating them in the most efficient way or terminating all the resources by rolling back changes automatically if any errors are identified.

You can treat your infrastructure just as code and create it with a code editor of your choice and can check it into a version control system and then review and deploy it into production. Creating and managing a set of AWS resources is made simple and easy by provisioning and updating them in a predictable order by your developers and systems administrators. AWS provides sample CloudFormation templates, or you can create custom templates that describe the AWS resources, dependencies, and runtime parameters. The AWS CloudFormation registry can be used to design, provision, and manage third-party application resources like incident management or version control tools. You can use the AWS CloudFormation Command Line Interface (CLI) to develop and test the infrastructure as code in a text file in either JSON or YAML format. AWS CloudFormation Designer can be used to design visually, and AWS Cloud Development Kit can be used to build your cloud application resources using programming languages like TypeScript, Python, Java, and .NET directly from your integrated development environment (IDE). AWS CloudFormation helps you avoid manual steps to provision the infrastructure, which helps minimize errors. Rollback triggers can be used to create a CloudWatch alarm that monitors the stack creation and update processes. It rolls back the entire stack operation to a previous deployed state when any of the alarms are breached.

The change sets can be used to preview the impact of proposed changes to determine whether they will delete or replace any of your critical resources. AWS CloudFormation makes the changes to your stack only after you decide to execute the change set. AWS CloudFormation automatically manages the AWS resource dependencies and the order in which resources are created, updated, or deleted during stack creation. AWS StackSets can be used to provision, update, and delete a common set of AWS resources across multiple accounts and regions with a single CloudFormation template, which determines the correct sequence of actions when performing stack operations. This provides the same level of automation, repeatability, and reliability to stack management operations across regions and accounts.

When architecting a highly scalable e-commerce web application that requires an Auto Scaling group to spin up an EC2 instance based on demand, use an Elastic Load Balancing load balancer to divert huge volumes of traffic, an Amazon Relational Database Service database instance for persistent storage, Amazon SQS to exchange data between applications, Amazon SNS for notification, Amazon S3 bucket and Amazon CloudFront to deliver static contents, Amazon Cognito for temporary access, and Amazon Route 53 for the domain name system. You can provision each individual service and configure them to work together in your AWS account for your development environment. By the time your e-commerce application is up and running, all these manual tasks become very complex and time consuming otherwise.

The AWS CloudFormation template can be used to define all these resources and create an AWS CloudFormation stack, which provisions all the AWS services you need for your e-commerce application along with handling the dependency for you. When your e-commerce application is up and running, you can manage, update, or delete the stack easily as a single unit. You can use the stack to create the same e-commerce application in any of your other environments or AWS accounts. If you have decided to create your application in different regions for high availability and disaster recovery, you can reuse your AWS CloudFormation template stack to provision the same resources consistently over and over in multiple regions. It is easy to update or upgrade any of the resources incrementally, like increasing the maximum number of instances in your Auto Scaling group, by simply tracking the differences in your templates and updating your infrastructure, like code. You can use any version control system for your templates to track changes and to know exactly when the changes were made, who made them, and what changes were made. You can easily reverse changes to your infrastructure by simply running the previous version of your template.

Templates

The AWS CloudFormation template uses the JSON and YAML format, which allows extensions like json, .yaml, .template, or .txt, and it uses these templates as blueprints for creating AWS resources. The following is the basic structure of a AWS CloudFormation template that describes which parameter is required and which parameters are optional ,along with descriptions of each.

```
{
1.   "AWSTemplateFormatVersion" : "version date",    ←——— Only valid value is
                                                          2010-09-09 (optional)

2.   "Description" : "string" ,←——————— Describes what the template will create (optional)

3.   "Metadata" : {
     metadata of template ←——————— Additional information about the template (optional)
   },

4.   "Parameters" : {
     set of parameters ←——————— Runtime values to be passed to your template (optional)
   },

5.   "Mappings" : {
     set of mappings ←——————— Conditional parameter values like lookup
   },                          table with keys and values (optional)

6.   "Conditions" : {
     set of conditions ←——————— Conditions to control whether to
   },                            create a specific resource (optional)

7.   "Transform" : {
     set of transforms ←——————— Declare and reuse resources that are
   },                            stored in the Amazon S3 bucket (optional)

8.   "Resources" : {           The only required parameter in the AWS CloudFormation
     set of resources ←——————— template where you can define resources like EC2 or S3, etc.,
   },                            that you want to create (required)

9.   "Outputs" : {
     set of outputs ←——————— Output values like your resource's host name, IP address, etc. (optional)
   }
}
```

Let us get started with practical AWS CloudFormation templates by creating simple templates using JSON, YAML, and Terraform formats. Since it's one of the important services for the exam and in your daily job, I will explain a few sample templates that teach and reinforce the AWS CloudFormation templates.

Use the JSON Template to Create a Single AWS Resource

In the following simple JSON template, the AWSTemplateFormatVersion parameter does not use the current date—it uses 2010-09-09, which is the only valid date that should be used for all your AWS CloudFormation templates. Then the self-explanatory Description parameter is where you can write a description/comment for the template like "My Sample S3 template." Resources is the only required parameter in a template, which describes what services will be created—for example, MyS3Bucket informs you that we are creating an S3 bucket. The Resource Type is AWS::S3::Bucket for creating an S3 bucket. The DeletionPolicy dictates whether to retain or delete the AWS after deleting the template stack, and Retain or Delete can be used. The Properties section contains relevant parameters to create the resource. The AccessControl parameter is defined as Private to keep it secure. The BucketEncryption parameter specifies what kind of encryption: Configuration or Algorithm. The BucketName parameter specifies the name for your bucket—for example, MyFirstS3Bucket. The VersioningConfiguration defines whether to keep different versions of the objects based on the Status parameter. Tags are another optional parameter, but it's one of the important parameters with Key and Value, and it can be used to manage and organize your AWS resources.

```json
{
  "AWSTemplateFormatVersion" : "2010-09-09",
  "Description" : "Sample S3 template",
  "Resources" : {
    "MyS3Bucket" : {
      "Type" : "AWS::S3::Bucket",
      "DeletionPolicy": "Retain",
      "Properties" : {
              "AccessControl" : "Private",
              "BucketEncryption": {
                "ServerSideEncryptionConfiguration": [{
                        "ServerSideEncryptionByDefault": {
                          "SSEAlgorithm": "AES256"
                        }
                }]
              },
              "BucketName" : "MyFirstS3Bucket",
              "VersioningConfiguration": {
                  "Status": "Enabled"
              },
              "Tags" : [
                      {
                        "Key" : "Name",
                        "Value" : "My S3 Bucket"
                      },
                      {
                        "Key" : "Owner",
                        "Value" : "Kamesh Ganesan"
                      }
              ]
      }
    }
  }
}
```

Use the YAML Template to Create a Single AWS Resource

The YAML template uses similar parameters as the JSON template to create an Amazon S3 bucket from the AWS Management Console or using CLI.

```
AWSTemplateFormatVersion: "2010-09-09"
Description: Sample S3 template
Resources:
  MyS3Bucket:
    Type: AWS::S3::Bucket
    DeletionPolicy: Delete
    Properties:
          AccessControl: PublicRead
          BucketEncryption:
            ServerSideEncryptionConfiguration:
              - ServerSideEncryptionByDefault:
                  SSEAlgorithm: AES256
          BucketName: MySecondS3Bucket
          VersioningConfiguration:
            Status: Enabled
          Tags:
            - Key: Name
              Value: 'My Second S3 Bucket'
            - Key: Owner
              Value: 'Kamesh Ganesan'
```

Use Terraform Script to Create a Single AWS Resource

HashiCorp's Terraform (terraform.io) is another famous infrastructure as code used for building, updating, and versioning your infrastructure by many enterprises and can be used for multicloud provisioning. You can download it from https://www.terraform.io/downloads.html and install Terraform based on your operating system. In this chapter, let us explore simple code that provisions an S3 bucket in AWS:

```
provider "aws" {
        region = "us-east-1"
        access_key = "ABCDEFGHIJKLMNOPQRST"
        secret_key = "a1b2c3d4e5f6g7h8i9j10K11L12M13N14o15P"
      }
```

First, you need to run "terraform init" using the earlier parameter to set the environment and configuration:

```
resource "aws_s3_bucket" "create" {
        bucket = "my-third-s3-bucket"
        acl    = "publicread"
        versioning {
          enabled = true
        }
        server_side_encryption_configuration {
          rule {
            apply_server_side_encryption_by_default {
              kms_master_key_id = "${aws_kms_key.mykey.arn}"
              sse_algorithm     = "aws:kms"
            }
          }
        }
      }
```

```
        tags = {
            "name"  = "My S3 Bucket"
            "owner" = "Kamesh Ganesan"
        }
}
```

Then use "terraform plan" to create the execution plan without making any changes to resources or to its state. This determines what actions are necessary to attain the desired state mentioned in the configuration files. Use "terraform apply" to apply the required changes to reach the desired state of your configuration. Finally, use "terraform destroy" to destroy the Terraform-managed resources, and you will be prompt for confirmation before deleting all the resources.

Use the JSON Template to Create Multiple AWS Resources

Now let us create multiple resources in a single template and configure how all the resources work together. The following template creates an Amazon EC2 instance and S3 bucket.

```
{
    "AWSTemplateFormatVersion": "2010-09-09",
    "Description": "Create S3 and EC2",
    "Resources": {
            "EC2Instance": {
                    "Type": "AWS::EC2::Instance",
                    "Properties": {
                      "ImageId": "ami-0gg9b82416f66f987",
                      "InstanceType": "t2.medium",
                      "KeyName": "my-ssh-login-key",
                      "BlockDeviceMappings": [
                          {
                             "DeviceName": "/dev/sda",
                             "Ebs": {
                               "VolumeType": "io1",
                               "Iops": "300",
                               "DeleteOnTermination": "true",
                               "VolumeSize": "30"
                             }
                          }
                      ]
                    }
            },
            "MyS3Bucket": {
                    "Type": "AWS::S3::Bucket",
                    "DeletionPolicy": "Delete",
                    "Properties": {
                      "AccessControl": "PublicRead",
                      "BucketEncryption": {
                        "ServerSideEncryptionConfiguration": [
                            {
                               "ServerSideEncryptionByDefault": {
                                 "SSEAlgorithm": "AES256"
                               }
                            }
                        ]
                    },
```

```json
      "BucketName": "MyFourthS3Bucket",
      "VersioningConfiguration": {
        "Status": "Enabled"
      },
      "Tags": [
        {
          "Key": "Name",
          "Value": "My 4th S3 Bucket"
        },
        {
          "Key": "Owner",
          "Value": "Kamesh Ganesan"
        },
        {
          "Key": "contact",
          "Value": "kamesh@example.com"
        }
      ]
    }
  }
 }
}
```

Use the YAML Template to Create Multiple AWS Resources

Here is a sample YAML template for creating multiple AWS resources:

```yaml
AWSTemplateFormatVersion: "2010-09-09"
Description: Sample JSON template to create an EC2 instance and S3 bucket
Resources:
        MyEC2Instance:
                Type: AWS::EC2::Instance
                Properties:
                   ImageId: ami-0gg9b89876f66f456
                   InstanceType: t2.medium
                   KeyName: my-ssh-login-key
                   BlockDeviceMappings:
                      - DeviceName: /dev/sda
                        Ebs:
                           VolumeType: io1
                           Iops: 300
                           DeleteOnTermination: true
                           VolumeSize: 30
        MyS3Bucket:
                Type: AWS::S3::Bucket
                DeletionPolicy: Delete
                Properties:
                   AccessControl: PublicRead
                   BucketEncryption:
                     ServerSideEncryptionConfiguration:
                        - ServerSideEncryptionByDefault:
                            SSEAlgorithm: AES256
                   BucketName: MySecondS3Bucket
                   VersioningConfiguration:
                     Status: Enabled
                   Tags:
                 - Key: Name
                   Value: 'My Second S3 Bucket'
```

```
            - Key: Owner
              Value: 'Kamesh Ganesan'
            - Key: Contact
              Value: 'kamesh@example.com'
```

In this sample using the YAML template, the AWSTemplateFormatVersion parameter uses 2010-09-09, which is the only valid date that should be used for all your AWS CloudFormation templates. Then the self-explanatory Description parameter is where you can write a description and comment for this template. Resources is the only mandatory parameter in a template, which describes what services will be created—for example, MyEC2Instance and MyS3Bucket specifies that we are creating an EC2 instance and S3 bucket. The Resource Types for this template are AWS::EC2::Instance and AWS::S3::Bucket for creating an EC2 instance and S3 bucket, respectively. The DeletionPolicy dictates whether to retain or delete the AWS after deleting the template stack. The Properties section contains relevant parameters to create the resource. The ImageId parameter specifies the image, and the InstanceType parameter specifies the instance size, like t2.medium. The KeyName specifies the key, like my-ssh-login-key that you already created, and can be used to log in to your new EC2 instance. The EBS volume BlockDeviceMappings specifies the DeviceName—for example, /dev/sda or /dev/sdb. The VolumeType specifies whether it is input/output optimized like io1. The Iops defines the Input Output per second, and DeleteOnTermination dictates whether to delete the volume. The VolumeSize parameter specifies the size of the volume. The AccessControl parameter is defined as Private to keep it secure. The BucketEncryption parameter specifies what kind of encryption: Configuration or Algorithm. The BucketName parameter specifies the name for your bucket—for example, MyFirstS3Bucket. The VersioningConfiguration defines whether to keep different versions of the objects based on the Status parameter. Tags are another optional parameter, but it's one of the important parameters with Key and Value, and it can be used to manage and organize your AWS resources.

Use the Terraform Script to Create Multiple AWS Resources

The Terraform script can be used to create an EC2 instance and S3 bucket by using the terraform init, plan, and apply commands:

```
provider "aws" {
        region = "us-east-1"
        access_key = "ABCDEFGHIJKLMNOPQRST"
        secret_key = "a1b2c3d4e5f6g7h8i9j10K11L12M13N14o15P"
    }
resource "aws_instance" "create" {
        ami                    = "ami-abcd4321"
        instance_type          = "t2.medium"
        key_name               = "my-ssh-login-key"
        tags = {
            "name"    = "My EC2 instance"
            "owner"   = "Kamesh Ganesan"
            "contact" = "kamesh@example.com"
          }
      }
```

```
resource "aws_s3_bucket" "create" {
        bucket = "my-third-s3-bucket"
        acl    = "publicread"
        versioning {
          enabled = true
        }
        server_side_encryption_configuration {
          rule {
            apply_server_side_encryption_by_default {
              kms_master_key_id = "${aws_kms_key.mykey.arn}"
              sse_algorithm     = "aws:kms"
            }
          }
        }
        tags = {
            "name"    = "My S3 Bucket"
            "owner"   = "Kamesh Ganesan"
            "contact" = "kamesh@example.com"
        }
}
```

The "terraform init" will set up the configuration of your AWS environment, and the "terraform plan" will be used to create the execution plan without making any changes to resources or to its existing state or creating new ones. In addition, "terraform plan" determines what actions are necessary to attain the desired state mentioned in the configuration files. Then run "terraform apply" to create a t2.medium EC2 instance and S3 bucket with versioning enabled. Both the EC2 instance and S3 bucket will have name, owner, and contact tags. You can use the AWS CloudFormation templates in JSON or YAML or use Terraform to build a complex set of resources with additional capabilities, and the templates can be reused to create multiple environments like Development, QA, Stage, and Production.

Stacks

AWS CloudFormation stacks can be used to create and manage related resources as a single unit. The collection of your AWS resources is defined in a stack, and AWS CloudFormation takes care of creating, updating, and deleting all stack resources. AWS CloudFormation either creates all the resources in a stack successfully or rolls back everything by deleting any resources that were created before the failure. You incur charges for the stack resources for its operation or uptime until it is completely deleted or terminated. You can create stacks based on the environment or application, based on how you want to relate the AWS resources. For example, if you are creating an e-commerce application that requires web servers, application servers, a database, a load balancer, and other networking services along with firewall rules, you can use an AWS Cloud-Formation stack to create all the e-commerce application resources, and they can be updated or deleted as a single unit. You can create, update, and delete the stack using the AWS CloudFormation console, API, or AWS CLI. You can create the e-commerce application resources in another environment by just submitting the template, and AWS CloudFormation provisions all the resources for you.

Updating a Stack

Often, you will need to update resources, but you can update the stack template instead of creating a new stack and deleting the old stack. You just need to submit the updated version of the original stack template, and AWS CloudFormation compares it with the original template and creates the change set, which lists all the proposed changes. You can execute the stack after reviewing the impact of your changes. AWS CloudFormation updates only the resources that you modified and restores the stack to the last known working state if there is any failure.

Deleting a Stack

When you no longer need your resources that you created—for example, your e-commerce application or proof of concept—then you can specify the stack to delete, and AWS CloudFormation deletes all the resources in that stack, including the stack itself. You can use the AWS CLI, API, or AWS CloudFormation console to delete the stack. The deletion policy Retain can be used to retain some resources in that stack if necessary. The stack will remain until all resources are successfully deleted. If any of the resources cannot be deleted or fail to delete, then the stack will not be deleted.

Change Sets

You can update the stack if you need to make changes to any of your running resources. A change set gives you a summary of the proposed changes to your resource before making any changes. This gives you the opportunity to check the impact to your critical resources, and you can implement the changes after the review. For example, if you want to change the instance type of your EC2 instance to increase the size, AWS CloudFormation will stop the instance, release its public IPv4 (unless you attached an elastic static IP), and move the instance to new hardware. The Amazon EC2 Auto Scaling service might mark the stopped EC2 instance as unhealthy and try launching a new replacement instance after terminating it. This instance start will fail if it's part of a cluster placement group, and your change set displays the impact so you will be able to plan accordingly. You can update your stack after validating the impact and reports after all the resources have been created. AWS CloudFormation rolls back your changes by deleting the resources it created when a failure occurs when updating a stack.

Export

You can share information between stacks in the same AWS account and region using the export function instead of hard-coding the values or using input parameters in the template. You need to use the Export field in the Output section of your template, and you can use the Fn::ImportValue function to import those values. You can use ListImports to delete or modify exported output values.

AWS CloudFormation Registry

You can use the CloudFormation registry to list the resources that are available to use in your AWS CloudFormation account. The resources can be either private ones that you created, as well as ones shared with you, or public resources provided by AWS. You need to register your private resources before you can use them. You can view resources in the CloudFormation registry after you have registered the resource provider and then you can start using them in your stack templates. You can use the submit command in the AWS CloudFormation CLI or the register-type command in the AWS CLI to register the resource provider.

Chapter Review

This chapter began by explaining what AWS CloudFormation is and how it is used as infrastructure as code. It then introduced templates, stacks, and change sets. The chapter provided examples using simple templates in JSON and YAML formats, in addition to a simple Terraform script that creates an S3 bucket. The AWS CloudFormation service enables you to design and create your AWS resources securely using automation. AWS CloudFormation handles the provision of your AWS resources, and it takes care of the dependencies of your AWS resources and third-party application resources. The AWS CloudFormation template uses the JSON and YAML format, which allows extensions like .json, .yaml, .template, or .txt, and it uses these templates as blueprints for creating AWS resources.

A AWS CloudFormation stack is the collection of your AWS resources, and AWS CloudFormation takes care of creating, updating, and deleting all stack resources in your AWS cloud environment across all regions and accounts. It either creates all the resources in a stack successfully or rolls back everything by deleting any resources that were created before the failure. You can create stacks based on the environment or application, based on how you want to relate the AWS resources. You can use an AWS CloudFormation stack to create e-commerce application resources, for example, and they can be updated or deleted as a single unit. You can create, update, and delete the stack using the AWS CloudFormation console, API, or AWS CLI. You can create the resources in another environment by just submitting the template, and AWS CloudFormation provisions all the resources.

A change set gives you a summary of the proposed changes to your resource before making any changes and to verify the impact to your critical resources before implementing them. You can execute your stack after validating the impact and reports after all the resources have been created. If a failure occurs when updating a stack, AWS CloudFormation rolls back your changes by deleting the resources it created.

Exercise

The following exercise will help you practice using AWS CloudFormation templates. You need to create an AWS account, as explained earlier, to perform these exercises. You can use the Free Tier when launching AWS resources, but make sure to terminate them at the end.

Exercise 18-1: Create an AWS CloudFormation Template Using the AWS Management Console

1. Use your AWS account e-mail address and password to sign in and then navigate to the AWS CloudFormation Designer console at https://console.aws.amazon .com/cloudformation/.

2. Verify the AWS region by using the Region selector in the upper-right corner of the page.

3. From the navigation pane on the left, choose Designer.

4. You will create a simple template using the Designer. From the list of resources available on the left side, select EC2 and expand as shown here.

5. Select Instance from the Designer and drop it to the center pane. The template is created in the bottom pane in JSON.

```json
{
    "AWSTemplateFormatVersion": "2010-09-09",
    "Metadata": {
        "AWS::CloudFormation::Designer": {
            "a5c5a0ce-6944-4fb4-adef-b152fa024811": {
                "size": {
                    "width": 60,
                    "height": 60
                },
                "position": {
                    "x": 200,
                    "y": 80
                },
                "z": 0,
                "embeds": []
            }
        }
    },
    "Resources": {
        "EC2I4MUN6": {
            "Type": "AWS::EC2::Instance",
            "Properties": {
                "ImageId": "ami-0fc61db8544a617ed",
                "InstanceType": "t2.micro"
            },
            "Metadata": {
                "AWS::CloudFormation::Designer": {
                    "id": "a5c5a0ce-6944-4fb4-adef-b152fa024811"
                }
            }
        }
    }
}
```

6. The template can be automatically converted to a YAML template from the Designer, as shown next, and click on the checkbox symbol on top-left side of the Designer to verify this. For the ImageId type **ami-0fc61db8544a617ed** and for the InstanceType type **t2.micro** to create the instance in the Free Tier to avoid any charges.

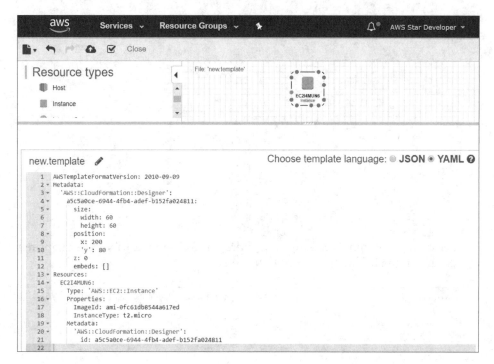

7. In order to create a stack, click on the up-arrow symbol on the top-left side of the Designer, which will take you to the next screen.

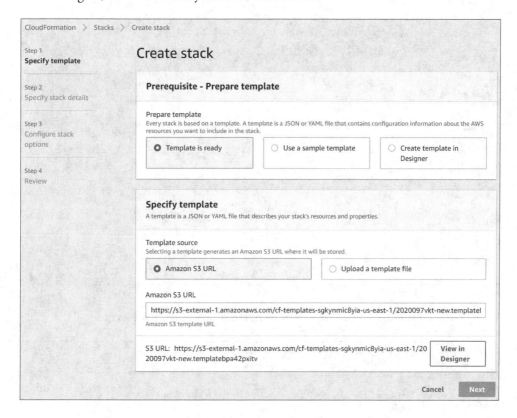

8. Click on the Next button. Enter **my-first-stack** for the stack name, and click the Next button again, as shown here.

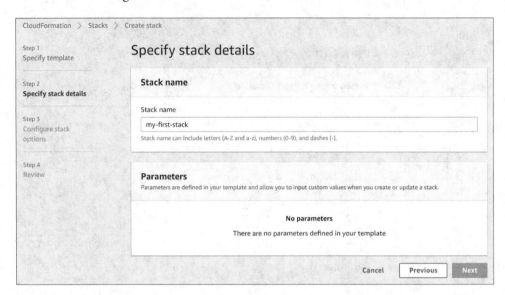

9. In the Configure Stack Options Screen, enter tags and click Next.

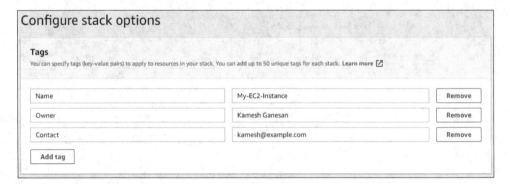

10. The Review page lists all the configurations for verification before creating it. The illustration here does not show the entire page, but you should be able to verify this in your console page. After reviewing the configurations, click on Create Stack.

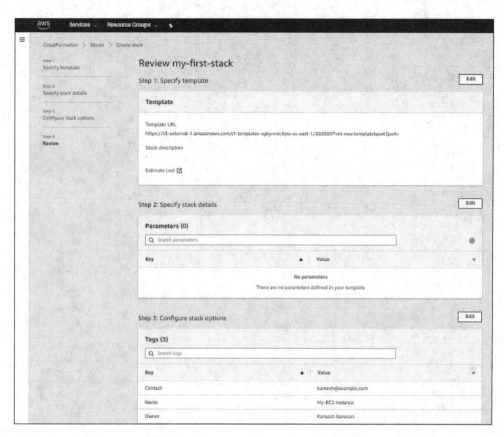

11. You can view the stack creation and its progress, as shown next.

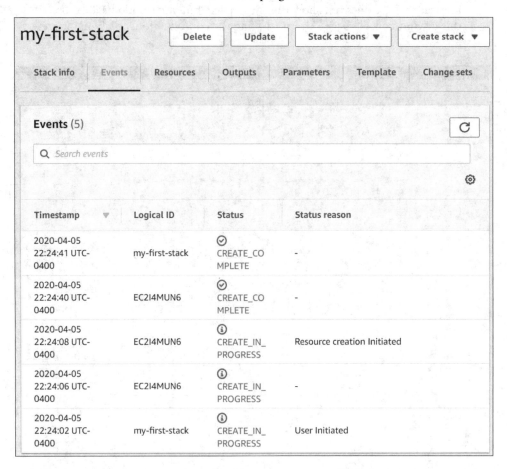

12. Now you can navigate to EC2 service and verify the new instance that you created using the CloudFormation Template (CFT) Designer.

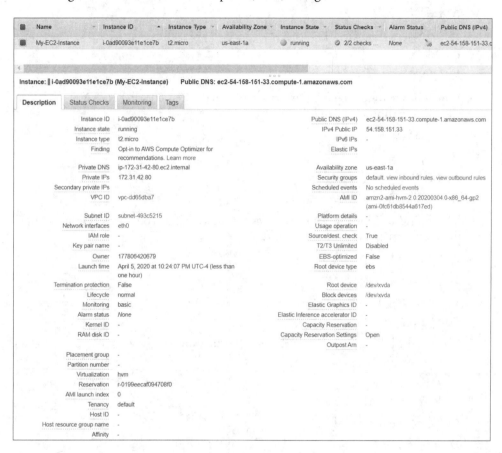

Questions

The following questions will help you gauge your understanding of the contents in this chapter. Read all the answers carefully because there might be more than one correct answer. Choose the best response for each question.

1. Which of the following services provides infrastructure as code in AWS?

    A. Amazon EC2

    B. Amazon S3

    C. Amazon RDS

    D. AWS CloudFormation

2. Which of the following two formats are supported in AWS CloudFormation? (Choose two.)

   A. JSON

   B. YAML

   C. PPTX

   D. XLSX

3. Which of the following parameters are required when creating an AWS CloudFormation template?

   A. Metadata

   B. Mappings

   C. Conditions

   D. Resources

4. Which of the following parameters return the values of your stack resources after the successful creation of your stack?

   A. Outputs

   B. Transform

   C. Description

   D. Mappings

5. What is the billing cycle for AWS CloudFormation, and how much you will need to pay?

   A. Pay as you go

   B. Reserved yearly

   C. Discounted monthly

   D. It is free

6. You are creating an EC2 instance using the AWS CloudFormation template, and you need to create a web server and admin user. Which of the following parameters can be used to execute the script?

   A. AdditionalInfo

   B. Tags

   C. User data

   D. LaunchTemplate

7. The AWS CloudFormation template can be used to bootstrap using which of the following configuration management tools to automate and deploy servers in your AWS environment? (Choose three.)

   A. Chef

   B. Puppet

   C. Ansible

   D. ELK

8. You deleted your stack successfully, and it returned a Delete_Complete state, but when you verify this, you notice a couple of resources were not deleted. What is the reason for this?

   A. You set DeletionPolicy to Delete

   B. You set DeletionPolicy to Retain

   C. You set DeletionPolicy to Snapshot

   D. You set DeletionPolicy to Keep

9. Which managed service enables you to discover, register, and use private third-party resource providers and public AWS resources?

   A. AWS CloudFormation registry

   B. AWS CloudFormation template

   C. AWS CloudFormation stack

   D. AWS CloudFormation change set

10. You need to create few resources and delete a few resources from an existing AWS CloudFormation stack. Your manager is concerned about the impact of these changes. How can you verify the impact of changes to the stack without actually executing them?

    A. Create a change set

    B. Use nested stacks

    C. Use the CloudFormation registry

    D. Use Windows stacks

Answers

1. **D.** The AWS CloudFormation service provides infrastructure as code in AWS.

2. **A, B.** JSON and YAML are the two formats supported in AWS CloudFormation.

3. **D.** Resources is the only required parameter in AWS CloudFormation.

4. **A.** The Outputs parameter returns the values of your stack resources after the successful creation of your stack.

5. **D.** There is no additional charge for using AWS CloudFormation; you pay only for the AWS resources you create.

6. **C.** User data can be used to execute the bootstrap script during the creation of your EC2 instance.

7. **A, B, C.** Chef, Puppet, and Ansible are the configuration management tools that can be used to bootstrap in the AWS environment.

8. **B.** If you set DeletionPolicy to Retain for any resource, it will be retained after the deletion of stack.

9. **A.** The AWS CloudFormation registry is a managed service that enables you to discover, register, and use private third-party resource providers and public AWS resources.

10. **A.** Change sets can be used to verify the impact of your changes to the stack without executing them.

Additional Resources

- **AWS CloudFormation**   The recommended documentation for any AWS services, including Amazon CloudFormation, is the official AWS documentation, where you always can get the most up-to-date information
  `https://docs.aws.amazon.com/cloudformation/index.html`

- **AWS CloudFormation Blog**   This is the official blog for AWS CloudFormation, which has all the latest information in one place.
  `https://aws.amazon.com/blogs/aws/category/management-tools/aws-cloudformation/`

PART VII

Developing Cloud Native Applications in AWS

- **Chapter 19** Developing Serverless Applications with Lambda
- **Chapter 20** Deploying a Static Website on Amazon S3 Bucket
- **Chapter 21** Deploying a Web Application Using AWS Elastic Beanstalk
- **Chapter 22** Migrating Your Application and Database to AWS

Developing Serverless Applications with Lambda

In this chapter, you will learn
- Lambda functions
- Lambda applications
- Lambda layers

This chapter will discuss how to develop serverless functions and applications using AWS Lambda.

AWS Lambda

AWS Lambda is a serverless compute service where you just provide your code to execute without having to provision any servers and pay only for the execution time. AWS Lambda manages the provision, scaling, and termination of servers automatically and charges only when your code is running. AWS Lambda supports Go, Node.js, Java, C#, Ruby, Python, and PowerShell to write your code for any application or backend services without the need for any underlying tasks, including code monitoring, logging, scaling, capacity provisioning, and server and operating system maintenance.

AWS Lambda can be automatically triggered based on events like data changes in an Amazon DynamoDB table, or changes to an Amazon S3 bucket, or AWS SDK API calls, or HTTP requests from the Amazon API Gateway, or data streaming data in Kinesis. You can also create your own serverless application or service composed of functions that can be triggered by events.

AWS Lambda Functions

The AWS Lambda function is an event-driven compute service that uses your code, chosen memory, timeout period, IAM role, and AWS service event to trigger the execution. The following are some of the key concepts that you need to understand before building your first serverless function and application:

- **Runtime**   This allows functions in various languages to use the same execution environment. You can use the runtime provided by Lambda or build your own runtime that sits in between the Lambda service and your function code, relaying responses between the two and invoking events.

- **Event**   Function uses the event, which is a JSON-format document to process, and then runtime converts it and sends it back to your function. The structure and contents of the event can be determined when invoking the function. For example, a custom event for timestamp data is as follows:

```
{
  "TimeFormat": 24,
  "TimeZone": EST,
  "Time": 15.35,
  "Year": 2020,
  "Month": 12,
  "Day": 25,
}
```

- **Concurrency**   This is the number of requests that a function can serve at any given time. Lambda provisions an instance when your function is invoked to process the event. The instance can process another event request when the current function is finished; if not, then another instance is provisioned to process the concurrent request. You can configure a specific level of concurrency to limit this.

- **Trigger**   This is a configuration that invokes your Lambda function, including any AWS service events, custom application events, or event source mapping, that reads from a stream or queue to invoke the function.

- **Versioning**   You can leverage versioning to store new code and configuration of your Lambda function. It will be used along with aliases to perform rolling or blue/green deployments.

- **Scaling**   Scaling is automatically handled by Lambda when your function receives a concurrent request while it's processing a request by launching another instance to handle the increased load.

- **High availability**   When you create your Lambda function to connect to a Virtual Private Cloud (VPC) and specify subnets in more than one Availability Zones, Lambda runs your function in multiple Availability Zones to ensure high availability.

- **Reserved concurrency**   You can reserve concurrency to handle additional requests, but you cannot exceed the specified number of concurrent invocations, which ensures that you have available concurrency when needed.

- **Retries**   Lambda retries the execution automatically, with delays between each invocation triggered by AWS services and other clients.

- **Dead-letter queue**   Lambda can be configured to send failed retry requests to a dead-letter queue, which can be an Amazon SQS queue or Amazon SNS topic that will be used for reprocessing or troubleshooting.

Let us create a function that logs the message pushed to the SNS topic.

1. Log in to your AWS Management Console and select Services from top-left screen. Choose AWS Lambda. The AWS Lambda console page will appear, as shown here.

2. Click on the Create Function button that will take you to the AWS Lambda Create Function screen.

3. Now select the s3-get-object-python function from the blueprint that will take you to the Basic Information page. Here you need to enter a name for your function, choose AWS Policy Templates, and then provide a role name. Choose Policy Templates from the dropdown and choose the S3 and SNS policies.

Basic information Info

Function name

```
my-first-lambda-function
```

Execution role
Choose a role that defines the permissions of your function. To create a custom role, go to the **IAM console**.

○ Create a new role with basic Lambda permissions

○ Use an existing role

● Create a new role from AWS policy templates

ⓘ Role creation might take a few minutes. Please do not delete the role or edit the trust or permissions policies in this role.

Role name
Enter a name for your new role.

```
my-aws-lambda-role
```

Use only letters, numbers, hyphens, or underscores with no spaces.

Policy templates - *optional* Info
Choose one or more policy templates.

| Amazon S3 object read-only permissions ✕ | Amazon SNS publish policy ✕ |
| S3 | SNS |

4. Now you need to configure the S3 trigger that can be run each time the defined event occurs. Choose your existing bucket from the dropdown menu, and select All Object Create Events. Provide the Prefix and Suffix as appropriate, and choose Enable Trigger.

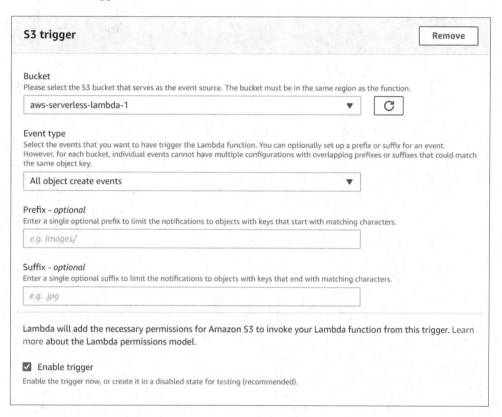

5. The last part is Lambda function code, which is preconfigured by the blueprint and can be updated after the function is created. This function uses Python 3.7. Click on the Create Function button.

```
Runtime
Python 3.7

1  import json
2  import urllib.parse
3  import boto3
4
5  print('Loading function')
6
7  s3 = boto3.client('s3')
8
9
10  def lambda_handler(event, context):
11      #print("Received event: " + json.dumps(event, indent=2))
12
13      # Get the object from the event and show its content type
14      bucket = event['Records'][0]['s3']['bucket']['name']
15      key = urllib.parse.unquote_plus(event['Records'][0]['s3']['object']['key'], encoding='ut
16      try:
17          response = s3.get_object(Bucket=bucket, Key=key)
18          print("CONTENT TYPE: " + response['ContentType'])
19          return response['ContentType']
20      except Exception as e:
21          print(e)
22          print('Error getting object {} from bucket {}. Make sure they exist and your bucket
23          raise e
24
```

Cancel   Create function

Your first AWS Lambda is successfully created, and you can explore testing different values and updating the code based on your need. This is the beginning of your exciting serverless journey. Explore many blueprint functions to quickly get started with creating and deploying AWS Lambda functions.

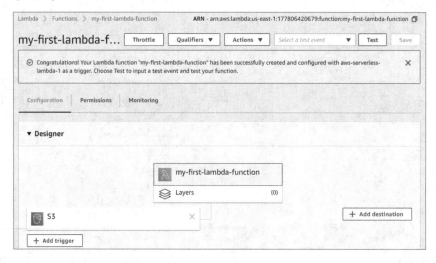

AWS Lambda Applications

An AWS Lambda application consists of Lambda functions, events, and triggers that work as a single package that you can deploy and manage as one resource. Lambda applications can be integrated with developer tools like the AWS SAM CLI. In addition, a collection of Lambda applications can be deployed easily with AWS CodePipeline for your projects. AWS CloudFormation, along with AWS SAM, provides a local testing platform for serverless application development by defining your application's resources and managing the application as a stack. This allows you to safely add and modify resources and roll back to the previous state of your application stack.

AWS Lambda Layers

A Lambda function can be configured to pull additional code in a ZIP archive format that contains a custom runtime, libraries, and content in the form of layers—up to five layers at a time. Custom layers, AWS, or third-party AWS customer published layers can be used like libraries in your function without including them in your deployment package. Resource-based policies can be used to grant layer usage permissions to specific AWS accounts or AWS organizations. The runtime uses libraries in a different location, under /opt, where layers are extracted in the function execution environment depending on the language. AWS SAM can be used to manage layers and its configurations.

AWS Lambda Security

AWS Lambda follows the AWS shared responsibility model, including compliance and regulations for data protection. AWS recommends using multifactor authentication (MFA) and SSL/TLS to communicate, capturing all user activity logging with AWS CloudTrail. AWS strongly recommends not using any sensitive identifying information in function names and freeform tags, since the metadata might get picked up in diagnostic logs, and never include external URL credential information.

All Lambda communication is encrypted with TLS, and the Lambda API endpoint supports only HTTPS secure connections. The environment variables can be used to store secrets securely because they are encrypted at rest. Environment variable values can be encrypted on the client side from the Lambda console before sending them to Lambda, which prevents secrets from being displayed unencrypted in the Lambda console or in the function configuration that's returned by the Lambda API. You can use customer-managed key to encrypt data in Amazon CloudWatch logs and AWS X-Ray, where the data is encrypted by default using the AWS-managed keys. All files that you upload are encrypted by default in Lambda, including deployment packages and layer archives.

PART VII

Chapter Review

This chapter began by explaining AWS Lambda, which is a serverless compute service where you execute your code without provisioning any servers and pay only for the execution time. It manages the provision, scaling, and termination of servers and supports Go, C#, Ruby, Python, Node.js, Java, and PowerShell to write your code for serverless functions and applications. AWS Lambda handles all the administration of underlying tasks, including code monitoring, logging, scaling, capacity provisioning, and server and operating system maintenance. The AWS Lambda function is an event-driven compute service that uses your code, chosen memory, timeout period, IAM role, and AWS service event to trigger the execution. You can use the runtime provided by Lambda or build your own runtime that sits in between the Lambda service and your function code, relaying responses between the two and invocating events.

AWS Lambda applications can be created from the AWS Management Console using the AWS SAM CLI, AWS CodeBuild, or AWS CodePipeline. An AWS Lambda application is a collection of Lambda applications that can be deployed easily with AWS CodePipeline for your projects. AWS CloudFormation, along with AWS SAM, provides a local testing platform for serverless application development by defining your application's resources and managing the application as a stack. A Lambda function can be configured with custom layers, AWS, or third-party AWS customer published layers, which can be used like libraries in your function without including them in your deployment package. Resource-based policies can be used to grant layer usage permissions to specific AWS accounts or AWS organizations. The runtime uses libraries in a different location, under /opt, where layers are extracted in the function execution environment depending on the language.

Exercise

The following exercise will help you practice creating an AWS Lambda serverless application using development tools. You need to create an AWS account, as explained earlier, before performing the exercises. You can use the Free Tier when launching AWS resources, but make sure to terminate them at the end.

Exercise 19-1: Create a AWS Lambda Serverless Application Using the AWS Management Console

1. Use your AWS account e-mail address and password to sign in and then navigate to the AWS Lambda console at https://console.aws.amazon.com/lambda/.

2. Verify the AWS region by using the Region selector in the upper-right corner of the page.

3. From the navigation pane on the left, choose Applications and click on the Create Application button.

4. The Create A Lambda application page has a few sample applications. I encourage you to create and test a few sample AWS Lambda applications before your exam. In this exercise, I chose Queue Processing, which uses Lambda to process messages from your Amazon SQS queue.

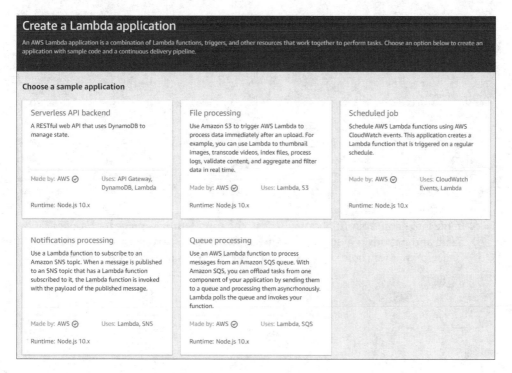

5. This sample AWS Lambda application uses Node.js and CodeCommit for source control. It uses CodeBuild for build and test and CodePipeline for continuous delivery. AWS CloudFormation is used in the background to deploy as an application template stack.

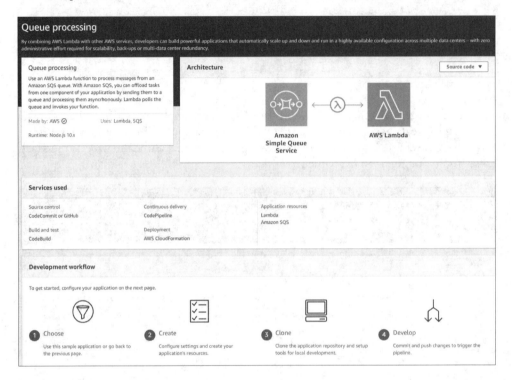

6. In the Configure Your Application screen, enter **my-lambda-queue** for the application name and provide a description. For Runtime, choose Node.js and choose CodeCommit for source control. For the Repository Name, type **my-lambda-queue**.

Also select Permissions to create an appropriate role and execute this AWS serverless application.

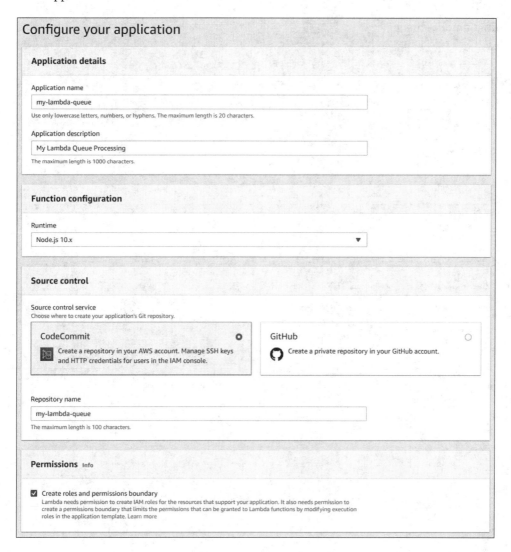

Configure your application

Application details

Application name

my-lambda-queue

Use only lowercase letters, numbers, or hyphens. The maximum length is 20 characters.

Application description

My Lambda Queue Processing

The maximum length is 1000 characters.

Function configuration

Runtime

Node.js 10.x ▼

Source control

Source control service
Choose where to create your application's Git repository.

CodeCommit ●
Create a repository in your AWS account. Manage SSH keys and HTTP credentials for users in the IAM console.

GitHub ○
Create a private repository in your GitHub account.

Repository name

my-lambda-queue

The maximum length is 100 characters.

Permissions Info

☑ Create roles and permissions boundary
Lambda needs permission to create IAM roles for the resources that support your application. It also needs permission to create a permissions boundary that limits the permissions that can be granted to Lambda functions by modifying execution roles in the application template. Learn more

7. When you click on the Create button, AWS Lambda starts provisioning all the resources you will need for this serverless application and shows you the progress.

8. In a few minutes, all the resources will be provisioned and the Application Created message appears.

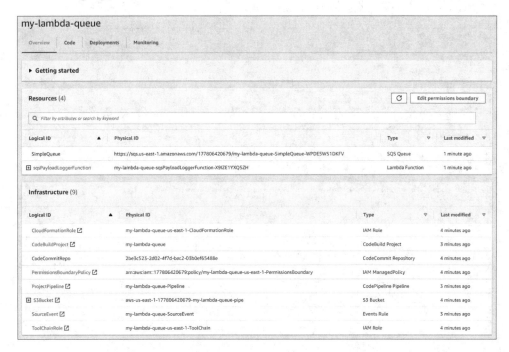

9. From the previous illustration, you can observe that four resources are created in addition to nine infrastructures for you, as shown at the bottom. On the Code tab, you can see the CodeCommit repository and option to clone the URL and SSH.

10. Now navigate to the Deployments tab, where you can find the CodePipeline application pipeline and its status, along with the SAM template that was used to create this serverless application.

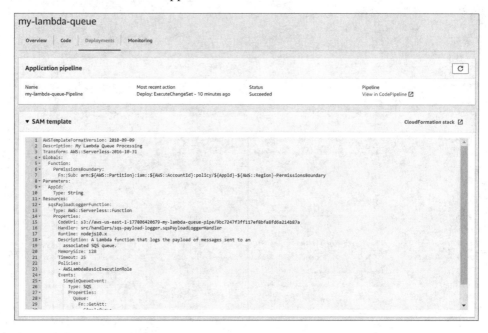

11. Now navigate to the Monitoring tab where you can see a couple of Dashboards, one for AWS Lambda, which has invocations, errors, duration, and concurrent executions as different charts.

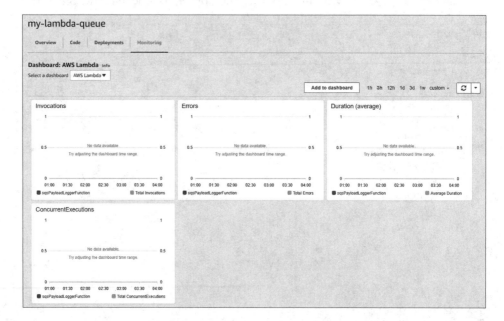

12. From the dropdown, choose Amazon SQS, which has charts for messages sent, received, deleted, visible, not visible, delayed, etc. You can create a queue and start seeing this serverless application in action, but do not forget to delete this once all the resources are completed.

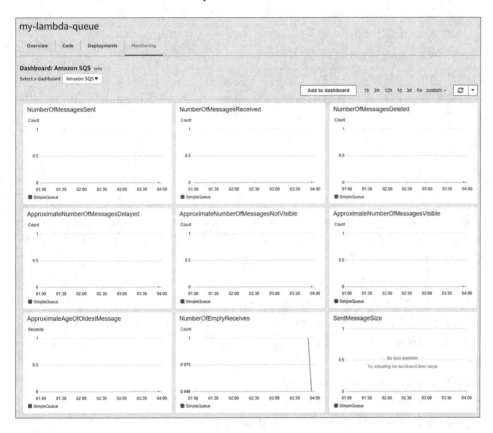

Questions

The following questions will help you gauge your understanding of the contents in this chapter. Read all the answers carefully because there might be more than one correct answer. Choose the best response for each question.

1. You have batch jobs that run every day and use a dedicated server on-premises. Your manager asked you to explore a AWS service that can be leveraged to replace the batch server and run all your jobs without provisioning any server in your cloud environment. Which of the following services satisfies your requirement?

　A. Amazon S3

　B. AWS Lambda

　C. Amazon EC2

　D. Amazon Athena

2. Your company asks you to stop and start your lower environment AWS EC2 instances and RDS databases during nonwork hours to save costs. Which AWS service can you leverage to create jobs that stop and start your instances and databases?

   A. Amazon SageMaker

   B. Amazon Kinesis

   C. AWS Amplify

   D. AWS Lambda

3. Which of the following languages are supported in AWS Lambda? (Choose all that apply.)

   A. Go

   B. Node.js

   C. Java

   D. C#

4. AWS Lambda provisioned an instance to execute your code, and before it finishes, you trigger the Lambda function again. What will happen in this scenario?

   A. Lambda will wait for the process to complete

   B. Lambda will fail

   C. Lambda will send a warning message

   D. Lambda will provision another instance to the handle additional request

5. What is the easiest way to develop, test locally, and deploy serverless applications in the AWS environment?

   A. Upload your code to Amazon S3

   B. Use the AWS Serverless Application Model (SAM)

   C. Provision an EC2 instance and develop your serverless application

   D. You can use the AWS Fargate service

6. Your serverless application is having issues, and you need to troubleshoot by tracing. Which AWS service will help you in this scenario?

   A. AWS X-Ray

   B. AWS Batch

   C. AWS Config

   D. Amazon CodeCommit

7. You created a serverless application using Python. Which of the following runtimes can you choose? (Choose all that apply.)

   A. Python 3.8

   B. Python 3.7

   C. Python 3.6

   D. Python 2.7

8. You have an Amazon S3 bucket that stores sensitive information. You need to monitor any changes to the bucket and send an alert to your security team. How can you achieve this cost-effectively?

   A. Create an AWS Lambda that can be triggered as soon as any changes to this bucket occur

   B. Hire an AWS engineer to monitor this Amazon bucket

   C. Use the Amazon SQS queue to monitor the Amazon S3 bucket

   D. Use the Amazon CloudSearch service to monitor it

9. Your company receives data from multiple sources that needs to be formatted before being stored in an OLTP database. The frequency of incoming data can be very low to high, depending on the day of the week and time of the day. What is an efficient way to format the data cost-effectively?

   A. Create new table and store unformatted data

   B. Ask your SQL developer to write a query to format the data

   C. Provision an EC2 instance and process the data using it

   D. Use AWS Lambda to format the data before storing it in the database

10. How do you provision instances for your AWS Lambda functions?

    A. Run your code, and AWS Lambda takes care of provisioning and managing the instances

    B. Provision the first instance, and AWS Lambda manages the rest of provisioning

    C. It is serverless, so it does not need any instance to run your code

    D. Select the auto-provision option

Answers

1. **B.** You can create AWS Lambda functions to run batch jobs.

2. **D.** AWS Lambda functions, along with Amazon CloudWatch, can be used to create, start, and stop jobs.

3. **A, B, C, D.** The supported languages are Go, Node.js, Java, and C# in addition to Ruby, Python, and PowerShell.

4. **D.** Lambda will provision another instance to handle the additional request concurrently.

5. **B.** The AWS SAM can be used to easily develop and test your serverless applications locally.

6. **A.** AWS X-Ray can be used to run tracing on your Lambda functions to troubleshoot.

7. **A, B, C, D.** Python 3.8, Python 3.7, Python 3.6, and Python 2.7 can be used as runtimes.

8. **A.** You can create an AWS Lambda that can be triggered as soon as any changes to this bucket occur.

9. **D.** You can use AWS Lambda to format the data before storing it in the database.

10. **A.** AWS Lambda takes care of all the provisioning and managing of instances.

Additional Resources

- **AWS Lambda**   The recommended documentation for any AWS services, including Amazon Lambda, is the official AWS documentation, where you can get the most up-to-date information.
  `https://docs.aws.amazon.com/lambda/index.html` and `https://docs.aws.amazon.com/serverless-application-model/index.html`

- **AWS Lambda Blog**   This is the official blog for AWS Lambda, which has all the latest information in one place for useful functions.
  `https://aws.amazon.com/blogs/compute/category/compute/aws-lambda/`

- **AWS SAM Blog**   This blog has all the latest information in one place for AWS SAM.
  `https://aws.amazon.com/blogs/compute/tag/aws-sam/`

Deploying a Static Website on Amazon S3 Bucket

In this chapter, you will learn
- Deploy a static website using Amazon S3
- Deploy a static website using Amazon S3 and Amazon Route 53
- Deploy a static website using Amazon S3, Amazon Route 53, and Amazon CloudFront

In this chapter, we will discuss various ways of creating static websites using Amazon S3.

Amazon S3

Chapter 8 explored Amazon S3 and its different components in detail. It is an object storage service that can be used to store objects in buckets. It can also be used to deploy static websites, which have the following advantages:

- It is easy to set up static websites in Amazon S3.
- It provides cost savings, as there are no web servers or databases to manage.
- You can host the static website using Amazon Route 53.
- You can deliver the contents locally using Amazon CloudFront.
- You can use Amazon Route 53 to manage your custom domain.
- You can deliver the contents securely using SSL from Amazon Certificate Manager.

Deploy a Static Website Using Amazon S3

It is easy and simple to create a static website in Amazon S3. The following will take you on a step-by-step journey of creating a simple website.

1. First log in to your AWS console, navigate to the Amazon S3 service page, and click Create Bucket.

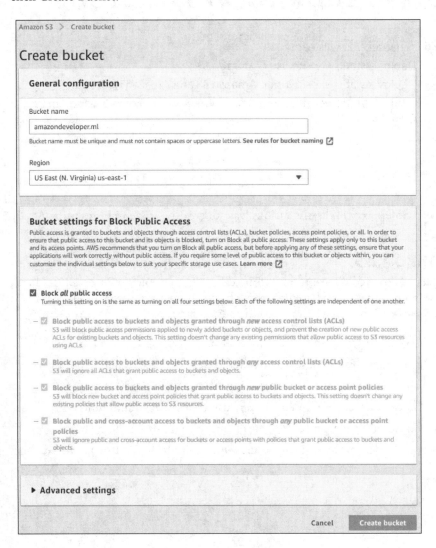

2. As shown next, a new Amazon S3 bucket called amazondeveloper.ml was created successfully.

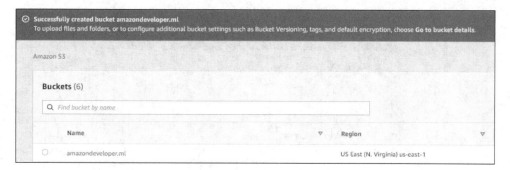

3. Click on the bucket name and select the Properties tab.

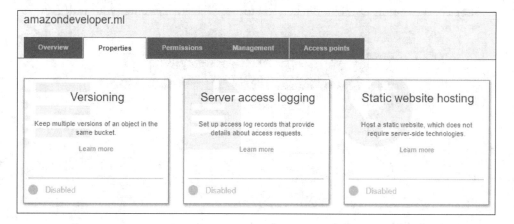

4. In order to make this Amazon S3 bucket a static website, select the Static Website Hosting box.

5. Select the option Use The Bucket To Host A Website and enter your index and error page.

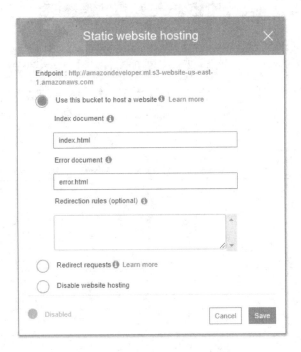

6. Now static website hosting is enabled. Click on the Permissions tab to give read-only access to your objects.

7. You can find the following Amazon read-only policy from the Amazon documentation (https://docs.aws.amazon.com/AmazonS3/latest/dev/example-bucket-policies.html#example-bucket-policies-use-case-2). You need to update the bucket name to the new Amazon S3 bucket name that we created in step 2.

```
{
  "Version":"2012-10-17",
  "Statement":[
    {
      "Sid":"PublicRead",
      "Effect":"Allow",
      "Principal": "*",
      "Action":["s3:GetObject"],
      "Resource":["arn:aws:s3:::amazondeveloper.ml/*"]
    }
  ]
}
```

8. Enter the policy and click Save.

 NOTE See the warning from AWS about granting public access to an Amazon S3 bucket, and never grant anonymous access unless it is absolutely necessary, such as when hosting a static website on Amazon S3.

9. You will see a warning in the Permissions tab regarding the bucket policy, since this bucket has public access.

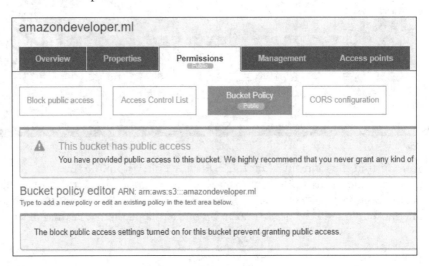

10. Now click the Overview tab to upload your HTML files and images.

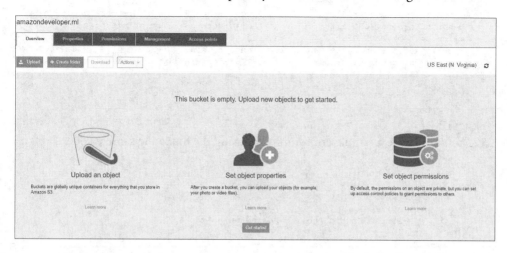

11. Create two simple HTML files in your local machine. You can use the following sample code to create your index.html file.

```
<!DOCTYPE html>
<html language="english">
    <head>
        <meta charset="utf-8">
        <title>
            A Simple Static Website Hosted on Amazon S3
        </title>
    </head>
    <body background="nature1.jpg">
        <br />
        <h1 align="center-left">
            <pre>
                <font face="Georgia" size="16" color="red"><span style="font-size:200%">SHOPPING UNLIMITED</span></font>    </pre>
        </h1>
        <br />
        <h2 align="center-left">
        <pre>
        <MARQUEE DIRECTION="down" BEHAVIOR="alternate" scrolldelay="200" scrollamount="3" STYLE="width:1400px; height:450px">
            <MARQUEE BEHAVIOR="alternate"><font face="Georgia" color="#FFFF00" size="12">A Simple Static Website Hosted on Amazon S3</font></MARQUEE>
        </MARQUEE>
```

```
        <h3 align="center"">
            <pre>
        <font face="Arial Bold" size="7" color="#FFFF00"><a href="#" style="text-
decoration:none;font-size:100%;font-family:verdana;color:orange;text-
align:bottom">PRODUCTS</a>        <a href="#" style="text-decoration:none;font-
size:100%;font-family:verdana;color:orange">CONTACT US</a>            <a href="#"
style="text-decoration:none;font-size:100%;font-family:verdana;color:orange">AB
OUT US</a>
                </font></pre>
        </h3>
    </body>
</html>
```

12. You can create a sample error.html page using the following sample code:

```
<!DOCTYPE html>
<html language="english">
    <head>
        <meta charset="utf-8">
        <title>
            A Simple Static Website Hosted on Amazon S3
        </title>
    </head>
    <body background="sky1.jpg">
        <br />
        <h1 align="center-left">
            <pre>
                <font face="Georgia" size="16" color="red"><span style="font-
size:200%">SHOPPING UNLIMITED</span></font>    </pre>
        </h1>
        <br />
        <h2 align="center">
        <pre>
        <MARQUEE DIRECTION="down" ONMOUSEOVER="this.stop()" ONMOUSEOUT="this.
start()"
BEHAVIOR="alternate" scrolldelay="100" STYLE="width:1400px; height:450px">
            <MARQUEE BEHAVIOR="alternate"><font face="Georgia" color="#FFFF00"
size="12">OOPS! Sorry For The Trouble!! We are working on it!!!</font></MARQUEE>
        </MARQUEE>
    </body>
</html>
```

13. Just replace nature1.jpg and sky1.jpg with pictures of your choice and upload them.

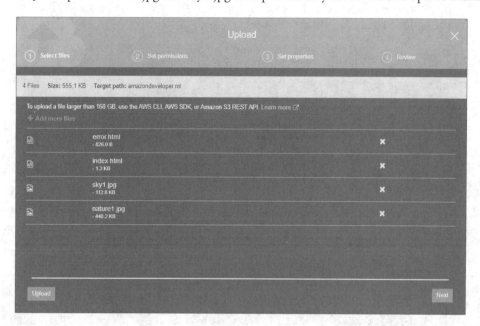

14. Choose the Standard storage class, since you will be frequently accessing this static site, as shown next. Note that here you have options to select Intelligent Tiering, Standard-IA, One Zone-IA, Glacier, Glacier Deep Archive, and Reduced Redundancy based on your requirements. Also, you have the option to encrypt the object using either the Amazon S3 master key or AWS KMS master key.

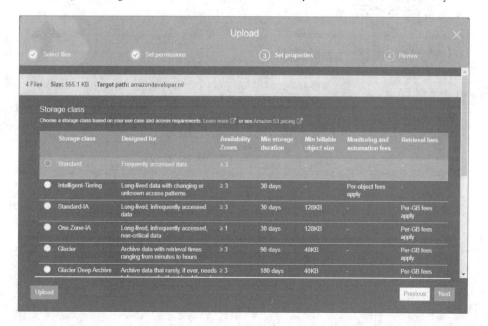

15. Here you can review all the options that you chose so far and update if necessary by clicking on the Previous button, shown next. If everything looks good, click the Upload button to upload the files.

16. Once the upload is successful, it will take you to the bucket, where you can view all the uploaded objects. Now the building of a simple static website is complete using Amazon S3.

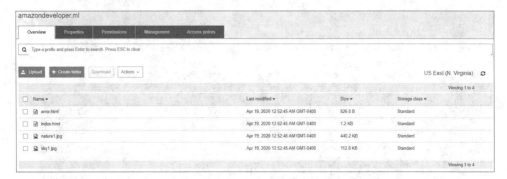

17. You can access your new static website using your bucket name URL—for example, amazondeveloper.ml.s3-website-us-east-1.amazonaws.com—without provisioning any web server or database.

18. You can also access your website using the index.html URL—for example, amazondeveloper.ml.s3-website-us-east-1.amazonaws.com/index.html.

19. Similarly, you can access your website error page using the error.html URL—for example, amazondeveloper.ml.s3-website-us-east-1.amazonaws.com/error.html.

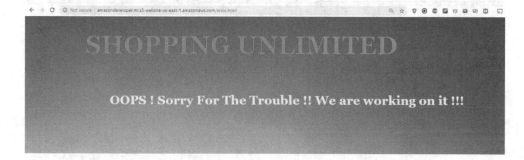

20. As a developer, you know very well that we need to test our implementation. So, let us enter the incorrect URL and see whether it displays the error page. You can add some word like "cloudy" at the end of the URL to test this—for example, amazondeveloper.ml.s3-website-us-east-1.amazonaws.com/cloudy.

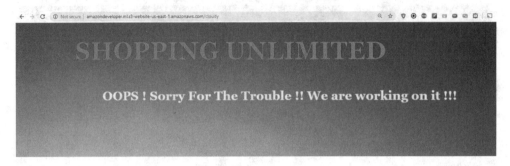

Deploy a Static Website Using Amazon S3 and Amazon Route 53

You can create the Amazon S3 static website using a custom URL and host it in Amazon Route 53. You can get a free domain from the freenom site that can be used for building your static website.

1. Go to https://www.freenom.com and look for any domain name of your choice—for example, I checked amazondeveloper.ml.

2. If the domain is available, you will see an option to select it.

3. When you click on Checkout after logging in, it will take you to the next page. Click Continue.

4. Next you will see the Review And Checkout page, where you can complete the order to get your new domain (which you will have to pay for after 12 months).

5. Now, you can go back to your AWS console and navigate to Amazon Route 53. Here you can see options for DNS management, traffic management, availability monitoring, and domain registration. Choose DNS Management to host your new domain.

6. The DNS management dashboard will appear, where you can create a hosted zone.

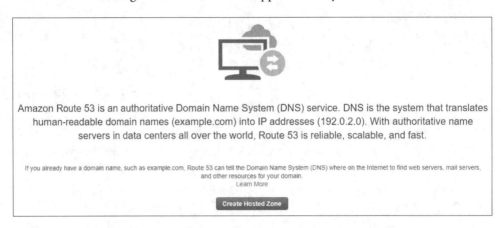

Amazon Route 53 is an authoritative Domain Name System (DNS) service. DNS is the system that translates human-readable domain names (example.com) into IP addresses (192.0.2.0). With authoritative name servers in data centers all over the world, Route 53 is reliable, scalable, and fast.

If you already have a domain name, such as example.com, Route 53 can tell the Domain Name System (DNS) where on the Internet to find web servers, mail servers, and other resources for your domain.
Learn More

Create Hosted Zone

7. Enter your domain name—for example, **amazondeveloper.ml**—in the Domain Name field, select Public Hosted Zone for the Type, and click the Create button.

8. Note the namespace values that you need to update in the https://www.freenom.com website.

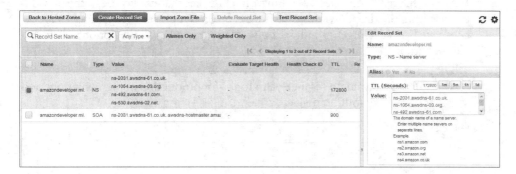

9. Now, go to https://wwwfreenom.com and navigate to Services | My Domains. Enter the namespace values from the previous step.

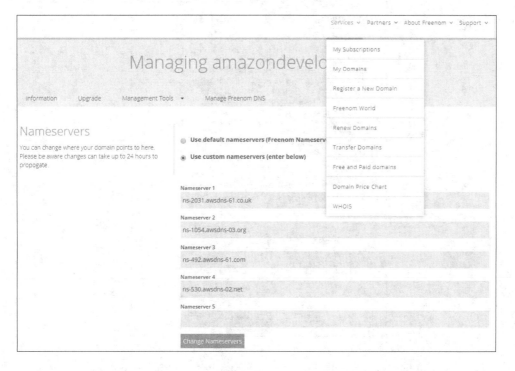

10. Navigate back to the AWS console and go to Amazon Route 53 DNS Management, and create Record Set, shown next. Select the Type as A and leave the name blank. For Alias, select Yes, and select the Amazon S3 bucket that we created in the previous exercise from the dropdown for Alias Target. Select Simple for the Routing Policy and leave Evaluate Target Health set to No. After reviewing all the options, click the Create button.

NOTE Set Evaluate Target Health to Yes for production implementations and for a failover routing policy.

11. Now you have successfully hosted your Amazon S3 static website using your custom domain in Amazon Route 53. You can type your custom URL in your browser and press ENTER to see your new site.

12. As you did before, test your implementation by adding any word at the end. The error.html page should appear and display the custom error message.

13. You also should be able to reach your website index.html page by entering **/index.html** at the end of your custom URL.

Deploy a Static Website Using Amazon S3, Amazon Route 53, and Amazon CloudFront

Your website has become very popular, and you have customers worldwide now. You can add Amazon CloudFront to deliver globally with low latency and high performance from the nearby points of presence (PoPs). Also, you can secure access to your site by using SSL.

1. Log in to your AWS console and navigate to the Amazon CloudFront service. Click Get Started under the Web delivery method.

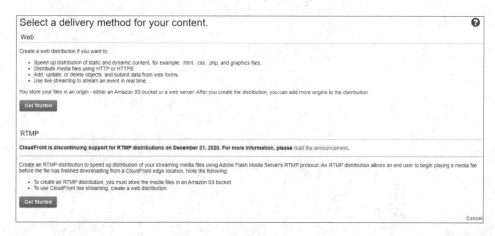

2. Enter your Amazon S3 bucket name in the Origin Domain Name field, and enter your domain name for the Origin ID—for example, amazondeveloper.ml— shown next. Restrict Bucket Access should be set to No for this exercise. Select Redirect HTTP to HTTPS for the Viewer Protocol policy, and allow only ready access by selecting GET in the Allowed HTTP Methods area.

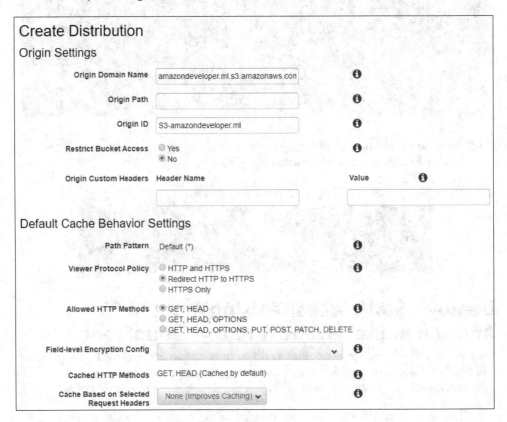

3. In the distribution settings, select Price Class for Use All Edge Locations. The CNAME should be your custom domain URL, and to create an SSL certificate, click the Request Or Import A Certificate With ACM button.

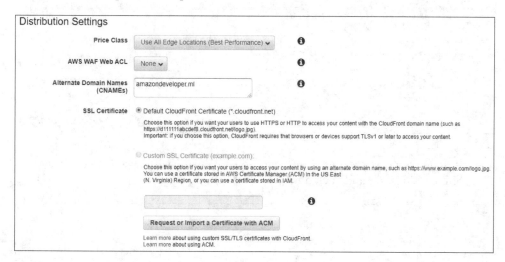

4. The Amazon Certificate Manager (ACM) page appears. Enter your domain name and click Next.

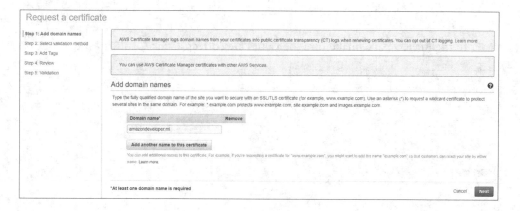

5. Select the DNS Validation method and click Next.

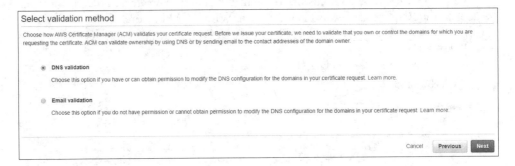

6. It is always a best practice to add tags, so add a name with a value like Website SSL Certification and click on the Review button.

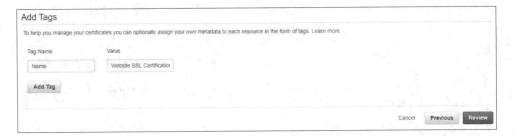

7. In the Review page, make sure the values are correct. Click Confirm And Request.

8. While the validation is in progress, you have an option to create a record in Amazon Route 53. Click on the Create Record In Route 53 button.

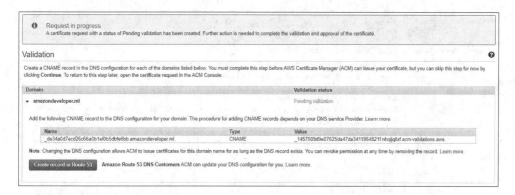

9. Here the values will be auto-populated for you to create the DNS record. Click the Create button to create the DNS record.

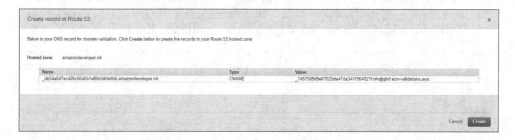

10. A success message appears. Since the validation status is in a pending state, you need to wait for couple of minutes.

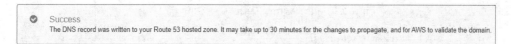

11. The SSL certificate status will be changed to Issued.

12. In the CloudFront page, select Custom SSL Certificate and select your ACM-issued SSL certificate.

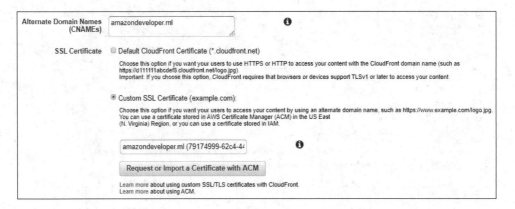

13. The Security Policy should be the recommended TLS. Select HTTP/2, HTTP/1.1, and HTTP/1.0 as supported HTTP versions, shown next. You can leave the logging off and select the Distributed state as Enabled. Click the Create Distribution button to create your Amazon CloudFront distribution.

 NOTE You need to enable logging for your production implementation and to troubleshoot any issues.

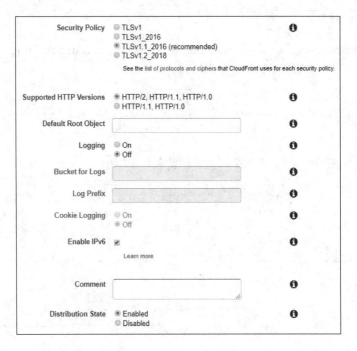

14. You will be redirected to the CloudFront Distributions page with your web distribution set to Enabled.

15. You may need to wait for a couple of minutes to see the status change from In Progress to Deployed.

16. Navigate to your Route 53 service page and update the A record, which is pointing to your Amazon S3 bucket in the Alias Target.

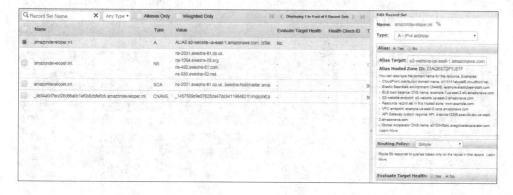

17. Update the Alias Target to your new CloudFront Web distribution from the dropdown and click Save Record Set.

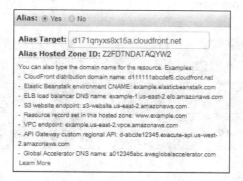

18. You can type your custom domain name—for example, amazondeveloper.ml—in your browser and press ENTER. Your Amazon S3 static website is now delivered through the Amazon CloudFront location nearest to you.

19. You can also reach your website using your index.html. For example, you can type **amazondeveloper.ml/index.html** and press ENTER to see the index page.

20. Similarly, you can directly reach your error page by appending **error.html** to your custom domain name.

21. As a best practice, let us test our implementation by inserting a random word like "cloudy" after the domain name. It should take you to the error.html page and display your custom error.

22. You can navigate to Amazon CloudWatch to see the performance of your CloudFront distribution.

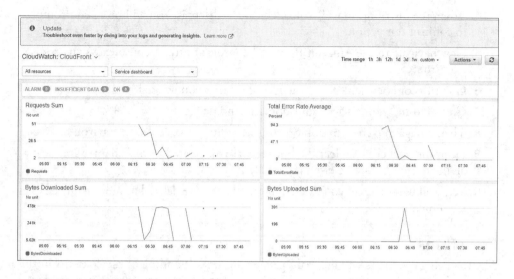

Chapter Review

This chapter began by explaining the advantages of using Amazon S3 to create a static website and then provided the detailed steps necessary to accomplish this. The chapter also provided the steps to create a custom domain and host it in Amazon Route 53 and then explained the steps to create a web distribution using Amazon CloudFront and the steps to create an SSL certificate using ACM. This experience will help you on the exam as well as in the real world.

Exercise

The following exercises will help you practice using Amazon S3 to deploy a website. You need to create an AWS account, as explained earlier, to perform these exercises. You can use the Free Tier when launching AWS resources, but make sure to terminate them at the end.

Exercise 20-1: Clean Up the Resources Created in This Chapter Using the AWS Management Console

1. Use your AWS account e-mail address and password to sign in and then navigate to the AWS CloudFront console at https://console.aws.amazon.com/cloudfront/.

2. Verify the AWS region by using the Region selector in the upper-right corner of the page.

3. From the navigation pane on the left, select the web distribution that you created in this chapter and choose to disable it. You will be prompted to confirm this action.

4. When the distribution is disabled, choose to delete it. You will be again prompted to confirm this action.

5. Now navigate to the Amazon Route 53 console at https://console.aws.amazon .com/route53/.

6. Go to Record Sets and delete the record set that you created in this chapter.

7. Go to Hosted Zone, select your domain, and delete it.

8. Then navigate to the Amazon S3 console at https://console.aws.amazon.com/s3/.

9. From the bucket list, select the bucket that you created in this chapter and delete all the objects before deleting the bucket.

10. Verify all the resources you created in this chapter are deleted to prevent any charges from incurring.

Questions

The following questions will help you gauge your understanding of the contents in this chapter. Read all the answers carefully because there might be more than one correct answer. Choose the best responses for each question.

1. You need to create a website in very short time. The website will have only static contents, including video and audio files. Which of the following options can you use to create a website quickly?

   A. Use AWS CloudFormation to create an EC2 instance and use RDS to deploy your website

   B. You can use Amazon S3 to upload HTML files, video files, and audio files and to host your static website

   C. Provision EC2 instances in each availability zone and use Elastic Load Balancer to route website requests

   D. Provision Amazon RDS with a read replica to host your website

2. You created and hosted a static website in Amazon S3, but you cannot access your website. What do you need to configure to make your static website hosted in Amazon S3 work? (Choose three.)

   A. You need to create and upload the index.html file

   B. You need to enable website hosting in Properties

   C. You need to add a bucket policy to make your bucket publically readable

   D. You need to upload video files to your Amazon S3 bucket

3. You created a static website hosted in Amazon S3, and your team want to use an existing URL instead of using the Amazon S3 URL. Which of the following AWS services can be used to achieve this?

    A. Amazon Athena

    B. AWS Lambda

    C. AWS Fargate

    D. Amazon Route 53

4. Your team hosts a static website using Amazon S3, and they want to display a user-friendly custom message when an error occurs. How can you achieve this?

    A. Delete the Amazon S3 bucket and create it again using the S3 Glacier storage class

    B. Encrypt your Amazon S3 bucket using Amazon S3 managed keys

    C. Upload a custom error.html page and enter the name in the Error Document box

    D. Create another Amazon S3 bucket to display the error message

5. Your customers are getting errors when accessing your static website, which is hosted on Amazon S3. How can you access the logs to perform analysis to troubleshoot and resolve this issue?

    A. Amazon S3 does not support logging

    B. Choose Enable Logging in Amazon S3 Properties Server Access Logging and provide the target bucket

    C. You need to delete the Amazon S3 bucket and create it with client-side encryption

    D. You need to set up a lifecycle policy to enable logging in Amazon S3

6. A company stores static web content in Amazon S3, and the security team requires the contents to be encrypted at rest. Amazon S3 provides which of the following options to encrypt the bucket objects? (Choose three.)

    A. Use server-side encryption with Amazon S3 managed keys (SSE-S3)

    B. Use server-side encryption with customer master keys (CMKs) stored in the AWS Key Management Service (SSE-KMS)

    C. Use server-side encryption with customer-provided keys (SSE-C)

    D. Use server-side encryption with an EC2 key pair (SSE-EC2)

7. Your team is planning to encrypt all static website objects being uploaded to Amazon S3, but they do not want to manage the encryption key. Which of the following options is available in Amazon S3 to achieve this?

    A. Amazon S3 Managed Keys (SSE-S3)

    B. AWS Key Management Service (SSE-KMS)

    C. Customer-provided keys (SSE-C)

    D. Client-provided keys (SSE-K)

8. Your security team wants to restrict access to your Amazon S3 bucket, which you have used for static website hosting. How can you restrict access to your bucket and still allow users to access your static website?

   A. Update your Amazon S3 bucket policy to deny access

   B. Create an IAM role that denies Amazon S3 access and attach it to this bucket

   C. You need to configure Amazon S3 to use SSL for more security

   D. Create a CloudFront web distribution with option Yes selected to restrict bucket access and use the origin access identity

9. You hosted a static website using Amazon S3 and used Amazon Route 53 to host your domain. You configured Amazon CloudFront to deliver the content. After reviewing the logs, you discovered that your website is being delivered from Amazon S3 and not from Amazon CloudFront. How can you fix this?

   A. Update the A record in Amazon Route 53 and choose Amazon CloudFront distribution as the Alias Target

   B. Delete the Amazon CloudFront web distribution and create an RTMP distribution

   C. Add a deny bucket policy to your Amazon S3 bucket

   D. You need to use the Amazon CloudFront URL

10. A global company has deployed their training website, which has thousands of large videos, using Amazon S3. Employees who are accessing content from a different country are complaining about video loading delays. How can you ensure that all employees have a seamless experience, regardless of which part of the world they log in from?

   A. Create a separate Amazon S3 bucket for training videos

   B. Use Amazon CloudFront to deliver the content

   C. Enable server-side encryption for the Amazon S3 bucket

   D. Upload the videos to Amazon DynamoDB

Answers

1. **B.** You can use Amazon S3 to upload HTML files, video files, and audio files and to host your static website.

2. **A, B, C.** You need to create and upload the index.html file and enable website hosting, and you need to add a bucket policy to make your bucket publicly readable.

3. **D.** You can use Amazon Route 53 to host your custom domain.

4. **C.** You can upload the custom error.html code and enter the name in the Error Document box.

5. **B.** Choose Enable Logging in Amazon S3 Properties Server Access Logging and provide the target bucket.

6. A, B, C. You can use SSE-S3, SSE-KMS, and SSE-C to encrypt your Amazon S3 bucket objects.

7. A. SSE-S3 is correct in this context.

8. D. You can create a CloudFront web distribution with Yes selected to restrict bucket access and use the origin access identity.

9. A. You need to update the A record in Amazon Route 53 and choose Amazon CloudFront distribution for the Alias Target.

10. B. You can use Amazon CloudFront to deliver the content.

Additional Resources

- **Amazon S3**   The recommended documentation for any AWS service, including Amazon S3, is the official AWS documentation, where you can always get the most up-to-date information.
  `https://docs.aws.amazon.com/s3/index.html`

- **Amazon S3 Blog**   This is the official blog for Amazon S3, which has all the latest information about different use cases in one place.
  `https://aws.amazon.com/blogs/aws/tag/amazon-s3/`

- **Amazon S3 Defense in Depth**   This blog shows you how to achieve defense in depth by applying multiple security controls to prevent data leakage.
  `https://twitter.com/Werner/status/971521075396751361` and
  `https://aws.amazon.com/blogs/security/how-to-use-bucket-policies-and-apply-defense-in-depth-to-help-secure-your-amazon-s3-data/`

CHAPTER 21

Deploying a Web Application Using AWS Elastic Beanstalk

In this chapter, you will learn
- Deploy a sample application in AWS Elastic Beanstalk
- Create, migrate, and deploy a custom application into AWS Elastic Beanstalk

This chapter will provide the steps to deploy a simple web application into the AWS Elastic Beanstalk service.

AWS Elastic Beanstalk

As a developer, you always want to spend more time developing applications for your customers instead of installing, configuring, and managing the infrastructure to run those applications. AWS Elastic Beanstalk enables you to deploy your application developed in Java, .NET, PHP, Python, Node.js, Ruby, and Go by just uploading the application source bundle, such as the .war file for Java. AWS Elastic Beanstalk automatically takes care of provisioning EC2 instances, the load balancer, database, scaling, and monitoring application health. You can use the Elastic Beanstalk CLI or AWS CLI or the AWS Elastic Beanstalk console to interact with AWS Elastic Beanstalk. It is free to use AWS Elastic Beanstalk, and you are charged only for the underlying AWS resources.

Deploy an Application in AWS Elastic Beanstalk

Let us deploy a sample application and explore the steps involved in using AWS Elastic Beanstalk.

1. Log in to your AWS console and navigate to AWS Elastic Beanstalk. You will see the list of environments and applications listed on this page if you provisioned them previously; if not, you will see the welcome page, shown next. Click on the Create Application button to get started.

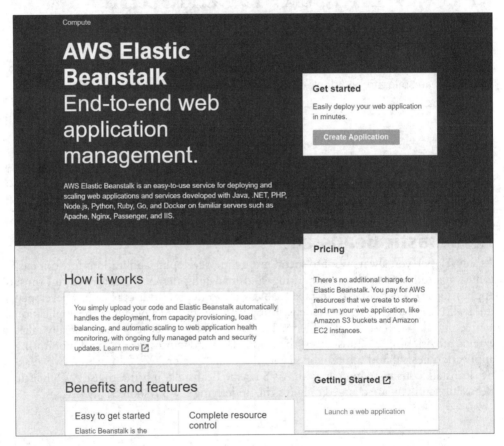

2. You will be provided with two options: Web Server Environment, which is the primary environment, and Worker Environment, which includes the Auto Scaling group and one or more Amazon EC2 instances to process additional requests using the SQS queue. Select Web Environment and enter **my-first-web-app** for

the application name and **sample** for the tag value. Select Java for the platform and leave the other values at their default settings. Click the Create Application button.

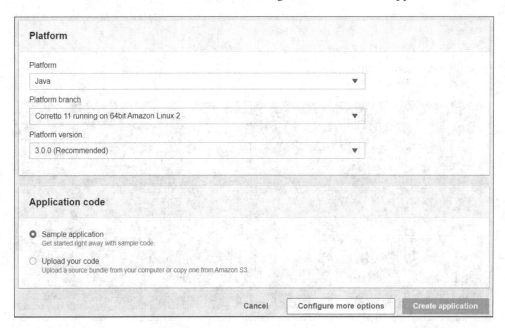

3. The environment provisioning begins by creating a security group and elastic IP. You can see that it uses an Amazon S3 bucket for environment data.

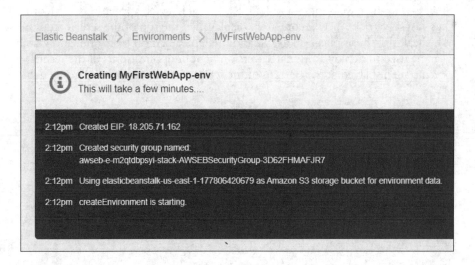

4. After few minutes, Elastic Beanstalk provisions EC2 instances and a load balancer if required. Once ready, you will see the message such as "Successfully launched."

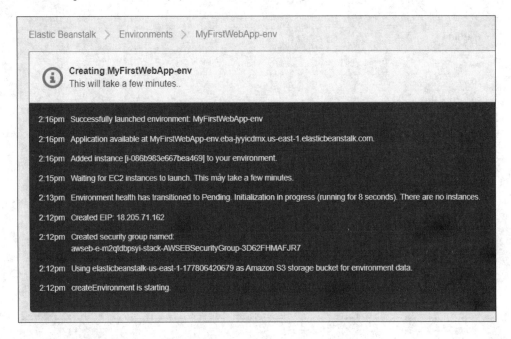

Elastic Beanstalk > Environments > MyFirstWebApp-env

ⓘ **Creating MyFirstWebApp-env**
This will take a few minutes..

2:16pm	Successfully launched environment: MyFirstWebApp-env
2:16pm	Application available at MyFirstWebApp-env.eba-jyyicdmx.us-east-1.elasticbeanstalk.com.
2:16pm	Added instance [i-086b983e667bea469] to your environment.
2:15pm	Waiting for EC2 instances to launch. This may take a few minutes.
2:13pm	Environment health has transitioned to Pending. Initialization in progress (running for 8 seconds). There are no instances.
2:12pm	Created EIP: 18.205.71.162
2:12pm	Created security group named: awseb-e-m2qtdbpsyi-stack-AWSEBSecurityGroup-3D62FHMAFJR7
2:12pm	Using elasticbeanstalk-us-east-1-177806420679 as Amazon S3 storage bucket for environment data.
2:12pm	createEnvironment is starting.

5. The environment page lists the configuration, logs, health, monitoring, alarms, managed updates, events, and tags of your new application. The application name—my-first-web-app—and its URL—MyFirstWebApp-env.eba-jyyicdmx .us-east-1.elasticbeanstalk.com—are displayed at the top of the screen. You can see the health of the application as Ok and the Upload And Deploy button, which can be used to deploy an updated version of your application. All the recent events are displayed at the bottom of the screen. You can access the newly deployed web application using the URL displayed—for example, MyFirstWebApp-env.eba-jyyicdmx.us-east-1.elasticbeanstalk.com.

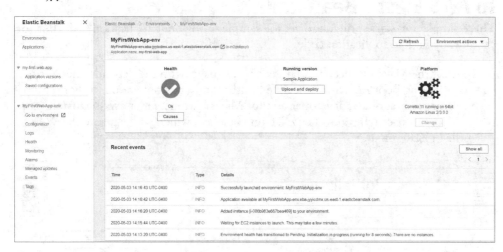

6. You will see the Congratulations message for the sample web application.

You have successfully deployed your first web application using AWS Elastic Beanstalk. Next we will migrate a sample application from your local machine to AWS Elastic Beanstalk.

Migrate and Deploy an Application to AWS Elastic Beanstalk

This example uses start.spring.io to get the sample spring boot application code, but you can use any sample application code.

1. Select the Maven Project and Java as the language, with the dependencies Spring and Spring Boot Actuator to see the health using a custom endpoint. For Group Name enter **com.awsdeveloper** and for Maven Artifact enter **aws-beanstalk-app**. Select war packaging and then click on Generate, which will generate the WAR file in ZIP format.

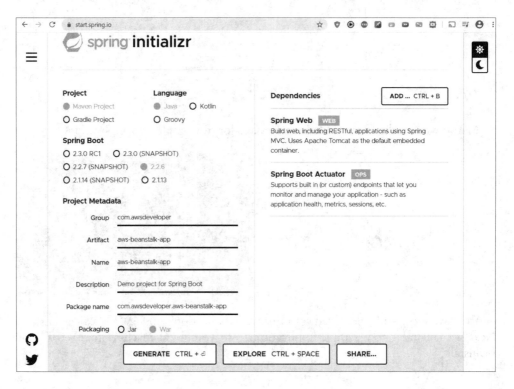

2. Go to the download location of the ZIP file in your local machine and unzip it. This example used IntelliJ IDEA, but you can use any IDE of your choice. Choose Open and select the location of the unzipped WAR folder.

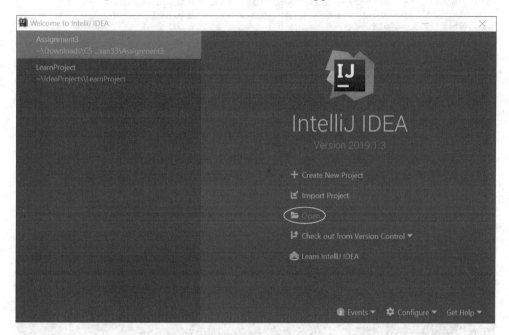

3. Explore the src, main, and java locations and see the standard Java files. Create another class by right-clicking com and selecting a new class for testing.

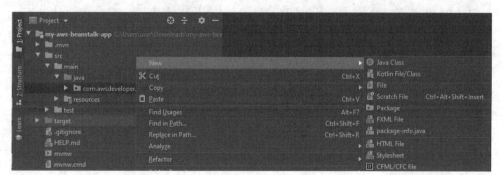

4. Create a new class called **HelloWorld.java** and enter the following code:

```
package com.awsdeveloper.myawsbeanstalkapp;

import org.springframework.web.bind.annotation.GetMapping;
import org.springframework.web.bind.annotation.RequestMapping;
import org.springframework.web.bind.annotation.RestController;

@RestController
@RequestMapping("/welcome")
public class HelloWorld {
    @GetMapping
    public String welcome() {
        return "Welcome to My AWS Elastic Beanstalk Application !!!";
    }
}
```

Then click the Maven on right side and select Package to create an updated WAR file. The WAR file location will be displayed at the bottom along with a build successful message.

```
[INFO] Assembling webapp [my-aws-beanstalk-app] in [C:\Users\user\Downloads\my-aws-beanstalk-app\my-aws-beanstalk-app\t
[INFO] Processing war project
[INFO] Webapp assembled in [559 msecs]
[INFO] Building war: C:\Users\user\Downloads\my-aws-beanstalk-app\my-aws-beanstalk-app\target\my-aws-beanstalk-app-0.0.
[INFO]
[INFO] --- spring-boot-maven-plugin:2.2.6.RELEASE:repackage (repackage) @ my-aws-beanstalk-app ---
[INFO] Replacing main artifact with repackaged archive
[INFO] ------------------------------------------------------------------------
[INFO] BUILD SUCCESS
[INFO] ------------------------------------------------------------------------
[INFO] Total time:  28.808 s
[INFO] Finished at: 2020-05-03T16:42:10-04:00
[INFO] ------------------------------------------------------------------------
```

5. Log in to your AWS console, navigate to the AWS Elastic Beanstalk service, and click on the Create Application button.

6. Enter **my-welcome-web-app** for the application name and add tags, which is a best practice to follow when creating any AWS resource. Select Tomcat for the platform and leave the other options at the default settings.

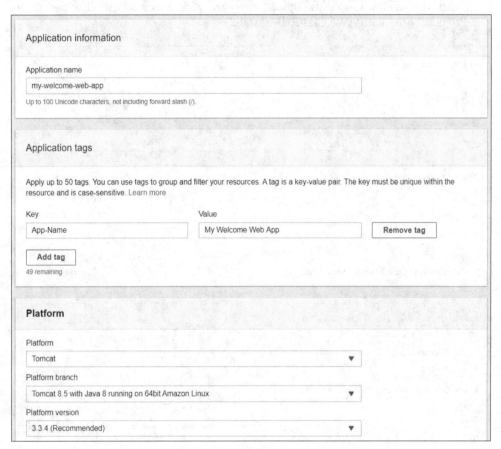

7. For the Application Code field, select the Upload Your Code option, which will display the source code origin. You can either use Amazon S3 bucket or upload your local file. Once you upload the WAR file that was generated in the previous step, you will see a successful upload message. Click the Create Application button to get started with AWS Elastic Beanstalk.

Application code

○ Sample application
Get started right away with sample code.

● Upload your code
Upload a source bundle from your computer or copy one from Amazon S3.

Source code origin

(Maximum size 512 MB)
● Local file
○ Public S3 URL

⌅ Choose file

File name : **my-aws-beanstalk-app-0.0.1-SNAPSHOT.war**
⊘ File successfully uploaded

Version label
Unique name for this version of your application code.

my-welcome-web-app-source

▸ **Application code tags**

Cancel   Configure more options   Create application

Within a few minutes, you will start seeing the resources like Elastic IP, EC2 instance, security group, and load balancer, if required. The application URL will also be displayed, along with the new application environment name.

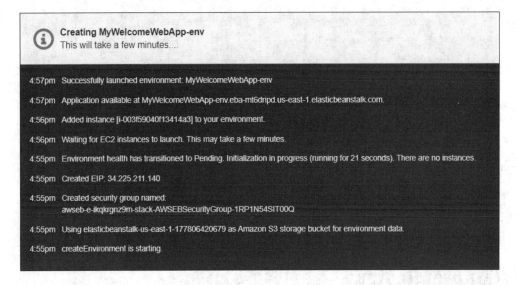

Once the provisioning is complete, it will display the environment page with health and platform details. You can deploy an updated version of your application using the Upload And Deploy button. You can view all the recent events at the bottom of the page. Also you have the option to explore configuration, logs, health, monitoring, alarms, managed updates, and events and tags.

8. Enter your new application URL—for example, **mywelcome.eba-mt6dripd .us-east-1.elasticbeanstalk.com/welcome**—in your browser. The welcome message that we set up in our HelloWorld.java will be displayed here.

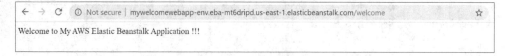

You can also see your application's health status using actuator in the URL—for example, mywelcome.eba-mt6dripd.us-east-1.elasticbeanstalk.com/welcome.

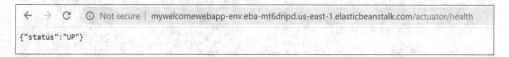

You have successfully created a Java Spring boot application and built it using Maven before packaging it as a WAR file. You then migrated the application to AWS Elastic Beanstalk using the upload option and deployed it successfully.

Chapter Review

This chapter began by explaining how developers can use AWS Elastic Beanstalk to easily deploy their application instead of spending time provisioning and managing its infrastructure. First, the chapter provided the steps to successfully create and deploy a sample Java application in AWS Elastic Beanstalk. It then explained the process to create a Java Spring boot application locally and upload it to AWS Elastic Beanstalk to build the web application.

Exercise

The following exercises will help you practice deleting the environments that you created in this chapter. There is no charge to use AWS Elastic Beanstalk, but you will need to pay for the underlying resources. You need to create an AWS account, as explained earlier, to perform these exercises. You can use the Free Tier when launching AWS resources, but make sure to terminate them at the end.

Exercise 21-1: Delete the AWS Elastic Beanstalk Environment Using the AWS Management Console

1. Use your AWS account e-mail address and password to sign in and then navigate to the AWS Elastic Beanstalk console at https://console.aws.amazon.com/ elasticbeanstalk/.

2. Verify the AWS region by using the Region selector in the upper-right corner of the page.

3. From the navigation pane on the left, choose Environments.

4. Select the environments that you created in this chapter.

5. Choose Actions, navigate to the bottom, and select Terminate.

6. Wait for a couple of minutes and then verify the environments are terminated.

7. Now select Applications and delete the applications that you created in this chapter.

8. Navigate to EC2 and verify the instances are terminated and the EIPs are released.

Questions

The following questions will help you gauge your understanding of the contents in this chapter. Read all the answers carefully because there might be more than one correct answer. Choose the best responses for each question.

1. Your developers are complaining that they are spending more time troubleshooting the application infrastructure then developing applications. Which AWS service can help your developers concentrate only on application development?

   A. Amazon EC2

   B. Amazon S3

   C. AWS Elastic Beanstalk

   D. Amazon DynamoDB

2. Your company security policy mandates that your application should not be accessible publicly. How can you make your AWS Elastic Beanstalk application private?

   A. You can use Amazon VPC, security group rules, network ACLs, and custom route tables to make it private

   B. You cannot make AWS Elastic Beanstalk applications private, so you need to use Amazon EC2

   C. By default, the AWS Elastic Beanstalk applications are private

   D. You can use AWS IAM to deny public access

3. Which of the following languages are supported in AWS Elastic Beanstalk? (Choose all that apply.)

   A. Java

   B. Node.js

   C. .NET

   D. Python

4. How do you provision EC2 instances, RDS databases, and a load balancer for your AWS Elastic Beanstalk application?

   A. Use the AWS CloudFormation template

   B. Use Terraform to deploy the infrastructure

   C. Use Ansible to provision those resources

   D. AWS Elastic Beanstalk automatically provisions the infrastructure

5. Your AWS Elastic Beanstalk application needs a database to store data. Which of the following databases are supported in AWS Elastic Beanstalk? (Choose two.)

   A. Amazon SageMaker

   B. Amazon RDS

   C. Amazon DynamoDB

   D. Amazon Cognito

6. Your company deployed applications in AWS Elastic Beanstalk and asked you to manage the platform updates. How can you manage the underlying platform to make sure it runs on the latest version?

   A. Opt in to automatically update the platform using AWS Elastic Beanstalk

   B. Set up a monitoring alarm to receive a notification when the new updates are available

   C. The AWS Elastic Beanstalk underlying platform cannot be updated

   D. You can use AWS CloudFormation to update the application platform

7. Your company is planning to migrate and deploy many applications in AWS Elastic Beanstalk. They asked you to find the cost of deploying 1,000 applications. Which is of the following is correct regarding the cost of AWS Elastic Beanstalk?

   A. It uses a pay-as-you-go pricing model

   B. You can use a reserved pricing model

   C. There is no cost; you pay only for the underlying AWS resources

   D. You can use a spot-pricing model

8. You have an application running in production that was deployed using AWS Elastic Beanstalk, and you added a new feature to your application in your local development environment. How can you deploy your updated application in AWS Elastic Beanstalk?

   A. You can use the Upload And Deploy button on the environment overview page

   B. You need to delete the existing application and deploy the updated application in AWS Elastic Beanstalk

   C. You cannot update your application in AWS Elastic Beanstalk

   D. You need to deploy the updated application in another region and use a load balancer

9. A company deployed many applications in AWS Elastic Beanstalk. One of the applications needs to be scaled using auto-scaling with minimum and maximum instances and a load balancer. How can you achieve this requirement?

   A. You need to delete and create the application again with a load balanced type

   B. You need to use Amazon EC2 instances to auto-scale your application

    C. You need to deploy another AWS Elastic Beanstalk and use Elastic Load Balancer

    D. You can edit the capacity configuration and update the environment type to load balanced by providing the required number of instances

10. Your company has deployed critical business application in AWS Elastic Beanstalk and tasked you with monitoring the application. How can you monitor this application and set up an alarm to alert you?

    A. You need to set up a cron job to monitor the application

    B. You need to set up Amazon CloudTrail for monitoring and to provide the alarm

    C. You can add an alarm from the AWS Elastic Beanstalk Environments page

    D. You cannot set up an alarm for the AWS Elastic Beanstalk application

Answers

1. **C.** AWS Elastic Beanstalk can be used to save your developers from carrying out infrastructure provisioning.

2. **A.** You can use Amazon VPC, security group rules, network ACLs, and custom route tables to make it private.

3. **A, B, C, D.** Java, Node.js, .NET, Python, PHP, Ruby, and Go are supported languages.

4. **D.** AWS Elastic Beanstalk automatically provisions the infrastructure for your application.

5. **B, C.** Amazon RDS and Amazon DynamoDB are supported.

6. **A.** You can opt in to automatically update the platform using AWS Elastic Beanstalk.

7. **C.** There is no cost to use AWS Elastic Beanstalk; you pay only for the underlying AWS resources.

8. **A.** You can use the Upload And Deploy option on the environment overview page to deploy the updated application.

9. **D.** You can edit the capacity configuration and update the environment type to load balanced by providing the required number of instances.

10. **C.** You can add an alarm from the AWS Elastic Beanstalk Environments page.

Additional Resources

- **AWS Elastic Beanstalk** The recommended documentation for any AWS service, including AWS Elastic Beanstalk, is the official AWS documentation, where you can always get the most up-to-date information.
  `https://docs.aws.amazon.com/elastic-beanstalk/index.html`

- **AWS Elastic Beanstalk Blog** This is the official blog of AWS Elastic Beanstalk, which has all the latest information about different use cases in one place.
  `https://aws.amazon.com/blogs/devops/tag/elastic-beanstalk/`

PART VII

Migrating Your Application and Database to AWS

In this chapter, you will learn
- Application migration
- Database migration

This chapter provides experience in performing real-time migration of an application and database from on-premises to AWS Cloud.

AWS Migration

Many organizations are migrating their on-premises workload, such as their business applications and databases, to the cloud. This chapter provides you with hands-on experience that will help you in the real world when performing migration, and includes information for the AWS certification. Enterprises follow many cloud migration strategies, including the 6R (Rehosting, Re-platforming, Repurchasing, Refactoring, Retain, and Retire) migration strategy. The first step in any migration strategy is the discovery of existing resources. The resources might be spread across many datacenters across the country, or across the globe, based on your business. Once you complete the discovery phase by finding all the resources and their dependencies, you need to split them into at least three categories, such as easy, medium, and complex. The easy resources might be simple applications and databases with less dependency, such as your development and proof-of-concept (POC) environments. The medium resources are applications and databases with fewer dependencies, such as your preproduction and user acceptance testing environments. The complex resources are often your business-critical applications and databases, which have many dependencies and a large impact on your business. Based on these classifications, you need plan your cloud migration strategy. Enterprises migrate the easy workloads first and gain experience with positive reinforcement of cloud migration. Next you can either migrate your medium or complex workload based on your experience and requirements.

The 6Rs of cloud migration and their advantages are as follows:

- **Rehosting** This is also called "lift and shift" because here you just take the image copy of your on-premises server and migrate it to AWS Cloud using AWS VM Import. It is the easiest migration option, since you are not changing the hosted application or database and there is either no change or few changes to this configuration. This option will provide the benefit of the cloud in terms of availability, scalability, and cost, but it does not offer the full potential of the native cloud and tools.

- **Re-platforming**   This is also called "lift, tinker, and shift" because you either migrate your application to Amazon Elastic Beanstalk or migrate your database to Amazon Relational Database Service (Amazon RDS). It will also provide the benefit of the cloud, but migrating large monolithic complex applications or databases requires more work.

- **Repurchasing**   This option involves purchasing and migrating to Software as a Service (SaaS) platforms such as Salesforce for customer relationship management (CRM) and Workday for human resource (HR) applications.

- **Refactoring**   This is also called "re-architecting" because it involves changing your big monolithic applications into small microservices or using a serverless architecture to improve business agility. It is the most expensive and complex migration strategy, but you get the full benefit of the cloud.

- **Retain**   This is also called "revisit" because you do nothing and revisit the issue at a later point in time. There are applications and databases that do not need to be migrated to the cloud because of a specific business requirement or a compliance and regulations requirement.

- **Retire**   You will be surprised to see how many resources are underutilized or not at all utilized in your datacenter, so you can shut down and move these out of your datacenter.

Application Migration

This section will take you through the step-by-step journey of "lift and shift" that you can practice using your AWS free account from your laptop or desktop. First you need to install VMware Workstation on your laptop or desktop and then create a virtual machine with any operating system. I created a Ubuntu Linux virtual machine and installed an Apache web server.

Log in to your Linux virtual machine and type **sudo apt install apache2** for Ubuntu or **sudo yum install apache2** for RedHat Linux. The Apache web server will be installed.

```
On-Premises-Linux  ×
Setting up apache2 (2.4.41-4ubuntu3) ...
Enabling module mpm_event.
Enabling module authz_core.
Enabling module authz_host.
Enabling module authn_core.
Enabling module auth_basic.
Enabling module access_compat.
Enabling module authn_file.
Enabling module authz_user.
Enabling module alias.
Enabling module dir.
Enabling module autoindex.
Enabling module env.
Enabling module mime.
Enabling module negotiation.
Enabling module setenvif.
Enabling module filter.
Enabling module deflate.
Enabling module status.
Enabling module reqtimeout.
Enabling conf charset.
Enabling conf localized-error-pages.
Enabling conf other-vhosts-access-log.
Enabling conf security.
Enabling conf serve-cgi-bin.
Enabling site 000-default.
Created symlink /etc/systemd/system/multi-user.target.wants/apache2.service → /lib/systemd/system/ap
ache2.service.
Created symlink /etc/systemd/system/multi-user.target.wants/apache-htcacheclean.service → /lib/syste
md/system/apache-htcacheclean.service.
Processing triggers for ufw (0.36-6) ...
Processing triggers for systemd (245.4-4ubuntu3) ...
Processing triggers for man-db (2.9.1-1) ...
Processing triggers for libc-bin (2.31-0ubuntu9) ...
root@ubuntu:/home/developer#
```

You can find the IPv4 IP address of your virtual machine using the ifconfig command. You need to note the IP address after the inet value to use in the next step.

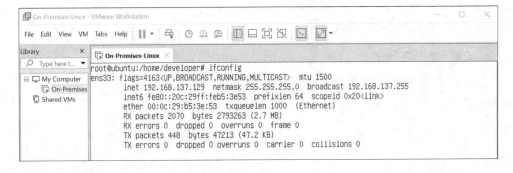

Open your browser and type the IPv4 IP address you noted in the previous step and press ENTER. You can see the default Apache page.

Apache2 Ubuntu Default Page

It works!

This is the default welcome page used to test the correct operation of the Apache2 server after installation on Ubuntu systems. It is based on the equivalent page on Debian, from which the Ubuntu Apache packaging is derived. If you can read this page, it means that the Apache HTTP server installed at this site is working properly. You should **replace this file** (located at /var/www/html/index.html) before continuing to operate your HTTP server.

If you are a normal user of this web site and don't know what this page is about, this probably means that the site is currently unavailable due to maintenance. If the problem persists, please contact the site's administrator.

Configuration Overview

Ubuntu's Apache2 default configuration is different from the upstream default configuration, and split into several files optimized for interaction with Ubuntu tools. The configuration system is **fully documented in /usr/share/doc/apache2/README.Debian.gz**. Refer to this for the full documentation. Documentation for the web server itself can be found by accessing the **manual** if the apache2-doc package was installed on this server.

The configuration layout for an Apache2 web server installation on Ubuntu systems is as follows:

```
/etc/apache2/
|-- apache2.conf
|       `--  ports.conf
|-- mods-enabled
|       |-- *.load
|       `-- *.conf
|-- conf-enabled
|       `-- *.conf
|-- sites-enabled
|       `-- *.conf
```

Open the /var/www/html/index.html file using Vim, and replace its content with the following sample HTML to display a custom page for the migration experiment.

```
<!DOCTYPE html>
<html language="english">
   <head>
      <meta charset="utf-8">
      <title>
         A Simple Apache Server Hosted on On-Premises
      </title>
   </head>
```

```
<body>
    <h1 align="left">
        <font face="Georgia" size="12" color="orange"><span style="font-
size:100%">AWS Migration from On-Premises</span></font>
    </h1>
    </body>
</html>
```

After saving the updated index.html file, you can either refresh the browser or type the IP address in another browser and press ENTER. You will see the custom page with "AWS Migration from On-Premises" in orange.

Now we are ready for the lift and shift migration. Select Export To OVF from the File menu of your VMware workstation to export the VM image for the migration.

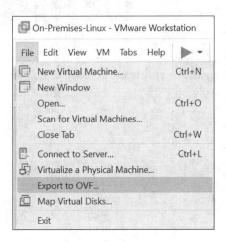

Three files are created, and we need the file with the .vmdk extension for our migration to AWS Cloud. This will take few minutes, based on the size of your virtual machine, and it exports the image in .vmdk format.

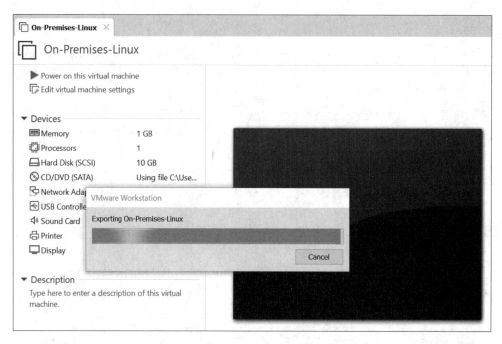

Log in to your AWS Management Console, navigate to the IAM service, and select Create Role. You need to create a vmimport role with the following trust policy, which provides the STS assume role access:

```
{
  "Version": "2012-10-17",
  "Statement": [
    {
      "Effect": "Allow",
      "Principal": {
        "Service": [
          "vmie.amazonaws.com",
          "ec2.amazonaws.com"
        ]
      },
      "Action": "sts:AssumeRole",
      "Condition": {
        "StringEquals": {
          "sts:Externalid": "vmimport"
        }
      }
    }
  ]
}
```

Once the role is created, attach the following policy to your newly created vmimport role, which grants Amazon S3 get access and Amazon EC2 copy image access:

```
{
    "Version":"2012-10-17",
    "Statement":[
        {
            "Effect":"Allow",
            "Action":[
                "s3:GetBucketLocation",
                "s3:GetObject",
                "s3:ListBucket"
            ],
            "Resource":[
                "arn:aws:s3:::'on-premises-migration'",
                "arn:aws:s3:::'on-premises-migration'/*"
            ]
        },
        {
            "Effect":"Allow",
            "Action":[
                "ec2:ModifySnapshotAttribute",
                "ec2:CopySnapshot",
                "ec2:RegisterImage",
                "ec2:Describe*"
            ],
            "Resource":"*"
        }
    ]
}
```

Once the policy is successfully attached to your vmimport role, navigate to the Amazon S3 console and create a bucket—for example, on-premises-migration—to upload the .vmdk file that was exported from the VMware workstation. Now choose the bucket and upload your .vmdk file.

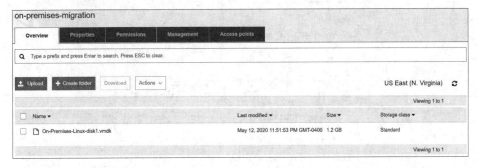

Create the following .json file as containers.json in your local machine:

```
[
    {
        "Description": "My On-Premises Server",
        "Format": "vmdk",
        "UserBucket": {
            "S3Bucket": "on-premises-migration",
            "S3Key": "On-Premises-Linux-disk1.vmdk"
        }
    }
]
```

PART VII

Execute the following command from your local machine using the AWS Command Line Interface (AWS CLI) by providing an appropriate file location for the .json file:
$ aws ec2 import-image

```
--description "My On-Premises server VM"
--disk-containers "file://C:\Users\user\Downloads\containers.json"
```

As soon as you enter the ec2 import-image command, you can see the status as "active" and the status message as "pending."

```
C:\Users\user>aws ec2 import-image --description "My On-Premises server VM" --disk-containers "file://C:\Users\user\Downloads\containers.json"
{
    "Description": "My On-Premises server VM",
    "ImportTaskId": "import-ami-053b01f85bea53c8e",
    "Progress": "2",
    "SnapshotDetails": [
        {
            "DiskImageSize": 0.0,
            "Format": "VMDK",
            "UserBucket": {
                "S3Bucket": "on-premises-migration",
                "S3Key": "On-Premises-Linux-disk1.vmdk"
            }
        }
    ],
    "Status": "active",
    "StatusMessage": "pending"
}

C:\Users\user>
```

After a few minutes, the status message will change to "validating" when AWS starts validating your image. You can see the status of your import-image using the aws ec2 describe-import-image-tasks command.

```
            }
        }
    ],
    "Status": "active",
    "StatusMessage": "pending"
}

C:\Users\user>aws ec2 describe-import-image-tasks
{
    "ImportImageTasks": [
        {
            "Description": "My On-Premises server VM",
            "ImportTaskId": "import-ami-053b01f85bea53c8e",
            "Progress": "19",
            "SnapshotDetails": [],
            "Status": "active",
            "StatusMessage": "converting"
        },
        {

            "Description": "My On-Premises server VM",
            "ImportTaskId": "import-ami-0fdd07b2eacef0f05",
            "Progress": "2",
            "SnapshotDetails": [],
            "Status": "active",
            "StatusMessage": "validating"
        }
    ]
}

C:\Users\user>
```

After a few minutes, the status message changes to "converting." The image validation is complete, and AWS starts converting your image.

```
C:\Users\user>aws ec2 describe-import-image-tasks
{
    "ImportImageTasks": [
        {
            "Description": "My On-Premises server VM",
            "ImportTaskId": "import-ami-053b01f85bea53c8e",
            "Progress": "19",
            "SnapshotDetails": [
                {
                    "Description": "My On-Premises Server",
                    "DiskImageSize": 1276295168.0,
                    "Format": "VMDK",
                    "Status": "active",
                    "UserBucket": {
                        "S3Bucket": "on-premises-migration",
                        "S3Key": "On-Premises-Linux-disk1.vmdk"
                    }
                }
            ],
            "Status": "active",
            "StatusMessage": "converting"
        },
        {
            "Description": "My On-Premises server VM",
            "ImportTaskId": "import-ami-0fdd07b2eacef0f05",
            "Progress": "19",
            "SnapshotDetails": [],
            "Status": "active",
            "StatusMessage": "converting"
        }
    ]
}

C:\Users\user>
```

The import status message will change to "updating" once the image conversion is complete.

```
C:\Users\user>aws ec2 describe-import-image-tasks
{
    "ImportImageTasks": [
        {
            "Description": "My On-Premises server VM",
            "ImportTaskId": "import-ami-053b01f85bea53c8e",
            "Progress": "20",
            "SnapshotDetails": [
                {
                    "Description": "My On-Premises Server",
                    "DiskImageSize": 1276295168.0,
                    "Format": "VMDK",
                    "Status": "completed",
                    "UserBucket": {
                        "S3Bucket": "on-premises-migration",
                        "S3Key": "On-Premises-Linux-disk1.vmdk"
                    }
                }
            ],
            "Status": "active",
            "StatusMessage": "updating"
        },
        {

            "Description": "My On-Premises server VM",
            "ImportTaskId": "import-ami-0fdd07b2eacef0f05",
            "Progress": "22",
            "SnapshotDetails": [
                {
                    "Description": "My On-Premises Server",
                    "DiskImageSize": 1276295168.0,
                    "Format": "VMDK",
                    "Status": "completed",
                    "UserBucket": {
                        "S3Bucket": "on-premises-migration",
                        "S3Key": "On-Premises-Linux-disk1.vmdk"
                    }
                }
            ],
            "Status": "active",
            "StatusMessage": "updating"
        }
    ]
}
```

The import task will end when the status is changed to "completed."

```
C:\Users\user>aws ec2 describe-import-image-tasks
{
    "ImportImageTasks": [
        {
            "Description": "My On-Premises server VM",
            "ImportTaskId": "import-ami-053b01f85bea53c8e",
            "Progress": "27",
            "SnapshotDetails": [
                {
                    "Description": "My On-Premises Server",
                    "DiskImageSize": 1276295168.0,
                    "Format": "VMDK",
                    "Status": "completed",
                    "UserBucket": {
                        "S3Bucket": "on-premises-migration",
                        "S3Key": "On-Premises-Linux-disk1.vmdk"
                    }
                }
            ],
            "Status": "active",
            "StatusMessage": "updating"
        },
        {

            "Description": "My On-Premises server VM",
            "ImportTaskId": "import-ami-0fdd07b2eacef0f05",
            "SnapshotDetails": [
                {
                    "Description": "My On-Premises Server",
                    "DiskImageSize": 1276295168.0,
                    "Format": "VMDK",
                    "Status": "completed",
                    "UserBucket": {
                        "S3Bucket": "on-premises-migration",
                        "S3Key": "On-Premises-Linux-disk1.vmdk"
                    }
                }
            }
        }
```

Navigate to the Amazon EC2 service page in the AWS Management Console and click on AMIs on the left pane below Images. You will see the new image that you imported. You need to select Owned By Me below the Launch button if the image is not displayed.

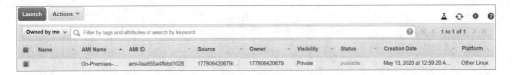

You have successfully migrated your application server to AWS, and you can create the server using the Launch button. In few seconds, your EC2 instance will be provisioned. You can view the EC2 instance from the EC2 instance page by clicking on Instances on the left navigation pane. Note the IPv4 public IP to launch the application and test the migration.

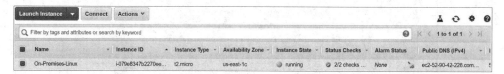

Enter the public IP in your browser, and you will see the custom message "AWS Migration from On-Premises" in orange. Open port 80 for the HTTP protocol to allow the ingress traffic in the EC2 security group if you get an access error.

You have migrated the server using the lift and shift strategy and tested it successfully. In the real world, you need to automate the process to migrate hundreds or thousands of application servers to AWS Cloud.

AWS Server Migration Service

You can also use AWS Server Migration Service or third-party migration tools to automate, schedule, and migrate your thousands of on-premises workloads to AWS Cloud. AWS Server Migration Service can be used to migrate instances from VMware-vSphere and Windows-Hyper-V to AWS. It provides automated, live replication that you can see from the AWS Management Console. AWS recommends using AWS Server Migration Service instead of using EC2 VM Import for migration, and it allows replication of your on-premises servers to AWS for up to 90 days for each server.

Database Migration

This section will demonstrate the "lift, tinker, and shift" strategy to migrate a PostgreSQL database from on-premises to AWS RDS. I have PostgreSQL database installed on my local machine, which has a database called northwind with 15 tables.

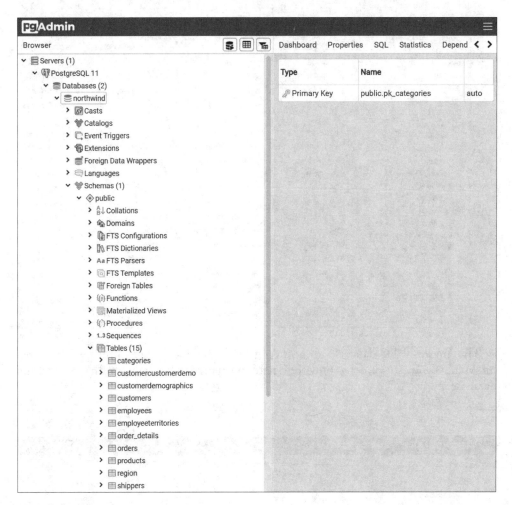

When I run a select query on the customer table in the northwind database, it displays 91 rows. I am planning to use AWS Database Migration Service to migrate the northwind PostgreSQL database into the Amazon RDS PostgreSQL database that I created using the AWS Management Console.

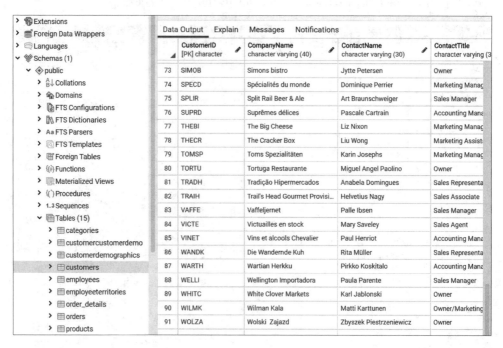

The Amazon RDS database connection is highlighted in orange in the pgAdmin tool browser. As you can see, it has only the default postgres database along with the rdsadmin database.

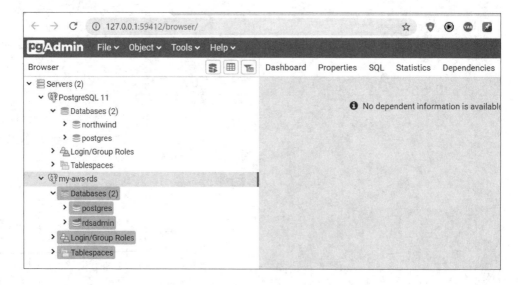

Log in to your AWS Management Console and navigate to the AWS Database Management Service. Select Replication Instances from the left pane, give it a name—for example, **my-db-replication**—and select the appropriate instance class based on your database size. You can leave the remaining values at the default settings and click the Create button.

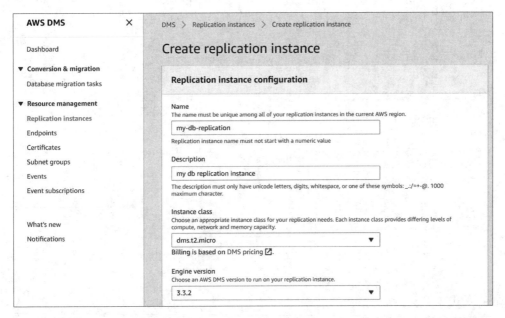

Next, create endpoints for both source and target databases. Select Endpoints from the left navigation pane. Select Source Endpoint and provide the endpoint identifier—for example, **my-onpremise-db**. Select Postgres for the source engine, and then enter the server name, port, username, and password along with the database name (in this case, northwind).

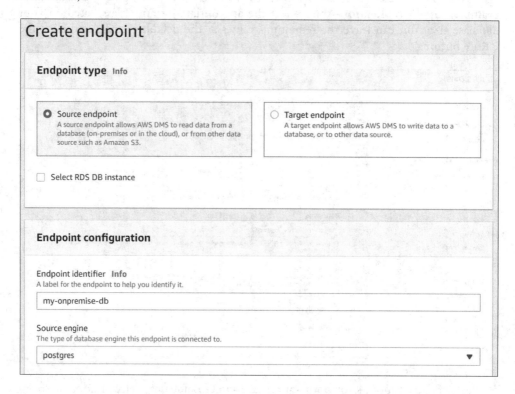

Again, select Endpoints from the left navigation pane and select Target Endpoint for the endpoint time. Select the Select RDS DB Instance checkbox. Select the RDS instance from the dropdown, and enter the name—such as, **my-aws-rds**—for the endpoint identifier. Select Postgres for the target engine from the dropdown and leave other options at their default settings.

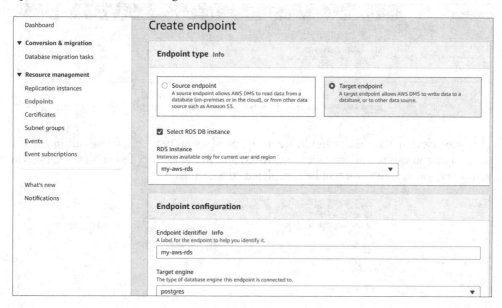

Now, you need to create the database migration tasks from the left navigation pane. For the task identifier, enter **on-prem-to-aws-db-migration** and choose Replication Instance from the dropdown. Select the previously created source database endpoint and target database endpoint from the dropdown. For migration type select Migrate Existing

Data, and you can select Replication if so desired. Leave the other options at their default settings, and click the Create Task button.

If you selected Start Task On Create in the previous step, then the task automatically starts, and you can see the overview, statistics, and metrics. After few minutes, based on your database size, the task will be completed successfully.

Now you can refresh the databases of your Amazon RDS DB connection and see the migrated northwind database. You can also see 15 tables are migrated along with the data.

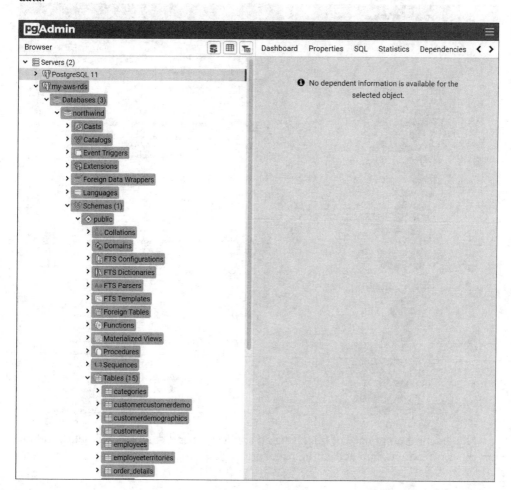

Now let us run the same select query on the customer table. As you can see, all the data migrated successfully.

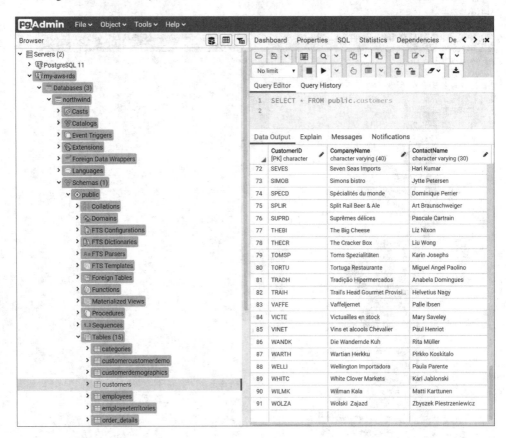

The practical experience of migrating an application and database will help you both on the certification exam and in the real world.

Chapter Review

This chapter began by explaining the 6Rs migration strategy that most enterprises follow. Then it explained step by step how to migrate a Linux web server from on-premises to AWS Cloud using the lift and shift migration strategy. And finally it provided the steps to migrate a PostgreSQL database from on-premises to Amazon RDS by using the lift, tinker, and shift migration strategy.

Exercises

The following exercises will help you delete all the resources that you created in this chapter. You need to create an AWS account, as explained earlier, to perform these exercises. You can use the Free Tier when launching AWS resources, but make sure to terminate them at the end.

Exercise 22-1: Delete the Amazon EC2 Instance Using the AWS Management Console

1. Use your AWS account e-mail address and password to sign in and then navigate to the AWS Elastic Compute Cloud Service (Amazon EC2) console at https://console.aws.amazon.com/ec2/.

2. Verify the AWS region by using the Region selector in the upper-right corner of the page.

3. From the navigation pane on the left, choose Instance.

4. In the center panel, select the instance. Then choose Actions and Instance State.

5. Select Terminate to terminate the instance.

Exercise 22-2: Delete Amazon RDS Using the AWS Management Console

1. Use your AWS account e-mail address and password to sign in and then navigate to the Amazon RDS console at https://console.aws.amazon.com/rds/.

2. Verify the AWS region by using the Region selector in the upper-right corner of the page.

3. From the navigation pane on the left, choose Databases.

4. In the center panel, select the database. Then choose Actions and then Delete to delete the database.

Exercise 22-3: Delete the Amazon S3 Bucket Using the AWS Management Console

1. Use your AWS account e-mail address and password to sign in and then navigate to the AWS Simple Storage Service (Amazon S3) console at https://console.aws.amazon.com/s3/.

2. From the navigation pane, choose Buckets.

3. In the center panel, select the bucket you want to delete.

4. First delete all the objects in the bucket, including the .vmdk image, then choose Delete Bucket.

Questions

The following questions will help you gauge your understanding of the contents in this chapter. Read all the answers carefully because there might be more than one correct answer. Choose the best responses for each question.

1. Your company has decided to migrate to AWS Cloud. What is the first thing they need to do to migrate all the resources, including applications and databases?

   A. Hire a cloud expert and expect him to migrate everything

   B. First migrate all the critical applications

   C. First migrate all the mission-critical databases

   D. Discover all your resources, like applications, databases, and dependencies

2. Your company plans to migrate their on-premises workload to AWS Cloud in two years. What kind of workload do you suggest migrating to AWS Cloud first?

   A. You suggest migating complex production applications that bring revenue to your company

   B. You suggest migrating production databases that have a high impact to your business first, followed by applications

   C. You suggest migrating all the resources from on-premises to the cloud at the same time

   D. You suggest migrating development and POC environments that have a minimum impact to your business to the cloud

3. Which of the following are part of the 6Rs of cloud migration? (Choose three.)

   A. Rehosting

   B. Re-platforming

   C. Relocation

   D. Refactoring

4. What service can you leverage to migrate your on-premises applications to AWS Cloud?

   A. AWS Server Migration Service

   B. AWS Ground Station

   C. AWS CloudHSM

   D. AWS Control Tower

5. Your company decided to quickly migrate the application and databases. Which of the following 6R migration strategies you would suggest to do the lift and shift?

   A. Re-platforming

   B. Rehosting

   C. Refactoring

   D. Retain

6. A company wants to take advantages of the cloud by using the Platform as a Service (PaaS) service from AWS but does not have time or resources to develop cloud-native applications. What migration strategy you would suggest?

A. Retire

B. Repurchasing

C. Rehosting

D. Re-platforming

7. Your company is planning to split all the big monolithic applications into microservices and serverless applications and leverage cloud-native development. What migration strategy you would suggest?

A. Repurchasing

B. Re-platforming

C. Refactoring

D. Rehosting

8. Your company has many legacy applications that are not supported in cloud environments and have stringent compliance regulations to keep the data on-premises. What migration strategy is suitable for this scenario?

A. Retain

B. Retire

C. Rehost

D. Repurchase

9. A company wants to migrate its customer relationship management (CRM), enterprise resource planning (ERP), and human resources (HR) software to the cloud instead of managing them on-premises. Which migration you would suggest for this scenario?

A. Rehosting

B. Refactoring

C. Re-platforming

D. Repurchasing

10. A company has discovered many redundant applications and databases during its cloud migration discovery phase. What kind of migration strategy you would suggest?

A. Retire

B. Repurchasing

C. Rehosting

D. Retain

Answers

1. **D.** You need to first discover all your resources, like applications, databases, and dependencies.

2. **D.** You need to migrate minimum-impact development and POC environments to the cloud and gain confidence.

3. **A, B, D.** Rehosting, re-platforming, and refactoring. (The other three are repurchasing, retain, and retire.)

4. **A.** You can use AWS Server Migration Service to migrate your on-premises applications to the cloud.

5. **B.** Rehosting, which is also known as lift and shift.

6. **D.** You can use re-platforming to migrate the application to AWS Elastic Beanstalk and the database to Amazon RDS.

7. **C.** The refactoring migration strategy allows you to build cloud-native and serverless applications.

8. **A.** When you have compliance regulations to keep some workload in on-premises, you can use the retain strategy.

9. **D.** The repurchasing strategy allows you to purchase CRM, ERP, or HR cloud-based solutions from the AWS marketplace.

10. **A.** You need to use the retire strategy to shut down and remove those servers from your datacenter.

Additional Resources

- **AWS Migration Whitepaper**   This whitepaper explains all the details you need to know to migrate your workload from on-premises to AWS Cloud.
  `https://d1.awsstatic.com/whitepapers/Migration/aws-migration-whitepaper.pdf`

- **AWS Enterprise Migration Strategy Blog**   These blogs provide all the best practices and steps to plan and migrate your enterprise workload.
  `https://aws.amazon.com/blogs/enterprise-strategy/category/enterprise-strategy/migration-enterprise-strategy/`

- **AWS Migration Best Practices**   This whitepaper explains all the best practices and strategies that you can follow for your cloud migration.
  `https://d1.awsstatic.com/Migration/migrating-to-aws-ebook.pdf`

PART VIII

Building, Deploying, and Debugging Cloud Applications

■ **Chapter 23** Hosting Secure Repositories Using AWS CodeCommit
■ **Chapter 24** Building an Application Using AWS CodeBuild
■ **Chapter 25** Deploying Applications Using CodeDeploy and CodePipeline
■ **Chapter 26** Building a Scalable and Fault-Tolerant CI/CD Pipeline

Hosting Secure Repositories Using AWS CodeCommit

In this chapter, you will learn
- AWS CodeCommit

This chapter will teach you how to create repository in AWS CodeCommit and pull, update, and commit changes from your local machine and AWS Cloud9.

AWS CodeCommit

As a developer, you often use a source code repository such as GitHub, GitLab, or other tools. AWS CodeCommit provides a private, secure, scalable, and managed source code repository that is closely integrated with other AWS services and third-party services. This section provides the step-by-step procedures to create a repository; pull code; create branches; and commit, compare, and merge your source code.

You need to access AWS CodeCommit from your local machine using either an HTTPS or SSH connection, so you need the relevant credentials. AWS recommends using a separate user instead of using your root credentials. So, first create a new user with required access, as shown in the following illustration. Log in to the AWS Management Console and navigate to the IAM service. Select Users from the pane on the left and click on the Add User button. Enter a username—for example, **Developer**—and choose the access type for both programmatic access and console access. Enter a password and click Next: Permissions.

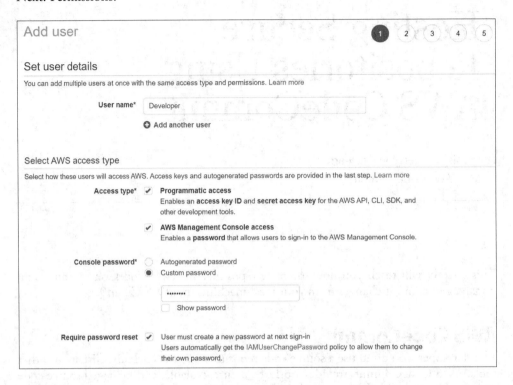

Here you can either create a custom policy or attach an existing policy directly. Search for CodeCommit in the filter policies, and choose AWSCodeCommitFullAccess. If you have a user with similar permissions, then you can select Copy Or Add This User To A group. Once you select the required permissions, click the Next: Tags button.

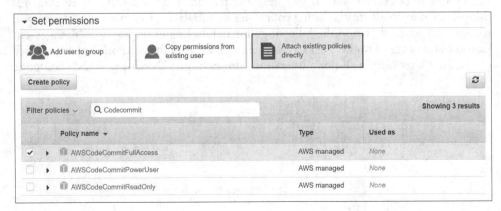

In accordance with the standard least-privilege security best practice, grant only the required permissions and click Create User.

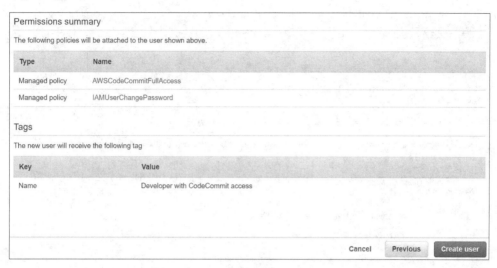

Once the user is created, click on the username, and scroll down. Upload your SSH public key and download the HTTPS Git credentials for AWS CodeCommit. You just need either one normally, but this example is using both HTTPS and SSH to access AWS CodeCommit.

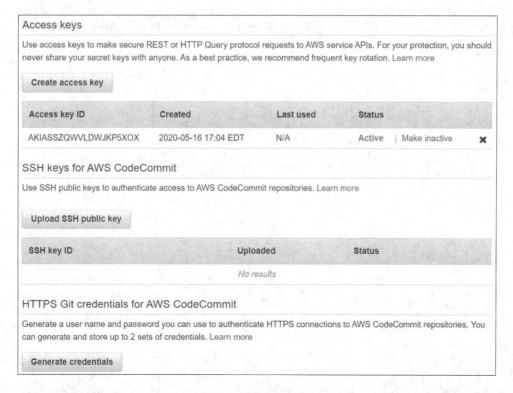

Click on Generate Credentials for HTTPS, and you will be prompted with the following screen. Here either copy the username and password or download the credentials.

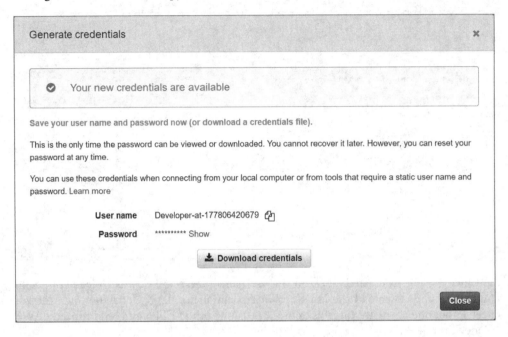

You can use Git Bash to simulate bash in Windows or use Terminal in Mac. Create and navigate to the .ssh folder and type **ssh-keygen -t rsa -b 2048 -C "aws-codecommit"**

and leave the defaults for other prompts. Now open your .pub file and copy the contents.

```
MINGW64:/c/Users/user/.ssh                                    —    □    ×

user@DESKTOP-5B87H96 MINGW64 ~/.ssh
$ ssh-keygen -t rsa -b 2048 -C "aws-codecommit"
Generating public/private rsa key pair.
Enter file in which to save the key (/c/Users/user/.ssh/id_rsa): aws-codecommit
Enter passphrase (empty for no passphrase):
Enter same passphrase again:
Your identification has been saved in aws-codecommit.
Your public key has been saved in aws-codecommit.pub.
The key fingerprint is:
SHA256:r/xeaXOlNYS/JbVXnNDD+SlOXrFR1/2WOK7nPsOjAkI aws-codecommit
The key's randomart image is:
+---[RSA 2048]----+
|            .+ B|
|            .oX=|
|            .oo&|
|     E    ooB*|
|    . S   + ===|
|     . o   = *=|
|      . o = =o.|
|      . . + + +o|
|      ooo . o.o|
+----[SHA256]-----+

user@DESKTOP-5B87H96 MINGW64 ~/.ssh
$ ls -al
total 25
drwxr-xr-x 1 user 197609    0 May 16 16:55 ./
drwxr-xr-x 1 user 197609    0 May 16 16:54 ../
-rw-r--r-- 1 user 197609 1823 May 16 16:55 aws-codecommit
-rw-r--r-- 1 user 197609  396 May 16 16:55 aws-codecommit.pub

user@DESKTOP-5B87H96 MINGW64 ~/.ssh
$ cat aws-codecommit.pub
ssh-rsa AAAAB3NzaC1yc2EAAAADAQABAAABAQDRcMyFm23hMC4NoNWZeEc+f8bIVAi7M95/FgrxSBv9J+O5OV9l2e
3PFnVQ/DSGMPQZoQlRAMM5BWtlZw3DAxwcFzffRzFwtOs7fZrM27ViMErAnRd1Oov9suty8lAgCRDIpgazBMAGMaqZ
C2YY5pGHao4xzE3NECf5//vAKxCKDxHFmNnuH8ny8hyzpcsmxoe5h4+Ng2jOVB7FiPqIjb19Er2+A6G5e5uVOOjqNM
uM5zqB5nzqdt/vXOsulpWArOzLlWVMOq3JSHF4seICEYZoxPSZwS/HBF/iwljtywLzeSLbTFbbTzhYuQM4ZCNvz2mD
dmVj9c/YoVzsny379QhL aws-codecommit

user@DESKTOP-5B87H96 MINGW64 ~/.ssh
$
```

Switch to your AWS Management Console and navigate to the IAM service. Select the Developer user and click Upload SSH Public Key. Paste your .pub content and click on Upload SSH Public Key. You can delegate repository access through the IAM role to other AWS accounts using AWS Security Token Service (STS), where an IAM user can assume the role when running commands.

Now log in to the AWS Management Console as the Developer user and navigate to the AWS CodeCommit service. Select Repositories on the left pane, and you will see the list of repositories that you created already.

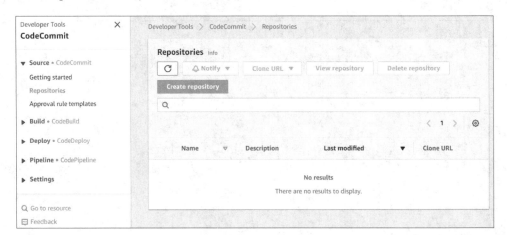

Enter **my-app-code-repository** for the name and provide a description. As a best practice add tags and click the Create button.

Repository settings

Repository name

my-app-code-repository

100 characters maximum. Other limits apply.

Description - *optional*

My Application Code Repository

1,000 characters maximum

Tags

Key	Value - *optional*	
Name	Apps	Remove

Add

Note the connection details for HTTPS.

HTTPS	SSH	HTTPS (GRC)

Step 1: Prerequisites

You must use a Git client that supports Git version 1.7.9 or later to connect to an AWS CodeCommit repository. If you do not have a Git client, you can install one from Git downloads. View Git downloads page ☑

You must have an AWS CodeCommit managed policy attached to your IAM user, belong to a CodeStar project team, or have the equivalent permissions. Learn how to create and configure an IAM user for accessing AWS CodeCommit. ☑ | Learn how to add team members to an AWS CodeStar Project. ☑

Step 2: Git credentials

Create Git credentials for your IAM user, if you do not already have them. Download the credentials and save them in a secure location. Generate Git Credentials ☑

Step 3: Clone the repository

Clone your repository to your local computer and start working on code. Run the following command:

git clone https://git-codecommit.us-east-1.amazonaws.com/v1/repos/my-app-   Copy 🗗

Additional details

You can find more detailed instructions in the documentation. View documentation ☑

Note the SSH connection details.

▼ **Windows**

Step 1: Prerequisites

You must use a Git client that supports Git version 1.7.9 or later to connect to an AWS CodeCommit repository. If you do not have a Git client, you can install one from Git downloads. View Git downloads page ⬚

You must have an AWS CodeCommit managed policy attached to your IAM user, belong to a CodeStar project team, or have the equivalent permissions. Learn how to create and configure an IAM user for accessing AWS CodeCommit. ⬚ | Learn how to add team members to an AWS CodeStar Project. ⬚

You must install a Bash emulator if you don't have one already installed.

You must have an SSH public-private key pair. Open the Bash emulator and create a public-private key pair using ssh-keygen. Learn how to generate public-private key pair ⬚

Step 2: Register SSH Public Key

Upload your SSH public key to your IAM user. Learn how to upload your SSH public key ⬚

Once you have uploaded your SSH public key, copy the SSH Key ID. You will need it in the next step.

Step 3: Edit Local SSH Configuration

Edit your SSH configuration file named "config" in your local ~/.ssh directory. Add the following lines to the file, where the value for User is the SSH Key ID you copied in Step 2.

```
Host git-codecommit.*.amazonaws.com
User Your-IAM-SSH-Key-ID-Here
IdentityFile ~/.ssh/Your-Private-Key-File-Name-Here
```

Step 4: Clone the repository

Clone your repository to your local computer and start working on code. Run the following command:

```
git clone ssh://git-codecommit.us-east-1.amazonaws.com/v1/repos/my-app-cc
```
Copy ⧉

Click on the Create File button to create your first example source code.

my-app-code-repository Info   Add file ▼

Name

Empty repository

Your repository is currently empty. You can add files to it directly from the console or by cloning the repository to your local computer, creating commits, and pushing content to the remote repository in AWS CodeCommit.

Create file

Type **welcome to your secure, private source code repository** and click Commit Changes.

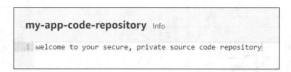

Now we are ready to clone our new repository using the HTTPS connection. From your local machine, type **git clone https://git-commit.us-east-1.amazoneaws.com/ v1/repos/my-app-code-repository** and press ENTER. Enter your HTTPS username and password and click OK.

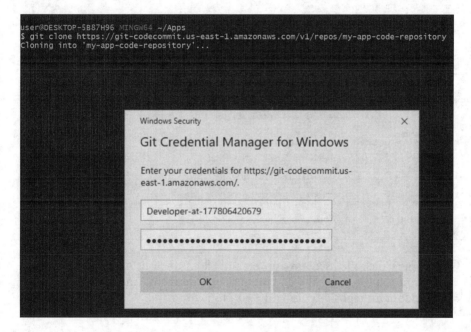

Navigate to your repository folder—for example, cd my-app-code-repository—and you can see the source file that we created earlier.

```
MINGW64:/c/Users/user/Apps/my-app-code-repository                          —    □    ×

user@DESKTOP-5B87H96 MINGW64 ~/Apps
$ git clone https://git-codecommit.us-east-1.amazonaws.com/v1/repos/my-app-code-repository
Cloning into 'my-app-code-repository'...
remote: Counting objects: 3, done.
Unpacking objects: 100% (3/3), done.

user@DESKTOP-5B87H96 MINGW64 ~/Apps
$ ls -al
total 20
drwxr-xr-x 1 user 197609 0 May 16 17:31 ./
drwxr-xr-x 1 user 197609 0 May 16 17:30 ../
drwxr-xr-x 1 user 197609 0 May 16 17:34 my-app-code-repository/

user@DESKTOP-5B87H96 MINGW64 ~/Apps
$ cd my-app-code-repository/

user@DESKTOP-5B87H96 MINGW64 ~/Apps/my-app-code-repository (master)
$ ls -al
total 5
drwxr-xr-x 1 user 197609   0 May 16 17:34 ./
drwxr-xr-x 1 user 197609   0 May 16 17:31 ../
drwxr-xr-x 1 user 197609   0 May 16 17:34 .git/
-rw-r--r-- 1 user 197609  54 May 16 17:34 first-app.txt

user@DESKTOP-5B87H96 MINGW64 ~/Apps/my-app-code-repository (master)
$ cat first-app.txt
welcome to your secure, private source code repository
user@DESKTOP-5B87H96 MINGW64 ~/Apps/my-app-code-repository (master)
$ git status
On branch master
Your branch is up to date with 'origin/master'.

nothing to commit, working tree clean

user@DESKTOP-5B87H96 MINGW64 ~/Apps/my-app-code-repository (master)
$ git remote -v
origin  https://git-codecommit.us-east-1.amazonaws.com/v1/repos/my-app-code-repository (fetch)
origin  https://git-codecommit.us-east-1.amazonaws.com/v1/repos/my-app-code-repository (push)

user@DESKTOP-5B87H96 MINGW64 ~/Apps/my-app-code-repository (master)
$
```

Create a new file called **second-app.txt** and add it to git using the git add command. Then commit the file using the git commit -m "comment" and push it to the remote AWS CodeCommit repository using the git push command.

```
MINGW64:/c/Users/user/Apps/my-app-code-repository                          —    □    ×

user@DESKTOP-5B87H96 MINGW64 ~/Apps/my-app-code-repository (master)
$ echo "Hello World, this is my second app source code" > second-app.txt

user@DESKTOP-5B87H96 MINGW64 ~/Apps/my-app-code-repository (master)
$ ls -al
total 10
drwxr-xr-x 1 user 197609  0 May 16 17:42 ./
drwxr-xr-x 1 user 197609  0 May 16 17:31 ../
drwxr-xr-x 1 user 197609  0 May 16 17:36 .git/
-rw-r--r-- 1 user 197609 54 May 16 17:34 first-app.txt
-rw-r--r-- 1 user 197609 47 May 16 17:42 second-app.txt

user@DESKTOP-5B87H96 MINGW64 ~/Apps/my-app-code-repository (master)
$ git status
On branch master
Your branch is up to date with 'origin/master'.

Untracked files:
  (use "git add <file>..." to include in what will be committed)

        second-app.txt

nothing added to commit but untracked files present (use "git add" to track)

user@DESKTOP-5B87H96 MINGW64 ~/Apps/my-app-code-repository (master)
$ git add .
warning: LF will be replaced by CRLF in second-app.txt.
The file will have its original line endings in your working directory

user@DESKTOP-5B87H96 MINGW64 ~/Apps/my-app-code-repository (master)
$ git commit -m "added my second app source code"
[master 1e956a5] added my second app source code
 1 file changed, 1 insertion(+)
 create mode 100644 second-app.txt

user@DESKTOP-5B87H96 MINGW64 ~/Apps/my-app-code-repository (master)
$ git push
Enumerating objects: 4, done.
Counting objects: 100% (4/4), done.
Delta compression using up to 4 threads
Compressing objects: 100% (2/2), done.
Writing objects: 100% (3/3), 340 bytes | 170.00 KiB/s, done.
Total 3 (delta 0), reused 0 (delta 0)
To https://git-codecommit.us-east-1.amazonaws.com/v1/repos/my-app-code-repository
   df7cd55..1e956a5  master -> master

user@DESKTOP-5B87H96 MINGW64 ~/Apps/my-app-code-repository (master)
$ |
```

Navigate to the AWS CodeCommit service in the AWS Management Console and select my-app-code-repository. You can see the new source code for second-app.txt that you pushed from your local machine.

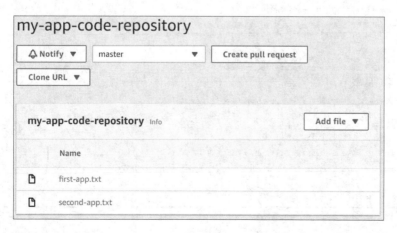

Click on the second-app.txt, and you can see the code.

Now, let us clone the AWS CodeCommit repository using SSH, where you do not need to enter your credentials each time.

```
Host git-codecommit.*.amazonaws.com
User ABCDEFGHIJKLMNOP (Your SSH username)
IdentityFile ~/.ssh/aws-codecommit (Your SSH keyname)
```

Navigate to the .ssh folder and create the config file, as shown here.

```
MINGW64:/c/Users/user/my-app-code-repository                                      —    □    ×

user@DESKTOP-5B87H96 MINGW64 ~/.ssh
$ cat config
Host git-codecommit.*.amazonaws.com
User APKASSZQWVLDVOAWDWET
IdentityFile ~/.ssh/aws-codecommit

user@DESKTOP-5B87H96 MINGW64 ~/.ssh
$ cd ..

user@DESKTOP-5B87H96 MINGW64 ~
$ git clone ssh://git-codecommit.us-east-1.amazonaws.com/v1/repos/my-app-code-repository
Cloning into 'my-app-code-repository'...
remote: Counting objects: 6, done.
Receiving objects: 100% (6/6), 598 bytes | 99.00 KiB/s, done.

user@DESKTOP-5B87H96 MINGW64 ~
$ cd my-app-code-repository/

user@DESKTOP-5B87H96 MINGW64 ~/my-app-code-repository (master)
$ ls -al
total 30
drwxr-xr-x 1 user 197609  0 May 16 18:33 ./
drwxr-xr-x 1 user 197609  0 May 16 18:33 ../
drwxr-xr-x 1 user 197609  0 May 16 18:33 .git/
-rw-r--r-- 1 user 197609 54 May 16 18:33 first-app.txt
-rw-r--r-- 1 user 197609 48 May 16 18:33 second-app.txt

user@DESKTOP-5B87H96 MINGW64 ~/my-app-code-repository (master)
$ echo "Hello All, this is my third application source code" > third-app.txt

user@DESKTOP-5B87H96 MINGW64 ~/my-app-code-repository (master)
$ git status
On branch master
Your branch is up to date with 'origin/master'.

Untracked files:
  (use "git add <file>..." to include in what will be committed)

        third-app.txt

nothing added to commit but untracked files present (use "git add" to track)

user@DESKTOP-5B87H96 MINGW64 ~/my-app-code-repository (master)
$ git add .
warning: LF will be replaced by CRLF in third-app.txt.
The file will have its original line endings in your working directory

user@DESKTOP-5B87H96 MINGW64 ~/my-app-code-repository (master)
$ git commit -m "adding my third app source code"
[master 6d39d15] adding my third app source code
 1 file changed, 1 insertion(+)
 create mode 100644 third-app.txt

user@DESKTOP-5B87H96 MINGW64 ~/my-app-code-repository (master)
$ git push
Enumerating objects: 4, done.
Counting objects: 100% (4/4), done.
Delta compression using up to 4 threads
Compressing objects: 100% (3/3), done.
Writing objects: 100% (3/3), 376 bytes | 188.00 KiB/s, done.
Total 3 (delta 0), reused 0 (delta 0)
To ssh://git-codecommit.us-east-1.amazonaws.com/v1/repos/my-app-code-repository
   1e956a5..6d39d15  master -> master

user@DESKTOP-5B87H96 MINGW64 ~/my-app-code-repository (master)
$
```

Create a new source code file called **third-app.txt** and add it using the git add command. Then you need to commit it using the git commit -m "comment" and push the new code to your AWS CodeCommit remote repository using the git push command.

Navigate to the AWS CodeCommit service in the AWS Management Console and select Code from the left pane. You can see third-app.txt is added to the repository.

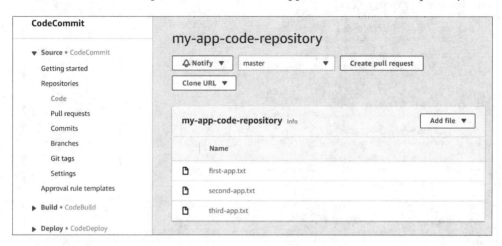

Now we will use AWS Cloud9, which is an integrated development environment (IDE), to work on your repository using a browser instead of using your local machine. Navigate to AWS Cloud9 from the AWS Management Console and click Create Environment. For the name, enter **my-cloud-ide** and click Next Step.

Leave all the default values selected and click Next Step.

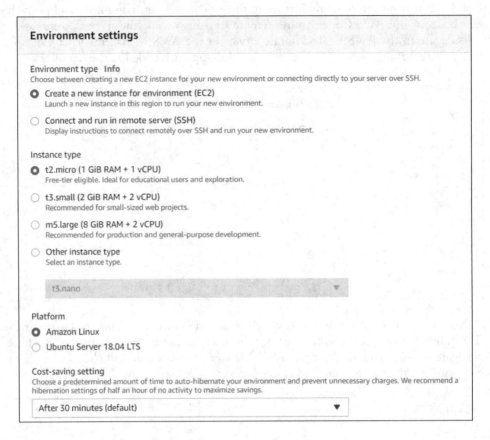

Review all the details and click Create Environment.

The AWS Cloud9 IDE environment creation is in progress.

AWS Cloud9 IDE is ready, and you are logged in as the Developer user by default. You can clone the repository using the git clone HTTPS command. Create a new branch using the git branch my-new-branch command and navigate to the new branch. Create a new source code my-cloud9-app.txt and add it using the git add command. You can commit the code using the git commit -m "comment" and use git push to push the new source code.

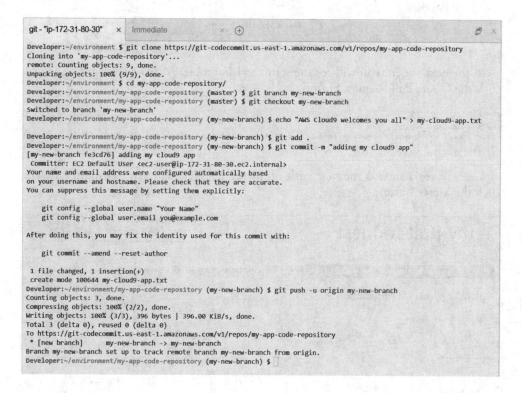

```
git - "ip-172-31-80-30"    ×    Immediate              ×   ⊕                                          ⊟  ×

Developer:~/environment $ git clone https://git-codecommit.us-east-1.amazonaws.com/v1/repos/my-app-code-repository
Cloning into 'my-app-code-repository'...
remote: Counting objects: 9, done.
Unpacking objects: 100% (9/9), done.
Developer:~/environment $ cd my-app-code-repository/
Developer:~/environment/my-app-code-repository (master) $ git branch my-new-branch
Developer:~/environment/my-app-code-repository (master) $ git checkout my-new-branch
Switched to branch 'my-new-branch'
Developer:~/environment/my-app-code-repository (my-new-branch) $ echo "AWS Cloud9 welcomes you all" > my-cloud9-app.txt

Developer:~/environment/my-app-code-repository (my-new-branch) $ git add .
Developer:~/environment/my-app-code-repository (my-new-branch) $ git commit -m "adding my cloud9 app"
[my-new-branch fe3cd76] adding my cloud9 app
 Committer: EC2 Default User <ec2-user@ip-172-31-80-30.ec2.internal>
Your name and email address were configured automatically based
on your username and hostname. Please check that they are accurate.
You can suppress this message by setting them explicitly:

    git config --global user.name "Your Name"
    git config --global user.email you@example.com

After doing this, you may fix the identity used for this commit with:

    git commit --amend --reset-author

 1 file changed, 1 insertion(+)
 create mode 100644 my-cloud9-app.txt
Developer:~/environment/my-app-code-repository (my-new-branch) $ git push -u origin my-new-branch
Counting objects: 3, done.
Compressing objects: 100% (2/2), done.
Writing objects: 100% (3/3), 396 bytes | 396.00 KiB/s, done.
Total 3 (delta 0), reused 0 (delta 0)
To https://git-codecommit.us-east-1.amazonaws.com/v1/repos/my-app-code-repository
 * [new branch]      my-new-branch -> my-new-branch
Branch my-new-branch set up to track remote branch my-new-branch from origin.
Developer:~/environment/my-app-code-repository (my-new-branch) $ ▯
```

Since we created the new source code in a branch, you need to create a pull request on the AWS CodeCommit page. Select the destination as master and the source as my-new-branch. Click the Compare button before creating the pull request.

In the next screen, you will see the status as Mergeable. After reviewing the changes, click the Create Pull Request button.

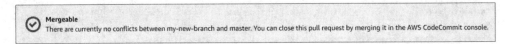

You will see a success message with no merge conflicts. After reviewing the details, click the Merge button.

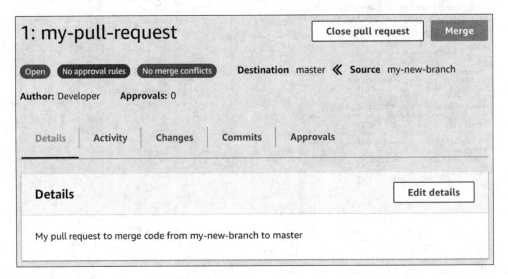

Here you have three merge options to select from. Choose Fast Forward Merge, which is the default git merge strategy, and click on the Merge Pull Request button. You can use other merge strategies, such as squash and merge or three-way merge, based on your requirements.

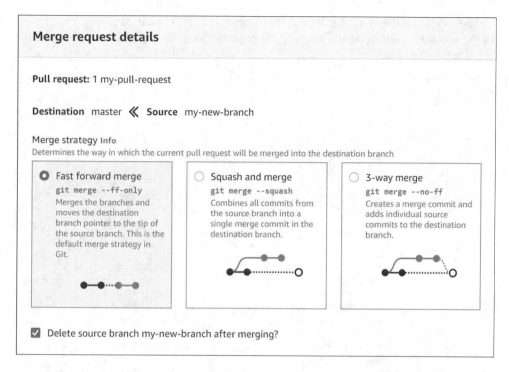

You can see that my-new-branch has been merged into the master with a success message.

When you click on Code on the left pane, you can see the new source code my-cloud9-app that we created using the AWS Cloud9 IDE.

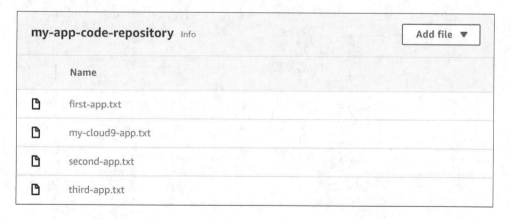

You can see all the commits by selecting Commits from the left pane. You can explore all the commits from here, and you can list commits from the master or from any of the branches.

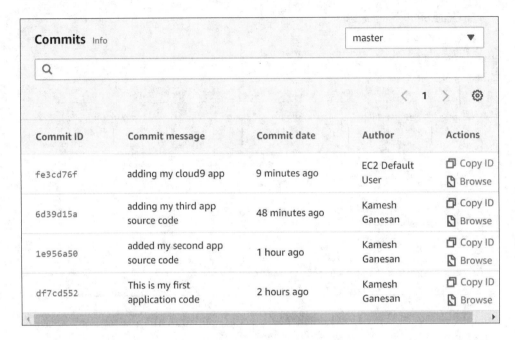

You can explore all your branches by choosing Branches from left navigation pane.

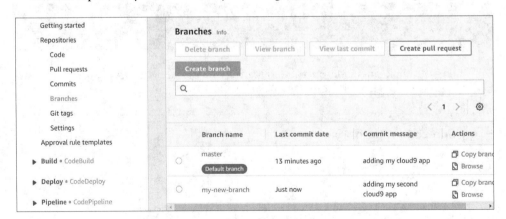

You can configure notification rules for a repository when comments are added to commits or pull requests. You also can set up a notification when a pull request is created or merged, in addition to the creation, deletion, or updating of branches. An Amazon CloudWatch Events rule and Amazon SNS topic can be configured for notifications. The existing Git repository can be migrated to the AWS CodeCommit repository. First, you need to create a repository in AWS CodeCommit. Then you need to clone the existing repository in your local machine and push it to AWS CodeCommit.

Chapter Review

This chapter began by explaining what AWS CodeCommit is. You created an IAM user with just AWS CodeCommit access. Then you went through the process of creating a repository; new source code; a new branch; and pull requests, as well as adding, committing, pushing, and comparing the source code using AWS CodeCommit from your local machine, as well as from the interactive development environment AWS Cloud9.

You gained the experience of creating a source code repository using AWS CodeCommit service and cloned it to your local machine as well as to AWS Cloud9 IDE. You also created sample source code from different places and pushed it to your AWS CodeCommit remote repository. This experience will help you in AWS Developer certification as well as in real world when you start working on AWS cloud environment.

Exercises

The following exercises will help you practice using AWS CodeCommit. You need to create an AWS account, as explained earlier, before performing these exercises. You can use the Free Tier when launching AWS resources, but make sure to terminate them at the end.

Exercise 23-1: Delete the AWS CodeCommit Repository Using the AWS Management Console

1. Use your AWS account e-mail address and password to sign in to the AWS account and then navigate to the AWS CodeCommit console at https://console .aws.amazon.com/codecommit/.

2. Verify the AWS region by using the Region selector in the upper-right corner of the page.

3. From the navigation pane on the left, choose Repositories.

4. Choose Settings.

5. Navigate to the Delete Repository on the General tab. Choose Delete Repository.

6. Enter delete in the popup window and choose to delete.

Exercise 23-2: Delete the AWS Cloud9 Environment Using the AWS Management Console

1. Use your AWS account e-mail address and password to sign in to the AWS account and then navigate to the AWS Cloud9 console at https://console.aws .amazon.com/cloud9/.

2. Verify the AWS region by using the Region selector in the upper-right corner of the page.

3. From the navigation pane on the left, choose Environments.

4. Choose the environment you want to delete and click on the Delete button.

5. Enter delete in the popup window and choose to delete. The Amazon EC2 instance will be terminated by AWS Cloud9.

Questions

The following questions will help you gauge your understanding of the contents in this chapter. Read all the answers carefully because there might be more than one correct answer. Choose the best responses for each question.

1. Your company security team directed you to find a solution for storing source code securely, which should be a managed solution for everyone in your team who is spread across the globe. They should be able to use their existing git tools. Which AWS service you will suggest?

   A. AWS CodeBuild

   B. AWS CodeDeploy

   C. AWS CodePipeline

   D. AWS CodeCommit

2. Your company security policy mandates that the source code should not be cloned to your local machine. Your company is using AWS CodeCommit to store and share the source code repository securely across the team. Which AWS service you would recommend to clone and work on your source code securely?

   A. Amazon Athena

   B. AWS Cloud9

   C. AWS Outposts

   D. AWS Config

3. Your company is developing a new product, and many teams are working on different features of this product. As a developer, how you will make sure each team can work on their feature set and merge the source code once ready in AWS CodeCommit?

   A. Create a new repository for each team and combine when ready

   B. Create a different branch for each team and merge to the master when ready

   C. Ask each team to work on their local machine and upload to AWS CodeCommit when ready

   D. AWS CodeCommit does not support merging the source code

4. A team member cloned the application source code repository to a local machine and made all the necessary changes. The team member is getting an error while pushing the code to AWS CodeCommit. What is the correct sequence of git command execution?

   A. Git add – Git commit – Git push

   B. Git add – Git push – Git commit

   C. Git commit – Git Push – Git add

   D. Git push – Git add – Git commit

5. Your development team should be able to push changes to only their branches but not allowed to push changes or create a merge pull request to the master branch in AWS CodeCommit. How can you achieve this in AWS?

   A. Create a policy with allow push, merge, and add to the master and attach it to the developer IAM group

   B. Enable server-side encryption for the master branch

   C. Enable client-side encryption for the master branch

   D. Create a policy with deny push, merge; add to the master; and attach it to the developer IAM group

6. Your company has many AWS accounts and created the AWS CodeCommit repository in the development AWS account. How can you allow cross-account access to the development account AWS CodeCommit repository?

   A. Create an IAM role to delegate access and use AWS STS to assume the role in another AWS accounts

   B. Create a VPN connection between all your AWS accounts to enable cross-account access

   C. Create VPC peering to connect all your AWS accounts to enable cross-account access

   D. Create an IAM user in each account and grant access directly from the development AWS account

7. What three merge strategies are available in AWS CodeCommit? (Choose three.)

   A. Two-way merge strategy

   B. Squash merge strategy

   C. Three-way merge strategy

   D. Fast-forward merge strategy

8. A DevOps team configured an AWS CodeCommit repository, and they want to receive a notification whenever a developer commits or merges changes to the master. Which of the following steps will alert the DevOps team of this?

   A. Set up an Amazon CloudWatch events rule to be triggered and add the Amazon SNS topic as the notification target

   B. Set up Amazon CloudTrail for repository changes and add the Amazon SNS topic as the notification target

   C. Set up AWS Lambda to be triggered every five minutes and add the Amazon SNS topic as the notification target

   D. Set up AWS Batch to be triggered and add the Amazon SNS topic as the notification target

9. What two protocols are supported in AWS CodeCommit to clone a repository? (Choose two.)

   A. TCP

   B. HTTPS

   C. HTTP

   D. SSH

10. You have an existing Git repository that you want to migrate to AWS CodeCommit. What migration steps do you need to perform? (Choose three.)

    A. Create an AWS CodeCommit repository

    B. Clone the existing Git repository in your local machine

    C. Delete the AWS CodeCommit repository

    D. Push the changes to your AWS CodeCommit repository

Answers

1. **D.** You can use AWS CodeCommit to collaborate on the source code with other team members.

2. **B.** AWS Cloud9 provides a secure integrated development environment in AWS Cloud.

3. **B.** You can create a different branch for each team and merge them to the master when ready.

4. **A.** You need add the files first using git add, then commit the changes using git commit, and finally push the changes to the remote repository using git push.

5. **D.** You can create a policy with deny access to push, merge, and add to the master and attach it to the developer IAM group.

6. **A.** You need to create an IAM role to delegate access and use AWS STS to assume the role in another AWS account.

7. **B, C, D.** The three merge strategies in AWS CodeCommit are fast-forward, squash, and three-way.

8. **A.** Set up an Amazon CloudWatch events rule to be triggered and add the Amazon SNS topic as the notification target.

9. **B, D.** HTTPS and SSH are the two protocols used in AWS CodeCommit.

10. **A, B, D.** First, create an AWS CodeCommit repository and then clone the existing Git repository in your local machine. Finally, push the changes to your AWS CodeCommit repository.

Additional Resources

- **AWS CodeCommit**   AWS official documentation is the only place where you will get up-to-date information about any AWS service, including AWS CodeCommit.
  `https://docs.aws.amazon.com/codecommit/index.html`

- **AWS CodeCommit Blog**   AWS blogs are another great source of information where you get step-by-step implementations of AWS CodeCommit along with other AWS services.
  `https://aws.amazon.com/blogs/devops/tag/aws-codecommit/`

Building an Application Using AWS CodeBuild

In this chapter, you will learn
- AWS CodeBuild
- Working with CodeBuild
- Test reporting

This chapter will show how to build a Docker image and store it in the Amazon Elastic Container Registry (Amazon ECR).

AWS CodeBuild

As a developer you might have code-building tools such as Gradle, Apache Ant, Apache Maven, Bamboo, CruiseControl, or Hudson that automates the process of building an application from your source code by compiling and packaging the code into an executable application. A typical build automation comprises scripting and automating different tasks that you as a developer perform in your daily life.

AWS CodeBuild service, which is a managed build service in AWS Cloud, compiles the source code and produces artifacts that can be used to deploy your application. AWS CodeBuild scales on demand without the need to provision or manage the build servers.

Build Projects

A build project contains all the required details that need to be provided to AWS CodeBuild as input, such as source code location (AWS CodeCommit, Amazon S3, GitHub, Bitbucket), the build environment to use, how to run a build, and where to store the build output.

Build Environment

A build environment consists of the runtime of your programming language, tools, and operating system that AWS CodeBuild uses to run any build. The nohup command is used to run the background tasks, and you can forcibly stop the running background tasks by using the disown command. AWS CodeBuild provides several environment variables, such as AWS_REGION, CODEBUILD_BUILD_IMAGE, and CODEBUILD_LOG_ PATH, and you can also provide custom environment variables. The printenv command lists all the available environment variables in your build environment.

Working with AWS CodeBuild

We are going to create a container image registry in Amazon ECR and build all the required specification configuration source code files using AWS CodeCommit and build the Docker application code using AWS CodeBuild. First, log in to your AWS management console, navigate to the Amazon ECR service, and choose Create Repository. Enter the repository name as **aws-codebuild** and click on the Create Repository button.

You will be directed to the ECR Repositories page, where you can see the repository name and ECR repository URI. Note down this URI, which we need during the source code configuration in later steps.

Since it is a new ECR repository, it will not contain any Docker images.

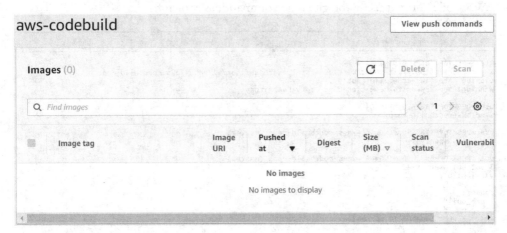

Now, navigate to AWS CodeCommit and choose Create Repository. Enter the repository name as **aws-codebuild-repo**, and then enter a description before clicking on the Create button.

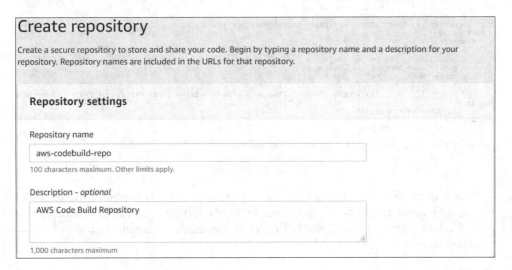

Now, from your local machine, clone the empty repository that you just created in AWS CodeCommit using the git clone command, as shown here.

```
MINGW64:/c/Users/user/aws-codebuild-repo                                          —   □   ✕

user@DESKTOP-5B87H96 MINGW64 ~
$ git clone https://git-codecommit.us-east-1.amazonaws.com/v1/repos/aws-codebuild-repo
Cloning into 'aws-codebuild-repo'...
warning: You appear to have cloned an empty repository.

user@DESKTOP-5B87H96 MINGW64 ~
$ cd aws-codebuild-repo/

user@DESKTOP-5B87H96 MINGW64 ~/aws-codebuild-repo (master)
$ vi buildspec.yml

user@DESKTOP-5B87H96 MINGW64 ~/aws-codebuild-repo (master)
$ cat buildspec.yml
version: 0.2

phases:
  pre_build:
    commands:
      - echo Logging in to Amazon ECR...
      - aws --version
      - $(aws ecr get-login --region $AWS_DEFAULT_REGION --no-include-email)
      - REPOSITORY_URI=177806420679.dkr.ecr.us-east-1.amazonaws.com/aws-codebuild
      - COMMIT_HASH=$(echo $CODEBUILD_RESOLVED_SOURCE_VERSION | cut -c 1-7)
      - IMAGE_TAG=build-$(echo $CODEBUILD_BUILD_ID | awk -F":" '{print $2}')
  build:
    commands:
      - echo Build started on 'date'
      - echo Building the Docker image...
      - docker build -t $REPOSITORY_URI:latest .
      - docker tag $REPOSITORY_URI:latest $REPOSITORY_URI:$IMAGE_TAG
  post_build:
    commands:
      - echo Build completed on 'date'
      - echo Pushing the Docker images...
      - docker push $REPOSITORY_URI:latest
      - docker push $REPOSITORY_URI:$IMAGE_TAG
      - echo Writing image definitions file...
      - printf '[{"name":"aws-codebuild-app","imageUri":"%s"}]' $REPOSITORY_URI:$IMAGE_TAG > codebuildim
age.json
      - cat codebuildimage.json
artifacts:
    files: codebuildimage.json

user@DESKTOP-5B87H96 MINGW64 ~/aws-codebuild-repo (master)
$ |
```

Your source code must have a buildspec file, which contains the build specifications that could include a set of build commands in YAML format and the related settings that AWS CodeBuild uses to run a build. To declare a buildspec, navigate to aws-codebuild-repo and create a buildspec YAML file:

```
version: 0.2

phases:
  pre_build:
    commands:
      - echo Logging in to Amazon ECR...
      - aws --version
      - $(aws ecr get-login --region $AWS_DEFAULT_REGION --no-include-email)
      - REPOSITORY_URI=177806420679.dkr.ecr.us-east-1.amazonaws.com/aws-codebuild
      - COMMIT_HASH=$(echo $CODEBUILD_RESOLVED_SOURCE_VERSION | cut -c 1-7)
      - IMAGE_TAG=build-$(echo $CODEBUILD_BUILD_ID | awk -F":" '{print $2}')
```

```
build:
  commands:
    - echo Build started on 'date'
    - echo Building the Docker image...
    - docker build -t $REPOSITORY_URI:latest .
    - docker tag $REPOSITORY_URI:latest $REPOSITORY_URI:$IMAGE_TAG
  post_build:
    commands:
    - echo Build completed on 'date'
    - echo Pushing the Docker images...
    - docker push $REPOSITORY_URI:latest
    - docker push $REPOSITORY_URI:$IMAGE_TAG
    - echo Writing image definitions file...
    - printf '[{"name":"aws-codebuild-app-v1.0","imageUri":"%s"}]' $REPOSITORY_
URI:$IMAGE_TAG > codebuildimage.json
    - cat codebuildimage.json
artifacts:
  files: codebuildimage.json
```

Next create another file called **Dockerfile** with source code:

```
FROM node:carbon
WORKDIR /usr/src/app
COPY package*.json ./
RUN npm install
COPY . .
EXPOSE 8080
CMD [ "npm", "start" ]
```

Then create a .json file called **package.json** using the source code:

```
{
  "name": "aws-codebuild-app",
  "version": "1.0.0",
  "description": "AWS CodeBuild Appln on Docker",
  "author": "Kamesh Ganesan <kamesh.ganesan@example.com>",
  "main": "server.js",
  "scripts": {
    "start": "node server.js"
    },
  "dependencies": {
    "express": "^4.16.1"
    }
}
```

Finally, create a JavaScript file called **server.js** with the following source:

```
const express = require('express');
// Constants used in this application
const PORT = 8080;
const HOST = '0.0.0.0';
// AWS CodeBuild Application
const app = express();
app.get('/', (req, res) => {
  res.send('<h1 style="color:green;">AWS CodeBuild Application v1.0</h1> \n');
});
app.listen(PORT, HOST);
console.log(`Running on http://${HOST}:${PORT}`);
```

Enter the git status to see the four files that you created.

```
MINGW64:/c/Users/user/aws-codebuild-repo                          —    □    ×
user@DESKTOP-5B87H96 MINGW64 ~/aws-codebuild-repo (master)
$ vi package.json

user@DESKTOP-5B87H96 MINGW64 ~/aws-codebuild-repo (master)
$ cat package.json
{
  "name": "aws-codebuild-app",
  "version": "1.0.0",
  "description": "AWS CodeBuild Appln on Docker",
  "author": "Kamesh Ganesan <kamesh.ganesan@example.com>",
  "main": "server.js",
  "scripts": {
    "start": "node server.js"
  },
  "dependencies": {
    "express": "^4.16.1"
  }
}

user@DESKTOP-5B87H96 MINGW64 ~/aws-codebuild-repo (master)
$ vi server.js

user@DESKTOP-5B87H96 MINGW64 ~/aws-codebuild-repo (master)
$ git status
On branch master

No commits yet

Untracked files:
  (use "git add <file>..." to include in what will be committed)

        Dockerfile
        buildspec.yml
        package.json
        server.js

nothing added to commit but untracked files present (use "git add" to track)

user@DESKTOP-5B87H96 MINGW64 ~/aws-codebuild-repo (master)
```

Add the files using the git add command and commit the changes using git commit -m "comment." When everything is successful, push the code to the remote repository using the git push command.

Next navigate to the AWS CodeCommit service using the AWS Management Console. Choose Repositories and then Code from the left pane. You can see all the source code has been pushed successfully.

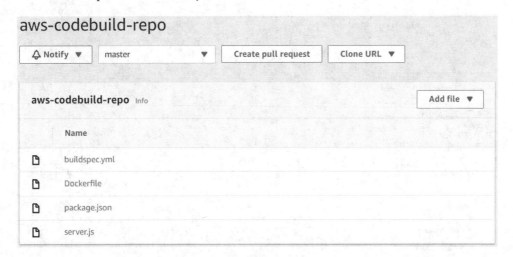

All the prerequisites are ready for us to build our Docker code. Navigate to the AWS CodeBuild service and choose Build Projects. Click the Create Build Project button.

Enter the project name as **docker-image-build** and provide a description. Next, you need to add the source, so choose AWS CodeCommit as the source provider from the dropdown and choose aws-codebuild-repo for the repository.

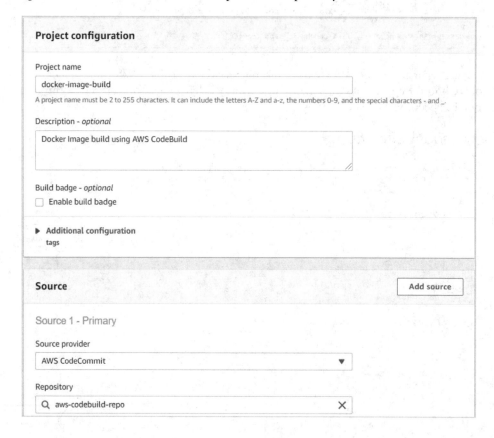

Now you can choose either a managed image or custom image for the environment image. Choose Managed Image and Ubuntu for the operating system, as shown next. Then choose Runtime as the standard and aws/codebuild/standard:1.0 for the image. The runtime is standard for Amazon Linux 2 and Ubuntu and base for the Windows operating system. You can either choose the image version from the dropdown menu or leave the default option to always use the latest image for this runtime version. Choose Linux as the environment type from the dropdown. You need to select the checkbox for Privileged to build Docker images.

Next, choose an existing service role with required access or create to create a new service role. If you require your AWS CodeBuild to access resources inside your Virtual Private Cloud (VPC), then choose Additional Configuration and provide the VPC, subnet, security group, etc. Because, typically AWS CodeBuild cannot access your resources like Amazon EC2, Amazon RDS is defined inside a VPC. By enabling VPC connectivity, you can test your build against data in your Amazon RDS database or interact with web services hosted on Amazon EC2 in a private subnet. In addition, you have the option to add a timeout between 5 minutes and 8 hours (the default timeout is 1 hour). Also, you can install a self-signed certificate or a certificate signed by a certification authority, which is stored on your Amazon S3 bucket.

Now you can either use the buildspec YAML file that was created already or insert build commands to create a new buildspec YAML file, and you will provided with a sample script template when you click on Switch To Editor. Since we created the YAML file already, choose Use A Buildspec File. Since you are pushing the Docker image to ECR, choose No Artifacts. Choose Build ID for the namespace and the packaging as None or Zip to compress the file before storing it in Amazon S3. If you select Amazon S3, you will also have an option to provide the encryption key. You can either supply the AWS KMS customer master key or leave the default setting. Finally, you have option to choose to store the build output logs. You can choose Amazon CloudWatch logs to upload build output logs to Amazon CloudWatch or choose Amazon S3 to upload build output logs to the Amazon S3 bucket. Click Create Build Project.

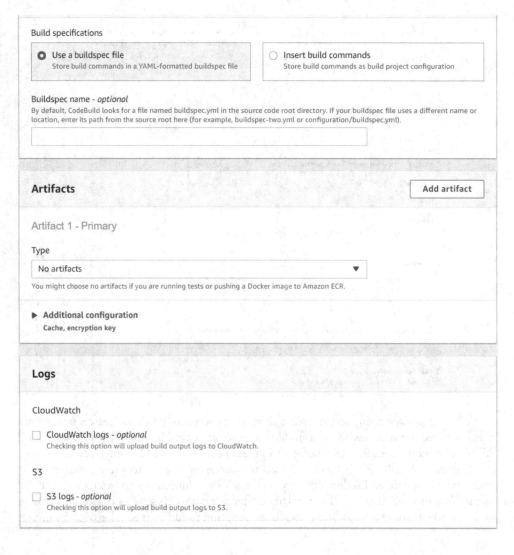

Now you are ready to build, so click Start Build.

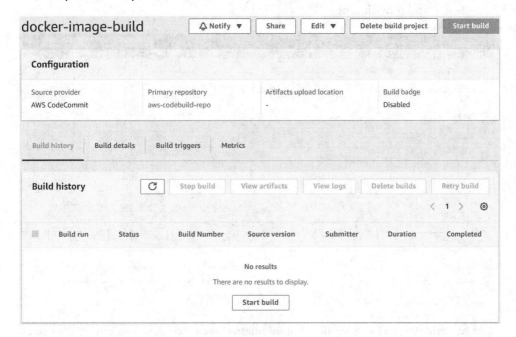

Provide the project name as **docker-image-build** and leave the other options at the default settings. Click the Start Build button again.

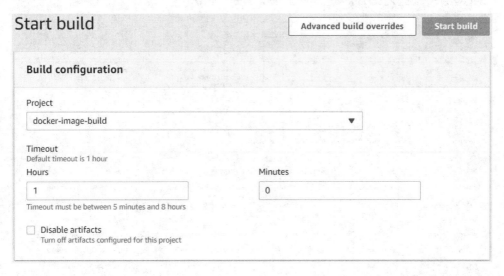

Your code build is successfully started, and you can see various stage names as submitted, queued, and provisioning.

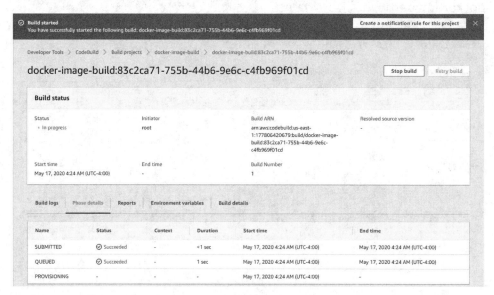

In few minutes, you can see all the build phases have succeeded. You can see the overall build status is "Succeeded" and the build number is 1.

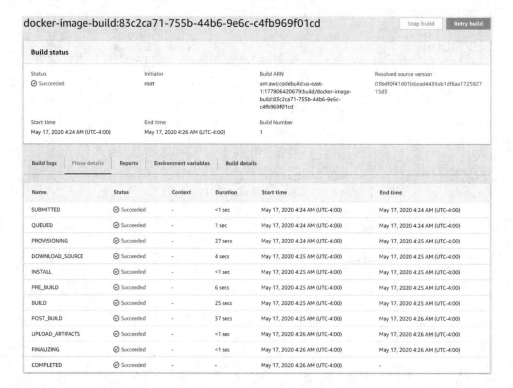

Now, navigate to the aws-codebuild repository in Amazon ECR and see a new image listed.

Let us make a simple change in the buildspec file from your local machine. Change the aws-codebuild-app-v1.0 to **aws-codebuild-app-v2.0** in the printf line.

```
MINGW64:/c/Users/user/aws-codebuild-repo                                    —   □   ×

user@DESKTOP-5B87H96 MINGW64 ~/aws-codebuild-repo (master)
$ vi buildspec.yml

user@DESKTOP-5B87H96 MINGW64 ~/aws-codebuild-repo (master)
$ cat buildspec.yml
version: 0.2

phases:
  pre_build:
    commands:
      - echo Logging in to Amazon ECR...
      - aws --version
      - $(aws ecr get-login --region $AWS_DEFAULT_REGION --no-include-email)
      - REPOSITORY_URI=177806420679.dkr.ecr.us-east-1.amazonaws.com/aws-codebuild
      - COMMIT_HASH=$(echo $CODEBUILD_RESOLVED_SOURCE_VERSION | cut -c 1-7)
      - IMAGE_TAG=build-$(echo $CODEBUILD_BUILD_ID | awk -F":" '{print $2}')
  build:
    commands:
      - echo Build started on 'date'
      - echo Building the Docker image...
      - docker build -t $REPOSITORY_URI:latest .
      - docker tag $REPOSITORY_URI:latest $REPOSITORY_URI:$IMAGE_TAG
  post_build:
    commands:
      - echo Build completed on 'date'
      - echo Pushing the Docker images...
      - docker push $REPOSITORY_URI:latest
      - docker push $REPOSITORY_URI:$IMAGE_TAG
      - echo Writing image definitions file...
      - printf '[{"name":"aws-codebuild-app-v2.0","imageUri":"%s"}]' $REPOSITORY_URI:$IMAGE_TAG > codebu
ildimage.json
      - cat codebuildimage.json
artifacts:
    files: codebuildimage.json

user@DESKTOP-5B87H96 MINGW64 ~/aws-codebuild-repo (master)
$ |
```

Add the updated buildspec file using the git add command and commit the changes using the git commit -m "comment" command. Then push the code to your remote repository in AWS CodeCommit using the git push command.

```
MINGW64:/c/Users/user/aws-codebuild-repo                          —   □   ×
user@DESKTOP-5B87H96 MINGW64 ~/aws-codebuild-repo (master)
$ git status
On branch master
Your branch is up to date with 'origin/master'.

Changes not staged for commit:
  (use "git add <file>..." to update what will be committed)
  (use "git checkout -- <file>..." to discard changes in working directory)

        modified:   buildspec.yml

no changes added to commit (use "git add" and/or "git commit -a")

user@DESKTOP-5B87H96 MINGW64 ~/aws-codebuild-repo (master)
$ git add .
warning: LF will be replaced by CRLF in buildspec.yml.
The file will have its original line endings in your working directory

user@DESKTOP-5B87H96 MINGW64 ~/aws-codebuild-repo (master)
$ git commit -m "application version 2.0"
[master b583f80] application version 2.0
 1 file changed, 1 insertion(+), 1 deletion(-)

user@DESKTOP-5B87H96 MINGW64 ~/aws-codebuild-repo (master)
$ git push
Enumerating objects: 5, done.
Counting objects: 100% (5/5), done.
Delta compression using up to 4 threads
Compressing objects: 100% (3/3), done.
Writing objects: 100% (3/3), 306 bytes | 306.00 KiB/s, done.
Total 3 (delta 2), reused 0 (delta 0)
To https://git-codecommit.us-east-1.amazonaws.com/v1/repos/aws-codebuild-repo
   03bdf0f..b583f80  master -> master

user@DESKTOP-5B87H96 MINGW64 ~/aws-codebuild-repo (master)
$ |
```

Navigate again to your build project in AWS CodeBuild and click on Start Build. In the next few minutes, the overall build status is "Succeeded" and the build number changes to 2.

Build status			
Status	Initiator	Build ARN	Resolved source version
⊘ Succeeded	root	arn:aws:codebuild:us-east-1:177806420679:build/docker-image-build:da83310c-716f-4611-8c4e-437a90bB6c94	b583f802d43a53a24740992ca0914fd2ff87b4f5
Start time	End time	Build Number	
May 17, 2020 4:32 AM (UTC-4:00)	May 17, 2020 4:33 AM (UTC-4:00)	2	

You can see the build history details by choosing Build History from the left pane.

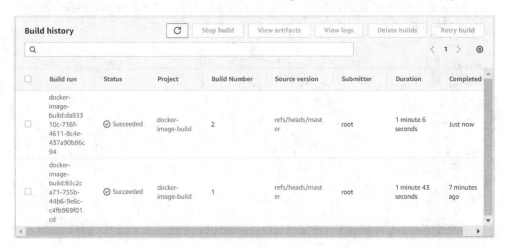

You can see the build metrics details on the Account metrics dashboard by choosing Account Metrics from the left navigation pane.

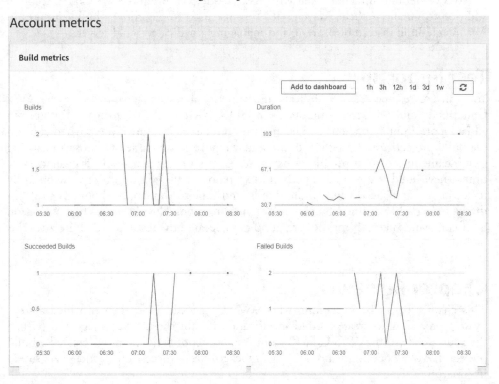

Finally, you can navigate to your aws-codebuild repository on the Amazon ECR service page. You can see that both the images you built using AWS CodeBuild are successfully stored here.

AWS CodeBuild integrates well with AWS CodeCommit and AWS CodeDeploy in addition to Gradle, Apache Maven, etc. You just need to pay for the build minutes in AWS CodeBuild instead of running and managing a dedicated build server.

Test Reporting

You can create reports for unit tests and functional tests that run during the AWS CodeBuild build, with test result details in JSON, XML, and TRX formats. You need to add a report group name in the buildspec file, and test reports are created when you run the build project. You can either specify a new report group name or choose an existing group name in the buildspec file. A new test report with the new results is created every time a new build is executed. The build test reports help you optimize your build by reviewing the test success and failure trends, and it helps you troubleshoot any problem that you encounter during a build run. You need to export the test results file to Amazon S3 if you want to keep it for more than 30 days because the test reports expire after this period.

Chapter Review

This chapter began by explaining what AWS CodeBuild is. It then provided a step-by-step procedure to create a build specification file for the Docker image and pushed the source code to the AWS CodeCommit remote repository. Then, we created a build project in AWS CodeBuild and built two Docker images successfully, which were stored in Amazon ECR.

Exercises

The following exercises will help you practice using AWS CodeBuild. You need to create an AWS account, as explained earlier, before performing these exercises. You can use the Free Tier when launching AWS resources, but make sure to terminate them at the end.

Exercise 24-1: Delete the AWS CodeBuild Project Using the AWS Management Console

1. Use your AWS account e-mail address and password to sign in to the AWS account and then navigate to the AWS CodeBuild console at https://console.aws.amazon .com/codebuild/.

2. Verify the AWS region by using the Region selector in the upper-right corner of the page.

3. From the navigation pane on the left, choose Build Projects.

4. Choose the radio button next to your build project.

5. Choose Delete to delete your build project.

Exercise 24-2: Delete Build Images from Amazon ECR Using the AWS Management Console

1. Use your AWS account e-mail address and password to sign in to the AWS account and then navigate to the AWS Amazon ECR console at https://console.aws.amazon .com/ecr/.

2. Verify the AWS region by using the Region selector in the upper-right corner of the page.

3. From the navigation pane on the left, choose Repositories.

4. From the Repositories page, choose your repository.

5. Choose Images from the left navigation pane.

6. Select all the images that you want to delete.

7. Choose Delete to delete your images.

Exercise 24-3: Delete the AWS CodeCommit Repository Using the AWS Management Console

1. Use your AWS account e-mail address and password to sign in to the AWS account and then navigate to the AWS CodeCommit console at https://console.aws.amazon .com/codecommit/.

2. Verify the AWS region by using the Region selector in the upper-right corner of the page.

3. From the navigation pane on the left, choose Repositories.

4. Choose Settings.

5. Navigate to Delete Repository on the General tab.

6. Choose Delete Repository.

7. Enter **delete** in the popup window and choose to delete.

Questions

The following questions will help you gauge your understanding of the contents in this chapter. Read all the answers carefully because there might be more than one correct answer. Choose the best responses for each question.

1. Your company is having issues managing its build server, which is hosted on an Amazon EC2 instance that is used by many teams. Which of the following AWS service provides a managed code build service?

   A. AWS CodeCommit

   B. AWS CodeDeploy

   C. AWS CodePipeline

   D. AWS CodeBuild

2. Your company security policy mandates that all the build artifacts be stored in an Amazon S3 bucket as encrypted using a client encryption key. How can you encrypt all the build artifacts using a client master AWS KMS key?

   A. Supply the customer master AWS KMS key in the Artifact section during build project creation

   B. Upload the customer encryption key during build project creation in AWS CodeBuild

   C. Check the enryption checkbox in AWS CodeCommit

   D. Supply the AWS KMS key during the build process

3. Your team is using AWS CodeBuild to compile source code, and when they try to run a test with their Amazon RDS hosted on their private subnet, they are having an access issue. How can you resolve this?

   A. Update the private subnet route table to allow AWS CodeBuild

   B. Update the private subnet security group to allow AWS CodeBuild

   C. Add an Internet Gateway to the VPC and access it through the Internet

   D. When creating a build project, they need to select appropriate VPC and private subnet in the Additional Configuration section.

4. What two environment image options are available during build project creation in AWS CodeBuild? (Choose two.)

   A. Managed image

   B. Docker image

   C. Custom image

   D. Windows image

5. What three operating systems are available when you choose managed image during build project creation in AWS CodeBuild? (Choose three.)

   A. Amazon Linux 2

   B. Ubuntu

   C. Windows Server

   D. CentOS

6. A DevOps engineer in your company created a build project in AWS CodeBuild to build Docker images and store them in Amazon ECR. The build is failing in the Docker build phase. How can you resolve this issue?

   A. The Privileged checkbox should be selected while creating build projects to provide the elevated privilege to run Docker commands

   B. Create an AWS IAM user and give it read-only access to the Amazon ECR service

   C. Create an AWS IAM user and give it full access to Amazon EC2

   D. Create an AWS IAM user and give it full access to the Amazon S3 service

7. Your team is running a build project, but they are getting a timeout error after 1 hour. They asked you to resolve the issue and requested that their build project not timeout even after 7 hours. How can you achieve this?

   A. Configure the timeout to 7 hours—the default is 1 hour

   B. Remove the timeout from the build project

   C. Update the timeout to 0—the default is 12 hours

   D. Create a support ticket in AWS

8. Your company audit team mandates all the build logs be stored in redundant places. What you can enable to store logs in multiple places during build project creation?

   A. Choose Amazon CloudWatch and Amazon RDS as your log destination

   B. Choose Amazon S3 and Amazon RDS as your log destination

   C. Choose Amazon S3 and AWS CodeCommit as your log destination

   D. Choose Amazon CloudWatch and Amazon S3 as your log destination

9. Your security engineer found that AWS CodeBuild runs all your build commands as the root user. What is the reason for this?

   A. AWS CodeBuild uses the root user to run all build commands by default

   B. You need to create new a AWS IAM user and grant it full AWS CodeBuild access

   C. Delete the root user from the AWS Management Console

   D. Use a different AWS account that does not have a root user

10. What pricing model is used by AWS CodeBuild?

   A. It is free to use for your entire workload

   B. Pay up-front pricing model

   C. Pay hourly pricing model

   D. Pay-as-you-go pricing model

Answers

1. **D.** AWS CodeBuild is the managed build service from AWS.

2. **A.** You can supply the customer master AWS KMS key in the Artifact section during build project creation.

3. **D.** When creating a build project, they need to select the appropriate VPC and private subnet in the Additional Configuration section.

4. **A, C.** AWS CodeBuild offers managed images and custom images.

5. **A, B, C.** Amazon Linux 2, Ubuntu, and Windows Server operating systems are available in AWS CodeBuild.

6. **A.** The Privileged checkbox should be selected when creating build projects to provide the elevated privilege to run Docker commands.

7. **A.** You need to add the timeout to 7 hours. The timeout can be set from 5 minutes to 8 hours (the default is 1 hour).

8. **D.** Choose Amazon CloudWatch and Amazon S3 as your log destination.

9. **A.** AWS CodeBuild uses the root user to run all build commands by default.

10. **D.** AWS CodeBuild uses a pay-as-you-go pricing model.

Additional Resources

- **AWS CodeBuild**   AWS CodeBuild official documentation is the place to get all the latest information about this service in addition to all the updates to its features and new features.
  `https://docs.aws.amazon.com/codebuild/index.html`

- **AWS CodeBuild Blogs**   These blogs help you with step-by-step details of using AWS CodeBuild for different use cases and security best practices.
  `https://aws.amazon.com/blogs/devops/category/developer-tools/aws-codebuild/`

Deploying Applications Using CodeDeploy and CodePipeline

In this chapter, you will learn
- AWS CodeDeploy
- AWS CodePipeline

This chapter will provide a practical approach to learn AWS CodeDeploy and AWS CodePipeline.

AWS CodeDeploy

As a developer, you might have used automated code deployment tools such as Jenkins, Bamboo, TeamCity, etc., including AWS CodeDeploy. AWS CodeDeploy automates your application deployments to Amazon EC2, Amazon ECS, AWS Lambda, and on-premises instances. You can deploy your application code, serverless functions, packages, executables, and web and configuration files from your git repositories and Amazon S3 buckets.

You need to provide an application name to uniquely identify the deployment and specify the compute platform as EC2/On-premises, AWS Lambda, or Amazon ECS. The CodeDeploy agent is necessary when you use the EC2/On-Premises compute platform, but it is not required for AWS Lambda or Amazon ECS. You also need to specify the deployment configuration, such as canary, linear, or all at once to indicate how the traffic is routed during the deployment.

The next component is the deployment, where you can choose either in-place deployment or blue/green deployment, based on whether your application needs to be available even during the application deployment. With in-place deployment, the application is stopped and the updated application is installed, tested, and started again. In blue/green deployment, the updated application is deployed to the deployment group while the application is online and the load balancer reroutes the traffic to the new deployment group without any downtime to the application. However, it works only with Amazon EC2 instances, not on-premises instances. The in-place deployment type is not available for Amazon ECS and AWS Lambda. AWS CodeDeploy APIs, AWS CLI, AWS SDKs, and AWS Management Console can be used to access and manage AWS CodeDeploy.

Now let us explore the step-by-step procedure to automatically deploy a sample application using AWS CodeDeploy and add AWS CodePipeline to automatically pull source code changes from the code repository, such as AWS CodeCommit, and deploy it to an Amazon EC2 instance using AWS CodeDeploy. You need to log in to your AWS account and navigate to the AWS Identity And Access Management (IAM) page. But you first need to create a CodeDeployRole and attach the AWS managed policy AWSCodeDeployRole.

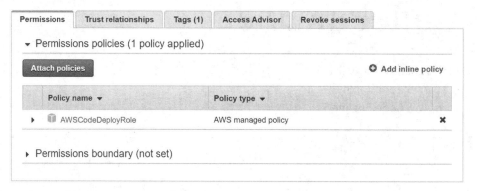

You need to create another service role—EC2-to-S3-Read-only—and attach the AWS managed policy AmazonS3ReadOnlyAccess to enable the Amazon EC2 instance to access Amazon S3 and read the objects.

You then need to navigate to the AWS CodeCommit service page and create a repository—for example, DevOps-Repo—and click the Create button.

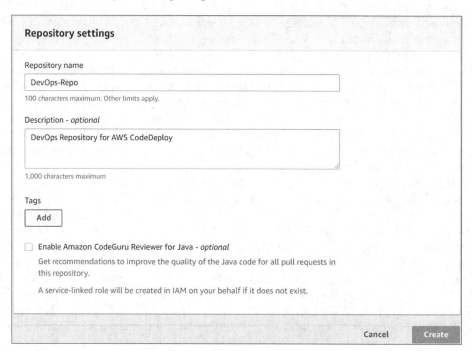

Note either the HTTPS or SSH URL from this page to clone it in your local machine. Click the Copy button.

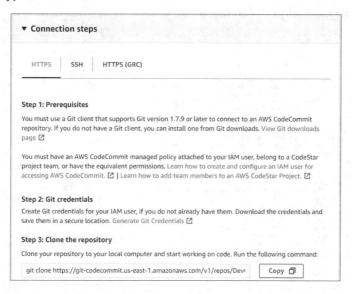

On your local machine, open git.bash, if it is Windows OS, or Terminal, if it is macOS. Clone the repository and then go to the DevOpsRepo directory. You can use any sample application code or use this Amazon sample application: https://s3.amazonaws.com/ aws-codedeploy-us-east-1/samples/latest/SampleApp_Linux.zip, and move the contents of this ZIP file to the DevOps-Repo folder.

```
MINGW64:/c/Users/user/DevOps-Repo                                          —    □    ×

user@DESKTOP-5B87H96 MINGW64 ~/.ssh
$ git clone ssh://git-codecommit.us-east-1.amazonaws.com/v1/repos/DevOps-Repo
Cloning into 'DevOps-Repo'...
Warning: Permanently added the RSA host key for IP address '52.94.229.29' to the list of known hosts.
warning: You appear to have cloned an empty repository.

user@DESKTOP-5B87H96 MINGW64 ~/.ssh
$ cd ..

user@DESKTOP-5B87H96 MINGW64 ~
$ cd DevOps-Repo

user@DESKTOP-5B87H96 MINGW64 ~/DevOps-Repo (master)
$ ls -al
total 24
drwxr-xr-x 1 user 197609 0 May 23 21:43 ./
drwxr-xr-x 1 user 197609 0 May 23 21:44 ../
drwxr-xr-x 1 user 197609 0 May 23 21:43 .git/

user@DESKTOP-5B87H96 MINGW64 ~/DevOps-Repo (master)
$ ls -al
total 45
drwxr-xr-x 1 user 197609     0 May 23 21:45 ./
drwxr-xr-x 1 user 197609     0 May 23 21:44 ../
drwxr-xr-x 1 user 197609     0 May 23 21:43 .git/
-rw-r--r-- 1 user 197609   359 May 23 21:45 appspec.yml
-rw-r--r-- 1 user 197609   717 May 23 21:45 index.html
-rw-r--r-- 1 user 197609 10884 May 23 21:45 LICENSE.txt
drwxr-xr-x 1 user 197609     0 May 23 21:45 scripts/

user@DESKTOP-5B87H96 MINGW64 ~/DevOps-Repo (master)
$ git status
On branch master

No commits yet

Untracked files:
  (use "git add <file>..." to include in what will be committed)

        LICENSE.txt
        appspec.yml
        index.html
        scripts/

nothing added to commit but untracked files present (use "git add" to track)

user@DESKTOP-5B87H96 MINGW64 ~/DevOps-Repo (master)
$ |
```

Add the new files to the remote repository using the git add command, and commit the changes using the git commit command. Then push the code to the AWS CodeCommit repository using the git push command.

```
MINGW64:/c/Users/user/DevOps-Repo                                    —    □    ✕

user@DESKTOP-5B87H96 MINGW64 ~/DevOps-Repo (master)
$ git add -A
warning: LF will be replaced by CRLF in LICENSE.txt.
The file will have its original line endings in your working directory
warning: LF will be replaced by CRLF in appspec.yml.
The file will have its original line endings in your working directory
warning: LF will be replaced by CRLF in index.html.
The file will have its original line endings in your working directory
warning: LF will be replaced by CRLF in scripts/install_dependencies.
The file will have its original line endings in your working directory
warning: LF will be replaced by CRLF in scripts/start_server.
The file will have its original line endings in your working directory
warning: LF will be replaced by CRLF in scripts/stop_server.
The file will have its original line endings in your working directory

user@DESKTOP-5B87H96 MINGW64 ~/DevOps-Repo (master)
$ git commit -m "uploading to remote DevOps Repo"
[master (root-commit) 4903fb9] uploading to remote DevOps Repo
 6 files changed, 266 insertions(+)
 create mode 100644 LICENSE.txt
 create mode 100644 appspec.yml
 create mode 100644 index.html
 create mode 100644 scripts/install_dependencies
 create mode 100644 scripts/start_server
 create mode 100644 scripts/stop_server

user@DESKTOP-5B87H96 MINGW64 ~/DevOps-Repo (master)
$ git push
Enumerating objects: 9, done.
Counting objects: 100% (9/9), done.
Delta compression using up to 4 threads
Compressing objects: 100% (7/7), done.
Writing objects: 100% (9/9), 5.04 KiB | 1.01 MiB/s, done.
Total 9 (delta 0), reused 0 (delta 0)
To ssh://git-codecommit.us-east-1.amazonaws.com/v1/repos/DevOps-Repo
 * [new branch]      master -> master

user@DESKTOP-5B87H96 MINGW64 ~/DevOps-Repo (master)
$
```

You can verify the source code changes by navigating to the AWS CodeCommit page and choosing Code Repository.

You need an Amazon EC2 instance to deploy the code. You can use your existing Amazon EC2 instance by just adding the tag Name with value DevOps or create a new instance by clicking the Launch Instance button.

Choose the latest Amazon Linux 2 AMI from the list and click Next.

We can use the Free Tier–eligible instance type for this example. Select t2.micro and click the Next: Configure Instance Details button.

Choose either your default VPC or custom VPC that you have in your account, and choose a public subnet, since we are going to deploy our sample web application. You need to attach the EC2-to-S3-Read-Only service role.

Scroll down and click on the Advanced Details section. Enter the following code in the user data to install the AWS CodeDeploy agent and click Next:

```
#!/bin/bash
yum -y update
yum install -y ruby
cd /home/ec2-user
curl -O https://aws-codedeploy-us-east-1.s3.us-east-1.amazonaws.com/latest/
install
chmod +x ./install
./install auto
```

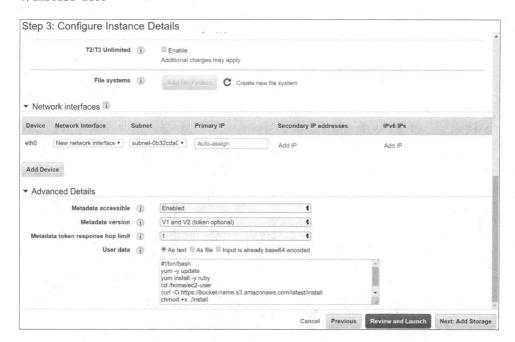

You can add more storage if needed, but make sure Delete On Termination is checked to ensure this storage volume will be deleted when you terminate the instance.

As per the best practice, you need to always add appropriate tags to each AWS resource. Here you must add a tag for the AWS CodeDeploy to identify your instance. Add a tag name with the value **DevOps**.

You can create a new security group or select an existing security group. It is not advisable to open the traffic to 0.0.0.0/0, which is open to the public in your enterprise environment. You do need to open HTTP and SSH in case you need to log in to the instance later.

Review all the options and click the Launch button.

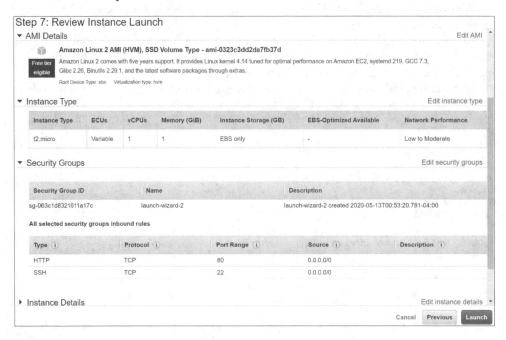

You can either use your existing key pair or create a new key pair, which will be used to log in to the instance later.

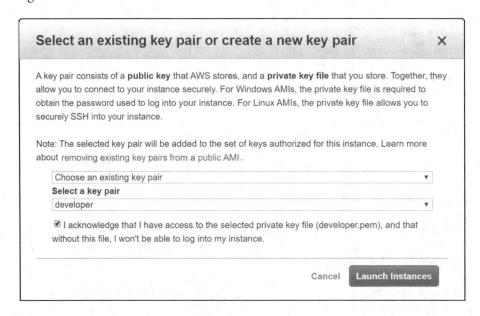

If everything is successful, you will see a message such as "your instances are now launching." Click the View Instances button to verify the status.

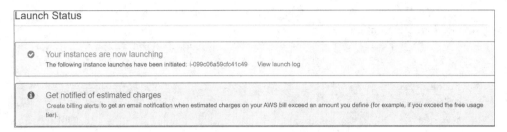

Note down your public IP and verify the status checks are okay.

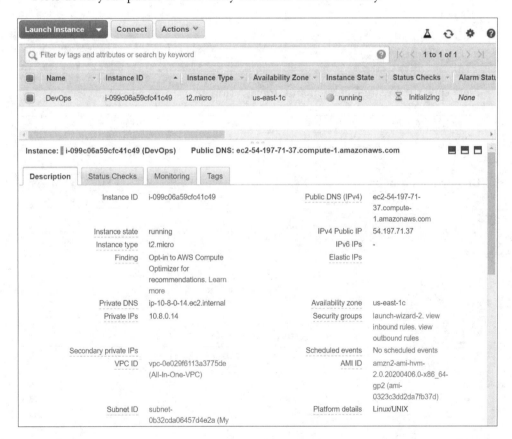

All the prerequisites are completed to get started with AWS CodeDeploy. Navigate to the AWS CodeDeploy service in the AWS Management Console and click the Create Application button.

Enter the application name as **CodeDeply-Appln** and select the compute platform as EC2/On-premises from the dropdown.

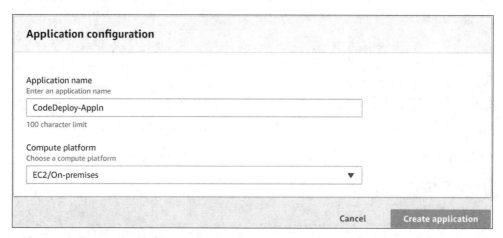

Next click the Create Deployment Group button.

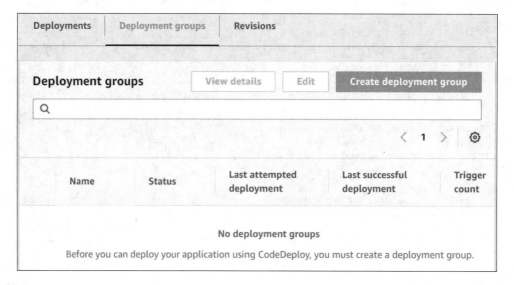

Enter the deployment group name as **CodeDeploy-Appln-group** and select the CodeDeployRole that you created initially.

Choose the in-place deployment type and select Amazon EC2 instances for the environment configuration. Enter the tag that you specified on the instance, and note that it identified the instance with a message such as "1 unique matched instance."

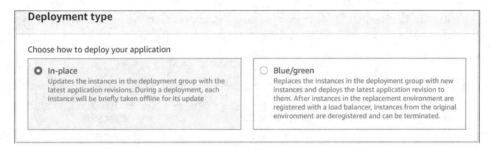

The deployment settings can be all at once, which is default, but you can also choose half at a time and one at a time based on your requirements. Also, you can place the deployment behind a load balancer if you choose. For simplicity, choose AllAtOnce for

Deployment Settings, uncheck Enable Load Balancing, and click Create Deployment Group.

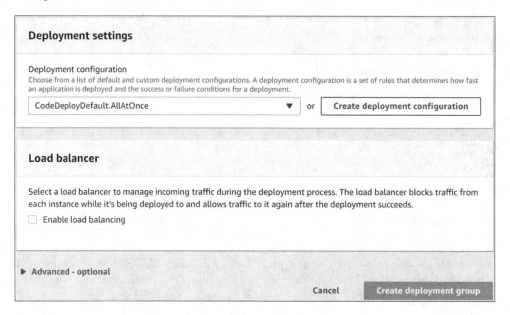

Verify the deployment group details, such as application name, deployment type, compute platform, service role, and deployment configuration.

Deployment group details

Deployment group name	Application name	Compute platform
CodeDeploy-Appln-Group	CodeDeploy-Appln	EC2/On-premises
Deployment type	Service role ARN	Deployment configuration
In-place	arn:aws:iam::177806420679:role /CodeDeployRole	CodeDeployDefault.AllAtOnce
Rollback enabled		
False		

Environment configuration: Amazon EC2 instances

Key	Value
Name	DevOps

AWS CodePipeline

Many tools are available for creating continuous integration/continuous delivery (CI/CD) pipelines, such as Jenkins, CircleCI, Spinnaker, Buddy, and Bamboo, to name a few. AWS CodePipeline provides easy integration with other AWS developer tools like AWS CodeCommit, AWS CodeBuild, and AWS CodeDeploy. You can configure, visualize, and automate different stages of your software release process, such as building, testing, and deployment, using AWS CodePipeline. You can use the AWS Management Console, AWS SDK, and AWS CLI to configure and manage your CI/CD pipeline in AWS CodePipeline. AWS CodePipeline provides a consistent set of release processes, which helps to speed up the delivery of new features to your application, resolve bug fixes with improved quality, and avoid manual errors.

You can use your existing source code repository or AWS CodeCommit to push source code changes, which will be picked up automatically by the build process using tools such as AWS CodeBuild. The release cycle then moves to the deploy and testing stage by using tools such as AWS CodeDeploy.

A stage is a logical unit, such as a build stage or deployment stage, which contains the actions that are performed on an application artifact, such as source code. An action is a group of operations that can be performed on your source code change or when deploying an application to instances. A transition is the point where the execution moves from one stage to another, like moving from commit to build to deploy. A pipeline can be defined as a workflow that specifies how the different stages progress in the software release process, and it tracks each execution. A pipeline can be triggered either manually or automatically when the source code is changed by your developer, or you can schedule pipeline execution using Amazon CloudWatch events. You can stop pipeline execution in two ways: stop and wait or stop and abandon. When you use stop and wait, the actions in progress will be completed and all the remaining actions will not be started. When you use stop and abandon, all the actions in progress, including any future actions, will be stopped. You can always use the retry option to start the pipeline execution again. The best practice is to group all the related actions for each application environment, such as development, QA, or production. You can create notification rules to alert you when any important changes, like pipeline execution, are completed.

Navigate to the AWS CodePipeline service in the AWS Management Console and click on Create Pipeline.

Enter a name for the pipeline—for example, **DevOps-Pipeline**—and choose a service role, if it already exists. If it does not, choose to create a new service role and check

Allow AWS CodePipeline To Create A Service Role So It Can Be Used With This New Pipeline.

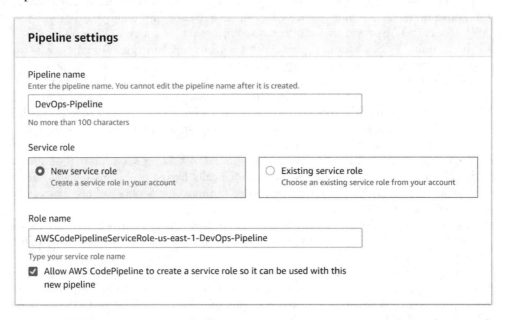

Now, add the source stage by choosing AWS CodeCommit from the dropdown and choose the repository name, DevOps-Repo, with its branch name. Choose Amazon CloudWatch Events to detect changes and click Next.

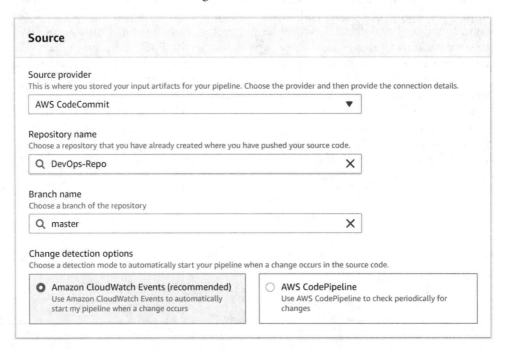

In this exercise you are not going to build using the pipeline, since you created the EC2 instance already. So, click the Skip Build Stage button.

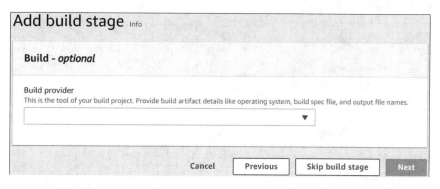

In the popup window, click Skip.

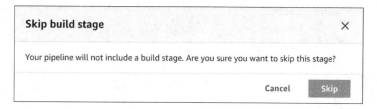

Add the deploy stage to your pipeline by selecting AWS CodeDeploy from the dropdown Deploy Provider menu. Select your region, select your AWS CodeDeploy application name as CodeDeploy-Appln and your deployment group as CodeDeploy-Appln-Group, and click Next.

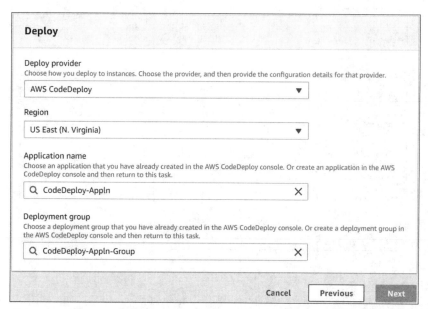

Review all the options that you selected and click Create Pipeline.

Review Info

Step 1: Choose pipeline settings

Pipeline settings

Pipeline name
DevOps-Pipeline
Artifact location
A new Amazon S3 bucket will be created as the default artifact store for your pipeline
Service role name
AWSCodePipelineServiceRole-us-east-1-DevOps-Pipeline

Step 2: Add source stage

Source action provider

Source action provider
AWS CodeCommit
RepositoryName
DevOps-Repo
BranchName
master
PollForSourceChanges
false

Step 3: Add build stage

Build action provider

Build stage
No build

Step 4: Add deploy stage

Deploy action provider

Deploy action provider
AWS CodeDeploy
ApplicationName
CodeDeploy-Appln
DeploymentGroupName
CodeDeploy-Appln-Group

Cancel   Previous   Create pipeline

The application source code is automatically pulled from AWS CodeCommit and the source stage is completed successfully. The deploy stage is in progress.

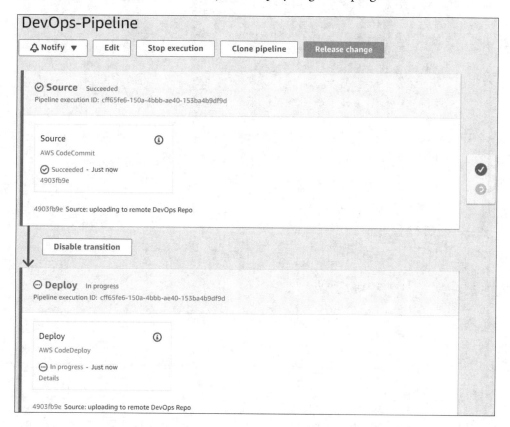

Within a minute, the deploy stage is also successfully completed.

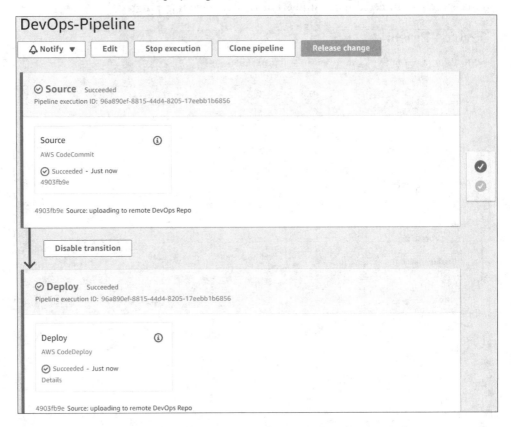

Open the browser of your choice and enter the public IP of your EC2 instance. When you press the ENTER key, you can see the "Congratulations" message.

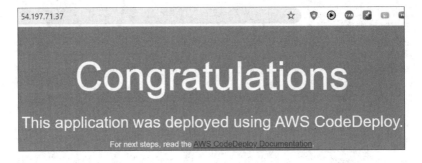

Now, go to your local machine and edit the index.html file to change the header-1 to **Hello World!** and header-2 to **This application was deployed using AWS CodeDeploy and AWS Pipeline.**

```
MINGW64:/c/Users/user/DevOps-Repo                                    —    □    ×
<!DOCTYPE html>
<html>
<head>
  <meta charset="utf-8">
  <title>Sample Deployment</title>
  <style>
    body {
      color: #ffffff;
      background-color: #FFA500;
      font-family: Arial, sans-serif;
      font-size: 14px;
    }

    h1 {
      font-size: 500%;
      font-weight: normal;
      margin-bottom: 0;
    }

    h2 {
      font-size: 200%;
      font-weight: normal;
      margin-bottom: 0;
    }
  </style>
</head>
<body>
  <div align="center">
    <h1>Hello World !</h1>
    <h2>This application was deployed using AWS CodeDeploy and AWS CodePipeline.</h2>
    <p>For next steps, read the <a href="http://aws.amazon.com/documentation/codedeploy">AWS CodeDeploy Documentation<
/a>.</p>
  </div>
</body>
</html>
~
~
index.html[+] [unix] (21:45 23/05/2020)                                9,31 All
:wq!
```

Save the source code change and add it to the repository using the git add command. Then commit the changes using the git commit command and push the updated source code to the remote repository using the git push command.

```
MINGW64:/c/Users/user/DevOps-Repo                                    —    □    ×
user@DESKTOP-5B87H96 MINGW64 ~/DevOps-Repo (master)
$ vi index.html

user@DESKTOP-5B87H96 MINGW64 ~/DevOps-Repo (master)
$ git status
On branch master
Your branch is up to date with 'origin/master'.

Changes not staged for commit:
  (use "git add <file>..." to update what will be committed)
  (use "git checkout -- <file>..." to discard changes in working directory)

        modified:   index.html

no changes added to commit (use "git add" and/or "git commit -a")

user@DESKTOP-5B87H96 MINGW64 ~/DevOps-Repo (master)
$ git add .
warning: LF will be replaced by CRLF in index.html.
The file will have its original line endings in your working directory

user@DESKTOP-5B87H96 MINGW64 ~/DevOps-Repo (master)
$ git commit -m "updated index file"
[master e613e68] updated index file
 1 file changed, 3 insertions(+), 3 deletions(-)

user@DESKTOP-5B87H96 MINGW64 ~/DevOps-Repo (master)
$ git push
Enumerating objects: 5, done.
Counting objects: 100% (5/5), done.
Delta compression using up to 4 threads
Compressing objects: 100% (3/3), done.
Writing objects: 100% (3/3), 356 bytes | 118.00 KiB/s, done.
Total 3 (delta 2), reused 0 (delta 0)
To ssh://git-codecommit.us-east-1.amazonaws.com/v1/repos/DevOps-Repo
   4903fb9..e613e68  master -> master

user@DESKTOP-5B87H96 MINGW64 ~/DevOps-Repo (master)
$
```

Navigate to the AWS CodePipeline and verify that the source for the updated index file has completed successfully. You will notice that the deploy stage is in progress for the updated index file.

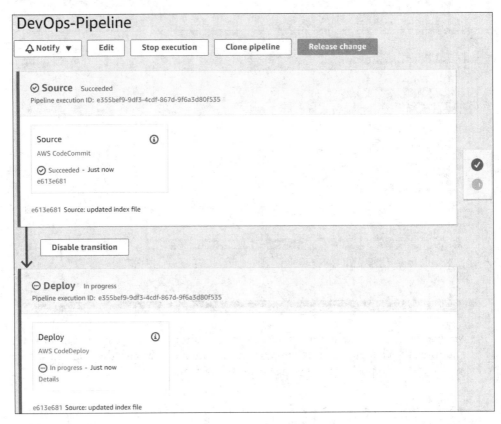

Within a few seconds, the deploy stage is completed successfully.

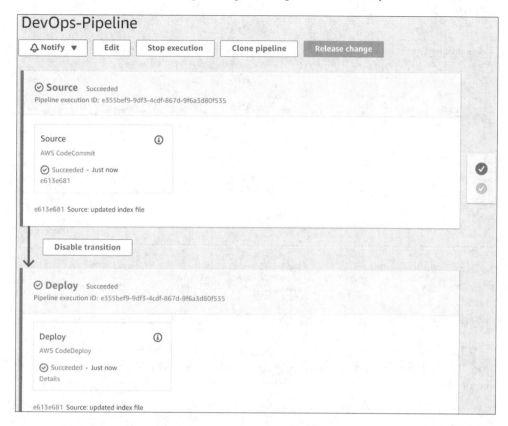

Open a browser and enter the public IP of your Amazon EC2 instance. You will see the updated application code deployed successfully.

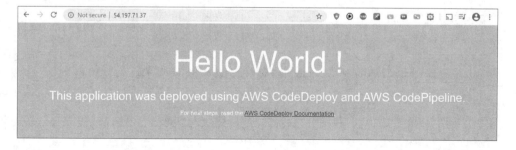

You can review the pipeline's execution history. It shows the source revisions, duration, and triggers, etc.

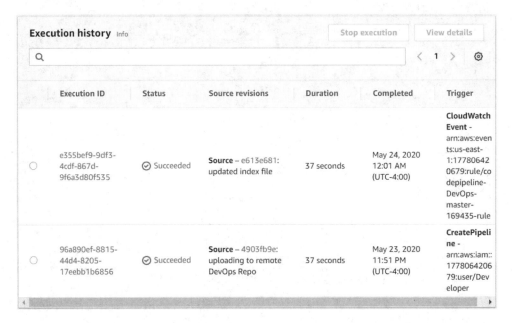

When you click on Settings for the pipeline, you can see the general details, notifications (if configured), and pipeline tags. You also can see the artifact store, version, and region details.

Navigate to the AWS CodeDeploy deployment history and review the deployment details.

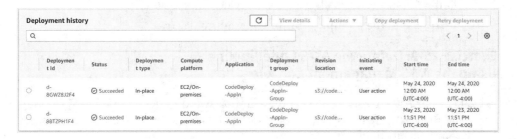

You have successfully created a pipeline and automatically deployed the changes. You need to clean up all the resources that you created as a best practice for your Free Tier to avoid any charges.

Chapter Review

This chapter began by describing AWS CodeDeploy and how it helps you automate application deployments to your Amazon EC2 instances. AWS CodePipeline was introduced, which is used to create continuous integration and continuous deployment pipelines and visualize the execution. This is another practical chapter where we created an Amazon EC2 instance and automatically deployed the sample application using AWS CodePipeline. Then we changed the source code and observed the automatic execution of source code deployment into the application. You gained important experience in terms of your certification and how it will relate to the real world in this chapter.

Exercises

The following exercises will help you practice using AWS CodeDeploy and AWS CodePipeline. You need to create an AWS account, as explained earlier, before performing these exercises. You can use the Free Tier when launching AWS resources, but make sure to terminate them at the end.

Exercise 25-1: Delete the AWS CodeDeploy Application Using the AWS Management Console

1. Use your AWS account email address and password to sign in to the AWS account and then navigate to the AWS CodeDeploy console at https://console.aws.amazon .com/codedeploy/.

2. Verify the AWS region by using the Region selector in the upper-right corner of the page.

3. From the navigation pane, expand Deploy. Then choose Applications.

4. Choose the DevOps-Appln that you created in this chapter and click on the application name.

5. On the Application Details page, click Delete Application.

6. In response to the prompt, confirm you want to delete.

Exercise 25-2: Delete the AWS CodePipeline Using the AWS Management Console

1. Use your AWS account e-mail address and password to sign in to the AWS account and then navigate to the AWS CodePipeline console at https://console.aws.amazon .com/codepipeline/.

2. Verify the AWS region by using the Region selector in the upper-right corner of the page.

3. From the navigation pane on the left, choose Name.

4. Choose the DevOps-Pipeline that you created in this chapter.

5. Click on Edit on the Details page.

6. Click on Delete from the Edit page.

7. In response to the prompt, confirm you want to delete the pipeline.

Exercise 25-3: Delete the AWS CodeCommit Repository Using the AWS Management Console

1. Use your AWS account e-mail address and password to sign in to the AWS account and then navigate to the AWS CodeCommit console at https://console .aws.amazon.com/codecommit/.

2. Verify the AWS region by using the Region selector in the upper-right corner of the page.

3. From the navigation pane on the left, choose Repositories.

4. Choose Settings.

5. Navigate to Delete Repository on the General tab.

6. Choose Delete Repository.

7. Enter **delete** in the popup window and choose to delete.

Exercise 25-4: Delete the Amazon EC2 Instance Using the AWS Management Console

1. Use your AWS account e-mail address and password to sign in to the AWS account and then navigate to the Amazon EC2 console at https://console.aws .amazon.com/ec2/.

2. Verify the AWS region by using the Region selector in the upper-right corner of the page.

3. From the navigation pane on the left, choose Instances.

4. Choose the DevOps instance and select Actions from the dropdown.

5. Click Instance State and choose Terminate.

6. When prompted, choose Yes to terminate the instance.

Questions

The following questions will help you gauge your understanding of the contents in this chapter. Read all the answers carefully because there might be more than one correct answer. Choose the best responses for each question.

1. Your company wants to improve the application deployment process in AWS and asked you to find an appropriate tool that makes it easy to rapidly release new features and avoid any downtime during deployment and scale the deployment to thousands of instances when required. Which of the following AWS service provides those features?

   A. AWS CodeCommit

   B. AWS CodeBuild

   C. AWS CodeDeploy

   D. AWS CodePipeline

2. Which of the following compute platforms does AWS CodeDeploy use to deploy applications? (Choose three.)

   A. AWS Lambda

   B. Amazon ECS

   C. Amazon EC2/On-Premises

   D. Amazon S3

3. Which of the following deployment configurations does AWS CodeDeploy use to specify how traffic is routed during deployment? (Choose three.)

   A. Canary

   B. Linear

   C. All-at-once

   D. Rolling

4. Which of the following compute platforms requires the CodeDeploy agent in AWS CodeDeploy deployment?

   A. Amazon EC2/On-Premises

   B. Amazon ECS

   C. AWS Lambda

   D. Amazon S3

5. What two deployment types are available in AWS CodeDeploy? (Choose two.)

    A. Reckless deployment

    B. In-place deployment

    C. Shadow deployment

    D. Blue/green deployment

6. A company started using AWS CodeDeploy to automate application deployments. Which of the following deployments cannot use an in-place deployment type? (Choose two.)

    A. Amazon EC2

    B. Amazon ECS

    C. AWS Lambda

    D. Amazon S3

7. Which of the following can be used to access and manage AWS CodeDeploy? (Choose all that apply.)

    A. AWS CodeDeploy API

    B. AWS SDK

    C. AWS Management Console

    D. AWS CLI

8. Your company has a hybrid environment and has applications with instances on both AWS Cloud and On-Premises. You enabled blue/green deployments on AWS CodeDeploy to make the applications highly available. Which of the following is true?

    A. Blue/green deployments work only with Amazon EC2 instances

    B. Blue/green deployments are not supported in the AWS Lambda compute platform

    C. Blue/green deployments work only with On-Premises instances

    D. Blue/green deployments are not supported in the Amazon ECS compute platform

9. A company wants to automate and visualize the continuous integration and continuous deployment pipeline to release software code to production. Which of the following AWS services has the functionality that provides this solution?

    A. AWS CodePipeline

    B. AWS CodeBuild

    C. AWS CodeDeploy

    D. AWS CodeCommit

10. Which of the following can be used to stop pipeline execution in AWS CodePipeline? (Choose two.)

   A. Stop and wait

   B. Stop and start

   C. Stop and abandon

   D. Stop and terminate

Answers

1. **C.** AWS CodeDeploy can be used to rapidly release new features to applications and avoid any downtime during deployment and scale the deployment to thousands of instances when required.

2. **A, B, C.** AWS Lambda, Amazon ECS, and Amazon EC2/On-Premises are the compute platforms available in AWS CodeDeploy.

3. **A, B, C.** All-at-once, canary, and linear are the deployment configurations that AWS CodeDeploy uses to specify how traffic is routed during deployment.

4. **A.** Amazon EC2/On-Premises requires the CodeDeploy agent in AWS CodeDeploy deployment.

5. **B, D.** In-place deployment and blue/green deployment are available in AWS CodeDeploy.

6. **B, C.** Amazon ECS and AWS Lambda cannot use an in-place deployment type in AWS CodeDeploy.

7. **A, B, C, D.** AWS CodeDeploy API, AWS SDK, AWS Management Console, and AWS CLI can be used to access and manage AWS CodeDeploy.

8. **A.** Blue/green deployments work only with Amazon EC2 instances.

9. **A.** AWS CodePipeline can be used to automate and visualize the end-to-end continuous integration and continuous delivery pipeline to release software code to production.

10. **A, C.** Stop and wait and stop and abandon are the two ways used to stop pipeline execution in AWS CodePipeline.

Additional Resources

- **AWS CodeDeploy**   The official AWS documentation is the best place to get the latest updates and new features for each service, including AWS CodeDeploy.
  `https://docs.aws.amazon.com/codedeploy/index.html`

- **AWS CodeDeploy Blogs**   These blogs will help you explore AWS CodeDeploy in more depth and include many best-practice architectures to practice and implement.
  `https://aws.amazon.com/blogs/devops/tag/codedeploy/`

- **AWS CodePipeline**   The official AWS documentation is the best place to get all the latest information on all the AWS services, including AWS CodePipeline. `https://docs.aws.amazon.com/codepipeline/index.html`

- **AWS CodePipeline Blogs**   These AWS DevOps blogs will help you explore many reference architectures and best practices that can be used for your proof of concept and to practice and implement in your own environment. `https://aws.amazon.com/blogs/devops/category/developer-tools/aws-codepipeline/`

Building a Scalable and Fault-Tolerant CI/CD Pipeline

In this chapter, you will learn
- Build a CI/CD pipeline using AWS developer tools

In this chapter, we are going to build highly available, scalable, and fault-tolerant application using AWS developer tools such as AWS CodeCommit, AWS CodeBuild, AWS CodeDeploy, and AWS CodePipeline.

CI/CD Pipeline

A typical CI/CD pipeline automates the entire software code builds, automated testing, and deployment to a production environment process using DevOps tools. We are going to use AWS developer tools such as AWS CodeCommit for storing application source code, or you can use another source code repository such as GitHub; AWS CodeBuild to build and test the application code; AWS CodeDeploy to automate code deployments using blue/green deployment; and AWS CodePipeline to automate the continuous delivery pipeline.

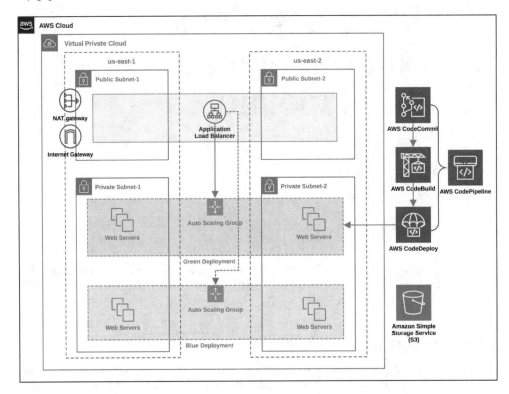

First, you need to log in to your AWS Management Console, navigate to the AWS CodeCommit service, and choose Create Repository. Enter the repository name—for example, **HAFT-App-Repo**—and provide a description of **Highly Available Fault Tolerant Web Application** and then click the Create button.

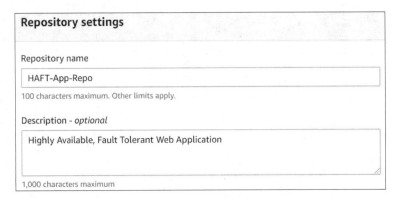

Note the clone URL for HTTPS or SSH.

Go to your local machine and use git.bash for Windows and Terminal for macOS. You need to clone the AWS CodeCommit repository using the git clone and go to the HAFT-App-Repo folder. Download the AWS sample web application from https://github.com/aws-samples/aws-cicd-bluegreen/raw/master/WebApp.zip and unzip it to the local repository. You also need to move and remove some files from it.

```
MINGW64:/c/Users/user/HAFT-App-Repo                              —    □    ×

user@DESKTOP-5B87H96 MINGW64 ~
$ git clone ssh://git-codecommit.us-east-1.amazonaws.com/v1/repos/HAFT-App-Repo
Cloning into 'HAFT-App-Repo'...
warning: You appear to have cloned an empty repository.

user@DESKTOP-5B87H96 MINGW64 ~
$ cd HAFT-App-Repo/

user@DESKTOP-5B87H96 MINGW64 ~/HAFT-App-Repo (master)
$ ls -al
total 40
drwxr-xr-x 1 user 197609     0 May 24 02:19 ./
drwxr-xr-x 1 user 197609     0 May 24 02:18 ../
drwxr-xr-x 1 user 197609     0 May 24 02:18 .git/
-rw-r--r-- 1 user 197609 16063 May 24 02:16 WebApp.zip

user@DESKTOP-5B87H96 MINGW64 ~/HAFT-App-Repo (master)
$ unzip WebApp.zip
Archive:  WebApp.zip
   creating: WebApp/
  inflating: WebApp/template.yml
  inflating: WebApp/appspec.yml
  inflating: WebApp/buildspec.yml
   creating: WebApp/tests/
  inflating: WebApp/tests/test.js
  inflating: WebApp/README.md
   creating: WebApp/public/
  inflating: WebApp/public/index.html
   creating: WebApp/public/css/
  inflating: WebApp/public/css/styles.css
  inflating: WebApp/public/css/gradients.css
   creating: WebApp/public/js/
  inflating: WebApp/public/js/set-background.js
   creating: WebApp/public/img/
  inflating: WebApp/public/img/tweet.svg
  inflating: WebApp/package.json
   creating: WebApp/scripts/
  inflating: WebApp/scripts/stop_server.sh
  inflating: WebApp/scripts/start_server.sh
  inflating: WebApp/scripts/beforeInstall.sh
  inflating: WebApp/app.js

user@DESKTOP-5B87H96 MINGW64 ~/HAFT-App-Repo (master)
$ mv WebApp/* .

user@DESKTOP-5B87H96 MINGW64 ~/HAFT-App-Repo (master)
$ rm -rf WebApp

user@DESKTOP-5B87H96 MINGW64 ~/HAFT-App-Repo (master)
$ rm WebApp.zip

user@DESKTOP-5B87H96 MINGW64 ~/HAFT-App-Repo (master)
$
```

Add the sample web application files to the repository using the git add command.

Commit the files using the git commit command, and use the git push command to push the AWS sample web application files to the remote repository in AWS CodeCommit.

Navigate to the AWS CodeCommit service in the AWS Management Console and verify your updated repository.

Next, you need to create the infrastructure using the template.yml file, which you extracted from WebApp.zip. Navigate to the AWS CloudFormation service in the AWS Management Console and click on Create Stack.

Choose Template Is Ready in the Prepare Template section and choose Upload A Template File for the Template Source. Upload template.yml from your local machine and click View In Designer.

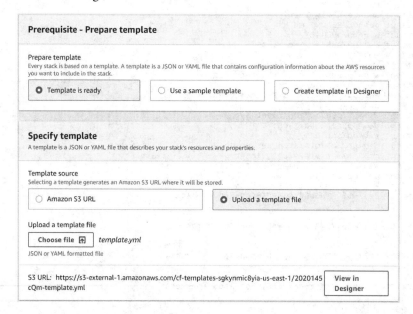

The AWS CloudFormation designer is a graphical tool used to visualize and modify resources using a drag-and-drop interface. You can verify all the resources that will be created as part of this template.

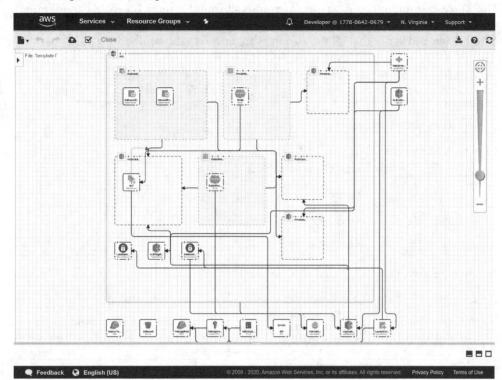

Enter a stack name—for example, **HAFT-Application**—and click Next.

Stack name

Stack name

HAFT-Application

Stack name can include letters (A-Z and a-z), numbers (0-9), and dashes (-).

As per best practices, add a tag of **Name** with value of **HAFT Application Stack** and leave other options at their default settings. Click Next to continue.

PART VIII

Review all the options that you selected, acknowledge that the AWS CloudFormation might create IAM resources, and click Create Stack.

Select the Events tab to see all the events in your template execution, which have a "Resource creation initiated" status. As you recall from Chapter 18, AWS CloudFormation takes care of the dependencies regarding which resource needs to be created first, etc. Scroll down and verify that all the resources are created successfully.

Timestamp	Logical ID	Status	Status reason
2020-05-24 02:42:13 UTC-0400	NAT	ⓘ CREATE_IN_PROGRESS	Resource creation Initiated
2020-05-24 02:42:13 UTC-0400	NAT	ⓘ CREATE_IN_PROGRESS	-
2020-05-24 02:42:11 UTC-0400	PublicSubnetNetworkAclAssociation01	⊘ CREATE_COMPLETE	-
2020-05-24 02:42:10 UTC-0400	PublicSubnetRTAssociation01	⊘ CREATE_COMPLETE	-
2020-05-24 02:42:10 UTC-0400	PrivateSubnetRTAssociation02	⊘ CREATE_COMPLETE	-
2020-05-24 02:42:10 UTC-0400	PrivateSubnetRTAssociation01	⊘ CREATE_COMPLETE	-
2020-05-24 02:42:09 UTC-0400	PublicSubnetRTAssociation02	⊘ CREATE_COMPLETE	-
2020-05-24 02:42:09 UTC-0400	PublicSubnetNetworkAclAssociation02	⊘ CREATE_COMPLETE	-
2020-05-24 02:41:56 UTC-0400	ApplicationLoadBalancer	ⓘ CREATE_IN_PROGRESS	Resource creation Initiated
2020-05-24 02:41:55 UTC-0400	PublicSubnetNetworkAclAssociation01	ⓘ CREATE_IN_PROGRESS	Resource creation Initiated
2020-05-24 02:41:55 UTC-0400	PublicSubnetRTAssociation01	ⓘ CREATE_IN_PROGRESS	Resource creation Initiated
2020-05-24 02:41:55 UTC-0400	PublicSubnetNetworkAclAssociation01	ⓘ CREATE_IN_PROGRESS	-

Next, click the Outputs tab and note the Application Load Balancer (ALB) URL.

ALBTargetGroup	BlueGreenTG	TargetGroup Name	-
ASGroup	BlueGreenASGroup	AutoScaling Group Name	-
DeployRoleArn	HAFT-Application-DeployTrustRole-1VF3NE39Y4SR9	CodeDeploy role Arn	-
S3BucketName	build-artifact-bluegreenbucket-us-east-1-177806420679	Bucket to for storing artifacts	-
URL	http://HAFT-Appli-ADS1WFMNE6TU-1931851748.us-east-1.elb.amazonaws.com	URL of the website	-

Open a browser on your local machine, enter the ALB URL, and press ENTER. You will see the Hello World! message. You have successfully created the infrastructure VPC, subnets, web servers, ALB, Internet Gateway, NAT Gateway, etc.

← → C ⓘ Not secure | haft-appli-ads1wfmne6tu-1931851748.us-east-1.elb.amazonaws.com ☆ 🛡

`Hello World!`

Navigate to the AWS CodeBuild service from the AWS Management Console and choose Create Build Project. Enter **HAFT-App-Build** for the project name and **Highly Available Fault Tolerant Application Build** for the description. In the Source section, choose AWS CodeCommit as the source provider and HAFT-App-Repo as the repository. Then select the reference type as Branch and choose Master.

Project configuration

Project name

```
HAFT-App-Build
```

A project name must be 2 to 255 characters. It can include the letters A-Z and a-z, the numbers 0-9, and the special characters - and _.

Description - *optional*

```
Highly Available Fault Tolerant Application Build
```

Build badge - *optional*

☐ Enable build badge

▶ **Additional configuration**
   tags

Source   [Add source]

Source 1 - Primary

Source provider

```
AWS CodeCommit                                  ▼
```

Repository

```
🔍  HAFT-App-Repo                                ✕
```

Reference type
Choose the source version reference type that contains your source code.

◉ Branch
◯ Git tag
◯ Commit ID

Branch   Commit ID - *optional*
Choose a branch that contains the code to build. Choose a commit ID. This can shorten the duration of your build.

```
master                          ▼                🔍
```

Select the environment image as Managed Image and the operating system as Ubuntu. Choose Runtime for the standard and aws/codebuild/standard:2.0 for the image. Choose Linux for the environment type as Linux and Always Use The Latest Image For This Runtime Version for the image version. Select Privileged if you want to build a Docker image (you can leave it unchecked for this application). Select New Service Role to create a new CodeBuild service role in your account.

In the Buildspec section, choose Use A Buildspec File. In the Artifacts section, choose Amazon S3 for the type and select the bucket name and filename. Choose Zip for the artifacts packaging to upload artifacts as a compressed file.

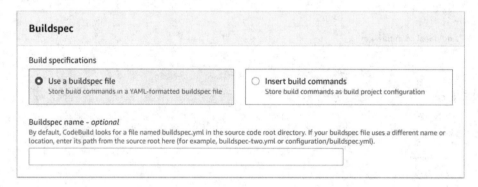

Enable logs and choose either CloudWatch Logs or Amazon S3, or both, which will be helpful to verify detailed steps and for troubleshooting if required. Enter a group name and stream name.

Logs

CloudWatch

☑ CloudWatch logs - *optional*
Checking this option will upload build output logs to CloudWatch.

Group name

/haft

Stream name

/app

S3

☐ S3 logs - *optional*
Checking this option will upload build output logs to S3.

Verify the build project details, such as source provider, primary repository, and artifacts upload location. Click the Start Build button.

Configuration

Source provider	Primary repository	Artifacts upload location	Build badge
AWS CodeCommit	HAFT-App-Repo	build-artifact-bluegreenbucket-us-east-1-177806420679	Disabled

---

Click the Start Build button again to start the initial build process of your application. Within a minute, the overall status is "Succeeded" and all the phases are listed, such as Submitted, Queued, Provisioning, Download_source, Install, Pre_build, Build,

Post_build, Upload_artifacts, Finalizing, and Completed. You can verify the build number, source version, start time, and end time.

Name	Status	Context	Duration	Start time	End time
SUBMITTED	⊘ Succeeded	-	<1 sec	May 24, 2020 3:18 AM (UTC-4:00)	May 24, 2020 3:18 AM (UTC-4:00)
QUEUED	⊘ Succeeded	-	1 sec	May 24, 2020 3:18 AM (UTC-4:00)	May 24, 2020 3:18 AM (UTC-4:00)
PROVISIONING	⊘ Succeeded	-	18 secs	May 24, 2020 3:18 AM (UTC-4:00)	May 24, 2020 3:18 AM (UTC-4:00)
DOWNLOAD_SOURCE	⊘ Succeeded	-	16 secs	May 24, 2020 3:18 AM (UTC-4:00)	May 24, 2020 3:19 AM (UTC-4:00)
INSTALL	⊘ Succeeded	-	22 secs	May 24, 2020 3:19 AM (UTC-4:00)	May 24, 2020 3:19 AM (UTC-4:00)
PRE_BUILD	⊘ Succeeded	-	<1 sec	May 24, 2020 3:19 AM (UTC-4:00)	May 24, 2020 3:19 AM (UTC-4:00)
BUILD	⊘ Succeeded	-	<1 sec	May 24, 2020 3:19 AM (UTC-4:00)	May 24, 2020 3:19 AM (UTC-4:00)
POST_BUILD	⊘ Succeeded	-	1 sec	May 24, 2020 3:19 AM (UTC-4:00)	May 24, 2020 3:19 AM (UTC-4:00)
UPLOAD_ARTIFACTS	⊘ Succeeded	-	<1 sec	May 24, 2020 3:19 AM (UTC-4:00)	May 24, 2020 3:19 AM (UTC-4:00)
FINALIZING	⊘ Succeeded	-	2 secs	May 24, 2020 3:19 AM (UTC-4:00)	May 24, 2020 3:19 AM (UTC-4:00)
COMPLETED	⊘ Succeeded	-	-	May 24, 2020 3:19 AM (UTC-4:00)	-

Navigate to AWS CodeDeploy and choose Create Application. Enter an application name, such as **HAFT-Appln**, and select the compute platform as EC2/On-Premises from the dropdown. Click the Create Application button.

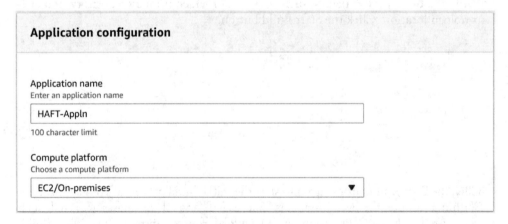

Create a deployment group by clicking the Create Deployment Group button.

Enter **HAFT-Appln-Group** for the deployment group name and choose a service role that has access to CodeDeploy. Choose Blue/Green for the deployment type, which replaces the instances in the deployment group with new instances that have the latest application revision. Once the new environment is registered with load balancer, the old environment will be deregistered and its instances terminated.

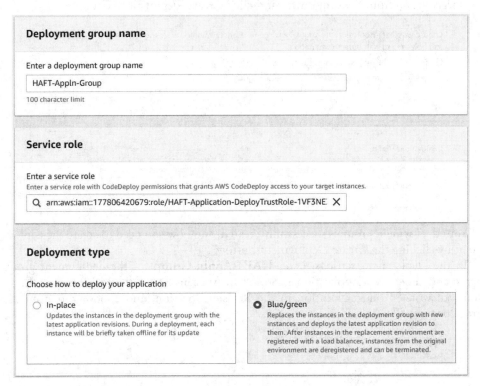

In the Environment Configuration area, choose Automatically Copy Amazon EC2 Auto Scaling Group to deploy the revised application to it. Choose the current Amazon EC2 Auto Scaling group name, such as BlueGreenAsGroup. In Deployment Settings, choose Reroute Traffic Immediately and choose Terminate The Original Instances In The Deployment Group.

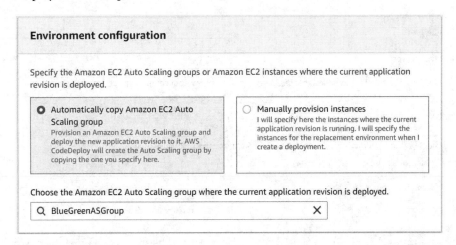

For the deployment configuration choose AllAtOnce, which is the default for CodeDeploy. In the Load Balancer section, choose Application Load Balancer, choose the target group from the dropdown, and click Create Deployment Group.

Choose whether instances in the original environment are terminated after the deployment is succeeds, and how long to wait before termination.

○ Terminate the original instances in the deployment group

○ Keep the original instances in the deployment group running

Days	Hours	Minutes
0 ▼	1 ▼	0 ▼

Deployment configuration
Choose from a list of default and custom deployment configurations. A deployment configuration is a set of rules that determines how fast an application is deployed and the success or failure conditions for a deployment.

CodeDeployDefault.AllAtOnce ▼	or	**Create deployment configuration**

Your deployment group is successfully created, and now you need to create the deployment by clicking the Create Deployment button.

In the Deployment settings, enter **HAFT-Appln-Group** for the deployment group name and choose My Application Is Stored In Amazon S3 for the revision type. Enter your Amazon S3 bucket location in the Revision location, and choose Zip from the dropdown for Revision Type.

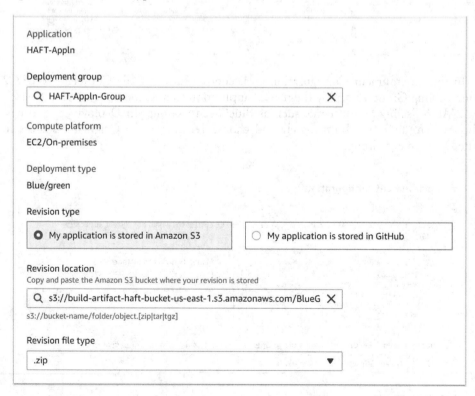

Application
HAFT-Appln

Deployment group

Q HAFT-Appln-Group   ✕

Compute platform
EC2/On-premises

Deployment type
Blue/green

Revision type

○ My application is stored in Amazon S3   ○ My application is stored in GitHub

Revision location
Copy and paste the Amazon S3 bucket where your revision is stored

Q s3://build-artifact-haft-bucket-us-east-1.s3.amazonaws.com/BlueG ✕

s3://bucket-name/folder/object.[zip|tar|tgz]

Revision file type

.zip ▼

On the next page you can enter additional deployment behavior settings. For this example, leave everything at the default settings and click the Create Deployment button.

In the Deployments section, you can see the status of provisioning replacement instances, installing application on the replacement instances, reroute traffic to replacement instances, and terminating the original instances. You can also view the traffic shifting progress here.

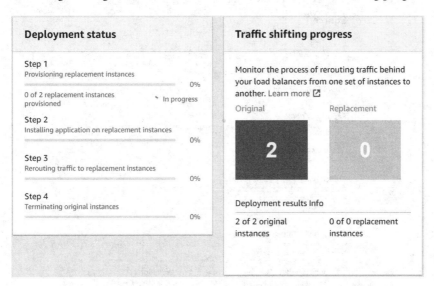

You have successfully configured AWS CodeDeploy, so navigate to AWS CodePipeline and click Create Pipeline.

Enter a name for your pipeline, such as **HAFT-APP-Pipeline**, and choose to create a new service role. Check Allow AWS CodePipeline To Create A New Service Role To Be Used In This Pipeline and click Next.

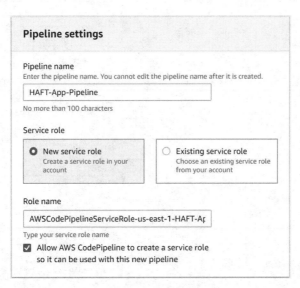

In the Add Source Stage area, choose AWS CodeCommit from the dropdown for the source provider. Enter **HAFT-App-Repo** for the Repository name and select Master for the branch name. Then select the recommended Amazon CloudWatch events for change detection options and click Next.

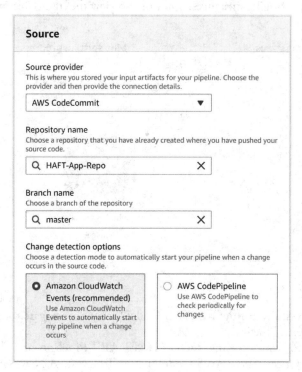

In the Add Build Stage area, choose AWS Codebuild as the build provider from the dropdown and choose your region. Enter the build project name, such as **HAFT-App-Build**, leave the other settings at their defaults, and click Next.

In the Add Deploy Stage area, choose AWS CodeDeploy as the deploy provider from the dropdown and choose your region. Then enter the CodeDeploy application name, such as **HAFT-Appln**, and enter **HAFT-Appln-Group** for the deployment group. Click Next to continue.

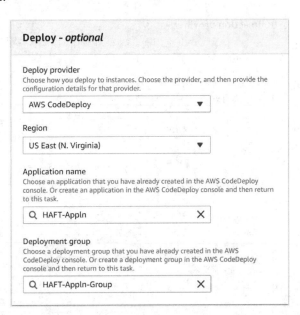

Review the pipeline settings and verify the source provider details.

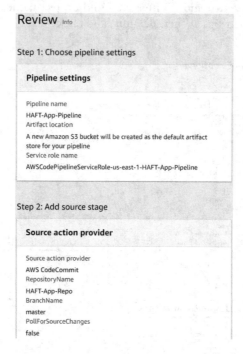

Review the build stage details and the deploy action provider details. Click Create Pipeline once you are done.

You have successfully created the HAFT-App-Pipeline, and you can visually see the progress of your CI/CD pipeline. The source stage is in progress and the build stage is waiting.

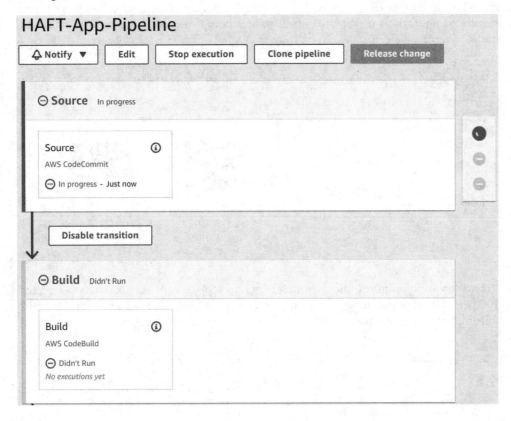

Within a few minutes the source stage and build stage have completed successfully. Now the deploy stage is in progress.

When you click Deploy Stage Details, you can visually see the traffic staging progress where the two instances are running in the original deployment and another two instances are provisioned as replacement instances. Also, you can see the deployment status and verify that the provisioning replacement instances completed 100 percent and installing applications on replacement instances completed 100 percent. The rerouting traffic to replacement instances is halfway through, with 50 percent progress.

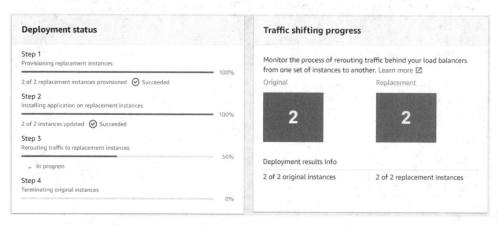

In a few more minutes, the rerouting traffic to replacement instances has completed 100 percent and terminating original instances is in progress. You can also view the traffic shifting progress is completed and moved to replacement instances.

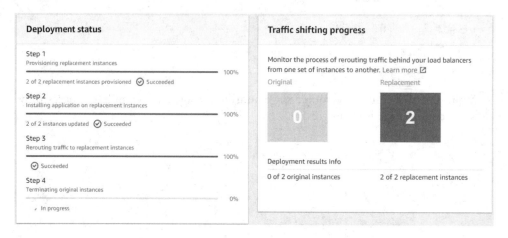

From your AWS Management Console, navigate to your ALB, which will be on the left navigation pane in the Amazon EC2 dashboard. Select your ALB and note the DNS name.

Now on your local machine, open a browser of your choice, enter the ALB DNS name, and press the ENTER key. Congratulations! You just created a scalable, highly available, fault-tolerant web application by using an automated software release pipeline.

It is easy to add a new feature or update your source code and deploy it in production automatically using the CI/CD pipeline that you created using AWS developer tools. Go to your source code repository in your local machine and edit index.html, which is stored in the public folder. For simplicity, change Congratulations to **Hello World!** and change the second line to **You just deployed HAFT Node.js web application V2 successfully!!**

Now add the index file using the git add command and commit the change using the git commit command. Next push your source code changes to your remote repository in AWS CodeCommit using the git push command.

```
MINGW64:/c/Users/user/HAFT-App-Repo                          —    □    ×

user@DESKTOP-5B87H96 MINGW64 ~/HAFT-App-Repo (master)
$ vi public/index.html

user@DESKTOP-5B87H96 MINGW64 ~/HAFT-App-Repo (master)
$ git status
On branch master
Your branch is up to date with 'origin/master'.

Changes not staged for commit:
  (use "git add <file>..." to update what will be committed)
  (use "git checkout -- <file>..." to discard changes in working directory)

        modified:   public/index.html

no changes added to commit (use "git add" and/or "git commit -a")

user@DESKTOP-5B87H96 MINGW64 ~/HAFT-App-Repo (master)
$ git add .
warning: LF will be replaced by CRLF in public/index.html.
The file will have its original line endings in your working directory

user@DESKTOP-5B87H96 MINGW64 ~/HAFT-App-Repo (master)
$ git commit -m "updated HAFT application"
[master 07576ae] updated HAFT application
 1 file changed, 2 insertions(+), 2 deletions(-)

user@DESKTOP-5B87H96 MINGW64 ~/HAFT-App-Repo (master)
$ git push
Enumerating objects: 7, done.
Counting objects: 100% (7/7), done.
Delta compression using up to 4 threads
Compressing objects: 100% (4/4), done.
Writing objects: 100% (4/4), 502 bytes | 100.00 KiB/s, done.
Total 4 (delta 2), reused 0 (delta 0)
To ssh://git-codecommit.us-east-1.amazonaws.com/v1/repos/HAFT-App-Repo
   414333d..07576ae  master -> master

user@DESKTOP-5B87H96 MINGW64 ~/HAFT-App-Repo (master)
$
```

Navigate to AWS CodeBuild in the AWS Management Console and verify the build history. You can see the build process is in progress using the updated source code from AWS Commit.

In few minutes, you can see that the traffic is shifted to new instances. Also, you can verify from the deployment status that all the steps are completed 100 percent successfully.

Next navigate to your CI/CD pipeline and verify that the updated HAFT application is in AWS CodeCommit. Next, you can see the build has succeeded using the updated HAFT application source. Finally, you can see the successful deployment in the deploy stage using the updated HAFT application.

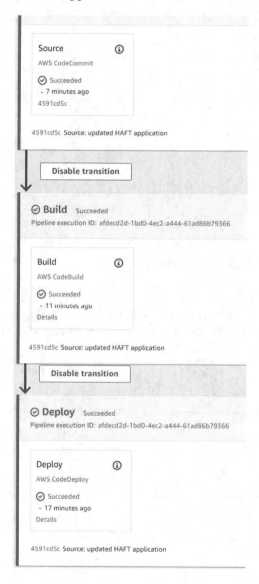

On your local machine, open a browser and enter the ALB URL that you noted down previously. When you press ENTER, you can see the updated application is displayed successfully.

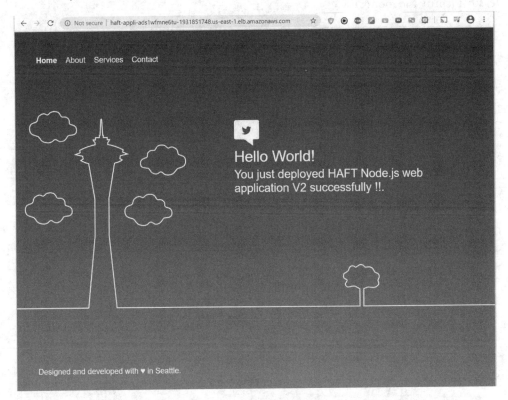

Navigate to Amazon CloudWatch and click on Logs in the navigation pane. Choose Log Groups and click on the haft log group. You can verify all the messages that were created during the execution. This is helpful when troubleshooting any issues later to easily identify the root cause.

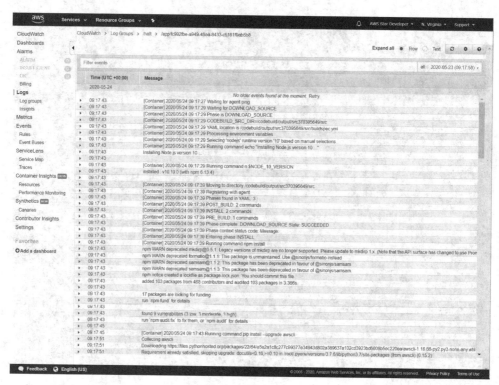

You have observed the demonstration of building a CI/CD pipeline using AWS CodeCommit, AWS CodeBuild, AWS CodeDeploy, and AWS CodePipeline. Using this CI/CD pipeline, you created a highly scalable, available, and fault-tolerant sample web application quickly. You also changed the application source code and observed from the AWS CodePipeline page the different stages of your software build, testing, and application deployment. This experience will help you in your certification exam, and you can practice in your test environment and possibly implement it in a real environment once you gain confidence. You can release new application software and additional features to your software rapidly by implementing continuous integration and continuous delivery using AWS developer tools, which accelerates your software development, testing, and release cycle.

Chapter Review

This chapter began by explaining what a CI/CD pipeline is and how it automates the entire software code build, automated testing, and deploying to a different environment. We then used AWS developer tools to build a CI/CD pipeline. The AWS CodeCommit service is used for storing sample application source code. We used AWS CodeBuild to build and test the web application code. We also used AWS CodeDeploy to automate code deployments using the blue/green deployment type. The chapter showed how to use AWS CodePipeline to automate the continuous delivery pipeline. You also learned how to host your application code, build, test, and automatically deploy applications in AWS Cloud in this chapter.

Exercises

The following exercises will help you practice using AWS development tools. You need to create an AWS account, as explained earlier, before performing these exercises. You can use the Free Tier when launching AWS resources, but make sure to terminate them at the end.

Exercise 26-1: Delete the AWS CodeCommit Repository Using the AWS Management Console

1. Use your AWS account e-mail address and password to sign in to the AWS account and then navigate to the AWS CodeCommit console at https://console.aws.amazon .com/codecommit/.

2. Verify the AWS region by using the Region selector in the upper-right corner of the page.

3. From the navigation pane on the left, choose Repositories.

4. Select HAFT-App-Repo and choose Settings.

5. Navigate to Delete Repository on the General tab.

6. Choose Delete Repository.

7. Enter delete in the popup window and choose to delete.

Exercise 26-2: Delete the AWS CodeBuild Project Using the AWS Management Console

1. Use your AWS account e-mail address and password to sign in to the AWS account and then navigate to the AWS CodeBuild console at https://console.aws.amazon .com/codebuild/.

2. Verify the AWS region by using the Region selector in the upper-right corner of the page.

3. From the navigation pane on the left, choose Build Projects.

4. Choose the radio button next to HAFT-App-Build project.

5. Choose Delete to delete your build project.

Exercise 26-3: Delete the AWS CodeDeploy Application Using the AWS Management Console

1. Use your AWS account e-mail address and password to sign in to the AWS account and then navigate to the AWS CodeDeploy console at https://console.aws.amazon .com/codedeploy/.

2. Verify the AWS region by using the Region selector in the upper-right corner of the page.

3. From the navigation pane on the left, expand Deploy. Then choose Applications.

4. Choose HAFT-Appln that you created in this chapter.

5. Click on the application name.

6. On the Application Details page, click Delete Application.

7. In response to the prompt, confirm that you want to delete.

Exercise 26-4: Delete the AWS CodePipeline Using the AWS Management Console

1. Use your AWS account e-mail address and password to sign in to the AWS account and then navigate to the AWS CodePipeline console at https://console .aws.amazon.com/codepipeline/.

2. Verify the AWS region by using the Region selector in the upper-right corner of the page.

3. From the navigation pane on the left, choose Name.

4. Choose the HAFT-App-Pipeline that you created in this chapter.

5. Click Edit on the Details page.

6. Click Delete from Edit page.

7. In response to the prompt, confirm you want to delete the pipeline.

Exercise 26-5: Delete the AWS CloudFormation Stack Using the AWS Management Console

1. Use your AWS account e-mail address and password to sign in to the AWS account and then navigate to the AWS CloudFormation console at https:// console.aws.amazon.com/cloudformation/.

2. Verify the AWS region by using the Region selector in the upper-right corner of the page.

3. From the navigation pane on the left, choose Stacks. Select the stack that you created in this chapter.

4. From the Stack Details page, choose Delete

5. When prompted, choose Delete Stack to delete the entire stack.

Questions

The following questions will help you gauge your understanding of the contents in this chapter. Read all the answers carefully because there might be more than one correct answer. Choose the best responses for each question.

1. What four AWS developer tools can be used to build a CI/CD pipeline? (Choose four.)

   A. AWS CodeCommit

   B. AWS CodeBuild

   C. AWS CodeDeploy

   D. AWS CodePipeline

2. Which of the following AWS developer tools provides a fully managed solution to host your application source code by creating a code repository and uses git commands to interact with your code repository?

   A. AWS CLI

   B. AWS Cloud9

   C. AWS CodeCommit

   D. AWS CodePipeline

3. Which of the following AWS developer tools provides the integrated development environment (IDE) for creating, executing, and debugging your source code from the AWS CodeCommit repository?

   A. Amazon Corretto

   B. AWS CDK

   C. AWS CLI

   D. AWS Cloud9

4. Which of the following AWS developer tools can be used to build your application and test your source code with continuous scaling?

   A. AWS Cloud9

   B. AWS CodeDeploy

   C. AWS CodeBuild

   D. AWS X-Ray

5. Which of the following AWS developer tools can be used to automate your application code deployment and maintain your application uptime using blue/green deployment?

   A. AWS CodeCommit

   B. AWS CodeBuild

   C. AWS CodeDeploy

   D. AWS Device Farm

6. Which of the following AWS developer tools can be used to automate the software delivery using automated continuous delivery pipelines and also used for fast and reliable software code updates by visually monitoring the flow?

   A. AWS CodeCommit

   B. AWS Cloud9

   C. AWS CodeDeploy

   D. AWS CodePipeline

7. Your company is planning to deploy an application to the production environment frequently using AWS CodeDeploy. The application, which is hosted on Amazon EC2, needs to be always available even during application code change implementations. How you can meet your company's requirement?

   A. Use in-place deployment

   B. Use blue/green deployment

   C. Use rolling deployment

   D. Use canary deployment

8. Your company uses the AWS Lambda platform and uses AWS CodeDeploy to deploy serverless applications to production. They want to direct the traffic in increments to the new AWS Lambda functions instead of directing all the traffic at once. How can you meet this requirement?

   A. Use an all-at-once deployment configuration

   B. Use a linear deployment configuration

   C. Use a canary deployment configuration

   D. Use a rolling deployment configuration

9. A company wants to remove the manual process in their software delivery process and use an automated process end to end from development, build, and deployment into production. They want to utilize AWS services to build the pipeline, and they use GitHub as their source code repository. What services stack do they need to build the CI/CD pipeline?

   A. GitHub, AWS CodeBuild, AWS CodeDeploy, AWS CodePipeline

   B. GitHub, AWS CodeBuild, AWS CodeDeploy, AWS CodeCommit

   C. AWS Cloud9, AWS CodeBuild, AWS CodeDeploy, AWS CodePipeline

   D. AWS CodeCommit, AWS CodeBuild, AWS CodeDeploy, AWS Cloud9

10. A company has enabled all the available options to store logs in AWS CodeDeploy. What are the two destinations where the logs will be stored? (Choose two.)

   A. Amazon CloudWatch logs

   B. Amazon EC2

   C. Amazon S3

   D. Amazon RDS

Answers

1. **A, B, C, D.** You can use AWS CodeCommit to store the code repository, AWS CodeBuild to build your application, AWS CodeDeploy to automatically deploy your application, and AWS CodePipeline to build the CI/CD pipeline.

2. **C.** AWS CodeCommit provides a fully managed service to host your application source code by creating a code repository, and you can use git commands to interact with your code repository.

3. **D.** AWS Cloud9 provides the IDE for creating, executing, and debugging your source code from the AWS CodeCommit repository.

4. **C.** AWS CodeBuild can be used to build your application and test your source code with continuous scaling.

5. **C.** AWS CodeBuild can be used to automate your application code deployment and maintain your application uptime using blue/green deployment.

6. **D.** AWS CodePipeline can be used to automate the software delivery using automated continuous delivery pipelines.

7. **B.** Use blue/green deployment when the application needs to be always available even during application code change implementations.

8. **C.** Use a canary deployment configuration to direct the traffic in increments to the new AWS Lambda functions.

9. **A.** You can use GitHub, AWS CodeBuild, AWS CodeDeploy, and AWS CodePipeline to build the pipeline.

10. **A, C.** You can use Amazon CloudWatch logs and Amazon S3 as log destinations.

Additional Resources

- **Blue/Green Deployment**   This reference deployment guide has a quick-start guide with an architecture diagram and scripts to quickly deploy the CI/CD pipeline using AWS CodePipeline.
  ```
  https://aws.amazon.com/quickstart/architecture/blue-
  green-deployment/
  ```

- **Automate Infrastructure Deployments** This blog demonstrates how to use AWS CodePipeline to orchestrate the end-to-end infrastructure and application deployment.
  https://aws.amazon.com/blogs/devops/bluegreen-infrastructure-application-deployment-blog/

- **Build Containers with AWS CodePipeline** This blog explains the approach to building Windows Server containers using the CI/CD pipeline.
  https://aws.amazon.com/blogs/devops/building-windows-containers-with-aws-codepipeline-and-custom-actions/

- **Continuous Kubernetes Deployment** This blog explains the steps to automatically build a Kubernetes cluster using AWS CodeCommit, AWS CodeBuild, and AWS CodePipeline.
  https://aws.amazon.com/blogs/devops/continuous-deployment-to-kubernetes-using-aws-codepipeline-aws-codecommit-aws-codebuild-amazon-ecr-and-aws-lambda/

PART IX

Appendixes and Acronyms and Glossary

- **Appendix A**   AWS Certified Developer - Associate Exam Objective Map (DVA-C01)
- **Appendix B**   About the Online Content
- **Acronyms and Glossary**

AWS Certified Developer - Associate Exam Objective Map (DVA-C01)

Exam Objective	All-in-One Exam Guide	Chapter #
Domain 1: Deployment		
1.1 Deploy written code in AWS using existing CI/CD pipelines, processes, and patterns	Hosting Secure Repositories Using AWS CodeCommit	23
	Building an Application AWS CodeBuild	24
	Building a Scalable and Fault-Tolerant CI/CD Pipeline	26
1.2 Deploy applications using Elastic Beanstalk	Deploying a Web Application Using AWS Elastic Beanstalk	21
1.3 Prepare the application deployment package to be deployed to AWS	Deploying Applications Using CodeDeploy and CodePipeline	25
1.4 Deploy serverless applications	Developing Serverless Applications with Lambda	19
Domain 2: Security		
2.1 Make authenticated calls to AWS services	Web Identity Federation and Amazon Cognito for User Authentication	11
2.2 Implement encryption using AWS services	Protecting Your Data Using Server-Side and Client-Side Encryption	12
2.3 Implement application authentication and authorization	Securing AWS Resources with Identity and Access Management	10

Exam Objective	All-in-One Exam Guide	Chapter #
Domain 3: Development with AWS Services		
3.1 Write code for serverless applications	Amazon Simple Workflow Service, Amazon API Gateway, and AWS Step Functions	16
3.2 Translate functional requirements into application design	Deploying a Static Website on Amazon S3 Bucket	20
3.3 Implement application design into application code	Distributing the Contents via AWS CloudFront Domain Name System and Amazon Route 53	6 7
3.4 Write code that interacts with AWS services by using APIs, SDKs, and AWS CLI	Interacting with AWS Using API, SDK, and CLI	2
	Working with Simple Storage Service	8
	Infrastructure as Code Using AWS CloudFormation	18
Domain 4: Refactoring		
4.1 Optimize applications to best use AWS services and features	Networking Using Amazon Virtual Private Cloud	3
	Creating a Virtual Machine Using EC2	4
	AWS Relational Database Services	13
	AWS NoSQL Database Service: Amazon DynamoDB	14
4.2 Migrate existing application code to run on AWS	Elastic Load Balancing and Auto Scaling	5
	Amazon EBS, Amazon EFS, and Amazon Glacier	9
	Migrating Your Application and Database to AWS	22
Domain 5: Monitoring and Troubleshooting		
5.1 Write code that can be monitored	Amazon Simple Queue Service and Simple Notification Service	15
	Simple Workflow Service, Amazon API Gateway, and AWS Step Functions	16
5.2 Perform root cause analysis on faults found in testing or production	Monitoring Using Amazon CloudWatch, AWS CloudTrail, and AWS Config	17

About the Online Content

This book comes complete with TotalTester Online customizable practice exam software with 130 practice exam questions.

System Requirements

The current and previous major versions of the following desktop browsers are recommended and supported: Chrome, Microsoft Edge, Firefox, and Safari. These browsers update frequently, and sometimes an update may cause compatibility issues with the TotalTester Online or other content hosted on the Training Hub. If you run into a problem using one of these browsers, please try using another until the problem is resolved.

Your Total Seminars Training Hub Account

To get access to the online content you will need to create an account on the Total Seminars Training Hub. Registration is free, and you will be able to track all your online content using your account. You may also opt in if you wish to receive marketing information from McGraw Hill or Total Seminars, but this is not required for you to gain access to the online content.

Privacy Notice

McGraw Hill values your privacy. Please be sure to read the Privacy Notice available during registration to see how the information you have provided will be used. You may view our Corporate Customer Privacy Policy by visiting the McGraw Hill Privacy Center. Visit the **mheducation.com** site and click **Privacy** at the bottom of the page.

Single User License Terms and Conditions

Online access to the digital content included with this book is governed by the McGraw Hill License Agreement outlined next. By using this digital content you agree to the terms of that license.

Access   To register and activate your Total Seminars Training Hub account, simply follow these easy steps.

1. Go to **hub.totalsem.com/mheclaim**

2. To Register and create a new Training Hub account, enter your e-mail address, name, and password. No further personal information (such as credit card number) is required to create an account.

   If you already have a Total Seminars Training Hub account, enter your e-mail address and password on the **Log in** tab.

3. Enter your Product Key: **640w-jwct-wvdw**

4. Click to accept the user license terms.

5. For new users, click the **Register and Claim** button to create your account. For existing users, click the **Log in and Claim** button.

You will be taken to the Training Hub and have access to the content for this book.

Duration of License   Access to your online content through the Total Seminars Training Hub will expire one year from the date the publisher declares the book out of print.

Your purchase of this McGraw Hill product, including its access code, through a retail store is subject to the refund policy of that store.

The Content is a copyrighted work of McGraw Hill, and McGraw Hill reserves all rights in and to the Content. The Work is © 2021 by McGraw Hill.

Restrictions on Transfer   The user is receiving only a limited right to use the Content for the user's own internal and personal use, dependent on purchase and continued ownership of this book. The user may not reproduce, forward, modify, create derivative works based upon, transmit, distribute, disseminate, sell, publish, or sublicense the Content or in any way commingle the Content with other third-party content without McGraw Hill's consent.

Limited Warranty   The McGraw Hill Content is provided on an "as is" basis. Neither McGraw Hill nor its licensors make any guarantees or warranties of any kind, either express or implied, including, but not limited to, implied warranties of merchantability or fitness for a particular purpose or use as to any McGraw Hill Content or the information therein or any warranties as to the accuracy, completeness, correctness, or results to be obtained from, accessing or using the McGraw Hill Content, or any material referenced in such Content or any information entered into licensee's product by users or other persons and/or any material available on or that can be accessed through the licensee's product (including via any hyperlink or otherwise) or as to non-infringement of third-party rights. Any warranties of any kind, whether express or implied, are disclaimed. Any material or data obtained through use of the McGraw Hill Content is at your own discretion and risk and user understands that it will be solely responsible for any resulting damage to its computer system or loss of data.

Neither McGraw Hill nor its licensors shall be liable to any subscriber or to any user or anyone else for any inaccuracy, delay, interruption in service, error or omission, regardless of cause, or for any damage resulting therefrom.

In no event will McGraw Hill or its licensors be liable for any indirect, special or consequential damages, including but not limited to, lost time, lost money, lost profits or good will, whether in contract, tort, strict liability or otherwise, and whether or not such damages are foreseen or unforeseen with respect to any use of the McGraw Hill Content.

TotalTester Online

TotalTester Online provides you with a simulation of the AWS Certified Developer Associate exam. Exams can be taken in Practice Mode or Exam Mode. Practice Mode provides an assistance window with hints, references to the book, explanations of the correct and incorrect answers, and the option to check your answer as you take the test. Exam Mode provides a simulation of the actual exam. The number of questions, the types of questions, and the time allowed are intended to be an accurate representation of the exam environment. The option to customize your quiz allows you to create custom exams from selected domains or chapters, and you can further customize the number of questions and time allowed.

To take a test, follow the instructions provided in the previous section to register and activate your Total Seminars Training Hub account. When you register you will be taken to the Total Seminars Training Hub. From the Training Hub Home page, select AWS Developer Assoc (DVA-C01) TotalTester from the Study drop-down menu at the top of the page, or from the list of Your Topics on the Home page. You can then select the option to customize your quiz and begin testing yourself in Practice Mode or Exam Mode. All exams provide an overall grade and a grade broken down by domain.

Technical Support

For questions regarding the TotalTester or operation of the Training Hub, visit **www .totalsem.com** or e-mail **support@totalsem.com**.

For questions regarding book content, visit **www.mheducation.com/customerservice**.

Acronyms

ACL   Access control list

ACM   AWS Certificate Manager

AES   Advanced Encryption Standard

ALB   Application load balancer

Amazon SWF   Amazon Simple Workflow Service

AMI   Amazon Machine Image

ASG   Auto-scaling group

AWS   Amazon Web Services

AZ   Availability Zone

BGP   Border Gateway Protocol

CAA   Certification authority authorization

CDN   Content delivery network

CIDR   Classless Inter-Domain Routing

CLI   Command-line interface

CNAME   Canonical name record

CPU   Central processing unit

CRR   Cross-regional replication

CSV   Comma-separated value

DaaS   Data as a Service

DBMS   Database management system

DDL   Data Definition Language

DDoS   Distributed denial of service

DHCP   Dynamic Host Configuration Protocol

DML   Data Manipulation Language

DMS   Database Migration Service

DoD   Department of Defense

ENI   Elastic Network Interface

ERP   Enterprise resource planning

ETL   Extract, transform, and load

FaaS   Function as a Service

FedRAMP   Federal Risk and Authorization Management Program

FIFO   First in, first out

GPU   Graphics processing unit

HA   High availability

HIPAA   Health Insurance Portability and Accountability Act

HTML   Hypertext Markup Language

HTTP   Hypertext Transfer Protocol

HTTPS   HTTP Secure

HVM   Hardware virtual machine

IaaS   Infrastructure as a Service

ICMP   Internet Control Message Protocol

IDE   Integrated development environment

IoT   Internet of Things

IP   Internet Protocol

ISO   International Organization for Standardization

IT   Information technology

JDBC   Java Database Connectivity

JSON   JavaScript Object Notation

LAMP stack   Linux, Apache, MySQL, and PHP stack

MAC   Media Access Control address

MFA   Multifactor authentication

NAT   Network Address Translation

NFS   Network File System

NIST   National Institute of Standards and Technology

NLB   Network load balancer

NS   Name server record

ODBC   Open Database Connectivity

OLAP   Online analytical processing

OLTP   Online transaction processing

PaaS   Platform as a Service

PCI   Payment Card Industry

PHP   Hypertext Preprocessor

PIOPS   Provisioned input/output operations per second

PV   Paravirtual

RDBMS   Relational database management system

REST   Representational State Transfer

RPM   Revolutions per minute

SaaS   Software as a Service

SAML   Security Assertion Markup Language

SDK   Software development kit

SLA   Service-level agreement

SOA   Service-oriented architecture

SOAP   Simple Object Access Protocol

SOC   System and organization controls

SQL   Structured Query Language

SSD   Solid-state drive

SSH   Secure Shell

SSL   Secure Sockets Layer

SSO   Single sign-on

STaaS   Storage as a Service

TCP/IP   Transmission Control Protocol/Internet Protocol

TDE   Transparent database encryption

TLS   Transport Layer Security

TXT   A text record

UDP   User Datagram Protocol

UPS   Uninterruptible power supply

VM   Virtual machine

VPG   Virtual private gateway

VPN   Virtual private network

WAF   Web Application Firewall

webACL   Web access control list

XML   Extensible Markup Language

XSS   Cross-site scripting

YAML   YAML Ain't Markup Language (originally known as Yet Another Markup Language)

Glossary

A (address) record   Points a domain or a subdomain to an IP address.

AAAA (quad A) record   Points a domain to an IPv6 address.

Alexa for Business   Organizations and employees use Alexa as their intelligent assistant to be more productive in their work.

Amazon API Gateway   A scalable managed service used to create, maintain, monitor, publish, and secure APIs.

Amazon AppStream 2.0   A managed application streaming service used to manage your desktop applications and securely deliver them to any computer.

Amazon Athena   A query service that enables users to query data in Amazon S3 using standard SQL.

Amazon Aurora   A relational database that supports two open-source engines such as MySQL and PostgreSQL.

Amazon CloudFront   The content delivery network service of AWS.

Amazon CloudSearch   A managed web service for search solutions.

Amazon CloudWatch   A monitoring service for AWS Cloud resources.

Amazon Cognito   A service that lets you easily manage users of your web and mobile apps.

Amazon DocumentDB   A managed document database service that supports MongoDB workloads and is used to store, manage, and retrieve semi-structured data.

Amazon DynamoDB   Amazon's NoSQL database.

Amazon Elastic Block Storage (Amazon EBS)   Provides persistent block storage for EC2 instances.

Amazon Elastic Compute Cloud (Amazon EC2)   Comprises secure and resizable virtual machines in the cloud.

Amazon Elastic Container Service (Amazon ECS)   A secure and scalable managed container orchestration service.

Amazon Elastic File System (Amazon EFS)   Provides a shared, scalable, cloud-native file system for EC2.

Amazon ElastiCache   A service that helps in deploying an in-memory cache or data store in the cloud.

Amazon Elasticsearch   A managed web service that hosts Elasticsearch clusters in the AWS Cloud.

Amazon Elastic MapReduce (Amazon EMR)   A managed, hosted Hadoop framework in the cloud.

Amazon FreeRTOS   Extends FreeRTOS, an open-source operating system for microcontrollers.

Amazon FSx for Lustre   A file system designed for fast processing of workloads.

Amazon FSx for Windows   A managed native Microsoft Windows file system to move Windows-based applications.

Amazon GuardDuty   Threat detection application that continuously monitors for unauthorized behavior and malicious activity to protect your AWS accounts.

Amazon Inspector   An automated security assessment tool to improve security and compliance.

Amazon Kinesis A service that allows you to ingest real-time data.

Amazon Lex A full service for building chatbots.

Amazon LightSail A simple virtual private server (VPS) solution in the cloud.

Amazon Neptune A managed graph database for storing relationships and querying the graph with millisecond latency.

Amazon Polly A managed service that converts text into realistic speech.

Amazon QuickSight A managed business analytics service.

Amazon RDS Amazon's relational database service in the cloud.

Amazon Redshift A managed petabyte-scale data warehouse service.

Amazon Rekognition A fully managed image recognition service.

Amazon Route 53 A Domain Name System (DNS) web service.

Amazon S3 Glacier Amazon's archival lowest-cost storage class that supports long-term retention that may be accessed once or twice in a year.

Amazon S3 Intelligent-Tiering automatically moves data to cost-effective tier, without impact or operational overhead.

Amazon S3 One Zone-Infrequent Access (S3 One Zone-IA) Used for data that is accessed less frequently and stores data in a single Availability Zone.

Amazon Simple Queue Service (SQS) A managed message queuing service used to decouple and scale distributed systems, microservices, and serverless applications.

Amazon SageMaker A managed service that provides the ability to build, deploy, and train machine learning models.

Amazon Simple Email Service (SES) A cloud-based service used to send e-mail.

Amazon Simple Notification Service (SNS) A managed publication/subscription messaging service for distributed systems, microservices, and serverless applications.

Amazon Simple Storage Service (S3) An object storage system used to store and retrieve any amount of data on the Web.

Amazon Simple Storage Service – Infrequent Access (S3-IA) Used to store infrequently accessed data.

Amazon Simple Storage Service – Reduced Redundancy Storage (S3-RRS) Used to store noncritical and reproducible data.

Amazon Virtual Private Cloud (VPC) A logically isolated section in a virtual network that you define.

Amazon VPC Flow Logs   Captures information of the IP traffic in your VPC.

Amazon WorkSpaces   A managed desktop service that provides desktops across the globe for either Windows or Linux.

Apache Cassandra   An open-source, distributed, wide column store, NoSQL database management system.

API Gateway   A managed service used to create, publish, and maintain APIs at scale.

Auto Scaling   A technology used by AWS to scale up and scale down EC2 instances.

AWS Backup   A managed backup service used to centralize and automate the backup of data from on-premises site using the AWS Storage Gateway and across AWS services.

AWS Batch   Used to run batch computing jobs on AWS.

AWS Budgets   Used to set up custom budgets to alert you when your costs, usage, or forecasted usage exceeds your budget.

AWS CloudFormation   A tool for deploying AWS resource stacks.

AWS CloudHSM   Hardware-based key storage for regulatory compliance.

AWS CloudTrail   A managed service that records all AWS API calls.

AWS CodeBuild   A managed service that builds and compiles source code.

AWS CodeCommit   A managed service where you can host source code repository.

AWS CodeDeploy   A managed service that automates code deployment.

AWS CodePipeline   A managed continuous integration and continuous delivery pipeline.

AWS Config   A managed service that tracks configuration changes.

AWS Cost Explorer   Used to visualize and manage your AWS costs and usage.

AWS Database Migration Service   Used to perform database migration securely.

AWS Device Farm   A service for testing mobile devices.

AWS Direct Connect   Used to establish private, dedicated network connectivity from your datacenter to AWS.

AWS Elastic Beanstalk   A service used for running and managing web applications.

AWS Fargate   Used to run containers without having to manage servers or clusters.

AWS Glue   A managed extract, transform, and load service.

AWS Identity and Access Management (IAM)   Used to manage access to AWS services and resources securely using roles, groups, and users.

AWS IoT 1-Click   Empowers services to trigger AWS Lambda functions that can execute an activity.

AWS IoT Analytics   A managed service offering that makes it simple to run and operationalize extremely large volumes of IoT information.

AWS IoT Button   Based on the Amazon Dash Button hardware and is programmable.

AWS IoT Core   A managed cloud service that can support billions of devices and trillions of messages with a lightweight communication protocol.

AWS IoT Greengrass   A managed service used for running IoT applications in the AWS Cloud.

AWS Key Management Service (KMS)   Used to create and manage cryptographic keys.

AWS Lambda   A serverless function that runs your code without you provisioning or managing any servers.

AWS Marketplace   A store where you can buy software that can be used on AWS.

AWS Mobile Hub   A service used for deploying mobile applications.

AWS OpsWorks   A configuration management service that provides support for Chef and Puppet.

AWS Outposts   A Native AWS service that enables your datacenter to remain on-premises due to low latency or compliance requirements by extending the AWS infrastructure and providing a hybrid environment.

AWS Organizations   A policy-based management system used to manage multiple AWS accounts from a single service.

AWS Personal Health Dashboard   A personalized view of your AWS service health in a dashboard form.

AWS Secrets Manager   Used to protect secrets that accesses your applications and IT databases.

AWS Security Hub   Provides a complete view of your compliance status and high-priority security alerts across AWS accounts.

AWS Security Token Service (STS)   Used to request temporary, limited-privilege credentials for AWS IAM users or for federated users.

AWS Server Migration Service (SMS)   An agentless service used to perform large-scale server migrations from on-premises to AWS.

AWS Serverless Application Model (SAM)   An open-source framework that is used to create serverless applications on AWS.

AWS Serverless Application Repository A managed repository for serverless applications to enable individual developers, teams, and organizations to store and share reusable applications.

AWS Service Catalog Used to create and manage IT services catalogs to complete multi-tier application architectures.

AWS Shield A managed protection service for distributed denial of service (DDoS) used to safeguard your applications running on AWS.

AWS Snowball A data transfer service with petabyte scale built as a secure suitcase-sized device to quickly move data in and out of the AWS Cloud.

AWS Snowball Edge A data transfer service with petabyte-scale capability along with a computing platform that helps you perform simple processing tasks.

AWS Snowmobile An exabyte-scale data transfer service that uses a 45-foot-long container, which is ideal for exabyte-scale migrations and datacenter shutdowns.

AWS Step Functions Provides a visual workflow of AWS services.

AWS Storage Gateway A service that helps to seamlessly integrate on-premises storage with AWS Cloud storage.

AWS Systems Manager Used to configure and control infrastructure on AWS.

AWS Transit Gateway Used to connect Amazon VPCs and on-premises networks to a single gateway.

AWS Trusted Advisor Used to help improve security and reduce costs by optimizing the AWS environment.

AWS Virtual Private Network A secure tunnel from your on-premises network to the AWS global network.

bucket A container for storing objects in Amazon S3.

Cloud Foundry An open-source cloud application platform used for building and deploying enterprise cloud applications.

CloudStack An open-source cloud computing software used for building and deploying infrastructure cloud services.

CockroachDB An open-source, relational database that is compatible with PostgreSQL.

CouchDB An open-source, document-oriented NoSQL database.

Cozy A personal data store used to host personal web apps.

dead-letter queue (DLQ) A dead-letter queue lets you set aside and isolate messages that cannot be processed correctly to determine why their processing failed.

dedicated host   A physical server with EC2 instance capacity fully dedicated to a single customer.

dedicated instance   A single customer runs on dedicated hardware even though it belongs to a different AWS account and is physically isolated at the hardware level.

Directory Service   A directory service built on Microsoft Active Directory in the cloud.

edge location   Used to serve content to end users.

elastic IP address (EIP)   An IP address that is reachable from the Internet.

Elastic Load Balancing (ELB)   Distributes incoming traffic across multiple targets, like Amazon EC2 instances, containers, and Lambda functions.

Fn project   An open-source, container-native, serverless platform that can run on any cloud or on-premises.

instance   Another term for an Amazon EC2 server.

instance store   Local storage on the EC2 server.

Internet gateway (IGW)   A component of VPC that allows it to communicate with the Internet.

Network Access Control List (NACL)   This acts as a firewall at the subnet level.

OpenPaaS   An open-source digital workplace.

OpenShift   An open-source container application platform based on Kubernetes.

OpenStack   A free, open-standard cloud computing platform.

OpenWhisk   An open-source, distributed, serverless platform that executes functions in response to events.

ownCloud   A client/server software system used for file hosting services.

point of presence (POP)   This is also known as an edge location.

point-to-site VPN   Used to securely access the instances in your VPC from your individual laptop or from a client computer.

region   The unique geographic area in the world where AWS datacenters are hosted.

root user   Owner of the AWS account.

root volume   Contains the software that is used to boot the instance.

route table   A table consisting of routes that determine where traffic is directed.

security group   A virtual firewall for EC2 instances.

service-level agreement (SLA)   A commitment between a client and service provider.

site-to-site VPN   Used to securely connect your VPC with your own (remote or on-premises) network.

subnet   A logical subdivision of a VPC network.

vault   Similar to a safe deposit box or locker in Amazon S3 Glacier where archives are stored.

VMware Cloud on AWS   Allows organizations to migrate and extend their on-premises, VMware vSphere-based environments to the AWS Cloud using EC2 bare-metal infrastructure.

INDEX

A

A records
  DNS, 189
  Route 53, 196
A1 EC2 instances, 111
AAAA records
  DNS, 189–190
  Route 53, 196
AAD (additional authenticated data), 328, 330
accelerated computing EC2 instances, 113
access
  Amazon CloudFront, 165–168
  Amazon SWF workflows, 419
  buckets, 223
  CloudTrail, 444–445
  IAM. *See* AWS Identity and Access
    Management (IAM) service
  Route 53, 194
access control lists (ACLs), 224, 236–237
access key IDs in Cognito, 313
AccessControl parameter, 460, 464
Account metrics dashboard, 609
accounts
  creating, 37–41
  exercise, 68
  questions, 74
  review, 67–68
  settings, 47
ACID (atomicity, consistency, isolation, and
  durability) properties, 375
ACLs (access control lists), 224, 236–237
ACM (AWS Certificate Manager)
  IAM, 288
  static website deployment, 517
acronyms, 679–682
actions
  application deployment, 625
  load balancer listener rules, 142

Active Directory (AD)
  identity federation, 310
  SAML 2.0, 318
Active Directory Federation Services, 318
active state in load balancers, 140
activities in Amazon SWF, 417
actors in Amazon SWF, 417
AD (Active Directory)
  identity federation, 310
  SAML 2.0, 318
Add Storage page, 124
Add Tags page, 124
additional authenticated data (AAD), 328, 330
administrator users, 299–300
Advanced Encryption Standard (AES-256)
  DynamoDB, 382
  EBS, 255–257
  RDS, 360
  server-side encryption, 333–335
  SSE-S3, 236
agents in CloudWatch, 442
aggregation metric in CloudWatch, 440
Alarm state
  CloudWatch alarms, 440
  Route 53, 204
alarms in CloudWatch, 383, 440, 449–450
ALBs (Application Load Balancers)
  CI/CD pipelines, 646, 659, 663
  creating, 154
  description, 138
alerts in Amazon SNS, 402
Alerts menu, 48
Alexa for Business, 23
algorithms, encryption, 328, 330
alias records in Route 53, 195
All Upfront reserved DB instances, 358
alternate domain names in CloudFront,
  170–171

Always Free option, 42
Amazon API Gateway
  Cognito user pools, 316
  description, 17
  Lambda integration, 423–424
  overview, 420–423
  questions, 432–435
  resources, 435
  REST API, 423–424
  review, 429–430
Amazon AppStream 2.0, 24
Amazon Athena query service, 23
Amazon Aurora database, 15
Amazon Certificate Manager (ACM) page, 517
Amazon CloudFront, 161–162
  alternate domain names, 170–171
  caching, 171–172
  content expiration, 172
  custom error pages, 173–174
  description, 17
  distributions, 168–170
  domain fronting, 173
  exercises, 175–178
  field-level encryption, 168
  HTTP, 165
  origin access identity, 167, 174
  origin groups, 173
  origin servers, 162–163
  pricing, 163
  questions, 178–183
  regional edge caches, 164
  resources, 183–184
  review, 174–175
  securing content, 164
  signed URLs, 165–167
  static website deployment on buckets,
    520–521
  static website deployment with Amazon S3
    and Route 53, 515–523
  WebSocket protocol, 171
Amazon CloudWatch
  agents, 442
  Amazon SNS messages, 406
  CI/CD pipelines, 654, 664
  CloudTrail, 444
  CodePipeline pipelines, 626
  dashboard, 48, 360
  data protection, 442

  description, 19
  DynamoDB, 383
  events in EFS, 267
  events in S3 Glacier, 274
  exercises, 449–450
  logs, 442
  metrics, 438–442
  overview, 437–438
  questions, 451–456
  resources, 456
  review, 448–449
Amazon Cognito
  Cognito Sync, 313
  description, 18
  exercises, 321–323
  identity federation, 310
  identity pools, 312, 316–317
  mobile apps, 313–317
  overview, 311
  questions, 323–326
  resources, 326
  review, 321
  user pools, 312, 314–317, 322
Amazon Cognito Sync, 313
Amazon DocumentDB, 16
Amazon DynamoDB
  auto-scaling, 379
  backup and recovery, 381
  Cognito tables, 313
  control plane operations, 373
  data distribution, 379
  data plane operations, 373–374
  data protection, 382–383
  data types, 373
  DAX, 376–379
  description, 16
  exercises, 386–389
  global tables, 381
  local, 379–380
  logging and monitoring, 383–384
  maintenance window, 383
  overview, 371–372
  questions, 389–391
  resources, 392
  review, 385–386
  secondary indexes, 380
  security, 384–385
  SQL vs. NoSQL, 374–375

streams, 380–381
transactions, 375–376
web, 380
Amazon EBS–backed Instances, 116–117
Amazon EC2 Auto Scaling, 146
advantages, 146–147
attaching and detaching, 148
CloudWatch, 437
description, 12
enter and exit standby, 148–149
exercises, 154–156
group monitoring, 152–153
groups, 149–150
instance management, 150–152
launch configurations, 149
launch templates, 149
lifecycle, 147
lifecycle hooks, 148
questions, 156–159
resources, 160
review, 153–154
scale out and in, 148
Amazon EC2 instances
application deployment, 615–616,
618–619, 623
CloudFormation templates, 462–465
connecting, 125–126
creating, 123–125
deleting, 565, 636–637
DynamoDB, 384
Elastic Beanstalk, 529–530, 532
hibernation, 121–122
key pairs, 53–54
lifecycle, 117–122
metadata, 120–121
protecting, 126–127
reboot, 122
retirement, 122
stop and restart, 121
store–backed instances, 116
termination, 122
types, 110–115
virtualization types, 115–116
Amazon Elastic Block Store (EBS)
AWS Config volumes, 446
best practices, 261–262
description, 14
elastic volumes, 256

encryption, 256–260
exercises, 275–278
metrics, 261
overview, 249–251
questions, 278–281
RAID configuration on Linux, 260–261
resources, 282
review, 274–275
snapshots, 253–256
volumes, 250–253
Amazon Elastic Compute Cloud (Amazon
EC2), 107
AMI, 108–109
auto scaling. See EC2 Auto Scaling
best practices, 127–128
CloudFront origins, 170
description, 11
EFS, 263–264
exercises, 129–131
IAM, 286
instances. See Amazon EC2 instances
launching, 123–126
pricing model, 113–115
questions, 131–133
resources, 134
review, 128–129
security groups, 126–127
security keys, 122–123
storage options, 116–117
Amazon Elastic Container Registry (ECR)
description, 12
repositories, 596–597
Amazon Elastic Container Service (ECS), 12
Amazon Elastic Container Service for
Kubernetes (Amazon EKS), 13
Amazon Elastic File System (EFS)
AWS Direct Connect and VPN,
264–265
backups, 266
best practices, 268
data consistency, 265
description, 14
EC2, 263–264
encryption, 266–267
exercises, 275
Lifecycle Management, 267
monitoring, 267
overview, 262–263

Amazon Elastic File System (EFS) (*cont.*)
    performance, 267–268
    questions, 278–281
    resources, 282
    review, 274–275
    storage classes, 266
Amazon Elastic MapReduce, 22
Amazon ElastiCache, 16
Amazon Elasticsearch Service, 23
Amazon FreeRTOS, 25
Amazon FSx for Lustre, 15
Amazon FSx for Windows File Server, 15
Amazon GuardDuty, 18
Amazon Inspector, 18
Amazon Kinesis, 22
Amazon Lightsail, 13
Amazon Machine Images (AMIs), 60
    bundle tasks, 108
    HVM, 115
    PV, 115–116
    tenancy options, 109–110
Amazon Neptune, 16
Amazon QuickSight, 23
Amazon Redshift, 16
Amazon Relational Database Service (RDS)
    ARN, 361
    backups, 358–359
    best practices, 361–362
    billing, 358
    description, 15
    encryption, 360
    exercises, 363–366
    high availability, 351–352
    lifecycle, 353–355
    monitoring, 360
    option groups, 356–357
    overview, 349–351
    questions, 366–368
    read replicas, 355–356
    resources, 369
    review, 363
    security, 359–360
    snapshots, 359
    storage, 357–358
    tagging, 361
Amazon Resource Names (ARNs)
    AWS Config, 446
    DAX controls, 378

RDS, 361
    session policies, 319
Amazon Route 53, 185–186
    access, 194
    concepts, 194–197
    description, 17
    domain registration, 197
    exercises, 205–215
    health checks, 202–204
    hosted zones, 199–200, 212–215
    questions, 215–217
    resources, 217–218
    review, 204–205
    routing policies, 201–202
    routing traffic, 198–200
    static website deployment with Amazon
        S3, 510–515
    static website deployment with Amazon S3
        and CloudFront, 515–523
Amazon SageMaker, 24
Amazon Simple Notification Service (Amazon
  SNS)
    alerts, 402
    architecture, 402
    AWS Config, 447
    buckets, 224
    CloudTrail, 443
    CloudWatch, 437
    DAX controls, 378
    dead-letter queues, 404
    delivery policies, 403–404
    delivery retries, 403
    delivery status, 403
    description, 21
    encryption, 405
    exercises, 410–411
    fanout, 402
    logs, 406–407
    message attributes, 405
    message durability, 403
    message filtering, 405
    monitoring, 406
    overview, 401
    push messages, 402–403
    push notifications, 403
    questions, 411–413
    resources, 413–414
    review, 407–408

S3 Glacier, 270–271
security, 406–407
tags, 405
Amazon Simple Queue Service (Amazon SQS)
architecture, 396
buckets, 224
description, 21
EC2 Auto Scaling, 152
encryption, 401
exercises, 408–410
inflight messages, 399–400
large messages, 400
message timers, 400
overview, 395–396
polling, 399
questions, 411–413
queues, dead-letter, 399
queues, delay, 400
queues, FIFO, 397–399
queues, lifecycle, 396
queues, standard, 396–397
queues, standard, migrating to FIFO, 398–399
queues, temporary, 400
queues, virtual, 400
resources, 413–414
review, 407–408
visibility timeouts, 399
Amazon Simple Storage Service (S3), 221
access tiers, 228
best practices, 238–239
buckets. *See* buckets
client-side encryption, 336
data protection, 236–237
description, 13, 222
exercises, 241–244
IAM, 234
object lifecycle management, 229–230
object operations, 234–236
object versioning, 230–234
objects, 226–227
overview, 499
questions, 244–247
resources, 247
review, 240–241
static website deployment, 500–510

static website deployment with Route 53, 510–515
static website deployment with Route 53 and CloudFront, 515–523
storage classes, 227–229
Amazon Simple Storage Service (S3) Glacier, 24, 228
archives, 269–270, 272
data protection, 273
data retrieval policies, 273
description, 14
exercises, 275
jobs, 270
logging and monitoring, 274
notification configuration, 270–271
operations, 271–273
overview, 268–269
questions, 278–281
resources, 282
review, 274–275
Vault Lock, 273
vaults, 269, 271–272
Amazon Simple Workflow Service (Amazon SWF)
development environment, 416–419
exercises, 430–432
logs, 420
monitoring, 419
overview, 415–416
questions, 432–435
resources, 435
review, 429–430
tags, 419
Amazon States Language, 426
Amazon Virtual Private Cloud (VPC)
Amazon SNS, 402, 407
Amazon SQS, 401
application deployment, 619
AWS Config, 446, 448
AWS Step Functions, 429
CodeBuild in, 603
creating, 69–70, 92–102
customer gateways, 89–90
DAX, 376
deleting, 71
description, 16
DHCP, 84

Amazon Virtual Private Cloud (VPC) (*cont.*)
  Direct Connect, 90
  DynamoDB, 384
  EFS, 263
  egress-only Internet gateways, 88
  elastic IP addresses, 85
  endpoints, 85–87
  Internet gateways, 83–84
  NACLs, 82
  NAT devices, 87–88
  overview, 80–81
  peering connections, 88–89
  questions, 103–105
  RDS, 349–350
  resources, 106
  review, 91–92
  route tables, 81–82
  security groups, 82–83
  subnets, 81
  transit gateways, 91
  virtual private gateways, 89
  virtual private networks, 89–90
Amazon Web Services (AWS) overview
  capabilities, 25–28
  history, 9
  questions, 28–35
  regions and availability zones, 9–11
  resources, 35–36
  review, 28
  services, 11–25
Amazon WorkSpaces, 24
AMIs (Amazon Machine Images), 60
  bundle tasks, 108
  HVM, 115
  PV, 115–116
  tenancy options, 109–110
anomaly detection in CloudWatch, 441–442
Apache Maven tool, 58
API Gateway. *See* Amazon API Gateway
API permissions in Amazon SWF
  workflows, 419
Application Load Balancers (ALBs)
  CI/CD pipelines, 646, 659, 663
  creating, 154
  description, 138
applications
  building. *See* AWS CodeBuild
  deleting, 635–636, 666
  deploying with AWS CodeDeploy, 615–624

deploying with AWS CodePipeline,
  625–635
deploying with Elastic Beanstalk, 530–533
Lambda functions, 487–495
migrating, 546–556
ApplyImmediately parameter for RDS, 353
archives in S3 Glacier, 229, 269–272, 275
ARNs (Amazon Resource Names)
  AWS Config, 446
  DAX controls, 378
  RDS, 361
  session policies, 319
AssumeRole API, 319
AssumeRoleWithSAML API, 319
AssumeRoleWithWebIdentity API, 310, 319
asymmetric encryption, 328, 331
atomicity, consistency, isolation, and
  durability (ACID) properties, 375
attaching EC2 Auto Scaling instances, 148
attributes
  Amazon SNS messages, 405
  Amazon SQS messages, 398–399
  DynamoDB, 372
authentication
  Amazon Cognito. *See* Amazon Cognito
  encryption for, 327
  IAM. *See* AWS Identity and Access
    Management (IAM) service
  identity federation. *See* identity federation
authoritative name servers in Route 53, 195
authorization in IAM, 287
auto scaling
  DynamoDB, 379
  EC2 Auto Scaling. *See* EC2 Auto Scaling
Auto Scaling policy in S3 Glacier, 274
availability zones (AZs)
  Classic Load Balancers, 140
  DAX controls, 378
  DynamoDB, 382
  EBS, 249–250, 254
  EC2 Auto Scaling, 146–147
  EFS, 262–265
  NAT, 87–88
  Network Load Balancers, 139
  overview, 9–11
  RDS, 350, 352
  S3 Glacier, 273
  VPCs, 95
average metric in CloudWatch, 439

AWS Backup
  description, 15
  EFS, 266
AWS Batch service, 13
AWS Budgets, 22
AWS Certificate Manager (ACM)
  IAM, 288
  static website deployment, 517
AWS Certified Developer - Associate Exam
  Objective Map, 673–674
AWS Cloud Development Kit, 458
AWS Cloud9, 583–590
AWS CloudFormation
  change sets, 466
  CI/CD pipelines, 644–646
  description, 20
  designer, 458
  exercises, 468–475
  export function, 466
  Lambda functions, 490
  overview, 457–459
  questions, 475–478
  registry, 467
  resources, 478
  review, 467
  stacks, 465–466
  templates, 459–465, 468–475
AWS CloudHSM, 18
AWS CloudTrail
  Amazon SNS messages, 406
  AWS Step Functions, 428–429
  control access, 444–445
  description, 19
  DynamoDB, 382–384
  EFS logs, 267
  exercises, 450–451
  IAM, 286
  lifecycle, 443–444
  overview, 442–443
  questions, 451–456
  resources, 456
  review, 448–449
  security, 443–445
AWS CodeBuild
  build environment, 595–596
  build projects, 595
  CI/CD pipelines, 647, 661
  description, 21
  exercises, 611–612
  Lambda functions, 490
  overview, 595
  questions, 612–614
  resources, 614
  review, 610
  test reporting, 610
  working with, 596–610
AWS CodeCommit
  application building, 597–598, 601
  application deployment, 616–618
  CI/CD pipelines, 644, 647, 654,
    660–662
  description, 21
  exercises, 589–590
  Lambda functions, 490
  overview, 571–572
  pipelines, 626
  questions, 590–593
  repositories, 572–589
  resources, 593
  review, 589
AWS CodeDeploy
  application deployment, 615–624
  CI/CD pipelines, 650–655
  description, 22
  exercises, 635
  pipelines, 627
  questions, 637–639
  resources, 639–640
  review, 635
AWS CodePipeline
  application deployment, 625–635
  description, 22
  exercises, 636–637
  Lambda functions, 487, 490, 494
  questions, 637–639
  resources, 639–640
  review, 635
AWS Config
  description, 20
  exercises, 451
  managing, 447
  monitoring, 448
  overview, 445–446
  questions, 451–456
  resources, 446–447, 456
  review, 448–449
  rules, 448
  security, 446

aws configure command, 51–52
AWS Cost Explorer, 22
AWS Database Migration Service, 21, 558–564
AWS_DEFAULT_PROFILE environment
  variable, 52
AWS Direct Connect
  description, 17
  EFS, 264–265
  overview, 90
  transit gateways, 91
  VPC endpoints, 85
aws dynamodb describe-table command, 379
AWS Elastic Beanstalk
  application deployment, 530–533
  application migration to, 534–540
  description, 12
  exercises, 540–541
  overview, 529
  questions, 541–543
  resources, 543
  review, 540–541
aws-encryption-cli command, 337–338
AWS Fargate, 13
AWS Glue, 23
AWS Identity and Access Management (IAM)
  service
  Amazon SNS, 406
  application deployment, 616
  application migration, 550
  AWS CodeCommit, 576
  AWS Config, 446–447
  AWS Step Functions, 428
  best practices, 297–298
  buckets, 224
  CloudTrail, 444
  Cognito, 313
  description, 17
  DynamoDB, 382
  EC2, 124
  exercises, 299–302
  groups, 290–291
  identity federation, 309–310, 319
  Java 2.0, 58
  multifactor authentication, 69, 289–290
  .NET, 59
  overview, 285–287
  passwords, 288–289
  policies and permissions, 293–296

questions, 303–306
RDS, 349
resources, 306–307
review, 298–299
roles, 291–292
S3, 234
setting up, 40–41
users, 288–289
VPC endpoints, 87
AWS IoT 1-Click, 25
AWS IoT Analytics, 25
AWS IoT Button, 25
AWS IoT Core, 24
AWS IoT Greengrass, 24
AWS Key Management Service (KMS)
  Amazon SQS, 395
  CLI encryption, 337
  client-side encryption, 335–336
  CloudTrail, 443, 445
  description, 18
  DynamoDB, 382
  EBS, 256
  encryption, 330
  RDS, 360
  server-side encryption, 332–333
AWS Lambda. See Lambda functions
AWS-managed policies in IAM, 294
AWS Management Console
  accounts, 44–49
  Amazon SNS, 410–411
  Amazon SQS, 408–410
  Amazon SWF, 416, 419, 430–432
  application deletion, 635–636, 666
  Application Load Balancers, 154–156
  application migration, 550, 555
  AWS Cloud9, 583, 590
  AWS CloudFormation templates, 461,
    468–475
  AWS CodeCommit, 576
  AWS CodePipeline, 625
  AWS Config, 451
  AWS SDK for .NET, 59–60
  bucket configuration, 211, 223
  bucket creation, 175–176, 209–210,
    241–242
  bucket deletion, 565
  CI/CD pipelines, 642, 664
  CloudFront distributions, 176–178

CloudTrail, 442, 450–451
CloudWatch, 438, 449–450
CMKs, 340–342
database deletion, 565
database migration, 559
DAX, 376
DB instances, 355–356, 358–359
description, 19
DynamoDB, 380, 386–389
EBS snapshots, 278
EBS volumes, 276–277
EC2 instance deletion, 565, 636–637
EC2 instance recovery, 119
Elastic Beanstalk environment deletion,
    540–541
exercise, 68
federation, 318
hosted zones, 212
IAM, 287–289, 299–302
IAM users, 58–59, 68
identity federation, 310
identity pools, 322
image deletion, 611
Lambda functions, 483–486, 488–495
pipeline deletion, 636, 666
project deletion, 611, 665–666
RDS, 350, 353–354, 363–366
repositories, 581
repository deletion, 589, 611–612,
    636, 665
resource cleanup, 523–524
S3 objects, 243–244
SAML 2.0, 318
server-side encryption, 334
services access, 93
stack deletion, 666–667
static website deployment, 500, 511,
    514–515, 520
user pools, 322–323
VPCs, 92–102
AWS Marketplace, 108–109
AWS OpsWorks, 20
AWS Organizations, 19
AWS Outposts, 13
AWS Personal Health Dashboard, 20
AWS PrivateLink, 218, 448
AWS_REGION environment variable, 59, 596
AWS Security Hub, 19

AWS Security Token Service (STS)
    Amazon SNS, 406
    AWS CodeCommit, 576
    DynamoDB, 384
    S3 Glacier, 273
AWS Server Migration Service, 556
AWS Serverless Application Model (SAM)
    Lambda functions, 487
    working with, 62–63
AWS Serverless Application Repository, 13
AWS Service Catalog, 20
AWS Services page, 40
AWS Shield, 18
AWS Snowball, 14
AWS Snowball Edge, 14
AWS Snowmobile, 14
AWS StackSets, 458
AWS Step Functions, 425
    local, 426–428
    logs, 428
    monitoring, 428
    questions, 432–435
    resources, 435
    review, 429–430
    security, 428–429
    tags, 428
    workflows, 425–426
AWS Storage Gateway, 15
AWS Systems Manager, 20
AWS Toolkit for Eclipse, 63–65
AWS Toolkit for PowerShell, 59–60
AWS Toolkit for Visual Studio
    installing and uninstalling, 65–66
    .NET, 60
AWS Tools for Microsoft Visual Studio Team
    Services, 66–67
AWS Tools for PowerShell Core
    Linux and macOSX, 61
    Windows, 60–61
AWS Tools for Windows PowerShell, 60–61
AWS Transit Gateway, 17
AWS Trusted Advisor, 21, 360
AWS Virtual Private Network (AWS VPN), 16
AWS Web Application Firewall (WAF)
    CloudFront, 167
    description, 19
AWSCodeDeployRole policy, 616
AWSTemplateFormatVersion parameter,
    460, 464

AXFR records, 190
AZs. *See* availability zones (AZs)

B

Backoff Phase in Amazon SNS policies, 404
backups
    AWS Backup, 15
    DynamoDB, 381
    EFS, 266
    RDS, 358–359
Basic metrics in EBS, 261
Basic Plan, 40, 42–44
BatchGetItem operation, 373
BatchWriteItem operation, 373–374
bell menu, 48
billing
    RDS, 358
    S3 buckets, 225
Billing and Cost Management dashboard, 48
binary attribute in Amazon SNS messages, 405
block ciphers, 329, 331
block-level storage. *See* Amazon Elastic Block
    Store (EBS)
BlockDeviceMappings parameter for AWS
    CloudFormation templates, 464
blue/green application deployment, 615
bootstrapping EC2 instances, 118
bring your own IP (BYOIP), 85
BucketEncryption parameter, 460, 464
BucketName parameter, 460, 464
buckets
    access, 223
    application building, 603
    application deployment, 531
    application migration, 551
    AWS CloudFormation templates, 460–465
    AWS Config, 446–447
    billing and usage reporting, 225
    CLI for, 57
    CloudFront, 169–170, 175–176
    CloudTrail, 444–445
    configuration options, 223–225
    creating, 223, 241–242
    cross-origin resource sharing, 223
    cross-region replication, 224
    deleting, 565
    description, 222

EC2, 119–120
event notifications, 224
folders, 226
IAM, 286
objects, 226–227
questions, 244–247
Requester Pays, 225–226
resources, 247
static website deployment with Amazon
    S3, 500–510
static website deployment with Amazon S3
    and Route 53, 510–515
static website deployment with Amazon
    S3, Route 53, and CloudFront, 515–523
transfer acceleration, 224–225
uploading folders and files to, 242–243
versioning, 231–234
website hosting, 209–211
build environment, 595–596
build projects, 595
buildspec files
    applications, 598–599, 604–605, 607–608
    CI/CD pipelines, 648
Bulk archive operations in S3 Glacier, 272
bundle tasks in AMI, 108
Burstable Performance instance class, 350 351
BurstBalance metric, 250
Business Plan, 40
BYOIP (bring your own IP), 85

C

CAA (Certification Authority Authorization)
    records
    DNS, 190
    Route 53, 196
caches in CloudFront, 164–165, 171–172
calculated health checks in Route 53, 204
callback URLs in Amazon API Gateway, 421
capabilities of AWS, 25–28
Catch failure template, 427
centralized routers, 91
certificates
    application building, 603
    CAA records, 190, 205
    ELB, 145
    server, 288
    static website deployment, 519–520

Certification Authority Authorization (CAA)
  records
    DNS, 190
    Route 53, 196
chaining IAM roles, 292
change sets in AWS CloudFormation, 466
charges, checking, 48
child health checks in Route 53, 204
child workflows in Amazon SWF, 419
chmod command, 53
Choice state in AWS Step Functions, 427
Choose an Amazon Machine Image page, 123
Choose An Instance Type page, 124
CI/CD pipelines
    building, 641–664
    exercises, 665–667
    questions, 667–669
    resources, 669–670
    review, 665
CIDR (Classless Inter-Domain Routing)
  blocks, 81, 92, 95
ciphertext, 329
Classic Load Balancers, 139–140
Classless Inter-Domain Routing (CIDR)
  blocks, 81, 92, 95
cleaning up resources, 523–524
CLI. See Command Line Interface (CLI)
client-side encryption
    CMKs, 335–336
    master keys, 336
client-side errors in Amazon SNS, 404
cloning repositories, 582
cloud computing overview, 3
    benefits, 4
    deployment models, 5–7
    questions, 28–35
    resources, 35–36
    review, 28
    service types, 7–8
CloudFormation. See AWS CloudFormation
CloudFront. See Amazon CloudFront
CloudTrail. See AWS CloudTrail
CloudWatch. See Amazon CloudWatch
clusters in DAX, 377–378
CMKs. See customer-managed keys (CMKs)
CNAME records
    CloudFront, 170, 178
    DNS, 190–191
    Route 53, 196

code for Lambda functions, 486
CodeBuild. See AWS CodeBuild
CODEBUILD_BUILD_IMAGE
  environment variable, 596
CODEBUILD_LOG_PATH environment
  variable, 596
CodeCommit. See AWS CodeCommit
CodeDeploy. See AWS CodeDeploy
CodePipeline. See AWS CodePipeline
Cognito. See Amazon Cognito
cold HDD (sc1) volumes in EBS, 250
command-completion feature, 53
Command Line Interface (CLI)
    buckets, 57
    CloudFormation, 458
    EC2 key pairs, 53–54
    EFS backups, 266
    encryption, 336–337
    exercise, 69–71
    help, 53
    identity federation, 310
    instance launching, 56
    overview, 49–50
    profile setup in, 50–52
    questions, 71–76
    RDS, 349–350, 352
    resources, 76
    review, 67–68
    SAM, 62–63
    security groups, 54–56
Comment field for AWS Step Functions
  states, 428
comments for repositories, 589
community clouds, 8
compliance mode in S3 Object Lock, 237
composite primary keys in DynamoDB, 372
compute-optimized EC2 instances, 111
concurrency in Lambda functions, 482
conditions in load balancer listener rules, 142
confidentiality, encryption for, 327
Config. See AWS Config
configuration
    AWS Config, 445–448
    buckets, 223–225
    EC2 Auto Scaling, 149
    Elastic Load Balancing routing, 143
    load balancer listeners, 141
    profiles, 51–52
    S3 Glacier notifications, 270–271

Configure Security Group page, 124
configure set outputtable command, 52
configure set region command, 52
connecting ED2 instances, 125–126
connection idle timeouts in load balancers, 141
connections for VPCs, 88–89
ConsumedReadCapacityUnits value, 383
ConsumedWriteCapacityUnits value, 383
consumers in Amazon SNS, 401
Contact Information page, 39
content
    CloudFront. *See* Amazon CloudFront
    S3 objects, 235
content expiration in CloudFront, 172
context in encryption, 329
control access in CloudTrail, 444–445
control plane operations in DynamoDB, 373
cookies
    CloudFront, 165–167, 172
    Elastic Load Balancing, 144
cooldown periods in EC2 Auto Scaling, 152
coordination logic in Amazon SWF, 418
COPY operations in server-side encryption,
    333–335
copying
    EBS snapshots, 255, 257–260
    S3 objects, 234–235, 243
CORS (cross-origin resource sharing), 223
cost allocation tags in Amazon SQS queues, 399
costs
    cloud computing, 4
    CloudFront, 163
    EC2, 113–115
    EC2 Auto Scaling savings, 146
create operations in DynamoDB, 373
CREATE TABLE statement in SQL, 374
CreateTable operation in DynamoDB, 373
credentials
    AWS CodeCommit, 574
    Cognito, 312
    IAM, 288
    Java 2.0, 58–59
    .NET, 59–60
credentials file, 51
cross-account access for IAM roles, 292
cross-origin resource sharing (CORS), 223
cross-region replication (CRR), 224

cross-zone load balancing, 140
cryptography. *See* encryption
curl command, 55
cURL tool, 120
custom error pages in CloudFront, 173–174
custom metrics in CloudWatch, 438
custom rules in AWS Config, 448
customer gateways
    point-to-site VPNs, 90
    site-to-site VPNs, 90
    VPCs, 89–90
customer-managed keys (CMKs)
    CLI encryption, 337
    client-side encryption, 335–336
    creating, 340–341
    disabling, 342
    DynamoDB, 382
    server-side encryption, 332–333
    tags, 342
customer-managed policies in IAM, 294
customer master keys (CMKs)
    EBS encryption, 256–260
    EFS encryption, 267
customer-provided keys (SSE-C), 332, 334–335

D

Data as a Service (DaaS), 6–7
data consistency in EFS, 265
Data Definition Language (DDL)
    operations, 350
data distribution in DynamoDB, 379
data encryption. *See* encryption
data in transit encryption
    Amazon SNS, 407
    CRR, 224
    EBS, 250–251, 255–256
    EFS, 266–268
    KMS, 382
    S3, 227–228, 236, 273
    Step Functions, 429
data in use encryption, 382
data integrity, encryption for, 327
data keys in encryption, 328
Data Lifecycle Manager (DLM), 255–256
Data Manipulation Language (DML)
    operations, 350
data plane operations in DynamoDB, 373–374

data protection
 CloudWatch, 442
 DynamoDB, 382–383
 encryption. *See* encryption
 S3, 236–237
 S3 Glacier, 273
data retrieval policies in S3 Glacier, 273
data types
 Amazon SNS messages, 405
 Amazon SQS message attributes, 398
 DynamoDB, 373
databases
 deleting, 565
 migrating, 557–564
DAX. *See* DynamoDB Accelerator (DAX)
DB instances
 billing, 358
 lifecycle, 353–356
 option groups, 356–357
 RDS, 349–352
 read replicas, 355–356
 snapshots, 359
 storage, 357–358
DDL (Data Definition Language)
 operations, 350
dead-letter queues
 Amazon SNS, 404
 Amazon SQS, 399
 Lambda functions, 482
deciders in Amazon SWF, 418
decision task lists in Amazon SWF, 417
decision tasks in Amazon SWF, 417
decisions in Amazon SWF, 418
decryption
 description, 328
 files, 338
dedicated hosts in EC2, 110, 115
dedicated instances in EC2, 110
dedicated tenancy in EC2, 110
deduplication IDs in Amazon SQS
 messages, 398
delay queues for Amazon SQS messages, 400
delays in FIFO queues, 398
delegation of IAM roles, 292
Delete On Termination option in application
 deployment, 619
delete operations in DynamoDB, 374
DELETE statement in SQL, 375

DeleteItem operation in DynamoDB, 374
DeleteOnTermination parameter for AWS
 CloudFormation templates, 464
DeleteTable operation in DynamoDB, 373
deleting
 Amazon SQS messages, 396
 applications, 635–636, 666
 AWS Cloud9 environment, 590
 AWS CloudFormation stacks, 466
 buckets, 57, 243–244, 565
 Cognito identity pools, 322–323
 Cognito user pools, 323
 databases, 565
 DB instances, 355
 DynamoDB items, 374–375
 EBS snapshots, 254, 278
 EBS volumes, 251–252, 277–278
 EC2 Auto Scaling policies, 152
 EC2 instances, 565, 636–637
 Elastic Beanstalk environment, 540–541
 images, 611
 load balancers, 156
 pipelines, 636, 666
 projects, 611, 665–666
 RDS snapshots, 359
 repositories, 589, 611–612, 636, 665
 S3 Glacier archives, 272
 S3 Glacier vaults, 271–272
 S3 objects, 231–235, 243
 security groups, 55–56
 shortcuts, 46
 stacks, 666–667
 VPCs, 71
deletion protection for load balancers, 141
DeletionPolicy parameter for AWS
 CloudFormation templates, 464
delivery policies in Amazon SNS messages,
 403–404
delivery retries in Amazon SNS messages,
 403–404
delivery status in Amazon SNS messages, 403
deployment
 applications with AWS CodeDeploy,
 615–624
 applications with AWS CodePipeline,
 625–635
 applications with Elastic Beanstalk, 530–533
 CI/CD pipelines groups, 652

deployment (*cont.*)
  cloud computing models, 5–7
  static websites with Amazon S3, 500–510
  static websites with Amazon S3 and Route
    53, 510–515
  static websites with Amazon S3, Route 53,
    and CloudFront, 515–523
deregistration delay in Elastic Load
  Balancing, 144
describe-db-instances command, 352
describe-import-image-tasks command, 552
DescribeStream operation in DynamoDB, 374
DescribeTable operation in DynamoDB, 373
detaching
  EBS volumes, 252, 277
  EC2 instances, 148
Detailed metrics in EBS, 261
Developer Plan, 40
development environment in Amazon SWF,
  416–419
DHCP (Dynamic Host Configuration
  Protocol), 84
dimensions metric in CloudWatch, 439, 441
dir command, 51
Direct Connect. *See* AWS Direct Connect
disabling CMKs, 342
distributions, CloudFront, 168–170
DKIM (Domain Keys Identified Mail)
  records, 191
DLM (Data Lifecycle Manager), 255–256
DML (Data Manipulation Language)
  operations, 350
DNS. *See* domain name system (DNS)
DNS Validation method for static website
  deployment, 518
Docker, installing on Linux, 63
document types in DynamoDB, 373
domain fronting in CloudFront, 173
Domain Keys Identified Mail (DKIM)
  records, 191
domain name system (DNS), 185–186
  description, 186
  domain names, 186–187
  exercises, 205–215
  name servers, 187
  questions, 215–217
  record types, 189–194

resolution, 187–188
  resources, 217–218
  review, 204–205
  Route 53, 195
  static website deployment, 512, 518–519
  zone files, 187–189
domain names
  CloudFront, 170–171
  Route 53, 194
  static website deployment, 512
domains
  Amazon SWF, 417
  Route 53, names, 194
  Route 53, registering, 197, 206–208
  Route 53, registrars, 195
  Route 53, registry, 195
  Route 53, resellers, 195
  SRV records, 193
durability of Amazon SNS messages, 403
Dynamic Host Configuration Protocol
  (DHCP), 84
dynamic labels in CloudWatch, 441
Dynamic Scaling in EC2 Auto Scaling, 151
DynamoDB. *See* Amazon DynamoDB
DynamoDB Accelerator (DAX)
  clusters and nodes, 377–378
  components, 377
  control, 378
  encryption, 379
  LRU, 377
  maintenance window, 383
  overview, 376–377
  reads, 377
  writes, 378

E

e-mail. *See* Amazon Simple Notification
  Service (Amazon SNS)
EarliestRestorableDateTime setting in
  DynamoDB, 381
EBS. *See* Amazon Elastic Block Store (EBS)
EBS-Optimized specification for DB Instance
  Class, 351
EC2. *See* Amazon Elastic Compute Cloud
  (Amazon EC2)
ec2 authorize-security-group-ingress
  command, 55

EC2 Auto Scaling. *See* Amazon EC2 Auto Scaling

ec2 create-key-pair command, 53–54

ec2 create-security-group command, 54

ec2 create-tags command, 53, 56

ec2 delete-key-pair command, 54

ec2 delete-security-group command, 55

ec2 describe-instances command, 56

ec2 describe-key-pairs command, 53–54

ec2 describe-security-groups command, 54–55

ec2 help command, 53

ec2 import-image command, 552

EC2_INSTANCE_LAUNCHING lifecycle hook, 148

EC2_INSTANCE_TERMINATING lifecycle hook, 148

ec2 run-instances command, 56

ec2 terminate-instances command, 56

EC2-to-S3-Read-only role, 616, 619

ECDHE (Elliptic Curve Diffie-Hellman Ephemeral) cipher, 384

Eclipse toolkit, 63–65

ECU specification for DB Instance Class, 351

edge caches in CloudFront, 164–165, 172

edge consolidators, 91

edge-optimized API endpoints in Amazon API Gateway, 421

effects in IAM policies, 295

EFS (Elastic File System). *See* Amazon Elastic File System (EFS)

EFS-to-EFS backups, 266

egress-only Internet gateways, 88

Elastic Beanstalk. *See* AWS Elastic Beanstalk

Elastic Block Store. *See* Amazon Elastic Block Store (EBS)

Elastic Compute Cloud (EC2). *See* Amazon Elastic Compute Cloud (Amazon EC2)

Elastic File System. *See* Amazon Elastic File System (EFS)

elastic IP addresses, 85, 99

Elastic Load Balancing (ELB), 137–138
   best practices, 145
   concepts, 140–141
   description, 12
   exercises, 154–156
   listeners, 141–143, 155
   monitoring, 145
   questions, 156–159
   resources, 160
   review, 153–154
   target groups, 143–144, 155
   testing, 156
   types, 138–140

elastic volumes in EBS, 256

Elliptic Curve Diffie-Hellman Ephemeral (ECDHE) cipher, 384

encryption
   Amazon SNS messages, 406–407
   Amazon SQS, 395, 401
   AWS Step Functions, 429
   best practices, 339
   buckets, 224
   client-side, 335–336
   CloudFormation templates, 460, 464
   CloudFront, 168
   CloudTrail, 443
   CloudWatch, 442
   command-line, 336–337
   data protection, 327–331
   DAX, 379
   decryption, 338
   DynamoDB, 382
   EBS, 251, 256–260
   EBS snapshots, 253, 255
   EFS, 266–267
   exercises, 340–342
   Lambda functions, 487
   questions, 342–345
   RDS, 360
   resources, 345
   review, 340
   S3, 236
   server-side, 331–335

encryption at rest
   AWS Step Functions, 429
   EFS, 266–267

encryption in transit
   Amazon SNS, 407
   CRR, 224
   EBS, 250–251, 255–256
   EFS, 266–268
   KMS, 382
   S3, 227–228, 236, 273
   Step Functions, 429

End field for AWS Step Functions states, 428

endpoints
Amazon API Gateway, 421–422
database migration, 559–562
VPCs, 85–87
enter and exit standby for EC2 Auto Scaling, 148–149
Enterprise Support plan, 40
entities in IAM, 287
envelopes in encryption, 329
environment variables
editing, 50
Lambda functions, 487
profiles, 52
environments
applications, 530–532
AWS Cloud9, 584–585
build, 595–596
CI/CD pipelines, 651
deleting, 540–541, 590
Ephemeral Diffie-Hellman (DHE), 384
error pages
CloudFront, 167, 173–174
static website deployment, 502, 506, 509–510, 522
Evaluate Target Health option, 514
events
Amazon SWF, 418
buckets, 224
CI/CD pipelines, 654
CloudTrail, 443–444
CloudWatch, 384
Lambda functions, 482
pipelines, 626
exam objective map, 673–674
execution in Amazon SWF workflows, 418
exit standby in EC2 Auto Scaling, 148–149
Expedited archive operations in S3 Glacier, 272
expiration
CloudFront content, 172
DynamoDB TTL, 372
S3 objects, 229–230
SOA records, 193
export AWS_ACCESS_KEY_ID command, 59
export AWS_DEFAULT_PROFILE command, 52
export AWS_REGION command, 59
export AWS_SECRET_ACCESS_KEY command, 59

export function in AWS CloudFormation, 466
express workflows in AWS Step Functions, 425–426

F

FaaS (Function as a Service), 7
Fail state in AWS Step Functions, 427
failed state in load balancers, 140
failover process in Multi-AZ, 352
failover routing policy in Route 53, 196, 201
failure threshold in Route 53, 204
fanout in Amazon SNS, 402
fault tolerance
availability zones, 139
CI/CD pipelines, 641–664
EC2 Auto Scaling, 146
Federal Risk and Authorization Management Program (FedRAMP), 274
federation. *See* identity federation
field-level encryption in CloudFront, 168
FIFO (first in/first out) queues in Amazon SQS, 395, 397–399, 409–410
files
decrypting, 338
encrypting, 336–337
filtering Amazon SNS messages, 405
first in/first out (FIFO) queues in Amazon SQS, 395, 397–399, 409–410
fixed-response actions in load balancer listener rules, 142
folders for buckets, 226
forward actions in load balancer listener rules, 142
frameworks in Amazon SWF, 416
Free Tier amount in EC2, 113
Free Tier Only policy in S3 Glacier, 273
free tiers, 42–44
Function as a Service (FaaS), 7

G

gateways
customer, 89–90
egress-only, 88
endpoints, 87
NAT, 87–88
transit, 91

virtual private, 89
VPCs, 7, 83–84, 98
general-purpose EC2 instances, 111
general-purpose SSD (gp2)
EBS volumes, 250
RDS, 357
geographic distribution restrictions in
CloudFront, 167
geolocation routing policy in Route 53,
196, 201
geoproximity routing policy in Route 53,
196, 201
Get-AWSPowerShellVersion cmdlet, 61
GET operations
S3 Glacier, 272
S3 objects, 234
server-side encryption, 333, 335
GetFederationToken API operation, 319
GetItem operation, 373
GetRecords operation, 374
GetShardIterator operation, 374
Glacier. *See* Amazon Simple Storage Service
(S3) Glacier
global scale in cloud computing, 4
global secondary indexes (GSIs) in
DynamoDB, 372, 380
global tables in DynamoDB, 381
glossary, 682–689
GNU Wget tool, 120
governance mode for S3 Object Lock, 237
GPU-based EC2 instances, 113
Gradle tool, 58
graphs in CloudWatch, 419, 438, 440–442
groups
CloudFront origins, 173
EC2 Auto Scaling, 149–150
Elastic Load Balancing targets, 143–144, 155
IAM, 286–287, 290–291, 293–294,
300–302
groups, security
application deployment, 619
CLI for, 54–56
EC2 instances, 126–127
load balancers, 140
VPCs, 82–83
GSIs (global secondary indexes) in
DynamoDB, 372, 380

H

hardware MFA devices in IAM, 290
hardware virtual machines (HVMs), 115
hash attributes in DynamoDB, 372
hash-based message authentication code
(HMAC) value, 334
HEAD operations in server-side encryption, 335
health checks in Route 53, 202–204
Health Insurance Portability and
Accountability Act (HIPAA)
Amazon API Gateway, 423
S3 Glacier, 274
Hello world template, 427
help for CLI commands, 53
hibernation, instance, 121–122
high availability
Amazon SQS, 396
CloudFront, 173
DynamoDB, 372
ELB, 145
Lambda functions, 482
RDS, 351–352
high memory instances in EC2, 112
high-resolution metrics in CloudWatch,
438–439
HIPAA (Health Insurance Portability and
Accountability Act)
Amazon API Gateway, 423
S3 Glacier, 274
history
Amazon SWF workflows, 417–418, 425
application building, 609, 661
AWS, 9
configuration changes, 424, 446
events, 443–444, 448–449
pipeline execution, 634–635
hit ratios in CloudFront caches, 171
HMAC (hash-based message authentication
code) value, 334
host-header conditions in load balancer
listener rules, 142
hosted zones
Route 53, 195, 199–200, 212–215
static website deployment, 512
hostnames in load balancer listener rules, 142
hosts in EC2, 110, 115

HTTP
    Amazon CloudFront, 165
    Amazon SWF, 416
http-header conditions in load balancer
    listener rules, 142
http-request-method conditions in load
    balancer listener rules, 142
HTTPS
    AWS Step Functions, 427
    CloudFront, 168
    Route 53 health checks, 204
    server-side encryption, 335
HVMs (hardware virtual machines), 115
hybrid clouds, 8

I

i3.metal instances, 112
IA class, 266
IaaS (Infrastructure as a Service), 5–6
IAM service. *See* AWS Identity and Access
    Management (IAM) service
ICMP (Internet Control Message Protocol), 88
identities in IAM, 287
Identity and Access Management service.
  See AWS Identity and Access Management
    (IAM) service
identity-based session policies, 319–320
identity federation
    exercises, 321–323
    IAM roles, 292
    providers, 309–310
    questions, 323–326
    resources, 326
    review, 321
    SAML 2.0, 318–319
    session policies, 319–321
    web, 310
identity pools
    Cognito, 312, 316–317
    user pools, 322
identity providers (IdPs)
    Cognito, 312–313
    identity federation, 310
IDEs. *See* Integrated Development
    Environments (IDEs)
ImageId parameter for AWS CloudFormation
    templates, 464

images
    applications, 603–604
    CI/CD pipelines, 648
    deleting, 611
Immediate Retry (No Delay) Phase in
    Amazon SNS policies, 403
Impaired status for EBS volumes, 253
Import-Module cmdlet, 61
in-place application deployment, 615, 623
Inbound Rules for VPCs, 100
index.html file for static website deployment,
    505–506
indexes in DynamoDB, 372, 380
inflight Amazon SQS messages, 399–400
Infrastructure as a Service (IaaS), 5–6
infrastructure security for DynamoDB, 384–385
ingress traffic limiting, 55
inline policies in IAM, 294
input/output metric for DB instances, 351
InputPath field for AWS Step Functions
    states, 428
INSERT statement in SQL, 375
Insights events in CloudTrail, 444–445
Install-Module cmdlet, 60–61
installing
    AWS Toolkit for Eclipse, 64
    AWS Toolkit for Visual Studio, 65
    Docker on Linux, 63
    profiles, 50–52
Instance Hibernation, 121–122
instances
    AMIs generated from, 109
    CLI, 56
    DB instances. *See* DB instances
    EC2. *See* Amazon EC2 instances
    EC2 Auto Scaling, 150–152
    Elastic Load Balancing, 143
    NAT, 88
    RDS, 349–350
InstanceType parameter for AWS
    CloudFormation templates, 464
INSUFFICIENT_DATA state for
    CloudWatch alarms, 440
Insufficient-data status for EBS volumes, 253
Integrated Development Environments
    (IDEs), 63
    AWS Toolkit for Eclipse, 63–65
    AWS Toolkit for Visual Studio, 65–66

AWS Tools for Microsoft Visual Studio
Team Services, 66–67
questions, 75
review, 67–68
integration requests in Amazon API
Gateway, 421
integration responses in Amazon API
Gateway, 421
integrity, encryption for, 327
intelligent-tiering in S3, 228
interface endpoints in VPCs, 86
Internet Control Message Protocol (ICMP), 88
Internet gateways
egress-only, 88
VPCs, 83–84, 98
Internet Protocol version 4 (IPv4) format, 198
Internet Protocol version 6 (IPv6) format, 198
internetwork traffic, Amazon SNS
security for, 406
Invoke-RestMethod command, 120
IOPS metric for DB instances, 351
Iops parameter for AWS CloudFormation
templates, 464
IP addresses
application migration, 547–549
DHCP, 84–85
DNS. *See* domain name system (DNS)
elastic, 85
Elastic Load Balancing, 143
Network Load Balancers, 139
Route 53, 195, 198–199
IPv4 (Internet Protocol version 4) format, 198
IPv6 (Internet Protocol version 6) format, 198
isolated routers, 91
isolation levels in DynamoDB, 376
items in DynamoDB, 372

J

Java 2.0 SDK, 58–59
Java Virtual Machine (JVM), 58
jobs in S3 Glacier, 270
JSON format
application migration, 551–552
authorization policies, 287
AWS CloudFormation templates, 459–460,
462–463, 465
DynamoDB documents, 373
IAM policies, 293–296

Lambda events, 482
notification configuration, 270
profiles, 52
signed cookies, 166
signed URLs, 165, 175
source code, 600
JSON web tokens (JWTs) in Cognito, 312

K

key encryption keys, 329
Key Management Service. *See* AWS Key
Management Service (KMS)
key pairs
application deployment, 620
CLI for, 53–54
creating, 70
EC2, 122–123
KeyName parameter for AWS
CloudFormation templates, 464
keys
Amazon API Gateway, 421
CLI encryption, 337
CloudTrail, 445
CodeCommit, 573, 576
DynamoDB, 372, 382
EBS encryption, 256–260
EFS encryption, 267
IAM, 288–289
S3 objects, 227, 235
types, 328–330
keys rotation, 341–342
KMS. *See* AWS Key Management Service
(KMS)
KmsKeyId parameter for EBS encryption,
257–258

L

labels in CloudWatch, 441
Lambda functions
Amazon SNS, 402
API Gateways, 316, 423–424
applications, 487–495
AWS Config, 448
concepts, 481–482
creating, 483–486
description, 12
Elastic Load Balancing targets, 143
exercises, 488–495

Lambda functions (*cont.*)
    layers, 487
    overview, 481
    questions, 495–498
    resources, 498
    review, 488
    SAM, 62
    security, 487
Lambda tasks in Amazon SWF, 417
Lambda@Edge, 174
large Amazon SQS messages, 400
Latency metric for DB instances, 351
latency routing policy for Route 53, 196, 201
LatestRestorableDateTime setting, 381
launch configurations in EC2 Auto Scaling, 149
launch templates in EC2 Auto Scaling, 149
launching EC2, 123–126
launching instances
    CLI, 56
    EC2, 118
layers in Lambda functions, 487
LDAP (Lightweight Directory Access
  Protocol), 318
least-privilege access in Amazon SNS, 406
least recently used (LRU)
  algorithm in DAX, 377
legal holds in S3 objects, 237
lifecycle hooks in EC2 Auto Scaling, 148
lifecycles
    Amazon SQS queues, 396
    CloudTrail, 443–444
    EBS snapshots, 255–256
    EC2, 117–122
    EC2 Auto Scaling, 147
    EFS policies, 267
    RDS, 353–355
    S3 objects, 229–230
lifetime
    CloudFront caches, 171
    CloudFront signed URLs and cookies, 166
lift and shift migration, 545–556
lift, tinker, and shift migration, 546
Lightweight Directory Access Protocol
  (LDAP), 318
Linux
    AWS Tools for PowerShell Core, 61
    Docker installation on, 63
    RAID configuration on, 260–261
    starting from, 49

listeners in Elastic Load Balancing,
  141–143, 155
listing
    buckets, 57
    object keys, 235
ListStreams operation in DynamoDB, 374
ListTables operation in DynamoDB, 373
load balancers
    ALB. *See* Application Load Balancers
    (ALBs)
    ELB. *See* Elastic Load Balancing (ELB)
local DynamoDB, 379–380
local secondary indexes (LSIs) in DynamoDB,
  372, 380
logs and logging
    Amazon SNS messages, 406
    Amazon SQS, 401
    Amazon SWF, 420
    AWS Step Functions, 428
    CI/CD pipelines, 649, 664
    CloudTrail, 444–445
    CloudWatch, 383, 442
    DynamoDB, 382–384
    EFS, 267
    Lambda functions, 487
    S3 Glacier, 274
    S3 server access, 226
long polling in Amazon SQS queues, 399
low-latency links in regions, 10–11
LRU (least recently used) algorithm
  in DAX, 377
ls command, 51
LSIs (local secondary indexes) in DynamoDB,
  372, 380

M

M5 EC2 instances, 111
macOSX, AWS Tools for PowerShell
  Core on, 61
Magnetic DB instances in RDS, 350
magnetic (standard) volumes in EBS, 250
magnetic storage in RDS, 357
Mail eXchange (MX) records in DNS, 191
main route tables in VPCs, 81–82
maintenance phase in RDS, 353
maintenance window in DynamoDB, 383
major upgrades in RDS, 353
managed policies in IAM, 294

managed rules in AWS Config, 448
Management Console. *See* AWS Management
  Console
manual EC2 Auto Scaling, 150
Map state in AWS Step Functions, 427
mapping templates in Amazon API
  Gateway, 421
markers in Amazon SWF workflows, 419
master keys in encryption, 328, 330
    CLI encryption, 337
    client-side encryption, 336
    EBS encryption, 256
Maven tool, 58
Max. Bandwidth (Mbps) specification, 351
Max Retrieval Rate policy, 273
MediaPackage in CloudFront, 170
MediaStore in CloudFront, 170
Memory (GiB) specification in DB Instance
  Class, 351
Memory Optimized instance class in RDS, 351
memory-optimized instances in EC2, 112
Message Deduplication ID token, 397–398
Message Group ID token, 397–398
messages
    Amazon SNS. *See* Amazon Simple
      Notification Service (Amazon SNS)
    Amazon SQS. *See* Amazon Simple Queue
      Service (Amazon SQS)
metadata
    adding, 56
    Amazon SNS messages, 405
    Amazon SQS messages, 398
    instances, 120–121
    S3 object keys, 227
methods requests and responses in Amazon
  API Gateway, 421
metric math in CloudWatch, 441
metrics
    application building, 609
    CloudWatch, 438–442
    EBS, 261
MFA. *See* multifactor authentication (MFA)
migration
    applications to Elastic Beanstalk, 534–540
    AWS Server Migration Service, 556
    databases, 557–564
    exercises, 565
    lift and shift, 546–556

questions, 566–568
requirements and advantages, 545–546
resources, 568
review, 564
standard queues to FIFO, 398–399
minimum TTL in SOA records, 193
minor RDS upgrades, 353–354
mobile apps in Cognito, 313–317
mock integration in Amazon API Gateway, 421
models in Amazon API Gateway, 422
modify-db-instance command, 354
modify phase in RDS lifecycle, 353
ModifyDBInstance action, 354
monitoring
    Amazon SNS messages, 406
    Amazon SQS, 401
    Amazon SWF, 419
    AWS Config, 448
    AWS Step Functions, 428
    with CloudTrail. *See* AWS CloudTrail
    with CloudWatch. *See* Amazon
      CloudWatch
    DynamoDB, 383–384
    EBS volumes, 252–253
    EC2 Auto Scaling groups, 152–153
    EFS, 267
    Elastic Load Balancing, 145
    RDS, 360
    read replicas, 356
    S3 Glacier, 274
moving S3 objects, 243
.msi installer, 60
Multi-AZ
    failover process, 352
    high availability, 351–352
    RDS, 349–350
multifactor authentication (MFA)
    AWS Step Functions, 429
    CloudTrail, 445
    CloudWatch, 442
    Cognito, 312
    enabling, 69
    IAM, 41, 286, 289–290
    Lambda functions, 487
    S3 objects, 231
multivalue answer routing policy in Route 53,
  196, 202
multivolume snapshots in EBS, 254

mvn clean install command, 58
mvn javadoc command, 58
MX records in Route 53, 197

N

NACLs (Network Access Control Lists), 80, 82
Name records in Route 53, 198
Name Server (NS) records
    DNS, 192
    Route 53, 197
name servers in Route 53, 195
names
    accounts, 37
    Amazon SNS messages, 405
    Amazon SQS queues, 398
    applications, 531, 615, 622–623
    ARN, 361
    buckets, 57, 170, 501, 503
    CloudFront domains, 170–171
    CloudWatch, 439
    DB instances, 350, 354
    domain, 186–187
    Elastic Beanstalk, 537
    Lambda functions, 484
    pipelines, 625
    profiles, 52
    repositories, 577
    S3 object keys, 227
    security groups, 82
    static website deployment, 512–513, 518
NAPTR records in Route 53, 197
NAT (network address translation) devices, 87
    gateways, 87–88
    instances, 88
nesting IAM groups, 290–291
.NET, SDK for, 59–60
Network Access Control Lists (NACLs), 80, 82
network address translation (NAT) devices, 87
    gateways, 87–88
    instances, 88
Network File System (NFS) version 4
    protocol, 262
Network Load Balancers, 138–139
Network Performance specification for DB
    Instance Class, 351
Network Time Protocol (NTP), 350
networking with VPCs. See Amazon Virtual
    Private Cloud (VPC)

Next field for AWS Step Functions states, 428
NFS (Network File System) version 4
    protocol, 262
No Retrieval Limit policy, 273
No Upfront reserved DB instances, 358
nodes in DAX, 377–378
nonrepudiation, encryption for, 327
NoSQL database service. See Amazon
    DynamoDB
NoSQL Workbench, 381
notifications
    Amazon SNS. See Amazon Simple
        Notification Service (Amazon SNS)
    AWS Config, 447
    CloudTrail, 443
    S3 Glacier, 270–271
NS (Name Server) records
    DNS, 192
    Route 53, 197
NTP (Network Time Protocol), 350
number attribute in Amazon SNS messages, 405

O

OAuth access tokens in Cognito, 313
Object Lock, 237
objects in S3, 226–227
    lifecycle management, 229–230
    operations, 234–236
    versioning, 230–234
OK state
    CloudWatch alarms, 440
    EBS volumes, 253
on-demand instances
    EC2, 114
    RDS, 358
One Zone-Infrequent Access, 228
Oomph plug-in, 65
Open Java Development Kit (OpenJDK), 58
operations in IAM, 287
optimized EC2 instances, 111–112
optimized HDD volumes, 250
optimizing CloudFront caching, 171–172
option groups in RDS, 356–357
origins in CloudFront, 169–170
    access identity, 167
    groups, 173
    servers, 162–163

Outbound Rules for VPCs, 101
OutputPath field for AWS Step Functions
    states, 428

P

PaaS (Platform as a Service), 6
Parallel state for AWS Step Functions, 427
Parallel template for AWS Step
    Functions, 427
paravirtual (PV) virtualization, 115–116
parent health checks in Route 53, 204
Partial Upfront reserved DB instances, 358
partition keys in DynamoDB, 372
Pass state for AWS Step Functions, 427
passwords
    AWS CodeCommit, 572, 574
    IAM, 288–289
    setting, 47
path-pattern conditions in load balancer
    listener rules, 143
PATH variable, 50
paths in load balancer listener rules, 142
Payment Card Industry (PCI) Data Security
    Standard (DSS)
    Amazon API Gateway, 423
    S3 Glacier, 274
    VPCs, 80
Payment Information page, 39
peering connections in VPCs, 88–89
per-second billing in EC2, 113
percentiles in CloudWatch, 440
performance
    cloud computing, 4
    EFS, 267–268
periods (.) in domain names, 187
periods metric in CloudWatch, 439–440
permissions
    Amazon SWF workflows, 419
    AWS CodeCommit, 572–573
    Cognito, 313
    IAM, 286, 293–296
    Lambda functions, 491
    session policies, 320
    static website deployment, 503–504
PIOPS (Provisioned IOPS) DB instances,
    350, 352
pip3 install awscli command, 50

pipelines
    AWS CodePipeline, 625–635
    CI/CD, 641–664
    deleting, 636, 666
plaintext, 328
Platform as a Service (PaaS), 6
point-to-site virtual private networks, 90
Pointer (PTR) records
    DNS, 192
    Route 53, 197
policies
    Amazon SNS messages, 403–404
    Amazon SWF, 419
    AWS CodeCommit, 572
    EC2 Auto Scaling, 151–152
    EFS lifecycle, 267
    IAM, 293–296, 302
    Lambda functions, 484
    passwords, 289
    Route 53 routing, 201–202
    S3 Glacier data retrieval, 273
    session, 319–321
polling
    Amazon SQS queues, 399
    Amazon SWF, 418
Portable Operating System Interface (POSIX),
    262–263
ports
    load balancer listener rules, 142
    load balancer listeners, 141
    SRV records, 194
POSIX (Portable Operating System Interface),
    262–263
Post-Backoff Phase in Amazon SNS policies, 404
POST requests
    CloudFront, 168, 170
    S3 Glacier, 272
    server-side encryption, 333, 335
PostgreSQL database, migrating, 557–564
Pre-Backoff Phase in Amazon SNS policies, 403
pricing
    Amazon API Gateway, 422–423
    cloud computing, 3
    CloudFront, 163
    EC2, 113–115
primary keys in DynamoDB, 372
primary name servers for SOA records, 192

primary route tables for VPCs, 81–82

principals in IAM, 287, 295

priority

    load balancer listener rules, 142

    MX records, 191

    SRV records, 194

private API endpoints in Amazon API Gateway, 422

private clouds, 8

private DNS in Route 53, 195

private hosted zones in Route 53, 200

private integration in Amazon API Gateway, 422

private keys, 328

private VPC subnets, 81

producers in Amazon SNS, 401

profiles

    configuring, 51–52

    installing and setting up, 50–52

promoting read replicas, 356

protocols

    load balancer listener rules, 142

    SRV records, 193

providers in identity federation, 309–310

Provisioned IOPS (PIOPS) DB instances, 350, 352

Provisioned IOPS SSD (io1)

    EBS, 250

    RDS, 357

provisioning state for load balancers, 140

proxy integration in Amazon API Gateway, 422

PTR (Pointer) records

    DNS, 192

    Route 53, 197

public accessibility in Amazon SNS security, 406

public clouds, 7–8

public hosted zones in Route 53, 200

public keys

    AWS CodeCommit, 573, 576

    description, 328

public VPC subnets, 81

publishers in Amazon SNS, 401–402

pull requests in repositories, 586, 589

push messages in Amazon SNS, 402–403

push notifications in Amazon SNS, 403

pushpin icon, 45

PUT requests

    CloudFront, 170

    server-side encryption, 333–335

PutItem operation in DynamoDB, 373

PutMetricData call in CloudWatch, 438–439

PuTTY sessions, 125

PV (paravirtual) virtualization, 115–116

Q

queries in load balancer listener rules, 142

Query operation in DynamoDB, 373

query-string conditions in load balancer listener rules, 143

query string parameters for CloudFront caching, 172

Queue Depth metric for DB instances, 351

queues. *See* Amazon Simple Queue Service (Amazon SQS)

R

r5.metal and r5d.metal instances, 112

RAID configuration on Linux, 260–261

range attributes in DynamoDB, 372

RCUs (read capacity units) in DAX, 378

RDS. *See* Amazon Relational Database Service (RDS)

re-architecting, migration for, 546

re-platforming, migration for, 546

read capacity units (RCUs) in DAX, 378

read consistency in DynamoDB, 376

read operations

    DAX, 377

    DynamoDB, 373

read replicas in RDS, 355–356

read/write capacity mode in DynamoDB, 376

ReadThrottleEvents value in DynamoDB, 383

Real-Time Messaging Protocol (RTMP) protocol, 162–163

rebooting

    DB instances, 354

    EC2 instances, 122

receipt handles for Amazon SQS messages, 398

Receive Request Attempt ID token, 397

receiving messages in FIFO queues, 398

records

    DNS, 189–194

    Route 53, 196

recovering EC2 instances, 119

recovery in DynamoDB, 381

recursive name servers in Route 53, 196

redirect actions in load balancer listener rules, 142

redundancy in regions, 10
refactoring, migration for, 546
refresh times for SOA records, 193
regional API endpoints in Amazon API
    Gateway, 422
regional edge caches, 164–165
regions
    overview, 9–11
    selecting, 46–47
registered targets for Elastic Load
    Balancing, 144
registering domains, 206–208
registry for AWS CloudFormation, 467
rehosting, migration for, 545–546
Relational Database Service. *See* Amazon
    Relational Database Service (RDS)
Remote Access, starting from, 49
removing CloudFront content, 164
renaming DB instances, 354
replacement instances in CI/CD pipelines, 653
replicas in RDS, 355–356
replication instances in database migration,
    559–561
reporting CodeBuild tests, 610
repositories
    application building, 596–598
    application deployment, 616–618
    AWS CodeBuild, 596–598, 601–602,
        607–608
    AWS CodeCommit. *See* AWS
        CodeCommit
    AWS CodeDeploy, 615–618
    AWS CodePipeline, 626–635
    CI/CD pipelines, 642–644, 647–649, 660
    deleting, 589, 611–612, 636, 665
Representational State Transfer (REST), 420,
    423–424
repurchasing, migration for, 546
request and response behavior in CloudFront,
    173–174
request headers in CloudFront caching, 172
Requester Pays buckets, 225–226
requests in IAM, 287
reserved concurrency in Lambda functions, 482
reserved DB instances, 358
reserved EC2 instances, 114
resource-based policies
    IAM, 294
    session policies, 319–320

Resource Groups menu, 48–49
resources
    Amazon SWF workflow permissions, 419
    AWS CloudFormation. *See* AWS
        CloudFormation
    AWS Config, 446–447
    cleanup, 523–524
    IAM, 287
response time in Route 53, 204
responsible party in SOA records, 192
REST (Representational State Transfer), 420,
    423–424
restarting EC2 instances, 121
restoring
    EBS snapshots, 257–260
    S3 objects, 236
restricting Amazon CloudFront access,
    165–168
retaining, migration for, 546
retention periods
    Amazon SQS messages, 396
    RDS backups, 358–359
    S3 objects, 237
retirement of EC2 instances, 122
retiring, migration for, 546
retries
    Amazon SNS messages, 403–404
    Lambda functions, 482
    SOA records, 193
Retry failure template in AWS Step
    Functions, 427
reusable delegation sets in Route 53, 196
revisiting, migration for, 546
roles
    application migration, 550–551
    IAM, 287, 291–292
root device types in AMI, 109
root servers operation, 186
Route 53. *See* Amazon Route 53
route tables in VPCs, 81–82, 97
routers in VPCs, 91
routes in Amazon API Gateway, 422
routing in Elastic Load Balancing, 143–144
routing policies in Route 53, 196, 201–202
routing traffic
    CI/CD pipelines, 658, 661
    Route 53, 198–200
RTMP (Real-Time Messaging Protocol)
    protocol, 162–163

rules
    AWS Config, 448
    CloudTrail, 444
    load balancer listeners, 142–143
    NACLs, 82
    security groups, 82–83, 126–127
runtime Lambda functions, 481–482

S

S3. *See* Amazon Simple Storage Service (S3)
s3 cp command, 51
S3 Glacier. *See* Amazon Simple Storage Service
    (S3) Glacier
S3 Glacier Deep Archive, 229
s3 ls command, 51–52, 57
s3 mb command, 57
s3 rb command, 57
S3–Managed Keys (SSE-S3), 331, 333–334
SaaS (Software as a Service), 7
SAML (Security Assertion Markup Language),
    287, 318–319
SampleCount metric in CloudWatch, 439
scalable CI/CD pipelines, 641–664
scalar types in DynamoDB, 373
scale out and in with EC2 Auto Scaling, 148
scaling
    EC2 Auto Scaling. *See* Amazon EC2 Auto
        Scaling
    Lambda functions, 482
Scan operation in DynamoDB, 373
scheduled EC2 Auto Scaling, 150–151
SDKs. *See* Software Development Kits (SDKs)
secondary indexes in DynamoDB, 372, 380
Secure Shell (SSH)
    EC2 instance connections, 125
    repositories, 578
    security groups, 54, 83
    static website deployment certificates,
        519–520
Secure Shell (SSH) keys
    AWS CodeCommit, 573–576
    IAM, 288
    RSA, 123
Secure Sockets Layer (SSL)
    Amazon SNS, 405
    Amazon SQS, 401
    buckets, 169, 224
    cross-region replication, 224

data protection, 331, 382
Elastic Load Balancing, 145
RDS, 360
S3, 227–228, 236
S3 Glacier, 273
static websites, 515, 517–520
Secure Sockets Layer/Transport Layer Security
    (SSL/TLS)
    AWS Step Functions, 429
    DynamoDB, 384
    Lambda functions, 487
    user credentials, 288
security
    Amazon SNS, 406–407
    application deployment, 619–620
    AWS Config, 446
    AWS Step Functions, 428–429
    cloud computing, 4
    CloudFront content, 164
    CloudTrail, 443–445
    CloudWatch, 442
    CodeCommit, 572–575
    DynamoDB, 382, 384–385
    IAM. *See* AWS Identity and Access
        Management (IAM) service
    Lambda functions, 487
    RDS, 359–360
    repositories, 578
    S3 Glacier, 273
    static website deployment, 503–504,
        519–520
Security Assertion Markup Language (SAML),
    287, 318–319
security groups
    application deployment, 619
    CLI for, 54–57, 70–71
    EC2 instances, 126–127
    load balancers, 140
    VPCs, 82–83
security keys in EC2, 122–123
Security Token Service (STS)
    Amazon SNS, 406
    AWS CodeCommit, 576
    DynamoDB, 384
    S3 Glacier, 273
Select A Support Plan page, 38, 40
SELECT statement in SQL, 375
selecting S3 object content, 235

self-signed certificates, 603
Sender Policy Framework (SPF) records
  DNS, 193
  Route 53, 197
sending messages with FIFO queues, 397
Sequence Number token in Amazon SQS, 397–398
serial numbers in SOA records, 193
server access logging for buckets, 226
server certificates in IAM, 288
server-side encryption
  Amazon SNS, 407
  CloudTrail, 443, 445
  CMKs, 332–333
  overview, 331–332
  SSE-C, 236, 334–335
  SSE-KMS, 236
  SSE-S3, 236, 333–334
server-side errors in Amazon SNS, 404
server-side resources for Cognito user pools, 315
Serverless Application Repository, 63
serverless applications with Lambda. See Lambda functions
serverless infrastructure in Amazon API Gateway, 420
service-linked roles in IAM, 292
service roles
  IAM, 292
  pipelines, 625–626
Service (SRV) records
  DNS, 193–194
  Route 53, 197
service types in cloud computing, 7–8
session policies in identity federation, 319–321
set AWS_ACCESS_KEY_ID command, 59
set AWS_REGION command, 59
set AWS_SECRET_ACCESS_KEY command, 59
Set-Cookie headers in CloudFront, 166
set types in DynamoDB, 373
setx command, 52
shared security responsibility, 359
shared tenancy in EC2, 110
Short Message Service (SMS), 402
short polling in Amazon SQS queues, 399
shortcuts, 45–46
sign-in page, 40–41
sign-up services in Cognito, 312

signals in Amazon SWF workflows, 419
signed URLs and cookies in CloudFront, 165–167
Simple Notification Service. See Amazon Simple Notification Service (Amazon SNS)
Simple Queue Service. See Amazon Simple Queue Service (Amazon SQS)
simple routing policy in Route 53, 196, 201
simple scaling policy in EC2 Auto Scaling, 151–152
Simple Storage Service. See Amazon Simple Storage Service (S3)
Simple Storage Service Glacier. See Amazon Simple Storage Service (S3) Glacier
Simple Workflow Service. See Amazon Simple Workflow Service (Amazon SWF)
single data points in CloudWatch, 441
single sign-on (SSO) in identity federation, 310
site-to-site virtual private networks, 90
slow start mode in Elastic Load Balancing, 144
SMS-based MFA, 290
snapshots
  AWS Config, 447
  RDS, 359
snapshots, EBS, 251–254
  copying, 255
  creating, 276, 278
  deleting, 254, 278
  lifecycle, 255–256
  multivolume, 254
  restoring and copying, 257–260
SNS. See Amazon Simple Notification Service (Amazon SNS)
SOA (Start of Authority) records
  DNS, 192–193
  Route 53, 197
SOC (System and Organization Controls) in S3 Glacier, 274
Software as a Service (SaaS), 7
Software Development Kits (SDKs), 57
  Amazon SWF, 416
  AWS Step Functions, 426
  Java 2.0, 58–59
  .NET, 59–60
  RDS, 350
  review, 67–68

solid-state disks (SSDs) for DynamoDB, 372
source code
    application building, 599–601
    applications with AWS CodePipeline,
        626–635
    AWS CodeCommit repositories. *See* AWS
        CodeCommit
source-ip conditions in load balancer listener
    rules, 143
speed in cloud computing, 4
SPF (Sender Policy Framework) records
    DNS, 193
    Route 53, 197
split-view DNS in Route 53, 200
spot instances in EC2, 114
SQL (Structured Query Language), 374–375
SQS. *See* Amazon Simple Queue Service
    (Amazon SQS)
SRV (Service) records
    DNS, 193–194
    Route 53, 197
SSDs (solid-state disks) for DynamoDB, 372
SSE-S3 (S3–Managed Keys), 331, 333–334
SSH. *See* Secure Shell (SSH)
SSL. *See* Secure Sockets Layer (SSL)
SSL/TLS (Secure Sockets Layer/Transport
    Layer Security)
    AWS Step Functions, 429
    DynamoDB, 384
    Lambda functions, 487
    user credentials, 288
SSO (single sign-on) in identity federation, 310
STaaS (Storage as a Service), 6
Stackery.io toolkit, 63
stacks
    CloudFormation, 465–466
    deleting, 666–667
stages
    Amazon API Gateway, 421
    application deployment, 625
Standard archive operations in S3 Glacier, 272
Standard class in EFS, 266
Standard-Infrequent Access in S3, 228
Standard instance class in RDS, 351
standard queues in Amazon SQS, 395–399,
    408–409
Standard S3 storage class, 227

standard workflows in AWS Step
    Functions, 425–426
Start of Authority (SOA) records
    DNS, 192–193
    Route 53, 197
starting DB instances, 355
stateful VPC security groups, 83
statements in IAM policies, 295
states
    AWS Step Functions, 427–428
    CloudWatch alarms, 440
    load balancers, 140
static website deployment
    Amazon S3, 500–510
    Amazon S3 and Route 53, 510–515
    Amazon S3, Route 53, and CloudFront,
        515–523
    exercises, 523–524
    questions, 524–527
    resources, 527
    review, 523
static websites on S3, 225
statistics metric in CloudWatch, 439
StatusCheckFailed_System alarm, 119
step functions. *See* AWS Step Functions
step scaling policy, 151
sticky sessions in Elastic Load Balancing, 144
stopping
    DB instances, 354–355
    EC2 instances, 121
    pipeline execution, 625
storage
    CloudFront charges, 163
    EBS. *See* Amazon Elastic Block Store (EBS)
    EC2 options, 116–117
    EFS. *See* Amazon Elastic File System (EFS)
    RDS, 357–358
    S3. *See* Amazon Simple Storage Service (S3)
    S3 Glacier. *See* Amazon Simple Storage
        Service (S3) Glacier
    static website deployment, 507
Storage as a Service (STaaS), 6
storage classes
    EFS, 266
    S3, 227–229
storage-optimized EC2 instances, 112
stream ciphers, 329, 331

streams in DynamoDB, 372, 374, 380–381

string attribute for Amazon SNS messages, 405

Structured Query Language (SQL), 374–375

STS (Security Token Service)

Amazon SNS, 406

AWS CodeCommit, 576

DynamoDB, 384

S3 Glacier, 273

subdomains in Route 53, 196, 200

subnets

load balancers, 140

VPCs, 81, 84, 101–102

subscribers in Amazon SNS, 401–402

Succeed state in AWS Step Functions, 427

sum metric in CloudWatch, 439

Support Center, 48

Support menu, 48

SWF. *See* Amazon Simple Workflow Service (Amazon SWF)

symmetric encryption, 328, 330

System and Organization Controls (SOC) in S3 Glacier, 274

system attributes for Amazon SQS messages, 399

SystemErrors value in DynamoDB, 383

T

T2, T3, and T3A EC2 instances, 111

TAB key command-completion feature, 53

tables in DynamoDB, 372, 386–389

Tag Editor, 49

tags

Amazon SNS messages, 405

Amazon SWF workflows, 419

applications, 531, 619

AWS Step Functions, 428

CloudFormation templates, 460, 464

CMKs, 342

Elastic Beanstalk, 537

RDS, 361

static website deployment, 518

target groups in Elastic Load Balancing, 143–144, 155

target tracking scaling policy in EC2 Auto Scaling, 151

targets in SRV records, 194

Task state in AWS Step Functions, 427

tasks in Amazon SWF

activities, 417

lists, 417

routing, 418

TCP (Transmission Control Protocol)

NAT gateways, 88

Network Load Balancers, 138–139

Route 53 health checks, 204

templates

Amazon API Gateway, 421

AWS Step Functions, 427

CI/CD pipelines, 644–645

CloudFormation, 459–465, 468–475

EC2 Auto Scaling, 149

temporary queues for Amazon SQS messages, 400

tenancy options in EC2, 109–110

terminating EC2 instances, 56, 122

Terraform format for AWS CloudFormation templates, 461–462, 464–465

tests, reporting, 610

Text (TXT) records

DNS, 194

Route 53, 197

third-party geolocation in CloudFront, 168

third-party identity providers in Cognito, 317

ThrottledRequests value in DynamoDB, 383

Throughput metric for DB instances, 351

throughput-optimized HDD (st1) volumes, 250

Time to Live (TTL) value

DAX reads, 377

DynamoDB, 372, 381, 383

Route 53, 196

SOA records, 193

timeouts

Amazon SQS messages, 399–400

CloudFront, 173

load balancers, 141

timers

Amazon SQS messages, 400

Amazon SWF workflows, 419

timestamps metric in CloudWatch, 439

TimeToLiveDeletedItemCount value in DynamoDB, 383

TLDs (top-level domains)

DNS, 187

Route 53, 195

TLS (Transport Layer Security)
    Amazon SNS, 406
    CloudWatch, 442
    RDS, 360
top-level domains (TLDs)
    DNS, 187
    Route 53, 195
TotalTester Online practice exam, 675–677
TPS (transactions per second) in Amazon
  SQS messages, 396
traffic routing
    CI/CD pipelines, 658, 661
    Route 53, 198–200
traffic shifting in CI/CD pipelines, 653
traffic staging in CI/CD pipelines, 658
TransactGetItems operations
    DAX, 378
    DynamoDB, 375
transactions in DynamoDB, 375–376
transactions per second (TPS) in Amazon
  SQS messages, 396
TransactWriteItems operations
    DAX, 378
    DynamoDB, 375
transfer acceleration in S3 buckets, 224–225
transit gateways, 91
transitions
    application deployment, 625
    S3 object lifecycle, 229
Transmission Control Protocol (TCP)
    NAT gateways, 88
    Network Load Balancers, 138–139
    Route 53 health checks, 204
Transport Layer Security (TLS)
    Amazon SNS, 406
    CloudWatch, 442
    RDS, 360
Trials option, 42
triggers for Lambda functions, 482, 485
TTL. *See* Time to Live (TTL) value
12 Months Free option, 42
TXT (Text) records
    DNS, 194
    Route 53, 197
Type field for AWS Step Functions
  states, 428
Type records in Route 53, 198

types
    Amazon EC2 instances, 110–116
    Amazon SWF workflows, 418
    DynamoDB documents, 373
    Elastic Load Balancing, 138–140

U

U2F security keys in IAM, 289
UDP (User Datagram Protocol)
    NAT gateways, 88
    Network Load Balancers, 139
Uninstall-Module cmdlet, 61
uninstalling AWS Toolkit for Visual Studio, 67
units metric in CloudWatch, 439
UPDATE statement in SQL, 375
UpdateItem operation in DynamoDB, 374
UpdateTable operation in DynamoDB, 373
updating
    AWS CloudFormation stacks, 466
    in DynamoDB, 374
    S3 Glacier archives, 272
upgrading
    AWS Toolkit for Eclipse, 65
    RDS, 353–354
uploading S3 objects, 234
URLs
    Amazon API Gateway, 421
    Amazon SQS queues, 398
    CloudFront, 165–167
usage plans in Amazon API Gateway, 422
usage reporting for buckets, 225
User Datagram Protocol (UDP)
    NAT gateways, 88
    Network Load Balancers, 139
user IDs in IAM, 288
user pools in Cognito, 312, 314–317, 322
usernames in AWS CodeCommit, 574
users in IAM, 286, 288–289, 300–301

V

validating application migration, 552–553
value attribute for Amazon SNS messages, 405
Value records for Route 53, 198
Vault Lock, 273
vaults, S3 Glacier, 269, 271–273
vCPU specification in DB Instance Class, 351

versioning
    Amazon SWF workflows, 418
    IAM policies, 295–296
    Lambda functions, 482
    S3 objects, 230–234
VersioningConfiguration parameter for
    CloudFormation templates, 460, 464
video on demand in CloudFront, 169
virtual MFA in IAM, 289
Virtual Private Cloud. *See* Amazon Virtual
    Private Cloud (VPC)
virtual private gateways, 89
virtual private networks (VPNs)
    DynamoDB, 384
    EFS, 264–265
    site-to-site, 90
virtual queues for Amazon SQS messages, 400
visibility timeouts in Amazon SQS
    messages, 399
Visual Studio
    .NET, 60
    toolkit, 65–67
Visual Studio Team Services (VSTS), 66
VM Import/Export service, 118–119
VMware Cloud on AWS, 13
volumes in EBS, 250
    attaching, 277
    creating, 251, 276
    deleting, 277
    detaching, 277
    elastic, 256
    monitoring, 252–253
    working with, 252
VolumeSize parameter for AWS
    CloudFormation templates, 464
VolumeType parameter for AWS
    CloudFormation templates, 464
VPC. *See* Amazon Virtual Private Cloud
    (VPC)
VPC Only specification in DB Instance
    Class, 351
VPC wizard, 94
VPNs (virtual private networks), 90
    DynamoDB, 384
    EFS, 264–265
    site-to-site, 90
VSTS (Visual Studio Team Services), 66

W

Wait state in AWS Step Functions, 427
WAR files in Elastic Beanstalk, 536, 538
Warning status for EBS volumes, 253
web
    CloudFront distributions, 169–170
    DynamoDB, 380
    identity federation, 310
Web Server Environment for application
    deployment, 530
website deployment
    Amazon S3, 500–510
    Amazon S3 and Route 53, 510–515
    Amazon S3, Route 53, and CloudFront,
        515–523
    exercises, 523–524
    questions, 524–527
    resources, 527
    review, 523
website hosting for buckets, 209–211
WebSocket protocol
    Amazon API Gateway, 421–423
    CloudFront, 171
weight in SRV records, 194
weighted routing policy in Route 53, 196, 202
where /R command, 50
Windows command line, starting from, 49
workers in Amazon SWF, 417
workflows
    Amazon SWF. *See* Amazon Simple
        Workflow Service (Amazon SWF)
    AWS Step Functions, 425–426
writes in DAX, 378
WriteThrottleEvents value for DynamoDB, 383

X

x-amz-server-side-encryption-aws-kms-key-id
    request header, 333
x-amz-server-side-encryption-customer-
    algorithm, 335
x-amz-server-side-encryption-customer-key, 335
x-amz-server-side-encryption request header,
    333–334
x-amz-server-side-encryption-customer-key-
    MD5, 335
x1 EC2 instances, 112

Y

YAML (YAML Ain't Markup Language)
    AWS CloudFormation templates, 459–461,
       463–465
    AWS Config, 447
    buildspec files, 598–599, 604–605

Z

z1d.metal EC2 instances, 112
zones
    DNS files, 187–189
    Route 53, 195, 199–200, 212–215
    static website deployment, 512